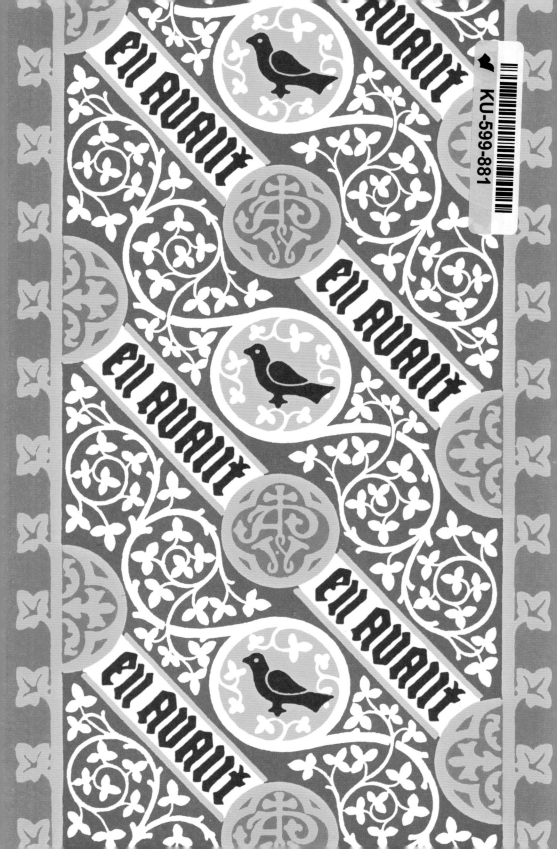

God's Architect

ROSEMARY HILL

God's Architect

Pugin and the Building of Romantic Britain

ALLEN LANE
an imprint of
PENGUIN BOOKS

ALLEN LANE

Published by the Penguin Group
Penguin Books Ltd, 80 Strand, London WC2R ORL, England
Penguin Group (USA) Inc., 375 Hudson Street, New York, New York 10014, USA
Penguin Group (Canada), 90 Eglinton Avenue East, Suite 700, Toronto, Ontario, Canada M4P 2Y3
(a division of Pearson Penguin Canada Inc.)
Penguin Ireland, 25 St Stephen's Green, Dublin 2, Ireland
(a division of Penguin Books Ltd)
Penguin Group (Australia), 250 Camberwell Road, Camberwell, Victoria 3124, Australia
(a division of Pearson Australia Group Pty Ltd)
Penguin Books India Pvt Ltd, 11 Community Centre, Panchsheel Park, New Delhi – 110 017, India
Penguin Group (NZ), 67 Apollo Drive, Rosedale, North Shore 0632, New Zealand
(a division of Pearson New Zealand Ltd)
Penguin Books (South Africa) (Pty) Ltd, 24 Sturdee Avenue, Rosebank, Johannesburg 2196, South Africa

Penguin Books Ltd, Registered Offices: 80 Strand, London WC2R ORL, England

www.penguin.com

First published 2007
2

Copyright © Rosemary Hill, 2007

The moral right of the author has been asserted

Set in 9/12.25 pt PostScript Adobe Sabon
Typeset by Rowland Phototypesetting Ltd, Bury St Edmunds, Suffolk
Printed in Great Britain by Clays Ltd, St Ives plc

A CIP catalogue record for this book is available from the British Library

ISBN: 978-0-713-99499-5

www.greenpenguin.co.uk

Penguin Books is committed to a sustainable future
for our business, our readers and our planet.
The book in your hands is made from paper
certified by the Forest Stewardship Council.

Even the loose stones that cover the high-way,
I gave a moral life, I saw them feel,
Or link'd them to some feeling: the great mass
Lay bedded in a quickening soul, and all
That I beheld respired with inward meaning

William Wordsworth, *The Prelude*,
Book III, ll. 125–9

Contents

CONTENTS

Part Four

Part Five

Part Six

List of Illustrations

Photographic acknowledgements are given in parentheses

1 A. W. N. Pugin by J. R. Herbert, 1845 (Palace of Westminster)
2 Auguste Charles Pugin, by an unknown artist (private collection)
3 Pugin as a child of two, drawn by his uncle in 1814
4 'The Pillory', from *The Microcosm of London*, illustrated by A. C. Pugin and Thomas Rowlandson
5 Design for a sideboard for Windsor Castle, 1827 (V&A)
6 'My first design', 1821 (British Museum)
7 Scarisbrick Hall, Lancashire (*Country Life*)
8 The Great Hall, Scarisbrick (*Country Life*)
9 St Marie's Grange, Alderbury, near Salisbury (Graham Miller)
10 Refectory table at Oscott College, Birmingham, *c.*1838 (Graham Miller)
11 The Grange, Ramsgate, from the garden side (Martin Charles)
12 'A True Prospect of St Augustine's', 1849 (private collection)
13 The Grange, Ramsgate (Martin Charles)
14 St Giles's, Cheadle, Staffordshire (Graham Miller)
15 The satire on the architectural profession from *Contrasts*, 1836
16 'St Edmund's Procession', from *The Shrine*, Pugin's Ideal Scheme of 1832 (V&A)
17 St Marie's College, an Ideal Scheme of 1834 (V&A)
18 John Hardman, Pugin's closest friend
19 George Myers, Pugin's builder (Patricia Spencer Silver)
20 Ambrose Phillipps
21 John Talbot, Sixteenth Earl of Shrewsbury, lithograph from a painting by Carl Blaas (Carlton Towers archive)
22 St Mary's, Derby, exterior

Prologue

Travelling through England on a train, or flying into London, low along the Thames and over the suburbs, the landscape is still, to a great extent, made up of little pitch-roofed houses and gardens. Sprinkled among them are the towers and spires of Gothic churches, while here and there are small village schools and big Victorian town halls. The architectural texture of our towns and of the countryside is still largely nineteenth-century and none of it would look, quite, as it does had A. W. N. Pugin never lived.

Pugin gave Britain's capital cities two of their greatest landmarks, the clock tower of the Palace of Westminster, generally, if inaccurately, known as Big Ben,[1] and, in Edinburgh, the spire of Tolbooth St John's. He built the first English cathedral since Wren's St Paul's and he reinvented the family house. But his influence depended not only, not even primarily, on his buildings, it was both wider and more elusive. He gave the nineteenth century a new idea about what architecture could be and mean. He saw it as a moral force in society and as a romantic art. 'He was our leader and our most able pioneer,' George Gilbert Scott, that most prolific and essentially Victorian architect, recalled.[2]

Like many who come to be seen as great men, Pugin seemed to his contemporaries at once typical and exceptional; he embodied the dilemma of his age and lived it out on a dramatic scale. To a generation sick of Georgian laissez-faire and frightened and excited in almost equal measures by the speed of its own steam-driven progress, Pugin offered a way forward – which was also a way back. He pointed to the Middle Ages as a model not just for architecture but for society, for a coherent, Christian civic order in which the poor would be fed, the old cared for, the children taught. As the Victorian age began it was a compelling image. The 1830s saw some of the worst civil unrest in English history.

There was disturbance and rioting in the countryside, while in the cities the factories and slums proliferated and misery and discontent grew with them.

So it was that the nineteenth century decided to revive Gothic architecture. What had been, for three generations, a style for rich men's houses, garden follies and the occasional church became a national style, a public principle, the proper form for the Houses of Parliament, for schools, shops, railway stations and for nearly every church. Pugin did not effect all this by himself, but he did more than any other individual to bring it about. He was the pivot around which the sensibility of nineteenth-century architecture turned. That he failed in his ideal of transforming England into a Catholic, Gothic kingdom is hardly surprising. What is surprising is the extent to which he succeeded. His was a romantic vision. If – as T. E. Hulme said – romanticism is 'spilt religion', then the Gothic Revival, as it came to be known, was a long, late attempt to contain Romanticism within a formal religious understanding of the world, to hold together art and God.[3]

Pugin, in many ways, fitted the type of the romantic hero. Born in 1812, the year of Byron's overnight success, he had a brilliant early career, going to work for George IV at Windsor when he was fifteen. By the time he was twenty-one he had been shipwrecked, imprisoned for debt and widowed. He had already lived 'a long life in a short one'.[4] Nineteen years and another lifetime later he died, still young, but disillusioned and insane.

In person Pugin himself was, as George Gilbert Scott discovered, often heartier and less intense than in print, 'tremendously jolly', with 'almost too much bonhomie' for his admirer's 'romantic expectations'.[5] Energetic, humorous, roughly spoken and often roughly dressed, he disconcerted many people. Yet his moods changed quickly. The jollity alternated with passionate dejection; he wept often and in public. He was susceptible to women, falling in love easily and often, somewhat more often than was in accordance with his ideal of Christian marriage. His unhappy love affairs and other, less romantic sexual adventures were a cause of scandal that marked and marred his adult life. Many people disliked him, notably Ruskin and John Henry Newman, but nobody doubted his importance. As the nineteenth century drew to a close, it seemed to those who remembered him that 'we should have had no Morris, no Street, no Burges, no Shaw, no Webb, no Bodley, no Rossetti, no Burne-Jones, no Crane but for Pugin'.[6]

Then, as he passed from living memory, Pugin's reputation began to pursue a tortuous course. At first he vanished altogether amid the general revulsion against the Victorians, and their age of 'crystal palaces, bassinettes, military helmets, memorial wreaths, trousers, whiskers, wedding cakes'.[7] There had never been, to Virginia Woolf, anything 'at once so indecent, so hideous and so monumental' as Victorian art.[8] It was in 1928, the same year Woolf wrote those words, that the young Kenneth Clark published a perceptive and witty book, *The Gothic Revival*, archly subtitled 'an essay in the history of taste'. The very idea of taking Victorian Gothic seriously was outré. Clark later recalled that it was then generally believed in Oxford not only that Keble College was 'the ugliest building in the world' but that it had somehow manifested itself out of the writings of Ruskin.[9] When Clark suggested that Keble was the work of William Butterfield he was called a liar in public by an 'eminent historian' of the University.

As the reaction against the nineteenth century worked itself out in the wholesale destruction of art and architecture and the incidental ruination of many towns and cities, others came to retrieve Pugin's fading reputation. To Nikolaus Pevsner, arguably England's greatest architectural historian, he seemed especially interesting because, in his writings, he had laid down rules for architecture that anticipated 'our functionalists of the twenties and thirties'.[10] The young Pevsner then saw architectural ideas as a Hegelian stream flowing on towards 'the ocean of the International Style of the 1930s'.[11] Pevsner's early idea of Pugin's importance as a 'pioneer of modernism', the discoverer of 'rational planning' and the designer of furniture that prefigures modernist designs of the twentieth century can still sometimes be found among those who hold to a teleological view of history, but it will not stand much examination. As Pevsner grew older and less doctrinaire he himself changed his mind about Pugin and found him less easy to admire. Throughout *The Buildings of England* there is a perceptible disillusionment with Pugin's work; 'antiquarianly correct' was Pevsner's final verdict on this curious man whose importance he sensed but could not, quite, pin down.[12]

His disappointment was not unfair, for, as an architect, Pugin was wildly uneven. Lack of money, lack of experience and his own volatile temperament led to more failures than successes. He built most in the early years of his career when he knew least. Pugin understood this. Nobody was ever more disappointed in his buildings than Pugin himself, but those who have found themselves at his churches in Dudley or Stockton on a winter afternoon will fully sympathize.

A later generation, faced with the undeniable inadequacy of Pugin's oeuvre to account for his equally undeniable importance, found another explanation, one which Pevsner had also suggested. Pugin, it was now said, was important as a theorist for introducing the French rationalist tradition of Cordemoy and Laugier to English architecture. No evidence that Pugin was aware of, let alone interested in, such a tradition has been offered, beyond the fact that 'his father was French'.[13] Nevertheless it was, by 1996, felt to have been a 'long . . . recognised' fact.[14] Pugin, who read little and that little unsystematically, formed his ideas from different sources and in different ways, as his biography reveals.

To see Pugin steadily means to see him whole and in his time. He himself never admitted any distinction between his work and his life any more than between his faith and his art. His importance was, as his contemporaries said, that he inspired, transformed and reinvigorated English architecture and design. To see him only as an architect, or as a writer or as a Catholic, will always produce a baffling and partial view. At the turn of another century it is easier perhaps to put Pugin together again, to sympathize with what he felt and wanted. The confidence of the post-war town planners has long since evaporated. We feel, once more, that there is something wrong with our cities and that perhaps this has something to do with ourselves. Fifty years ago the association of religion with art and politics seemed peculiarly Victorian. But 'the God question' does not go away and a new millennium poses it again.[15] The passage of time has not made Pugin's bad buildings any better, but it has yielded a fuller appreciation of the best and revealed new qualities of insight and daring in buildings that were little considered in the nineteenth century, obscure village schools, country parsonages and unrealized designs for churches. His work contains, like a densely packed capsule, almost everything that followed with the High Victorians, the Arts and Crafts movement and in the works of Ruskin and Morris. Working in every medium, in glass and metal and stone and as a pattern designer of Mozartian facility, it would take three generations to develop all that was implicit in Pugin's short career.

Pugin's story begins with his parents'. He lived with them for half his life and their deaths propelled him into the central crisis of his life. His father, Auguste Charles (whom I shall call Auguste for clarity), was a French émigré, the *soi-disant* Comte de Pugin. When Kenneth Clark wrote *The Gothic Revival* it was A. C. Pugin, the artist of *The Microcosm of London*, who was better remembered than his son. Pugin's early work grew seamlessly out of his father's, while his clever, caustic mother, Catherine Welby, largely shaped his peculiar cast of mind. It was she who gave him the idea for *Contrasts*, his first important book.

Catherine and Auguste Pugin were Georgians, born before the French Revolution, and already in their forties in 1812. They belonged to a different age from that in which their son reached adulthood. 'From the England of Miss Austen,' Froude wrote, soon after Pugin's death, 'to the England of Railways and Free-trade, how vast the change . . . The world moves faster and faster . . . The temper of each new generation is a continual surprise.'[16] It was essential to Pugin's character and to his place in history that he belonged as much to the England of Jane Austen as to the Victorian age. He articulated and in part he brought about the change of temper from one to the other. That gave him his importance and his success. It accounted also for the bitterness of his last years. Formed by the Georgian age he violently rejected, he was never wholly at ease with the Victorian ethos he helped to form.

In one of Pugin's sketchbooks there is a note, written by his widow, Jane, in 1867. She was forty then and had been widowed for fifteen years. Her marriage, the most vivid experience of her life, had lasted four.

Who has used this pencil? Old Mr Pugin and Augustus at least 40 years old!! & here I am writing on the sofa in my room on Monday April 27th '67 Kate is singing in the attic 'I dreamt I dwelt in marble halls' Mary and Peter are in the library I do not feel well I do not think I shall long be here . . . I have nothing to live for.[17]

It is a scene from Dickens, or Millais; the still handsome but melancholy widow repining on the sofa, the parlour ballad floating down the stairs. Outside, beyond the heavy curtains, the rattle of railways and free trade is audible. Turning the pages of the same sketchbook we are suddenly in the England of Miss Austen, among 'old Mr Pugin's' drawings of the trial of Queen Caroline.

Pugin's biography begins there, with his father, Auguste Charles, who first picked up his pencil in Paris, before the Revolution.

Part One

I

Auguste Charles Pugin

In the 1820s, when Auguste Pugin ran a drawing school, he liked to amuse his teenage pupils, and no doubt himself, with stories of his early life, his aristocratic connections and his hair's-breadth escape from the French Revolution. One of his pupils was Benjamin Ferrey, who later became an architect and, in 1861, wrote the first biography of the Pugins, father and son. Ferrey set down as much as he could remember of what Auguste had told him some forty years before.

The elder Pugin was born in France, in the year 1762; his birthplace is unknown, but he was descended from a family of distinction, his ancestor being a nobleman who raised a hundred soldiers for the service of Fribourg ... in 1477. Pugin witnessed many of the fearful scenes in the French Revolution, and it is said that he fell fighting for the king, and was thrown with some hundred bodies into a pit near the Place de la Bastille, whence he managed to escape by swimming across the Seine, flying to Rouen, and embarking from that place to England.[1]

It is hard to imagine who could have said all this other than Auguste himself, but it has the ring of a tall tale, unaccountable in some details, suspiciously familiar in others. There were several variations: that he had fought a duel, that he was in fact 'le Comte de Pugin', that he had rowed across the Channel with some friends. Auguste was not in any serious sense an impostor. If he allowed the boys in the drawing school to think he was the Comte de Pugin he never made any attempt to claim the title. It is clear, however, from his wife's letters and his son's later efforts to trace the family history that he led them to believe that the Pugins were of the nobility and had been ruined in the Revolution. He concealed many facts about his origins and elaborated others. A humorous man, sceptical about politics, uninterested in religion and no snob, he simply realized, like many exiles, that given a fresh start it was easier to rise in the world if one implied that one had, in fact, come down. The legend of the émigré Count wandering the streets of London in his tricorn hat, with his muff and gold-topped cane, was handed on by his pupils and passed into myth. It became entwined with the romance of the Gothic Revival, where history and fiction mingle easily. Among the possessions still preserved by Auguste's descendants is a ring said to bear the secret sign of the Scarlet Pimpernel. What emerges from the surviving records is as follows.

Auguste Pugin was born in Paris in 1767 or '68 in the parish of St Sulpice, one of seven children of Joseph Nabor Pugin and his second wife, Marie Marguérite Duchène.[2] Pugin is a French Swiss name, originating from Fribourg, and Auguste may well have been distantly related to the hero of 1477. By the mid eighteenth century, however, it was a tenuous connection. Fribourg was then, in all but name, French. The frontier was open and many of the Fribourgeois had settled in France. Most, including Joseph Pugin, came as mercenary soldiers. Swiss mercenaries had fought in France since the Middle Ages and they had a reputation for courage and bravado in keeping with the spirit at least of Auguste's anecdotes. Under Louis XIV they were formed into regular regiments and acquired their distinctive uniform with the tricorn hat. By 1789 there were eleven Swiss regiments in the regular French army. In addition to these there were the Swiss guards, the elite corps who served the King personally.

Joseph Nabor, who described himself at the time of his first marriage in 1752 as the son of Jean-Claude Pugin, a labourer, had, like many of his countrymen, become a soldier in hopes of improving his fortune.[3] Later, he settled in Paris and became a 'Suisse de l'ambassadeur de l'empire'.[4] 'Suisse' described both his nationality and his job in the household of the Imperial Ambassador. He was a 'huissier', something between a guard and an usher, a sort of military footman who would have stood at the door, announcing visitors and showing them in. Joseph's first wife must have died some time during the next fifteen years and at the time of his second marriage Joseph was performing the same function on the staff of the Prince de Salm Salm.[5]

Both his wives were Parisian. The first, Marie Anne Carmentrar, was the daughter of a tinsmith. Of the parents of the second, Auguste's mother, there seems to be no trace. Her sister, however, was the wife of one Michel Dufort, a 'fruitier oranger', or fruit and butter seller, also of

St Sulpice.[6] Elsewhere in the archives there are references to a number of Pugins.[7] Many of them must have been related. They are listed as retired soldiers, household guards like Joseph, a goldbeater, two French polishers, a post office official, a cloth merchant and one notary. They represent in essence the solid petite bourgeoisie, the class that Louis-Sébastien Mercier described in his great portrait of the city before the Revolution, *Le Tableau de Paris*, as the happiest. He thought them the most productive and contented of the eight ranks into which he divided society, and, ironically in the light of Auguste's later elaborations, the least socially pretentious.

The Paris of the 1780s, in which Auguste reached adolescence, was a hectic, teeming city. Mercier found it in many ways exasperating, light-minded and narcissistic. One aspect of Parisian life that irritated him particularly was the obsession with fashion. He railed against the craze for hats and elaborate headdresses, the latest so tall that they had to be made with built-in springs so that they could be lowered to get into a carriage. Among those who fed the rapidly succeeding passions for clothes, carriages and interior decoration were the editors of a small fortnightly magazine, first published in November 1785, *Le Cabinet des Modes*. It is here, in April the following year, that Auguste first becomes visible in history, making his debut as an illustrator with a drawing of a fashionable carriage, the 'vis-à-vis à l'Angloise'.[8] In May he drew four designs for hats as delightful and impractical as anything Mercier describes, with feathers and enormous brims.

Auguste became a regular contributor to the *Cabinet*, providing drawings, engraved for publication, of luxury goods. His pictures of waistcoats in 'spring yellow' velvet, of panelled boudoirs, elegant shoe buckles and costumes 'à la Turque' are all that remains of this part of his life. That he was working at eighteen suggests financial need as much as talent. As the months passed the perspective in his work became noticeably steadier and the line stronger. Who taught him to draw or whether he had anything so formal as lessons is not known, although there were a number of schools of design in Paris, notably the Ecole Royale, which were free to pupils. By now Auguste seems to have been moving on the fringes of the commercial art world, for it was about this time that he met the painter Louis Lafitte. It was to be a lifelong friendship. Lafitte later married one of Auguste's sisters and, like Auguste, went on to greater things, but at this time his family were among the 'artisans obscurs' with whom the dissolute but charming painter Simon Mathurin Lantara would lodge.[9]

The *Cabinet des Modes* bubbled on happily over the next few years. After the storming of the Bastille it appeared several days late, with apologies for the delay 'due to circumstances too well-known and unfortunate' to need explanation.[10] In November Auguste published a fold-out plate of an elegant salon interior hung with blue taffeta. Then at the beginning of the next year the *Cabinet* changed hands. It ceased to credit the illustrators and Auguste disappears, once more, from view. The *Cabinet* kept up with the changing times, offering outfits with tricolours and a costume for a 'femme patriote en négligée'.[11] Gradually, however, events overwhelmed it. The quality of the paper declined and in the dark days of February 1793 its cheery little light was snuffed out.

By then Auguste had left Paris. Exactly when he went and whether alone or not remains a mystery. The mutable city was changing once again in the greatest upheaval it had ever known; everyone was on the move, while in the background could be heard 'the dull roar of a vanishing world, the distant noise of a crumbling society'.[12] Chateaubriand remembered that: 'Those who had lost sight of one another for twenty-four hours could not be sure of ever meeting again. Some took the road of revolution; others made plans for civil war; others set off for Ohio, sending on ahead plans of country houses to be built among the savages . . . all this cheerfully and often without a sou in their pockets.'[13] Louis Lafitte won the Prix de Rome in 1791, the last artist to receive it from Louis XVI, and left for Italy. His departure may have prompted Auguste to make his own way out of Paris. Whatever his reason for crossing the Channel, he was in London on 27 March 1792, when he enrolled in the Royal Academy Schools. On 20 April France declared war on Austria. Nearly a quarter of a century of conflict in Europe followed. It was almost thirty years before he saw Paris again.

One of the more believable parts of Auguste's story is his assertion that he found his early days in London difficult. He never learned to speak English fluently and probably knew none when he arrived. Neither can he have had much money. Yet he was an engaging, gregarious young man, still in his early twenties, well used to the ways of a big city and with some proven ability as an artist. He had, too, a gift, which he passed on to his son, for falling easily into conversation with anyone who interested him, and a great directness and warmth of manner. It was typical of him, many years later, when writing a bread-and-butter letter to his landlord about repairs to the family home, to conclude, 'I am sure you will hear with interest that your house has been a very successful one to me having met with a great deal of encouragement professionally, since I am in it ... wishing you ... every success and happiness you deserve.'[14]

There was by now a significant émigré community in London. Auguste met, or already knew, the engraver Paul Condé and together they drank tea in Soho (a centre of émigré life), talked of art and followed 'les chemins de l'académie'.[15] A reproachful letter from one of his sisters in Paris, complaining that he has made no effort to keep in touch, suggests that Auguste settled down quickly and suffered little from homesickness. The Academy, then in Somerset House in the Strand, was the focus of English artistic life and taste. Classes were free but entry was competitive. Auguste must have produced a sufficiently impressive portfolio to gain his letter of admission. Once accepted, his studies would have included lectures on painting, architecture, anatomy and geometry, life classes and drawing from casts and models. He enrolled just a month after the death of the Academy's first President, Joshua Reynolds, whose influence was still pre-eminent in the English view of art. This was the classical, Enlightenment view, that the artist was to represent a higher truth, transcending what Reynolds called the 'little and mean' world of direct sensory experience.[16] The most highly regarded genre – in theory, though in practice it was the least popular – was history painting, idealized, heroic scenes. There were already, however, signs of a change of taste, of romantic sensibility, a different view of nature and of what was suitable subject matter for art. It was apparent in the growing popularity of landscape painting and in the rising taste for watercolours by Thomas Hearne, Michael 'Angelo' Rooker, Paul Sandby and many others, which favoured more evocative, emotional depictions of nature, emphasizing light and shade over line and form.

At the Academy Auguste would have encountered this view of art not so much in the painting classes as in the lectures on architecture. The professor was a watercolour painter, Thomas Sandby, who, through his teaching, effected a revolution in architectural drawing. He encouraged his students to make not merely plans and sections of a design but to create an imaginary portrait of a building as it would look in its setting.

With this 'perspective view' patrons might begin to imagine how they would feel about living in it or walking past it, to consider qualities more abstract and subjective than elevations alone could convey. Unrolling one of his great teaching drawings, 'The Bridge of Magnificence', Sandby told the students to consider 'how much more Picturesque than a Geometrical Elevation' such a perspective was and how much better calculated to show their designs to advantage.[17] The effect was instant. The 'powerful impression the sight of that beautiful work' made on the young John Soane was typical.[18] The perspective became an established feature in architectural drawing. It called for something of the illustrator's skill as well as an ability to paint in watercolour, and these were talents which many architects lacked. Thus a new profession emerged, one that suited Auguste precisely, and it was there that he was to find his niche in England, as one of the first generation of architectural perspectivists.

Some time over the next two years he got a job as a draughtsman, working for John Nash. Nash went on to become one of the most successful architects of his or any other day. To him we owe some of the most characteristic buildings of late Georgian England – the Brighton Pavilion, Regent Street, Regent's Park, All Souls, Langham Place, and Buckingham Palace. In the early 1790s, however, things were not going so well. Nash was in his forties and already had one, disastrous, career behind him. At a time when divorce was rare and expensive he had instituted proceedings against his wife in particularly sensational circumstances.[19] He had also been bankrupt. Later he wrote his rackety early life out of his autobiography, claiming that he had lived as a private gentleman on his estate in Wales for many years before discovering that he had a talent for architecture. It was a less ambitious tale than Auguste's but one more seriously calculated to deceive. In the 1790s, when both of them were trying to put a respectable front on an obscure background, they must have had some fellow feeling. Certainly both had a flair for self-dramatization.

Down in Carmarthen, where he was rebuilding his career, Nash had taken a lease on the local theatre. This allowed him to indulge his passion for acting and to mingle on easy terms with the local gentry. In 1795 Charles Mathews, on the verge of a career as one of the greatest comic actors of his day, found himself appearing there. He acted with Nash in *The School for Scandal*. The scenery, which he thought 'capital', was painted by Auguste.[20] Auguste later claimed to have been the original of Mathews's popular character, M. Mallet, a comic French émigré. In fact Mallet was based on an episode Mathews witnessed in America. It seems more likely that the inspiration went the other way and Auguste took something of his own flamboyant style from 'the very finest part' Mathews ever had, an Englishman's idea of a Frenchman, 'almost serious, perfectly tragic in some scenes' and at the same time richly comic.[21]

Over the years that followed Auguste made different kinds of drawings for Nash, but his special strength – which he later put at the disposal of other architects and engineers – was the evocative perspective view. He bodied forth and glamorized designs, setting them in perfect light and modulating them with subtle shadow, refining details. He flattered and improved them so much that his pupil Ferrey felt in many cases they 'might in strictness claim him as their author', a remark that has prompted more than one fruitless attempt to reattribute the works of Nash and others to Auguste.[22] In fact he never developed a career as an architect. The occasional garden building, gateway or little villa was as far as his talents or his luck ever took him in that direction. It was in the interstices between art, design and architecture that he found his place, primarily as an illustrator. Auguste's fate was always to be close to great events, but never at their centre. When taste or fashion turned a corner, when a peace treaty was signed or a monarch crowned, he was usually there, no more than a figure in the crowd but near the front and holding a pencil. Now his introduction to Nash put him instantly in touch with the most advanced aesthetic theory of the day.

Carmarthen was a 'very flourishing place' which offered plenty of opportunities for an architect. There was a large number of 'respectable and opulent individuals' among the commercial middle class who were anxious to improve the town.[23] In his work in Wales, however, Nash did more than consolidate his practice. It was here that he encountered men and ideas which prompted him to develop a style that was quite original, both architecturally and in its conception of the relation of buildings to landscape. This was the Picturesque, whose leading architect he became. The Picturesque was England's most significant contribution to aesthetic theory. It had its effect on literature, on theatre and on art, but its most enduring influence was in architecture and landscape design. In so far as Pugin himself has a place in the history of aesthetic ideas, the idea that matters is the Picturesque, which he was to absorb from his father and, in time, to transform. It was the single most important theme in English architecture until modernism, and modernism, in its English form, was still haunted by the Picturesque.

The word itself was not new when Nash came to Carmarthen; it had been popularized by William Gilpin, who defined it first simply enough as 'that kind of beauty which is agreeable in a picture'.[24] In 1782 Gilpin published his *Observations on the River Wye*, the first of many guidebooks to encourage visitors to appreciate the qualities of the scenery they were passing through. In the last decade of the century, however, the Picturesque took on a new and more complex significance. Circumstances combined to transform it from a general term into a vital idea. The most important circumstance was the war, for after 1793 nobody, however rich, could take a Continental tour, so the wealthy and cultivated, and the less wealthy but enterprising, began to turn their eyes and sketchbooks towards local scenery and sights. The already popular trip down the Wye Valley was established as Everyman's Grand Tour. Out of this new interest in native landscape an unlikely quartet of pioneers emerged. They were two Whig squires, Uvedale Price and Richard Payne Knight, whose estates lay in the Picturesque heartland on the Welsh borders; Humphry Repton, the son of an excise man, the first person to call himself a landscape gardener; and John Nash.

The Picturesque developed in their hands into the aesthetic branch of Romanticism. It was a theory of art that put the personal and the particular above the powerful and the public. It dealt in the semitones of experience, its moods were meditative, 'it neither tenses nor relaxes', Price wrote.[25] Its preferred season was autumn, its time of day twilight, which 'connects what before was scattered'.[26] The Picturesque fed on the power of memory and association, the interchange of subjective and objective experience. In their subject matter, like Wordsworth and Coleridge slightly later, its proponents saw interest 'where a common eye sees nothing but ruts and rubbish'.[27] In architecture and landscape they favoured the asymmetric, the rough and the vernacular. The cottage and the barn were to them what the Cumberland Beggar and the Idiot Boy were to the poets. Knight and Price, the theorists, were well aware of the social and political implications of their arguments about land and nature. The Clee hills in Herefordshire were rich in coal and iron ore. Knight's own fortune came from Bringewood Ford, owned by his grandfather, an ironmaster. Yet industrialization disturbed him. He feared for the 'wild, rich and solitary' landscape that he loved and in his writings his aesthetic theories were worked out in a critique that was as much political as philosophical.[28] Burke, the proponent of the Sublime and the opponent of the French Revolution, was his particular target, for Knight was not only a Whig but a pantheist and one of those supporters of the Revolution who thought even the Terror justified. Nash and Repton, the practitioners, were less philosophical. Nash was not philosophical at all, while Repton was pragmatically conservative. From a professional point of view he could not subscribe to doctrines that left nature as little altered as the squires would have liked, for there would have been no scope for him, and since landscape gardening was expensive he was dependent on the upper classes. He did not want to see his clientele guillotined. He did, however, write and his *Sketches and Hints on Landscape Gardening* which appeared in 1795 did much to popularize the Picturesque. Its terminology of 'variety', 'pleasing association' and the all-seeing 'eye of taste' was soon the smart slang of the cultivated classes.

Nash met Uvedale Price in about 1790, when Price was building himself a small summer retreat in Aberystwyth in a romantic spot between the sea and the castle ruins. Nash at once persuaded him he needed an architect and proposed a typical villa of the time, symmetrical and four-square on the outside. Price objected that he wanted a building that reflected his own ideas. It was to face in several directions, its plan dictated not by symmetry but by the various views, 'the rooms turned to particular points'.[29] He also wanted the house close to the sea, showing Nash 'the effect of the broken foreground and its varied line, and how by that means the foreground was connected with the rocks in the second ground'.[30] In other words he suggested building with the landscape rather than merely imposing upon it. Nash built Castle House perched above the shore with turrets and angles, 'a strange geometrical experiment', long since demolished.[31] It broke rules of architectural propriety that had prevailed for generations. Its asymmetric shape and appearance were dictated by personal preference, by the light at certain times of day and by the landscape. It did not oppose art to the 'little and mean' experience of nature but embraced nature and formed itself in relation, in conversation, with it. Nash developed the possibilities suggested by Castle House with rapidity and daring over the following years in a succession of houses and villas. Soon after he met Price he was introduced to Repton. 'We were charmed with each other,' Repton recalled. 'Two such congenial minds were never brought together since the days of David and Jonathan!'[32] For a while, until Repton discovered that Nash was not to be trusted, especially not with money, they collaborated very happily, with Repton bringing several important clients Nash's way.

So it was that from 1790 onwards Knight, Price, Repton and Nash developed the theory and the practice of the Picturesque. Between themselves they formed alliances, built houses, created landscapes and published books. By the time the century turned they had all quarrelled, but by then the Picturesque was established in the national imagination as a way of describing the relationship of interior mood to exterior stimulus, of understanding the effects of light and colour, in nature and in architecture, on human sensibility. It had its texts and its terminology. After 1800 every educated person knew why an open view was soul-expanding and why autumn made one sad.

Auguste meanwhile bobbed along in Nash's wake. He made drawings of Nash's schemes and indeed exhibited a design of his own for a villa at the Royal Academy. No trace of it survives, but in about 1796 he wrote a letter to a client which gives an idea of what it must have been like. Sending his patron plans for a modestly scaled house, he explained that if they were satisfactory then the actual appearance of it, the elevations, could be decided later, 'being a matter of taste and particular fancy we can vary it at pleasure without varying the ground plan'.[33] Here, quite casually set out, was the idea of designing from plan to elevation with which his son was later supposed to have overturned every principle of Georgian architecture.[34] Auguste's letter went on, with an almost audible clearing of the throat, to a disquisition on the Picturesque which he preferred to write down, he said, because 'I always feel a mistrust of my language in speaking.'[35] What follows has so much the air of a prepared piece that he was possibly also afraid of forgetting it:

Rustic architecture now . . . so fashionable in this country in constructing what is called the gentleman's cottage had its rise from the eye of taste observing how beautifully the strait uniformity of the horizon is broken and relieved by the picturesque irregularity of outline formed only from motives of convenience in building the farm house the millers house, the husbandman's cottage the fisherman's hut and the play of light and shadow caught by their irregular masses: Science has refined upon these circumstances and reducing them to regular principles has formed the rustic into a separate branch of architecture . . . its ground principles are variety in the out line, irregularity in the masses . . .[36]

And so he went on at considerable length, paraphrasing Repton, about the approach, the view – where an analogy between the unresting eye and the dove from Noah's ark led him into some syntactical confusion – and the setting. He concluded on a note of reassurance, the importance of which he had no doubt learned from Nash: 'I will only allow myself to say one thing more, which is perhaps not the least material – it is my opinion such a cottage as I have designed, with the grounds and every part formed complete would be finished for less rather than above the sum you mentioned.'[37] The patter of the Picturesque became for many architects, including Auguste, something of a sales pitch. Yet for all the persiflage it was in these 'regular principles' that the origins of Pugin's own true principles, pronounced a generation later, lay. Nash and Auguste designed from plan to elevation and Nash believed, as Pugin did later, that ornamental details should 'be essential parts of the construction . . . growing out of the necessity of the things themselves'.[38]

The theories that Auguste was boiling down for his patrons were in implication much wider. Knight especially, the most intellectually original of the quartet, made suggestions about the psychology of perception and the symbolic nature of art that looked forward to the next century. Pevsner could find no other word for them than 'psychoanalytical'.[39] Knight also described the essential quality of Gothic architecture in a way that looks forward to Pugin: 'Dim and discoloured light diffused . . . through unequal varieties of space, divided but not separated . . . thus effects more imposing have been produced, than are, perhaps, to be found in any other works of man.'[40] With the singular exception of John Soane, however, it would be the next generation who felt and built like that. For the moment the architecture of the Picturesque remained largely pragmatic, a matter of refined taste rather than passion.

As Nash prepared for his return to London he put his draughtsmen to work on a set of drawings showing his restoration of St Davids cathedral. These, he hoped, would advertise his impending arrival and make a favourable impression with the Society of Antiquaries. They did not, but they did bring Auguste for the first time in touch with the growing enthusiasm for medieval architecture.

While the English were obliged to stay at home they began to look more closely not just at their landscape but also at its ancient buildings, with their obviously Picturesque qualities of rough irregularity and pleasing association. It requires an effort of historical imagination now to realize what a change this was, how neglected and how little respected the architecture of the Middle Ages had generally been in the eighteenth century. Most people thought it crude and primitive. Churches either fell into ruin or were adapted to modern use regardless of their historic fabric. Restoration or 'improvement' took little account of archaeological accuracy, and Nash was one of the most cavalier restorers. He had patched and added to the cathedral with abandon. Auguste made a perspective for him showing 'The Ancient City of St David's' that set the cathedral at the centre, obscuring the town itself, which was generally agreed at the time to be a 'most grievous disappointment' to visitors, and of a 'wretched and sickening appearance'.[41] There was no hint of that in the drawing. The question of whether or not the Antiquaries would agree to have the watercolours engraved disappears quietly from the minutes of the Society's meetings.[42] A flavour of the unminuted discussion can be had, however, from the article on St Davids later published in the *Gentleman's Magazine*. Its author was John Carter, a prominent antiquary and energetic journalist. He was immensely sarcastic about Nash's 'tasteful performance' as a restorer, which he thought vulgar and 'ridiculous beyond expression'.[43]

At this level of magazine journalism a general, educated readership was beginning to be increasingly disquieted by the barbaric treatment of historic buildings by contemporary architects. The worst offender was James Wyatt, but he was largely typical of his time in seeing medieval cathedrals as untidy and decrepit buildings in need of reorganization. Wyatt had taken medieval stained glass out of Salisbury to lighten it and was just now proposing to demolish the twelfth-century galilee porch of Durham to make way for a carriage drive for the bishop. Carter was determined to stop him and he succeeded. Such campaigns to save medieval buildings gathered momentum over the following decades and in time Auguste became much involved with the documenting of Gothic architecture. For the moment, however, neither he nor Nash seems to have taken the disappointment with the Antiquaries too hard.

In 1798 at the Royal Academy Nash showed a group of pictures, 'Three Cottages and Three Entrances' (the 'entrances' would have been lodges or gatehouses). They were designs intended to flush out a client who might commission a picturesque estate village. It seems likely that the pictures and possibly the designs themselves were by Auguste.[44] He was also beginning to branch out on his own and was now invited to the Earl of Essex's estate at Cassiobury to make drawings. Wyatt was busy here too, Gothicizing the house, and Repton was improving the grounds with a lake and a canal. A number of artists, including Turner, received a similar invitation. Such entrées to aristocratic patrons were not uncommon, for the artist enjoyed a socially ambiguous status that allowed him to cross the barriers of class. Auguste, whose charmingly broken English made him especially unplaceable, cultivated from now on something of a sideline as a semi-professional country house guest and typically took advantage of his visit to Cassiobury to propose to the Earl a little improvement to a garden building.

Nash was now ready to move on. His performance as Peter Teazle must have been one of his last in Carmarthen. Later that year he took a lease on two sites in Dover Street in London and by the following Christmas had built two houses, one for himself and one to rent. His own, number twenty-nine, proclaimed Nash's arrival in the capital as a man of property and importance. It had a front as bold as its designer, wider than the other houses in the street with a three-bay colonnade, 'impudence in bricks and mortar – and stucco', his biographer called it.[45]

Nash was on his way to fame and success. He had left his debts and his wife behind and was soon to leave Repton with as little compunction, sailing smoothly on as the century turned. In 1801 he submitted designs for a new building at Magdalen College, Oxford. Auguste made the perspective and no doubt devised much of the profuse detail in this glamorous, 'somewhat fantastic' and unrealized scheme.[46] He too was now settled in London, more modestly than his employer, in lodgings off Hanover Square, a part of London thick with minor artists. He seems to have continued to piece together a makeshift living out of freelance work for Nash and others. Repton's son George, who remained in Nash's office after his father's quarrel with him, was now training to become an architect in his own right, but Auguste could probably not afford such a formal apprenticeship even had he wanted one.

In 1800 he published his first known etchings, adding another technical string to his bow.[47] He had many friends and connections now among the commercial artists and illustrators in London, but he was not exactly thriving. Professionally he was doing little more than keeping his head above water, and he had turned thirty. As the war moved on towards its second decade and the prospect of invasion threatened, there was a mood of caution and retrenchment. Commissions were not easily come by. Auguste seems to have moved several times. In 1801 he drew the back of 6 Elkins Road, Bayswater, a very humble, not to say shabby-looking place which may have been his lodgings in what was then still a village outside London.[48] At the beginning of the next year he was in Marylebone. That was where he was living in February 1802, when he married Catherine Welby.

2

Catherine Welby

There was never any question about the origins of the Welby family. The stained-glass figure of Johannes de Welby, armed cap-à-pie, had knelt in the north-east window of Ropsley church in Lincolnshire since the thirteenth century.[1] The name, like the church, was older still, Saxon in origin. There had been Welbys in Lincolnshire before the Conquest.[2]

Over the generations they had married into other local landowning families, the Cholmeleys of Easton, the Halls at Westborough, the Gregorys, the Earles and the Glynnes.[3] They had still, in the eighteenth century, to achieve a baronetcy but they were immovably fixed at the solid centre of county society. Their principal seat was – and still is – at Denton. A forceful impression of the Welbys' sense of their place in this world and the next is conveyed by the monument there to Richard Welby, who died in 1713. Carved in marble he stands, life size, in the parish church, in a full-bottom wig framed by a Baroque portico. Tiny putti weep over his large head, on which they place a heavenly crown.[4]

Catherine Welby's father, one of many Williams, belonged to a junior branch of the family. He owned land but it was not enough to allow him to live in any style on his estates. He became instead an attorney, practising in King's Bench.[5] He was admitted to Middle Temple in 1759 at the age of thirty-five, but although Benjamin Ferrey – or perhaps Catherine herself – promoted him to a 'distinguished barrister', he was never called to the Bar.[6]

William Welby took a house in Islington, which was then still a village about a mile to the north of London. It seems he married twice. His first wife, Elizabeth Caesar, apparently died soon after the birth of a daughter, Selina, in 1764. Three years later he married another Elizabeth, Twyford. She was also from Lincolnshire and she brought him some more small landholdings. They had three children, Catherine, Montagu

William and Adlard. No record of Catherine's birth has come to light but she must have been born in 1768 or '69, making her almost exactly Auguste's contemporary.[7] Montagu, who died in infancy, was born in 1773 and Adlard, the youngest, in 1776. Nothing more telling than a small silhouette has survived to record Catherine's appearance. A poem written to her by an admirer refers to a Roman nose and auburn hair. Even Ferrey, who was frightened of her as a boy and portrayed her as a hysteric and a martinet, agreed that she was good-looking. She was also, as he acknowledged, acutely intelligent and unusually well read. She gave her husband the idea for his most successful book and hers was the dominating influence on her son for the first half of his life.

Catherine Welby grew up between two worlds, equally attached to both, and her temperament developed as a result into a volatile mixture of conservatism and independence, in which her son took after her. An avowed respect for certain social and intellectual principles never overrode her passionate attachment to her own ideas, a passion bordering at times on obsession. In Lincolnshire the Welbys inhabited the England of Jane Austen. The county was not much touched by the industrialization that struck Knight and Price in Herefordshire. Isolated from its neighbours by the Humber, the Trent and by the undrained fens to the south, it had no centre of population large enough to breed an intellectual community. London news reached Lincolnshire late and made no great impression when it arrived. The young Welbys had a widespread network of cousins, from whom, when they were in Islington, there came frequent letters. The eighteenth-century idea of family 'connexion' extended ties of obligation through many degrees of kinship, to second and third cousins. This broad but finely nuanced sense of family was the essence of social identity in county life.

Catherine and her brother and half-sister were well aware that they were poor relations. Through her correspondence Catherine might hear about the fireworks at Belvoir Castle and catch a glimpse of the Prince of Wales at dinner. She could join her cousins' mockery of Mrs Welby of Denton, with her sycophancy, her extravagance and her unfortunate hair, but she would never herself take part in such scenes. She grew up to be touchy about questions of social distinction and something of a snob. A witty woman and a sharp observer of character, she was never fond of jokes against herself.

At home in Islington, growing up through the 1780s and '90s, she inhabited a very different milieu. The house where the Welbys lived is now 88 Islington High Street; it was then Number 3 Pullins Row.[8] Mr Welby had rented it from Mr Pullin himself, a dairy farmer, and Islington was still rural enough for dairy farming to be the mainspring of its economy. But among the population of 6,500 there was already a noticeable number of intellectuals – writers, Radicals, dissenters and antiquaries. Living a short distance from the Green and an even shorter one from the Angel Inn, the Welbys counted among their neighbours over the years Charles and Mary Lamb, Coleridge (briefly), the engraver Richard Earlam, Grimaldi the clown, Rousseau's publisher, the translator of Handel's *Messiah*, the co-founder of the Royal Humane Society and any number of dissenting divines. Thomas Paine was living at the Angel when he wrote *The Rights of Man*.

Neither the age nor the place was entirely stable, or refined. Going to his rooms in Essex Court in Middle Temple Mr Welby would have seen on Temple Bar the rotting heads of Jacobites, executed after the rising of 1745. During the Gordon Riots in 1780 Clerkenwell jail was broken open and the prisoners flooded on to Islington Green. Catherine was twenty at the time of the French Revolution and with her brother Adlard entered with enthusiasm into the debate it engendered in England. They inclined towards the Radical line and later they clubbed together to buy Paine's *The Age of Reason*.

Catherine's letters show her to have been as accurate a barometer of advanced opinion as ever lived in Islington. She was for women's rights and for the better treatment of animals, especially the cattle she saw regularly driven down the hill to Smithfield. In religious matters she and Adlard inclined towards deism, the belief that human beings have a natural moral sense which if cultivated will tend towards the common good, and that reason rather than revelation is the basis of faith. They were suspicious of organized religion and critical of the monarchy.

In Lincolnshire of course the Welbys were Tory. At elections the toast was drunk to the 'Wel-by-ing' of the borough, a family joke that was handed down as carefully as the silver. Possibly some resentment of the Denton relations' condescension was mixed up in Catherine and Adlard's youthful radicalism, some vague consoling thought of Mrs Welby in a tumbrel. Elsewhere, however, they found kindred spirits among their relations. The Cholmeleys of Easton were Whigs, and at Cleve in Devon they had a cousin by marriage who was a real Radical,

Thomas Northmore. Catherine later gave his name to her son, in a characteristic gesture of both social and intellectual aspiration. Northmore, who was three years older than her, was kind to his young relatives if somewhat impatient with them, for he was a figure on an altogether larger stage, a free-thinking gentleman in the mould of Knight and Price. Northmore was a founder member of the Hampden Club; he was a linguist, a scientist and an inventor.[9] Faraday acknowledged his work, and he earned a footnote in the history of evolutionary theory by befriending the young Catholic priest John MacEnery and showing him Kent's Cave in Torquay.[10]

Catherine found Northmore intimidating, for her experience was much narrower than her reading. The chief companion of her intellectual adventures was Adlard. They were both deeply attached, Catherine especially, to their elder half-sister, Selina, but Selina's role was always to be the admiring audience. It seems to have been tacitly agreed within the family that Catherine and Adlard were the clever ones. Selina, who never married, stayed at home worrying about everybody's comfort but her own. Often her goodness was presumed on, but her letters never hint at any resentment. They speak consistently of a truly kind, unselfish nature. She became to Pugin one of the heroic maiden aunts in which the nineteenth century was rich.

Family life in Pullins Row, as it is glimpsed through the correspondence of the 1790s, was for the most part lively and cheerful. There are references to dinner parties, assemblies and plays as well as local deaths and marriages. Mr Welby is usually off stage, referred and sometimes deferred to, locked in his study 'as if . . . in prison' during the spring cleaning, playing cards with friends or away in Essex Court.[11] William Welby had not been to university and neither was it, apparently, suggested that his son should go. In 1797 Adlard turned twenty-one and the question of his future had to be considered. Before that, however, to finish his education he set off on the now popular domestic grand tour. From Bristol he went over to Chepstow and sketched the view from the castle, before going on into the Wye Valley and across Wales to Aberystwyth. He and Catherine were as up to date with the Picturesque as with every other intellectual movement.

Adlard felt a suitable melancholy wandering in the remoter mountains, where the only sound was the pleasingly appropriate one of 'a distant bagpipe from some shepherd'.[12] Catherine, who enjoyed a discussion on the relative merits of spring and autumn, wrote back lengthy accounts of her thoughts and impressions. Adlard encouraged the literary skills of 'friend Cath' as he called her: 'above all the description of the storm I admire I thought I saw it all as completely as if present.'[13] In the Welbys' minds, as in many people's, the Picturesque and the Gothic were associated; the sensitive romantic traveller was also expected to be something of an antiquary. Adlard compared the qualities of medieval ruins. Catherine knew John Nichols and Richard Gough's *Biblioteca Topographica Britannica*, which reprinted in ten volumes a wealth of historic documents relating to topographical subjects, and she transcribed extracts from it.

Adlard had, as he admitted, 'an insatiable . . . mania for roving'.[14] As time went by the tour seemed to be stretching on indefinitely, taking him to other popular romantic spots as far afield as Cumbria and the lakes. The following year he was still admiring ruins and sending to Islington for money. A certain anxiety, not to say exasperation – on Mr Welby's part at least – begins to be felt in the correspondence. Rather than settle down to the law, which bored him, Adlard mooted another idea. He wanted to find a remote spot and take a cottage where he would live with like-minded friends; 'I hope one day to collect a little commonwealth,' he wrote and, a few months later, in the autumn of 1798, he and his sister embarked on a scheme for doing just that.[15] This was Adlard and Catherine's attempt to put into practice the social ideals of William Godwin, what Southey and Coleridge called 'pantisocracy', and it would merit them a line or two in the history of Romanticism even if they had no part to play in Pugin's story. Their experiment was brief and only a partial success, but after all Coleridge and Southey, who planned to go to America, never even set sail.

Pantisocracy developed from Godwin's *Political Justice*, which argued that within small groups, withdrawn from the world, a new social order might arise. As Adlard put it: 'The stream of the mind (tho' it receives some good) in society is kept muddy by a flood of error, folly and extravagance . . . retirement alone can purge it and let it flow smoothly as the Derwent which runs by my window.'[16] How urgently Adlard really needed relief from 'the tumult of the political world' is questionable but he was determined to try the experiment.[17] For Catherine, who complained to her brother of the limited scope for action available to women, it was a chance of freedom.

Mr and Mrs Welby gave their headstrong children their way. Adlard rented a cottage at Hasingham in Norfolk, and he and his sister remained there for a year. Catherine, who now talked of writing a novel, practised her descriptive skills in letters to Selina. 'The ground rising so immediately from the house brings our horizon to a very small compass, & often makes me fancy I am an inhabitant of some lesser planet than formerly when I look at our hemisphere on a fine starlight night . . . The prospect over the common would be dreary but for two or three cottages which bounds it to us, which, with the trees that surround the house softens it into a very agreeable pensiveness.'[18] Catherine's letter makes a pair with Auguste's to his client. He was the professional, she the amateur practitioner of the Picturesque.

Norfolk offered Catherine another romantic possibility, the chance she had longed for to see the sea for the first time. They waited for appropriate weather. ' "The morning lowered, & heavily in clouds brought on the day" our sturdy oaks could scarcely brave the wind, while not one drop of moisture fell – a storm's at hand, said Adlard, the very time for Yarmouth.'[19] They set off at once and when she saw it the long-imagined 'world of waters' did not disappoint. Catherine stood on the shore 'lost in admiration in wonder & delight'.[20] There is something touching at this moment about the brother and sister, almost exact contemporaries of William and Dorothy Wordsworth, staring out to sea in their own attempt to reach towards the infinite and the eternal.

Life at Hasingham, however, was not without its privations. Discussions of the pleasures of solitude were interspersed in letters home with urgent requests for bottled water, fly powder and sausages. It was Selina of course who was responsible for organizing all this. Catherine and Adlard did not preserve her letters with the same care with which she kept theirs. One survival from about this time, however, catches her tone, that of a young Miss Bates, kindly, anxious and full of small news: 'I should have wrote again before this but first I waited to hear . . . if the trunk arrived safe, then my father would write in this paper, then changed his mind, and then I thought you would not wish to have two letters from home in one day. Mary left me on Thursday, you recollect telling me Miss White, where Mrs Brooke lodged was married, very well, it is there Mary is going to live . . .'[21]

While Adlard went back to Islington to discuss the ever more tender topic of his future employment, Catherine stayed at Hasingham. She had her brother's pistols ready and was not afraid, she said, to use them. Brooding alone, she wrote a letter on the subject of female courage and the subjugation of women that was so 'wild' that Adlard and Selina hardly dared read it to her parents.[22] If, as is perfectly likely, she had read Mary Wollstonecraft's *Vindication of the Rights of Woman*, she was prepared to go much further, certainly in terms of rhetoric:[23] 'what rage! what indignation! what shrieks! what howling and lamentation was heard on earth and cast to heaven when first a conquered sex they felt themselves defenceless. I think I see the mother of a family struggling with the father of her children now her oppressor . . . look round yourself upon the female world & however the spirit of their Fore-Mother may be degenerated in them in regard to object its restless violence may be discovered every where . . .'[24] This capacity for passionate, indeed hysterical tirades was the side of Catherine that later frightened Benjamin Ferrey, and it was the side of her son that variously frightened, repelled or inspired his contemporaries.

The 'commonwealth' never materialized. It was decided to give up the cottage when the year was out, 'just when I had begun to reap the benefits of our labour', Catherine lamented, though there was an unmistakable note of relief at the thought of coming home.[25] Before she did so, however, she had several 'questions', which were in fact somewhat peremptory requests, to which she wanted answers from Selina 'by next Saturday'.[26] Chief among them was that she should have a room of her own, as well as her bedroom, 'and be allowed to fit it up according to my own ideas of comfort'.[27]

She had turned thirty and was, perhaps, resigned to the idea that she would never marry. 'When we are to spend all our time at home, it becomes necessary that we should find our happiness there in the comforts it affords us, and the not having a room I could positively call my own I have always felt a great inconvenience.'[28] The room duly became hers. Adlard was less easily settled. Catherine had already tartly suggested that he take their father's advice and become an attorney, for 'it would be agreeable to [his] wishes you should pursue the law, as being better than the laws pursuing you'.[29] However, he still prevaricated. In 1801 he married a cousin, Elizabeth Hall, one of the Halls of Westborough. The marriage neither eased his wanderlust nor brought him happiness for very long. It was decided that he should go to Lincolnshire and farm, which he did with no very good grace, settling, about now, at Rauceby.

Catherine returned to Islington, to her own room, her piano, her books and her friends. Some time soon afterwards she met Auguste Pugin, possibly at one of the many supper parties to which the Welbys seem to have been invited. To a woman of her tastes and temperament, with a vivid imagination but a limited and in certain ways naïve view of the world, he must have presented a figure of tremendous glamour. Engaging in himself, he trailed clouds of reflected glory – a witness of the Revolution, an acquaintance of the famous Mr Repton and the increasingly famous Mr Nash, an artist and a man of taste. She saw someone with whom she might live out her ideas about the relations between the sexes, an intellectual companion as well as a husband. What Auguste told her of his earlier life at this stage is not clear. Much wiser in the ways of the world than she, he probably realized that however much she was a Radical in theory she was too much of a Welby to relish the idea of marrying the son of a freelance soldier turned footman.

Her father was less easily charmed. If he had ceased to hope that his daughter would settle safely into the Lincolnshire gentry, he can never have imagined as a son-in-law a penniless French émigré with no background and no prospects. Whatever Auguste told him about his origins, Mr Welby, whose professional experience in King's Bench had no doubt made him sceptical of elaborate autobiographies, had his doubts. His younger daughter was of age, however, and of very determined character. He did what he could. He remade his will, putting Catherine's modest inheritance, £2,000 of government stock with 4 per cent interest, into Adlard's care, for her 'use and benefit . . . Not to be subject to the debts, [or] countroul . . . of any husband whatsoever.'[30]

It was perhaps because of this *froideur* that Catherine and Auguste were not married, as convention would have dictated, in her parish church but in his, St Mary, Marylebone. Loyal Selina, of course, attended the service on 2 February 1802. Mr Welby, it would seem, did not, for Catherine wrote him a dignified if somewhat high-flown letter:

Dear and most respected sir

I cannot leave my paternal roof without reflecting upon the many blessings I have enjoyed under it, or think of them, without having my mind filled with the most grateful sentiments towards yourself & my mother from whom they have flowed . . . I this morning give my hand to Mr Pugin, after which the first wish of my heart will be, to be allowed with my husband, to give our personal respects to yourself & my mother, for I must ever remain, under all changes of circumstances,

your gratefully affectionate daughter
Catherine Welby[31]

It was only figuratively that Catherine was leaving the paternal roof. Although Auguste had taken a room in Edward Street near Portman Square for professional purposes, the newly married couple could not contemplate a house of their own. They returned after the wedding to begin their married life in Pullins Row.

3

The Microcosm of London

1802 to 1812

The household adjusted in time to the newcomer. There were at first 'some conversations' which Selina feared upset her sister, but these passed and life duly settled into a pattern.[1] Auguste worked in Edward Street and returned to Islington, where Mrs Welby and Selina spoiled him, according to Catherine, particularly with regard to food. If Mr Welby's doubts persisted, or if he felt irritated by so much fuss made of his son-in-law, he kept his feelings to himself. From a social and material point of view Auguste had done well in marrying Catherine. But the evidence of their letters is that they were in love. The first years of their marriage were happy and companionable, if overshadowed sometimes by anxieties about money and health and by Catherine's desire, much greater than her husband's, that he should make a name for himself. It was almost certainly she who conceived the idea that they should combine their talents in genteel popular journalism.

The month after their wedding the Peace of Amiens was signed. After nearly a decade of war it brought only a fragile truce, one, as Sheridan said, 'which all men are glad of, but no man can be proud of'.[2] Nevertheless, there were celebrations across London. The house of the French minister in Portman Square was brilliantly illuminated with coloured oil lamps and a great 'transparency', a painting on linen lit from behind, which showed 'England and France . . . in the act of uniting their hands in token of amity, before an altar dedicated to humanity'.[3] An orchestra played in the square and crowds gathered to admire the 'taste and novelty' of the scene.[4] Displays of light on such a scale were unimaginably exciting in the days before gas, when streets were only poorly and erratically lit. The transparency was emblazoned with the words 'Peace' and 'Concord'. There was briefly some trouble about this when a group of sailors in the crowd, whose spelling was weak, took it to mean that they had been 'conquered' by the French and began to riot. 'Concord' was hurriedly changed to the unambiguous 'Victory' and the celebrations went on. Catherine made a note of this incident because it obliged Auguste to alter the drawing he was making of the scene. It was to be engraved and Catherine was writing an accompanying description.[5] Cheap prints of this sort with text or 'letterpress' as it was known sold well. When newspapers were still unillustrated it was to the print shops that Londoners went for political satire, for the vicious cartoons of Gillray and the bawdy ones of Rowlandson, and where they bought engraved portraits of prominent people, pictures of current events and the ever more popular topographical views.

The years that followed offered considerable scope for graphic journalism. Catherine and Auguste covered the impeachment of Lord Melville in 1806, which took place in Westminster Hall, the scene of the trials of Thomas More, Guy Fawkes and Charles I. 'That very beautiful specimen of Gothic architecture' was drawn by Auguste 'on the spot from actual observation' packed to the hammerbeams with the famous and the fashionable.[6] 'Within its eventful walls,' Catherine wrote, at her most orotund, 'human greatness has experienced the extreme of vicissitudes: the human heart has suffered all the excess of its various emotions: has now bounded with festive joy; now swelled with triumphant pride; anon palpitated tremulous with fear, or, leaden with grief, has scarcely beat at all.'[7]

Earlier that year Auguste, without Catherine this time, had been commissioned to make watercolours of the greatest state occasion of the decade – for which *The Times* published its first illustration – the funeral of Nelson. This was some of Auguste's best work. In his drawing of the scene at Greenwich, as the coffin set off upriver to St Paul's, the Thames is broken into grey and choppy waves. Everywhere flags at half-mast blow stiff in the January gale, but while clouds overshadow the foreground a great burst of watery sunshine breaks over Wren's Royal Hospital. Auguste knew by now how to create in light and shade and weather that mood of intermingled grief and triumph suitable to the occasion, what Ruskin, much later, would call the 'pathetic fallacy'.

Catherine had made efforts in the first year of their marriage to advance her husband's career through family connections, explaining to the Cholmeleys that he was now 'desirous that he should appear under his own name' as an architect.[8] But when the unsatisfactory peace broke down the threat of invasion loomed and the Cholmeleys, like most landowners, had been reluctant to build. Richard Welby commissioned some pictures, but his letter acknowledging receipt of them suggests that he saw it as a favour and one that he was unlikely to repeat. 'I thank you for the sketches and the care you have taken in executing the views; the smaller one is much warped and will not go into the Frame . . . it is not of great consequence . . . I send you a Draft . . . Pray make my compliments acceptable to the family at Islington.'[9]

Without doubt it was Catherine who set the pace in the Pugins' marriage. She was energetic and ambitious, her husband much less forceful and more indolent. But their differences were for the moment more a subject of teasing and jokes than argument. 'Madame Pugin is a wonderful woman,' Auguste told the young artist Frederick Goodall and his father, even if, as he went on to explain, she insisted on sleeping with the windows open in the middle of winter 'while I . . . am shivering with cold under the blankets'.[10] When they were apart Auguste applied to his wife for advice, which she readily gave, urging him to assert himself, to 'take care to be *handsomely* indemnified' and to calculate his expenses carefully.[11] He, in turn, confided in her the difficulties of the aspirant gentleman artist, angling for opportunities without seeming to presume.

On an exploratory visit to Lincoln he reported on his pursuit of Lord Brownlow: 'At last I catched [sic] his Lordship in the Minster, but surrounded by so many people that it was really a difficult matter to speak . . . he afterwards repeated his invitation to Belton but as he did not pressed it I answered in the negative thinking it would be loosing time and encreasing my expenses for no purpose . . . his ugly wife was with him.'[12] Catherine cherished her husband's affection. If she could not resist theorizing about marriage in the abstract, as 'an union of minds', she was also fond of him in a more ordinary, physical way. Visiting Adlard she wrote home: '. . . by our separation all my pleasures are diminished half and all my pains increased to the whole, since you cannot share either with me . . . Selina says you are cold at night (a kiss) there is something to warm you from yours and ever yours . . .'[13]

Yet her support was not always an unmixed blessing. She found the realities of the professional world at times distasteful. She was easily offended and seems to have fallen out with Nash and his wife when, soon after their marriage, the Pugins went to visit them on the Isle of

Wight. Catherine had hoped that Nash would put some small architectural commission in Auguste's way. When he did not and there was a misunderstanding and an exchange of notes between Nash's East Cowes Castle and the Pugins' lodgings, Catherine was plunged into despair. She had already suffered two early miscarriages and now this disappointment, she thought, brought on a third. She raged against the Nashes and wrote home, saying that she feared she might die, begging Selina to make sure that Mr and Mrs Welby would be kind to Auguste.

It was a sad incident, but telling and not untypical. Catherine was always at the mercy of her intense emotions, and so were those around her. Selina wrote from Islington: 'My thoughts are frequently engaged in regulating your mind as the principal seat of all your troubles . . . it has been a great misfortune to us my dear C. to have been born of too good a family for our fortune, refining our sentiments till we are unfit to bustle with an unfeeling world, or one that appears so when viewed with this refinement of feeling; for in the general way Mr and Mrs N's conduct has been very obliging . . . do not let your mind be so easily agitated.'[14] It was not in Catherine's nature, any more than it was later to be in her son's, to bustle easily with the unfeeling world. In Pugin's case, too, his friends and family would often find it hard to tell how much his episodes of illness and bodily collapse were extrapolations of a state of mind. On this occasion, however, Catherine was soon well enough to enjoy letters and relish the news that Mrs Welby of Denton had appeared at a ball with her hair 'dressed in the french fashion of little wormy sort of ringlets' and had 'never looked worse'.[15] But although Auguste continued to work for Nash after this, the Pugins' relationship with him developed no further, either privately or professionally. It seemed that, after all, commercial art, topical scenes, views and watercolours, offered Auguste his best hope of earning a living. It was as an artist that he listed himself in *Holden's Directory*, a smart, somewhat social publication that gave the London addresses of the gentry as well as those of members of the more select professions. He began to exhibit occasionally at the Royal Academy and he was elected to the newly formed Society of Painters in Water Colour.

The Society was a snook cocked at the Academy and its hierarchy of genres, and it was a confirmation of the standing which watercolour had attained over the previous twenty-five years. The great flowering that produced Turner, Cotman, Girtin, Paul Sandby, and others, gave England a rare moment of supremacy in European art. A generation earlier the watercolour drawing had been, was indeed still considered by the Academy, merely a by-product, a preparatory study for a painting or engraving. Now, the watercolourists declared it a work of art in its own right, on a par with oil painting, and they held their own exhibitions. The founders of the Society, Auguste's occasional collaborator John Claude Nattes, Cornelius Varley, William Pyne and seven others, were not perhaps the best artists, but those who felt the greatest need to promote themselves and their métier. They catered for a middling sort of taste but their work sold well, and it was a great help to Auguste in his still uncertain career to be elected.

His other piece of good fortune was his introduction, probably as a result of his work on Nelson's funeral, to Rudolph Ackermann. Ackermann was a German immigrant, four years Pugin's senior. A tall man, powerfully built and physically and personally imposing, he had, like Pugin, married an Englishwoman. A Lutheran, who took his religion seriously without being stuffy, he stood out in the busy and often unscrupulous world of commercial art and journalism as a beacon of honesty, generosity and entrepreneurial genius. He had premises at 101 Strand, which he called The Repository of the Arts, a suitably capacious name for a place that was at the same time a bookshop, art gallery, tearoom, publishing house and salon, from which he also ran a drawing school. Arguably the first picture dealer of the modern sort, Ackermann saw the potential of watercolour. He sold works by the young Turner, Rowlandson and the apocalyptic painter John Martin, whose career he was largely responsible for launching. He commissioned illustrations from Auguste and probably sold his pictures too.

Auguste later drew the interior of the Repository as it must have looked on a typical morning. The spacious top-lit gallery accommodates a group of shoppers and browsers, leafing through prints, choosing 'fancy goods' for home decoration and passing the time of day. Women are in the majority, for Ackermann catered especially for polite female taste. His strictly moral view of art and business made the Repository utterly respectable and Ackermann understood his clientele because he was one of them. Although he was upright he was also cosmopolitan, with a passion for inventions, especially in print technology, and a belief in progress that was combined with a fondness for the Gothic in art and literature.

So Auguste continued to maintain himself more or less, but between his lack of business sense and his undoubted inclination towards laissez-faire, funds were tight. Catherine, who always felt the uncomfortable gap between her refined breeding and her inadequate fortune, was inclined to overspend. She liked clothes and jewellery and Auguste liked books. Selina's neatly kept accounts show how modest her own wants were and she was always able to spare something from her allowance. She was 'very very kind' in subsidizing her sister and brother-in-law and Adlard too lent them money, which he could ill afford as his own family began to expand, while all such transactions were carefully concealed from the Welby parents.[16] It was after about four years of this unsteady professional existence that Catherine had another idea for her husband and herself. Although it did not make them rich, it was the basis of Auguste's reputation in the twentieth century and it led to the creation of one of the most original and enduring picture books ever produced, *The Microcosm of London*. The *Microcosm*, conceived on the eve of the Regency itself, is, for many more people than know it by name, the quintessential image of Regency London.

Catherine's idea was to produce a variation on the usual sequence of topographical views which 'afforded little more than a representation of . . . public buildings, churches etc.'.[17] This would be a full 'portrait . . . of the metropolis of England'.[18] It would show 'the picturesque and characteristic', the shops, the marketplaces and the schools.[19] More especially, the scenes would not appear as usual with just a few figures included for scale, but would feature equally the 'animate' scenery, 'the modes and customs of streets thronged by men and women . . . hurrying to and fro in the pursuit of pleasure the concerns of business or toiling in the meaner occupations of life'.[20] In other words it would show what London was like, not just what it looked like. According to Catherine's prospectus 'Mr Pugin' had had such a work in contemplation for some time. He would draw the pictures and she would write the text.

Technically and artistically it was a very ambitious project and it was not until they met Ackermann that the Pugins found someone capable of realizing such an elaborate scheme. Ackermann is usually given the credit for creating *The Microcosm of London* and certainly, without him, it would never have appeared. It was he who co-ordinated the production of 104 illustrations, published over three years between 1808 and 1810 with accompanying text. It must soon have been apparent, however, that Catherine lacked the experience and the stamina to produce the letterpress and the task was given to the watercolourist William Pyne, a long-standing friend of Ackermann, who was later replaced by a seasoned hack, William Combe.[21] When it came to the plates Ackermann decided to divide the task between Auguste, who would draw the architectural settings, and Thomas Rowlandson, who put in the figures. Rowlandson was not only hugely popular, he worked quickly, and his involvement in the *Microcosm* considerably increased the chances of its commercial success.

The mechanics – and the tactics – of working with two such different artists presented their own difficulties. Rowlandson was the more versatile and experienced but the burden of the work fell on Auguste, who first provided outlines for approval, then sketches and then finished drawings before Rowlandson put the figures in. It was his most important commission to date and it had been partly his idea, so he fussed over it, asking Rowlandson for numerous changes. Rowlandson's only note in reply suggests laconic exasperation: 'With submission to Mr Pugin's better judgement Mr Rowlandson conceives if the light came in the other side of ye Picture, the figures would be sett off to better advantage.'[22] Ackermann mediated between the artists. This gave him editorial control, very necessary in the case of the irrepressible Rowlandson. Ever since his days at the Royal Academy, 'where he deployed a pea shooter to great effect in the life class, causing the model to lose her pose', he had taken a sceptical view of life and art.[23] He liked teasing Ackermann, who, with his polite clientele in mind, made urgent requests for Rowlandson to raise the necklines of the ladies and tone down the political caricatures.

Technically the *Microcosm* was a landmark in illustrated book production. The plates set the standard by which aquatint has been judged ever since. A technique which 'came in with the romantic era, and wedded itself to the picturesque', it was perfectly suited to reproducing the subtle effects of watercolour.[24] The great triumph of the *Microcosm*, however, is that it achieved exactly what Catherine hoped, it caught the mood of a great city at a single historical moment. 'The metropolis of England at the beginning of the nineteenth century' was, as she and many others knew at the time, a remarkable place.[25] It was the largest city that anyone had ever seen. It was stable and prosperous, while the Continent was in constant upheaval and the spoils of war and revolution flowed into London.

Louis Simond, the Frenchman whose account of his English travels is best known for his meetings with De Quincey and Wordsworth, was struck, in the capital, by the opulence of the shops and the variety of the amusements. He noted the popular interest in science and the number of ladies who attended the lectures of Humphry Davy. He was overawed by the vast West India Dock, where gigantic cargoes of rum and sugar were landed. Visitors also commented on a certain brash philistinism in London life, on the noise, the smoke and the fact that, as Simond put it, if the inhabitants were not exactly dirty, they never appeared to be quite clean either. All of this is captured in the *Microcosm*, along with a great deal else: the courthouses and the prisons, the workhouse, the madhouse and Billingsgate fish market. In scene after scene Auguste's meticulous, tight sense of proportion is the foil for Rowlandson's comic dispro- portion. Everywhere in the plates is the mixture of high taste and low life. Pyne, describing the Pantheon during a masked ball, noted that the company in Rowlandson's drawing is composed 'as these scenes usually are, of . . . peers and pickpockets, honourables and dishonourables'.[26] The same pragmatic scepticism governs the organization of the book itself. The plates being arranged in simple alphabetical order, the reader passes directly from St James's Palace to St Luke's Lunatic Asylum. Since Ackermann took such care to avoid offending polite taste, the *Microcosm* can be read as a fair barometer of a middle-class morality that was tolerant, not to say indifferent. The Freemasons' Hall, the Houndsditch synagogue, the Roman Catholic chapel and the Quaker meeting house are all presented without prejudice, as objects of legiti- mate interest. But so, too, are the condemned prisoners at Newgate, sitting round a coffin to hear their last sermon. A fire, a circus, the House of Lords, everything is spectacle, there for the beholder to enjoy.

Ackermann never produced anything else like the *Microcosm*. It was immediately followed by other illustrated books, on which Auguste was regularly employed. The handsome volumes on Westminster Abbey and the colleges of Oxford and Cambridge are, however, purely descriptive; they have no organizing idea and no humour. The *Microcosm* owes its unique interest to the Pugins' conception.

Just as the third volume was starting to appear in 1809, Catherine's father died. William Welby was eighty-four; his death was not unexpected. He was buried in the family vault he had bought 'in perpetuity' in St Mary's church, Islington.[27] He had seen no reason to change his will and Catherine's inheritance was left in trust to her brother. Adlard, however, made no difficulty about releasing £400 to Catherine and Auguste, with which they took a lease on a new house and, for the first time, could look forward to an establishment of their own. Number 39 Keppel Street, Bloomsbury, was one of hundreds of terraced houses then being built by James Burton, 'the most enterprising and successful London builder of his time', on land belonging to the Duke of Bedford.[28] The Duke had abandoned his town house in 1800 and had been developing the site ever since. Burton bought more of the plots than anyone else. He built many of the plain, stock-brick terraces that give Bloomsbury its architectural character, as well as the larger and more elaborate houses of Russell Square and Woburn Place.

The Pugins, as was usual, took the house as a shell and chose the finishes and fittings themselves. Catherine and Auguste went up to Lincolnshire, where Auguste had undertaken to arrange a jubilee monument to George III for the Earl of Buckinghamshire. Selina was left to deal with Mr Prosser, the foreman, and the many small but critical decisions involved in finishing a house; whether or not register grates were necessary to stop the fires from smoking, whether to have oil paint or distemper and the 'sad expensive job' of buying bells.[29] Selina wrote to her sister for instructions. 'The only value of your letter,' Catherine replied crushingly, 'was that it was sent me by the Countess of Buckinghamshire, Pugin having been at the Earl's seat . . . they always most politely convey him backwards and forwards in one of their carriages.'[30]

After this momentary propulsion into aristocratic circles Catherine descended once more to Keppel Street and the unsatisfactory Mr Prosser, who in her absence distempered the hall, against her express wishes, and whose men, 'if they worked three days stayed away four'.[31] Eventually they were able to move in. At forty Catherine was mistress at last of her own household. Auguste's career was modestly flourishing. He never earned large sums, but he was fairly constantly employed; there are regular payments to him from now on in Ackermann's accounts.[32] His name was becoming known. Louis Simond commented, as many did, on the quality of the English watercolourists, and singled out from the Society's annual exhibition one of the views of Cassiobury: 'l'intérieur d'une bibliothèque, par Pugin, d'un effet prodigieux.'[33]

Auguste was starting work on Ackermann's *Westminster Abbey*, and he had another outlet as a contributor to the magazine Ackermann started in 1809, named after his shop, *The Repository of the Arts*. With this more sophisticated version of *Le Cabinet des Modes* Auguste came in a sense full circle. The difference between the *Cabinet* and the *Repository*, however, was not only the difference in fashion over twenty years, but the difference between the frivolity of pre-revolutionary Paris and the more various and vigorous taste of contemporary London. *The Repository*'s index featured typically:

> Furniture, fashionable;
> Homer, his genius traced to its real source;
> Rousseau, anecdote of him
> Scotch haymakers, song of;
> Smoke conductor, patent, description of etc.

In art and decoration, as elsewhere, Ackermann's preference was for middle-class furnishings. The Repository specialized in the 'schönen Englischen simplicität' that was the closest Britain came to the Biedermeier style.[34]

It was not long after Auguste's jubilee monument to George III was unveiled that the King became ill with another bout of what is now thought to have been porphyria. This time there seemed little hope of his recovery. In February 1811 the Prince of Wales was created Prince Regent. Auguste and Catherine had been married nearly nine years. They were middle-aged and established where they would remain, on the shabbier fringes of artistic and intellectual London life. Bloomsbury was respectable but, as Anthony Trollope, who was born there six years later, wrote, 'Keppel Street cannot be called fashionable and Russell Square is not much affected by the nobility.'[35] The Pugins clung, sometimes with difficulty, to their gentility. Debt was an ever-present fear in the circles in which they moved. Ackermann was just now delivering Rowlandson's illustrations for his satire on the Picturesque, *Dr Syntax*, having weeded out the many he thought indecent, to William Combe, who wrote the accompanying verses in King's Bench prison. The annual exhibition of the Society of Painters in Water Colour came to a sudden halt when the pictures were seized in lieu of rent on the gallery. The Trollopes were eventually obliged to flee to France to avoid their creditors.

The commercial wealth of London and a taxation system that favoured the rich and the luxury trades did nothing to alleviate the poverty and degradation that festered a few streets away from Blooms-bury in the rookeries of St Giles and the brothels of Covent Garden. It did, however, create particular opportunities in art, architecture and decoration. The work that came Auguste's way kept him afloat while his wife's intellectual pursuits continued to mirror the age. She drafted an 'Address to the people of fashion and demi-fashion of Great Britain on the immorality folly and dangerous impolicy of their contemptuous conduct towards their inferiors'. It shows her moving, like many of her contemporaries, most famously Coleridge, from a radical to a radical-conservative point of view. Increasingly pessimistic in her view of human nature and society, she looked still to radical means, but invoked them for reactionary ends.

By the autumn of 1811 Catherine would have been sure that she was once again pregnant. It must have been a surprise. She was now in her early forties. She had been married for nearly a decade and her correspondence suggests that there had been no more pregnancies after the miscarriage she thought she suffered on the Isle of Wight. She had probably given up any idea of children. Some years earlier, with characteristic candour, she wrote from a visit to Adlard that 'while with a small family in a small house, with a small income, I must say I cannot wish for children'.[36] She and Auguste were no doubt apprehensive. But on 1 March 1812, in London, she gave birth safely to their son, Augustus Welby Northmore.[37]

Part Two

4

Waverley

1812 to 1821

'. . . my dear Lovel, you shall have full notes . . . we will revive the good old forms so disgracefully neglected in modern times . . . I'll annihilate Ossian.'

'But we must consider the expense of publication,' said Lovel.

'Expense!' said Mr Oldbuck pausing, and mechanically fumbling in his pocket – 'that is true . . . – but you would not like to publish by subscription?'

– Walter Scott, The Antiquary, *1816*

Named for his father, his mother and his distant Radical cousin, Pugin was, from the moment of his birth, the 'pride of papa's and the anxious joy of mama's heart'.[1] As well as his parents he had his aunt Selina, who was almost a second mother, to adore him, and on her unselfish love he, like the rest of her family, came to rely. Only Adlard, whose own children continued to appear at regular intervals, while he made half-hearted jokes about selling them off to rich neighbours, sounded a note of mild scepticism. 'Never boy was better nursed perhaps,' he wrote to Catherine. 'I think the Duke of Rutland would do well to send the young marquis of Granby to you.'[2] Catherine was, from the first, passionately devoted to her son. As on all subjects in which she was interested, she kept notes. He was her latest and greatest project. For the next two years he seems to have absorbed almost her entire attention. She recorded his various sayings and a list of the words he could spell before he was a year and nine months old.

The sole focus of so much benign interest, Pugin could not but be spoiled. He was not excessively indulged but he had no rival. He was so much loved and so attended to in childhood that for the rest of his life he found opposition hard to bear and malice incomprehensible. His upbringing bred a temperament in which precocious self-confidence was combined with an enduring innocence and vulnerability. The only child of middle-aged parents, he grew up, in some ways, very fast and in others not at all. A drawing by Louis Lafitte shows Pugin at about two, the rounded forehead and somewhat bulbous chin already evident, a serious, watchful child, in whom great hopes were vested.[3]

Lafitte was in London because, in May 1814, the Treaty of Paris had brought another, apparently more secure, end to the war. There was immediately a rush across the Channel in both directions of tourists, artists, exiles and long-separated friends and relatives. One of the first boats from France to England brought Auguste's old friend. Lafitte had married Auguste's sister, Jeanne Adelaide, in 1795 and he brought her and their daughter Antonia with him. In the twenty years since they had parted Lafitte had fared rather well. He had had one narrow escape in Italy when Roman rioters set fire to the French Academy and he was forced to leap from the roof across a courtyard, catch hold of a balcony, and hang there until the occupants hauled him in. After that he had been more careful. Back in France he managed to stay on the right side of each succeeding regime.[4] 'Une âme douce et paisible', noted for his good nature and as indifferent as Auguste to politics or religion, he adapted himself and his pleasing neo-classicism to changing times.[5] He drew the *Calendrier Républicain* for the revolutionary decimal year, painted murals in the dining room at Malmaison for Josephine and designed bas-reliefs for the Arc de Triomphe de l'Etoile. He had most recently been engaged on a series of medals, the Histoire Métallique, portraying the victories of the Emperor. For the moment his career had come to a halt with Napoleon's.

There must have been a great deal of news to exchange at this long-delayed reunion and presumably some understanding was reached about what, exactly, should be said about the Pugin family history. Auguste's father was dead and, it seems, his mother.[6] One brother survived and at least one other sister, Sophie, now Madame Bernard. But by this time Pugin and Lafitte's youth in the Paris of the *ancien régime* must have seemed to belong not merely to another century, but to another world. The family history had already begun to take on a romantic glow. The Lafittes' daughter was brought up in the belief that the Pugins had been a wealthy and noble family, impoverished over the generations, whose surviving estates had been compulsorily purchased during the Revolution.[7] The payment being in '*assignats*', the revolutionary currency, they had been ruined. Many people did lose everything in *assignats*. The amount of the original wealth and the size of the estate, however, grew with time. Joseph Pugin became a knight and the Prince de Salm Salm his great friend and patron, rather than simply his employer. So it was that tall tales of derring-do, narrow escapes, revolution and dramatic reversals of fortune were among the first that Pugin heard in his immediate family circle. They left him with a permanent terror of war and civil disorder and a tendency of his own towards exaggeration.

On a personal level Auguste and Lafitte took up their friendship where they had left it and fell easily into a pattern of regular visits and professional co-operation. Lafitte was the more talented, the more cultivated and more diligent, but since they were not competitive this seems to have caused no rancour. Catherine found him 'a dear goodnatured soul' and pleasant company, if somewhat garrulous.[8] The Peace, as in 1802, meant public festivities, and festivities, with Nash now installed as the Prince Regent's architect, meant work for Auguste and, fortuitously, his brother-in-law. Nash designed a suite of temporary rooms for the celebrations in the gardens of Carlton House and Lafitte, who was as happy to celebrate Napoleon's defeats as his victories, made, with Auguste, a group of large allegorical transparencies on such suitable themes as 'The Union of the Seine and the Thames' and 'Agriculture in England' to decorate them.[9] Then, on Pugin's third birthday, 1 March 1815, Napoleon escaped from Elba. The Lafittes were obliged to stay on in London for the duration of the Hundred Days until after Waterloo.

It was some time during his extended visit that Lafitte made the pencil study of his young nephew. He had a gift for portraiture and Pugin is depicted with as much attention as if he were the Emperor himself. This obscure child in Bloomsbury sitting to a French court artist makes a telling image. Pugin was never daunted, even as a very young man, by important personages or by entering directly into public affairs. He had felt close to the great events of the age all his life and grew up believing himself the equal of anybody.

Lafitte returned to Paris later that year, where he continued to ride the tide of events and in due course was appointed *peintre du cabinet du roi* to Louis XVIII. Auguste's professional life went on much as before. He exhibited watercolour views at the Royal Academy and elsewhere, receiving favourable notices in the *Repository* magazine. The reviewer was quite carried away by his *Christ Church Oxford*: 'the correctness of the perspective, the truth of light and shade, the beauty of details and the purity of colouring' were so wonderfully rendered 'that we are astonished at the power of an art that can thus, in so small a space, produce an imitation so illusive'.[10] It was considerably higher praise than Turner got for his view of Windsor Castle in the same show. England, however, after the war, was restless. Peace brought a sense of anticlimax. Over the decades of conflict Britain had lost about a third of a million men. In Parliament 'a discredited Opposition' was facing 'a discredited Government'.[11] There was radical agitation throughout the country and pressure to extend the franchise. From Manchester the weavers, threatened by mechanization, marched on London. In London itself there were riots. The Prince Regent, going to open Parliament in 1816, was watched by hostile, silent crowds. As he returned to Carlton House he was hissed. Then somebody took a shot at him, or possibly two, or at least a stone was thrown. The incident provoked panic and legislation. By March habeas corpus was suspended.

At Brighton, quite undeterred by his unpopularity, the Prince, with Nash, was getting to work expanding his seaside palace, the Pavilion. For admirers and detractors alike it was the *ne plus ultra* of Regency architecture. In the glittering interiors golden Chinese dragons hovered, appearing to hold the silk draperies up against domed ceilings; light glowed from crystal lotus flowers and chandeliers. The walls and wood-work were gilded, painted, trellised, grained and bambooed while in the new, steam-heated kitchens the great French chef Carême created his own architectural fantasies in pastry. While the country chafed under the repressive measures of the government, the Prince and his guests sat down, in a building that looked like a giant pudding, to enjoy puddings that looked like little buildings. The next year Nash began to add the famous 'hindoo' domes that give the Pavilion its silhouette and some time after that Auguste drew the interior and exterior in a series of views that captured it for ever in its heyday.

The autumn of 1818, when Pugin was six, was the first part of his childhood of which he could afterwards 'remember particulars'; it was a time that he never forgot, for it planted in him ideas and impressions that would last all his life.[12] It was to be a turning point for his parents

too. The family went on a tour up through Huntingdonshire to Lincolnshire and Yorkshire: 'visited Lincoln, York, Boston, Tatershall, Grantham, Peterbrough, Hull etc', Pugin recorded later.[13] They then went on
to stay for some weeks with Adlard at Rauceby. It was the first of the
autumn tours, lasting several weeks, which now became an annual
feature of family life. By the time he was twenty and making his note of
this first trip, Pugin was so familiar with the Gothic architecture of
England that it seemed unnecessary to specify the 'etc', which included
Beverley certainly and possibly Louth and Stamford. It was an impressive
introduction to the subject. Lincoln and York Minster are two of the
greatest medieval cathedrals. Boston, Grantham and Beverley have
between them four of the most imposing parish churches in England
and at Tattershall the tall, fifteenth-century keep, with its sturdy corner
turrets and machicolated battlements, satisfies every child's requirements
of a castle.

At their Lincoln lodgings, Mrs Hudson's, Castleyard, part of the
cellars, Pugin remembered, was found to have been 'formerly the vaults
of the castle'.[14] At six he was already learning, with Auguste's help
presumably, to explore buildings and to discover their history by careful
examination of the fabric. These were the empirical methods he would
use all his life. The buildings he saw in 1818 'much delighted' him.[15]
They remained among his favourites and formed his first and most
enduring idea of the Gothic. The years that followed from now until his
late teens, as he explored the medieval buildings of England, and later
France, in the company of his parents, were, he later recalled, a time of
great 'mental happiness', perhaps the happiest of his life.[16]

Auguste probably did not intend that the tour of 1818 would be the
beginning of a new professional departure, but such it was. He had a
commission to make drawings at Lincoln and Beverley. These were not
his usual watercolour views but scaled drawings and he was making them
for John Britton, editor and publisher of *The Architectural Antiquities of
Great Britain*. It was through Britton, and Britton's friend Edward
Willson, whom he now also came to know, that Auguste became involved with the Gothic Revival – not that anybody had yet coined that
term to describe the steadily growing interest in the Middle Ages. Britton,
now in his late forties, was a publisher and self-taught scholar. Born in
Wiltshire in 1771, he had begun life working in his father's baker's

shop. After he came to London he got a job as a cellar man in Clerken-well, reading at night for hour after hour to satisfy his craving for knowledge and advancement. He later escaped from drudgery into show business when he found a role as a compère, writing, performing and singing the commentary to an artificial light show designed by the painter P.J. de Loutherbourg and known as the Eidophusikon. It was described as 'the picturesque of sound' and it played on the audience's suscepti-bilities to moonlight and ruins. Here, in a milieu where art and learning mingled with theatre and circus, he met other would-be scholars, such as Belzoni, the professional strong man and noted Egyptologist. Gradually Britton turned himself into an expert on architecture and then into an author and publisher, without ever losing his fairground barker style. He was a pompous man, overbearing and pathologically long-winded. As he explained to a friend without irony: 'I wish to be short but cannot accomplish my own intentions – I must, however, skip over and abstain from many things – occurrences – events . . .'[17] The expedient of not saying everything three times never occurred to him.

His ten-year association with Auguste was not always happy and it ended in a quarrel. Yet Britton had all the virtues of his faults. He was determined, brave and inexhaustible in the pursuit of his projects. Not until Nikolaus Pevsner began work on *The Buildings of England* did another individual attempt a survey of the national architecture on the scale of Britton's *Beauties of England and Wales*, begun in 1801. In the perilous world of late Georgian publishing (not to mention late Georgian transport) it was an even more remarkable feat. Britton's idea was to build on the enthusiasm for popular topography something more scholarly and comprehensive. He wanted illustrations which, while they appealed to the Picturesque sensibility, took care to be accurate and for his latest series, *The Architectural Antiquities of Great Britain*, he wanted ground plans, sections and details as well as perspective views. He had already recruited many of Auguste's fellow watercolourists, indeed he used most of the best topographical artists and engravers of the day. Through his insistence on accuracy as well as art and by the sheer scale of his operations he put into the public mind a more vivid picture of medieval architecture than had existed before. As he was the first to point out, his work 'greatly assisted in rendering local history an object of fashionable study'.[18]

Britton was catering for a taste that grew over the next decade almost to a mania. A change was coming over the public sensibility, a new feeling for history and a thirst for information about the past. The Middle Ages no longer seemed merely dark and primitive, they were picturesque and romantic. Gothic architecture was not exclusively a taste for the wealthy and maverick like Horace Walpole and William Beckford. If this new enthusiasm had been at first propelled by 'a new taste in literature', as Edward Willson put it, by now each fed the other.[19] Britton's books were the topographical equivalent of the Waverley novels, the first of which appeared in 1814, and Walter Scott, a keen topographer, contributed to Britton's works. Both offered their readers the material reality of the past. In Scott's novels it was the food, the furniture, the clothes that they were asked to savour, along with the authentic terminology: 'hangings of sky-blue velvet and silver . . . chairs of ebony richly carved . . . silver sconces . . . Spanish foot cloth . . . Old English oak . . . a large . . . court cupboard . . . finest tapestry [from] the looms of Flanders' and so on.[20] In Britton's *Architectural Antiquities* they could see the vaults of the cathedrals, the battlements of castles and the tracery of Gothic windows in detail. Strawberry Hill Gothic now began to look very stagy, 'a heap of inconsistencies', as Willson put it: the ossianic mist that had hung over the Middle Ages began to lift, revealing a detailed, if still highly coloured panorama.[21]

The drawings Auguste made for Britton were a success and between the two of them another idea was mooted. This was that Auguste should produce a book of his own of architectural 'specimens', illustrating details of medieval buildings, doors, mouldings and tracery, presented with measurements. These could be used by architects to copy when they were asked, as they were with increasing frequency, to design a church or a house in the Gothic style. The more that people knew about the real architecture of the past, the more critical they became of what Scott called the 'monotonous stone pepper boxes' of modern Gothic.[22] They wanted more than a few applied crockets to find a building convincing. But most architects had no idea where to begin to study or analyse medieval buildings. *Specimens of Gothic Architecture* marked a new phase of the Gothic Revival and a permanent change in the Pugins' domestic life. From now on the two were intimately connected.

In 1819 the Pugins moved to Store Street, on the other side of Gower Street. The new house was like the old, a four-storey, stock-brick terrace.

The reason for the change was apparently the advantage of a large, light attic room, suitable or perhaps already fitted out as a drawing office. Auguste was preparing to take on pupils to help him with the *Specimens*. From now on he ran a regular drawing school, which with its fluctuating population of teenage boys and young men became a permanent and for Catherine often an annoying presence in the household. She found them noisy and sometimes uncouth and insisted on a separate office door bell so that business need not sully too much the gentility of family life.

The vagaries of the publishing world and Auguste's own flamboyant style meant that despite the success of its endeavours, there was always an element of the theatrical and comic about his drawing school. Frederick Goodall recalled hearing of the occasion when Auguste, who was drawing the medieval buildings of Oxford for *Specimens*, arranged to hire a carriage to sit in, out of the wind. 'He had some difficulty in explaining that he did not want any horses, and when he had the carriage placed in the street and began to draw, he flattered himself on the clever idea ... But in the middle of the day the undergraduates came around, and were so amused at his sketching from the window that they thought they would have a lark, and rocked his carriage about. This made Pugin very angry.' A small crowd gathered to watch the furious Frenchman shouting and waving his fists out of the windows until about twenty of them got between the shafts and pulled the vocally protesting Auguste several miles out of the city – where they left him. Many other anecdotes were told of the drawing school and there were many anecdotalists to tell them, for among the first pupils were the sixteen-year-old Charles Mathews, son of the actor whom Auguste had met in Wales in the 1790s, who later became an actor himself, and James d'Egville, the son of a ballet master at the Italian Opera.

Despite these diversions the first volume of *Specimens* appeared in 1821, with a dedication to John Nash, who had almost no interest in historic architecture but was happy to lend his name to help the work on its way in fashionable circles. It was a well-drawn, if not a well-organized book. Despite its shortcomings, however, there was plenty of solid information and, as Britton promised in his Preface, *Specimens* provided 'genuine materials for the Architect to work from'.[23] It was a success. So scarce still was detailed technical information on Gothic architecture that *Specimens* and its succeeding volumes were repeated ad nauseam and the chimneys of Hampton Court, the pinnacles of York Minster and the oriel window of Magdalen College, Oxford, began to sprout all over England.

The text of *Specimens* was written by Edward Willson, who was to figure large in Pugin's life. An architect, living at Newport near Lincoln, Willson was a thoughtful man, more complex than Britton and although, like him, self-taught, much more intellectually sophisticated. Willson was thirty-three when *Specimens* was published. Slight, pale, mild-mannered and often unwell, he had almost literally grown up in Lincoln cathedral, where his father was retained as a carpenter; every detail of the building had been impressed on his imagination in childhood, as it was now being impressed on Pugin's, and Willson loved it. His under-standing of the Gothic was imbued with a romantic empathy for the buildings of the past and the society that had created them. He was a cradle Catholic and he was also that peculiar creature of the Gothic Revival, 'the antiquary'. Antiquaries, historians who dealt with the physical remains of the past, as well as written records, had existed for centuries, but as a figure the antiquary broke the surface of the public imagination with Scott's novel of 1816 and its protagonist Jonathan Oldbuck. Antiquaries were often caricatured in the popular press as Oldbucks, bumbling eccentrics and collectors of rubbish, but their scholarship was real – they studied Gothic buildings stone by stone, climbed spires, dug trenches and dredged lakes. It was in this empirical tradition, profound if often unsystematic, that Pugin got his education.

Willson was a judiciously critical reader of Payne Knight and he brought Picturesque theory to bear on his studies. To achieve the 'ex-quisite sublimity' that Willson loved in his cathedral it was essential, he said, having once learned the vocabulary of Gothic, to articulate it from within. To make the dead language speak again to the nineteenth century, to make it sing, the architect must inhabit it entirely and 'endeavour to think in the manner of the original inventors'.[24] This was the view, or rather the vision, that Pugin would later adopt as his own. In his notes and correspondence Willson talks, or murmurs, principally to himself in the peculiar tone of the antiquary:

Local notes by Parishes and Wapentakes . . . Quaere how these towns came into the possession of the Danes? By Doctor Henry's History it would seem that King Alfred gave them up as places of refuge to the Danes who remained in England . . . Quaere whether this is expressly recorded in any good authority . . . Inscription on a sword, found in the River Witham[?] . . . mem. to have an exact drawing made of this . . . account of the opening of Bishop Fox's tomb, no ring found . . . notes on the Roman Altar and fragments on my Terrace Walk in Lincoln . . . the larger spur was found amongst some old brass in an ironmongers shop here . . . it will be several months yet before I get my treatise on the proportions of bells finished . . . notes collected from the remembrance of old people . . . mem. I suppose that the incident of the skeleton was only an imaginary circumstance . . .[25]

Part archaeologist, part collector, self-taught scholar and de facto dealer in real and supposed antiquities, he was typical of his species, not least in preferring research and note-taking to actual production. He liked to fuss and hated to finish. His work on bells was never completed. Only collaboration could force a text out of him – and even then it was difficult. Although he was the most obscure of the contributors to *Specimens*, Willson was the one who spoke for the rising generation as it became increasingly impatient with the frivolities of the Prince Regent and his architect. In the second volume, which was not dedicated to Nash, Willson attacked him, the great architect of the Picturesque, for travestying its principles in so undignified a building as the Brighton Pavilion. Auguste, however, had no such qualms. He and his pupils were busy by then with views of the seaside palace for a lavish colour plate book, published by Ackermann. The visits to Brighton were much discussed and the occasion on which the Regent knocked over Auguste's paints and afterwards apologized to him was never forgotten in the drawing school.

In January 1820 George III died. The Prince Regent became George IV and immediately started planning the most expensive coronation in history. Some years before he had enjoyed a 'snug little dinner' with Walter Scott and had been persuaded (quite easily) to see himself as an heroic figure in the Waverley tradition, a king of the olden times.[26] He wanted a coronation that evoked every historic association. Auguste was of course commissioned to draw the scene, capturing the intention, the 'gorgeous splendour of ancient chivalry' combining with 'the intense heroic interest of modern times', rather than the somewhat comic reality.[27]

By 1821, as he entered his fifties, Auguste was busier than ever. Artist, draughtsman, engraver, watercolourist and occasional architect, he was also a publisher, print dealer, drawing master and designer of furnishings in the Gothic style, which he published in the *Repository*. He was a well-placed cog in the great commercial art machine whose mechanism connected, within a few revolutions, the King and his architect at the top, with Ackermann and the Society of Painters in Water Colour in the middle and the small Soho galleries and brokers' shops somewhat nearer the bottom. His connections extended across the Channel to Paris, where the craze for the Gothic and for Waverley was raging among the Bourbon Ultra-Royalists. Lafitte, still in favour, was happy to introduce Auguste to the Duchesses de Berry and d'Angoulême, both of whom were great patrons of the arts and admirers of Scott. Auguste was soon supplying them with prints and illustrated books from London.

Catherine's visit to Paris in 1819 was probably her first. She learned French easily and took a great liking to her Parisian relatives by marriage and to 'the never-failing amusements of France'.[28] The Pugins' life in London and Paris was busy and cosmopolitan. Visitors were frequent and work, family and friendships naturally intertwined. 'I send you 71 prints various subjects for which you will fix yourself the price,' Auguste wrote to Ackermann when the family had just returned from France. 'The six numbers after Raphael as you said you had 25 sets of them I thought it was of no consequence about mine and Mr Stephanoff [an artist] having called on me fell in love with it, and I sold him for four Guineas.'[29] Catherine seems to have given up publishing her work, but she continued to pursue the intellectual life. A letter from the father of one of Auguste's pupils about some missing luggage is covered with her jottings on the subject of property rights and 'the moderate dependence' necessary for a peasant.[30]

Perhaps she and Auguste were less close than in the early days of their marriage, when they worked together and had more leisure. Perhaps her intense preoccupation with her baby had produced some temporary estrangement. It has been suggested that Auguste had an affair shortly after his son's birth with the poet Margaret Harries, who lived nearby in Bloomsbury, and that he fathered an illegitimate son.[31] Catherine's notes include some caustic remarks on the subject of women, matrimony and disillusionment. But if there was a certain tension the letters hint at no positive disharmony, nothing like the rows between the increasingly restless and misanthropic Adlard and his wife, who were now on the brink of separation after years of quarrelling which had at times embroiled the Pugins. Auguste did his best to keep the peace and not take sides but Catherine, typically, was less restrained and her protests on behalf of her sister-in-law infuriated her brother. A wedge was driven between the once devoted pair.

Pugin was nine in 1821. His parents could not have afforded a nursemaid, but nor would they have wanted one. They kept their son with them as much as they could, as he too, despite the conventions of the Victorian age, would keep his children about him. Thus stimulated, encouraged and naturally precocious, Pugin begins to emerge as a distinct personality.

5

'My first design'

1821 to 1824

'You see,' said Mr Pecksniff, passing the candle rapidly from roll to roll of paper, 'some traces of our doings here. Salisbury Cathedral from the north. From the south. From the east. From the west. From the south-east. From the nor'west. A bridge. An alms-house. A jail. A church. A powder-magazine. A wine-cellar. A portico. A summer-house. An ice-house. Plans, elevations, sections, every kind of thing.'
– Charles Dickens, *Martin Chuzzlewit*, 1843–4[1]

Immediately after the coronation, in a sweltering August, the Pugins, with several pupils in tow, set off for a working visit to Paris. At Dover there was a muddle. Catherine was too nervous to go by steamboat, which was still a novel and she thought unsafe means of transport, but the luggage was already on board. Auguste, 'white as . . . paper and dripping with heat', could not find his wife's bags to bring them back on shore but then, at the last moment, 'in came my boy with an air of triumph, at the head of two porters & the commissioner, saying "mama I saw your luggage as soon as I went to the side of the vessel and told the commissioner I was sure it was yours, and he must bring it . . . directly" and so it was'.[2] Even allowing for a fond mother's partiality Pugin must have been a very commanding nine-year-old, already possessed of the natural authority in practical matters that later made people generally do what he wanted. It was a great advantage for an architect. Workmen, almost always, respected and liked him and he in turn got on with them.

When the party finally reached Paris, where the 'stage effect of life' Catherine noticed came naturally to the French, there were constant

57

amusements and interesting sights.[3] Pugin and his mother went to the Chapel Royal, where they managed to glimpse Lafitte's patron, the Duchesse d'Angoulême. The Duchesse, a daughter of Louis XVI and Marie Antoinette, was a figure of great romantic interest and in appearance put Catherine in mind of one of the Cholmeley cousins. Mother and son also went to Mass. Catherine had apparently ceased to be a deist – deism was now intellectually rather passé – but she remained deeply engaged in religious questions. A mixture of courtesy and curiosity led her, unlike Auguste, who came 'neither for high mass or low at home or abroad', to accompany the Lafittes to church, but if the experience of the Mass made any particular impression on Pugin he seems never to have referred to it afterwards.[4] It was Catherine who, despite misgivings about the role of 'superstition' in the Roman Catholic Church, found the gloom of St Roche, lit here and there by glimmering tapers, 'inconceivably affecting'.[5]

France, now, for all its amusements, was uneasy. Louis XVIII's nephew, the Duc de Berry, had been assassinated the year before. The King himself was ill and rarely seen in public and the military presence made itself felt oppressively. The Lafittes prospered, but the past still cast mysterious and unhappy shadows. Auguste's brother had died, leaving a wife and two children, whom the Lafittes would have nothing to do with. His marriage had been 'imprudent' and the destitute children too great a financial burden for their relatives to accept.[6] Catherine was distressed by the situation but helpless. Despite bitter family quarrels nothing was ever done and the children recede from view through the correspondence into some unspecified outer darkness. Such was the fate of Pugin's first cousins. He was safe within his own adoring family, but it was all that stood between him and a very unfeeling world.

At home he began to have drawing lessons from Auguste. 'I was very fond of Perspective,' he recalled, 'and made a good proficiency of it'; adding airily, 'began to design buildings etc.'[7] A somewhat shaky drawing of a church with a west tower and spire survives from 1821. Shortly before his death Pugin annotated the picture: 'my first design'.[8] A careful exercise in perspective, made at about the same time, shows his father's drawing office with two rather wooden-looking pupils surrounded by set squares and T-squares, plaster casts for copying and watercolour paints. On the back of the door hangs the separate office bell. Pugin went out with the older boys to Hampton Court, where they were making drawings for the second volume of the *Specimens*. On a trip to Hastings he made studies of tumble-down cottages emphasizing their Picturesque qualities, the unevenness of rubble stone and the twisting of ancient half-timbering. Outside office hours he entertained his parents with fantastical drawings of scenes from the Arabian Nights in which long processions wind their way through gorgeous tented interiors. Later he could remember being impressed only by medieval buildings, but the Brighton Pavilion obviously appealed to him at the time.

He had virtually no formal schooling. He learned French from his family and on later visits to Paris he had lessons and was soon fluent but, as is often the case with bilingual children, his spelling in both languages suffered. Catherine oversaw his reading and writing, making him compose a weekly essay on a moral or religious theme, over which he laboured without much pleasure. It was a lopsided education, intense in some areas, neglected in others. Like the hero of *Waverley* he was allowed 'to learn as he pleased, what he pleased, and when he pleased', with the result that his energy and ability were never modified by much mental self-discipline; 'the art of controlling . . . the powers of his mind' always eluded him.[9]

When he was eleven an attempt was made to round out his education by sending him as a private pupil to Christ's Hospital, the Bluecoat School. Christ's Hospital had a reputation for nurturing what John Britton, with his gift for the unhappy phrase, called 'the germs of genius', including Coleridge and Charles Lamb.[10] It got little chance to nurture Pugin. He was never formally enrolled and four years of desultory lessons made almost no impression. Although his master, Mr Adams, was, he recalled, 'a most clever, excellent, good man' who 'paid every attention to me', the subjects never caught his imagination.[11] Mathematics, he recalled, 'was not to my liking' and Latin 'much too dry a study'.[12] Benjamin Ferrey insisted that his friend had shown outstanding academic ability, but Pugin's own, frank account is the truth. He never applied himself to anything that bored him, he disliked sitting still and found most sustained intellectual effort 'dry'. Later he had cause to regret his lack of Latin and made efforts to improve, but he never mastered it. Mistakes crept into inscriptions on his metalwork and even the title pages of his books. At Christ's Hospital he did not, it was noticed, mix much with the other children, preferring adult company, such as he was used to. If he had gone away to school he might have acquired more self-discipline. It might have made him wiser in the ways of the unfeeling world and less emotionally dependent on his parents. As it was he stayed at home, and found his education, his recreation and his friendships there.

In 1823 the family moved again, another few hundred yards, to a larger house in Great Russell Street. Like Keppel Street it was new, built by another of the great speculative builders of the age, Thomas Cubitt. The move was a small step up, the house was bigger than its immediate neighbours, the rent £50 a year. Great Russell Street heralded an expansion of the drawing school and a period of professional buoyancy for Auguste. As Pugin himself drew closer in age to the young men who came to study with his father they became his daily companions. Over the years the pupils included Edward Cooke, later a well-known painter of seascapes; one of Nash's adopted children, James Pennethorne, who became a successful architect; Joseph Nash, no relation, who became a painter and architectural illustrator through whose eyes we still see much of early Victorian art and design; Talbot Bury, architect, engraver and a lifelong friend of Pugin. Benjamin Ferrey arrived in 1826.

The pupils learned drawing, perspective and the use of the camera obscura. They helped with whatever work was in hand. Auguste would have taught them the principles of picturesque composition as he had picked them up from Nash and Repton and they had the run of his ever-expanding library of English and French works on architecture, but he was not in a position to teach them much about construction or the preparation of working drawings, for he had almost no experience in those areas himself. Those of the pupils who later became architects nearly all went on to study in an architectural office. One of the exceptions was Talbot Bury, another was Pugin himself. The Great Russell Street school's principal purpose, as far as Auguste was concerned, was to get the drawings made for his books. Talbot Bury remembered that Auguste would write to the boys' parents and say that their sons were looking sickly and required fresh air. He would then take them off to draw for twelve hours a day, at whichever building he needed, making sketches which he would then correct and they would finish. Bury also recalled that the parents had to pay hefty fees for their children's hard work. James Pennethorne's bill suggests this was true.

By Boarding from the 25th March to the 25th June £3-13-od
  " premium for the third quarter £26-5-od
  " expenses at Hampton Court £2-13-4d
  " pencils colours and brushes 19/9d
Total £43-11-1d
Deduct time absent £2-16-00d
  Total £40-15-od[13]

Despite his general good nature Auguste was prone to outbursts of impatience and temperament, while Catherine, whose chief concern was to keep the 'young folk' in order, ran the household on a strict routine and endeavoured to maintain high standards of behaviour at table. Pugin drew for his fellow students a weekly Wheel of Fortune, showing who was in favour and who was out with his variously volatile parents. It says a great deal for his good nature that he was popular in the school and made lasting friendships there. The adored son of the house, he might have been insufferable, a sneak or a cry-baby. In fact he spent as much time as he could with the other pupils, while Catherine struggled, outside office hours, to keep him away from company she regarded as rough and socially inferior.

In the time he spent with his mother they were companionable. She shared his enthusiasms, learning about architecture, admiring his drawings and encouraging his precocious talent. She poured her energies into his efforts as she had once poured them into Auguste's and with more success. Her son had inherited her emotional intensity and energy. Where his mind was engaged his heart and soul went with it. He, for his part, would sit with her if she was ill when they were travelling, reading to her while Auguste worked. He grew up to enjoy female company, depending on it for approval and reinforcement. His closeness to his mother and his aunt gave him a sensitivity towards women and their needs that later made him very attractive to them. Good-natured, optimistic and self-confident, his was, in early adolescence, a happy disposition, whose happiness spread easily to others.

If Ferrey remembered life at Great Russell Street as 'severe and restrictive in the extreme' and Catherine as an austere martinet, who punished 'the smallest want of punctuality or infringement of domestic rules', that was perhaps because he was homesick, the only one of the boys who lived too far away to go home for weekends.[14] Other pupils remembered things differently. Catherine's letters reveal that there were outings and amusements in London and in Paris, and they also suggest that some of her severity was the result of anxiety at so much responsibility for other people's children. The boys were often boisterous and out of order. When Talbot Bury got lost at Versailles she was frantic.

Undoubtedly, however, the working hours were long. They started at six in the morning, with no breakfast until half past eight. To Ferrey, grammar-school educated, the son of a country draper, it seemed punishing. But it was not an unusual working day in the 1820s. Nearby in Lincoln's Inn Fields Sir John Soane's pupils were working twelve hours a day six days a week. Edward Cooke, who had grown up in Soho and been a professional illustrator since he was nine, probably did not find it such an exorbitant regime, and it was a routine that Pugin kept up all the rest of his life.

6

Metropolitan Improvements

1824 to 1826

We are so far advanced in the Arts and Sciences, that we live in retrospect.

— William Hazlitt, *The Spirit of the Age*, 1825

The autumn tour of 1824 took the drawing school back across the Channel in preparation for a book on the medieval architecture of Normandy, a subject of increasing interest in Britain, later to be published as *Specimens of the Antiquities of Normandy*. They went first to Rouen, the site of some of the most spectacular late Gothic architecture in France. The Palais de Justice, the churches of St Ouen and St Maclou and the archbishop's palace were set then among winding streets of timber houses whose upper storeys overhung the road. 'Meshed like gossamer with inextricable tracery', the buildings of Rouen were a gift to watercolourists, especially Cotman and Samuel Prout, the epitome of romantic Gothic.[1] Young Ruskin, looking at Rouen through Prout's eyes, saw in it 'one labyrinth of delight . . . grey and fretted towers . . . letting the sky like blue enamel through the foiled spaces of their crowns of Work'.[2] Pugin, seeing Rouen at first hand, was similarly entranced. The city became for him, too, a touchstone.

He was growing up architecturally as well as verbally bilingual. In the three months he spent in France that year he 'worked very hard all the time and measured a great deal'.[3] The party travelled at a considerable pace in the large French stagecoaches, the Pugins inside and the pupils out. They would undertake a round trip of 100 miles in three days, drawing the buildings as they went. Catherine found that 'like the king I may die, but I must not be ill'.[4] They visited Caen and Bayeux and the church at Caudebec, where, in order to find out how the pendant vault was constructed, Auguste had a hole made in the roof above it and lowered some of the smaller boys inside to draw what they saw. At that time it was perfectly easy – if hazardous – to interfere structurally with medieval buildings in this ad hoc way. Ferrey, who was one of those who went in, remembered that getting out again was difficult. It was by such direct methods, rather than by poring over the treatises of Laugier, that Pugin learned the underlying principles of Gothic building.

Everywhere they went the party would have seen the scars of the Revolution, the terrible destruction for which the word 'vandalisme' was coined. The statues on the front of Notre Dame in Paris had been smashed, in the mistaken belief that they depicted kings of France. Medieval monasteries had been used as quarries. At St Denis, where the royal tombs had been removed by order of the Committee of Public Safety, Dom Germain Poirier, the Benedictine historian, had stood helpless while 'in three days they destroyed the work of twelve centuries'.[5] It was early impressed on Pugin that radical and revolutionary ideas were inimical to Gothic architecture. Out of the revulsion against such violence a French Society of Antiquaries had been founded in 1815 and by the 1820s there was a considerable exchange of ideas and information between Normandy and England. Britton had a friend, Arcisse de Caumont, still a student at Caen, but already an expert in medieval history, who was deputed to help Auguste and the pupils with the latest work. De Caumont was the great synthesizer of French archaeological studies. Through him Pugin could know all that was then known about the Gothic in France; a better guide, Ferrey recalled, could not have directed them.

Of the other antiquary they got to know, E. H. Langlois, Ferrey was not able to speak so well. 'He was the type of a class of men who rank high in French estimation,' the young draper's son wrote, guardedly. 'In this country things are rather different; it must be admitted that, in general, a man of talent unfortunately placed in M Langlois' circumstances could not mix in society on equal terms.'[6] The peculiarities to which Ferrey made such oblique reference had no deterrent effect on Pugin, who became a friend of Langlois for the rest of Langlois's life. Erudite and caustically witty, Langlois was just then engaged on a study of the stalls of Rouen cathedral. What troubled Ferrey was that he lived in virtual destitution, with his alcoholic wife and seven children, in an abandoned convent. Literally out of the ruins of the Revolution he had made a museum of objects he had rescued: carvings, statuary, pieces of stained glass and illuminated manuscripts. He inhabited it as Quasimodo inhabited Notre Dame, the external expression of a private obsession.

Pugin too had begun to collect antiquities. He 'purchased some tiles from the Ducal Palace Caen, and got some fragments of stained glass from the circular window at the end of Hall'.[7] There was beginning to be a resistance in France to the selling off of fragments of buildings, but Pugin was quite happy at this stage to buy anything he could afford. He went on collecting and dealing in antiques all his life and his purchases are now in the Victoria and Albert, the British Museum and the Metropolitan in New York. In the first half of the nineteenth century it was possible, even with the limited pocket money of a twelve-year-old, to buy world-class works of medieval art, for few people knew or cared about them. Pugin soon learned to rummage in brokers' shops, pick up unconsidered trifles in churches under repair and sort through rubbish on building sites.

In Paris, where the visit ended in October, there was yet another shift in the political wind. The fat and feeble Louis XVIII had died and his brother, the Comte d'Artois, became Charles X. He was an Ultra-Royalist, determined to restore the majesty of the Bourbon line, the 'forty kings who in a thousand years created France', and of whom Louis had been such an unsatisfactory representative.[8] Charles believed in the divine right of kings, the power of history and the glory of the medieval past, which he saw, to a great extent, through the magnifying lens of Waverley. Charles's coronation, like George IV's, was a pageant. It took place at Rheims and was, as Victor Hugo noted, 'another sign of the progress of Romantic ideas'.[9] The decorations, which Hugo thought flimsy, were by the ever-present Louis Lafitte and the new regime rewarded the one-time designer of the Calendrier Républicain with the Légion d'honneur. Catherine was delighted. It put him, almost, on a par with the Welbys of Denton so that, as she explained to Selina, 'hereafter when my son may visit France his family connections will be very respectable'.[10]

The Lafittes now claimed, or as they put it had restored to them, the Pugin family 'arms' which, they told Catherine, had had to be burned during the Revolution. It was this crest – it was never a full coat of arms – that established or at least asserted their connection with the fifteenth-century Pugin of Fribourg. The badge was the sort of device that can be found for any family if the search is cast wide enough and far enough back in time, and the Pugins and the Lafittes were by no means alone or unusual in their pretensions in the 1820s. Under the Empire it had been more than respectable to be a self-made bourgeois. Now the Bourbons' fatal nostalgia for the *ancien régime* made lineage important again. Many pedigrees were polished up or rewritten and many tenuous or optimistic family connections asserted. It was the same in England, where the craze for the Middle Ages spawned applications to the College of Heralds by claimants to long-dormant titles. Some people claimed several at a time and there were professional genealogists, like Disraeli's Baptist Hatton in *Sybil*, who were prepared to guarantee a peerage in return for 'a paltry twenty or thirty thousand pounds'.[11] Even among those who had no need to worry about their social position it became fashionable to Gothicize one's name. The English ambassador to France became Stuart 'de Rothsay'. Pugin – on occasion – would later style himself, with no justification other than euphony, 'de Pugin'.

The Pugin 'arms', which he later used throughout his work, on everything from title pages to floor tiles, meant a great deal to him. Like Thackeray's Pendennis he believed his chivalrous ancestors to be 'real and actual beings', as real as ' – whom shall we say? Robinson Crusoe'.[12] He was no snob – he was, from his mother's point of view, alarmingly oblivious of social distinctions – but his arms connected him with the world of knights and castles that the novels of Scott, which he was now reading eagerly, and his study of architecture made ever more vivid in his imagination. Most excitingly his aunt Lafitte told him that the arms entitled him, if he returned to Switzerland, to claim a piece of land on which to build a château of his own.

Apart from architecture and Gothic novels, Pugin's chief enthusiasm as he entered his teens was for the theatre. He had by now also acquired his enduring fascination with sensational gossip and disasters. Storms, fires and the scandals of the popular press all made their way into his memoranda. 'Mr Hughes Ball elopes with Mademoiselle Mercandotti of the Kings Theatre ... Hon F Ashley Cooper, son of the Earl of Shaftesbury died in consequence of a fight between him and another school fellow at Eton ... Comet Steamer from Inverness to Fort William run down by the steamboat Ayr – 60 lives lost.'[13] With more consistency he commented on the openings at Covent Garden, Drury Lane and the Haymarket and the reception of new works. 'Augusta Blind Girl drama not very sucessfull'; 'the White Maid of Avenal musical drama sucessful' and so forth.[14] Ferrey claimed that Catherine prevented her son from ever going to the theatre, but it seems unlikely that he would, or could, have made so many notes of performances without seeing any.

The other theme that runs through Pugin's adolescent diary notes, later collected in the short *Autobiography*, written when he was about nineteen, is one that preoccupied the whole of London in the 1820s, the great 'metropolitan improvements'. All his life the capital had been expanding. New bridges crossed the Thames at Waterloo, Southwark, Hammersmith and Vauxhall, while beneath it, at Rotherhithe, Marc Brunel was building his tunnel. On the south bank the trickles of brick that had flowed into Kent and Surrey in the eighteenth century began to form pools; factory developments, modest housing and further south substantial villas and suburbs. Ackermann moved to Camberwell in 1817. Six years later the Pugins' Bloomsbury neighbours, the Ruskins, went to Herne Hill. For those who could afford a carriage the commuter age had arrived.

The Pugins could not. They stayed in Bloomsbury, surrounded by building. When they had come to Keppel Street the land to the east had still lain undeveloped. Tavistock Square, Gordon Square, Woburn Place and much of Great Russell Street had all been built in Pugin's lifetime. Ten thousand new houses were being run up every year, many of them cheap. Visitors were often depressed by the monotony of these new streets and Soane, now professor of architecture at the Royal Academy, used pictures of Burton's Bloomsbury housing to exemplify what his students should avoid. Among the houses there were also new churches, intended to impose order and identity on the rapidly expanding city. The Church Building Commission, set up in 1818 with a fund of £1,000,000, removed the necessity to pass an Act of Parliament for each new Anglican church. In the 1820s about thirty-five were built in London and more than 150 elsewhere.[15] Guidelines for the new churches were set out by Soane, Nash and Robert Smirke, the three architects officially attached to the government Office of Works, but inevitably with such a number of buildings going up so fast many were perfunctory, especially those that attempted the new Gothic style. To aficionados such as the Pugins and the drawing school, 'Commissioners' Gothic' was soon a term of abuse.

Outside London the provincial cities too were growing and indus-trializing fast. A crust of cheap and shoddy building overlay the squalor and discontent of the urban working class. The problem of 'the city' in the nineteenth century, the creation of a way of life on a scale and of a kind that had never been known before in the history of the world, was to be a central theme in Pugin's life and work. Already the Prussian architect Schinkel, who came to Britain on a discreet spying trip in 1826, was shocked by the way the English allowed their urban centres to grow without control, the factories, 'monstrous shapeless buildings put up only by foremen without architecture . . . and out of red brick', sprawling unplanned.[16] He saw that it boded ill, and not only for architecture. He noticed also the great 'military presence' in Manchester.[17]

In contrast to such ramshackle development there was also, in the capital, a great programme of public works in hand. A few dozen yards from the Pugins' house Robert Smirke was rebuilding the British Museum. The site of Trafalgar Square was being cleared and there was talk of a new National Gallery, while in the West End Nash's great ceremonial route from Carlton House up to Regent's Park was under way. Auguste was still sometimes employed by Nash. He designed for him the building in Park Square East to house the Diorama, Daguerre's picturesque light show. With Britton he embarked on a two-volume survey with measured drawings and descriptions, *Illustrations of the Public Buildings of London*. The Great Russell Street drawing office and Pugin himself were as well informed about modern architecture as medieval.

Driving many of these developments was a great urge to make up for the slack years of the Napoleonic wars. 'Reform', 'improvement' and 'the march of intellect' were the catchphrases of the press. It was generally agreed that these were stirring times 'pregnant with change', but whether for good or ill was unclear.[18] Many who had been Radicals in their youth began to look more pessimistically on human society. Catherine Pugin's view of humanity continued to darken and as ever she had her finger on the increasingly feverish pulse of the times. In her mid-fifties she had lost none of her gusto for life. Having always been critical of the Anglican Church, which was now increasingly influenced by Evangelicals, though dominated by the High Church party, she found a stimulating alternative in the preaching of Edward Irving. Irving was a minister of the Church of Scotland who suddenly sprang to fame in 1823 when Canning praised his sermons in Parliament. He was to cast a long shadow across Pugin's life. At that time he presided over a grim little brick chapel in Hatton Garden, where, after Canning's endorsement, hundreds crammed themselves into the pews to hear him. Tall and handsome, with brilliant dark eyes and a vivid, theatrical manner, he was the Edmund Kean of the pulpit. The admired friend of Coleridge and the Carlyles, Irving had, at least in his early days in London, a pure desire to re-animate the Christian lives of his congregation. Thus the young Pugin and Ferrey found themselves seized, like Dickens – figuratively – by a female hand and 'dragged by the hair' to sit through interminable preaching, services 'at which no human child . . . could possibly keep its eyes open'.[19]

Ferrey, who disliked Pugin's later conversion to Catholicism as thoroughly as he disliked Catherine, tried to link the two in his biography by suggesting that Irving's preaching actually drove Pugin into the arms of Rome out of sheer boredom. Pugin certainly conceived a great dislike of preachers and 'preaching box' chapels, but the immediate effect on him was a strong reflection of 'what are called Evangelical views' in his weekly essays and although he abandoned the views, the dramatic rhetoric of Hatton Garden left a permanent mark on his prose.[20] At home there were now heated debates about religion. Catherine, 'never happier than when she could find somebody willing to engage in controversy', would become passionate on religious doctrine.[21] 'Leave the house, sir, leave the house, sir, you dare to rob my SAVIOUR of His Divinity?' Ferrey, lurking on the stairs, remembered hearing her haranguing a visitor. The library door was thrown open, the front door slammed and 'Thus unceremoniously was the gentleman expelled the premises.'[22] One of the pupils, mentioning to Auguste at breakfast that he had not yet seen Mrs Pugin that day, received the reply, ''ow 'appy is that man.'[23] This latest of Catherine's enthusiasms clearly put a strain on domestic relations.

In 1825, when he was thirteen, Pugin was ill for some time and in September his mother took him to convalesce in the country. They went to Christchurch and Salisbury. Both places made a deep impression. The Augustinian Priory at Christchurch, 'as grand as a cathedral', dates mostly from the twelfth century.[24] It stands on a rise from which, in the 1820s, there was a fine view to the sea across the water meadows at the junction of the Avon and the Stour. Pugin was drawn back again to Christchurch and even more to Salisbury, where the cathedral, despite Wyatt, still offered a beau idéal of Early English Gothic and one that was taking on a particular, symbolic resonance in the troubled 1820s. Constable painted Salisbury Cathedral, showing it under a rainbow against a stormy sky, and Cobbett, who was there on his *Rural Rides* the year after the Pugins, looked at the spire and reflected that he lived in 'degenerate times' for 'such a thing could never be made now'.[25] Pugin was one of many who came to see in Salisbury something bigger and better than the nineteenth century. He returned to London in full health and with 'two large chests full of antiquities beside a very ancient chair' which, Catherine reported, he had 'talked and coaxed the old lady out of with whom we lodged'.[26]

On 21 December Pugin noted that 'The tower of Fonthill Abbey fell with a tremendous crash at ½ past 3PM.'[27] Wyatt's great house for William Beckford had indeed collapsed, confirming the contemptuous opinion of the architect held by John Carter and most of his fellow antiquaries. 'Wyatt the destroyer', as he was remembered, he who had dared to meddle with Salisbury and Durham, was punished posthumously by the destruction of his own hubristic monument. Pugin also noted 'panic in the city'.[28] For the first four months of 1826 his memoranda consist entirely of lists of bankruptcies. The financial crash was spectacular. Walter Scott was one of many to be ruined and everyone felt the effects. The Pugins were already used to tight funds. In sanguine resignation Auguste had totted up his account with Ackermann's clerk the year before and concluded: 'I am now indebted to Mr Ackermann of £7.6s 9d which I regret to say it is not in my power to send you – having not a guinea in my house.'[29] Ackermann himself had now to explain to his butcher, whose bill was overdue, 'the dreadful-times is the cause, not a day passes but I have bills of my customers returned, not less than two today'.[30]

As Pugin turned fourteen he was itching for his independence. He decided to write a book on castles and set off with Ferrey to Rochester Castle, which was then being restored, to undertake some antiquarian investigations along the lines he had learned from his father and Willson. He had himself lowered down the castle well in hope of finding treasure but was disappointed. He then hired some men to dig a trench in order to discover how the foundations were formed. A minute after he had climbed out the trench collapsed. He would not have been the first antiquary to die in the course of his investigations. The book on castles never appeared but this unpromising start marked nevertheless the beginning of his working life. His childhood, in a world closer to trade than to the professions where childhood was short, had come to an end. The next year he undertook his first independent commission.

7

The King's Pleasure

1827

*& what do you mean about my being unfit to manage a manu-
factury have I not managed ten times the men you ever saw . . .
had I not 700 men, cabinet makers, chair makers ebonisers,
carvers, gilders, etc etc for the Windsor job!!*
– Pugin to John Hardman, February 1850[1]

Pugin had now given up lessons at Christ's Hospital and was only
an occasional attender at his father's office. Characteristically, having
mastered what Auguste had to teach, he had no desire to go on repeating
it. He worked quickly but loathed reworking or anything finicky. Ferrey
recalled that he was not much help with Auguste's books. 'The labour
of drawing out the details . . . in a strictly geometrical manner . . . little
suited his active habits or mental energy. Sedentary occupations were
distasteful to him.'[2] It was already difficult to persuade Pugin to do
anything he found distasteful.

Instead of labouring over the drawing boards at Great Russell Street
he went about London looking at buildings, meeting people and making
friends. He was now beginning to know the brokers' shops in and
around Soho and Bond Street where the carved wood, stained glass
and other antiquities shaken loose by war and vandalism in France and
the Netherlands poured in to be auctioned in the vast and widely advertised 'importation sales'. There was also new furniture in the 'ancient
style' and made-up pieces, composed of old and new in a process
known as 'sophisticating'. It was not, exactly, faking because in the
1820s authenticity still mattered less, to most people, than what an
object looked like and the associations it evoked. Pugin was soon
not only buying but also selling antiquities, and Edward Hull, a broker

whose shop was then in St Martin's Lane, became a particular friend.

Pugin got on easily with people of his parents' age. He had his father's habit of contriving to know anybody if he wanted to and Auguste's name, as well as his example, was a help. David Roberts, the Scottish artist, who was then most famous as a brilliant scenery painter, was an object of the stage-struck Pugin's interest and when Pugin discovered that a decorator he knew was making curtains for Roberts he saw an opportunity. Roberts later recalled coming into his drawing room one day to find a youth up a ladder who said to him, 'You know my father,' to which Roberts said he replied, 'Wha the deil is your father?' and got the answer, 'I am the son of Augustus Pugin, and wanted to have the honour of hanging up David Roberts's curtains.'[3]

It was by similarly direct means no doubt that he got to know J. T. Smith, keeper of prints and drawings at the British Museum. 'Rainy Day' Smith, a noted raconteur and gossip, ran the print room as a personal salon. He liked to have lively company while he dried out mouldy Rembrandts by the fire. Anyone he found boring was told there was no room. Pugin would have felt at home in this atmosphere of art and conviviality, for it was indeed like his own home and it was probably Smith who introduced him to the work of Dürer, which he began to copy. The heavy, intricate lines, as well as the Gothic subject matter, appealed to him at once. *Knight, Death and the Devil*, with its entanglement of rocks, skulls and armour, became a particular favourite, of which he later owned an example. It was perhaps also in the print room that Pugin met John Bridge of the royal goldsmiths Rundell Bridge and Rundell. On 19 March he went with Bridge to Christie's auction rooms for 'the sale of the Duke of York's plate'.[4] The Duke, George IV's younger brother and heir apparent, had died on 5 January. Pugin had watched the cortège pass along Knightsbridge and noted that 'the funeral was not very splendid'.[5] Indeed the Duke was not extravagantly mourned. Many people agreed with Wellington that he and his brother were the 'damn'dest millstone about the neck of any government that can be imagined'.[6] After his death he was found to have been hugely in debt. Now his possessions were being auctioned off.

The King, however, seemed still oblivious to disapproval. He was very unpopular and constitutionally he was less powerful than any of his predecessors. In his architectural projects, however, he was an absolute monarch whom nobody, not even Wellington, who made strenuous efforts, could withstand. The current royal hobby-horse was the re-building of Windsor Castle. Most monarchs since Charles II had avoided Windsor, but George III had made extensive improvements and his successor also liked it. What had once been its drawbacks, the fact that it was old and inconvenient, now appeared, to the eye of modern taste, to be advantages. It had a 'quaint rurality', it was picturesque, it was medieval.[7] Nash had adapted a house in the park for the King, making 'The Cottage' (now Royal Lodge) into a residence of charm and enor-mously expensive simplicity, and next, of course, he hoped to get the job of recasting the Castle itself. Auguste and Frederick Mackenzie worked every morning at Mackenzie's office in Holborn to produce perspective views for Nash to tempt the King, but in this case without success. The commission went to Jeffry Wyatt, nephew of the late James. Wyatt later Gothicized not just the Castle but himself, changing his name to Wyatville, which was very slightly more credible than 'de Wyatt'. He carried out the work well enough, was knighted for his efforts and withdrew.

Wyatville believed that an architect's responsibility stopped with the fabric of the building. Decoration and furnishing he considered too liable to change to be worth taking great trouble over. It was a limiting view of architecture and one that was to be vigorously challenged by the rising generation. It suited the King, however, who had ideas of his own. He wanted some Gothic rooms and some Louis XV and much else besides. In both style and scale the fitting out of Windsor Castle was the last great display of Georgian splendour, a final burst of unashamed extravagance before a more sober and more thoughtful age began to dawn. It came to epitomize everything the young Victorians despised. Even after the King's death nobody was ever sure exactly how much it had cost. Nicholas Morel, an 'upholsterer', or decorator, of French extraction, was put in charge of the job and was at once applied to on all sides by suppliers and designers hoping for a share of the spoils. Morel, who had worked at the Brighton Pavilion, was already an acquaintance of Auguste and so the Pugins were well placed to take part in the great enterprise.

The King had decided that 'those portions of the interior which retained a mediaeval character should be furnished with objects in a corresponding style'.[8] It was an apparently straightforward suggestion that raised difficult questions about what did correspond to the medieval character. As the shops of Wardour Street demonstrated, very little real 'Gothic' furniture survived. In the Middle Ages furniture was sparse and what did exist was considered too heavy and inconvenient for nineteenth-century houses. Auguste had, over the last few years, developed another of his sidelines as a designer of modern Gothic furniture.[9] Architects including William Porden and C.R. Cockerell had employed him, and for the last three years he had been publishing in Ackermann's *Repository* a series of designs 'in the general style of the fifteenth century' which evoked the Gothic, while offering genteel patrons 'those improved forms and elegant contrivances which the superiority of modern art and ingenuity have introduced'.[10] The accompanying text made up in confidence for what it lacked in consistency. To the general view that Gothic was a style suitable for halls and dining rooms, Auguste added designs for the boudoir and the library, arguing over the months that Gothic could be variously scholarly, decorative, feminine, masculine, ecclesiastical, fashionable, modern, historic, convenient, magnificent, economical and patriotic. The designs were similarly mixed. The 'celebrated Château Fontaine le Henri' which he had drawn in Normandy became a bookcase.[11] The lectern at King's College Cambridge in a version 'more easy of removal' became a music stand, with 'Cherry Ripe' open on it.[12] Some of the pieces have a spiky, elegant charm. Others, like the full-length dressing mirror with flying buttresses on castors, are 'a complete burlesque', as Pugin later put it, of medieval art.[13] Overall the effect was still much closer to Strawberry Hill than to anything that had existed in the Middle Ages.

Auguste, as the articles made clear, had his eye on 'the great and magnificent works in progress at Windsor Castle'.[14] Morel duly asked him to provide some drawings. Having made a number of designs, including a sideboard and dining chairs, Auguste for some reason decided to hand the project over to his son. Pugin had perhaps been contributing to his father's work for the *Repository*. His collecting had given him an interest in furniture design and this was an area, unlike the detail drawings, where he was happy to assist. Thus it was that Pugin, at the age of fifteen, came to design furniture for George IV at Windsor. This brilliant debut became part of the myth that grew up around him. He himself, over twenty years later, had got it somewhat out of proportion, for he was never in charge of 700 men, or even seven. He went to work, for a guinea a day, designing the furniture and supervising its manufacture at the workshops in Aldersgate Street in the City. Pugin had no hesitation in modifying his father's ideas. In the surviving drawings and in the furniture itself there is a telling, rather touching contrast between father and son, the former more sophisticated in technique, the latter, already, more inventive in design. Auguste's watercolours are delicate and finely coloured. His son's thick line, showing the influence of Dürer, where it is coloured in at all, is filled out with a splashy casualness. Auguste's designs are elegant, iterative; his son's bolder, more solid and assertive. Pugin removed finials, avoided crockets and reduced the amount of piercing through of wood.

Although Pugin later repudiated his work at Windsor, the designs show him thinking ahead of his elders about what it meant to design in a 'corresponding' style to the medieval. At the same time this caused a difficulty. It brought him up against a problem that would dog him all his life. For to be, conceptually, so far ahead meant that when it came to carrying out his ideas he was hampered by technical ignorance, his own as much as other people's. Nobody had seen, let alone built, anything like this before and not everyone was persuaded that the effort was worthwhile. Many of the furniture makers at Windsor were French; George IV, like many of his contemporaries, being wildly Francophile in his taste. These were the best craftsmen in the world, men of immense skill and experience in a long, conservative tradition of cabinet-making. The *ébénistes* who had made exquisite Empire pieces for Malmaison found the whole idea of 'Gothic' furniture ridiculous. Pugin thought that François-Honoré-Georges Jacob-Desmalter, who had run his family's business in Paris for twenty-five years, was 'a very ignorant conceited man, and extremely unpleasant to be connected with'.[15] What Desmalter thought of the child designer can only be imagined. With both style and designer still in their infancy the results were bound to be uneven. The plainer items, the stools and benches, display a practicality and confidence that looks forward to Pugin's maturity. The sideboard, however, destroyed by the fire of 1992, was massively over-engineered and the dining chairs are so heavy that it requires two footmen to lift each one. They have scarcely ever been used.[16] Yet the momentum of informed taste was behind Pugin and turning against the light, elegant Gothic of his father.

In 1827 Auguste showed at the Royal Academy one of his designs for a chapel, in the new cemetery being planned by Marc Brunel. The

Gentleman's Magazine complained that the polygonal 'sepulchral chapel in the Norman style' looked 'far more like a summer house'.[17] Propriety, gravity, the very qualities that Pugin was emphasizing in his furniture, were increasingly sought after. Some time during that year Pugin also designed a set of altar plate for Mr Bridge, probably for Windsor. It was another joint effort with his father.[18] Auguste's single candlestick, a gorgeous confection of nodding ogee arches and soaring crockets, would have looked at home in Fonthill. His son's designs for a paten and chalice look like medieval metalwork.

Pugin's share in the work at Windsor came to a close with the summer. In mid August the family and the pupils set off again for France. There were the usual amusements. Family visits, dinner parties, a trip to the Jardin des Plantes to see 'this newly discovered animal called the giraffe' and a visit to the Swiss Mountain, a sort of fairground ride, 'where cars roll down with the rapidity of lightning'.[19] One day Joseph Nash alarmed Catherine by bringing her son home from Notre Dame, where they had been sketching, having had an attack of what sounds like migraine: 'The whole building,' Catherine reported, 'seemed breaking and tumbling to pieces, and the pavement so agitated he could not stand.'[20] Catherine applied castor oil and camomile and he soon recovered, but it was indicative. The intensity of his enthusiasms always led him to push his strength to the limit and his passions were not balanced by any steadying round of school or office work, by self or any other control.

In many ways he was still a child, getting into pillow fights with his father's pupils and unable to dress properly without his mother's supervision. His handwriting was wobbly, his spelling erratic. Professionally, however, he was now on equal terms in the family enterprise. 'We go to Bouvae [sic],' Catherine wrote, 'how long we shall stay . . . depends very much on what Mr Pugin and son find to interest them.'[21] Pugin and Son, however, was to be an uneasy partnership.

8

Beginning the World

October 1827 to July 1831

. . . those who look into the matter strictly will be surprized to find how much our ordinary language and ordinary ideas are modified by what we have seen and heard on the stage.
– Walter Scott, *Quarterly Review*, June 1826

Ha, Mr Editor I have you on the hip. Look to yourself.
– Pugin, Letter to the *Rambler*, 1850

Although he was excited by the glamour of the Windsor commission, Pugin took no direct advantage of it. His course over the next four years was not so much that of a rising star as of a Catherine wheel, spending his tremendous energy in all directions and becoming increasingly a worry to his parents, who also had worries of their own. Auguste's next project was to be a trip to Germany to 'take documents & sketches to publish a work on the German style of architecture of the Middle Ages' along the lines of *Antiquities of Normandy*.[1] Catherine began making up a list of useful German words and phrases, but the visit never took place and no book of German 'specimens' was begun.

The reason why is not certain, but it was probably because Auguste and John Britton now, finally, quarrelled. Britton was overbearing and, his artists often thought, mean. He protested, not unreasonably, that he took all the risks and was under constant financial pressure. The other sponsors of *Antiquities of Normandy* besides Auguste were two of the best engravers of the day, the brothers John and Henry Le Keux. They had worked often for Britton and had each put up a quarter of the costs of the book. They were hoping now, as was Auguste, to make up the accounts. Britton, however, was being evasive and was no doubt short of ready cash. Despite 'having called several times', Auguste could not get an answer.[2] He lost patience, which was unfortunate, for Britton was, if exasperating, not dishonest and he would eventually have got his money. However, 'harassed' beyond endurance and possibly urged on by Catherine, Auguste forced the issue and went to court.[3] As a result of the case and the costs, control of his share of both *Antiquities of Normandy* and *The Public Buildings of London*, the fruit of several years' work, a vast investment of time and money, passed out of Auguste's possession. It was a professional disaster. The publications from which he might have expected, at last, to receive a regular income earned him nothing.

From this point there began to be a perceptible decline in the Pugins' financial fortunes. The buoyant years that had begun with the move to Great Russell Street were coming to an end: 'there is not remaining a whole hat, coat or gown, shoe or boot amongst us,' Catherine informed Selina, adding that Auguste said that they were, as a result, 'the more picturesque'.[4] She worried not only about money but, increasingly, about her wayward teenage son, her 'extraordinary boy' with his intense enthusiasms: '[he] works so hard,' she observed, 'I fear he goes beyond his strength.'[5] Then in the summer of 1828 there came another blow, personal and professional. After a short illness Louis Lafitte died, leaving his widow inconsolable and his brother-in-law without one of his oldest friends and most loyal professional allies.

In September the Pugins were back in Paris, working on a hastily conceived potboiler, *Paris and its Environs*. Designed to fill the gap in their programme left by the abandoned German project, it was one of the 'cheap topographical works' now so common that the *Gentleman's Magazine* merely listed them. Auguste gave his son a greater role than before in overseeing operations. 'A. Pugin jn.' contributed a number of views, though he was not, then or later, especially gifted as a water-colourist or a topographical artist. He chose the buildings that he liked best, including the Gothic highlights, Notre Dame, the Hôtel de Cluny and the Sainte-Chapelle.

Returning to London, Auguste found business slow. He was not alone. Ackermann, now in his late fifties, was ailing and thinking of retirement. At the end of 1828 he closed the *Repository* magazine, a decision that further limited Auguste's income. The demise of the *Repository* was a sign, too, that a generation was passing. The year before, Ackermann had followed Rowlandson's coffin to the churchyard at St Paul's, Covent Garden. The world of the *Microcosm* went with it. Auguste felt the change. Later that year Nash, whose work at Buckingham Palace had run wildly over its budget, began to face awkward questions. The end of his career was in sight. Writing to Ackermann's cashier, Auguste asked to have his account made up to date, as he was 'particularly anxious to know the exact state of my affairs in regard to money matters'. 'I much regret having nothing to do now for Mr Ackermann,' he went on, 'having much leisure.'[6] He was still dealing in prints, sending copies of John Martin's popular apocalyptic scenes *Belshazzar's Feast* and *Joshua Stopping the Sun* to Paris, but there was not much money in that. He decided to embark on another book of Gothic architecture, based, like *Specimens*, on English buildings. By February he had almost enough plates for a first volume. These *Examples of Gothic Architecture*, as he decided to call them, were taken from a selection of sacred and secular buildings in the later Gothic styles. If, as reviewers pointed out, it was a somewhat random selection, this was because there were constraints of time and access. Random or not, *Examples* was another substantial addition to the available knowledge of Gothic buildings. The subscribers included nearly all the leading architects of the day, as well as the sculptor Francis Chantery and the painter John Constable.

Pugin was of little help with his father's difficulties. He was seldom in the office. Still desperately stage-struck, he preferred to hang around in Covent Garden. He was not alone in his enthusiasm for the theatre. His generation grew up in an age of huge auditoria, where spectacle took over from acting, and many of them, including Ruskin and Dickens, were as spellbound as Pugin. This was the heyday of Paganini and Taglioni, of romantic ballet, melodrama and pantomime. It was the moment when stage design became for the first time a profession in its own right, and Pugin decided it was the one for him, a resolution confirmed by his meeting with George Dayes, an occasional scene-shifter whom Pugin had encountered in the Aldersgate Street workshop while he was making the furniture for Windsor. Dayes had entertained him hugely with anecdotes of theatrical life and that summer Pugin managed to get himself a job at the English Opera House just off the Strand, as a super-flyman for a revival of *Der Freischütz*. Super-flymen worked above the stage managing the special effects. The job required a good head for heights, physical strength, and a sure sense of balance, for the gantries in the fly loft were narrow and the heavy flats and flying 'cars' went up and down at speed. It was rough, physical work and stage mechanics were a rough and transient population, many of them ex-sailors, who were good with ropes and had a head for heights. It was about as déclassé an occupation as Pugin could have found for himself within the law.

Der Freischütz was advertised more for the scenery than the music, which must have been barely audible. The playbill promised 'A storm and a Hurricane – The Daemon of the Hartz Mountains appears . . . the Rattle of Wheels and the Tramp of Horses are heard and a Fiery Phantom passes through the Glen' and so on through a 'tremendous explosion' and a meteorite storm until, at the end, 'all the horrors of the preceding scene are accumulated'.[7] Despite which, Pugin noted the production was 'not remarkably sucessful'.[8] The notebook that he kept when he worked at the English Opera House is the first example of what became his habitual approach to a new subject, whether stage carpentry or church ritual. A list of terms is interspersed with sketches and practical observations: '. . . swing block. oak. bad for hanging borders. always use fixed block nailed or screwed against the joists . . . for heavy things ¾" rope . . . for flying cars loose rope ¼".' He drew cleats, sheaves and blocks and, in some detail, the construction of a dowel strong enough to 'run 30 foot long without sagging . . . best for country stages'.[9] Clearly he was expecting to continue in the business for some time.

In the autumn he was briefly down in Sussex with Ferrey, drawing Herstmonceux Castle for his father's *Examples*. By now there was a marked tension in his relations with his parents, especially his father, who could have done with more of his assistance. Neither he nor Catherine liked their son working in the theatre, for although there were respected artists among the scene-painters the milieu was not a salubrious one. As well as the low-class company he might fall into in the fly loft, the theatres were notorious for immorality on both sides of the curtain. The lobbies at Covent Garden were openly used for soliciting, and the prostitutes, when the house was not full, used the boxes for business. Actresses and dancers were thought of as little better than prostitutes themselves, and while this was a slander in many cases, backstage mores were certainly very different from those of Great Russell Street. Venereal disease was endemic. Pugin, so confident, so headstrong, so naïve and at seventeen beginning to be curious about women, was running risks of which, unlike his parents, he was utterly unaware. But if Auguste was inclined to try to curb his son's activities, Catherine, however much she worried, could deny him nothing. At home he was allowed to turn the top floor of Great Russell Street into an elaborate model theatre with working scenery in which he tried out his own designs. This was done 'at much expense', as it involved taking out the attic ceilings and 'cutting away the roof' in order to install cisterns for the water effects.[10] Theatre design enabled him to work, for the first time, in three dimensions, to discover the effects of light and shade and, at home at least, to control the entire performance down to the smallest detail. Throughout his career there was perhaps a part of Pugin that would always remain an only child with a toy theatre in the attic.

From now on he applied himself to one venture after another. As well as draughtsmanship and scenery the autumn brought another new friendship, with the Scottish architect James Gillespie Graham. Graham, at fifty-three, had a well-established practice with more than three dozen country houses and twenty-eight churches to his name as well as parts of the New Town in Edinburgh. He had established himself by a mixture of talent and the necessary push, and he was, like Auguste and his son, not quite a gentleman: his illegitimate half-brother had lately been hanged at Aberdeen for forgery. Graham himself, however, was a kindly man and, like many people, took an instant liking to the young Pugin with his enthusiasm, his precocious knowledge and his warmth. Graham had come to London to arrange fittings for a house he was building at Murthly in Perthshire for John Stewart of Grantully. The Scots were as entranced by the myth of themselves propounded by their great national poet as were the English and the French. Stewart wanted a Jacobean palace from the pages of *Waverley*, with a great hall and ancient carvings and, for the sake perhaps of comparison with Windsor, a French drawing room.

Among the brokers' shops in London Graham found a man who had a collection of 'heaps of interior carving'.[11] The man was probably John Swaby, a collector and dealer who had a shop in Wardour Street and who introduced him to Pugin. Soon after he had met Graham, Pugin was working for him. He was off at Hatfield House drawing details for him to copy in his own Jacobean creation. Within a month, Pugin was using his Wardour Street connections to supply antique carvings for Murthly and he continued to do so for two years, along with casts, models and drawings.

In October he was back at the theatre admiring Fanny Kemble, who made her debut at Covent Garden as Juliet. Anxious for a better job than super-flyman, he applied to Thomas Grieve, who ran the scenery department at Covent Garden, and 'entreated to be employed'.[12] The Grieve family were the leading scene-painters of the day. Even so they were surprised that Pugin, whom they knew by repute as his father's son, should want such a menial job. 'Knowing that [Auguste] was in a good position,' Grieve recalled, 'I was astonished at [Pugin's] coming to me, and I heard afterwards that, at the office, he could knock out work at the rate of £10 a day.'[13] Nevertheless Grieve took him on, and Pugin started work in October on *The Devil's Elixir*, 'a musical tale of romance' whose special attractions included the spectacular collapse of the shrine of St Anthony.

For the rest of the season Pugin divided his attentions between Covent Garden and drawings for Murthly, for which he designed a suite of interiors: a great hall, with a hammerbeam ceiling, as well as a 'chapel, entrance hall and staircase, anti-room, Library and Drawing room', this last in the style of Louis XIV.[14] Little survives. The palace at Murthly was a *folie de grandeur* which, having stood incomplete and increasingly ruinous for over 120 years, was blown up after the Second World War. Some of the fittings were put into a new wing of the old house. It is probably there, looking up into the hammerbeams of the hall, that we see Pugin's first independent and quite creditable essay in Gothic architecture. For the most part, however, the interiors have vanished as completely as the shrine of St Anthony.

Pugin got on well at Covent Garden. The Grieves were now his friends and they were impressed, as everyone always was, by the speed with which he worked. 'From first to last he rarely, if ever, painted,' Grieve recalled, 'but that was of no consequence to me, as all I wanted was his designs. After he left me, he would often come into my painting room, and in a few hours (if there was anything Gothic going on) do a surprising quantity of work.'[15] There was often something Gothic going on, for the theatre, like everything else, was saturated with the passion for the Middle Ages. Scott's novels were the basis for dozens of ballets and plays. There were new historic dramas as well as a revived enthusiasm for neglected works, such as Shakespeare and Fletcher's *Henry VIII*, in which the trial scene offered scenic opportunities. Theatregoers, like tourists, were becoming better informed about the past and beginning to expect authenticity in scenery and costumes, so Pugin was in demand both as a draughtsman and as an antiquary able to provide 'documents' from his own collection and Auguste's, drawings and actual objects, from which designers and prop-makers could work. Wardour Street was not far in any sense from Covent Garden. The Gothic Revival and the art of illusion were common to both.

Pugin learned a great deal from the theatre that he would apply and develop in architecture. One thing in particular he learned from the Grieves was about the interior division of large three-dimensional spaces. By the time he was working at Covent Garden the stage was 68 feet deep and 82' 6" wide, the size, if not the shape, of a substantial church. To manage it the designers had begun to use techniques borrowed from Picturesque landscape painting, the wings and flats arranged with irregular masses in receding fields. To complicate further the bare space the Grieves had developed their trademark 'three-door' device, especially useful for ceremonial scenes. A three-arched structure divided the stage half-way down to define an interior playing area. It might represent doors or windows; in one case at least, it was actually a Gothic rood screen.[16] The space within a space, the Picturesque ideal of revelation by partial concealment, became one of Pugin's favourite architectural devices.

Intellectually too, despite its determined populism, the theatre had its effect on him. It was a good place, in the 1830s, to develop a critical view of architecture, for, as *The Times* put it, 'If comedy holds the mirror up to nature, it is pantomime, with her concave glass, that should, peculiarly, caricature the deformities of the town.'[17] With the vast resources that Covent Garden and Drury Lane poured into their efforts to outdo each other and the scale of the stages, buildings could be created almost full size. The Brighton Pavilion was a particular favourite, invoked for any exotic scene and turning up typically as the Sultan Bahama's Castle of the Hundred Gates. The continuing 'improvements' were also popular topics: the New Cemetery Company, Nash's buildings for the peace celebrations, all these and many more appeared in character or simply as themselves on the enormous London stages. Pugin saw architecture dramatized, satirized, given narrative meaning.

From the scene-painting room at Covent Garden a flight of stairs led to the stage door, which opened into Hart Street. In November of 1829

Pugin took a lease on the upper loft of Number 12, where he set up his own business, 'in the carving and joinering' line.[18] It was, no doubt, the receipt in October of £163 12s. 6d. from Gillespie Graham, for carvings for Murthly, that made this possible. Pugin proposed to supply furniture, metalwork and interior fittings in a number of styles and on an apparently immense scale. He produced a catalogue which survives in a hand-drawn version, which may in fact have been the only version, offering Gothic and Jacobean chairs, tables and stools. The scope, quantity and variety of the models suggests an enterprise much larger than the reality, which was a workshop 15' by 30' 6", two carvers and a seventeen-year-old designer. The carvers were probably recruited from brokers' workshops. What little survives of the furniture they made for Pugin has mostly been much simplified from the designs. His ambitions ran to silverware as well. The title page of the designs is inscribed with the names of his heroes, 'Albertus Durer' and 'Benvenuto Chetini'.

In June 1830 George IV, who had been ailing for two years, died. He was largely unlamented (except by John Nash, who had been on the point of receiving a baronetcy from him). A royal death, however, meant the closure of the theatres and Pugin, temporarily unwanted in the scenery department, concentrated his efforts on the furniture designs he had begun for Mrs Gough of Perry Hall in Warwickshire. Mrs Gough, through whose commission the history of the Hart Street works is principally told, must have been a tolerant woman and not without humour. Through the summer and into the autumn Pugin worked on her order. Enclosing sketches of chairs and sideboards in Gothic and Jacobean variations he wrote:

I have consulted with my foreman and do not think that it would be possible to execute the subjoined designs under the price mentioned with them without simplyfiring so much as to destroy all the effect of the composition. I have taken the Liberty of making another design of a sideboard in a totally different composition which I am of opinion would be preferable in the situation in which it is to be placed.

I remain madam your obedient servant

A. Pugin Junr.[19]

In this attempt at the kind of business letter he had seen his father write, Auguste's prose sits on his son as his top coat might have done, too large and somewhat out of date.

The drawings show two alternative sideboards and eight designs for chairs suitable for Perry Hall, a house that had been made over in the Old English style. They demonstrate how much Pugin had learned by now, from the theatre, the brokers' shops and his own experiments, about wooden construction. The difficulty of the decoration remained, but he had solved for himself the problem he had faced at Morel's, when nobody knew how to build his designs. He had either learned from looking at antique furniture, or worked out independently, how to construct furniture that could be assembled without glue or nails and could be put together on site. When it was ready he dispatched the sideboard 'flat packed' in numbered pieces, with instructions for putting it up when it arrived. He told Mrs Gough to tell her carpenters there was 'no occasion to Glue' the pieces together, 'as they are sufficiently firm without it'.[20]

Some of the furniture was ready in September and Pugin sent with it a letter that is an artless self-portrait:

I have the honour to inform you that the following articles of your furniture are compleated . . .

I trust by this time you have recovered from your indisposition with which you was suffering when I took the liberty of Calling at Perry Hall when Last in the Country . . . I hope it has so proved or I should not wenture to trouble you with this letter on business . . .

the tables have not come to so much as I originally expected but the sidebard has much exceeded my estimate.[21]

He wrote again, the next day, explaining that he had 'an unexpected payment to make on saturday' and wondering if Mrs Gough might let him have ten pounds straight away.[22] She sent him twenty. No doubt she was pleased with the furniture, but she must also have felt an affection for Pugin, with his wobbly spelling, his cockney 'wenture' and 'warnish', his desire to please and his transparent delusions of grandeur. The register of his letters swoops and crashes as his professional voice breaks, from the high-flown to the colloquial, between frequent requests for money. By October Pugin was telling Mrs Gough that his premises were too small. At the same time he was asking for £100, 'this being our flat time of year', and Pugin having 'Lately sustained a heavy Loss in business'.[23] He was applying too to Gillespie Graham, who was telling John Stewart that the model maker in London was 'urgent for payt'.[24]

Pugin took more space in the same building. He would never learn to bend with the financial wind; when money was short he would still extend his operations and his expenses. He learned to cost his materials more accurately, but not his time.

Legally Pugin was still a minor, and this by now gave Auguste his only control over his son. With his business expanding, albeit on such an unsteady basis, Pugin was longing for his own house, which of course he intended to design. It was to be a place where he might retire 'apart from the turmoil of business in London'.[25] The area he favoured was Christchurch. The town with its priory and castle had continued to draw him back since his visit as a convalescent. He found a picturesque spot and placed an offer for a piece of land, but he needed his father's consent as guarantor for the purchase and this Auguste refused. Pugin's love for Christchurch was expressed instead by the gift to the Priory of an altar table which he had made. It was one of his more elaborate designs, much simplified in execution, and it is the gesture, perhaps, that is more revealing than the object itself. Where Pugin's interests and affections were engaged, whether with people, or buildings, or with a whole field of work, like theatre design, he held back nothing of himself. He wanted to be involved, as intimately as possible. He wanted to put some expression of himself into Christchurch, a place he loved. There is little evidence at this date about his religious feelings, which were not, apparently, especially intense, but the implication of the gift is that already the sacred was closely linked for him with the personal; the power of architecture and of association moved him deeply.

Anyone who was fond of Pugin, as many people were, must have feared for him as they watched him throw himself at such a headlong pitch into life. In 1830 Gillespie Graham had his own architect's compasses inscribed as a present to his young friend. Perhaps he was trying with this gift to suggest that it was time Pugin began to concentrate his energies and consider his future more seriously. When, fifteen years later, Pugin sat reluctantly for his portrait he chose to hold Graham's compasses as a sign of his vocation. At the time that he was given them, however, the vocation had yet to emerge. His love of architecture was only one of several loves, and his ambitions to build one of many ambitions and not yet within reach. If Graham had hoped Pugin might take the conventional way into the profession by becoming a pupil in his office he was disappointed. Pugin was too used to his independence, too restless and too busy.

That summer saw a revolution in France, a short revolution but one that terrified Europe by its implications. As Pugin put it, 'In 3 days the citizens posses themselves of Paris. Charles the X obliged to abdicate and fly to England.'[26] Lafitte's former patron the Duchesse de Berry fled to Scotland. The Ultra-Royalists proclaimed her son, the Duc de Bordeaux, Henry V, while in Paris the Duc d'Orléans became the 'citizen king', Louis Philippe. Among the consequences, for the Pugins, was the loss of the last remnants of their network of French patronage. 'I am now in a very different situation to what I was,' Auguste explained to an acquaintance who was hoping for help to promote some work in France.[27] The July Revolution had its effect on England. There too there was unrest. Agrarian riots, attributed to the mythical 'Captain Swing', raged close to London and far beyond, filling many minds with foreboding. Some argued for reform, others for repression. In November Wellington's government fell and the Whigs came to power. In March 1831 Macaulay introduced a Reform Bill, which proposed to extend the right to vote more widely than ever before into the middle classes. He warned Parliament not to put up 'a hopeless struggle against the spirit of the age now, while the crash of the proudest throne of the continent is still resounding in our ears', but to act before 'that last and most dreadful paroxysm of popular rage' swept away Parliament, monarch and all.[28]

He was defeated, and as the debate went on the unrest continued. 'We have had some rioting here,' Gillespie Graham wrote from Edinburgh on 6 May, 'but very little harm done. I hope this great political question will soon be . . . set at rest.'[29] He was also, he remarked, once again, in receipt of a 'pressing letter' from Pugin asking for money.[30] Pugin meanwhile was having trouble supplying Mrs Gough with her armchairs, having become involved in 'a dispute with the person employed in the stuffing' over which he had been obliged to take legal measures 'which . . . cost me much time money & uneasiness'.[31]

At the theatre things were going better. He made designs for Deshayes's ballet *Kenilworth* and provided 'authorities' for costumes. Princess Victoria, now heir to her uncle William IV, copied some of them for her dolls. The production was a great success.[32] The *Athenaeum* thought it 'magnificent beyond description'.[33] Pugin's next job was on

L'ultimo Giorno di Pompeii, with its spectacular volcanic effects. Frustrated in his ambition to build a house, he decided to buy a boat instead, a step which probably worried and annoyed his parents even more. It was no doubt in the fly-tower of the theatre where so many sailors worked that he got the idea and the know-how. Sailing, which was to be a lifelong passion, combined his love of mechanisms, of wooden construction and the sea. It satisfied his restlessness and need to be physically active. The *Elizabeth*, his first boat, was bought in May 1831 and he sailed from Westminster Bridge 'for an excusion on the water' lasting five days down the Thames and up the Medway. 'A man named Ward accompanied me all the way and we only landed once the whole time.'[34] He soon became a confident sailor and took to wearing nautical dress even when ashore. By nineteen he had, as Ferrey noted with disapproval, changed considerably from the 'refined boy and polished gentleman' he had been when 'under his parents' care'.[35] The delicate child of Lafitte's drawing was transformed into a broad-shouldered, somewhat roughly-spoken young man. His behaviour was now 'a source of much pain and anguish' to his family and friends, 'more especially to the refined tastes of his father'.[36] Some of this was adolescent affectation which passed, some of it was not and did not. Indeed, some of his rougher habits became more entrenched with time. Pugin's appearance always caused comment. He later wore working clothes of his own design which were based on sailing gear and were, he argued, simply practical. He never lost the personal untidiness of which his mother had complained when he was a child, and his dishevelment became at times uncleanliness. Although he never picked up the nautical taste for tobacco or strong drink, he would swear, 'freely and unconsciously', while he worked, and Ferrey was not the only one of his contemporaries to be disconcerted or repelled by Pugin's lack of gentility.[37]

Once he had some experience as a sailor he began to use his boat for trips to the Continent, especially to Flanders and Holland. He seems to have carried various cargoes but his chief purpose was to buy antiquities, which, with his fluent French and well-developed bargaining skills, he was able to pick up at sales and brokers' shops. The trade was booming. Pugin's was only one of the 'small vessels . . . wholly freighted' with art and artefacts that plied a regular trade across the Channel.[38] Imported antiquities were heavily taxed. Immediately after the Napoleonic wars manuscripts cost a shilling per pound weight, and although by the time Pugin was working duty had gone down, he still, according to Talbot Bury, preferred to land out of the way and avoid the necessity of paying anything at all. Some of his haul he kept for himself, to make the foundation of a museum that he was planning. Other pieces he would sell to dealers or to architects, like Graham, who had uses for them.

On one of these trips he was shipwrecked, driven ashore and only just saved with his crew. Ferrey tells a curious tale of him blowing into Leith and walking, dripping wet, to Gillespie Graham in Edinburgh. Pugin's son-in-law was later told a more likely story, that it was an old woman who had taken Pugin in and that Pugin sent a present of food to her at Christmas every year afterwards. However, exactly, it came about, his shipwreck taught him a lesson as perhaps only an elemental force could have taught him at this point in his life. Thereafter he was a cautious sailor.

At Great Russell Street, meanwhile, family life continued its peculiar course. Pugin had his model theatre in the attic. Catherine had her religious disputes in the library and in the drawing school there were several projects in hand. Auguste made one of his last and most effective perspectives this year, for the Brunels. Marc Brunel was his exact contemporary, another French refugee with an English wife and a prodigiously talented son, and he had made use of Auguste's services before for designs for his cemetery company. This time he and Isambard wanted assistance with the Clifton suspension bridge in Bristol, or rather they wanted help to persuade the building committee in charge that the architectural appearance of this great landscape feature would be of a high enough standard. Like most people of taste just now the committee were in dispute about the relative merits of Gothic and classical: 'the committee is much divided about the stile of the Porticos', Marc Brunel noted in his diary, adding pragmatically, 'the Egyptian is likely to settle the difference'.[39] He paid Auguste ten guineas for drawing out a handsome pharaonic creation which was published as a lithograph. Like Auguste's earliest work for Nash the purpose of the drawing was largely rhetorical. It succeeded in delighting the committee and winning the day for the Brunels, but it was never built in the elaborate form he depicted.

The name of Pugin was now well enough known to make a convenient umbrella under which the pupils, as they grew up, might make their own first excursions into authorship with Auguste as publisher. The

Great Russell Street school was beginning to bear fruit. Benjamin Ferrey produced a book of 'ornamental gables' and Joseph Nash launched himself with a series of *Views Illustrative of Pugin's Examples of Gothic Architecture*. These were lithographs that took the buildings from the *Examples*, Croydon Palace, Oxburgh Hall and the rest and reconstructed them as they might have looked in the past with scenes such as 'Queen Elizabeth's visit to Archbishop Matthew Parker'. Nash went on to develop this idea into a hugely popular series, *The Mansions of England in the Olden Times*.

As Willson wrote, the century had already seen a great change in attitudes to medieval buildings. 'The study of ancient architecture is not now confined to the mere antiquary, but has become almost a part of polite education.'[40] In theatre and art and architecture itself there was a growing demand for more historical accuracy on the one hand and on the other for heightened emotion: the purer the illusion, the greater the artistic truth. Literal truth was also increasingly admired. As the scepticism of the Regency faded, a more rigorous age was coming in, inclined to ask questions and to expect explanations. With George IV dead and a Whig government in office, John Nash had no powerful friends left and plenty of enemies. He was called upon by the Treasury to account in detail for what had gone wrong at Buckingham Palace, something which he could not convincingly do. A Select Committee found him guilty of 'inexcusable irregularity and great negligence' and he retired in disgrace to the Isle of Wight, as little lamented as his king.[41]

At nineteen, with his own business, his own boat, many friends and a growing collection of antiquities, Pugin felt ready to assemble material for an autobiography. The book he took up for the purpose has 'Designs for Furniture' written on the spine. About half the pages are covered with the fitful journalizing of adolescence. Whole years are skipped, some months chronicled in detail. Many of the entries are on slips of paper noting newsworthy events and theatrical performances in his childhood, made, perhaps, from almanacks. Most of it must have been assembled that year; how much was copied from earlier notes is impossible to tell. In July 1831, after a note of the death of a retired theatrical manager, the journal breaks off. That is probably because it was about now that Pugin embarked on one of the experiences of adult life that he had not yet attempted. He fell in love.

9

A Very Short Courtship

July 1831 to May 1832

O Lady! we receive but what we give,
And in our life alone does Nature live:
Ours is her wedding garment, ours her shroud!
  – Samuel Taylor Coleridge, *Dejection: An Ode*, 1802

Sarah Anne Garnett (or Garnet) was the younger half-sister of George
Dayes, Pugin's scene-shifting friend. Dayes's father had been the watercolourist, Edward, a troubled and unpopular man who committed
suicide. His mother, Sarah Parker, a miniaturist, had remarried; her
second husband was Joseph Garnett, a tailor with a shop in Museum
Street. The family was neither wealthy nor well-placed.[1] Their circumstances were, Pugin noted, with some defensiveness, 'much reduced'.[2]
Ferrey described Dayes merely as 'a person of inferior position'.[3] He
was humorous, though, with a fund of theatrical anecdotes, and he and
Pugin remained friends. Dayes's half-sister was a pretty girl, twenty-two
in the summer of 1831, some three years older than Pugin, gentle and
sweet-natured. She may well have been a dancer, one of the girls Leigh
Hunt described, destined to 'bloom out their short lives in the borders
and vindicate their common humanity between disgrace and daring'.[4]
Or Pugin may simply have met her with Dayes. In any event Anne,
obscure and penniless, came from exactly that socially and morally
dubious world of tradesmen and theatre mechanics in which his parents
were so anxious that Pugin should not mix.

Flirtation was not in his nature, with women or with anything else.
He was soon in love and passionately attached to Anne, whose family
put no restrictions on the time she spent with him. Pugin took her to
Christchurch to show her the Priory and the water-meadows. He liked

female company and with his mother and his aunt he was used to finding in it a source of support and shared enthusiasm for all his own endeavours. From a lover he would always want and expect the same complete devotion, as well as a perfect soulmate. Not surprisingly while he was so preoccupied, the business at Hart Street, already on a shaky footing, reached a crisis. On 1 September Pugin wrote to Mrs Gough to explain that he was giving up furniture manufacture. His reasons, if not elegantly set out, were unanswerable: 'I have never spare any money in ... execution, and as in most cases my prime cost has far exceeded my estimate ... in no work in which I have been hitherto engaged in have I ever been able to clear any remuneration.' In view of which, he concluded, with a flying clutch at dignity: 'I have at Length determined to ... confine my-self entirely to my original profession of an architect and designer.'[5]

Pugin had been unable to cost his work or manage the business side of his enterprise. In the end, despite the gloss he put on it, the decision to discontinue trading was not his but his landlords'. He had got behind with the rent and was arrested for non-payment and put into the sponging house. Such episodes were not uncommon in the Pugins' circles, but it was a shock and, in his parents' eyes, certainly a disgrace when the spectre of financial ruin that had long haunted them manifested. Auguste asked Weale and Hogarth, the architectural publishers, to underwrite a bond for his son. Pugin was released and the money was found to pay off the debt, possibly with the help of the ever-generous Selina. The whole incident was over in a matter of days at most. But its implications were not so easily dispelled. It was the first time Pugin had been grazed by the unfeeling world beyond Great Russell Street and it made a considerable impression.

While he could scarcely justify his claim to be returning to architecture, he was not entirely distracted by love. He was determined to pay back the money he owed and he was capable of earning, if not of managing, considerable sums. The fitting up of Murthly went on until the end of the year and at Covent Garden he was busy for the Grieves. Four new scenes were needed for a revival of *Henry VIII*, which opened in October with Charles Kemble in the lead. Pugin was useful to the Grieves in helping them re-create, in wood and canvas, the choir and west front of Westminster Abbey. It was reconstructed in detail as it would have appeared in 1533, without Hawksmoor's towers. A theatre audience, by now, would have noticed and objected to any anachronism of that sort. For the interior scenes, the apartments encrusted with Gothic sculpture that Leigh Hunt noted in his review, Pugin relied on his Wardour Street experience of the made-up rooms supplied for collectors.

As Christmas approached there were pantomimes. He was at work on *Hop o'My Thumb*, which was not a great success, but this, by now, was not the most pressing of Pugin's difficulties.[6] Even his debts must have taken second place in his mind to a new anxiety. By November it would have been apparent to them both that Anne Garnett was pregnant. Pugin, who sometimes spent the night at the theatre, sleeping in one of the boxes when he was working late, had not always, it seems, been alone. Older than he, more experienced and brought up in a very different milieu, Anne had clearly been willing to enter into a sexual relationship more rapidly and with less security than a girl of his own class would have been. But her compliance did not mean that she ran no risk; the moral laxity of the world in and around Covent Garden should not be mistaken for tolerance. Girls of Anne's type often found themselves in her situation and men in Pugin's position might pay them off or, if they chose and could afford to, set them up as mistresses, but often they merely abandoned them. After that a woman's prospects were bleak. An illegitimate child almost invariably deprived her of any chance of an ordinary respectable life, whatever her class. *Harris's List*, one of several published guides to prostitutes, which described them alphabetically by name with details of their prices, services and personal attractions, included many whose careers had started with an accident like Anne's. A few ended happily with a rich keeper, even a husband. Most ended in the gutter, diseased and gin-sodden.

Pugin had by now been long enough at Covent Garden to have no illusions about what would happen to her if he abandoned Anne. He was headstrong and spoiled, wildly egotistical, but not in any narrow sense selfish. In the thousands of letters and papers that survive to document his life in his own words and those of others there is no suggestion, for all his impetuosity and his sometimes exaggerated emotionalism, that he ever did a mean or a cowardly thing. Now his impetuosity and his honesty propelled him in the same direction. He had no hesitation in deciding that he and Anne should be married and he resolved to tell his parents nothing until it was a fait accompli. He was still under age and unable to marry without the parental consent which he had reason to doubt would be forthcoming. The banns could not be read in Bloomsbury, where a 'just cause or impediment' might well be declared. So he and Anne went, instead, to St Mary's, Whitechapel, a seventeenth-century brick church serving a vast parish with a poverty-stricken population. Remote from the fragile respectability of Blooms-bury, it was a place where few questions were asked. The couple declared themselves to be of age and to be resident there – as Anne may have been. The last months of 1831 must have been tense. While he waited for his banns to be read on three successive Sundays in November, Pugin, whose nature was frank and who had always been in his parents' confidence, no doubt felt his secret weighing on him. His father was becoming increasingly concerned about money and as his anxieties grew his health declined; he was beginning to develop a tremor in his hands, disastrous for an artist, and to suffer from pains in his feet.

Outside the Pugin household there were other signs of unease which no doubt found an echo across the family dinner table. Edward Irving, whose services Catherine still apparently attended, had moved to a new, much larger, Gothic church in Regent Square where 1,000 people at a time could gather to hear him. In October there was the first outbreak of 'glossolalia', or speaking in tongues, among the London congregation. These 'manifestations', among other things, would eventually lead to Irving's expulsion from the Church of Scotland and the establishment of his own breakaway 'Catholic Apostolic' or 'Irvingite' church. To the general public it was largely a matter of bewildered amusement. One of the scenes in *Hop o'My Thumb* was a skit on the Irvingites, as they began to be known. A large Unknown Tongue, made out of cardboard, appeared on stage and held a conversation with Pantaloon. Not all the satire was so mild. In a heavily censored theatre it was pantomime that gave scope for political comment and dissent. The theme of *Hop o'My Thumb* is the story of poor Jack, who takes his son to the forest and leaves him to starve because there is no food at home. It was a resonant one in the autumn of 1831 and not an accidental choice. The Reform Bill was still struggling to pass into law. In October it was defeated in the House of Lords by the votes of the bishops, a move which prompted general civil unrest directed especially at the clergy. In Bristol the bishop's palace was destroyed, at Nottingham the castle was burned down. Everywhere there was a growing mood of alarm and pessimism.

As the Pugins drank to the turn of the new year Auguste said, only half jokingly, that he thought 1832 would be the last he would see in.

On 12 January, after what Ferrey tactfully referred to as their 'very short courtship', Pugin and Anne, now five months pregnant, were married in Whitechapel and came back to Bloomsbury to face the consequences.[7] It cannot have been an easy moment for anyone. In an age when class was, very largely, destiny, it was not mere snobbery that would have caused his parents pain. Just when he might have been about to rise in the world, their talented son appeared to have sunk irretrievably. Committed to a wife who brought him nothing but obligations, who his parents might have suspected of deliberately trapping their naïve and warm-hearted son into marriage, it would have seemed that a vast spectrum of social and professional possibilities was placed, at a stroke, beyond his reach before he was twenty-one. At the same time they were not prudes. Catherine's consciousness of her Welby inheritance had never outweighed her affections. She herself had married, thirty years earlier almost to the day, in the teeth of her own father's objections. Auguste, who had, perhaps, an illegitimate child of his own, may have had private reasons to sympathize with his son's predicament. In any event there was no course open to them, as affectionate parents, but to accept the inevitable and welcome Anne into their home with a good grace, and they seem to have become genuinely fond of her. If Anne's own family played any part in her marriage or her new life, they left no record of it.

Two weeks after the wedding the couple set off on a six-week honeymoon. It was a long and somewhat strenuous journey for a pregnant woman, but Pugin was by now a seasoned traveller. He wanted to show Anne more of what he loved of the landscape and architecture of England and Scotland, and he was never particularly sensitive to the needs or physical comforts of others. He wanted to introduce her to some of his friends and, perhaps, he preferred to be out of his parents' way for a while. It was in some respects a bleak voyage, undertaken in a bitter winter. The country was in the grip of disease. The first outbreak of cholera to reach Britain was spreading rapidly. As the question of reform continued to cause unrest, there was talk in Parliament of divine displeasure and calls for a day of public atonement. The Irvingites and other independent groups multiplied. There was unease within the Established Church and a note, there too, of millenarian prophecy. On 22 January

Pugin's former Bloomsbury neighbour John Henry Newman preached at Oxford a university sermon on the theme of personal influence, in which he predicted that there would arise a 'few highly-endowed men' who, like the apostles, 'will rescue the world for centuries to come'.[8] It was seen, later, as the first expression of what became the Oxford Movement. On that same day Pugin left London for Leith on board the *Royal Sovereign* to visit Gillespie Graham. Off the 'Fern' Islands, as he called them, the ship was hit by a squall, losing, Pugin noted with precision, her topmast, gaff, topsail and flybynight.[9] He arrived at Edinburgh to find the cholera there and the city in 'great alarm . . . almost at a stand' as the authorities tried to enforce a *cordon sanitaire*, preventing the citizens from leaving.[10] Policemen were stationed on the Musselburgh Road to hold back the 'great number of families' who were attempting to flee.[11]

Pugin remained, working on drawings for Graham. He was, probably, designing the first of two great spires he would contribute to his friend's oeuvre. This one, destined for Graham's church at Montrose, was modelled on that most perfect of Perpendicular steeples, St James's, Louth, in Lincolnshire, which Pugin had known since childhood. Two weeks later, as they made their way south via Newcastle, Durham, York, Beverley, Hull and Lincoln, the weather improved and the reports of cholera grew less alarming. Pugin was back among the buildings that had first awoken his love of architecture and the Middle Ages. In each place he spent the hours of daylight drawing and measuring. How Anne's time was passed he did not record in the journal he kept of the trip. He did, however, record his thoughts about the architecture. He had by now well formed and decided opinions. At York Minster, where the damage caused by the artist John Martin's mad arsonist brother was still in course of repair, under the supervision of Robert Smirke, Pugin admired the wood carving by local craftsmen but found the new stalls, made in London, wanted 'spirit and variety of character'.[12] The new stained glass he thought abominable and 'the whole business', he concluded, had been 'conducted in a jobbing manner and is just what might be expected from so ignorant a man in Gothic as Mr Smirke'.[13]

This may have been the first time Pugin set such thoughts down on paper, but they were clearly well established in his mind. He had written off men like Smirke, in fact the whole of the late-Georgian architectural establishment, just as he dismissed Desmalter the *ébéniste*. In the 1830s there was a genuine distinction between, on the one hand, professional architects, trained in offices and working in a variety of styles including Gothic, and, on the other, antiquaries like Willson, who were deeply versed in Gothic by virtue of their studies, which in turn informed their own buildings. For Pugin this was by now more than a difference in practice. It was a moral difference. The professional architects were 'jobbing', ignorant, working for the money. The antiquaries had a scholarly devotion to what they did. Craftsmen too, he began to observe, imparted life and variety to their work which machines could not reproduce. His vision of architecture and the applied arts was beginning to coalesce. As Pugin went along he was, as usual, making friends with like-minded people, antiquaries and workmen. At Beverley he fell in with Mr Cummings, the head mason, who treated his enthusiastic visitor as he treated the buildings in his care, 'most kindly'.[14]

The stay in Lincoln in February was the last visit that Pugin recorded in his journal. The city was his home from home, long known and loved. Its cathedral, perched on a hill, visible for miles, is a masterpiece of, mostly, Early English Gothic. In St Hugh's Choir the rhythm and counter-rhythm of asymmetric vaulting is played out, as pleasingly to an eye like Pugin's as music to a trained ear. It kept him absorbed day after day. He had no fear of heights and sat drawing, perched up against the roof while the winter daylight lasted, until he became such a fixture that the woman who took the guided tours pointed him out to visitors. In Lincoln, as well as the cathedral, Pugin had the pleasure of visiting Willson and his wife, who liked and were kind to Anne. Willson, though he wrote so slowly, read widely and deeply. He was gentle but critical in his mild way. He and Pugin talked about the buildings they loved, about their collections of books and antiquities, and deplored together the crimes of modern architects.

In his recent introductory essay to the first volume of Auguste's *Examples*, Willson had made his own contribution to the debate that continued to rage, albeit in sedate and heavily footnoted form, among antiquaries about the correct term for medieval buildings. 'Gothic' had originated as a pejorative term, meaning merely crude. John Britton had suggested 'Christian' and this was now widely in use by initiates. Willson, quietly, in a footnote, put the point that Christian and Gothic were not really synonymous. 'If a term were to be borrowed from religion, it might be more properly denominated "Catholic Architecture" in as much as the sublimest productions of this style were originally dedicated to the solemnities of the Catholic liturgy; and, on the other hand, its destruction immediately followed the subversion of Catholicity.'[15]

Willson, himself a Catholic, was devout but undogmatic in his faith. It was a scholarly, not a polemical suggestion. And in any event, he added, 'it is too late now to expect' any change in terminology.[16] There he was wrong. Pugin took up the point almost at once. That same year, in a sketchbook, he drew an imaginary chapel, a densely decorated little chantry, developed through a sequence of views and details. Underneath it he wrote 'Catholic chapel', the first time he seems to have used the word.[17] What exactly he meant by it is unclear, probably no more than an endorsement of his friend Willson's opinion, as against that of Britton whom he now, like his father, heartily disliked. His religious ideas would seem at this stage still to have been less formed than his architectural opinions. The journal of his honeymoon is the first surviving record of his religious practice, and while his attendance at church was clearly more than formal, it was not perhaps much more. In a life of constant and mostly cheerful activity, marred only by the boredom of Irving's sermons, his churchgoing, when he could get to a church he liked, had been one of many sources of happiness.

The last entry in the journal is for 26 February. The couple must have returned to London soon afterwards. There they would have found that the cholera had arrived before them. March 21 was proclaimed by Parliament a day of fasting and penitence. In Westminster Abbey a large crowd fidgeted, more curious than penitent, through an austere service. The spring saw the Reform Bill reach the Lords again. It was amended in May to preserve the anomalous 'pocket' boroughs, seats whose representation was in the gift of individuals. After the amendment the death bells tolled all night at Birmingham. The King and Queen were booed when they appeared in public. All agreed the times were ominous. Sir Robert Peel, who was in opposition and against the Reform Bill, gave it as his opinion that the monarchy would not last more than five years. Even so sober a man as Thomas Arnold felt that 'an epoch of the human race' was ending.[18] He was himself briefly inclined to follow Irving, who was now expelled from his church in Regent Square, the prophesying of his congregation having reached a point that was considered by his superiors heretical. Many others did follow him.

On 20 May in the afternoon, after a twelve-hour labour, Anne Pugin gave birth to a daughter at Great Russell Street. 'Thank god it is perfectly healthy,' Catherine wrote to Selina, 'and we all think a very sweet creature.'[19] Anne herself was 'like puss with her first kittens "was never so proud or so pleased in her life" she seems never tired of looking at it and thinks it better than all her fourteen dolls together'.[20] If there was a note of impatience in Catherine's description of her daughter-in-law, it was, perhaps, understandable. Selina sent money to buy baby clothes. Adlard came round with a bottle of champagne, of which Catherine took 'a modest glass'.[21] But then, some time over the next day or so, Anne became ill. Presumably she had contracted post-puerperal fever, which claimed so many women's lives in childbirth even into the twentieth century. After several days of restless agony, during which her mother-in-law nursed her as best she could, Pugin's young wife died. No doubt it was Auguste who found, among his artist friends, someone who could make a death mask. It survives, with a cast of her hand and the scrap of a baby's smock that she had been sewing. It was not much. There was no picture of her. None of the people among whom she died, even her own husband, had known her so much as a year. In his misery Pugin scratched an inscription on his watch: 'This day, May 27, 1832, my dearest Anne died unto this world, but lived unto God.'[22] His wife had died, Pugin later told Edward Willson, 'supported . . . in her Last moments with wonderful fortitude' by her 'strict religious feelings'.[23] It was his only consolation.

When she realized that she was dying Anne had asked to be buried at Christchurch Priory. The visits to Christchurch that summer when she and Pugin first knew one another were perhaps the most vivid experiences in a short life passed mostly in drab, urban poverty. Pugin was determined to do as she wished, although it was an expensive and elaborate matter to take a body so far by horse-drawn carriage. The funeral could not take place for nearly three weeks. In the interval his family did what they could for him. Selina sent more money for a nurse and Catherine sat all night, every night, by her son's bed in case he should wake and be alone at 'the dreadful hour'.[24] He was thin and ill 'what with grief and working', for he was still at the theatre.[25] It was now that his mother said of him at twenty what others said of him at forty, that he seemed to have lived at an unnatural pace and had 'already experienced a long life in a short one'; 'may almighty god', she added, 'of his infinite mercy sanctify unto him all his sorrows.'[26]

On 12 June Pugin went down to Christchurch and Auguste followed. Catherine stayed in London with the baby. Anne's funeral took place two days later. It was the first of many funerals that Pugin would arrange. The rites of death became, to him, among the most important of the Church. In his imaginary landscapes, even in a drawing of his own house, funeral processions of varying kinds wind their way. He did all he could to give some dignity to this first, modest, burial. Clearly and characteristically he had enough sway with the clergy at Christchurch to organize matters as he wished. He had the coffin placed in the centre of the choir instead of the nave and the service was held in the evening, at eight o'clock, in the midsummer dusk. Anne was laid to rest under the north aisle of the priory and he returned to London, a father and a widower at twenty.

10

'Gothic for ever'

June 1832 to April 1833

The poorest Day that passes over us is the conflux of two
Eternities; it is made up of currents that issue from the remotest
Past and flow onwards into the remotest Future.
– Thomas Carlyle, *Signs of the Times*, 1829

It was decided to name the baby after her mother. Selina stood god-mother with one of Adlard's sons and another friend. Catherine was relieved that all the sponsors were 'seriously disposed', for her son's distress was such that, always inclined to imagine the worst, she feared for his life too, and 'who shall say my poor little Anne may not be left an orphan'.[1] The baby herself at least was a healthy, endearing child and, Catherine told Selina, she had inherited her 'mamma's leg and foot with very long fingers' (that these were considered striking features suggests that Anne Garnett had, indeed, been a dancer).[2] The problem of nursing was still unsolved. Fifty pounds a year, which was what the present nurse asked, was more than they could afford. It was with a mixture of pleasure and weariness that Catherine found herself 'plung-ing' once more, in her early sixties and racked by rheumatism, into 'the loves and anxieties of the nursery'.[3]

Pugin, it was decided, should go to stay with his aunt to 'recruit in health and spirits'.[4] Old Mrs Welby had died in 1815 and the house in Pullins Row had been given up. Selina had spent much of her time since her stepmother's death on extended visits to relatives, but had now taken a cottage at Ramsgate. The prospect of being there was Pugin's 'only pleasurable thought'.[5] After his mother's intense, but highly emo-tional sympathy, Selina's gentler presence was no doubt a soothing contrast. This was possibly Pugin's first visit to Ramsgate, the town that eventually became his home. In the early 1830s it was a small, genteel resort that had grown up just south of the medieval village of St Lawrence. The period of its first expansion is told in the names of the streets: Royal Crescent, Nelson Crescent, the Plains of Waterloo. The young Princess Victoria came to stay there with her mother, and for a maiden lady in Selina Welby's situation it was a highly suitable residence. She had taken Rose Cottage, just a little way back from the sea. The sea always attracted Pugin and to some extent comforted him. The surrounding Isle of Thanet had many Gothic churches and monastic ruins to explore. But he was, for once, inclined to more sedentary pursuits. It was probably now that he began to draw the first of his Ideal Schemes.

These remarkable, dream-like sequences of drawings flowed from him over the next three years as he passed through the determining crisis of his life. They tell, more vividly than anything he wrote, of the formation of that vision of Gothic architecture and its meaning that established itself during this time until it was the pivot of his existence. The schemes are made up of densely detailed pen and ink drawings, most bound together into books. They have titles, typically with the definite article as if they were novels or plays. Some might have been the sort of melodramas Pugin worked on at Covent Garden. The first, twenty-six pages long, is *The Chest*. Inside the cover Pugin drew, apparently for the first time, his 'arms', the shield which his aunt Lafitte had given the Pugins when he was twelve, 'gules, on a bend or, a martlet sable', with his monogram above.[6] The chest itself, a richly carved piece of fifteenth-century woodwork, is shown first, followed by its contents. Vestments, sacred vessels, jewels, pass across the pages. A second inner casket of ivory contains its own store of secular treasure. On the final page is an hourglass, the last sand running through. As drawings the images make plain how much Pugin knew by now about medieval design. His visits to the sacristies of Flemish churches, his browsing among the dealers' shops and the print room are the principal sources. He knew a great deal but, as he later noted himself, the Ideal Schemes are marked also by anachronisms and mistakes, pieces of Renaissance design and inauthentic details. More important, however, than its elements is the kind of artefact that *The Chest* itself represents. It is a romance in pictures, a narrative fiction told through objects and their associative power. The use of the definite article in the titles of the schemes insists on their reality, their specific, rather than their general, existence, but the truth they convey is not a literal one.

Back in London family life was gradually resumed. Pugin went home to Great Russell Street and to work in the scenery room, where he was constantly employed. His reputation was growing and although, as his mother noted, 'his name does not come forward', it was 'well known behind the scenes', so well known that he was approached by the manager of the Paris opera house to see if he would work there.[7] Auguste was not faring so well. He had few commissions and his health was poor. His hands shook more than ever, and his hands and feet were sometimes numb. Despite constant bathing, on medical advice, by late summer he could hardly draw. He found it so difficult to hold a pen that his writing was all but illegible; his letters went astray and made business even more difficult. He determined, nevertheless, to go on with the second volume of the *Examples* and a visit was planned to the West Country for the pupils to draw and measure suitable buildings. It was to be the last of the family tours that had marked each year of Pugin's life for as long as he could remember.

He and Catherine went down first to Salisbury. Here Pugin made friends with a stonemason, William Osmond, a local man in his forties, who worked at the cathedral. Pugin teased Osmond about his neo-classical memorial tablets which, he said, looked like 'blisters' on the Gothic walls. Osmond was charmed and amused by the argumentative young man and they remained friends for some years. Auguste meanwhile was unable to leave London: 'still short of £25 to assist ... in defraying the expences [sic] attending the journey', he could not set off until he had raised it.[8] He wrote with instructions to his son to organize the others when they arrived. Pugin was working for his father only reluctantly. Auguste assured Catherine, with an earnestness that suggests it was a point of dispute, that it was his 'full wish and intention' to pay his son 'so much per day' at whatever rate he specified.[9] Half was to be in cash, half to discount his debts, which hung over from the wreck of the Hart Street business. In fact Pugin only sketched and measured.[10] The finished drawings were left to Ferrey and the rest to work up.

The city of Wells, where they all eventually met, was a revelation. Both mother and son were overwhelmed by the beauty of the place. It was 'the most delightfully situated town in the world', Catherine thought, and with so many medieval buildings that she and Pugin could only 'stand suspended which to admire most many a Cathedral I have seen but none so lovely as this . . . tears of admiration rushed into the eyes of Augustus'.[11] For Pugin, as for his mother, the step from grief to euphoria was short: 'if you want to be delighted if you want to be astonished if you want to be half as mad as I at present am, for Gods sake come over to wells,'[12] Pugin wrote to William Osmond; 'the Most magnificent thing for detail that can be seen . . . I am well acquainted with every thing here and have got introductions to all the most secret corners . . . Gothic for ever.'[13]

In 1832 the town was scarcely any bigger than it had been in the Middle Ages. Even today the heart of Wells is essentially unchanged. The cathedral, the moated bishop's palace, the deanery and the Vicars' Close, a pair of medieval terraces that offer a chance to walk along a complete 'planned street of the mid C14', presented to Pugin a vision of a whole Gothic town, sacred and domestic, humble and palatial all together.[14] It also gave him, and his mother, cause to reflect on the contrast between that medieval society and the present. The cathedral was not in good repair, the clergy far from exemplary. Catherine, always curious about the mood and social composition of any place she visited, analysed Wells and its difficulties:

The superior class of the society are all connected with the diocese and are high church, the lower and more numerous are mostly petty tradesmen and rank Methodists . . . who wish for nothing so much as to see the whole edifice in ruin while the churchmen, having no one to jog them, eat drink and sleep in perfect inattention to the ruin which daily threatens . . . to destroy this wondrous pile . . . and when they do bring forward a few pounds they employ such ignorant blockheads . . . that when in the confession they chant forth we have done what we ought not to have done and left undone what we ought to have done we can scarcely forbear casting our eyes around and responding – you have indeed.[15]

At the top of his letter to Osmond, with whom he was debating the relative merits of classical and Gothic art, Pugin drew two memorials, one a stark little 'blister' tablet marked 1832, the other a richly canopied tomb captioned 1532. In this and his mother's mordant criticisms were sown the seeds of Pugin's first important book, Contrasts. Like The Microcosm of London, his father's best-known work, it owed its first conception to what Ferrey reluctantly conceded was Catherine's 'suggestive imagination'.[16]

In the autumn of 1832, as Pugin and his mother cast their critical eyes around Wells, there was all over England an uneasy sense of suspense between the past and an uncertain future. The Reform Bill had finally passed into law that summer. The next election would bring in a new sort of Parliament, chosen by a new sort of electorate. Was this 'the conclusion of a crisis . . . or . . . only the prelude to fresh upheavals'?[17] There was a sense of *entre deux guerres*, an awareness that, in John Stuart Mill's words, 'the old doctrines have gone out, and the new ones have not yet come in'.[18] In her own life Catherine, full of fears, some exaggerated, some not, was also looking for signs of the times: '1802 married me,' she wrote, '1812 gave me my boy 1832 has made him miserable.'[19]

Back in London in October Auguste made a will. It is a somewhat pathetic document, for he had little to leave except the rights to the *Examples* and five shares in Brunel's cemetery company which he bequeathed to his wife. His anxiety that Catherine might be left badly off and that his son would squander any money he got his hands on are palpable. So, too, is his hard-won experience of private publishing. The chief duty of the executors was to raise as much as they could from the copyright of the *Examples*. Pugin was charged with the completion of the work if his father did not live to do it. In November, knowing he would never exhibit again, Auguste resigned from the Society of Painters in Water Colour. Soon afterwards his illness became acute. He took to his bed and lay in terrible pain for week after week.

Pugin meanwhile worked on another Ideal Scheme, *The Shrine*. *The Shrine* is shorter but vastly more complex than *The Chest*. The book itself is sumptuous. Pugin had the twenty-six pages of drawings bound in dark green leather stamped in gilt with Gothic motifs. It is an opulent, jewel-like creation. The viewer's progress through *The Shrine* begins in the transept of a great thirteenth-century church. The scene, unlike any in *The Chest*, is populated. Priests and monks pay homage. Over successive pages, the eye is drawn in through a series of views. As he composed the scenes, Pugin was restoring on paper what had been lost in reality at Wells and the other great English churches he knew, the furnishings, the vestments and the liturgy. He was following his friend Willson's logic. The great age of Gothic was the age of Catholicity. To show a Gothic church complete, its windows filled with coloured glass, its statuary unvandalized, its sacred vessels in use, meant showing a Catholic church.

The Ideal Schemes portray a complete world order, architecturally and socially harmonious. Another drawing Pugin made this year, while his father was ill and now, without doubt, dying, shows a bishop on his throne in a great hall, surrounded by priests. The bishop is looking attentively at the designs which an architect is spreading out before him. This was the world that Pugin wanted to inhabit, a world of completeness and order, beauty and permanence, where his own talents would be recognized. It was far from the reality that faced him. On 19 December Auguste died, aged (probably) sixty-four, 'well-known' as the *Annual Register* remarked, 'to all admirers of the fine arts'. 'A life . . . more of labour and anxiety than of pleasure and comfort', his brother-in-law, Adlard Welby, thought, and that, perhaps, was true by the end.[20] But happier days and the popularity which his easy-going charm and warmth had won him were evoked by the number of mourners, his fellow watercolourists prominent among them, who followed his coffin to St Mary's church, Islington, where it was placed in the Welby family vault.

Auguste's death left Pugin and his mother, who was worn out with nursing her husband as well as her granddaughter, ill with grief. At Great Russell Street the household was terribly diminished. The drawing school disbanded, leaving only Pugin, Catherine and the seven-month-old Anne. It was imperative that Pugin settle on some plan of practical action to support them. He was in 'great uncertainty' about the manner in which to proceed.[21] But once his father's affairs were settled and he had consulted his 'best friends', he came to a decision.[22] He wrote to Edward Willson in February 1833 to explain that he had 'resolved to give up my theatrical connection altogether and to devote *myself – entirely* to the pursuit of Gothic architecture and particularly to the prosecution and compleation of the works commenced or intended by My Late Father'.[23] He was hoping to publish the next part of the *Examples* in May and asked Willson to let him have the text as soon as possible.

Pugin went on:

I greive to inform you that my Mother is at this moment most dangerously ill with the jaundice brough on by continued greif & anxiety . . . the continued afflictions we have suffered scince I Last saw you has been dreadful . . . all I can now hope is that the Litle girl which is Left me will prove half as great a blessing as her mother was to me while alive – but for this I must wait. give my most grateful remembrances to Mrs Wilson and tell her I never shall forget both your & her kindness to my poor Anne.[24]

He had scarcely time to take stock of his altered situation, and turn his mind to his new and not especially congenial occupation, before he received another shattering blow. His twenty-first birthday on 1 March fell at one of the most desolate moments of his life. Catherine could not rally. She had complained for years of liver trouble. Possibly the underlying cause was cancer. On 28 April, scarcely more than four months after her husband, she, too, died and was buried with him, and her parents, in Islington. For Pugin it was a brutal coming of age. The household that had been his only home, his school, the place where he had met his first friends, lived with his wife and where his daughter had been born, was now entirely broken up. The long life encompassed in his first twenty-one years was over. He was left, with Anne, to begin the world again.

Part Three

11

Beginning the World Again

May 1833 to October 1834

That time is past,
And all its aching joys are now no more . . .
                    . . . other gifts
Have followed; for such loss, I would believe,
Abundant recompense . . .
        – William Wordsworth, *Lines written a few miles above*
                                    Tintern Abbey, 1798

At twelve noon on 4 June 1833, at the rooms of Mr Wheatley the bookseller in Piccadilly, bidding began for 'the property of the late Augustus Pugin Esq.'.[1] It took three days to clear the 690 lots of books, prints and drawings, as well as 'an exceedingly fine & perfectly unique collection of basso relievo casts from Rouen Cathedral'. The quartos and folios – Palladio, Derand's *L'architecture des Voûtes* and Philibert de L'Orme – went on the first day. They were interspersed with Catherine's manuscripts, including 'A christian and Sober Testimony against Sinfull [sic] Compliance' and copies of the *Monthly Register*. The books were followed by the prints, engravings and Auguste's own watercolours, the illustrations of Nelson's funeral, views of Louth and St Paul's cathedral. The work and the beliefs, enthusiasms, friendships and associations of thirty years all came under the hammer. There were copies of Louis Lafitte's designs for the Duc d'Angoulême, an edition of Byron, Catherine's collection of the works of Edward Irving (which fetched 4/6d), five boxes of casts from Christchurch Priory and a copy of *Healthful Sports for Young Ladies*. The life of the Great Russell Street household, in which pre-revolutionary France had been a living memory, 'the England of Miss Austen' still a palpable reality, passed before the auctioneer's desk and was gone. The sale realized £808 16s.

Pugin was not in Piccadilly when Mr Wheatley opened the bidding. He was in St Andrew's, Holborn, a medieval church later rebuilt by Wren, getting married. His second wife was Louisa Button and he can have known her for only a matter of months.[2] She was another denizen of the less than respectable world of Covent Garden, an actress or a dancer. Their marriage was a sudden, almost a desperate, step. Pugin's uncle Adlard was exasperated by this latest piece of rashness on the part of his headstrong nephew. 'Surely the less we say the less we may censure,' he wrote to Selina. 'His repeating such a blunder in matrimony however excusable the first time, is to speak mildly a great misfortune and bad move for a second.'[3] Adlard, who had now retreated to Italy with some eleven of his fifteen children in order to live cheaply with his mistress Mary Hutchinson after the breakdown of his own marriage, was in no position to criticize. Personal unhappiness, however, had made him bitter. Professionally too he was disappointed. He had travelled to America and published an account of his impressions of the new world which had made no great impact. No doubt this also added to his resentment of his talented, over-indulged nephew.

Pugin did not care what his uncle thought and cared even less about his new wife's social position. In the wreckage of his life he needed a fixed point of affection, some token of future happiness. To marry on the very day his parents' effects were sold was a gesture both of hope and of defiance. From now on he would always be looking forward. The trauma of the twelve months that began with his first wife's death in May 1832 and ended with his second marriage resonated throughout his life. He could never bear to look back at it directly, but the past, though he scarcely ever spoke of it, found expression, obliquely, throughout his work. He had now to start a new life and to do it alone would have been unbearable. He needed a stepmother for his daughter, but what he needed most of all, much more than when he had met Anne Garnett, was a female companion, a woman who would be all in all to him. To the warmth and sexual energy that were Pugin's nature and which attracted him easily to women, and they to him, there was from now on added an undercurrent of fear, a dread of being alone that would haunt him for the rest of his life. Like many only children Pugin was fated to be lonely, not in childhood, but as an adult when nothing could replace the completeness of the bond he had shared with his parents. From now on the 'one faithful heart', the female eye in which to see himself reflected, was a necessity. Without it he would lose his equilibrium, almost his sense of self. Louisa was to take the place of all that he had lost of human love and sympathy. It was a great deal to hope for from anyone.

Some of this his aunt and dying mother had understood. Selina assured Adlard that Catherine had spoken 'without disapprobation' of Pugin's attachment to Louisa, adding that the wedding itself had been precipitated by Catherine's death.[4] Adlard pretended not to know what she meant. Surely, he wrote, priggishly, a mother's death should be a reason for postponing rather than bringing forward a marriage. Then, with that Welby family talent, of which Pugin himself was not devoid, for stating the uncomfortably obvious in the most platitudinous terms, he concluded with the hope that 'this hasty step may prove a fortunate one and that the old saying "marry in haste repent at leisure" he may not experience'.[5] Adlard was not to be entirely disappointed in his ill-natured predictions. Almost every trace of Louisa has disappeared. No letters, no jewellery, not even a lock of her hair apparently survives. Later events make it seem likely, though not certain, that Pugin himself destroyed their correspondence. The only picture of her is a little posthumous pencil drawing. It shows a handsome face. Pugin, though oblivious to nuances of class, was always sensitive to beauty. He was, his son-in-law Hardman Powell recalled, 'artistic' in his choice of wives.[6] It was Hardman Powell, who met Louisa eleven years later, when he was himself still a boy, who left the only written account of her. It is a striking one and suggests a very different person from the delicate, self-effacing Anne Garnett.

She was short, broadly but compactly built, quick in her movements, and with that peculiar grace which is the result of perfect freedom of action; her features were clearly cut and regular though not refined, her eyes brown and sparkling with good humour when pleased, but of that kind appears [sic] to become almost black when angered, her eyebrows well marked and slightly tightened to the front, it might be with occasional fierce temper, her nose straight and rather pointed with delicate open nostrils, her mouth small well arched with thin and expressive lips, her forehead and cheeks smooth with an observable artificial bloom on the latter.[7]

This 'strange lady', with her rouge and her hint of temperament, impressed the young Hardman Powell. The clothes she wore that morning were designed, almost certainly, by her husband. Her dress was made of eighteenth-century brocade, and it recalls the costume that Zoë Beaupré wore in the *Kenilworth* on which Pugin had worked. Louisa's skirts were cut short to show her 'well-made' feet, her shoulders bare except for massive jewellery, also of her husband's creation. She presented 'a figure that arrested every eye by its singularity and beauty'. Hardman Powell remembered Pugin bending to kiss her on the shoulder. He remembered also thinking that either she was on her way to some extraordinary party or 'that my notions on the subject of ladies' costume were very provincial'.[8] Clearly to the provincial, the conventional or the socially discriminating eye the second Mrs Pugin, like her husband, presented a disconcerting sight, operatic, over-dressed for that hour of the morning, and, with her 'artificial bloom', barely respectable. On her wedding day in 1833 Louisa, a little younger than her husband, would have been twenty or just twenty-one. No doubt she was less broadly built than when Hardman Powell saw her, after a decade of childbearing. She and Pugin were both then slighter, less vivid figures than they would become.

With the proceeds of the sale, Pugin, Louisa and Anne, who had just passed her first birthday, set up home. They went to Ramsgate, to be near Pugin's beloved aunt, the only survivor of the old days, 'my only refuge and comfort', as he described her, even after his marriage.[9] Selina became 'quite a mother' to them and they were young enough to welcome a maternal presence as they started life in circumstances strange to both.[10] Pugin found a house at St Lawrence, the medieval village inland from Ramsgate. Only a short walk from Rose Cottage, Ellington Cottage was small, cheap and happily ancient. The modern terraces and crescents of the resort town were out of sight from this 'retired house' and Pugin enjoyed 'a magnificent view of the channel'.[11] Soon he had installed his collection of antiquities, his books and whatever he had kept of his parents' possessions. By the late summer Louisa would have known that she was pregnant and in the autumn Pugin set off on the usual annual drawing tour, but now for the first time without companions.

Travel was both stimulating and consoling to him. Like sailing, or the

1. Pugin, by his friend J. R. Herbert, 1845.

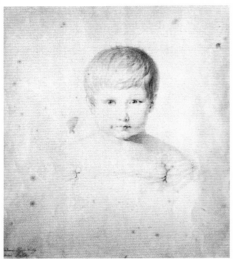

2. (*above left*) Pugin's father, Auguste Charles, the self-styled Comte de Pugin.

3. (*above right*) Pugin at two in 1814, a pencil drawing by his uncle, the French court painter Louis Lafitte.

4. (*above*) 'The Pillory', aquatint from a drawing by Pugin's father, A. C. Pugin, and Thomas Rowlandson in *The Microcosm of London*. This was the book which best captured the high taste and low morals of the Regency city into which Pugin was born.

5. (*above*) Watercolour of a sideboard for Windsor Castle designed by Pugin in 1827. This was his first major commission, at the age of fifteen, for George IV.

6. (*right*) 'My first design', 1821. At nine, Pugin was already hoping to build Gothic churches.

A design for a Church   A pugin 1821 9 years old

7. (*above*) Scarisbrick Hall, Lancashire. Here, within an existing house, Pugin made his first attempt to create a Catholic Mansion of the Olden Times. His designs were continued by his son, Edward, who built the massive tower.

8. (*left*) The Great Hall, Scarisbrick. The interior was assembled out of antique wood carvings, some of the many thousands stripped from Continental churches and imported to England in the aftermath of the Napoleonic Wars.

9. (*above*) Watercolour by Pugin of about 1835 showing his first house, St Marie's Grange at Alderbury, Wiltshire. A wildly original building that caused a scandal locally, it was a romance in red brick.

10. (*right*) Refectory table, designed for Oscott College in about 1838, the sort of plain structural furniture that earned Pugin a reputation as a proto-modernist. Powerful as it is, it is closely based on medieval models and looks back as much as forward.

11. (*above left*) The Grange, Ramsgate, Pugin's second house for himself, designed in 1844. In it he reinvented the Gothic as a new style for the nineteenth century. This was to be the prototype for hundreds of country rectories and suburban houses.

12. (*below left*) 'A True Prospect of St Augustine's', a watercolour Pugin showed at the Royal Academy in 1849. It represents his house and church in the manner of a Victorian book of hours, with the cycle of life and death set in a tranquil Kentish landscape.

13. (*above*) The Grange. Pugin planned his house around a central staircase living hall, a daring idea in the 1840s which later became the characteristic feature of the English Arts and Crafts house. He also designed the wallpaper, incorporating his crest and motto.

14. St Giles's, Cheadle, completed in 1846. A work of high Romantic art with a
dazzling interior, this was the building that marked the high point of Pugin's career.

mere presence of the sea, the sense of physical movement relieved his own restlessness. Much as the idea of home was necessary to him, he still saw it in a childlike way as a fixed point, a safe harbour, from which he could depart and to which he could return. Louisa would have to accustom herself to a marriage punctuated by long periods of separation. When he was especially anxious or unhappy Pugin would travel relent-lessly. Over the next two years he was on the move for weeks and months on end. This, his first solo excursion, was both a pursuit and at the same time a flight. He was escaping from the sorrows of the recent past and his quest, he told William Osmond, was not for information, or not at least for information alone. He was in search of 'the picturesque & beautiful', and he went looking for it in a surprisingly conventional place.[12] He headed west to Taunton, then by coach to Bristol, from where he took a steamer to Chepstow. From there he walked to Tintern, 'distant about 8 miles' to 'view the far-famed abbey'.[13] It was the route his uncle had taken in his own wandering years at the same age in 1797, through the heartland of the Picturesque, the ground in which the theories of Knight and Price had first taken root. By 1833 the Wye Valley was well trodden both in fact and in the national imagination. The year after Adlard's visit Wordsworth had composed his *Lines written a few miles above Tintern Abbey*, and the year after Pugin was there Tennyson came and wrote 'Tears, idle tears'.

Pugin's reaction was different from the poets'. Himself mourning so many deaths, he might well have shared Tennyson's melancholy and regret and found in 'the yellowing autumn-tide at Tintern', 'the sense of the abiding in the transient', a powerful reminder of 'the days that are no more'. But he did not. Pugin was determined only to look forward. He was duly impressed by the landscape of the Wye Valley, but by Tintern itself he was disappointed: 'the situation is beautiful, as a ruin the building is too,' he wrote, 'but dare I oppose the torrent of popular opinion and not admire tintern abbey as a building? yes I dare – and I say as a building it is anything but admirable . . . the plan, mouldings, windows &c are very common place . . .'; 'to express this opinion to the . . . general observer I should be set down . . . for . . . an opinionated upstart,' he noted with satisfaction.[14]

In his failure to find the Beautiful at Tintern, in his insistence on looking not at a picturesque ruin but at a building, and on judging it critically as architecture, lay the beginnings of the revolution in taste that Pugin was to precipitate. On the one hand he was saturated in the Picturesque as he had absorbed it from both his parents. His emotional responses to light and weather, to the associations of place and the power of the sea, were profound, integral to his temperament and personality. Yet while he was steeped in the Picturesque he was also sick of it, sick of it at least in its late Georgian form, of the now hackneyed vocabulary of Repton and Nash and the tired conventions of the guidebooks. He was ready to reinvent it for a new generation. In his rejection of the conventional view of Tintern he was taking the abbey more seriously, in a sense, than either Wordsworth or Tennyson. He was certainly taking it more literally, and the Victorian Picturesque, which Pugin invented, was to be a more serious and in some ways a more literal business than the Georgian. Over the months that followed, in between his travels, as he drew more Ideal Schemes, read more about the architecture of the Middle Ages and explored more of the ancient churches and cathedrals, so, out of the wreckage of his past life, a new vision emerged. It was a vision of Gothic, the one love that had not failed him, as a sacred style infused with inner truth, an architecture that did not merely evoke 'pleasing associations' but that embodied, in its very fabric, a metaphysical, divine reality.

This was the belief that was to transform Pugin's life and, when he published it, to transform English architecture. To understand why such an idea should take so deep and rapid hold in the public mind it is necessary to see how closely Pugin's particular experience in this first part of his adult life mirrored that of his generation. His anxieties, his discontents and above all the sense of imminent spiritual and moral crisis which he developed during the travels of 1833–4 were widely felt throughout Britain. The spectacle of Wells, the decay of both the physical and the spiritual fabric of the Established Church and the connection between the two, which had given Pugin and his mother such cause for comment and complaint, were apparent to many people. The Church of England had been under review and to some extent under attack for the whole of Pugin's life. Until now he had had little reason to take account of the criticisms levelled at the Establishment, but suddenly, as he looked over the wreckage of his own life, its weaknesses seemed to explain everything. The Anglican Establishment was much more still, in the 1830s, than a religious denomination and the debates that surrounded its future were more than narrowly sectarian. The powers of the Church had been interwoven for centuries with those of the State at almost every level of national life. Since the Reformation the 'vestry' or parish had been the unit of local government and 'church rates' or local taxes were levied on Church land. All holders of crown office, all university entrants and members of municipal corporations had had to subscribe to the Anglican faith. Only the Church of England could perform legal marriages and to be buried other than by the Church was difficult. In 1831 a quarter of all magistrates were still clergymen.

Yet while it continued to wield enormous power, the Church had declined in influence among the population at large. In 1790 perhaps 90 per cent of people had been, nominally at least, Anglican. By 1815 a third were dissenters. New ideas of social justice, the revolutions in America and France, new ways of life in an industrializing nation gave scope to the rapidly multiplying groups of nonconformists. Even those who wanted to be Anglicans were sometimes unable to get to church, for the parish boundaries no longer fitted the population. Many country parishes were sparsely inhabited, while the ever greater numbers moving to the cities found no church when they arrived. The Church Commissioners had already begun to address the problem but it was still far from resolved. In addition to which the clergy themselves in certain cases did little to inspire respect. Some held multiple livings and did no more than collect the revenue and live as gentry. They were seldom seen in clerical dress and were often observed out on the hunting field, while those who did their work, the poorly paid and shabby curates, commanded even less regard.

These abuses were by no means universal and by 1834 reforms were well under way. Much of the legislation restricting the rights of non-Anglicans had been removed. The Test and Corporation Acts were repealed in 1828, allowing Protestant dissenters to hold public office, and in 1829 Catholic Emancipation had extended most of the same rights to Catholics as well as allowing them to worship openly and build churches. New Anglican parishes were being made in the towns, new churches were being built, however unsatisfactory most of them looked to discriminating critics such as Pugin, and steps were being taken to prevent the clergy from simply farming their livings for as much as they could get. Nevertheless there was still plenty to criticize, not only in the details of church administration but in the fact of the Established Church itself. Why, many dissenters wondered, should they pay a church rate?

Why should so much power be vested in a body so little representative and why, after Parliament had been reformed, should the Church not similarly be purged and disestablished? Within the Church those who sought to defend it and the old social order it represented were equally anxious, highly vocal and deeply divided.

As he continued on his quest for truth and beauty, going on to Hereford and then to Worcester, Pugin became increasingly incensed with the state of modern England and of the Anglican Church, making notes, not only of the Beautiful but also of the Disgraceful. The neglect that he and Catherine had deplored struck him now on every side. In his sketchbook the compactly drawn details, fitted like pieces of a puzzle on to every quarter inch of paper, are interspersed with scandalized notes. 'Revd Wm. Cooper' wore 'top boots & white breeches on Sundays'. At Worcester 'divine service' was suspended to accommodate the local music festival. In Hereford Cathedral the Lady Chapel was full of bookcases. Hereford, like Lichfield where he went next, had been 'improved' by James Wyatt: 'yes – this monster of architectural depravity, this pest of Cathedral architecture has been here. need I say more,' he reported to Osmond.[15] Wherever he went Pugin saw confirmation of his growing convictions. Among his notes he drew the Puritan iconoclasts, smashing sacred sculpture. From the moment the Church seceded from Rome, from the Reformation to Cromwell to Wyatt and the Revd William Cooper, it was all, he now realized, the same sad story of destruction and decline. The ultimate crash must, surely, come soon. At Birmingham, 'Greek buildings & Smoking chimneys – radicals & disenters' were 'blended together'.[16] Disturbance of the social order, unchristian architecture, ugliness in the physical world, it was all one thing.

This was not a carefully balanced view. Nor, however, was it peculiar to Pugin. He was not the only person looking back to the Middle Ages not merely for its art or as a source of historical fiction but for a model, a solution to the problems of the present troubled age. Since Cobbett on his *Rural Rides* had gazed at Salisbury Cathedral and thought that he lived in degenerate times, the growing criticism of modern society had increasingly been cast in terms of comparison with the Middle Ages, so often indeed that John Stuart Mill thought it now the 'dominant idea' of the age.[17] It was common to Radicals and conservatives alike. Mill himself found in the medieval world a model of a progressive society, while Pugin saw in it an ideal of order and beauty, an ideal that he was now becoming determined to revive.

Here too, in his belief that time might somehow be reversed, he was not alone. Not everyone who looked for a solution to the evils of the present day looked to the historic past for a solution. Many were turning to the Bible, especially to the books of prophecy. The belief that the French Revolution had marked the beginning of the millennium, that the end of the world was nigh, was not confined in the early 1830s to eccentrics or those on the margins of society. Those who lived to the end of the nineteenth century looked back on these years almost with disbelief, as a time of feverish intellectual and religious turmoil. Newman's brother-in-law, Tom Mozley, a writer and a clergyman who later became one of Pugin's most constructive critics, recalled that at the time 'the whole fabric of English and indeed of European society, was trembling to the foundations'.[18] Everyone had a theory and many had a vision. 'Every clique, every sect, almost every middle-class family, believed itself [to be the] Truth, and felt no doubt that if any one of its members were to have the management of public affairs but for a very short period, it could and would entirely regenerate the world.' The belief, 'monstrous as we may deem it', Mozley explained, was not quite unnatural, for there was no confidence left in the old established order. 'At that time all who held office in the State, in the Church, in our county and municipal institutions and in the management of the army . . . in a word, the entire administration of the country, had long been under a load of depreciation amounting to the bitterness and weight of an anathema.'[19] This loss of confidence in the very fabric of society made the end of the world, the end of time, or time thrown into reverse, all seem possible; 'a thousand projectors were screaming from a thousand platforms' until 'all England was dinned with philanthropy and revolution'.[20] Carlyle's prophetic *Signs of the Times* was followed by more than two dozen books and pamphlets of the same title. Their authors included Robert Owen, Edward Irving and the Revd Patrick Brontë of Haworth. Prophecy was by now 'an ordinary intellectual activity' in England.[21]

As he travelled, Pugin was entirely absorbed in his own intense experiences, quite unaware of any connection between these and the broader current of national events. When he got away from Birmingham and arrived at Oxford, with its wealth of medieval architecture, 'where at every turning you meet a buttress and face an oriel window', he felt happy again.[22] He was oblivious to the great religious debate just now stirring in the great Gothic city. Yet of all the manifestations of discontent within and outside the Church of England, one of the most prominent, and the one which would come to affect Pugin most nearly, was the Oxford Movement. It began as a reaction to the reforms limiting the power of the Church and it had been launched just months before his visit, in July, when John Keble preached an assize sermon on the theme of National Apostasy, prompted by a government bill intended to reduce the number of dioceses and parishes of the Established Church in Ireland. Keble's argument was that the State had no right to interfere with such matters and that the Church was about to be 'forsaken, degraded, nay trampled on and despoiled by the State and people of England'.[23] Soon after the sermon the first three of the *Tracts for the Times*, their title a variant on the many 'Signs', were published. Though anonymous, all three were the work of John Henry Newman. Newman was to have a curious and ultimately hostile relationship with Pugin, complicated not least by what they had in common, for the piety of both men was deeply infused with Romanticism and driven by a fear of Radicals and 'liberalism'. Newman, who himself made calculations of the date of the apocalypse, believed in the immanence of the sacred in the visible world, in 'material phenomena' as 'both types and the instruments of real things unseen'.[24] It was a theological but also a romantic idea, a Coleridgean belief in the living symbol, the thing that might both be and mean itself. Pugin would never have constructed such an account of his own ideas, but that was what he now began to believe about Gothic architecture, that in its physical reality was embodied a communicable spiritual truth.

The intention of the Oxford Movement, the Tractarians as they became known, was to reform the Church from within, to reinvigorate it. By November Newman was talking of allies 'in Leicestershire, Cheshire, Hants, Oxford, and Northamptonshire'. 'We are in motion,' he wrote, 'from the Isle of Wight to Durham and from Cornwall to Kent.'[25] But this was a network of clergymen, university men. For the moment, down in his own corner of Kent, Pugin remained oblivious. He was working on more Ideal Schemes. In *St Margaret's Chapel* he reassembled details of his West Country tour into a dense, strange little building, mostly in the Decorated style of Gothic. Pugin picked the most dramatic features of what he had seen, the free-floating ribs of the Berkeley ante-chapel at

Bristol, the steep, heavy batter of the Hereford Lady Chapel, the convex triangular windows of Lichfield, and composed them in a sequence that shows him poised on the cusp of archaeology and invention. Nor had he forgotten the idea that he and his mother had discussed at Wells for a book comparing past and present. He made a series of drawings which he entitled 'Contrasts'.[26] Arranged in pairs, medieval buildings beside modern, they are invented compositions, showing the actual and conceptual flimsiness of the present day. They make their point, but in a somewhat diffuse way. The idea had yet to find a focus and a plan.

In January he was off again, at Ely on his way to Lincoln. The logic of his position was becoming clear to him. Everything had gone wrong at the Reformation and had been getting worse ever since. The only answer was to begin again from the point where the rot set in. Impulsive, intolerant of ambivalence, Pugin came in months to the conclusion it would take Newman another twelve years to reach. He told Osmond what he had decided:

I can assure you after a most close & impartial investigation I feel perfectly convinced the roman Catholick church is the only true one – and the only one in which the grand & sublime style of church architecture can ever be restored – A very good chapel is now building in the north & when compleat I certainly think I shall recant. I know you will blame me but I am internally convicted – that it is right.[27]

This laconic account is almost all that Pugin ever said about his decision to become a Roman Catholic. He repeated it from time to time with variations, but he never questioned or retracted it, he never denied the connection between his faith and his feelings for architecture, nor did he represent his conversion as explicitly spiritual. In his approach to his faith, if not in his faith itself, he was still his mother's son, using reasoned argument, 'impartial investigation' and his own judgement to arrive at a right conclusion. Like Newman later he was to find difficulty in accommodating such a degree of intellectual independence within a church founded on authority. Of the interior, spiritual experience of these months and the years that followed, Pugin himself, who was not by nature introspective, said nothing, and there is nothing that a biographer can properly say either. Only the expression of his faith and its consequences are visible in history. The latter, for the moment, were slight. Pugin asked Osmond not to mention what he had told him. Selina and Louisa were obviously not yet in his confidence. No doubt he was apprehensive of their reaction, for Catholics, despite Emancipation, were still a small and marginal group in England. There was considerable prejudice against them, partly historical, partly religious and partly social.

Still Pugin travelled on. By now he had settled into the sketching habits he would never change, covering the pages of small, leather-bound books with little, rapidly drawn details. He seldom drew a whole build-ing. Occasionally he made a perspective view of a street or a landscape, but most of the surviving thousands of closely covered pages show precisely jotted details, measured mouldings, tracery and corbel heads in profile and sometimes section, a staircase, a pulpit, chalices, locks or any other Gothic thing that had survived the Reformation. Clearly Pugin as he drew was thinking about building. He considered himself an architect in waiting. But what this meant to him was still, as in the Ideal Schemes, an accumulation of detail. He had no training and as yet apparently little interest in the planning or analysis of three-dimensional space. The exaggerated, dream-like quality of the schemes is closer to theatre design still than architecture, their peculiar power owing to an element of naïvety as well as originality.

In among the architectural notes are others: 'missal', 'mass book', 'The seven penetential psalms'. Just as he had taught himself the rudiments of stage design, so Pugin now began to learn about Catholicism. He learned it mostly from the antiquarian texts his father had used for his books on architecture. Catholicism was for Pugin the faith of England in the Middle Ages. Of the modern Catholic Church he, like most of his English contemporaries, knew almost nothing. The only Catholic he knew personally was Edward Willson, who was steeped in the same English antiquarian tradition and who had taught him to call the archi-tecture of the Middle Ages 'Catholic'. Pugin talked to Willson at length and borrowed rare books from his extensive library. The pursuit of truth led him to read more deeply now than ever before, but not more widely. As he read he became absorbed, unconsciously, in a tradition of histori-cal writing that had, like Gothic architecture, lain around him all his life but which now began to take on new significance.

The association between Gothic buildings and Catholicism, which had come to Pugin in his conversations with Willson, was centuries old, as Willson knew. It went back to the Reformation itself, after which antiquarian studies had blossomed, in an attempt to salvage as much as possible from the Dissolution of the Monasteries, that 'unparalleled catastrophe', as antiquaries saw it, that had 'arrested the stream of English life'.[28] Antiquarianism had not always had the cosy, bumbling associations of Waverley about it. Some of the antiquaries Pugin read were Protestant but many more were High Anglican or covertly Catholic. All of them were consciously political writers and some, like John Stow, had been penalized as Catholic subversives. Walter Raleigh complained in his *Historie of the World* that 'all cost and care bestowed and had of the church, whereby God is to be served and worshiped' was 'acounted . . . a kinde of Popery', and as recently as 1797 George III had denounced the Society of Antiquaries, when it declined to elect Wyatt, as 'a Popish cabal'.[29] Reading Henry Spelman's *History and Fate of Sacrilege* and the works of William Dugdale, Pugin was absorbing a highly tendentious view of history. In these accounts – and even in the works of pro-Reformation Anglicans such as John Strype and Camden – the Reformation was the defining event in English history, bringing about the transformation of the social fabric and with it the physical fabric of the Church. To many it had been, as Willson put it, 'a terrible blow' to the arts that 'adorn and soften life'.[30]

It was Dugdale who made the deepest and most lasting impression on Pugin.[31] One of the greatest of the seventeenth-century antiquaries, his *Monasticon Anglicanum* is a great lament for the lost treasures of the monasteries. It portrays pre-Reformation England as a landscape of Gothic churches and abbeys, a world of social harmony and piety, brutally and illegally violated by Henry VIII. Dugdale, who fought at the battle of Edgehill and wrote the *Monasticon* at Oxford, in exile with Charles I, was a far from neutral historian. A royalist and a High Church man, he took the view that the English Church, despite Henry's intervention, remained Catholic, but independent of Rome. It had continued after the Reformation, by direct apostolic descent. This was the ideal, an English Catholic Church, to which Pugin was from now on committed. That it was essentially an Anglican, not a Roman Catholic ideal, did not, yet, occur to him.

In the early 1830s such High Church ideas hung heavy in the air, especially at Oxford. The members of the Oxford Movement believed in exactly the same thing, a continuous English Catholic Church. John Bowden, Newman's closest friend, wrote to him that year that 'we,

Churchmen, are the Catholics of England', 'unless we can wrest the monopoly of the term from the Papists, we do nothing. We must disabuse our fellow churchmen of the idea that we belong to a Church, comparatively new, which, some 300 years ago, supplanted the old Catholic Church of these realms. Let us then bear, by all means, our Catholic title on our front; though there is, I admit, an inconvenience – it might mislead some people.'[32] It did. The dream of a restored English Catholic Church was, from the beginning, riven with contradictions that over the years would prove irreconcilable. Pugin and many of his contemporaries would discover that the 'Catholic' ideal meant fatally different, painfully incompatible things to those who espoused it, and indeed those who write about it now find themselves uncomfortably obliged to make distinctions between 'Catholics' and 'Roman Catholics', for the sake of clarity that would have offended those to whom they refer.

For the moment, however, it all seemed simple enough to Pugin as he settled down to study at St Lawrence. He had fitted up his house with 'antiquities of warious sorts from William the Conqueror to henry the 8'.[33] He bought books and 'carvings in Ivory . . . Bernard Pallisy ware of the time of Francis I'.[34] He loved a bargain. 'I have bought a copy of the *golden Legend* in Latin with 300 or more woodcuts in the original binding with brass clasps for 5s 6d theres Luck,' he told Willson.[35] Salvage was even better. At Norwich he found the remains of a 'beautiful Brass Lectorium' but unfortunately was 'too narrowly watched to be able to carry any of it off'.[36]

Like every true antiquary, Pugin found a ruin in his garden and dug up the 'great part of the tracery' of an ancient chapel.[37] In Ellington Cottage he lived like Langlois at Rouen inside his own imagination. Here in this self-generated world Pugin would devote himself to 'the study and delineation of . . . architecture'.[38] He had arranged a chapel in the house. It would be interesting to know who, if anybody, consecrated it. Perhaps nobody, for Pugin's beliefs were still highly personal, and his was still a largely private faith that found its expression in art rather than in liturgy.

He now began to haunt his own drawings both in the persona of 'the architect' and as himself, reading or writing by a window in a book-lined room. It was as if, having looked on glass, he had passed through it into the *hortus conclusus* of the Gothic world, invulnerable now to death and the passage of time. These drawings were romantic as much as religious images, projections of the self that recall Keats's letter to his sister describing his own ideal room: 'There I'd sit and read all day,' he wrote, 'like the picture of somebody reading.'[39] Such a sense of the divided self, of the individual both watching and at the same time acting out the drama of experience, is typical of the romantic consciousness. The romantic portrait often puts the sitter at a window, as Pugin put himself, at the symbolic meeting point of inner and outer realities. What Pugin experienced in 1833–4, over the months that followed his visit to Tintern, as he reshaped his own world and found his artistic voice, was perhaps the closest that English architecture ever came to a romantic epiphany.

But however much Pugin liked the idea of living a quiet antiquarian life, neither his temperament nor his circumstances allowed him to do so for long. One instalment of *Examples of Gothic Architecture* had appeared since Auguste's death and another, Pugin hoped, would be out in the spring, to complete Volume Two. In London his father's pupils Thomas Larkins Walker and Benjamin Ferrey were seeing the plates through the press. Pugin was obliged to go up and find out how they were getting on. He was discovering, as his father had before him, that co-ordinating all the various parties in serial publication was a tiring and frustrating job.

On 11 March Louisa gave birth to a son, Edward Welby. He was a healthy baby but Louisa was ill for weeks. Pugin's recently regained peace of mind was tried as he waited to see what course events would take. In time his wife recovered. The household economy, however, remained in an uncertain state. Until a second whole volume of *Examples* appeared, Pugin could not claim the subscribers' money and in the meantime the expenses of printing and engraving had to be paid. He reckoned they had cost £500 to date. His travels, or 'reshearches' as he called them, filled his sketchbooks with promising 'documents' for a sequel but they earned nothing.[40] At twenty-two, despite having a wife and two children, he could hardly to be said to have settled down. He was often away from home. He had no profession. He still had reason to be grateful for Selina's constant generosity with money. As Adlard observed piously, 'Matrimony', though 'generally a great steadier and turns many a man into a man of business who would not otherwise have become so', was not having this desirable effect on his nephew.[41]

It was not Pugin's fault that the *Examples* had stalled. Nothing would budge Willson, who, between ill health, preoccupation and a general reluctance to put pen to paper, still failed to deliver a text. Pugin made jokes about being chased down Great Russell Street by the enraged subscribers; he made a frank appeal: 'I have all my fathers former reputation to support and the foundations of my own to Lay. every excuse has been given from number to number for the non appearance of the promised portion of the Letter press ... my fortune is in your hands.'[42]

But in vain. They missed the early summer season. Having done all he could with Willson, Pugin set off again in May, this time for the Continent. 'I shall soon be up to my ears in delapidated chateus Ruined abbeys ancient libraries venerable Cathedrals ancient towns and splendid remains of every description,' he wrote to Osmond. 'Leave your blisters leave your Doric porticos leave all & follow me. when I return I will unfold such a tale.'[43]

For three months he travelled across France, into Germany and back via the Netherlands. He was perhaps following the route his father had outlined for his own projected tour. He returned at the end of August laden with antiquarian treasures and sketches and with his vision of the Gothic transformed. What he saw at Strasbourg, Louvain and, above all, in the church of St Lawrence at Nuremberg had been a revelation. It was the 'finest journey' he had ever known.[44] In Germany, he discovered, the Lutheran reformers had not been iconoclasts, the statues had not been smashed nor the altars stripped nor the windows broken. When he went into the Lorenzkirche for the first time it was as if he had been transported in reality back to the Middle Ages. Everything was still there: the thirteen Gothic altars, the stained glass, the candlesticks and, hanging in the choir, the Angelic Salutation, the two life-size figures of the Virgin and the Angel Gabriel, suspended, as in a vision, amid the soaring piers. Entering the church, Pugin wrote to Willson on his return, 'I could have repeated the song of Simeon without profanation.'[45] The song of Simeon, the 'Nunc Dimittis', begins: 'Lord now lettest thou thy servant depart in peace according to thy word, For mine eyes have seen thy salvation.' Pugin's dream of a revived Christendom, made manifest in art and architecture, was all at once before him.

The soaring German Gothic of steep roofs and massive towers impressed itself deeply on him. The immense height of the arcades, compared with English Gothic, seized his imagination. The vastness of these columniated spaces, their thin piers offering long vistas and complicated cross views, marked his own architectural imagination for years to come. 'I have seen the house of albert Durer, I have sketched his tomb. I have ascended the spires of Strasbourg chartres Antwerp & the Great tower of Malines. I have got precise information on many points which the cursed reformation has precluded the possibility of discovery in England,' he wrote excitedly to Willson on his return.

Then, yet again, just as he settled into his antiquarian idyll, came another shocking blow. On 4 September, after a few hours' illness, a stroke perhaps, his aunt Selina Welby died, a 'very heavy and tottally unexpected Loss'.[46] When her will was read it was discovered that, in response to his repeated appeals for money, Adlard received a legacy of £1,100. The bulk of the estate went to Pugin. It amounted to £3,050, a lifetime of modest savings. It was a last gesture of generosity that he never forgot. Selina Welby's was truly one of the hidden lives on which 'the growing good of the world depends', and much later Pugin recalled this self-effacing aunt 'who was kind in her life', who gave everything she had to her family and the poor and by her example 'made me a Catholic without knowing it'.[47] She was buried, as she had asked to be, with her family in Islington.

Adlard's letter about Pugin's poor business sense arrived after Selina's death and so he would have read it, setting the final seal on his estrangement from his petulant uncle. Adlard, so long used to being the favourite younger brother, had perhaps always been a little jealous of his nephew. As his own youthful vigour and restlessness curdled into discontent he came to dislike him. He and Pugin henceforth went their separate ways, and so with Selina passed Pugin's last personal connection to the gentry of Lincolnshire. The ties with the old days loosened further. Telling Willson of his aunt's death, Pugin reiterated his decision to become a Catholic. 'I can see the time . . . rapidly approaching when there will be only the catholick & the infidel, the power of the church of England is rapidly on the decline,' he explained.[48] Its power over him was appreciably lessened now that he need not fear troubling his aunt. Yet still he hung back. Louisa, it seems, was either unaware of his intentions or unsympathetic to them. In June, during his absence, his baby son had been baptized at St Lawrence, into the Anglican Church.

A few weeks after his aunt's death Pugin went to London, where there were reminders on every side of his earlier life. John Britton was still vigorous, though, Pugin thought, *'thinner & shorter'*.[49] 'He . . . complains of want of encouragement wishes he never had attached himself to litterary pursuits and rings the sovereigns in his pockets with the exclamations of horrid bad times.'[50] No love was lost on either side. It was while Pugin was still in London, on 16 October 1834 at about six o'clock in the evening, that Mrs Mullencamp, wife of a doorkeeper at the Palace of Westminster, ran to the deputy housekeeper shouting, as an enquiry later heard: 'Good God, the House of Lords is on fire.'[51] The housekeeper, seeing that it was so, ran into the street followed by her maid, who had molten lead running down her shoulders. The burning of old tally sticks had started a fire which now spread unstoppably through the Palace. The original medieval building, expanded, infilled, adapted and partitioned over centuries into the agglomeration of buildings that had become the Houses of Parliament, had already been described by Soane as 'an extensive assemblage of combustible materials'.[52] He had predicted that if a fire once broke out it would be impossible to contain. He was right. The flames were not extinguished until two o'clock the next morning, by which time the Palace was in ruins.

The destruction by fire of the old Palace of Westminster was seen, even at the time, to mark a period in national life. Huge crowds watched from Westminster Bridge and from the boats that packed the river until it was possible to walk from one bank to the other. Everyone knew that they were witnessing a historic moment. The old Palace, like the old Parliament before the Reform Act, like so much of the old order in England, had been ripe for destruction. There was something rotten in it that was being swept away for ever. Pugin was in the crowd, as were Turner and Constable, both of whom painted the fire. John Britton watched, already calculating which of his draughtsmen he should send to draw the ruins. Charles Barry, returning from Brighton by coach, saw the glow on the horizon. On hearing what it was, he is supposed to have said, 'What a chance for an architect.'[53]

All the capital was mesmerized by the 'grandeur and the terror' of the spectacle, the last great show of Georgian London.[54] Britton described the 'strong glittering of the flames' playing on Westminster Abbey. Pugin too saw something of John Martin's apocalyptic dioramas in the outlines of the tracery backlit by fire, 'truly curious & awfully grand'.[55] For him it was a practical and metaphorical vindication of everything he now believed. He saw 'nothing much to regret & a great deal to rejoice in', for the modern parts of the building had burned while the medieval fabric survived in Westminster Hall and the walls of St Stephen's Chapel.[56] 'A vast quantity of Soanes mixtures & Wyatts heresies have been effectually consigned to oblivion,' he wrote to Willson; 'oh it was a glorious sight to see his composition mullions & cement pinnacles & battlements flying & cracking . . . while his 2.6 turrets were smoaking Like so many manufacturing chimnies till the heat shivered them into a thousand peices the old walls stood triumphantly amidst this scene of ruin while brick walls & framed sashes slate roofs etc. fell faster than a pack of cards.'[57]

12

The New World Begun

October 1834 to May 1835

The building ... will be regarded as a part and parcel of the intellect of the age, as the model par excellence, the example in character, art and decoration of what is to come after.
– William Hamilton to the Earl of Elgin, 1836[1]

The question of what should replace the old Palace was being discussed even while the ruins smouldered. What the new Parliament should look like, its meaning as a seat of government, its appearance, were topics for the press and for public and private debate. The morning after the fire John Britton was on the site making sketches. *The Times* called for 'a noble Parliamentary edifice worthy of a great nation', to be designed with more room and better access for the public.[2] The *Westminster Review* put the Utilitarian argument that this was 'not ... a question of four walls placed here or there, built by this architect or that ... but the question by what machinery shall the legislative functions be best performed'.[3]

Robert Smirke, the only one of the Office of Works architects still active enough, was asked to report: 'he seems to attend burnt buildings Like a fireman,' Pugin complained – thinking of Smirke's efforts at York.[4] At first he assumed that the opportunity offered by the fire would be thrown away and wrote to Willson: 'I am afraid the rebuilding will be made a compleat job – as that execrable designer smirke has already been *giving* his opinions which May be reasonably supposed to be a prelude to his *Selling* his diabolical plans & detestable details.'[5] Pugin, however, was not alone in his distaste for 'jobbery', the fixing up of public commissions among a closed group of favoured candidates. The extravaganza of Windsor and the scandal of Buckingham Palace were still fresh in the public memory and reform was in the air, not only of Parliament but of public life and public building. The *Morning Herald* spoke for many in announcing that this time 'the British people intend to have the choosing of the architects'.[6]

Thus a debate was launched that made architecture a subject of popular interest as never before in Britain. Nor, until the present Prince of Wales's Hampton Court speech a hundred and fifty years later provoked a similar discussion of modernism, was it ever again so topical. Journalists, architects, men of taste and pamphleteers, even politicians, were ready to pitch themselves into the fray. Pugin, despite his pessimism about the likely outcome, was promising himself a 'few remarks' in print about Smirke.[7] For the present, however, the discussion of the Palace formed the backdrop to other events in Pugin's life which began to unfold rapidly. With his aunt's legacy he had sufficient funds to build a house for himself, and that was what, more than anything, he wanted to do. Since her death Ramsgate had not enough attractions to hold him. He decided to leave. It was to Salisbury, which he had first loved as a boy and where he now had a group of friends, that he decided to move.

Typically it was a mixture of the personal, the architectural and the sacred that drew him. The Osmonds were the kind of plain-spoken people, respectable rather than genteel, of an artisan class just below the middle, among whom Pugin felt most at ease. William, with his stonemason's yard in St John's Street, had come increasingly under Pugin's influence. He had all but given up his neo-classical 'blisters'. Salisbury Cathedral still bears witness, in more than a dozen Gothic monuments, to his artistic conversion. He and his wife Charity welcomed Pugin into their own large family with some of that parental kindness whose lack he still felt. Charity told him off in a motherly way about his scruffy appearance and he smartened himself up for her. William introduced him around the town. Among his acquaintance were others in the same line of work: the surveyor and builder Frederick Fisher, whose business premises were in the High Street, and the Peniston family, who had been architects and surveyors in Wiltshire for three generations.

The Penistons were also Catholics. Through them Pugin, whose resolution to leave the Church of England had neither diminished nor yet brought him to the point of action, met the small Catholic community of Salisbury. It was his first introduction to modern Catholic life. John Peniston was one of the leading members of the congregation. Mass had been said under licence in the Penistons' house in the Close for some years in the 1790s, and although a small chapel had since been built Peniston continued to bear the chief burden of administering the congregation's affairs, which were troublesome in ways that were typical of local Catholic life in the 1830s. The Emancipation Act had removed many of the disabilities previously placed on Catholics. They could now worship openly, sit in Parliament and – if otherwise qualified – vote. All this had made Peniston feel 'really a free man' at last, but in many more mundane ways little had changed for the Catholic population.[8] Funds were generally short and English priests hard to come by. The generation of French clergy who had fled to England in the 1790s was passing. The previous priest at Salisbury, Fr Begin, had been one of their number and had been in office for thirty years when he died in 1826 leaving substantial debts. There was no priest in 1834. The other difficulty the Catholics had to contend with was anti-Catholicism. Peniston's religion did not impede him professionally. Like Willson he was often employed to restore Anglican churches. Indeed religious hostility to individuals was rare and it was a long time since Catholics had been actively persecuted. But there was a deeply-rooted, if often ill-defined, dislike of 'papistry'. Most English people knew little about it; many of them had never met a Catholic, for Catholics had been, for centuries, a small minority. The anti-Catholics largely formed their dark impressions, as Pugin had formed his ideal, from a combination of history and highly coloured fiction. The rhetoric of anti-popery leaned heavily on Guy Fawkes, Bloody Mary and the Spanish Inquisition. Such prejudice was noticeable in the conservative society of Salisbury, a city dominated by the cathedral and its affairs, where, some years later, strolling through the Close, Anthony Trollope conceived the idea of Barchester. Mass had ceased to be said in the Penistons' house on the insistence of the Dean. The Catholic population must at times have felt beleaguered and their chapel was now rather run down.

Another of those who frequented it, and was prominent and well-respected in Salisbury, was John Lambert, a solicitor and gentleman of independent means, as well as an authority on church music. He, too, became a friend and lifelong supporter of Pugin, who, with his enthusiasm and warmth, seems to have made a welcome addition to the small circle. Pugin was now, for the first time in his life, among Catholics, and he found them congenial. Reasoning that for purposes of 'business' it was of no 'very great importance where I am so as a post can reach me', he bought a half acre of land, just outside the city at Alderbury, for £150.⁹ It was expensive. Land was hard to come by, for most of it belonged to large estates or the Church and this was the 'only peice . . . to be had near there for Love or money'.¹⁰ Situation, however, as Pugin and Osmond agreed, was everything and the site was perfect. It was sloping and close enough to Salisbury to command 'a magnificent view of the cathedral and city with the river avon winding through the beautiful valley'.¹¹ 'Under me,' he explained to Willson, 'is Longford castle seat of Lord Radnor with its turrets & chimney shafts rising among the venerable oak & elms.'¹²

Pugin's criteria were those of the textbook Picturesque. He had chosen a spot that Humphry Repton would have approved of for its rise and fall, its view and its noble associations, but the house Pugin built there, St Marie's Grange, would have scandalized Repton, as it did nearly everyone who saw it. As its name and dedication to the Virgin declared, Pugin intended his home to be a manifesto. It marked the start of a new life, a new profession and a new faith. It was the first demonstration of his vision of the Gothic as a revived, living style. To the astonishment and often undisguised mirth of passers-by, a turreted, fortified, red-brick house, apparently blown out of the pages of a book of hours, began to rise rapidly next to the main Southampton road. The Grange, which though altered still survives, was the fruit of Pugin's peculiar education, a mixture of Picturesque cottage and fifteenth-century house. In designing it he took the theories of Price and Repton and applied them with radical logic. He started with a ground plan, as his father would have done, creating an L-shaped pattern of interconnecting rooms on three floors. The stairs were in a corner tower, water closets for each floor in another tower. Behind these, rising through two storeys, was a chapel with a little bellcote on top.

The different parts of the building, chapel, sacristy, stair tower, were all adapted 'to the various purposes for which they were required', as Picturesque theory dictated.¹³ The irregular exterior appearance was 'formed only', as his father had put it, 'from motives of convenience in building'.¹⁴ This meant that Pugin put windows only where he needed light or wanted a view. His library looked out to the north-west and the south-west, towards the spire of Salisbury Cathedral. Towards the road the house presented a completely blank face. There was no visible door and no window. Not only was the façade blank, it was defended. Between the raised ground floor and the road there was a dry moat with a working drawbridge, overlooked by a watchtower. No other architect, however strictly Picturesque, would have had such a disregard for convention as to present a brick wall to the outside world. But Pugin had no hesitation. It was an eloquent gesture, for his house was both a retreat from the world and an assault on it.

After his parents' death Pugin was increasingly prey to nightmares, fear of burglary and other fears, less rational: the paraphernalia of the Gothic, in all its most clichéd forms, ghosts, sleepwalkers and all the assembled terrors of the night. His fortified house expressed his subjective dread, and also his strong streak of self-dramatization. The thickness of the walls, three feet, he told Willson, the moat, the lookout, were more necessary for his peace of mind than physical safety. He went so far as to conceal the well, as was common in the Middle Ages, to prevent tampering by enemies.[15] Like a medieval jewel case, the Grange was rebarbative on the outside while within all was to be richness, intimacy and glowing colour. Pugin's collections of antiquities, 'fine old damask. stone chimney oak furniture', made the rooms luxurious in a solemn way.[16] He bought a 'gilt Chalice of the 15th Cent.' for his chapel and medieval embroidery for his altar which he picked up for the price of the silver thread.[17] The bedrooms interconnected. The parlour led into the library, from which the chapel opened out. Parents and children, work and love and worship, were all to be contained inside the Gothic fastness. Servants, whose kitchen and scullery were on the lower ground floor, would use the same entrance as the family. It was a highly eccentric domestic arrangement. The Grange certainly 'formed a striking contrast to the class of modern suburban houses generally erected', as the more conventional Ferrey put it, with a smirk.[18]

The high-pitched roofs with gilded weather vanes and cresting, the stone casement windows with mullions instead of wooden sashes, made the house conspicuous and, to many people, ridiculous. Pugin chose red brick because he could not afford stone, and red brick had many medieval precedents, but to most people in Georgian England it was principally associated with modern warehouses and factory workers' cottages. Repton's view was that while brick was acceptable for a large, historic building such as Hampton Court, 'A compact red house displeases from the meanness of its materials', and most people agreed with him that it was barely decent for a gentleman's villa.[19] Among the red Pugin set black bricks to mark out a cross and the initial letter 'M', for Marie (always his preferred spelling of Mary). When the house was finished it bore two inscriptions: 'Laus Deo' (Praise the Lord) and 'Hanc domum cum capella edificavit Augustus de Pugin 1835' (This house and chapel were built by Augustus de Pugin 1835). Thus, though no passer-by could see into the house, travellers on the six coaches a day between Salisbury and Southampton could literally read its meaning. They were, Pugin reported, 'astonished beyond measure'.[20] This first house was a work of romantic art, a building with which its creator was entirely, subjectively identified. In it Gothic was realized as a total, organizing belief, running through both conception and construction, the appearance of the building and the kind of life that would be lived in it. This, Pugin believed, was what architecture could and should do. It was his own answer to the questions being debated in London about the design of the new Parliament, his personal attempt to mould 'the intellect of the age'.

It was also very much a young man's building, trying to do too much at once. It was not entirely practical. With its spiral staircase, drawbridge, watchtowers, sacristy and chapel, the Grange had only two bedrooms. In one sense it was not an important building, for it influenced nobody. Ferrey thought it 'tended rather to show the eccentricity of its owner than his superior skill in design', and even a sympathetic Nikolaus Pevsner diagnosed it as 'a case of extreme medievalism'.[21] Yet while it remains to some extent a cul-de-sac in English architecture, it was prescient, not least in the elements of its design that seemed most scandalous to Georgian eyes. In the 1830s a respectable villa had sash windows, pediments and either stone or stuccoed walls. Today's 'modern suburban house' will, like St Marie's, have casement windows, may well be built of red brick and will almost certainly have a pitched roof.

Work on the Grange began in January 1835 and went ahead fast. Pugin, though he knew a great deal about medieval architecture and construction, had no training as an architect. He never considered this a handicap and it was not, in 1835, so unusual. The profession had yet to organize and formalize. Many aspiring architects did train in architectural offices, but it was not a requirement and in Pugin's view such an education was worse than useless. Nevertheless he was faced with the need to create a modus operandi. Only one perspective drawing and a ground plan of St Marie's Grange survive. Although there may once have been more drawings, there is no reason to think that they were more detailed. Pugin had begun as he would go on, making only the briefest possible outline plans and sketches. Later he did make more detailed drawings for some of his buildings, but he always disliked doing it. He found the process as irritating and fiddly as his father's books. What Pugin wanted was a builder who understood medieval construction and could grasp what he wanted from little more than outlines. In this case his collaborator was one of the Penistons, probably John's eldest son John Michael. Pugin, impatient as ever, was constantly at his side as the work went on.

From 1835 most of Pugin's diaries survive. They are little appointment books, erratically filled with notes of accounts, work, addresses and laconic references to events. The personal, the newsworthy and the sensational are as freely interspersed as ever. 'Harlequin Steamer burnt in London' is the first entry.[22] From then on the early months of 1835 describe a round of visits from Ramsgate to London and Salisbury, sometimes with 'my dear Louisa', more often alone.[23] As work on the house went forward there are numerous purchases: oak, pictures and unspecified antiquities from Edward Hull. Among jottings of weather, removal arrangements and shipping, there are references, equally brief, to his religious life. 'Fast of Lent begins,' he noted on 4 March and on the 7th, cryptically, 'St Thomas Aquinas.'[24] He seems to have regarded himself now as a Catholic, writing to Willson about 'our faith' as if he had in fact converted. Yet he still held back from the final step. It was probably about now that he re-used the journal of his first honeymoon with Anne Garnett, writing on the blank pages in a smaller, better-formed hand a personal manual of Catholicism. He wrote out prayers, lists of vestments, notes of the meanings of ember days, the cardinal virtues, 'fasting days'. He was also trying to make good his lack of Latin, copying inscriptions and parts of the liturgy. The symbolic meaning of vestments interested him particularly.

Professionally he began to apply himself. That winter he told Willson, 'I have had as much business & more than I can do.'[25] He was often on the move but the restless wanderings of the last year or so were over. The 'reshearches' were turned to account, the contents of his sketchbooks and some of the Ideal Schemes were being worked up for books of designs, in the style of his father's *Gothic Furniture*, to be published by Ackermann and Co. Rudolph Ackermann had died the year before. His son was running the business and Ackermann Jun. and Pugin Jun. produced their first joint effort, *Gothic Furniture in the style of the 15th century*, in April. For Pugin it was a pragmatic venture. 'I am paid a certain sum for each plate,' he explained to Willson, '& as it is a useful cheap work I expect it will sell well.'[26] Unlike his father's *Gothic Furniture*, which attempted to replicate the entire contents of a Regency drawing room in the style of the Middle Ages, this was a collection of pieces that could more plausibly suggest the fifteenth century. The designs were richly carved but simple in outline. Pugin wrote in the prospectus that he had 'preserved inviolate . . . the principal features' of medieval design.[27] Later he repudiated these designs, which came to seem to him almost as bad as Strawberry Hill, but in many of them he had managed to make a critical transition. He was beginning to imitate medieval furniture as it had been, rather than applying medieval motifs, taken from architecture or window tracery, to modern furniture. It was a decided step towards integrity of design.

Gillespie Graham, Pugin's Scottish friend, was also employing him. Pugin was making drawings for a number of Graham's works, one of them an Ursuline convent in Edinburgh. Such an establishment would have been not only illegal but inconceivable in Scotland a decade earlier. Its inspiration had been in part that of Louis Lafitte's former patron, the Duchesse d'Angoulême. During her exile at Holyrood she had encouraged a Catholic priest, James Gillis, the future bishop, to attempt the convent. The Duchesse had taken a great liking to Gillis and so, in time, would Pugin. St Margaret's Convent was one of the earliest buildings of the Catholic revival, a flower of the Waverley age, now bearing fruit.

As the winter came to an end Pugin's house progressed. He was concerned with every aspect of it. He proposed to carve the stone himself, he wanted coloured glass for the windows and began to learn glass painting. He designed candlesticks and had them made in London, as well as bookcases to fit into the deep recesses beside the chimney-breasts. He wove the fabric of his life into the decoration with his own and Louisa's initials in the spandrels of doors and chimney-pieces. He had texts painted on the cornices: 'Gloriam Excelsis' was written over the chapel door. It was about now, according to Talbot Bury, who engraved the plates for some of Pugin's books of designs, that Pugin added the motto, which was entirely his own invention, 'en avant' to his coat of arms and from now on certainly he plunged into life again at a frantic pace. He had much to look forward to and, perhaps, a fear of looking back. For the rest of his life he worked like a man driven, or pursued.

At the beginning of May, when the house was nearly finished, he and Louisa packed their belongings, handed over the keys and, leaving Ellington Cottage for the last time, set off for Salisbury.

13

Salisbury and Sarum

Summer 1835

*I am much annoyed frequently by ... dreams the result of
continual excitement on the subject of antient architecture.*
 – Pugin to Edward Willson, 16 August 1835[1]

At Salisbury, which had already struck Cobbett and Constable as the
embodiment of all that was right and all that was wrong in nineteenth-
century England, Pugin was well placed to continue his comparative
inquiries into the medieval and the modern social orders. Sarum, as he
usually called it, using its ancient name, had been first founded nearby,
at Old Sarum, by the saint bishop Osmund in the eleventh century.
Osmund's foundation documents survive in the cathedral library, where
Pugin was now often to be found reading. He could see there too the
texts of the Sarum Rite. This 'Use of Sarum', compiled by Osmund
initially to determine the forms of liturgy and other practices of his own
cathedral, became established in the Middle Ages as the principal model
for secular (that is non-monastic) worship throughout Britain. Only
after the Reformation, in the reign of Mary I, was the Roman Breviary
introduced. In the Sarum Rite was embodied that continuous, native
Catholic tradition, a tradition in communion with but independent from
Rome, for which Pugin was searching. Salisbury was now confirmed as
the hub not just of his own world but of the true English Church, past
and soon to come.

Meanwhile the modern city was marked by the signs of the times. Old
Sarum had been one of the most notorious rotten boroughs, sending
members to Parliament long after it ceased to be inhabited, and its name
was often invoked in the debates on electoral reform as a byword for
corruption. Salisbury had seen its share of violence in 1830 and 1831.

The Established Church, here as everywhere else, was a subject of controversy and criticism. The year that Pugin arrived the Municipal Reform Act redrew the boundaries of the city and removed the last vestiges of secular power from the bishop. Everyday life was modernizing. The streets were lit by gas. Seven coaches a day ran to London. There were frequent popular balloon ascents, of which Pugin took note in his diary.[2] Charles Macready appeared at the local theatre in *Hamlet* (a performance described as 'tame almost to insipidity' by the *Salisbury and Winchester Journal*) and among the lectures at the Mechanics' Institute was one by John Peniston on 'The Progress of Architecture as connected with History', a subject on which he had no doubt received a great deal of advice from his client.[3]

Until their house was ready the Pugins went into lodgings in the High Street, Pugin using William Osmond's office for his work. Having bought his land, Pugin was qualified to vote and he duly registered. He was as happy to bustle with the new world as the old, for he saw no real distinction between them. He looked forward to the return of the old faith, which though old was not past. Meanwhile he was extending his local connections. Mr Payne, a glass and china merchant, employed him to restore a fifteenth-century merchant's house in the city, the Hall of John Halle. The house, as Pugin restored it, survives today and, by one of the more peculiar coincidences of ancient and modern to have overtaken his work, is now a cinema foyer. Pugin rapidly assumed a leading role among the Catholic congregation, even before his reception into the Church. The child who had commandeered the porters at Dover had grown into a young man of dramatic presence. He was of only medium height but broad-shouldered and solidly built, with a pale oval face, clear dark eyes, sometimes described as grey, sometimes as black, and longish hair swept back. He dressed, for work, usually in sailing clothes. His voice was loud but sonorous, he spoke fast and laughed easily, his manner was friendly and intense. Those who warmed to him found themselves wanting to do what he wanted. He was soon proposing alterations to the chapel. A new priest, Charles Cooke, arrived in March and presumably Pugin received some instruction to prepare him to become a Catholic, though he made no mention of it. Cooke's was destined to be a short incumbency. After five years his drinking obliged him to give up the priesthood. But Pugin, whose exaggerated fear of the world at large was matched by an equally undiscriminating trust in all individuals, was delighted with him. He thought his 'manner of saying mass . . . the most impressive I ever heard'.[4]

A much greater influence, however, as he prepared himself both as a Catholic and as an author was the work of John Milner, which he now began to read in depth. Milner, a Catholic bishop, antiquary and controversialist who had died nine years before, was Pugin's immediate intellectual predecessor. He had been a friend of Willson and it was no doubt he who recommended the books which 'delighted' Pugin with their mixture of history, religious polemic and Romanticism.[5] Milner had built his own little chapel at Winchester, with his friend the antiquary John Carter, the sworn enemy of Wyatt, who had been so dismissive of Nash's work at St Davids. Milner believed not only in the history but in the spiritual power of Gothic architecture, in the 'artificial infinite' created in the mind by the 'aspiring form of the pointed arches'.[6] He despised the 'small sashed windows and fashionable decorations, hardly to be distinguished . . . from common assembly rooms' of modern churches.[7] His own 'beloved chapel' was probably the first to be built with that faith in architecture as a living symbol which Pugin was about to preach to the world. Milner was also, like Pugin, humorous. Of Bishop Hoadly, that 'champion of liberty and the low church' whose monument was – and still is – cut deep into a shaft of Winchester Cathedral, Milner noted: 'It may be said of Hoadly' that 'both living and dying he undermined the church of which he was a prelate'.[8] Though often splenetic, Milner could also maintain a mildness in his writing that only infuriated his Anglican opponents the more. 'If [the clergy] will not be good Catholics,' he coolly explained, 'I am desirous that they should remain good Church of England men . . . I wish to prevent them from frittering away their religion.'[9] 'What a triumphant publication,' Pugin wrote to Willson when he read it, 'what a tremendous blow . . . I never read a finer peice of reasoning in my Life.'[10]

As he settled himself in Salisbury the pace of his working life accelerated. He had not yet put pen to paper on the subject of the new Parliament buildings but he had been to dine with Sir Edward Cust in London. Cust, 'a courtier and a man of taste', led the campaign to prevent Smirke's designs from being accepted unchallenged.[11] In an open letter to Sir Robert Peel, who was now, briefly, Prime Minister, Cust condemned the 'poverty' of Smirke's taste and recommended a public commission and a competition.[12] The press soon took up the cry. How Pugin had got himself on such terms with Cust is not clear, but he never had trouble meeting people when he wanted to. Cust knew several architects including Charles Barry, whom he had employed on his London house, and it may have been Cust who introduced Barry to Pugin. In any event three weeks later Pugin noted in his diary: 'dine with Mr Barry.'[13] It was the first time he mentioned the man with whose work and reputation his own was to become inextricably entwined.

Barry was forty, the son of a stationer. He had spent some time working in a surveyor's office; otherwise, like Pugin, he was largely self-taught. Already his talent, hard work and easy manners had taken him far. He was on intimate terms with the Whig intellectuals of the Holland House set and he was marked out as a rising star. Much later, when both men were dead, it was said that Pugin had made all Barry's designs for him, that he was the real architect of the Palace of Westminster and that Barry had stolen the credit. A bitter controversy was played out between the two men's families and friends through pamphlets, letters and newspaper articles in the autumn and winter of 1867-8. The controversy prompted editorials in *The Times* and an intervention by Gladstone, and it has hung over their reputations ever since. The true story of their working relationship is a complicated, delicate one that raises questions about the nature of authorship in architecture. It is best told in context as it developed. But Barry was no plagiarist and in 1835 it would have seemed laughable that the architect of so sophisticated a building as the Travellers' Club in Pall Mall could have been professionally indebted to the creator of St Marie's Grange.

What Barry wanted from Pugin when they met that spring was what any architect might expect to get from Auguste Pugin's clever young son, designs in the Gothic style that showed a scholarly grasp of detail and a practical sense of its application to a modern building. Barry wanted help with the finishing and furnishing of the Edward VI Grammar School at Birmingham, a commission for which he had successfully competed. The competition made no requirements about style and Barry's submission of a Gothic design was his own choice. It was logical, given the school's sixteenth-century origins, and its success also reflected the general movement of taste. Barry would never feel entirely at ease with Gothic, the classical was his natural idiom, but the grammar school in New Street was a strong, lucid design. It was also expensive, with stone vaulting and tracery, buttresses and oriels. For this he was already, in a sense, indebted to Pugin. Barry was a subscriber to Auguste's *Examples* and he made use of them. The Birmingham school sported windows from All Souls College and the popular oriel from Magdalen. But the composition, which was impressive, was entirely his own.

Pugin's first drawings for Barry show him applying his repertoire of detail to the existing structure to add depth and texture in panelling, chimney-pieces and corbels. It seems to have been an easy, if pleasant, job that required little more of him than his natural fluency. In designing the furniture for the school he stretched himself a little. It had to be simpler than the pieces that Ackermann could offer as models to wealthy private patrons. For the first time, Pugin developed an idea he had drawn in an Ideal Scheme, *St John's Hospital*, in which he used timber bracing, borrowed from roof construction, to make plain, adaptable furniture. He designed a table for the headmaster's house to seat 'eight persons to enlarge to accommodate 24' – a table still in use – made on those principles and constructed in sections.[14] Pugin 'began Mr Barry's drawings' ten days after their dinner and through the early summer they met several times.[15] They developed a warm and friendly working relationship, in which Pugin was unquestionably the junior partner. Barry signed his drawings (as architect), just as Gillespie Graham signed the work Pugin did for him and as most architects then and now sign the work of their assistants. For all his egotism and rebelliousness, Pugin always accepted Barry's authority. He respected him and in any practical situation which demanded it, sailing, scene-shifting, building, Pugin could work as part of a team.

At the same time he was making drawings for Graham for another school, Heriot's Hospital in Edinburgh. Although he did nothing without commitment, he clearly saw his work for Barry and Graham, like the plates for Ackermann, as bread and butter. He drew and thought rapidly, quarrying his sketchbooks and Ideal Schemes. His ideas came to him, almost always, in a single insight. He could not bear to redraw and hardly ever needed to. At the speed he could work he was earning useful sums of money and the income was grist to his own, great mill, the building of St Marie's Grange, which was nearing completion.

No doubt he and Barry talked when they met about the Palace of Westminster and Edward Cust's proposals for a commission to oversee the choice of an architect. This suggestion had now been adopted, in a much modified form, and on 2 June the terms were announced for a competition for designs. The style of the new building was to be either Gothic or 'Elizabethan', the latter to most people, including architects, a vague, Waverley term. The choice of style, as at Birmingham and Edinburgh, was a mixture of the obviously appropriate, so close to Westminster Abbey and Westminster Hall, and the increasingly popular. In so far as the building was to embody the 'intellect of the age', it would mark the 1830s as the turning point of the Gothic Revival, the moment in which the medieval began to become a national style.

There were no professional architects among the judges, who included Cust and the Radical MP Joseph Hume. The chairman was Charles Hanbury Tracy, who had built himself a Gothic manor house, Todding-ton, in Gloucestershire, for which, like Barry at Birmingham, he had leaned heavily on Auguste Pugin's works. Another judge was Thomas Liddell, who had used the *Specimens* to help his father Gothicize the family seat at Ravensworth. In 1835, in fact, almost everyone with an informed interest in Gothic architecture saw it, knowingly or not, through the eyes of the Pugin family. Barry asked Pugin for his assistance in preparing an entry for the Westminster competition. So did Gillespie Graham.

Pugin was in Salisbury at the time, completing his improvements to the local Catholic chapel. On 6 June, Whitsunday, he made a typically laconic entry in his diary: 'Finished alterations at Chapel received into Holy Catholic Church.'[16] It was a step he never reconsidered or regretted, a new beginning and at the same time a conclusion. The transformation that had begun with the first Ideal Schemes was now complete. The interior world of those schemes, 'the embodiment of his daydreams for years', was now to be externalized.[17] He had stopped dreaming, or rather he was ready to make the world inhabit his vision. He was ready to build Jerusalem.

14

Contrasts

Summer 1835 to August 1836

The historian is a prophet looking backwards.
                                                    – Friedrich Schlegel[1]

As the spring and summer went on, St Marie's Grange was being made ready. The finishing was done, like everything else, at top speed. 'Trees planted and walks laid out,' Pugin noted on 13 April.[2] The garden was in a formal, architectural style, with walls and regular beds, in keeping with a medieval or Elizabethan house. It is one irony of his re-interpretation of the Picturesque that Pugin could not abide picturesque gardens, which seemed to him modern and contrived. On 10 July he 'bought brewing utensils'.[3] More furniture and carpets followed. Although he and Louisa, who had not followed him into the Catholic Church, were still in lodgings, they were settling into life in the town. They dined with the Osmonds and the Fishers. Pugin made himself known to the local nobility and gentry, not least in hopes of getting patronage. He dined with Lord Radnor and prepared drawings for remodelling the façade of Longford Castle, a scheme which was never carried out. He had more luck with Sir Frederick Hervey-Bathurst, whose house, Clarendon Park, was near St Marie's Grange and for whom he designed a small lodge.

'My house is now nearly compleated,' he told Willson, 'the minutest details have been attended to and the whole effect is very good.'[4] At the same time he noted that it was causing a stir: 'the reports respecting my building here are truly rediculous'.[5] He had no doubts about it himself. The little house sparkled. Borrowing an idea from Repton, Pugin had added a gilded 'chrest of fleur de Lis' to the top of the roof and glittering weathervanes '(turning with every Wind)' which had 'a very good effect'.[6] In July he went to France and 'purchased some magnificent things' for his chapel.[7] But by now Pugin, like his house, was a conspicuous local talking point, gossiped about more and more wildly than he realized. He never had much sense of how he struck other people. His extravagance attracted notice and perhaps it was this combined with his rough and ready manners and the sailing clothes that caused rumours to reach Willson in Lincoln that his young friend was running a smuggling gang. 'I cannot conceive how such reports as that ... can be set afloat,' Pugin wrote back, horrified.

Once back in England he began to turn his attentions to the competition for the Palace of Westminster. The deadline had been extended from November to 1 December, but time was still short. The sequence of events that summer and autumn would later be much disputed when Edward Pugin launched his attack on the Barry family. William Osmond, Thomas Grieve and Talbot Bury were among those who struggled to remember what exactly had been done and said thirty years before. Their flatly contradictory evidence on points where none had a reason to lie is sufficient to remind a biographer how fragile memory is and how partial the most honest testimony. Even at the time, with everyone working up until the last minute, the order of events must have been confused, and for Pugin the competition drawings, if urgent, were not terribly important. The Palace, though it was destined to become his best-known work, never meant as much to him as his own designs. He told Grieve that he thought it all a great 'joke': 'Here are these two rivals competing for one prize and I am making the designs for both.'[8] It was a profitable joke. Barry paid him 400 guineas and Graham 300.

Most of the drawings Barry submitted to the judges have one way and another disappeared. It seems they were all, except for the plan, from Pugin's hand. Like his father before him working for Nash, Pugin's job was to present to an amateur eye a vision of what the building would be like, an evocation as much as a projection. The question raised in 1867 was how much he had contributed to what he drew and how far he merely followed instructions. Those drawings that survive from the two entries on which he worked tell a coherent and plausible story. With Graham Pugin had the upper hand, with Barry he did not. Graham, an old friend and something of a father figure, who can have had little real hope of winning the competition, let Pugin have his head. The entries submitted under Graham's pseudonymous device, the letters

'H.R.' with a rose and coronet, were barely modified Ideal Schemes. The
Great Hall of *St Marie's College* (one of the last schemes of 1834), with
its elaborate trefoil arched roof stretched even wider, became the House
of Commons. Overall the effect of these drawings was scenic, densely
elaborate and very church-like. In the opinion of Charles Hanbury Tracy
the Graham scheme as a work of art 'never has been and . . . never will
be surpassed'.[9] But as a workable proposal it was flawed. Only one
elevation survives, showing the river front. This immensely long façade
was the most difficult aspect of the problematic site. Pugin and Graham's
solution was an attractive looking but muddled agglomeration of separate sections.

The scheme exhibited by Barry under the badge 'Portcullis' displayed
his skill in planning. It took the late Gothic Perpendicular style and gave
it what Pugin described to Talbot Bury at the time as 'an Italian outline'.[10] To this Pugin added the Gothic details, culled from his sketchbooks and his Ideal Schemes. The drawings he made are lost, but the
copies that survive of some of them show what Edward Pugin was
anxious to point out, a strong echo of the *St Marie's College* scheme.
Even after the many alterations and simplifications made to the drawings
and then during construction, the resemblance is still apparent at some
points in the Houses of Parliament as they stand. Undoubtedly these
evocative drawings and the 'taste and knowledge of Gothic Architecture'
that they revealed weighed heavily with the Commissioners who judged
them.[11] Yet even at the time some critics complained of their unstructural
quality and the fact that they were not consistently related to the plan.
The answer to the question raised in 1867 must be that while Barry might
not have won the competition without Pugin, Pugin could certainly not
have won on his own. Barry's plan was coherent beyond anything Pugin
could have devised and Pugin must have known that. Bury recalled that
he admired it and 'anticipated a decision in Mr Barry's favour' from the
outset.[12] Pugin seems not to have thought of entering in his own name
as an architect. He did, however, seize the moment and the attendant
controversy to fire off a pamphlet, the first shot in his campaign to
change the face of England.

There had been a flurry of open letters after Cust's. One was by Arthur
Hakewill, an architect from a family of architects, whose father James
had broken the rules of the competition by submitting a classical design.
Hakewill Jun.'s pamphlet protested that Gothic was ugly and outdated

and that Westminster Abbey looked like nothing so much as a 'clump of thistles'.[13] Pugin decided that this was to be his *point d'appui*. *A Letter to A. W. Hakewill, architect, in answer to his reflections on the style for rebuilding the houses of parliament by A. W. Pugin architect* brought Pugin before the reading public for the first time as a polemicist. The pamphlet was, as *Contrasts* would be, sharply argued on the attack, broadly allusive and rhetorical on the defence. The style was passionately high-flown in some places, with echoes of his mother, journalistic in others and shot through with satirical humour. Hakewill raised the usual objection to Gothic that it was a dead style that should be left in the past. Yet the classical, Pugin pointed out, had been 'in vogue about 2,000 years ago among natives whose climate, religion, government and manners were totally dissimilar to our own'.[14] He defended Gothic partly in the old style of the *Repository* as being, in unspecified ways, everything at once, 'exquisite ... bold ... scientific ... light ... solid', but also for its associative powers, for creating buildings that would fill the mind of the beholder with admiration for 'the skill and perseverance of the ages in which they were built'.[15]

Pugin drew out the implications of his comparison to have a crack at the modern architectural profession and its system of education. Gothic was best and Gothic was best learned, as Pugin had learned it, empirically. He compared the 'foolish education of many architectural students who, after idling a few years on the classic soils of Greece and Italy, having measured for the hundredth time the remains of some fractured column, or restored a whole amphitheatre from a few feet of stone seat, return to their countries and venture to attempt the styles which the masterminds of a Steinback or a Wykeham carried to such perfection' with 'those who study this sublime style in all its ramifications, who seek it from the stupendous cathedral to the simple station chapel – from the massive crypt to the elaborate and gorgeous chantry – from the towered castle to the gabled and turreted mansion – these feel its beauties and learn to practice them. The chisels of many a humble mason, whose only school has been the cathedral of the city in which he dwells, have lately produced stonework scarcely inferior to the finest specimens of the olden time.'[16] Thus in a leap, or a lunge, Pugin, typically, reached conclusions, almost in passing, about the importance of craftsmanship and tradition in architecture that it would take the rest of the century and the combined efforts of Ruskin and Morris to work out in detail. On the back of his pamphlet he advertised his next work 'in progress and will be published as soon as completed', the long-considered *Contrasts*.

The scheme of 1833 had lain dormant amid the activity of the last two years. Now Pugin revived it. One day in August, while he was in London, working with Charles Barry on the Birmingham Grammar School, he took one of his father's old sketchbooks and walked around the capital singling out targets for his attack. He drew All Souls, Langham Place, the bandbox church that epitomized Regency taste and fashionable religion, designed by John Nash, who, long out of sight and mind, had died in May. He drew the new entry to King's College in the Strand, by the detested Smirke, which he would publish next to the magnificent entrance front of Christ Church Oxford. He drew George Dance's curious façade at the Guildhall, exaggerating its quasi-Indian features and lengthening the windows until it wore an expression of perpetual surprise, and he picked on one of the silliest new buildings in London, Stephen Geary's King's Cross, a statue of George IV with a police station in the pedestal, and later paired it with the medieval market cross at Chichester. It was no dispassionate survey. It was ammunition for an assault on modern architecture. No longer was Pugin content, as he had been in the first scheme, to make general points. He chose specific buildings and named names. He drew Soane's own peculiar house in Lincoln's Inn Fields to show what the Professor of Architecture at the Royal Academy was capable of. By the time he returned in mid-August to Salisbury he had an example for each of his points.

St Marie's Grange was near enough finished to be habitable in September and Pugin, as he took possession of his fortress, was ready for battle on several fronts. He was now an established, indeed a leading member of the congregation at St Martin Street, where, with Lambert, he officiated as an acolyte at Mass. They wore the robes that he had designed for them and which, he reported to Willson, were 'handsome and quite correct . . . worked by the Ladies of the Chapel'.[17] In fact, he added with a note of theatricality, 'I assure you you would hardly know me when issuing from the sacristy door in full cannonicals.'[18] He had no conception of comporting himself tactfully towards his fellow townspeople on religious matters and told Willson that he had 'to sustain a heavy attack continually on the score of religion – In which however I consider I always come off victorious.'[19] It was, after all, merely a matter of time before the Church of England was disestablished. Then the Catholic Church would take back into her care the great treasures so abused since the Reformation. Pugin would 'never rest satisfied' until he could 'follow the processional cross through the western doors of the cathedral', but he did not believe he had long to wait.[20]

Such thoughts were not confined to the young, the passionate or the recently converted. Since May the local papers had been noticing 'religious disputes' in Salisbury, and in August the Archdeacon and clergy published a letter to the King stating their 'deep apprehension' on behalf of the Established Church.[21] They, as the true 'successors of the illustrious martyrs and Christian patriots of former times', protested at 'degrading and unconstitutional' concessions to 'Roman Catholic influence and agitation' by the present government.[22] These were indeed, as the Dean said, 'times of rebuke and blasphemy, division and excitement'.[23] Pugin found himself, with some pleasure, 'in the thick of . . . controversy' with abuse 'thick as hail' flying in all directions.[24] Louisa was not, perhaps, so sanguine. She remained an Anglican, aloof therefore from what was now the mainspring of her husband's life and work. Pugin noted in passing that she 'does not have good health' at St Marie's Grange.[25]

As the deadline for the Westminster competition approached he put aside *Contrasts*. Talbot Bury came down to help him with the competition drawings and Pugin's diary records a frenetic pace, as he and Bury, Barry and Graham all shuttled between London and Salisbury working on the two separate schemes. On 24 September 'Mr Barry came':

25 Sent off 5 drawings to Mr Barry
26 worked all night
27 Parliament H
29 Sent to Mr Barry 14 drawings

And in October:

9 Sent off Mr Barry's drawings
10 Left London via Winchester
11 Gale all night
11–19 drew at Mr B
18 Returned to Sarum

20 Began Mr G Elevations
21 Ditto Ditto
22 Ditto Ditto
23 Ditto Ditto[26]

On 2 November Barry came back, and so it went on. There was only one, ominous, hiatus. On 6 November, while Barry was staying in Salisbury, Pugin noted, 'Ill all day. Sight very bad.'[27] This eye trouble, which he blamed on overwork and drawing by lamplight, was the first of his neurological symptoms to manifest and it would recur. He was twenty-three. It was some four or five years since his rackety days in the theatre world, about the length of time that it would take for the first symptoms of syphilis to appear. On this occasion, however, his sight recovered as suddenly as it had failed.

A Mr J. Hogarth, who mounted the drawings for both schemes, recalled that Pugin was working on the Graham scheme until six o'clock on the evening the entries were due. 'When he left he was most anxious that I should follow him to Mr Barry's as quickly as possible, which I did; and it was past 11 before I had the drawings finished, and the corrections were made in the office up to the last minute.'[28] Two days later Pugin was back at St Marie's Grange sending drawings to Willson for the *Examples*, of the Vicars' Close at Wells. The summer of 1832 when he had been so enchanted with the buildings of Wells, the last of the summer tours with his parents, must have seemed by now an age away, yet still Willson had not finished the text, still the next volume of *Examples* could not appear and the 'unfortunate and never ending subject' of which Pugin was so sick came between him and his old friend;[29] 'the whole blame is thron on me,' he protested, 'my pocket has been drained and my reputation compromised.' But still only a trickle of words issued, drop by drop, from Lincoln.[30]

The winter brought two new restoration schemes from Gillespie Graham, which further delayed the progress of *Contrasts*. Pugin would never find it easy to refuse work, or to refuse a friend. He took on almost anything that offered and while he looked forward, urgently, to the realization of his millenarian hopes for England, he made no systematic attempt to establish himself in practice. He would make a stage design for the Grieves or design a fountain for his neighbour Colonel Baker. His was a temperament that lent itself readily to the grand vision, but was incapable of medium-term planning. There is something of a parable at this point in the comparison between Pugin and his former fellow pupils from Great Russell Street. Talbot Bury was beginning to establish a practice in London. Walker was doing the same, overseeing the engravings of the *Examples* with Benjamin Ferrey. Ferrey, the amiable tortoise, inched along beside Pugin's hare, directing his less spectacular talents to more concentrated effect. He entered the Palace of Westminster competition. He cannot have thought he would win but took the chance to show what he could do and get his name in print when the results were announced. He soon received a commission to lay out an estate of villas at Bournemouth and was planning, on the strength of this, to get married. Pugin meanwhile poured out his ingenuity and creative energy on his own house, for which of course he paid, and on other architects' projects which brought him no direct credit. For Graham he designed a reconstruction of the ruined chapel at Holyrood. The plan, never realized, was to rebuild it as a meeting place for the Assembly of the Church of Scotland. To rebuild Holyrood, that prime site of the Gothic imagination, was much more to Pugin's taste, if less to his professional advantage, than Bournemouth villas.

In January the Commissioners overseeing the competition for the new Palace of Westminster reached its decision in favour of 'Portcullis'. Pugin made no mention of this in his diary. He was busy with the drawings for his next Ackermann publication, *Designs for Gold and Silversmiths*. He undoubtedly followed, however, the row that broke out as soon as the decision was made public. Barry had been so widely tipped to win that there were immediate allegations of 'jobbery'. The newly formed Institute of British Architects (later the Royal Institute) called for an exhibition of all the entries in order to 'allay any apprehension in the public mind, with respect to the propriety of the decision'.[31] The real intention was of course to open, rather than to close the question. As committees in both Lords and Commons were convened to consider the entries and report to Parliament, campaigns were launched to have the decision overturned. Charles Barry was questioned about his scheme, the likely cost, the length of time it would take, the models and precedents he had used. It was the first of innumerable cross-examinations he would face from time to time over the coming decades, many of them exhausting and hostile.

Meanwhile on 23 February, in his library at St Marie's Grange, Pugin

noted that he at last began 'drawings of work of Contrasts', the book
that would, more than any other, catch the wave of public opinion on
the subject of modern architecture about to break in London.[32] On
1 March, his twenty-fourth birthday, he sent the title page to Talbot
Bury to engrave. Four days later he delivered more drawings to him in
London and then set off on a week-long tour to the north, returning to
Salisbury via Wales. He visited Willson in Lincoln, to urge him on with
the *Examples*, and he made drawings for the medieval buildings he
would illustrate in *Contrasts*. His idea for the graphic part of the book
was now formed. Not only were all the buildings to be real, they were
to be urban. *Contrasts* had developed in his mind into an early treatment
of one of the great themes of the nineteenth century, the city. The
sprawling industrial centres that had disturbed Schinkel in 1826 with
their moral and physical squalor were increasingly troubling to the
English too. Pugin wanted to show what a good city could look like. He
wanted to show that the Gothic could offer models for more than
churches, that it could be applied to every modern building type, the
inn, the public conduit, the university, the family house.

Pugin had learned how to make visual jokes from the popular prints
at the Repository and the graphic satire of the pantomime, while from
his father's watercolours he knew how to stir the deeper emotions. The
illustrations were a mixture of comic cuts and Ideal Schemes, anti-
quarianism and topical cartoon. The medieval buildings were made to
appear rich, 'soften perspective' he noted to himself; the modern thin
and ridiculous.[33] *Contrasts* spoke with the voice of the rising generation.
It was the equal and opposite reaction to his parents' *Microcosm of
London*. Where that had been sceptical, inclusive and lavish, *Contrasts*
was tendentious, passionate and plain, morally and literally black and
white. It was an attack on the world of the Regency, that Vanity Fair of
stucco-fronted manners, high taste and low principles. Pugin, however,
made use of his parents' most original idea by using the figures in the
plates to make his argument. A disorderly crowd bursts out of the
modern chapel, desperate to get home. At the medieval parish church,
St Mary Redcliffe in Bristol, a solemn procession makes its dignified
way up the steps. In choosing Bristol Pugin evoked another contrast,
fresh in most minds, with the city's recent past, the anticlerical riots,
the bishop's palace in flames. Occasionally Pugin's point was entirely
social. At the modern pump, in Soho, its handle chained up, he drew a

thirsty boy being chased away by a policeman. It had little to do with architecture but it struck a sympathetic note in the year before *Oliver Twist*.

While Barry, up in London, was being pressed by the committee for detailed information about how, exactly, he proposed to carry out his enticing-looking scheme of Gothic decoration and in particular how much it would cost, Pugin was cheerfully caricaturing the whole competition. He drew a special plate for the front of *Contrasts*: 'dedicated without permission to the trade'.[34] At the top was an advertisement for a 'new church competition', 'Gothic or Elisabethan estimate must not exceed £1500 and style plain.' Busts of Nash and Soane appeared in a shop window – a glazing bar running impudently through Nash's nose – surrounded by advertisements for '2nd hand designs', 'norman gothic garden seats . . . at reduced prices' and 'a moorish fish market with a literary room over'. Thus *Contrasts* opened on a note of burlesque, but it concluded with a prophecy of doom, the tailpiece a massive scale, pivoted on the eye of truth. On one side was the nineteenth century, with the works of the most established modern architects in the balance. Outweighing it on the other were those of the fourteenth, of William of Wyckham and Adam Kraft. Round the scale was inscribed, 'They are weighed in the balance and found wanting,' the writing on the wall at Balshazzar's feast from the Book of Daniel.

In April Pugin went to London to get the plates etched. He also went to look at the exhibition of winning and commended designs for the Palace of Westminster competition. This had finally been mounted at William Wilkins's new and much-criticized National Gallery in Trafalgar Square after some delay, during which Barry had modified his own plan and, according to some of his rivals, stolen their better ideas. The Preface to the exhibition catalogue proclaimed a great moment in national life, when 'all England' (no mention was made of the rest of the United Kingdom), being 'jealous of her reputation in fine art', was, after a period of struggle in war and politics, 'at leisure to deliberate' the rebuilding of her seat of government.[35] In fact there was a great deal of struggling to come. A subcommittee of defeated architects had already petitioned the Commons for a commission of enquiry. The catalogue contained a hint of the controversy in its note of the committee's decision 'considerably' to abridge William Wilkins's description of his own rejected entry. Wilkins had the double annoyance of seeing his defeated scheme exhibited in his own unpopular building. Recently described by Thackeray as 'a little gin shop', it was seen to exemplify all the faults of the classical style.[36] It, as much as the exhibition, became a part of the debate. Wilkins arranged to have the full text of his 'description', a bitterly sarcastic attack on the whole competition, handed out at the door. Pugin must by now have been itching to join in the national row. In May he wrote the text for *Contrasts*.

The boy who had laboured so unwillingly over the weekly essays his mother set him, had not grown up to be a natural writer. Most of his books and pamphlets were composed at a single stretch, when he was 'worked up into a fever' of over-excitement, in which state he would write for hours, sometimes days on end, the dogmatic, often strident tone of his prose propelling him over internal contradictions.[37] Like a typical antiquary, notoriously his friend Langlois, he avoided revision by adding his afterthoughts in footnotes and appendices which grew and multiplied until they threatened to overwhelm the text. 'I have been indefatigable early & Late,' he told Willson, pointedly, when it was done, 'Letter press & plates have all been done *scince I saw you* thats what I call expedition.'[38]

The text of *Contrasts* comprised a preface, five chapters, a conclusion and twenty-one appendices, the whole purporting to show 'how intimately the fall of architectural art in this country, is connected with the rise of the established religion'.[39] Although Pugin claimed in his Preface to have 'conducted the comparison with the greatest candour',[40] the first sentence of the principal text dispelled any illusion of impartiality: 'On comparing the Architectural Works of the present Century with those of the Middle Ages, the wonderful superiority of the latter must strike every attentive observer.'[41] 'Who can regard those stupendous Ecclesiastical Edifices of the Middle Ages (the more special objects of this work),' Pugin went on,

without feeling this observation in its full force? Here every portion of the sacred fabric bespeaks its origin; the very plan of the edifice is the emblem of human redemption – each portion is destined for the performance of some solemn rite of the Christian church. Here is the brazen font where the waters of baptism wash away the stain of original sin; there stands the gigantic pulpit, from which the sacred truths and ordinances are from time to time proclaimed to the congregated people; behold yonder, resplendent with precious gems is the high altar, the seat of the most holy mysteries, and the tabernacle of the Highest! It is, indeed, a sacred place; and well does the fabric speak its destined purpose: the eye is carried up and lost in the height of the vaulting and the intricacy of the aisles; the rich and varied hues of the stained windows, the modulated light, the gleam of the tapers, the richness of the altars, the venerable images of the departed just, all alike conspire to fill the mind with veneration for the place, and to make it feel the sublimity of Christian worship. And when the deep intonations of the bells from the lofty campaniles, which summon the people to the house of prayer, have ceased, and the solemn chant of the choir swells through the vast edifice, – cold, indeed, must be the heart of that man who does not cry out with Psalmist, Domine delixi decorem domus tuae, et locum habitationis gloriae tuae.

Such effects as these can only be produced on the mind by buildings, the composition of which has emanated from men who were thoroughly embued with devotion for, and faith in, the religion for whose worship they were erected.[42]

In so far as *Contrasts* had an argument this was it, a combination of Picturesque theory about the way in which a building should express its function with antiquarian learning, of a romantic belief in the power of association and the need for the artist to be identified with his work, set in the context of the ancient Catholic faith, the whole laid out in the richly descriptive manner of Walter Scott. Pugin went on to outline the history of England as he had learned it from the antiquaries. The Reformation was of course the decisive event, the moment when the social and cultural fabric was shattered as Henry VIII, 'established in his new dignity' as head of the Established Church, brought about 'the total overthrow of art' by dissolving the monasteries, laying waste the buildings, dispersing 'the exquisite and precious ornaments with which they were filled' and breaking up the institutions which had 'formed alike the places for the instruction of youth, and the quiet retreat of a mature age'.[43]

When he came to deal with the present Pugin was just as angry, about many things, including the 'wretched state of architecture', but he was more sceptical and humorous at the expense of 'This great age of improvement and increased intellect' in which medieval churches were neglected and if seen then little understood.[44] He was withering about the picturesque tourists he must have seen in Herefordshire who 'go to see every thing that is to be seen, therefore they see the church – *id est*, they walk round, read the epitaphs, think it very pretty, very romantic, very old, suppose it was built in superstitious times, pace the length of the nave, write their names on a pillar, and whisk out, as they have a great deal more to see and very little time'.[45] The Georgian clergyman fared even worse: 'Do we see him perambulating in study and contemplation those vaulted cloisters, which were erected solely for the mediation of ecclesiastical persons? No; he only enters the church when his duty compels him; he quits it the instant he is able; he regards the fabric but as the source of his income; he lives by religion – 'tis his trade.'[46] Meanwhile the ancient buildings were either mutilated, like Salisbury in the hands of Wyatt 'of execrable memory', or neglected.[47] At Ely Pugin deplored

the water, pouring through unclosed apertures in the covering, conveying ruin into the heart of the fabric; the opening fissures of the great western tower, which, unheeded and unobserved, are rapidly extending . . . [while] what was once the Lady Chapel, [is] now filled with pews and vile fittings, brought from the parish church the chapter refused to repair; see how the matchless canopies have been pared down and whitewashed. Look on the decay of the whole church, and then remember Ely is yet rich in its revenues. What must be the hearts of those men forming the chapter? And yet they are but a fair type of most of the others; I only cite them in particular, because Ely is one of the most interesting churches in existence, and it is decidedly in a vile state of repair.[48]

There was, Pugin pointed out, 'no sympathy between these vast edifices and the Protestant worship'; the Established Church itself, 'so badly put together', a 'jumble of ancient church government with modern opinions and temporal jurisdiction', had never, he argued, either loved its buildings or commanded respect 'and from present appearances we may judge it will ere long be entirely changed'.[49]

In his 'Conclusion', trenchantly entitled 'On the Wretched State of Architecture at the Present Day', he laid about him liberally at the eccentricities of the Regency. 'We have Swiss cottages in a flat country; Italian villas in the coldest situations; a Turkish kremlin for a royal residence; Greek temples in crowded lanes; Egyptian auction rooms . . . It is hardly possible to conceive that a person, who had made the art of Architecture the least part of their study, could have committed such enormities.'[50] He condemned the National Gallery, the British Museum and the Gothic interiors at Windsor, on which he himself had worked, with their 'elongated or extended quatrefoil and never-ending set of six pateras ... the work of the plasterer and the putty presser, instead of the sculptor and the artist'.[51] Interestingly some of his deepest contempt was reserved for his father's employer and patron, Nash, for his work at Brighton, at Buckingham Palace and in the 'nests of monstrosities' in Regent's Park.[52]

None of the individual elements of *Contrasts* was original, it was the totality that was new. Only Pugin was prepared to project the romantic, retrospective vision of the medieval world on to the present and the future, to urge a complete revival of the Church and the arts of the Middle Ages. Carlyle said that the writing of history had become in the nineteenth century a form of prophecy. If ever there was an example of such a genre it was *Contrasts*. Overall the book was shaped by Pugin's knowledge and by his ignorance. Both were remarkable. He knew almost as much as anyone alive about medieval art and architecture, but he had never heard of the Renaissance, he could not spell 'parallel' or 'marriage' and his grasp of Roman numerals was shaky, as was his literary taste. He added a cheerful dollop of verse to his text in the form of Ward's *Reformation*, a rollicking doggerel which supplied his epigraphs:

> I sing the deeds of great King Harry,
> Of Ned his son, and daughter Mary;
> The old religion's alteration,
> The Church of England's first foundation;
> And how the King became its head;
> How Abbeys fell, what blood was shed;
> Of rapine, sacrilege, and theft,
> And Church of gold and land bereft.[53]

Although rapid in execution, *Contrasts* had been long in gestation. It was a kind of autobiography in so far as it was composed of everything Pugin had known. John Martin's apocalyptic scenes for sale at Ackermann's Repository, the rhetoric of Irving's pulpit, the stage of Covent Garden, Willson's library and A. C. Pugin's drawing school were all reflected in it. The long hours of his childhood summers, spent in the parish churches and cathedrals of England, his mother's caustic satire, his own humour and his fervent, millenarian hope for the future, were whirled together to make up his manifesto. When it was complete Pugin decided to publish it himself because, Ferrey later said, nobody else would undertake it. This perhaps makes the situation more dramatic than it was. It was clearly too controversial for Ackermann, and self-publication, of which Pugin had had experience all his life, was probably the next best option. There was, however, one final obstacle, the completion of the next volume of *Examples*. Pugin had decided that this would be his last. He had sold the next set of drawings to Thomas Larkins Walker to carry on the work. The present part only needed Willson's introduction: 'for heavens sake send the rest and cut it short,' he wrote to him, '. . . pray do sit down and finish it off . . . it is impossible to wait any Longer . . . the extreme time I can wait is the Latter end of next week . . . – I have wished the work at bottom of the sea fifty times.'[54]

Not only did he want to discharge his obligations, Pugin must have realized that he had to publish the *Examples* before *Contrasts*. The list of his own targets was almost identical to the list of his father's distinguished but now much irritated subscribers. He had already attacked the Hakewills in his pamphlet, Robert Smirke was satirized in the frontispiece of *Contrasts* as the author of the 'new square style', while among those 'weighed in the balance' on the final page and found lamentably wanting were Decimus Burton, William Wilkins and George Basevi, every one of them a subscriber to *Examples*. Pugin would find it embarrassing and possibly difficult to collect their money once they knew what he thought of them. Willson did, at last, finish. His essay is a warm tribute to his late friend Auguste Pugin. Of the 'various circumstances' that occurred to 'retard the accomplishment' of this part of the work, Willson avoided detailed explanation.[55] Pugin wrote a short Preface alluding brusquely to his collaborator's 'illness' and emphasizing that the delay 'has not been caused by any neglect or inattention on my part'.[56]

The second volume of Pugin's *Examples* was finally published in July 1836. *Contrasts* appeared on 4 August, a date that marked the beginning of Pugin's public career and the effective end of Georgian architecture.

Part Four

15

Entre Deux Guerres

Autumn 1836

*I have stated nothing but truth undisguised truth and I am
happy in the position I have taken.*
— Pugin to Edward Willson, August 1836

Nothing much happened at first. The rest of August passed peacefully.
Pugin experimented with oil painting, a medium with which he never
developed much affinity. Louisa was pregnant again, the baby expected
in September. Pugin began etching the plates for his next book for
Ackermann, *Details of Antient Timber Houses*, which showed measured
elevations of the fifteenth- and sixteenth-century wooden houses he had
seen in France. Timber construction, whether of buildings, furniture or
boats, always fascinated him, and he believed that he had discovered in
these houses, which were then rapidly disappearing, 'a most important
but unknown principle of ancient design' which he was hoping to apply.[1]
This was the last of Pugin's books that Ackermann would publish, a
hybrid of his father's style and his own, in which the polemicist overtook
the topographer on the last page. The final plate is a protest against the
demolition of wooden houses, showing a bonfire of 'antient carpentry'
blazing before a row of mean modern buildings, the one surviving timber
house placarded as 'Lot 2 Firewood for sale.'[2] At the foot of the page is
a tablet with the words 'The End'. It marked, also, the end of the career
of 'Pugin Jun.'

On 20 August Pugin went up to London. Gillespie Graham was there
and they worked on the Holyrood scheme. Charles Barry also wanted
Pugin's services, this time for the estimate drawings for the Palace of
Westminster. His scheme had not been, despite the protests, set aside
and the parliamentary Select Committee, anxious as ever about expense,

had given Barry five months to produce detail drawings, from which quantity surveyors could calculate the cost. Pugin was to provide suggestions for interior fittings – panelling, chimney-pieces, vaulting, door frames and much else. It was a perfect exercise for his well-stocked memory, a gigantic Ideal Scheme spun out of his sketchbooks, although Barry was anxious to remind him that 'simplex' must be the watchword.[3] Barry gave him plans with details of scale, from which Pugin, with astonishing speed and a versatility that had developed through the Ideal Schemes and never afterwards failed him, turned out 'windows, turrets', 'eight different sorts of doors', whole sheets of fireplaces.[4] Barry was hugely impressed and grateful for his '50-horsepower of creation'.[5]

By the time Pugin came home in early September, people in Salisbury had read *Contrasts* and 'certain parties' were, naturally, outraged.[6] 'I am a marked man,' Pugin wrote excitedly to Willson.[7] The first of his antagonists to break into print was a young Anglican clergyman, the Revd Arthur Fane. He wrote to the *Salisbury and Wiltshire Herald* to complain about this 'violent attack' on the nation's 'faith and discipline'.[8] Fane admired the engravings in *Contrasts* but came down hard on the 'extreme folly and puerile misrepresentation of the accompanying text'.[9] He pointed to its central flaw, that in his 'unlettered zeal' Pugin had misunderstood the history, both of art and of religion.[10] 'The grand blow to the Gothic style of architecture,' Fane wrote, 'was given by the taste for the Grecian style which arose at Rome in the pontificate of Leo.'[11] In other words the Renaissance came before the Reformation and the architecture of the Catholic Church, at its heart, was classical not Gothic. Fane's main contention was unanswerable and Pugin would have to concede it, but he was not ready to do so yet.

The editor of the *Herald*, a stoutly Tory paper, added a paragraph to 'A F's' letter, concurring with it and urging any of his readers foolish enough to think that Popery was 'altered in spirit' from the days of the Inquisition to look at *Contrasts* and see how wrong they were.[12] 'The Church of England may well exclaim,' he went on, ' "oh that mine adversary would write a book." '[13] The wisdom of publicizing the adversary's book quite so widely seems not to have troubled him. The *Herald* gave *Contrasts* more free advertising than a private publisher could have dreamed of and, Pugin told Willson, it was at once effective: 'Before this attack on me not a single copy had been sold here . . . I am now reduced to one.'[14] He wrote a lengthy reply to Fane in the *Herald*'s Liberal rival, the *Salisbury and Winchester Journal*. He claimed, untruthfully, that there was nothing in *Contrasts* to suggest he did not admire 'the Italian grandeur' of St Peter's in Rome.[15] He accused Fane of 'spite' and of mentioning Pugin's house, St Marie's Grange, 'no less than three times' and 'in a sarcastic manner'.[16] Fane hit back in the *Herald*, Pugin in the *Journal*. Letters, public and private, went to and fro, but nobody, except his friend John Peniston, supported Pugin in print. The curiosity and resentment he had been unwittingly arousing ever since his arrival in this somewhat staid provincial city now boiled over. The attacks on his house were numerous. Nobody who criticized *Contrasts* failed to refer to that 'singular red building on the road to Southampton', which was mocked for its colour, its 'distorted taste', the 'miserable vanity' of its name, and, interestingly, its foreignness: 'like a miniature bastile . . . fit for an inquisition'.[17] Fane called it Tudor, the editor of the *Herald* called it a 'nondescript pile'.[18]

To its Salisbury readers *Contrasts* was primarily a religious, rather than an architectural book. Some of them had opinions on architecture, but almost all were developing decided views on religion. The debate that had begun in Oxford three years before was now sending the 'vibration of an intellectual movement' across England.[19] The works of the Tractarians circulated in the diocese. The Revd Mr Fulford of Trowbridge was giving away hundreds of copies of the *Tracts for the Times*, and at Devizes Mr Patterson was preaching on the controversial subject of Apostolic Succession. The catholicizing implications of the Oxford Movement were obvious and to many alarming. The fear that their own Church might be 'Romanized' was what lay behind the violent anti-popery of the *Herald* and others. That same month the chaplain of New College, visiting the recently built church at Newman's parish of Littlemore, just outside Oxford, felt 'an indescribable horror' creeping over him at the sight of a piece of Romish idolatry, a stone cross at the East end.[20] The horror was 'indescribable' perhaps because Catholicism was, to most of the English, so largely an unknown quantity. This meant that it could be invoked to stand for any kind of menace, and over the next decades it was made to represent from time to time both the barbarian at the gates and the enemy within.

The years that followed the publication of *Contrasts* saw a revival of Catholicism and of anti-Catholicism, although the latter, with some dramatic exceptions, remained mostly sound and fury. The *Herald* might publish Fane's claim that 'Roman catholic and traitor were synonymous words', but it could also report with equanimity that John Lambert had taken first prize for a hothouse plant in the horticultural show.[21] Lambert later became mayor of Salisbury. At Lincoln, Edward Willson had recently been appointed a Justice of the Peace, one of the first Catholics to hold such an office. It was Pugin's abusive outspokenness about the Church of England as much as his religion that attracted personal hostility, and this both surprised and hurt him. He was willing to be a martyr but he did not like to be disliked. *Contrasts* was, he explained to Willson, 'aimed at the system and not at individuals'.[22] But naturally individuals were offended. Thomas Larkins Walker was annoyed. So was 'A Protestant', who wrote to the Salisbury papers. It was clear from his letter that the author knew Pugin and knew that he had been 'sanctioned and treated with every kindness and confidence' at the cathedral library when he was pursuing his researches.[23]

Pugin made many enemies in these early years of his new, Catholic life. He was not, by nature, aggressive. He disliked personal quarrels and had very few. He had simply not considered how the cathedral clergy, having encouraged and helped him in his enquiries, might feel when the enthusiastic young man whom they had shown round the archives turned on their Church like Savonarola. How much of the violence of his early writings was fuelled by that particular anger that sometimes accompanies bereavement is unknowable. Pugin's texts dwelt at length on the sufferings of Catholics and the loss and destruction of art and architecture. Perhaps their intensity owed something to his own experiences of pain and loss. It was not long before he would regret his more brutal pronouncements against the Established Church, but by then the damage was done. In Salisbury the authorities banned him from drawing in the cathedral. It was a slap in the face, the first sign that the course he had set out on with such hopes of reconciliation between the old faith and the new might involve loss as well as gain.

What Louisa felt at the public scandal surrounding her husband can only be imagined. The commotion went on and so did her pregnancy. September, when the baby was expected, passed. At last, on 13 October, she gave birth to a daughter, Agnes. Both survived the experience in good health, but Louisa remained an Anglican. Pugin baptized his second daughter himself. His glee at the completion of *Contrasts* was now mingled with anxiety and, he told Barry, illness. Having announced in the *Journal* that he had 'neither leisure nor inclination' to go on with the debate, he turned his attention back to his work in hand.[24] He was producing designs at a rate that gave Barry, pleased as he was with them, some anxiety. 'I am not surprised that your health suffers,' he wrote. 'Do not, however, I beseech you, carry too great a press of sail, but take in a reef or two if you find it necessary.'[25] The tone is typical of the way Barry dealt with Pugin, warm, at times protective, tactful, the nautical phrasing a friendly parody of Pugin's own. He was genuinely fond of him but also, just now, reliant on him. Nobody else could have provided Barry with the same service.

The estimate drawings set the pattern for their collaboration. Barry would outline what he wanted, Pugin would send back designs, Barry would either accept them or, more usually, ask for alterations. 'The design of this part of the building should, I think, be of a simple and massive character, and a pillar in the centre of the tower must be avoided,' Barry wrote of the King's entrance.[26] It was a typical instruction, clear but general, leaving Pugin plenty of scope for the 'glorious efforts' that Barry acknowledged were entirely his own.[27] Drawings for the House of Lords, the King's Stairs, galleries, lobbies and libraries flowed from St Marie's Grange day after day. Pugin was not Barry's only assistant. Barry had technical advisers and at least three more draughtsmen. He was unquestionably in command. The structure, the plan of the Palace, every final decision was his. Yet Barry's Italianate principles – 'symmetry, regularity, and unity' – were ill-suited to a Gothic design, at least as Gothic was understood in the 1830s.[28] It was Pugin's details that gave the drawings, and later the building, their character. It is they which create the first and the most lasting visual impression.

That winter one of the Covent Garden pantomimes was *Harlequin and George Barnwell*. It featured a transformation scene in which a box of Barry's drawings for the New Palace was changed into 'The office of the Society of Yarn Spinners'.[29] It is quite possible that Pugin lent a hand with the scenery and even more likely that it was he who gave the Grieves the impression that the estimate drawings included an element of yarn-spinning. In truth he and Barry (who was always notoriously inaccurate with his budgets) were on thin ice. It was one thing to draw Gothic doorplates and overmantels; quite another, in 1836, to know who, if anybody, could manufacture them or what they would cost, as Pugin had already learned from the painful experience of running his own manufacturing business. They must both have known the drawings were wildly speculative. But Pugin could afford to take a humorous view, for his part in the business was over once they were complete. From then on he gave the Palace little thought for the next seven years.

In the autumn he designed his second building, the lodge for his neighbour, Sir Frederick Hervey-Bathurst of Clarendon Park. A white brick gatehouse in a Jacobean style that could have passed unnoticed in any pattern book, it was scarcely enough to justify his description of himself as an architect, let alone the prophet of an architectural revolution. It was *Contrasts* that made Pugin's reputation. He was energetically dispatching it to friends and booksellers in London and Paris. He sent, in some cases personally delivered, review copies to the London magazines and, between his own and his father's old connections, was able to place it in the hands of a large number of dealers, antiquaries and critics. The first friendly response outside his own circle of acquaintance was from a Catholic priest, Daniel Rock. Rock was thirty-seven in 1836 and employed as chaplain to the Earl of Shrewsbury. Like Willson and Milner he was an antiquary, a scholar of the English Catholic tradition and particularly interested in the Sarum Rite. He too believed in the sacred power of art and architecture; they were, he thought, to the Mass itself as the body was to the soul, the physical expression of a spiritual reality.

Pugin knew Rock's writings and was thrilled to get a letter from him about his metalwork designs. He sent a copy of *Contrasts* in return to Lord Shrewsbury's Staffordshire seat, Alton Towers. 'To say your work pleased me,' Rock replied, 'would be cold tame praise it enchanted it delighted me every page is full of glorious sentiments.'[30] Rock showed *Contrasts* to the Earl, who got in touch with Pugin. So began the connection that was to be of central importance to both men for the rest of their lives.

16

Romantic Catholics

In a valley, not far from the margin of a beautiful river, raised on a lofty and artificial terrace at the base of a range of wooded heights, was a pile of modern building in the finest style of Christian architecture . . . built of a white and glittering stone.[1]
– Benjamin Disraeli, *Coningsby*, 1844

Contrasts was a violent push at an open door. Once through it Pugin found himself in touch with a section of English Catholic society to which his views were already familiar, among men and women who had come by various routes to similar conclusions. Most, but not all, were like himself converts. They were as saturated as he in the sensibility of the Picturesque and the romance of Waverley and they, too, were in revolt against utilitarianism and the modern city. They wanted, out of the flux of the 1830s, physically and morally to build a new England, peaceful, humane and Catholic. In the face of such unprecedented social change they were only one of many groups and sects who believed at that time that 'everything was wrong, yet capable of being effectually, and almost instantly rectified'.[2] Of the many visions and philosophies fomented in those years, theirs was not the most fantastic and it was one of the most benign.

The Romantic Catholics, to give them a name, were a small group, virtually a coterie, whose members were powerful and well connected in England and beyond. Although they have been largely forgotten and virtually written out of history, in 1836 and for a decade after they had an influence out of all proportion to their numbers. It was they who launched Pugin's career. At their centre was John Talbot, 16th Earl of Shrewsbury, the most prominent Catholic layman in England. Shrewsbury was forty-five in 1836. A tall man with a pale oval face, sloping shoulders and features more affable than handsome or strongly marked, his philanthropy made him a figure in Catholic folklore, the 'Good Earl John', the 'millionaire saint'. The reality was not so simple but nor was it essentially different. Modest, unselfish and pious, Shrewsbury felt keenly the responsibilities of his position in national and religious life, the first of his family since the Reformation to be able to take his seat, as a Catholic, in the House of Lords. Although he was not a convert, he had looked to the world of Waverley to invent a persona, not just as an emancipated Catholic, but as an Earl, for he had grown up, not very happily, as plain John Talbot, the younger son of a younger son. His mother had died the year after his birth in 1791 – it is striking and perhaps significant that many of the Romantic Catholics had suffered bereavement early in life – and on his father's remarriage John and his elder brother Charles were sent to live with a great-aunt at Lacock Abbey in Wiltshire. Lacock had been an Augustinian convent, built in the thirteenth century and partly rebuilt in the 1750s by Sanderson Miller into one of the most significant houses of the early Gothic Revival. Shrewsbury, like Pugin, therefore, had formed his early impressions of the world in the shadow of pointed architecture reading the novels of Walter Scott by the richly coloured light of stained glass.

John and his brother were sent away to school with the Benedictines at Vernon Hall in Lancashire, where Charles died. After an interval at Stonyhurst he was sent to another Catholic school, St Edmund's at Ware in Hertfordshire, where this 'most gentle, obedient and amiable' boy organized a pupils' rebellion and was expelled.[3] Conditions in public schools, in the years before Thomas Arnold arrived at Rugby, were often chaotic, rough and unsanitary. John had already lost his brother and he later maintained that what he suffered at St Edmund's had been 'beyond all endurance'.[4] The years after his abruptly concluded schooling were spent with tutors, then travelling in Portugal, Africa and the Mediterranean, often 'in the very wake of the British army', an experience that left him with a horror of war.[5] His father died in 1815 and with no fortune of his own John settled in a small house at Hampton-on-the-Hill, near Warwick, given to him by another old Catholic family, the Dormers. He lived there until, in 1827, his childless uncle died and the patchily educated, socially somewhat displaced John Talbot became 16th Earl of Shrewsbury, with property valued at £347,511 13s. od.

He had married, in 1814, a cousin, Maria Theresa Talbot of Wexford. The Countess was pretty, humorous, sharper than her husband and more worldly. She liked 'diamonds and going out'.[6] Her few surviving letters bear out the view of her as a good-tempered, talkative woman, but a gossip and a snob, over-awed by the position in which her marriage had placed her and inclined to domineer over her easy-going husband. In Rome her co-religionist Lady Mary Arundell, who liked her well enough in private, observed her with embarrassment 'acting fine' in society. 'She was so vulgar, and talked of her riches and estates, and of all the Kings and Queens she was intimate with . . .' that sometimes she 'had hardly left the room' before the laughter broke out.[7] It was, Lady Mary thought, 'a thousand pities that Lord S lets her govern so entirely and does not interpose his real good plain sense'.[8] Having lost her only son in infancy, Lady Shrewsbury's main ambition was the procurement of aristocratic Catholic husbands for her two daughters.

From the cottage on Lord Dormer's estate the new Earl and Countess were translated to the Shrewsbury family seat in Staffordshire. The house had been improved by succeeding generations in step with the forward march of taste. It had begun as Alton Lodge, a hunting pavilion in a remote spot above the Churnet Valley. When such a setting began to be picturesque, the lodge was magnified by the 15th Earl into his principal home, Alton Abbey, a Georgian Gothic exercise in landscaping. He had created gardens filled, or rather stuffed, with architectural features: Indian temples, pagodas and a model of Stonehenge. The effect was peculiar rather than attractive. Local people commented on the 15th Earl's epitaph, 'he made the desert smile', that it was 'a very polite desert not to laugh out loud'.[9] The new Earl updated Alton Abbey at a stroke by renaming it Alton Towers, a more historically correct title. He then employed two architects, Robert Abraham and Thomas Fradgley, to double the size of the house. Shrewsbury's ambitions for his faith and his wife's for herself coincided in a desire to make their home a spectacular showpiece, a place where national and international Catholic society would mingle on equal terms with the English ruling class. In his personal style the Earl (who used the word 'knightly' with approval) combined, in a chivalrous manner, the public flamboyance suitable to his rank with a modest private austerity. A great enfilade of public rooms was added to the Towers, through which the visitor passed as if through a succession of scenes from *Ivanhoe*; there was a blind harper, Edward Jervis, who lived on the estate. There was an armoury and a picture gallery and an octagon chamber with stained glass windows. It was all rather old-fashioned architecturally, looking back to Wyatt's Fonthill. Shrewsbury was committed to the idea of Gothic architecture as peculiarly Catholic and had already commissioned several churches, but he was not especially sophisticated in his taste. As a collector he was omnivorous. Despite Pugin's efforts over the years to dispose of the odder and shoddier items, the route to the chapel remained lined with a diverse mixture of cabinets of minerals, antique banners, a rhinoceros head, a rosary that had belonged to Mary, Queen of Scots, and a tomahawk. There was also a waxwork room, where the life-sized tableaux included a chimney sweeps' race. The young Princess Victoria thought Alton Towers 'an extraordinary house', and was surprised to have her luncheon on 'splendid gold plate'.[10] There was perhaps always something a little flashy about it. It stands now a ruin, the contents dispersed, the windows blank, the great chimney-pieces hanging in mid-air. The grounds, not inappropriately, are a theme park, owned by Tussauds.[11]

Shrewsbury was not an intellectual or an aesthete. Pugin and the 'clever good-humoured, smirking' Dr Rock were often exasperated by his erratic taste and his failure to grasp the essentials of Christian architecture.[12] The Earl good-naturedly did his best to keep up. 'What part of the church is the feretory,' he wrote once to Rock. 'Miss Phillpotts . . . wishes much to know . . . I promised to find out for her, tho' I really forget it myself. What is it?'[13] (A feretory is a shrine, usually portable and so not strictly part of a church at all.) At other times Shrewsbury's 'good plain sense' made him stand up for himself against the pedantry of his chaplain and the wilder flights of his architect's imagination. He and Pugin seem to have taken to each other at once. Both were enthusiasts and both were warm and direct in manner. Pugin, much as he deferred to the Earl's nobility in theory, was in practice as frank with him as with everyone else. Shrewsbury's letters show no patrician aloofness. He treated Pugin – almost always – as a friend on equal terms: 'I am dying to see you again. I have so much to talk about' is typical of his tone.[14]

Among the group that had gathered around Shrewsbury, Pugin's closest friendship was to be with Ambrose and Laura Phillipps. Ambrose, three years older than Pugin, and the model for Disraeli's Eustace Lyle, was a convert and the living embodiment of the romantic Catholic ideal.

A pale, slight young man with full lips, hooded eyes and an expression inclined to melancholy, he was highly-strung, at times hysterical, given to moods of depression and elation as extreme as Pugin's. Phillipps was driven both by a desire to do good and by a millenarian sense of divine destiny. He believed he was living in the Latter Times of prophecy, and of England's imminent return to the true faith he had no doubt. From a Leicestershire family of Whig gentry, Phillipps, who had also lost his mother in childhood, had known nothing about the Catholic Church beyond his own reading. It was this and the sight of Mass being celebrated in Paris that effected his conversion. When he was sixteen he had a dream in which God reproached him for failing to act on what he knew to be the truth. Phillipps arranged to meet a Catholic priest at the cottage of an Irish paviour and in these poignant surroundings 'received for the first time the Bread of Life'.[15]

He was not without a sense of the theatrical. In this and in their enthusiasm to confront the older generation, Pugin and Phillipps were typical of the angry young Catholics of the 1830s. At this distance in time the religious idealists of that generation look not unlike the social idealists of the 1930s, passionate if not always well informed about the cause they were espousing. Certainly a conversion to Catholicism in late Georgian England had a similar effect on one's parents to becoming a communist 100 years later. Phillipps had outraged his father and had even caused a ripple of consternation on a national scale when he converted his friend, the Hon. George Spencer. Spencer, an Anglican priest and the younger brother of Lord Althorp, had since been ordained in the Catholic Church and embarked on a strenuous prayer campaign for the conversion of England. To Phillipps the sound of plainchant echoing once more through vaulted aisles was to be the sound of a great awakening, 'an epoch in the Catholick history of England'.[16] He and his wife, Laura Clifford, the daughter of an old Catholic family, had embarked on married life as a shared endeavour to build this vision in reality in Leicestershire.

Phillipps's father struggled to control his irritation with his son's plans and the persistent attempts to convert his father. It was his daughter-in-law, whom he thought 'neither rich, nor pretty' with a 'Saxon' face and only a tolerable dress sense, who managed to reconcile father and son.[17] The couple lived on the Phillipps estate, at Grace Dieu. Near it were the remains of a thirteenth-century priory, that 'interesting spot', described by Wordsworth, with its 'ivied ruins'.[18] Twenty-five years later Phillipps proposed to re-animate the past, not in a Wordsworthian spirit, but literally. His father thought the idea 'preposterous'.[19] At Grace Dieu the little couple (many people commented on their slightness) built a mansion with a chapel. They started a school and acquired 227 acres of land on which to build a Cistercian monastery in the remote Charnwood Forest. Until they met Pugin they had no particular knowledge of architects, and these early buildings, in a bland Tudor style, were by William Railton. Thus the first rood screen and the first new monastery to be built in England since the Reformation were not the work of a Catholic idealist but of the architect best known for Nelson's Column.

There were other incongruities in this vision of Christendom revived among the industrializing Midlands, and not a few moments of bathos. The postal address of the monastery was 'Coalville'. The Phillippses were mocked as much as they were admired. Yet they worked, physically, extremely hard, driven apparently as Pugin was driven, to tax to the utmost their health, their strength and their substantial but not limitless income in the attempt to hold up a better model to an uncertain world than that offered by the new poor law, the workhouse, the factories and the slums. At the centre of their ideal society was their own marriage. For Ambrose and Laura – as for Pugin – it was a mark of the superiority of medieval civilization over classical that it set a high value on women and married love: 'The husband lived in the castle with his wife and children around him.'[20] Their model was a benign, paternalistic hierarchy, in which each rank deferred to those above and took responsibility for those below. This, they believed, was the only alternative to Radicalism, which they saw as meaning chaos and the destruction of the social fabric of civilization. The female sphere in their world was circumscribed, complementary to the male rather than equal, yet essential to the health of society. Pugin, for whom family life and female companionship were also indispensable, found this ethos at once appealing. He had not before thought much, perhaps, about the social implications of his ideas beyond a general notion of 'charity', but he was strongly influenced by the Phillippses' energetic philanthropy.

It was also through them and the Shrewsburys that he became aware of a wider revival of Catholic art and faith, spreading across the Continent. Although they were a small group in England, the Romantic Catholics were part of an international movement. Many Catholics of means, especially in the years before Emancipation, spent long periods abroad, often in Rome, where they could enjoy complete religious freedom. Some had been educated in Europe, several were at least bilingual. (Laura Phillipps's first language was German.) It was in Germany and Italy that English romantic Catholicism was developed. At Rome, where they spent long periods after their marriage, the Shrewsburys and their circle mixed with two generations of Catholic idealists. Among the older were Chateaubriand and the widow of Friedrich Schlegel. The younger included the Comte de Montalembert, who was campaigning with Victor Hugo to restore the historic monuments of France, his friend the art critic François Rio and the group of German painters who called themselves the Nazarenes. The Nazarenes, who became widely popular in England a decade later, had a view of art comparable to Pugin's of architecture. They had rediscovered the 'primitive' pre-Renaissance painters and were reviving both the style and the faith of the period of Giotto, in the belief that: 'Anything that is really alive acquires its outward shape from inner conditions; it develops organically'; thus their art was a direct expression of faith, as Pugin believed his architecture to be.[21] Shrewsbury, in his support for the German painters, whose work he brought to Alton Towers, was for once prescient in his taste.

If the Nazarenes were their artists and Pugin, from now on, their architect, the author who best expressed the Catholic romantic ideal was the curious figure of Kenelm Digby.[22] Digby, an older and long-standing friend of Phillipps, had unleashed the full force of Continental romantic Catholicism on the English reading public ten years before, with the second volume of his *Broadstone of Honour*, subtitled 'the true sense and practice of chivalry'. Digby, an Irish Protestant convert who was much under the spell of Byron, was an endearing combination of Don Juan and Don Quixote. He had travelled widely, he had fought a lion and once dived into the Rhine, yet he was a gentle, slender man, inclined to disparage himself, whose extravagance in print contrasted with a retired and bookish private life with his wife and children. Digby's manual of chivalry, which was followed by the much longer sequence of *Mores Catholici*, was read by the ageing Wordsworth and the young Burne-Jones. Few can have found it so practically useful as Shrewsbury, thrust as he was into an unprecedented chivalric role, but it was widely admired. Digby, too, believed in the 'spirit of family connexion and the high importance of women' as well as the civilizing power of Catholicism in the face of modern industrial society.[23] 'Had England continued in communion with the Catholic church,' he suggested, 'it is possible that Birmingham and Manchester might not have attained to their present character, for merciless inhuman industry would not have been tolerated.'[24] Like the Phillippses, Digby, who came to entertain an 'infinite regard & respect' for Pugin, showed him in return the wider social implications of the argument of *Contrasts*.[25]

Pugin was soon on terms with most of the Shrewsburys' circle. They brought him many opportunities and gave him a deeply sympathetic but very partial view of Catholicism. The Romantic Catholics, especially the converts, knew little of the Church. Theirs, like Pugin's, was a highly personal form of religion, a faith expressed through solitary pilgrimages among mountains and ruins, interspersed with moments of epiphanic insight in picturesque landscapes. What Pugin had felt at Nuremberg came to Phillipps in the Campagna in the autumn of 1828. 'The Appenines in the furthest distance wore a hue of violet tinged with pink . . . the majestic plains . . . broken here and there with a solitary pine, or a ruined tomb or tower.' To the romantic temperament, seeking affinities between the interior self and the eternal, the Catholicism of the Middle Ages offered the intimate, expressive spirituality it craved. The narratives of stained glass windows, the devotion to personal saints, the beauty of the Latin Mass, were refreshing to souls left parched by a State religion of sermons and commandment boards. This Gothic vision, however, with its emphasis on a powerful laity, an English Church and medieval forms of worship and charity, had little to do with the Church of the nineteenth century. The Romantic Catholics' part in the history of the Roman Catholic Church was ultimately destined to be small, yet to dismiss it as 'chiefly mediaeval play-acting' is crude and inaccurate, for in the religious and social debates that focused the mind and shaped the culture of early Victorian England, Shrewsbury and his circle played a significant part.[26] Their role was acted out between the existing English Catholic community and the Oxford Movement, and they have been largely forgotten or ignored by historians of both, yet their charitable efforts, if they did not solve the growing social problems of those years, were more effective than many and their influence, for a while, was considerable.

In 1836 Pugin had yet to discover how particular a section of Catholic life he had entered. For the moment he was delighted to find such patronage and so much sympathy.

17

The Professor of
Ecclesiastical Antiquities

1837

*In the story books of that date, the good man, the right man
. . . has only to show himself and to say a few words and he
carries all before him.*

Tom Mozley, remembering the 1830s[1]

Pugin's diary began to record new names. He dined with Kenelm Digby,
with George Spencer and with Spencer's father, the Earl, who was
rumoured – wrongly – to have converted. He began drawing the illustrations for Rock's projected work *The Church of Our Fathers*. It was
typical of both men that the drawings were finished in a matter of
months and the text took twelve years. The new circles in which Pugin
now began to move overlapped in many places with the old. Lord
Shrewsbury was familiar with the brokers' shops of Soho and Bond
Street, where he was a much-solicited customer. Montalembert knew
Pugin's French antiquarian associates, de Caumont and Langlois.
Authorship and architecture, antiquities and theology made up the
Romantic Catholics' ethos as much as they did Pugin's. He continued
to see his old Great Russell Street friends, Talbot Bury, Joseph Nash
and the disgruntled Thomas Larkins Walker, who had set up in practice
in Great Russell Street with Ferrey. Pugin's first independent step
towards an architectural career came in March with a visit to Oscott,
the Catholic school and seminary near Birmingham.

The Catholic Church in England was divided, for administrative purposes, into four districts. As a Protestant country it was regarded by
Rome as a 'mission' and each district had a Vicar Apostolic, who was a
bishop, presiding, technically, over an otherwise extinct early Christian
see. Lord Shrewsbury's influence was greatest and his charitable efforts

most concentrated near his home in the Midland District, where the Vicar Apostolic was Thomas Walsh, Bishop of Cambysopolis. Shrewsbury was helping Walsh to expand and rebuild Oscott. In the wake of Emancipation Walsh was confident that 'with Divine blessing' he could make 'numerous' converts.[2] The college later became 'the centre of the world' to Victorian Catholics, 'a great engine' for 'England's regeneration', where in 1852 Newman preached a famous sermon, the Second Spring.[3] In 1837, however, the habits of the penal days still lingered. The President was Dr Weedall, a cleric in the old Georgian style, 'the primmest possible little divine, with hair powder and every hair in its place, and having neat little shoes in a chronic state of high polish'.[4] Weedall was popular with the students, who enjoyed a benign regime. Their education was provided by a staff who reflected the peculiarities of the English Catholic community. French was taught by Baron de Saussey, 'an old legitimist in a snuff brown coat'.[5] Fencing was the province of Mr Parker, who was past seventy but still spry and often to be seen 'tripping along the ambulacrum in his padded jacket'.[6]

On to this quiet, somewhat antiquated scene Pugin burst. The impression he created was immense and instant. He was young, at twenty-five scarcely older than some of the seminarians, he was passionately enthusiastic, and as reviews of *Contrasts* began to appear in the national press he was becoming famous. With exactly what purpose he first went, or was sent, to Oscott, whether to teach or to build, is not clear, but from the moment he arrived the days of Joseph Potter, the architect in charge, were numbered. Weedall warmed to Pugin at once, while in John Moore, who taught philosophy and loved medieval art, he found a friend for life. The pupils hero-worshipped him and he got on with them easily, as he did with workmen, taking them on equal terms and drawing them into his ideas. One of the boys, Kerril Amherst, later a bishop, who became a friend of Pugin, recalled him then: 'Beardless, with long thick straight black hair, an eye that took in everything . . . a striking figure, though rather below ordinary stature and thick set.'[7] He wore a wide-skirted black dress coat, loose trousers, shapeless shoes 'tied anyhow' and a black silk handkerchief 'thrown' around his neck. The overall effect was 'inclined to that of a dissenting minister of that day, with a touch of the sailor'.[8]

Pugin's first visit to Oscott on 27 March was followed by others. Soon he was given a room of his own and established as Professor of

Ecclesiastical Antiquities, a subject new to any academic syllabus. Pugin was the only layman among the Oscott teaching staff, yet the power of his personality was such that he met with little resistance. Weedall honoured him with his 'entire confidence' and fell in with all his ideas.[9] Soon the staff and pupils grew accustomed to the sound of Pugin's 'loud voice as he gave directions, sounding through the corridors, or his rising laugh when he was struck by some ridiculous idea'.[10] His intention was to train up a generation of priests to understand the art and liturgy of the English Catholic Church – as he himself understood it. He was highly pleased with his appointment. Oscott gave him a base, a field of action and a professorship, of which he made frequent mention.

It was over a year before Potter received his final payment and decamped 'in high dudgeon', but Pugin had begun furnishing the college and fitting up the still unfinished chapel as soon as he arrived.[11] Within two months the Oscott accounts began to record substantial payments to Edward Hull and another dealer, John Webb of Bond Street. Flemish choir stalls, communion rails, enamels and an astonishing Baroque Spanish confessional were among the objects 'Torn by heretical and revolutionary violence from their original position', as Pugin put it, and now redeemed and collected for sacred use once more at Oscott.[12] He had yet to realize – or to acknowledge – what Montalembert knew and loudly complained of, that the trade in 'salvaged' antiquities had become an organized racket, with dealers willing to pay priests and others handsomely for as much as they could get their hands on. Not only were these objects of dubious provenance, none of them was medieval. Pugin was still oblivious visually as well as historically to the Renaissance; his idea of 'Gothic' was quite elastic enough to stretch far into the sixteenth century and occasionally beyond.

Potter's unfinished chapel was far from contemptible. Pugin was able to improve it with minor adjustments. He seems to have added the polygonal apse and he probably modified the shape of the windows. What made the final effect remarkable was the decoration. The walls were painted to imitate stone, a Georgian habit that Pugin would later think deceitful but which, for the moment, did not trouble him. The wings of the altarpiece were painted by John Rogers Herbert, a follower of the Nazarenes who now became a friend of Pugin. In the reredos antique carvings were set among Pugin's own designs. The impressions of his German tour resonate through the chapel in the woodwork and also in the windows, his first ecclesiastical stained glass, for which the figures of the apostles are taken from paintings in the Altes Pinakothek in Munich. These first windows showed Pugin's immediate affinity for glass design. Though he would develop far and fast beyond them, they exude a confidence and integrity that the chapel as a whole never quite achieved. The antiquities he bought were too disparate a collection not to appear incongruous. The Oscott chapel, Pugin's first ecclesiastical interior, still had a strong flavour of antiquarian bricolage.

Not only in the chapel but throughout the entire college Pugin 'left the impression of his artistic presence in almost every room'.[13] Over the two years following his first visit he designed all the internal fittings, the furniture, 'even the professors' gowns and the iron ink-pots'.[14] Ideas that had developed in Ideal Schemes and the drawings for Barry now began to be realized and to spread through libraries, bedrooms and attics. The most significant element in the scheme, in terms of Pugin's artistic development, was the furniture. He began by producing designs that bore an obvious relation to those in his book *Gothic Furniture* of the year before. Linenfold panelling, carved embellishment, decorative hinges and lock plates created a general appearance of richness. When he came to the more workaday parts of the building, however, the refectory, library and kitchen, both economy and propriety demanded something plainer.

The large 'constructional' tables that he first designed for Oscott, and which he later produced in variations for houses, convents and the Palace of Westminster, were central to his twentieth-century reputation as a proto-modernist. Seen from the far side of international modernism they indeed look uncannily prescient, but hindsight is not always an advantage. Pugin did not reconsider the form *de novo*, he did exactly what he said he did, he looked to medieval models. He based his designs on the sort of plain, pegged furniture that appears in paintings, such as Cranach's *Allegory of Melancholy*, and on surviving medieval tables, like those at Belvoir Castle, where his father had worked, with their massive pairs of scissor trusses. To draw directly on such models in the 1830s was as bold as the decision to build St Marie's Grange in red brick. The furniture was highly original and later influential, but it was the product of antiquarian knowledge and daring, both of which Pugin had in abundance, rather than abstract logic, which he almost entirely lacked. He would always work out theory from practice, rather than vice versa. His first tables, for the library, have a certain heaviness. They are over-engineered, as if Pugin was unsure still of the principles on which they worked. Probably he was. Soon this bottom-heaviness gave way to 'a more agile . . . structural self-consciousness', the elements of each piece held together in a 'stressed rigidity'.[15] The tables are massive yet poised, they have a monolithic drama and a strong, sculptural quality.

By the time it was complete, Oscott made as bold a statement as Lord Shrewsbury could desire of the reviving strength of the post-Emancipation Catholic Church. It was built and furnished on a grand scale, at a total cost of £52,145 8s. 6½d., of which Pugin's bills amounted to £3,576 13s. 10d. Paintings came from Lord Shrewsbury and other donors gave silver and antiquities. Bishop Walsh, who became quite carried away with the project, bought two whole libraries for Oscott, including that of the Marchese Luigi Marini, 18,000 books for £3,000. It was a wild extravagance, far beyond the college's means, of which Walsh had formed only the vaguest idea. The transformation that came over Oscott was mirrored by a similar change in its Professor of Ecclesiastical Antiquities. So sudden and such great recognition for his ideas and abilities was overwhelming, even for someone of Pugin's buoyant temperament. For all his egotism he was not, usually, boastful. Briefly, however, he became rather bumptious. 'Could you but see me at Oscott,' he told Willson, 'you would hardly credit me to be the same individual you remember.'

Reviews of Contrasts had been slow to appear in the national press, but once the book had been taken up interest in it grew rapidly. As the debate about the new Palace of Westminster had gone on it had developed into a general discussion of architecture and a battle of the styles between classicists and admirers of the medieval. 'The Greeks appear at an almost interminable feud with the Goths,' the Quarterly Review noted, in a round-up of ten publications on the subject, to which the author added his own views on the 'irresponsible appointments and uncontrolled presumption' of recent years and the decadent 'marine pavilions and royal cottages' of George IV.[16] Another factor in Contrasts' success was the expansion of magazine publishing. A drop in stamp duty had made publication cheaper just as steam presses were making it faster, producing a boom in titles catering for the middle-class readers, both general and specialist, who made up that ever more powerful force in national life, 'public opinion'. The *Civil Engineer and Architect's Journal*, the re-launched *Edinburgh Catholic Magazine* and the *Dublin Review* were among the new periodicals to notice *Contrasts*.

The national press did not indulge in the provincial bigotry of the *Salisbury Journal*. *Contrasts* was seen more as an architectural satire than a religious tract. Its main success was with the educated general readers, like those of the *Quarterly* and the *Gentleman's Magazine*, who shared in the growing popular admiration for and interest in the Gothic. To them *Contrasts* appealed as any popular polemic will. It told its readers what they already more or less thought, giving back to them their own half-formed ideas in a gratifyingly pointed and memorable way. *Contrasts* dealt the death blow to Georgian architecture because it was dying already to informed opinion and its protagonists were dying in fact as well. John Soane's death was announced while William Leeds's review for *Fraser's Magazine* was 'actually with the printer'.[17] To a man like Leeds – who was perhaps the first architectural critic in the modern sense – *Contrasts* seemed an exasperatingly overrated statement of the obvious. Everybody now agreed about the philistinism of Wyatt and the 'whimmery' of Soane. As another critic protested: 'it is too late in the day to claim superior taste . . . the country teems with those who are sharing the feelings in which [Pugin] pretends superiority.'[18]

To the cognoscenti, the older generation, the antiquaries, the eminent architects he had insulted and those who remembered his father, young Pugin was a prophet without honour. Leeds knew him and had known Auguste. He was infuriated by his young 'friend Welby' and his presumption. Such 'graphic sarcasm' did not, Leeds thought, 'come with the best possible grace from one who is known to the world, chiefly as a draughtsman' and as the author of the now mildly notorious St Marie's Grange, which, Leeds noted, Pugin failed to illustrate.[19] Pugin wrote a pamphlet in response to Leeds's review: 'oh greatly injured Welby,' the *Civil Engineer* snapped back.[20] It was all good knockabout stuff and it went on for nearly three years, by which time many more people than actually saw *Contrasts* were thoroughly familiar with it. Pugin became a household name. At the same time he burned his boats with the establishment, the increasingly well-organized architectural profession in which he would never now have, or seek, a place.

His career began to speed along, but it was propelled – still – by nothing more deliberate than chance, inclination and opportunity. He would do anything for a friend. Readers of *Contrasts* might have been surprised to know that its author was designing the front of a Unitarian chapel in Manchester for Charles Barry. His other important commission that year came to him through the Wardour Street antiques trade, via Edward Hull, who introduced him to a strange man called Charles Scarisbrick. All Scarisbrick wanted at first, apparently, was a Gothic garden seat and a chimney-piece, but Pugin immediately began trying to rebuild his house, the eponymous Scarisbrick Hall near Ormskirk in Lancashire. Charles Scarisbrick was eleven years Pugin's senior, a man of saturnine good looks, solitary temperament and vast wealth from a family that had remained Catholic ever since the Reformation. His fortune had come partly from his sisters, whom he had sued for their share of the family inheritance as far as the House of Lords. The rest came from mining and the development of Southport as a resort. Coal and boarding-houses were the raw material from which was spun the romantic fantasy of Scarisbrick Hall.

Scarisbrick was known to Hull, and every other dealer in London and beyond, as the greatest single collector of imported carving in England, the worst of those 'Elginists' condemned by the French for buying up looted antiques for their 'châteaux' just so that they could play 'au Moyen Age à la Walter Scott'.[21] He was a patron, too, of John Martin, twenty-one of whose apocalyptic canvases hung at the Hall, including *The Fall of Nineveh*. In 1837, a year of commercial crisis and unemployment in the Lancashire mills, his house must have presented a spectacle of dark opulence, with Martin's lurid visions hanging among the displaced choir stalls and looted altarpieces. Scarisbrick's was one of those flinty natures from whom Pugin's enthusiasm struck a rare spark. Pugin worked for him on and off for more than half of his career, and the house, despite several brushes with destruction, survives, a curious chronicle of nineteenth-century taste and of Pugin's own development.

In theory Pugin strongly disapproved of 'what is called fitting up old carvings', by people who would 'mutilate fine things . . . to suit [their] own caprice'.[22] But in practice he was prepared to compromise. He created for Scarisbrick a suite of rooms at the heart of his house, the Great Hall, the Oak Room and the King's Room, 'encrusted' with woodwork, like the sets for *Henry VIII*. Two great pairs of altar wings make doors into the libraries. In the Great Hall, which seems positively to drip with carving, a massive relief of Christ crowned with thorns faces the minstrels' gallery. The gallery itself, like the screen and the throne at its east end, were Pugin's own designs. This was the temptation for which Pugin swallowed his principles, the chance to create a real interior, an Ideal Scheme in three dimensions. Pugin wanted to transform the Hall into a Catholic Mansion of the Olden Times. Unfortunately his client had no such idea. Scarisbrick's family having been recusant since the Reformation, Catholicism had come to him not as something medieval, but as a continuous tradition. He saw no connection between his religion and his style of interior decoration. A semi-recluse with an irregular private life, he did not want his house to be a centre of hospitality, nor did he want pictures of Catholic martyrs on the library ceiling, or a chapel, or a large clock-tower. This last feature, which Pugin was particularly anxious to build, would have been highly unusual at that date and of no practical use for a country house in extensive grounds. It was almost certainly the work on the Palace of Westminster drawings that had put clock-towers into his mind, and it was typical of Pugin (and of many architects) that once he had seized on an idea he would try to build it into whatever job was in hand. He designed several versions of the tower, none of which was built in Ormskirk but one of which foreshadows very closely the tower at Westminster.

Otherwise Scarisbrick gave Pugin a remarkably free hand in his first exercise in country house architecture. Obliged to fit his designs within an existing fabric, he treated space, as has been pointed out, as 'something continuous in which he erected a series of frameworks'.[23] That, of course, was what he had learned to do in the theatre. The results are at times ingenious, in places gawky. To stand in the narrow runway connecting the minstrels' gallery with the south gallery and look down on the Great Hall feels, unmistakably, like perching in the flies looking down on a stage. Behind his polemical certainties Pugin's ideas were still unformed, his taste unsure and his practical experience limited. Yet he was full of confidence. His defences of *Contrasts* held out a vision of architectural and religious triumph like one of Martin's paintings:

... never has a greater step been made towards advancement by any class of persons in history, than that accomplished by the English Catholics during the last few years. Colleges have been founded; schools for the education of the poor erected; hundreds of new missions established ... These have enabled the Catholics, aided by the strong arm of Omnipotence, to raise themselves from the dust ... notwithstanding the exactions they are compelled to pay for the support of their enemies, who unremittingly assail them with the most violent slander and abuse. But in vain! 'the gates of hell shall not prevail against *my* Church,' said He who cannot lie; and the darts of its assailants fall harmless to the ground. The night of sorrow is far spent; the brightness of returning glory is seen.[24]

Pugin wrote his pamphlets in the short spells at home that punctuated his months on the road, travelling between Salisbury, London, Oscott and Scarisbrick. On 20 June, four days after he finished his *Apology for a Work Called Contrasts*, he noted in his diary, 'King died William 4th'.[25] The Victorian age was a week old when he set off for a summer tour of France and Belgium.

18

'My first church'

July 1837 to May 1838

Hear ye not the hum
Of mighty workings?
Listen awhile ye nations and be dumb
         – John Keats, 'Sonnet to Haydon', 1817

Pugin was abroad for the whole of July. His journey took him in two great loops through Bruges, Ghent, Antwerp and Brussels, then down to Paris and from there to Chartres, Evreux, Rouen, Honfleur, Lisieux, Coutances and Caen. On the 31st he sailed home from Le Havre. As always he travelled fast, mostly by coach, though from Bruges to Ghent he took a barge across the plains of Flanders, the flatness of the landscape made picturesque by the towers of cathedrals and town halls. Much of the journey was over well-trodden ground. At Rouen he visited Langlois, whose strange life was drawing to its bitter end. Langlois was depressed, sitting for days in his museum without speaking, refusing to see even old friends. But he let Pugin in. Both no doubt realized it would be their last meeting.

Pugin was as active and restless as Langlois was lethargic. Everywhere he went he drew. In Rouen his eye and mind ranged up and down the scale from the cathedral itself to the metalwork in Langlois's collection and the manuscripts in the public library, seizing rapidly on what he wanted. In the scenes in illuminated texts he could find the details of colour and pattern and furnishings, the living texture of medieval design, that had long since gone from the buildings themselves. Pugin copied them in watercolour and gold, accumulating elements from which, later, he would create designs for painted decoration, carpets, textiles and wallpapers. The modern mingled with the medieval in his notes – the play of coloured sunlight through stained glass on the stone of Chartres, the building of an iron bridge at Rouen, both were of interest. On the roof of Rouen cathedral he drew the new iron spire – so disliked by Ruskin – and the builders' scaffold with as much attention as the Gothic details.

On 1 August he was home and ten days later he was off again. The rest of the summer passed at Oscott, at Scarisbrick and on a tour, with Dr Weedall, of the midland Catholic missions. He must have written many letters to Louisa in Salisbury, but not one, it seems, survives. Louisa, often alone with three young children, was still an Anglican, a member of that Church against which her husband was pouring out such vitriol. She cannot have been happy. Pugin must have been urging her to convert and she, very probably, was urging him to spend more time at home. The disappearance of their correspondence implies that some of it at least was acrimonious. It also means, for Pugin's biographer, that in these early years of his career, when he was most completely in the grip of his vision of revival, Pugin is largely mute as a private man, his domestic life all but invisible behind his loudly audible, polemical public self.

In September he paid his first visit to Alton Towers, where he spent four days in Lord Shrewsbury's great house. Here, unlike Scarisbrick, was a real Catholic mansion, a semi-public building visited by about 12,000 tourists every year, its chapel serving as a parish church. This was the country house as social and religious force. The visit must have been tantalizing. Shrewsbury's new west wing was almost finished; as at Oscott, Pugin had come slightly too late. It would only be a matter of time, however, before he began to interest the Earl in more building.

He returned to London having been away from Salisbury for nearly a month. Three days later he noted in his diary 'Mrs P arrived.'[1] She was not, on this occasion, 'my dear Louisa', and if there was some strain between them it was scarcely surprising. Louisa may have protested about the inconvenience of life at St Marie's Grange, and Pugin himself was realizing that as his work took him ever more often to the Midlands he would find it difficult to be there. So, less than three months after the last of the gilding had been added to the vanes on the roof of the Grange, Pugin left his odd, original house still unfinished and took lodgings for himself and his family in Chelsea.

Chelsea was not smart in the 1830s, and Number 3 Prospect Place was not Gothic, it was one of a row of late-seventeenth-century houses near the Old Church, but at least it stood 'on the ground formerly occupied by the Mansion of Sir T More'.[2] The Pugins shared Jane Carlyle's 'noble contempt for fashion – Chelsea being highly unfashionable', which meant that they too could afford a large house 'quite to our humour'.[3] Before the Thames was embanked the character of Chelsea and the nature of its residents were largely determined by the river. Thomas Carlyle described Cheyne Walk in terms that make the area's appeal to Pugin obvious. It was 'a broad highway with huge shady trees . . . and a smell of shipping and tar . . . with white-shirted white trousered Cockneys dashing by like arrows in their long canoes' and 'beyond, the green beautiful knolls of Surrey with their villages. On the whole a most artificial green-painted yet lively fresh almost opera-looking business.'[4] The water, the bustle, the touch of the theatrical bordering on the brash, would have suited Pugin and no doubt Louisa, placing her, when she must be alone, in more congenial circumstances. The modest houses were interspersed with coffee shops, pawnbrokers, a printer and other small trade premises. Wherries were drawn up on the foreshore and just beyond Battersea Bridge there was a boatyard belonging to the Greaves, the family of boatmen who ferried Turner.

It was the artisan Greaves rather than the cerebral Carlyles that Pugin and Louisa got to know. Other old London friends and acquaintances, the painters William Etty and Clarkson Stanfield, could visit more easily, and Pugin, who had grown up in a house full of people, always welcomed visitors. The 'retired life' had never, in practice, suited him, and whatever pang he felt at leaving behind his first work of architecture he was not given to retrospection. Although the lodgings in Chelsea were intended at first to be temporary, he made only four visits to Salisbury over the next two years. After that he never saw St Marie's Grange again. The new quarters were convenient and congenial. Notes of freak tides, river traffic and accidents to barges began to appear in his diary. He was at home all the autumn, making drawings for Rock and Lord Shrewsbury and consulting with Gillespie Graham, who was in London.

Graham wanted designs for Taymouth Castle in Perthshire, home of the 2nd Marquis of Breadalbane. Taymouth was, and is, an enormous castle, one of the grandest relics of the Gothic Revival. It had begun life as a tower house. The eighteenth century had classicized it. The nineteenth had so far been devoted to turning it into a Gothic citadel, a process which had begun with the destruction of all that remained of the original fabric and the importation of a particularly motley selection of carvings and curiosities. The improvement and expansion went on for years, rising to a furious climax of expenditure five years later with Taymouth's apotheosis, the visit of Victoria and Albert. Pugin gave the castle two romantic rooms, the Library and the Banner Hall, which delighted the Queen, who chose to use the Library as her private drawing room during her stay. The interiors have the dark glamour of Scarisbrick without its clotted decoration or occasional incoherence. In the Library, a delicate composition of carving, panelling and a ceiling copied from Crosby Hall in London, Pugin created a bay window which could be cut off from the main room with a pierced wooden screen. It was the type of framed room within a room in which a figure would appear half seen and half concealed that he had learned to create in the theatre, the picturesque-romantic space between interior and exterior, in which Pugin had drawn himself in his Ideal Schemes.

In November he set off on the now familiar round of Scarisbrick, Oscott and Alton. At Oscott he was preparing to teach. He intended to do it by lecture and illustration, which did 'infinitely more good', he explained to Willson, who had two sons at Oscott, 'than wasting time in some modern architects office'.[5] It was the way that he himself had been taught by Auguste, from a collection of 'architectural prints speci- mens of architectural detail', casts and carvings and antique objects that the students could examine and draw.[6] That month he gave his first lecture. The lectures never amounted to anything so formal as a course but were 'irregularly delivered', veering over a number of subjects and, like all Pugin's intellectual efforts, the product of intense but fitful bursts of activity.[7] Despite this, they had a great effect on 'the plastic minds of the students'.[8] The first, which was published in the *Orthodox Journal*, must have gained much of its impact from Pugin's delivery. In a style reminiscent of his mother in her defence of the rights of women, he told his students of the wrongs of the Catholics: 'by a tyrannical apostate were they first wrested from the church of God; by villany were they kept from it; by oppression and cruel persecution has the heresy which robbed them been maintained.'[9]

Against this litany of wrongs was weighed once more the Picturesque account of Gothic as a series of sequential views, in which 'a varied aspect is assumed at every step' in gigantic churches, 'A whole quarry sunk beneath the ground for the foundation! Thousands of tons carried to a prodigious height! Buttress above buttress, pinnacle over pinnacle, arch over arch!'[10] 'Frothy and foaming', the by now much irritated William Leeds called this production, and indeed there was no argument in it.[11] Leeds found Pugin's 'new character' as 'Professor' ridiculous, his lecture lacking in any 'intelligible criticism', and he predicted, wrongly, that there would be no need ever to notice 'the man of St Marie's Grange' again.[12]

After the lecture Pugin travelled to Leicestershire for his first visit to the Phillippses at Grace Dieu Manor. Their house was complete and the school over which Laura presided was flourishing. In the first week 200 children came. The state at that time made no provision for education and free schooling was a central element in the many philanthropic and religious campaigns of the 1830s and 40s. As well as lessons pupils were given, usually, one meal and sometimes free shoes. To working people, mostly indifferent to or ignorant about religion, a school was a great draw. Some were truly converted. Many were happy to go to Mass in exchange for soup and lessons for their children. Relief was much needed, for in rural Leicestershire as elsewhere there was a great deal of poverty. The autumn of 1837 saw the first of the bad harvests that continued for the next five years, bringing in 'the grimmest period in . . . the 19th century'.[13] In the area round Grace Dieu those who did not work in agriculture were miners or self-employed stocking weavers. All of them suffered badly. The Phillippses' was a social as much as a religious campaign. They wanted to keep the people on the land, to arrest that drift towards the infernal city that swelled the slums, bred support for Radicalism and threatened to undermine the old rural hierarchy of squire and tenantry. They also wanted to keep their people out of the workhouses, products of the new poor law, passed three years earlier in 1834. Under its provisions there was no 'outdoor relief'. To get assistance it was necessary for the poor to leave their homes and go to the workhouse, where conditions were harsh and husbands and wives, often elderly, were separated. Against this cold modern charity the romantic Catholic ideal opposed the medieval monastery, which gave out aid to the poor in their homes. This, however, was more complicated to organize than a school. There had been a Cistercian monastery at Grace Dieu until the Dissolution, and Phillipps wanted to bring the order back, to restore it physically to the land of which it had been dispossessed. It was part of his mystical belief in the spirit of place, which for him was a divine spirit. But his somewhat vague and idealized mental picture of monks travelling through the countryside, visiting the sick, took no account of the reality of the Cistercian rule. The Cistercians are an enclosed, contemplative order; they do not go out. Lord Shrewsbury attempted to explain this to his young convert friend and suggested pastoral brothers would be more useful, but Phillipps was set on Cistercians. He made it a condition when the monks accepted the land that they should undertake mission work. In his assumption that the monastic rule could be modified to suit the requirements of a landlord he was still an Anglican, used to the ways of county gentry, where the parson was expected to accommodate the squire. Like Pugin, Phillipps had a lot to learn about the Catholic Church.

For the moment, however, he got his way. Shrewsbury donated vestments and Kenelm Digby promised to give the profits from his next book. Seven Cistercians duly arrived at Mount St Bernard's, as the monastery was called, and began to do what they could in such strange circumstances. Most of them were English and in the end they muddled through. Bernard Palmer, later the Abbot, found himself travelling for two and a half days a week over three parishes, which was 'quite contrary to our state'.[14] He consoled himself with the thought that 'St Anthony went out of his seel to encourage the faithful in the time of persecution, therefore, to refuse the poor peopel instructions that desier it and ask, it would be cruel . . .' [sic][15] Palmer himself, as his spelling suggests, was a self-educated, working-class man. He seems to have found an easy rapport with the local people and his converts were gratifyingly numerous.

The month before Pugin's visit, on three consecutive days, three new chapels at Grace Dieu, Mount St Bernard and the nearby village of Whitwick were consecrated. It was, to the people of Leicestershire, an almost incredible scene and the local newspapers reported it at length. Not for centuries had anything been witnessed in England like the procession that wound its way through the open countryside in brilliant autumn sunshine for two miles from Grace Dieu to the monastery. Led by a crucifer and six acolytes, Bishop Walsh walked in full pontificals, followed by a choir of monks in white, lay brothers in brown and Phillipps himself in his uniform as Deputy Lieutenant of the County. The sight of the crucifix, the sound of the chanting, the smell of the

incense – it was the vision of Catholic England that Pugin evoked in his
Apology for Contrasts apparently coming to pass. Bernard Palmer was
moved. Later he recalled: 'The sun cast a dazzling brightness . . . and as
the procession slowly and majestically ascended the hill . . . I was carried
back in imagination to the age when all England was Catholic.'[16] A
precisely similar thought came into the mind of the Revd Francis Merewether, Anglican vicar of Whitwick, though to him it was anything but
pleasant. Merewether wrote in alarm to his fellow clergymen. Soon
word reached Newman at Oxford that there was a 'large body of Roman
Catholics' in the Charnwood forest, preying on an ignorant population,
'withdrawing [them] from the profession of the Protestant faith and
rendering [them] violent and . . . successful opponents to the granting
of a church rate'.[17]

The Catholic revival had begun, and with it Pugin's career. From now
on commissions began to come to him rapidly. In January 1838 the
Edinburgh Catholic Magazine informed readers that Mr Pugin was
'actively engaged . . . in preparing drawings for several Catholic chapels,
to be commenced forthwith, or early in the ensuing spring. Reading,
Derby, Uttoxeter, Scarisbrick etc. are to be the theatre of his labours.'[18]
Under 'etc' came, or would come soon, schemes in Manchester, Birmingham, Solihull, Keighley, Bermondsey and Southwark. Over the next
two years he built or designed eighteen churches, two cathedrals, three
convents, two monasteries, several schools and about half a dozen
houses. With his architectural practice was also launched the pattern of
frantic, dangerous overwork. 'I have been obliged to work night and
day during the week,' he told Willson in February, 'and on sundays all
the time not occupied in devotion is filled up With writing Lectures and
articles for furthering the great cause.'[19]

What Pugin wanted to build, more than anything, was churches. A
Gothic church was for him the peak of architecture and of experience.
The aesthetic and the symbolic, the spiritual and the material, were all
present at once, and in this, too, Pugin spoke for the rising generation.
The church was to be the great Victorian building type, embodying the
ethos of the age as the country house did the eighteenth century and
Nash's Picturesque the Regency. The first foundation stone to be laid
was at Reading. In November Pugin went down to visit James Wheble,
a Catholic antiquary, who had bought the ruins of the twelfth-century

Reading Abbey, first consecrated by Thomas Becket but ruinous since the Civil War. Wheble had excavated the site and salvaged 'a quantity of stone facings' which he now wanted to incorporate into a new church on part of the Abbey grounds.[20] This was to be, even more literally than Phillipps's Cistercian monastery, a rebuilding of the past. The church of St James was in the Norman style 'as best suiting the situation, being contiguous to the ruins of an ancient abbey'.[21] It was small and its design was simple. His other new churches were, Pugin announced, to be 'in the early pointed style of Germany, which is used in preference to the corresponding style of our own country, because it may be made to produce a much richer effect with a great deal less money'.[22] The art-lessness of the last remark shows how little he had considered, yet, a theory of Gothic. He mixed the styles of different countries and different periods as he chose.

The most important of these first churches was at Derby, where the local priest, with the support of Bishop Walsh and the Earl of Shrews-bury, had bought a piece of land on the edge of the town. Such was usually the fate of the new Catholic churches, for land in town centres was scarce and expensive, in addition to which, Pugin claimed, 'every engine of prejudice and opposition' was used to keep them out.[23] A good Gothic church, he told his students at Oscott, should be 'at a distance . . . one great imposing mass' to 'astonish . . . the beholder, before a single feature or detail is distinctly visible'.[24] Had the spire of St Mary's, Derby, been built it would have soared 200 feet and redeemed the church's marginal position, inserting itself in the townscape on equal terms with the medieval churches of St Alkmund and All Saints. The spire, however, like most he designed, remained unbuilt, and today the church teeters on the edge of the ring road that swept past in 1967, taking St Alkmund's with it.

Pugin designed a church that was Germanic in the interior, English and late Gothic (although he later described it as 'early decorated') on the outside. This mixture did not, yet, worry him. What mattered was that St Mary's (or St Marie's as he spelled it) was arranged like a medieval church, rather than a modern 'preaching box'. Each separate part proclaimed its function – the nave for the laity, the chancel for the clergy. The altar, not the pulpit, was the focus. In the interior every element seems under tension, as if on the point of springing yet further upward. The rood beam, on which the crucifix is set, is bent like a wishbone into the chancel arch. With a massive west tower and delicate arcades it was by far the largest and most complicated building, in constructional terms, that he had yet designed. Even the blithely confident Pugin must have wondered how exactly he was going to build it. When contractors came to tender for the job he was greatly relieved to see a familiar florid face among them, that of George Myers. Pugin apparently threw his arms round Myers, who was nine years older and a head taller, and announced as he hugged him, 'You are the very man I want, you shall execute all my buildings.'[25]

The two had met at Beverley when Myers was a stonemason there, and Pugin had got into conversation with him, in his usual way, on one of his visits to the town whose great medieval churches he had first seen with his parents in 1818. Since then Myers had gone into business on his own account. He was the sort of craftsman builder Pugin admired, a man who understood Gothic construction from the inside better than any nineteenth-century architect. Myers was to be the rock on which Pugin built his architectural career. Phlegmatic, hard-working, with a square jaw, a high complexion and a forehead that seems to have worn a perpetual frown of concentration, he worked for Pugin for the rest of Pugin's life. In time he became one of the most important Victorian master builders. George Gilbert Scott, from the eminence of a knighthood, later recalled Myers as 'a strange rough mason from Hull'.[26] Pugin – for whom he was usually 'Mr Myers' – valued him as masons had been valued in the Middle Ages. He relied on him heavily and made no secret of his dependence. Myers and his family were personally as well as professionally loyal to Pugin over the years. When the two men quarrelled, which in the nature of things happened occasionally, they quarrelled as equals. Pugin more than once called Myers a 'pig', both on account of his enormous appetite, which devastated the table d'hôte at any inn, and for his refusal to be hurried. Myers was not intimidated. He was the immovable object that Pugin's irresistible force at times required. He was given the contract for Derby. The church was to be built in stone and Myers began sinking substantial foundations.

Pugin was at his best working with friends, with Shrewsbury behind him and Myers at his side. He was never good with committees. He generally got on better, too, in the smaller towns and the countryside. The ethos of the modern city did not suit him temperamentally any more than it did morally. In Manchester, famous and notorious already for

its mills and its 'rioting propensities', he had an early and revealing
failure.[27] Invited to design a Catholic church for a site near the Ashton
canal, amid factories and warehouses, Pugin drew out a scheme with a
massive west front and a north-west tower and spire. Had it been built,
his church would have commanded its dingy, difficult site, but it took
no account of cost. In his notes to the building committee Pugin
explained that although the scheme looked 'infinitely too extensive for
execution', it could be built in stages, as medieval churches were. 'It is
a most absurd idea to contemplate the entire completion of a building
for the sum that can be obtained at first.'[28] This argument, that it was
better to have the beginnings of a great building than a meagre one
complete, was one that Pugin put many times and seldom won. The
Manchester committee had £6,000 and they wanted a whole church for
their money. They decided to hold a competition. Lord Shrewsbury was
shocked at the idea of one of the '3 rate class of Protestant architects'
getting the job and the money being thrown away on some 'miserable
abortion'.[29] He exerted pressure to get Pugin employed:

Pugin is decidedly the Catholic architect of the day, with more zeal talent,
judgement, & experience than perhaps any man, so young, has hitherto acquired
. . . His object is to do honour & credit to our Religion . . . in the most disinterested manner . . . so that if Economy be the object of the Committee they
cannot I am sure so readily succeed as by employing him. He would be willing
to lay his plans before the Committee . . . without any remuneration & if adopted
to undertake the superintendence of the building for a very small charge perhaps
for 2 or 3 per cent, instead of five.[30]

But the Earl's writ did not run so absolutely in Manchester and his idea
of 'Economy' could not be reconciled with the committee's. Pugin made
revised designs, but nothing could be agreed and nothing was built.

By now Pugin was learning a great deal very fast. He could build
cheaply when he understood the necessity, and the churches he designed
in the first half of 1838, St Anne's, Keighley, St Augustine's, Solihull,
and St Marie's, Uttoxeter, were all cheap, plain and compact. Between
them they comprised a model to which Pugin returned often, and they
were the original of many copies in England and later in America,
Australia and throughout the Empire. Such little brick churches, many
of them a single space, divided internally only by a rood beam, were
often, when copied, no more than boxes. Pugin's own, however, were

never drab. Forced to invent, he began quickly to find by experiment the techniques that the next generation of architects would make their creed. He learned to do without elaboration, to strip away mouldings, to pare back the wall plane in layers to create relief and use the simplest rise and fall of outline to effect. He took the principles of the Picturesque – variety, irregularity, narrative – and pared them to the bone. The simplicity of the exteriors of these little churches, often relieved by the austere rhythm of buttress and lancet windows, was intended to ensure that some richness was possible in the interior, especially at the altar. Pugin's description of his church at Uttoxeter dwells almost entirely on the furnishings and their symbolism. A silver pyx in the form of a dove held the Blessed Sacrament suspended over the altar. He gave his little church at Solihull, for which he charged no fee, a sixteenth-century Flemish triptych, a spectacular enrichment for such a simple building.

Meanwhile work went on at Oscott, where Dr Weedall admired and encouraged him in everything. The moment for the opening of the chapel was approaching and in the background could be heard other more mechanical notes of preparation. The Liverpool and Manchester Railway was being extended and near Oscott a cutting for the Grand Junction Railway was being dug. From the college young Amherst and his friends could hear the work and 'one object for a walk was to see the uncouth-looking engine, with a chimney sticking out in front with a bend upwards'.[31] By April the London to Birmingham line was open almost throughout, and on 2 May Pugin, always eager to save time, noted that he had returned to London 'by railroad'.[32] The railways and the Gothic Revival, those two great Victorian enterprises, were gathering steam together. The address of Pugin's church at Solihull was 'St Augustine's, Station Road'. As the railways became, in Dickens's phrase, 'a new kind of religion', so religion felt the effects of the railway. The more that people travelled the more comparisons they made. They saw at first hand the slums, the mills and the factories. They read about the fossil remains discovered in the new cuttings and they pondered the modern human condition.

The consecration of Oscott chapel took place on 31 May. It was celebrated with a Pontifical High Mass, something few English people had ever seen and no one in living memory, the Staffordshire Examiner noted, had seen on such a scale. There were sixty-eight robed clergy, 'the gorgeous number and richness of official dresses, flickering with gold, contrasting with purple and the altar lit up with its massy candle-sticks'.[33] It was, Pugin said, 'the first great day for England since the Reformation'.[34] The length and solemnity of the ritual, the antique furnishings, the brilliant colours of the vestments and the clouds of incense penetrated by shafts of sunlight, filtering through stained glass, must have astonished Catholics as much as Protestants. After centuries in modest chapels and borrowed upper rooms, of referring to the Mass discreetly as 'prayers', of keeping its head down and minding its manners, English Catholicism had re-awoken. This was 'the brightness of returning glory' that Pugin had prophesied, it was the Middle Ages come to life again, it was religion as art and as sacred drama. Pugin, frantic with excitement, oversaw the ceremonies, his dark eyes, one bishop noted, 'flashing through . . . tears'.[35]

He was particularly proud of the vestments, designed in consultation with Dr Rock. The chasubles fell 'gracefully from the shoulders' in the medieval manner rather than following the stiff 'fiddle-back' design of contemporary convention.[36] Pugin had learned at Covent Garden the effect of costume on moving figures. Flowing fabric caught the light, and with sacred subjects embroidered on the vestments 'in the passing of a procession a complete series of sacred history' would be presented to the view, like a liturgical diorama.[37] Not everybody thought that such displays were entirely appropriate. There were, among those officiating at the consecration, some who questioned Pugin's prominent role, a layman within the sanctuary – and a convert. The chasubles were not orthodox, neither were all the rubrics. Complaints began to be heard.

19

Birmingham and Oxford

May 1838 to May 1839

> *If any nation is to be lost or saved by the character of its great*
> *cities, our own is that nation.*
>   – Robert Vaughan, *The Age of Great Cities*, 1843

No hint of dissent was apparent yet to Pugin. He was now, indisputably, famous. As trains passed Oscott on the new line the passengers could read in their copies of *Roscoe's Railway Guide* all about the 'magnificent pile' they could see from the window, with descriptions of the furnishings of its chapel and of the 'energy, talents, and taste of this extraordinary man Augustus Welby Pugin Esq.'[1] who was responsible. His reputation had spread to the Continent. In France Montalembert was writing of the great progress of Christian art across the Channel signified by the 'vaste collège avec une belle église' at Oscott.[2]

At the same time Pugin was making enemies and upsetting old friends and acquaintances. John Britton wrote to him referring to his Catholicism as 'My new hobby'; 'I dare say', Pugin added, ingenuously, 'he meant to be very civil'.[3] Britton, like Leeds, was irritated by so much attention being paid to Auguste Pugin's bumptious son. Even the gentle Edward Willson was piqued. He had hoped to get the job at Derby but found himself put aside in favour of his young friend. Pugin was surely telling the truth when he said he had 'no idea' that Willson had been in the running, but his brusque refusal to intervene on the older man's behalf – 'it is not for me to start difficulties and I can do nothing in the matter' – must have been hurtful.[4] Their friendship, from now on, began to be more distant. In May Pugin severed the last link with the Great Russell Street school, selling the copyright of *Examples of Gothic Architecture* outright to Larkins Walker. In June he made his first visit to Ireland.

Lord Shrewsbury numbered among his titles the earldom of Wexford and Waterford, and through his influence, and that of Lady Shrewsbury's uncle John Hyacinth Talbot MP, there would be many Irish commissions.

Although it suited Pugin to work fast, the hectic rate took a toll. His tearful over-excitement at Oscott was remarked. Twice in April he described himself as 'very ill' and again in the autumn 'taken ill', 'very ill all day'.[5] Whatever the illness was, it came and went suddenly. He was in London on 28 June for Victoria's coronation, the third in his lifetime. After the extravaganza of George IV had come the subdued enthronement of his brother William. Now 'the last son of George III' to reign in England was gone.[6] For the first time in the lives of even middle-aged men and women there was an enthusiasm for the monarchy and in the young Queen a figure of purity and hope. The Liberal cabinet decided to abandon the traditional banquet and organized a procession instead to show the monarch to her people. Victoria drove along a two-mile route from Buckingham Palace to Westminster Abbey, watched by a cheering crowd a million strong. As the cavalcade was passing through the streets of the capital, a smaller but equally solemn procession made its way across Derby to lay the foundation stone of St Mary's. In Pugin's absence it was George Myers, walking between a group of 150 local schoolchildren and the town band, who carried – perhaps a little self-consciously, for he had none of Pugin's theatricality – the silver trowel on a crimson cushion.

In July Pugin set off for the Continent. He wanted to revisit Germany. It was four years since he had seen the buildings that had so inspired him. He was away for nearly seven weeks on a tour from Rotterdam down the Rhine to Cologne. Here the Prussians were deliberating the greatest project of the continental Gothic Revival, the completion of Cologne Cathedral. The cathedral had been left unfinished since the fourteenth century, a builders' crane still perched evocatively above it. This enormous fragment, so eloquent of the romantic sense of time suspended, was now being repaired, and work was soon to start on the finishing of Meister Gerhard's masterpiece. It was what Pugin hoped to see in England, the Middle Ages set going again, like a clock that had merely been stopped.

On 20 August he took a boat across the Bodensee from Friedrichshaven into Switzerland. It was his first visit to the homeland of his father's

family, where, he had been told as a child when he was given the family
'arms', he had the right to claim a piece of land and build a castle.
Switzerland was the essential romantic landscape. Tourists in search of
the Picturesque had been coming to the Alps since the end of the war
and the mountains were not, by the 1830s, as unvisited as they had been
in Shelley's day. Mountains had passed into art and literature. The
paintings of Caspar David Friedrich, with their snow-covered Gothic
ruins and lonely crosses, expressed that sense of longing and melancholy
solitude that inspired the wanderings of Montalembert and Ambrose
Phillipps. Perhaps it was their influence that made Pugin decide to climb
mountains on this journey – something he seems never to have done
before or since, for natural scenery never interested or moved him as
much as architecture. Now, however, he went up Mount Salève and
slept a night on Mount Rigi. He made two uncharacteristic drawings
with Friedrich-like subjects, mountain passes, one with a wayside cross
wreathed in flowers.

He also made some enquiries after his father's family. Any relatives
he might find in Fribourg, where, according to Digby, there had once
been 'a solitary castle with a chapel on the rock over the Sarine, in the
midst of a vast Forest', would have suited him much better than the
Lincolnshire gentry.[7] But his efforts, not surprisingly, met with no success. Even if his grandfather had been from Fribourg itself, for which
there is no evidence, he had left by 1752 and there could hardly be
anyone left alive, more than eighty years later, who remembered anything about him. At the end of August Pugin left Switzerland and came
home by way of Paris and Rouen. Back in London for a night in
September, he was off again the next day to Alton, Derby and Oscott.

On 6 October he noted, 'My dear Louisa returned,' so, wherever she
had been while he was away, she had not spent the whole summer alone
in Chelsea.[8] For the rest of the autumn and winter he was more often at
home, taking stock of the summer's harvest of drawings and beginning
to turn it to use as new commissions arrived, hoping to build, if not
Jerusalem, then medieval Germany in the English industrial Midlands.
Before the end of the year he had designed three more churches, a
convent and his first cathedral. The Earl of Shrewsbury continued to
work energetically on his behalf. At Macclesfield in Cheshire a piece of
land had been bought for a new church and designs obtained from
Matthew Hadfield, a Catholic architect, Pugin's exact contemporary. In

September, when Pugin was at Alton Towers, the parish priest received a letter from the Earl containing the 'happy' news that 'Mr Pugin is just returned. He will call on you ... some day next week; should the committee agree to avail themselves of Mr Pugin's talents, I will add Fifty Pounds a year to my subscription ...'[9] It was not an offer a poor Catholic parish could refuse. Hadfield was dismissed and in December Pugin produced the designs for St Alban's, Macclesfield, one of the best and best-preserved of his early churches.

As at Derby he combined English and German Gothic, and it is the interior that comes from Germany, the arcades with their slender clustered piers rising to simple capitals. Once again the emphasis is upward, but the impression of height is less, or less dizzying; the eye does not simply shoot upwards to the roof. Capitals punctuate the vertical lines. The space is better articulated, more clearly divided between nave and raised chancel so that the emphasis, the sense of aspiration, is directed towards the sanctuary. At Macclesfield Pugin introduced for the first time a rood screen. Screens were to become a great point of controversy both for Pugin and for the whole nineteenth-century Gothic Revival, their importance both theological and aesthetic. A screen, partially veiling the sanctuary, attracts the gaze and at the same time resists it, emphasizing both the centrality and the impenetrable mystery of the Mass. It is medieval but also picturesque, creating the views between 'unequal varieties of space, divided but not separate' that Payne Knight defined as the essence of the Picturesque in Gothic buildings.[10] The passions aroused by liturgical furnishings were, sometimes still are, extreme. To the romantic medievalist a properly composed church was a living symbol, a diagram of divine purpose, it could not be chopped about to suit taste or convenience. The screen marks the division between laity and clergy. On it stands the rood itself, the crucifix with the Virgin and St John. At Macclesfield the rood almost fills the chancel arch; the figures, fifteenth-century carvings, recoloured by Pugin, appear to float above the screen. Originally the chancel arch was painted with a Last Judgement, as medieval churches were. Then the rood would have taken its place in a scheme depicting the four last things, death, judgement, heaven and hell, which lie between the human world and the divine.

As architecture Macclesfield represented both a step forward from Derby and a step back. Its architectural ideas are more sophisticated but the elements do not compose harmoniously. It suffered from the absence of George Myers. Another builder – William Smith – got the job on the basis of a low estimate. There was trouble with the foundations. Pugin complained that the church was 'shamefully worked' and 'settled in all directions'.[11] In the nave the roof corbels are off-centre in relation to the clerestory because no allowance was made for the width of the roof timbers. It was just the kind of mistake from which Myers would have saved Pugin and in the end he was brought in to sort things out. The tower of St Alban's was never completed, the spire never built. The combined inexperience of architect and builder no doubt contributed to the rising costs, which went beyond what Lord Shrewsbury or anybody else was prepared to meet. Although the church was dedicated and opened in 1841 it was not consecrated until all the debts were paid, and that was not until October 1931.

Pugin was not only inexperienced, he was artistically far from mature. 'Which,' the American historian Henry Russell Hitchcock asked of his early buildings, 'is the truer Pugin – the still somewhat Late Georgian master of volumes ... or [the] experimenter with articulated massing who was the inventor of the "realistic" or functional version of the Picturesque?'[12] The answer is certainly the former. When Pugin could find a medieval model he copied it. If he could make his churches symmetrical he did. He painted the walls to look like stone with *trompe l'œil* joints, he stained the timbers chestnut colour. Thinness and height and the elaboration of the Perpendicular were what he loved.

In December it was a year since the first stone of St James's, Reading, had been laid. Pugin had become in the meantime a national figure, a hero at Alton Towers and a villain in the *Civil Engineer and Architect's Journal*. Between the extremes of admiration and contempt, between images of himself as genius and gibbering bigot, Pugin would pass the rest of his life. His own moods were as variable. A single gust of good fortune might inflate his confidence to titanic proportions; the smallest blow might explode it again. At the end of 1838, despite his success, he was worried and unhappy, anxious about his children. The family was 'full of domestic trouble'. Edward was ill and Agnes, now two years old, 'almost blind', though in later life she seems to have had perfectly good sight.[13] Louisa remained a member of the Church of England. After Agnes's birth there was a four-year interval in Louisa's otherwise regular biennial pregnancies, another indication, perhaps, that relations between husband and wife at this point were less intimate. Pugin was also worried about money. Large sums passed through his hands as he acted as intermediary between the London dealers, Hull and Webb, and his clients at Scarisbrick and Oscott. His own earnings amounted to as much as £2,000 a year at a time when an income of £200 would qualify a family as middle-class. On 4 December he was paid £909 7s. 5d. for work at Oscott and he invested £400 in stock a few months later. But money always made him anxious and his income was never enough, or regular enough, to allay his fears. 'People send to me and think I make an immense fortune,' he wrote testily. 'I have had one offer from a person to keep my accounts for *a salary of some hundreds a year* when one sheet of writing paper would contain all my receipts.'[14] He no more wanted an accountant than he wanted a clerk or an office. He continued to work alone and at home. He was mostly in Chelsea in January, his diary a record of small payments and winter weather: 'high tide . . . high tide . . . heavy gale'.[15]

Absorbed in his work and his family anxieties, he seems, still, to have been oblivious of developments at Oxford. Within the university Newman's influence on the undergraduates and fellows was growing. More and more of the young Victorians found a welcome alternative to the familiar dry religion of their childhood in 'the charm' of Newman. All their lives they would remember him as Matthew Arnold evoked him, 'that spiritual apparition gliding in the dim afternoon light through the aisles of St Mary's' and that 'most entrancing of voices breaking the silence . . . subtle, sweet mournful'.[16] Outside Oxford the *Tracts for the Times* were selling, Newman noted, 'faster than they can print them', and the 'Puseyites' as they were called after one of their most prominent members, Edward Pusey, Oxford Professor of Hebrew, were becoming household names.[17] The *Tracts* were now less argumentative and more theoretical. 'A vista' began to open up before Newman of what it might all imply. Among Pugin's friends several, including Shrewsbury and Rock, were well aware of the potential of the Oxford Movement for the re-animation of Catholicism in England. Rock was in correspondence with several Tractarians on matters of Church history, while the less subtle Shrewsbury was merely impatient: 'it is extraordinary we cannot catch a few Puseyites,' he complained to his chaplain. 'Has even one of them come over?'[18]

The Earl was writing from Rome, where he had gone for his daughter Mary's wedding to Prince Doria. The alliance was the culmination of

his wife's strenuous manoeuvrings, which had ended in failure at home
with Lord Fitzalan, who was, disappointingly, in 'full pursuit' of 'Miss
Coutts . . . and her thousands'.[19] 'Poor Lady Mary', whose sister Gwendalyn had already been married to an Italian noble, the Prince Borghese,
was now, according to Lady Arundell, to have an arranged marriage to
a man who 'proposed . . . before he had seen her because he heard of
her fortune'.[20] As his wife and daughter got on with the preparations,
the Earl spent his time in Rome reporting to the Pope on the state of
religious affairs in England. Pugin sent him long accounts of his own
efforts. 'Half stupified' with overwork, he thought nothing of Oxford
except as the ideal Gothic city, for which he had felt a proprietorial love
since childhood.[21]

He spent the beginning of January writing an open letter of protest
against the proposal to erect a Martyrs' Memorial at Oxford to Cranmer,
Ridley and Latimer, the three bishops burned at the stake by Mary
Tudor. The scheme for the memorial was a calculated challenge to the
Tractarians. The monument affirmed a Protestant view of the Established Church as the product of the Reformation. The Tractarians did
not believe this. They thought that, as Pusey had put it, the Church of
England was no new creation, but merely the old faith 'purified'.[22] After
some deliberation Newman and Pusey decided that they would neither
support the memorial nor be drawn into opposing it. In Oxford small
gestures spoke loudly. A visit returned, a letter left unanswered, such
was the finely inflected language in which the debate was carried on. For
those taking part a great deal was at stake. The future of the Established
Church, the fabric of national life with which that Church had been
intricately interwoven over centuries, the livelihoods of many individuals, perhaps the soul of England itself, hung in the balance. Pugin,
quite unaware of all this, settled down to compose a pamphlet in his
now customary mixture of messianic rhetoric, antiquarian footnotes
and popular verse. Remembering the mistakes of *Contrasts*, he decided
to proceed 'with every caution', to make sure of his authorities and to
check his facts ready *'for every evasion'*.[23] Nevertheless he could not
resist prefacing the text with more lines from Ward's *Reformation* –
'Cranmer could tune his reverend song/To Harry's fancy, right or
wrong'[24] and so forth – thus playing straight into the hands of critics
such as the Revd Thomas Lathbury, author of *A History of the English
Episcopacy*, who by now were waiting for him.[25]

Pugin's argument, supported by many notes and quotations from Dugdale, was not at all consistent. But his line ran, as it always had, along essentially the same course as the Tractarians', that the true English Church was Catholic and the Protestant Establishment was merely 'a great state engine' built to serve a political purpose.[26] His tone, however, ensured that few of his intended readers would get beyond the first page: 'I must suppose you either utterly ignorant of the history of your establishment . . . or, that you have so long tried to delude others in these matters, that you have at length deceived yourselves,' he began.[27] Any of the clergy who stayed the course were informed at the end that they should 'Remember the same power that created can destroy: you are only tenants-at-will . . .' 'Go on, erect your puny memorial,' he concluded, 'it will cut but a sorry appearance among the venerable remains of ancient days that will surround it.'[28]

In the event the memorial was not puny. It stands today in Magdalen Street as a monument to several things besides the bishops. It commemorates one skirmish in the religious battles of the early Victorian years, and it is a monument, in a negative sense, to Pugin. Built two years after his insolent and intemperate letter, it was designed by the young George Gilbert Scott, one of Pugin's greatest and earliest admirers. Scott designed a version of an Eleanor cross of 'strict archaeological accuracy' that poignantly illustrates both Pugin's influence on the mainstream of English architecture and his simultaneous exclusion from it.[29] On 29 January, the day before a public meeting to raise support for the memorial, Pugin travelled to Oxford with his newly-printed pamphlet and 'went to all the bigwigs at the colleges', delivering it to them personally.[30] This, as he noticed, 'perfectly astonished them'.[31] At the same time the information he was sending to Rome was being compiled by Shrewsbury and Nicholas Wiseman, the Rector of the English College there, with material from Phillipps, Rock and others, to present the case to the Vatican for re-establishing English bishoprics. For the moment Rome was reluctant to do this. 'The pope', Shrewsbury found to his annoyance, was 'very decided in his opinions' and too inclined to listen to the clergy, who 'with the Exception of Dr Walsh . . . seem to throw every obstacle in the way of improvement . . . spoiling everything they meddle with'.[32]

In truth the English Catholics were deeply divided. The realities of the early Victorian Church, of which Pugin was becoming increasingly aware, were very different from what visitors to Alton Towers or Grace Dieu might suppose. There were, in 1839, probably about 700,000 Catholics in England.[33] Of these only the minority, fewer than 200,000, were English. The rest were immigrants, the 'Crowds of miserable Irish [who] darken all our towns'.[34] Many people shared Carlyle's mixed feelings of pity, fear and guilt for the 'false ingenuity, restlessness, unreason, misery and mockery' of these swarms, driven, after 'fifteen generations of wrong doing' by the English in Ireland, to swell the slums and undercut the wages of the workforce on the mainland.[35] The English Catholics were especially divided about Ireland, and would be for decades. Some felt sympathy for the Irish on religious grounds, but many did not. 'Scum', one Birmingham priest called them, resenting their vast numbers and even vaster poverty which drained the Church's scant funds and reinforced the impression among the wider English population that Catholicism was a religion of the poor and the ignorant.

There were divisions along other lines as well. The clergy, with some exceptions, resented the influence of laymen, as Shrewsbury was discovering. The secular clergy disliked the regulars (those in orders), especially the Jesuits, and these 'jealousies of ecclesiastics' in turn exasperated the laity.[36] 'One might think England was a field wide enough for all,' Kenelm Digby complained to Ambrose Phillipps.[37] The Romantic Catholics, especially the converts, were not for their part popular with those who had been Catholic for generations and who, educated in the same schools, marrying into the same families, had found a stable niche in society, albeit one that was something of a backwater. They did not want a revival or an influx of converts and medievalizing enthusiasts criticizing their chapels and altering their practices, many of which had grown into their own local and rather low-church forms over the centuries that England had been a 'mission' remote from Rome. It was true that the Catholics lacked a substantial middle class and an intelligentsia, but the converts' frequent, somewhat tactless, insistence on these points did not advance their cause.

Although Pugin was beginning to observe some of this, he was not prepared to accept it, or any of its implications. Now, when he was asked to design a church for London, intended in time to be a cathedral, he looked at the example of Westminster Abbey, but not at the poverty of Southwark. The great cruciform church he proposed for the site at St George's Fields was, he told his friends in Rome, to be 'a perfect catholic church', 220 feet long with a crossing tower 250 feet high.[38] His plans included a chapterhouse, a cloister, schools and a convent. For months he had been discussing the scheme with its instigator, the Revd Thomas Doyle, who was determined to do something for the huge and poorly served Catholic population of south London. In his holidays Doyle travelled round Europe asking for money from anyone who had it, including King Ludwig of Bavaria. He had managed to buy the land, but his enthusiasm and Pugin's were not yet matched by anything like sufficient funds for such a building as they proposed.

When the building committee met to look at Pugin's drawings they admired them but asked if they could know what all this was to cost. Pugin rolled up his plans and prepared to walk out. When asked for an explanation he gave the same one that had served him so badly in Manchester: 'Who ever heard of a complete cathedral being built in the life of one man? . . . How could I possibly frame an estimate for a building, a small portion of which might possibly only be raised during my lifetime? . . . Common sense should have taught the Committee not to put such absurd questions to me.'[39] Common sense is a subjective quality. As far as the committee was concerned, it dictated that they must have costings before they could proceed. Plans were suspended. There was still a vast gap between Pugin's aspirations, indeed his claims – for he told Wiseman that his church at Manchester was to be built and to be 'four feet wider than York Minster' – and the reality.[40] The first of his churches actually to be opened was little St Augustine's, Solihull, on 6 February 1839. Pugin carried the cross, and the 'plain, pure, Gothic' chapel was 'well and respectably filled' according to the *Orthodox Journal*, though 'chiefly by Protestants' consumed with curiosity.[41]

Neither London nor Oxford would ever respond to Pugin as he hoped, or offer him the opportunities he craved. His first cathedral, the first in England since Wren's St Paul's, was not to be in the capital or in one of the ancient Gothic cities that he loved, but in Birmingham, which he hated. It was indeed the home of 'Greek buildings & Smoking chimnies – radicals and disenters', but it was also the city of mercantile self-confidence, of the new railway and all-round Brummagem bounce, of which the Catholic population had its fair share.[42] 'A commodious and splendid Catholic church' was felt necessary to reflect the importance of 'a town which for the numbers, the wealth and the spirit of its inhabitants is justly termed the metropolis of the Midland district.'[43]

Although Pugin never liked Birmingham, he found friends there whom he came to love and the personal, as ever, determined the professional. The Hardman family were prominent local manufacturers whom Pugin had met at Oscott. Catholic since the penal days, they had come originally from Lancashire. The elder John Hardman, now in his seventies, had established a prosperous button-making business and gave generously from its profits to Catholic causes. His son John Hardman Jun., Pugin's exact contemporary, became his closest friend and collaborator. Even before plans for the cathedral were in hand, the button works was advertising 'Ecclesiastical ornaments, designed from Ancient Authorities and Examples, by A W Pugin Architect . . . Executed in a very superior style, and with scrupulous regard to Canonical Laws, by JOHN HARDMAN, Jun.' The business began in an ad hoc way with no separate manufactory; likely craftsmen were simply recruited individually to make small items such as candlesticks, hanging lamps and chalices. The goods were available in Birmingham, or in London at Edward Hull's shop in Wardour Street.

In time many of the extended Hardman family found themselves working with or for Pugin, on textiles, on stained glass and as modellers. Their lives and fortunes were transformed by him and his by them. They offered him what he had been looking for since his parents died, sympathy, unwavering loyalty and a collaboration in which work was interwoven with ties of personal affection and the security of family life. In friendship Pugin had no sense of reserve, and the younger John Hardman did not flinch from the role of confidant, though it must have been sometimes burdensome, for Pugin's emotions were torrential and Hardman, naturally, had occasional worries of his own. So few of Hardman's letters survive that his character must be deduced from the thousands Pugin wrote to him. Steady, practical and tolerant he must have been, as well as self-effacing, though not servile. In his pragmatic way he was as great an enthusiast as Pugin, and he offered the persistence and application his more brilliant collaborator lacked. Theirs was to be a friendship for life, 'almost brotherly', and 'undisturbed during fifteen years of daily correspondence and frequent personal converse'.

Pugin's cathedral was to replace the Georgian chapel, the 'filthy hole', as he called it, of St Chad's in Shadwell Street. Pugin and Myers began work on the drawings.[44] The design was German in style and brick. Pugin explained to Hardman that the advantage of this was that it was 'cheap and effective and Likewise because it is totally different from any *protestant* erection any person would be aware this was a catholic church ... and though it is very plain it will have a majestic appearance from its Lofty proportions and will be readilly distinguished at a distance'.[45] St Chad's was designed to have twin west towers with spires and a central spire at the crossing. The site slopes precipitously to the east, a fact which Pugin exploited by creating a deep crypt, intended at first for a school. The result was, indeed, majestic, although the crossing spire was never built. The planes of brickwork soar up as the ground falls away below. Looking as if it might tower above the Rhine, when built St Chad's towered instead above the Birmingham canal. A clutter of barges, bridges, wharves and the workshops of the gunsmiths' quarter washed around its feet. The view of it from the east, complicated by the facets of the chancel, is still spectacular. High-pitched roofs climb like a range of hills, taking the eye ever further up and on to the spires and their crosses. With the help of Lord Shrewsbury and the Hardmans, father and son, who gave £1,800 and paid for the rood screen and the high altar, Pugin obtained some of the best antiquarian fittings he put into any of his churches. The fifteenth-century pulpit is from Louvain, on its panels the four doctors of the Church, Jerome, Ambrose, Gregory and Augustine. Lord Shrewsbury gave St Chad's its grandest possession, the great brass lectern also from Louvain, confiscated by the French in 1798. This particular piece of international booty, however, was not destined to rest for long in England. The Birmingham Archdiocese later sold it off and it is for the moment in Manhattan.

In the spring of 1839, as the ground was being cleared in Birmingham, Lord Shrewsbury was still in Rome, buying paintings for Oscott and lobbying Propaganda – the department of the Vatican in charge of regulating Catholic affairs in non-Catholic or 'mission' countries – who were proving 'very difficult to deal with'.[46] The Pope himself would 'not hear of' English bishoprics, fearing that the English government would make diplomatic demands in return on the Papal States.[47] The news from England was not entirely good either. Pugin's pace of work was giving cause for concern. Walsh, who took a kindly personal interest in the young architect, listened patiently to his lectures on liturgy, and responded to his signing all his letters with a cross as if he were a bishop by occasionally referring to him as Bishop Pugin, had nevertheless used his authority to forbid him to fast during Lent. 'You cannot, my dear

Lord, be more concerned for the preservation of his valuable health than I am,' Walsh wrote to Shrewsbury, 'I consider him to be an extraordinary genius raised up for these times.'[48] Despite which, the bishop noted, the church at Derby was proving expensive. He had, he confessed to Shrewsbury, been making 'promises which I shall find it difficult to comply with' in regard to money.[49] Dispassionate observers had also noticed the cost of Derby, where, it was rumoured, Pugin had 'sunk £1200' in the foundations.[50] Even sympathizers began to fear that 'Pugin don't understand book-keeping by single entry'.[51] Shrewsbury wrote back to Rock urging him to animate the clergy and laity towards fund-raising.

On 2 April Pugin laid and Rock blessed the first stone of St Alban's, Macclesfield. Once again a large and peaceful crowd of more than 600 gathered to watch. The Revd Richard Gillow in his address assured the mostly non-Catholic spectators that he would not utter 'one sentiment . . . to wound their religious sensibilities'.[52] George Spencer, however, followed him and announced that for his part he was going on with his prayer campaign and would never rest 'till the Catholic religion is again the religion, not of a part, but of the whole of England'.[53] Dr Rock, having blessed the stone, followed Shrewsbury's advice and made an urgent appeal for money.

On 6 May Pugin 'left London with dear Louisa' for Birmingham and then Alton Towers.[54] He had confided to Dr Rock some weeks earlier that it was now 'finally settled' that she would be received into the Catholic Church. 'I am overjoyed at this glorious result to all my prayers & anxieties on this all-important subject,' he told him, 'it is in fact the greatest blessing which could befal me at the present juncture of affairs.'[55] What depth of reservation Louisa must have felt about taking this step can only be deduced from the fact that she waited four years to do so under what must have been intense pressure. To live with Pugin was to live in his world and on his terms. Yet these had changed unimaginably. In 1833, as a young actress or dancer, she had married a stage designer and draughtsman with ambitions to be an architect. She had found herself in the vanguard of a religious revival. Her husband was famous and successful, but if she had imagined a brilliant career for him, it would not have been this.

Louisa's reception into the Church was in dramatic contrast to her hasty wedding in Holborn. The spectacularly staged ceremony in the chapel at Alton Towers made 'an indelible impression' on her and she talked of it, Pugin reported, for long after. She was the centrepiece of a scene as gorgeous as anything at Covent Garden. A crowd, mostly, as usual, curious Protestants, filled the chapel for the High Mass, celebrated according to the Sarum Rite. A festoon was hung from one side of the chapel to the other, from which hung a crown of flowers suspended over Louisa's head. Dr Rock and two other priests officiated in vestments of cloth of gold. A large candle, decorated with Gothic patterns and surrounded by flowers at the base, was lit and given to Louisa to hold while she made her recantation. After which a Te Deum was sung and 'a solemn benediction was pronounced ... over the deeply affected convert, whose mind and soul seemed wholly absorbed with the momentous proceedings in which she was taking so prominent a part'.[56]

20

Young Victorians

May 1839 to February 1840

... and all the people cried,
'Arthur is come again: he cannot die'
– Alfred, Lord Tennyson, Morte d'Arthur, 1842

The ceremony at Alton Towers was not the only or the most elaborate medieval ritual enacted that summer. The passion for the past and its literal re-creation was stirring large parts of Britain. In Ayrshire Pugin's exact contemporary, the Earl of Eglinton, staged a famous tournament. Tens of thousands of people, many in home-made medieval costume, travelled by train to Liverpool and then on to Ardrossan by one of the first two iron steamers, the *Royal Sovereign* and the *Royal George*. They came to see real knights in real armour, brought up by Samuel Pratt from his shop in Bond Street, jousting while their ladies in gowns and wimples watched. The occasion was magnificent and even the torrential rain did not dim the impression made by the Eglinton Tournament. Daniel Maclise's painting *Merry Christmas in the Baron's Hall*, shown at the Royal Academy, Tennyson's *Morte d'Arthur* (written but not yet published), the *Tracts for the Times*, Pugin's new cathedral at Birmingham, all were the works of the children of Waverley. Neither Newman nor Pugin would have seen a connection between their spiritual campaigns and the muddy joust at Eglinton, but later ages can and some contemporaries saw it too. Gladstone gave Walter Scott credit for his part in the Catholic revival, for 'his writings in verse and prose . . . did much to break down anti-Catholic prejudice and to prepare the way for Newman and the Oxford Movement'.[1]

These were years of revivalism in the positive sense, not of nostalgia or lack of confidence in the present but a time when for many the past was experienced as a living source of inspiration from which England could regenerate itself, like Arthur come to life again. Everything seemed possible. Those who were later to be the great Victorians were still young, and youth was in the ascendant across Europe. Pugin at twenty-seven was four years younger than Henry Manning, three years younger than Gladstone and Tennyson, the exact contemporary of Dickens and seven years older than the Queen. The coming decade would see a movement called Young England. There would also be a Young Ireland and a Young Italy. Of varying degrees of significance and quite different in their intentions, together they bore witness to the dominance of youth and its ideals that characterized the early Victorian years, a dominance not seen again in Europe until the 1960s.

What the rising generation prized most was 'reality', the word that now began to replace, in letters and journals, the newspaper clichés of 'improvement' and 'the march of intellect'. Reality meant something more complex, more intellectual and at the same time spiritual. It stood for integrity and solidity, for high seriousness, for everything the Georgians seemed to their children to have lacked, in religion, in architecture and in life. Newman, just about to take on the editorship of the *British Critic and Quarterly Theological Review*, wrote to his sister Jemima that whatever the paper turned out to be in his hands, 'dull or lively, obscure or striking . . . if I can help it it shall not be unreal'.[2] Manning, a little later, sizing up W. F. Hook, the author of *The Gospel and the Gospel Only*, noted that he had 'the best mind I have yet seen among opponents and has *reality* about him'.[3]

'Reality' became a term of approval among architects some time later, but already the same enthusiasm for seriousness was being felt within the Gothic Revival. The desire to get to grips with buildings and their history was growing. Antiquaries, too, were getting younger. March 1839 saw the establishment of the Oxford Architectural Society and in May, at Cambridge, that of the more influential Camden Society, which took its name from the great Elizabethan historian and antiquary William Camden. Formed for the study of church architecture, it was, like many student societies, a dynamic and opinionated little body. Unlike most, however, it took the nation by storm and its effect on the style of new buildings, especially churches, was immediate. 'Few changes in our history can have been more sudden, more rapid, and more complete,' Tom Mozley recalled, 'than that from the Greek and Roman styles in church building to . . . the mediaeval.'⁴ Within three years the Society's membership included sixteen bishops and thirty-one peers and MPs, and it was dictating ecclesiastical taste to the nation.

'Reality', however, was the watchword of a generation saturated with romanticism. They were practical but also passionate. One of Maclise's less likely chivalric subjects was a group portrait of the campaigning journalists of *Fraser's Magazine*, who made their names in the 1830s with attacks on laissez-faire Utilitarianism, a view which accepted indus-trial slums, disease, child poverty and pollution as the inevitable result of surplus labour, a problem that should be left to work itself out. They called instead for urgent action. Maclise depicted the writers seated, as they worked, at their own Round Table, symbolizing their role as latter-day knights of the pen, chivalrously defending the rights of the poor. There was a general longing for such noble quests and, amid the opti-mism, a fondness for lost causes. At Oxford Tom Mozley was 'a Bour-bonist, knowing next to nothing of the Bourbons', while at Cambridge the future members of Young England, Lord John Manners and George Smythe, spent the long vacation of 1838 wandering in the Lake District.⁵ As they passed through the Wordsworthian landscape they too felt the need for a mission and like Pugin were willing, even keen, to be martyrs. Manners noted in his journal that after a long day's passionate conver-sation he and Smythe had pledged themselves 'to attempt to restore what? I hardly know – but still it is a glorious attempt and [Smythe] is well qualified to take the lead in it, but what rebuffs, sneers and oppo-sition must we expect: however, I think a change is working for the better and all, or nearly all, the enthusiasm of the young spirits of Britain is with us.'⁶ Theirs was a profoundly Christian quest and they felt, even in Cambridge, the powerful attraction of Newman, in whose preaching an 'ardent zeal and fine poetical imagination' smouldered beneath the surface of calm 'reality'.⁷ When this passion burst through, the effect of such a release of dramatic tension 'was irresistible, and carried his hearers beyond themselves at once'.⁸

With such emotions in the pulpit and in the press, the ideals of chivalry came to seem terribly modern. Thus to take a steam train to a Gothic tournament was to enter fully into the spirit of this particular age. Pugin too liked trains. The letters he wrote on his journeys record the new lines as they opened in rapid succession through the next decade. His own temperamental sense of urgency was heightened by the general sense of gathering speed as the vocabulary of the railways passed into everyday speech. 'I am such a Locomotive being,' he wrote to the artist David Read in Salisbury.[9] The great phrase, soon the cliché, of the railway age was 'the annihilation of space by time', and Ferrey remembered Pugin himself in these days as a kind of steam engine, his 'iron frame' enabling him 'absolutely to annihilate space'.[10] He was typical of the young Victorians, too, in that he was driven by anxiety as much as optimism, the fear of social disorder and breakdown. In the Radicals and dissenters that made him so dislike Birmingham he saw the heirs of the Calvinist iconoclasts and of 'the dreadful Revolution of 1790 . . . which swept away most of the remains of ancient art' in France, whose traces had still been fresh when he first went as a child to the Continent.[11] Now, as the poor harvests continued, discontent was growing among the poor and among the thinking classes. At the end of 1839 Carlyle published his pamphlet *On Chartism*. The first edition of 1,000 copies sold out immediately; its theme, 'the condition of England', was taken up by the press and the phrase passed into the language. In his essay Carlyle, a prominent contributor to *Fraser's Magazine*, appealed against the poverty of those masses who comprised the 'working class', the injustices of the new poor law, the workhouses and the clumsy and inadequate attempts of government merely to repress dissent rather than address it. Chartism, the first British working-class mass movement, whose Charter included a demand for universal manhood suffrage, was, he argued, symptomatic: a 'rather ominous matter' about which 'if something be not done, something will do itself one day, and in a fashion that will please nobody'.[12] Other popular writers similarly 'urged the rising generation to choose their lines of reformation at once, and pursue them obstinately to the end'.[13]

The Romantic Catholics did just that. Pugin and Shrewsbury developed a project in the summer for Alton. St John's Hospital was to be a 'hospital' in the medieval sense, a place where help would be given to all needy people, not only the sick. It was to be a complex of buildings sited next to the ruins of the ancient Alton Castle on the Earl's estate, just across the valley from the Towers. It would comprise a chapel, lodgings for twelve poor men, six elderly priests, for whose use a library was provided as well as a dining hall, and there would also be a school, open to an 'unlimited number of poor scholars'.[14] In the design of St John's Victorian reality and romance met on equal terms. The several parts of the building, set around three sides of a quadrangle, were disposed to reveal their function, in the picturesque manner in conscious contrast to the monotony of workhouse and factory architecture. The chapel was the most prominent feature, the community hall the next, while the range of poor men's lodgings was humbly uniform but marked by sturdy chimneys. The hospital was never completed as Pugin intended, but even as it stands it speaks of his, and Shrewsbury's, ideals. Opposite the castle 'with its overshadowed moat and winding paths', it perches on the edge of the Churnet Valley.[15] Today the graveyard behind the chapel is full. It slopes away until it merges with the edge of the forest. The crosses, which have settled at angles, are outlined against distant banks of trees, a Nazarene vision.

Architecturally the hospital was tougher than Pugin's earlier designs. There was a new robustness in some of the details. Two massive chimney stacks balance each other on either side of the site, one on the kitchen, the other, for no very practical reason, on the warden's house. Pugin based several of the chimneys at St John's on one of the first ancient buildings he had ever known, the Jew's House in Lincoln, which his father and Willson had included in their *Specimens*. Willson as an antiquary admired the 'curious' chimney stack which stands out on the front of the house and divides round the door, but it had seemed too peculiar, too outré, to Auguste to be worth drawing. Pugin now seized on it as the kind of strong, strange detail that would help to give Gothic character to a small building, or one without an obvious medieval precedent. In choosing what had seemed to his father's generation crude and heavy, even freakish, Pugin was taking another firm stride away from the Georgian elegance that still pervaded his church work. It was one of those sudden insights with which he pointed the direction that nineteenth-century architecture would go, towards the tougher, more dramatic, buildings of the High Victorian years. In cases such as this where he could not imitate and was forced to invent, Pugin was now becoming very inventive indeed. Yet still for the moment he preferred to imitate.

With so much work in hand at once, all under his direct supervision, he was constantly on the move. He made designs and decisions fast, and although his ideas developed swiftly, they developed erratically. His churches in progress now included Birmingham, Derby and Macclesfield, Keighley and Uttoxeter. He was still helping Gillespie Graham with the decoration of Taymouth. In Ireland there was a church beginning at

Gorey, a chapel in the convent at Rathfarnham and another at Wexford. At Dudley he was about to design a church for George Spencer. It was a very mixed bag. Different builders, various patrons, often limited funds and Pugin's fluid ideas all made for unevenness. The best he could say about Our Lady and St Thomas, Dudley, was that it was cheap: 'A small, simple but complete church' for only £3,165 including vestments, fittings and decoration.[16] 'A disappointment', Pevsner called it with justice.[17] Though Pugin gave thought to the siting, the church seems to slump. It has since been much altered and, to quote a recent incumbent, 'ruined'. At Keighley, where Myers was not in charge, there were structural difficulties. Pugin noted tersely in his diary: 'belfry fell'.[18] At Alton Towers he was now in sole architectural command. Thomas Fradgely, who had been working there since 1819, adding to the building, had been, like Potter at Oscott, seen off, and Pugin was designing apartments for the Shrewsburys' new son-in-law and his bride, as well as another gallery to lengthen, still further, the enormous enfilade. While he was at Alton that summer Thomas Doyle, the priest from Southwark, was also a guest and he persuaded Pugin to make another design for the pro-cathedral of St George's. There was to be a competition but Doyle promised that if Pugin entered it he would win.

Pugin and Myers took longer than usual drawing out the new scheme. Pugin hated to rework anything and it was a challenge to re-imagine the awkward, triangular site. His second scheme was for a hall church, a nave and two aisles of equal height with pitched roofs, its details Decorated Gothic. The shape of the plot meant that it had to be long and narrow. The nearly equal height of the three pitched roofs went some way to balance this by emphasizing such breadth as there was, but even with a massive and elaborate west tower it was oddly proportioned. Pugin came in time to be disappointed with nearly all his buildings, but at Southwark, where the stakes were so high, there was disappointment from the beginning. Here, in the capital, close to Westminster Abbey, where both the architect and the Catholic Church should have appeared to greatest advantage, the opportunity was never seized. He had been arrogant in his first renunciation of the job, but his instinct was right. It was too compromised by lack of money and his commitment to it was, in the end, to cost his reputation dear.

From Alton Pugin and Shrewsbury went to Grace Dieu, where the vision of Victorian Christendom was also gaining reality, at some cost.

Mary Arundell thought Laura looked thin, and Laura's guardian had complained that too much of Ambrose's money was being spent on charity and not enough on his wife and children, of whom there were now four. Yet Laura was as committed as her husband and the two of them were as active, as driven, as Pugin. Montalembert, who had visited in the summer, had been moved and impressed by them. He and Phillipps had been on a tour of the Cistercian abbeys, Kirkstall, Rievaulx and Fountains, which had cemented their friendship. It also had the more troubling effect of making Phillipps's own monastery look highly unsatisfactory when he came back. He determined that Pugin should build a new one. Cistercian monasteries are built to a pattern, established by the first foundation at Cîteaux in Burgundy in 1098. Neither Phillipps nor Railton had apparently known this in 1835, but Montalembert would have known. Phillipps now set about persuading Shrewsbury to pay for a proper monastery. Shrewsbury was reluctant. He was a good and generous man, 'a rare example of riches and charity united',[19] and he had embraced the idea of the hospital, with its obvious practical uses, but he was doubtful from the beginning about a 'monkery' as he called it, for a contemplative order.[20] The monks were not suited to Leicestershire, he argued, and suggested sending them to Italy. Phillipps threw such a hysterical fit at the suggestion that Shrewsbury was frightened into promising him £2,000. Pugin gave his services free. Passions always ran high in this intense little group of friends. Perhaps no two individuals had quite the same vision of the revival.

From the outset there were differences in politics, theology and culture. For one thing the converts, in reaction against the laxness of the Established Church and the politics of their parents, were Tory, while the old Catholics like Shrewsbury were mostly Whig, because the Whigs had supported Emancipation. Divisions over Ireland were deep. In April 1840 Daniel O'Connell founded the Repeal Association to campaign against the 1801 Act of Union which had drawn Ireland into the new United Kingdom. A lawyer from County Kerry who had led the movement for Catholic Emancipation, O'Connell, Great Dan, the Emancipator, was a hero to many of the Irish in England, like Mary Arundell, who was half Irish and firmly behind 'glorious Dan'.[21] To Pugin, as to Shrewsbury, the dismembering of the Union seemed to pose a threat to all they held dear. Phillipps, though he disliked and mistrusted O'Connell, was more pragmatic: 'on the principles of the British constitution I do not see how our government can much longer refuse . . . At any rate, if we yield nothing, we shall lose all.'[22] Thus among Catholics in England loyalty to their Irish co-religionists was pitched against concerns for national self-interest, while more generally even the most sympathetic of the clergy, like Walsh, having never worshipped in the ancient English parish churches, were sometimes baffled by the medievalism of the laymen.

The opening of St Mary's, Derby, in October 1839 was a telling fiasco. The priest, the aptly named Mr Sing, had not considered that it would be anything other than a tribute to the occasion to bring in M. Guynemer of the London Philharmonic Society to conduct a performance of a Beethoven Mass with a full choir and orchestra. For Pugin, as for Phillipps and Shrewsbury, the form of the Mass was of the essence. It had to be medieval plainchant. To revive the architecture, furniture, vestments and other attributes of medieval Catholic worship was to create the true, authentic setting. If the Mass itself was modern, it made a nonsense of the whole thing. Pugin and Shrewsbury demanded the music be changed. Bishop Walsh, who was to preach, pointed out that the musicians were already in their places. In that case, Shrewsbury said, they could not use the gold cope he had donated. Walsh, who was wearing it, took it off and the Earl, the architect and the rest of their party loaded up their vestments and left. It was not a dignified scene. Even Walsh, who wholeheartedly supported Pugin, was disconcerted. He wrote to Shrewsbury saying he had no idea there would be any objection to an orchestra, adding, rather unkindly, that 'Mr Sing himself has no ear for music'.[23] Moreover Sing, who was terribly dejected by the failure of his grand opening, ought to be consoled, as he had been called upon by the committee judging the St George's competition to give his opinion of Pugin as an architect.

It was an absurd incident, but also a flashpoint, one of several that autumn in which the growing tensions within and around the Catholic revival and the Tractarian Movement broke out. At Oxford, Newman was engaged in correspondence with his bishop to explain the actions of his curate at Littlemore, John Rouse Bloxam. Bloxam had been at Alton in the summer, visiting Dr Rock, and was reported to have attended Mass and bowed his head at the elevation of the host. This might be taken to imply that he subscribed to the doctrine of tran-substantiation, the belief that Christ's body and blood are corporally present in the Mass. Transubstantiation was one of the central articles of faith rejected by the English Church at the Reformation and it was a matter on which Bishop Bagot required assurance. Feelings were running high and such apparently small gestures loomed large, for by now a kind of magnetic attraction was drawing the romantic Catholics and the Tractarians into the same orbit. At last even Pugin began to be aware of what was going on. 'I wish you to read the British critic or Teological review for April,' he wrote to Willson, in June, 'you will find some capital articles especially on the internal decorations of churches which may easily be supposed to have been written by a catholic did not the cloven foot appear in the word *Romanist* etc there is a Long review of my contrasts . . . it is written by some very clever man & I suspect a Puseyite.'[24]

The *British Critic*, now under Newman's editorship, was, as all its other readers knew, the de facto house magazine of the Tractarians. The 'very clever man' was Tom Mozley. Pugin at once became an avid reader. In the *British Critic*, for the first time, he encountered Anglicans who knew as much about medieval architecture as he did and a great deal more about history. They knew and understood the intellectual and theological tradition which Pugin had absorbed as part of his upbringing. He was astonished to find how much they had in common. To the *British Critic* the tradition of Dugdale was as familiar as the 'Catholic' nature of Gothic. The contributors saw in the medieval architecture of England and Europe a proof that the 'Church of England is not an English, national, institution, but the English branch of that Catholic institution which was founded by our Lord'.[25] Mozley's essay on *Contrasts* was nineteen pages long. His line was firm and fair. He accepted Pugin as 'a first-rate architect' but thought 'the written part of his work . . . childish both in style and argument'.[26] He not only pointed out that the 'corruption' of English architecture began before the Reformation, but went on to note that Pugin had set his golden age in the middle of the Wars of the Roses and that Christ Church, his ideal college, was partly built with money raised from the suppression of religious houses. Yet Mozley's tone was friendly. He wrote with sympathy of the English Catholic tradition, which he was careful to distinguish from 'Romish novelties'.

The *British Critic* had an enormous influence on Pugin's still unformed ideas. He found in its pages the material to fill the gaps in his own, patchy, view of history and saw so many of his own ideas reflected in the articles that he was sure it could be only a matter of time before a 'reunion' between the Roman and English Catholic Churches would be achieved. He was not alone. The *Catholic Magazine* also looked forward confidently to reunion with that 'bright . . . body of learned and pious men' the Tractarians.[27] Others on both sides had their doubts. Kenelm Digby, who was irritated by Pugin's insistence that he should start reading the *British Critic*, written by a lot of 'parsons', noted that for all their 'writing genius, learning (of a certain kind) eloquence, profound thought' these clever, argumentative Oxford men showed 'not the least glimmering trace of the light of humility'.[28]

Nineteen days after the consecration of Derby the foundation stone was laid at Birmingham for St Chad's. After the ceremony Pugin made a long speech that was partly a manifesto, partly an apologia. He began by emphasizing how little his architecture owed to his own invention; 'there is not a single detail which has not been faithfully imitated,' he assured his hearers.[29] The only credit he deserved was that 'due to one who had reprinted an excellent but forgotten book'.[30] He urged them all to pray, with Spencer, for the conversion of England, to reject the claims of the Established Church and while placing their trust in God to act 'as if everything depended on our own individual exertions'.[31] It was his personal creed. His identification of God's work with his own was what gave Pugin his irresistible combination of self-effacement and self-promotion. He concluded with a long description of St Chad's as it was to be, a call to arms that echoed Blake's *Jerusalem* and foreshadowed William Morris. The battle for the soul of the cities, a battle already joined by *Contrasts*, was now carried into the heart of the Midlands: '. . . never shall I rest satisfied,' he concluded, 'till I see the cross raised high above every chimney in Birmingham, and hear the sound of St Chad's bells drowning the steam whistle and the proving of the gun barrels.'[32] He sat down to tremendous applause.

Pugin insisted on his unoriginality for two reasons. First because he believed it, and second because there were now many among his fellow Catholics who saw his Gothic vestments, hanging pyxes and other medieval revivals as unorthodox innovations. The resentments and complaints among the clergy which had first arisen at the consecration of Oscott had continued and Pugin had done nothing to appease them. He was never tactful. He had been horrified to find how perfunctory and at times vulgar the practices of the Catholic Church were, outside the Midland District. In London, during the season, the presence of the Italian opera company made the Mass into a popular entertainment, and within a year of his conversion Pugin had begun making satirical drawings of fashionable Catholic services as sharp as anything he levelled against the Church of England. He complained, loudly, in the *Catholic Magazine* of 'vile and contemptible' modern chapels, arranged like theatres, hosting 'a set of dissipated musicians taken from the theatre and the ball-room'.[33] His particularly violent distaste for the theatricals was perhaps intensified by memories of some 'dissipiated' episodes in his own past, but his satire was barely exaggerated. The fashionable Warwick Street chapel was generally known as the Shilling Opera. Not only were tickets for the Mass sold in advance, reviews appeared afterwards. 'To say the most of the Credo,' the *Orthodox Journal* enthused typically, 'it excelled the Gloria and was supported by Madame Persiani and Signor Tamborini, who came in during the sermon.'[34] Not all the clergy were complacent, but they had learned to be pragmatic. Neither Phillipps nor Pugin ever really grasped the fact that the Catholic Church in England was chronically short of funds. It had no lands, no endowments, no church rate. It was still difficult to make a legal will leaving money to the Catholic Church. And if the Catholic population was rising, it was mostly through Irish immigration, not through conversions.

By now it was becoming increasingly apparent that between those who expected the total conversion of England and the revival of medieval Christendom and those who wanted simply to build, on the gains of Emancipation, a sturdy and respectable Catholic communion there could be no meeting of minds. The pages of the hitherto friendly *Orthodox Journal* began to include protests against the expense of Pugin's buildings, making unfavourable comparisons with the simple arrangements of the Methodists – 'deluded followers' of a 'mushroom creed', as Pugin called them in a long, intemperate answer.[35] Matters came to a head when Bishop Baines, Vicar Apostolic of the Western District, enlisted the support of the other Vicars Apostolic, except of course Walsh, in declaring Pugin's flowing medieval-style chasubles 'illegal'. He sent a scale drawing of one to Griffiths, who agreed to ban them in the London District. Bishop Briggs, of the Northern District, thought that they looked like something from a 'Greek church'. He also resented being told what to wear by

Pugin, a mere 'tradesman'. Baines then went further and took the drastic step of complaining to Rome about Pugin's designs.

In November Walsh wrote to Shrewsbury, who was in Rome himself, with some 'very annoying information'.[36] He had received a letter from Propaganda alleging 'that I have allowed a certain architect a convert from Protestantism to introduce into the Midland District a new kind of vestments & that, as they understand, other innovations in contemplation, and calling on me to watch over the district and to prevent such changes. The language of the document is very strong.'[37] Walsh urged Shrewsbury to write to Pugin 'not to suffer his feelings to be too much excited' by this development 'but to be quiet & to continue cheerfully & zealously to prosecute plans for his new churches etc.'.[38] In the meantime Walsh banned the vestments. There was little chance of Pugin taking the news in the spirit the bishop advised. His reaction was intense and extreme. He was dismayed and not in any doubt that it was Baines's doing: 'what a farce,' he wrote to Rock, 'the opposition to the restoration of antient Catholic glory in England proceeds from the Clery we have nothing whatever to fear from protestant oppisition . . . if this decision of the propaganda is carried out I have done. I shall give up every hope. I am sick at heart.'[39]

In December Walsh picked up his pen with even more reluctance to write another difficult letter to Lord Shrewsbury. 'Humbly but most earnestly,' he began, 'do I entreat your Lordship in spirit at the foot of the cross.'[40] Poor Walsh had been going through his accounts and the results were alarming. The costs of Oscott, especially the purchase of the Marini Library, had brought him to the brink of ruin and disgrace. He blamed nobody but himself. He saw no way out but Shrewsbury's generosity. 'In this my distress my dear Lord I fly to you.'[41] The Earl paid the bills, but the following month Walsh had to tell Pugin that work at St Chad's and St Mary's, Dudley, would have to be delayed. 'The church at Derby alone cost me nearly double the sum I had proposed to expend on that building,' he wrote to the Earl. In these times of 'serious distress and great poverty occasioned by the want of trade . . . The priests in many places cannot . . . make up their minds to call on the poor for their pence.'[42] It was a desperate situation all round. At Southwark, where his competition designs had been duly selected, Mr Sing having been sufficiently mollified to praise him fulsomely, Pugin at once found himself caught up in meetings and misunderstandings. Bishop

Griffiths, having no doubt heard of the difficulties in the Midland District, was terrified that the expense would get out of control. The bishop, who struck Lord Shrewsbury as an 'excellent creature, but . . . somewhat wanting in energy and activity', became briefly very active indeed.[43] He wrote to the building committee twice and made Pugin sign a letter certifying that: 'I do not expect to receive any money whatever from the Right Revd. Dr Griffiths – on account of St Georges church Southwark.'[44]

Pugin reacted to these checks on his hitherto headlong progress with alternate declarations that he would carry on regardless and that he would give up entirely. In fact he continued to draw and design at the same torrential rate. Yet the dawning realization that within the Catholic Church there were many, perhaps a majority, who either opposed him or would not positively support him had the effect of bringing him closer to Phillipps and of making both men take a minute interest in developments at Oxford. Here they saw events progressing rapidly along lines more sympathetic to their own vision of the English Catholic Church.

That winter, restless as ever and with Louisa expecting another baby in June, Pugin took lodgings in Ramsgate for himself and his family, in a house in the Plains of Waterloo. The air was healthier, he thought, for the children than at Chelsea, and he and Louisa still had friends in the town. Perhaps chiefly it was the appeal of the sea that drew Pugin back, not only to sail, but to run over to France when he felt like it and simply to be near the English Channel in all its moods and colours, to be out in a storm, which he loved. His diary was often annotated while he was there with details of marine events: 'Heavy gale . . . Barque lost . . . Brigantine lost on the goodwins. Crew saved by Deal boat.'[45] He was close once again to the familiar landscape of Thanet, with its medieval monuments and ruins, and away from London where much that he found most oppressive was inescapable. He had by now given up any idea of living at St Marie's Grange again. Reluctant to sell his first building, he asked the Salisbury builder Frederick Fisher what to do. 'It cannot go on in this manner . . . My whole prospects are entirely changed since I built it . . . but I do not like so much money sunk without any return whatever.'[46] He made alterations and tried to rent it out, but there were still no takers for so eccentric a place.

Later in January Pugin went from Ramsgate, by way of London,

Birmingham, Alton and Macclesfield, where St Alban's was nearing completion, down to Grace Dieu and Garendon for five days. On the 17th he set out the ground for the new monastery. He had brought his drawings for St Chad's to show the Phillippses. They must have talked about the state of affairs in the Midland District and the censure from Propaganda. Pugin's moments of despair contrasted with Phillipps's millenarian sense that great forces were at work, destined to restore England to the Catholic Church. Phillipps now believed that 'reunion' of the English Catholic Church with the wider Roman Church was God's will. Dr Rock had been at Oxford that month, as had Spencer. Catholics who did not belong to what Newman called 'the party' were welcomed by the Tractarians, for in their politics the Romantic Catholics and the Oxford men were even closer than in their theology. 'The party' were the Liberals and Radicals, especially those who supported O'Connell and were thus, according to the *British Critic*, 'associated . . . with . . . low democracy' and 'pandering to the spirit of rebellion'.

Spencer went to urge his prayer campaign on the Oxford men and met with a varied response. Newman felt he could not meet an apostate priest, at least he could not *go* to meet him. It was settled that if Spencer called on Newman, Newman would receive him. In 1862 he annotated his correspondence to the effect that he had been so 'moved and drawn by Mr Spencer's coming, that . . . I with difficulty kept myself from laughing for joy while he talked to me'.[47] At the time he described the amiable Spencer as a typical Catholic priest, 'sadly smooth'.[48] Spencer felt the visit was a failure: 'The result was very different from what I expected,' he wrote forlornly to Phillipps, 'I shall not go there again.'[49] Intellectually he had been outclassed and out-argued. Chastened, he made no more sorties. Young Bloxam, meanwhile, was very cast down about the reprimand from his bishop for his behaviour at Alton and set on resigning the curacy of Littlemore. Phillipps was right to think that such a degree of disturbance must soon lead to something.

21

A Vision for England

March to December 1840

. . . the revival of our national antiquities must be our cry.
– Pugin to Dr Rock, March 1840

It was in the spring of 1840 that Pugin's ideas about church architecture came, quite suddenly, into focus. His conversations with Rock and his reading of the *British Critic*, which he now considered 'the most Catholic Publication of the Day', had encouraged him to think more about history and more discriminatingly about the Gothic and its various local and historical forms.[1] The immediate stimulus to concentrate his mind was the Earl of Shrewsbury's decision to commission a new church for the little town of Cheadle in Staffordshire, near Alton. St Giles's was to be the Romantic Catholics' manifesto. With no committees and no penny-pinching, it was to be 'as perfect a specimen as we can make it'.[2] Pugin was so excited by the prospect that Shrewsbury had to remind him about St John's: 'we . . . must not do too much,' the Earl wrote nervously from Rome, 'we must finish our present job at the Hospital first.'[3]

With St Giles's Pugin made two important decisions. The first was to work in English Gothic. Rock had persuaded him that national styles should be respected and so Pugin, whose dogmatism never prevented him from changing his mind, often with disconcerting suddenness, abandoned the German models that had hitherto inspired him and began to look more closely at English precedents. 'I will never perpratrate anything foreign in England again – you are quite right,' he told Rock, 'I am y day more satisfied of it . . . I am heartily ashamed of 9 tenth of what I have done . . . the revival of our national antiquities must be our cry.'[4] His other decision was to give up the elaborate late Gothic that he had first preferred. He knew by now that architecture had not continued in a seamless flow up until the Reformation. It had rather, according to most antiquaries, developed to a peak in the late thirteenth to early fourteenth centuries, and then declined. 'It was not long,' as the *British Critic* put it, ' – not much longer than the term assigned by the Psalmist as the measure of human existence – that the architecture of the North maintained the high and palmy state of its perfection.'[5] Pugin, too, prompted perhaps by the *Critic* or by Rock, now took this to be the ideal period, the moment at which the Gothic achieved the greatest variety and beauty, having developed beyond the simplicity of the Early English but not yet become florid, exaggerated or infected with symmetry and intimations of the Renaissance, as the later Perpendicular style was thought to be.

At Cheadle, and in the design he made at about the same time for the church of St Oswald, at Old Swan near Liverpool, Pugin lit on the type, the 'complete English parish church of the time of Edward I' that was to embody his new vision and soon that of the whole Gothic Revival. His church at Cheadle, despite its location in a small country town, remains one of the most admired and visited of all Victorian buildings. In St Giles's and St Oswald's there was a new 'reality' in the proportions and the massing. The last trace of Georgian thinness had gone; the interiors were intended to be dark, enfolding and complex. Typically Pugin's ideal parish church as it emerged had a nave and two aisles and was distinguished, externally, by a broach spire. A broach spire is complicated to describe but easy to recognize; the silhouette is repeated on a thousand skylines across the British Isles and far beyond. The 'broaches' are pyramidal sections that turn a square tower into an octagonal spire and the form allows for many variations: it can be small and snub on a village church or tall and elegant and punctuated with lucarnes. Broach spires are typical of the churches near Sleaford in Lincolnshire. They are found at Ewerby, Carlby and at Welby itself, the villages where Pugin's childhood summers were spent. Though perhaps with no conscious intent, it would seem that when he began to consider the perfect English church the image that rose in his mind was that of rural Lincolnshire in 1818, on the first journey of which he could 'remember particulars'. Though always hurtling *en avant*, disinclined, to Ferrey's disappointment, to reminisce about the old days, Pugin carried his lost childhood with him and now projected it on to the future, across the whole of England.

Meanwhile the campaign against him and his friends went on. In a pastoral letter to mark the beginning of Lent, Bishop Baines made a thinly disguised attack on him, along with Phillipps, Spencer and Digby. Baines accused the converts 'of an enthusiastic turn of mind' – enthusiastic, at that time, meaning more or less deluded or fanatical – and complained that they were 'perpetually hankering after new ideal wonders' and listening to 'old wives fables . . . about the approaching end of the world etc.'[6] The conversion of England he thought was 'a moral impossibility', and the chief effect of all this vehemence and abuse of 'hereticks' was to cause dissent. 'Almost all the little divisions which exist among us,' Baines wrote, disingenuously, 'and thank God they are not many – may be traced to those who have been recently called to the faith . . .'[7] The Pastoral infuriated many people, beyond its intended targets. The Shrewsburys were deeply upset. It was important, however, to avoid a public row. Kenelm Digby wrote to Phillipps imploring him to be 'sage' and to get Spencer and Pugin to be so too. 'Let us grieve and be silent. My impression [is] that Dr Baines has now dished himself . . . Let us leave it to others to serve him up . . . The thing is a slap on the face for us all four converts . . . but I think silent contempt is the proper treatment.'[8]

Shrewsbury, in Rome, thought it a 'sad' business and was inclined to attribute it to a disordered liver on Baines's part. Nevertheless, he did not quite like to leave the bishop to dish himself so he decided to serve him up by sending a copy of the Pastoral to Propaganda and arranging for it to be translated. As a result Baines was summoned to Rome, where he spent ten uncomfortable months trying to account for himself. If Propaganda found it difficult in these years to understand what was going on in England they could scarcely be blamed. Pugin thought Baines's pastoral 'outrageous' but he was too excited about his new church to dwell on it.[9] Shrewsbury, who was expecting to pay £1,000 for the land at Cheadle alone, was trying to instil some sense of restraint. 'I am most anxious to get on as quick as possible & to profit to the utmost of my power by your great taste & talent, but we cannot go beyond our means – I promise to go their full length.'[10] At the same time he was almost as excited himself. 'I have so much to talk about,' he went on, 'you must be at Alton as much as possible this summer.'[11]

The rapid focusing of his architectural ideas coincided with the moment when Pugin's technical resources were beginning to catch up with them. From Myers he had learned a great deal about construction and he was also pursuing the applied arts. He had designed furniture and metalwork before he became an architect and he had never doubted that the Gothic Revival must be a revival of all the crafts. To be complete, a building must engage every human sense; every surface and detail must be considered. Hardman was now making his metalwork; William Warrington, a pupil of Pugin's first glassmaker, Thomas Willement, for the moment made his stained glass. In Thomas Roddis, a stonemason working at Oscott, he had found a carver worth training up and now he discovered, in Herbert Minton of Stoke, 'at length', a man who had 'Suceeded in restablishing the manufacture of church paving tiles'.[12] Minton had been making these 'encaustic' tiles for several years and Pugin now began to make designs for him to use in Pugin's own churches. Minton was the epitome of the Victorian antiquarian-industrialist, a man who brought to the revival of the Middle Ages all the resources and the energy of the steam age. Though never so close to Pugin as Hardman and Myers, Minton became a friend and lifelong collaborator. He was an inspired technician who arrived at his factory before any of the employees to pursue his researches into the chemistry of ceramics. He had followed recent excavations of medieval kilns and been able to overcome the principal difficulty of encaustic, which is to make the different coloured clays, which fire at different temperatures, bond in the kiln. Encaustic tiles are hard-wearing because the pattern is not applied to the surface, it is integral (encaustic literally means 'burned in'), but if the clays fire at different times the result is nothing but a heap of fragments. Once Minton had mastered it the results were a rapid success. Practical, hygienic and authentically Gothic, encaustic flooring, most often in buff and red, was – and remains in thousands of churches, schools and domestic hallways – the essence of Victorian decoration.

Yet while he made great progress, Pugin's inexperience still told in some areas. He still depended on Myers for estimates and working drawings and he found it difficult to plan larger buildings for which there was no obvious model. At the back of St John's Hospital and in his drawings for the Phillippses' monastery there were untidy joins and awkward spaces. His first convent, built for the Sisters of Mercy in Bermondsey in 1838, had been a failure. Catherine McAuley, foundress of the order, a forthright practical woman, complained that it was 'not well-suited'.[13] 'The sleeping rooms are too large, the other rooms too small, the corridors confined and not well lighted.'[14] When, that year, the Hardman family offered to pay for another convent near their home at Handsworth, a village then just outside Birmingham, Mother McAuley took matters into her own hands. She told Pugin she wanted 'a plain simple durable building', not more than two storeys high with the refectory close to the kitchen.[15] She specified the exact dimensions of the rooms, which Pugin duly noted down and followed.[16] The convent, Hardman's Hospital as he called it, was a success. It is a cheerful, pretty building, feminine in scale yet robust. But the credit Pugin has been given for its 'rational approach' to planning should really go to Mother McAuley.[17]

In London, on 2 June, Pugin noted: 'My son Cuthbert born this day at 20 past 1pm.'[18] Cuthbert was named for the seventh-century Northumbrian who is one of the best-loved of the English saints. He survived to see the First World War and is a figure in living memory at the time of writing. Soon after his birth Louisa was ill with 'that most dreadful malady the Milk fever', which left her 'dreadfully reduced and weakened' and terrified her husband, 'for the fever was as violent as sudden & unexpected'.[19] She recovered, and on the 24th 'Dear little Cuthbert' was baptized at Margate at the small Catholic chapel there, a building so uncongenial to Pugin that he knelt on the gallery stairs, out of sight of the worst of the interior. He was a fond father but at this time a distant and intensely preoccupied one. His daughter Agnes, who was four in 1840, later told her granddaughter that she remembered Pugin saying that for her birthday that year he had designed a cathedral. She also remembered being very disappointed.[20]

Between Cuthbert's birth and his baptism, even while Louisa was ill, Pugin was up at Alton. The Shrewsburys were back from Italy and Pugin happily fell in with the suggestion that he should be there as much as possible. His addition to the great enfilade, the Talbot Gallery, was nearly complete. It brought the length of the whole range to 480 feet and was entered from the Octagon through a screen, Pugin's favourite device, designed to tantalize the eye, relieving the long vista of monotony. The interior was a celebration of the Talbot line, the blaze of heraldry and innumerable quarterings of his ancestors spelling out, for those who knew how to read them, the Earl's descent from William the Conqueror. The centrepiece was to be an equestrian figure of the 1st Earl, the Great Talbot, armed and dressed in his Garter robes. In that summer of 1840 Alton was at its zenith. Queen Adelaide, widow of William IV, honoured it with a three-day visit for which Pugin brought the expertise of the Covent Garden scenery department to the estate workshops. He had been 'indefatigable', the Countess reported to Laura Phillipps. 'He was . . . morning and night . . . making pennants, banners triumphal works, and really they did him credit and the coup d'oeil was really and truly worthy of a Gothic eye.'[21] The Queen Dowager arrived in the late afternoon, accompanied from the lodge by a procession of 300 local gentlemen. In the evening the company enjoyed a soirée dansante while a feast was provided for the tenantry. Such substantial pageants, and Pugin orchestrated several at Alton Towers, were as close as reality could come to the vision of Catholic England as Merrie England, the benign Gothic kingdom in which all ranks observed their station and were cared for, or took care of others, accordingly.

After the royal visit Pugin and the Shrewsburys made their way down to visit the Phillippses at Grace Dieu, where there was a conspicuous and not entirely happy addition to the household. The Italian priest Luigi Gentili was an ambivalent participant in the great programme of revival. He was a member of the Institute of Charity, a new order established in Italy in 1828 by Antonio Rosmini. Rosmini was a liberal intellectual in the mould of Montalembert, an admirer of the Nazarenes, a man whose huge correspondence cast a network of religious and moral sympathy across Europe. Gentili, who was forty, had none of Rosmini's temperance and where Rosmini was liberal, Gentili was radical. He was ascetic, intellectual, a lawyer by training and a linguist. He was also strikingly handsome, tall and pale with blue eyes and black hair. He had lived in England before and had a low opinion of English Catholics. 'For my part, I consider the English Mission the most difficult in Europe,' he had written on his first encounter with it, 'the scandals, the softness, the immorality.'[22] Phillipps, who seemed fated to mistake the character of religious orders, had invited the Rosminians to Leicestershire. Gentili was under the impression that Phillipps would establish a Rosminian house nearby. In fact Phillipps had promised more than he could afford.

The depression was now hitting rural Leicestershire hard. The Phillippses' income from rents fell just as demands on their charity rose. 'In the Eastern parts . . . and in Rutlandshire . . . there is now nothing at all but grazing farms,' Ambrose told Shrewsbury, 'the villages are dying away . . . turn all England into grass, and you will almost root out the whole rural population ... The masses would be all congregated together in Towns, the whole influence of the Gentry would be destroyed, the Trade and the Towns would swallow up all.'[23] He started allotment gardens at agricultural rents in the neighbouring villages. Gentili was as concerned about the poverty as Phillipps, but he knew nothing and cared less about Merrie England and the olden times and he had no wish to preserve the gentry. While Phillipps wanted Gentili to act as a private chaplain and draw people to Grace Dieu, Gentili wanted to go out into the villages and work directly with the poor. He was appalled by the condition of England. The reports he sent back to Italy painted a desperate picture of a working class both pitiable and exasperating, too poor even to afford shoes, yet oddly complacent. 'People shout at you that they are free, but they are slaves to a nobility that wallows in opulence. This idea of independence which in fact they have not got, acts like a drug and hides from them their temporal and spiritual ruin.'[24] Phillipps was soon dismayed by the nature of the beast he had imported. Gentili hardly ate. He slept on a board and his asceticism extended to a disdain for washing and shaving. Phillipps told him that 'In England it is the custom for men of the rank of Gentleman to shave every day. Hence when a man in that rank of Life . . . neglects this custom he is looked upon as a man of slovenly or dirty habits . . . Lord and Lady Shrewsbury made the same remark . . . and I can see that their thinking so makes them esteem your judgement less.'[25] Gentili, a lawyer in argument, replied that beards were medieval.

Gentili was to be a spoke in many wheels, including Pugin's, and his life and work in England a critique of much that characterized the early Victorian years. He looked at the English Catholics and saw decadence, complacency and play-acting. They looked back and saw a dirty Italian who would confirm the anti-papists' worst suspicions about the Church. Despite which, and to the credit of all, the mission made progress. For several years Phillipps and Gentili worked from opposite points of view towards the same ends of Catholic charity and evangelism. Gentili won Phillipps round to the idea of missionary stations and, following urgent instructions from Rosmini to keep his temper, he did his best to fit in with English manners. Shrewsbury was never persuaded, although the Countess, like many women, found something compelling about Gentili, especially the low sweet quality of his voice. Pugin felt the power of his personality, too, and confided in him, unaware how little

personal friendships mattered to a man like Gentili beside his sense of
the divine will.

The autumn brought more commissions. By now even the *Civil Engineer
and Architect's Journal*, which had so confidently written him off in
1836, was taking notice of Pugin. Usually it was hostile, but the hostility
seemed less and less justified. One reader wrote in to complain that the
paper was unfair for, 'with all his eccentricities', Pugin was 'beyond
comparison the first Ecclesiastical Architect of the day'.[26] The most
important building in the last part of the year was the bishop's house
for Birmingham, to stand opposite St Chad's. This was Pugin's first, and
one of his most successful attempts, to create an urban Gothic idiom. It
was an answer to the monotonous Georgian terraces he so disliked, and
it was an ingenious one, for buildings on a street line usually show only
one face from one angle and it is difficult to make them picturesque.
Pugin had based the design on French courtyard houses – before his
self-imposed ban on foreign models. This allowed him to fill the site
without a single flat front. The main part of the house was set back
behind a boundary wall that rose to the full height of the building,
descended to a single-storey cloister, rose again then dropped to a gate.
The chimney stack from the Jew's House, massively elaborated, and
oriels from the buildings at Wells, used in mirror image, created variety
within the compact space. Built in red brick, with black brick inset to
spell out Bishop Walsh's initials, the Birmingham 'Palace', as Pugin
referred to it, was of 'solid, solemn and scholastic character'. Photographs show it looking imposing and mysterious in the grey Birmingham
light. Its demolition after the Second World War, to make way for the
ring road, was one of the worst losses not only among Pugin's work,
but to Victorian architecture.

All this time the uneasy attraction between the Romantic Catholics
and the Tractarians was increasing. Daniel Rock was now regularly in
touch with John Bloxam, Newman's curate, who had so compromised
himself at Alton Towers. Bloxam, at thirty-three, was five years older
than Pugin, a knowledgeable antiquary and a member of the Oxford
Architectural Society. By September he could not resist an overture to
Pugin. He sent Rock a note asking for advice about liturgical arrangements which Rock passed on. Pugin wrote back at once. He said he
would be happy to help and he said much more. He rushed to embrace

the chance of an introduction at Oxford: 'Allow me to take this opportunity of assuring you that I have *Longed* for the honour of your personal acquaintance for some time,' he wrote in his first letter to Bloxam. 'I feel assured that in all that regards catholic art and architecture we have but one opinion.'[27] Eager, always, for friendship and sympathy, quick to imagine he had found it, Pugin began to write to Bloxam at length.

Bloxam, luckily, was a trustworthy recipient for such confidences. He was a man of integrity, a thoughtful admirer of Pugin's work and one who had no desire to make capital out of the divisions among the Catholics that Pugin artlessly laid bare. At the same time Bloxam thought it his duty to keep Newman informed of the correspondence. Pugin made a kind of apologia to Bloxam in these first letters. He told him how, since childhood, he had 'wept over the mutilated remains' of medieval buildings and how he had 'ever considered ecclesiastical architecture & faith inseperably connected'.[28] 'I never found any sympathy whatever for these very feelings when I was member of the Established church,' he went on. 'I had all your ideas within my breast but I found no one to share them with me. disgusted with all around me . . . I became a desperate enemy to the English church – but I am so no Longer.'[29] Of his own work he wrote: 'I strive to *revive* not *invent* and when I have done my best . . . I have produce a striking effect yet how terribly do my best efforts sink when tested by the scale of antient excellence.'[30]

Pugin's view of the present situation was passionate but wildly simplistic. He wanted the best of both worlds. 'The truth is, that devout & sincere men of both parties should meet – and instead of expending our resources against each other – should turn them against the common enemy of Liberalism and infidelty . . . I write this to you because I hold that Truth cannot be injured by Truth.'[31] On 29 October Pugin went to meet Bloxam at Oxford and Bloxam took him to dine at Exeter College as a guest of Pusey's assistant, John Brande Morris. The party were all Tractarians, invited with an injunction (unnecessary in Pugin's case) to 'talk strong'.[32] Among the company were George Bowyer, a lawyer who later converted and became a prominent Catholic MP, and W. G. Ward, who was to become a friend of Pugin. He represented the more radical element among the younger generation of Newman's admirers, for whom the desire to remain on terms with the Established Church weighed less heavily. These young men leaned ever further towards Rome. The talk was strong indeed. R. W. Church reported the evening in a letter that conveys the emotionalism, with the thick vein of hysteria that ran through Oxford then: 'Ward is said to have repeatedly jumped up and almost screamed in ecstasy at what was said, and Bowyer and Pugin had a fight about Gothic and Italian architecture.'[33]

Not everyone was taken with Pugin. Morris disliked him and thought he was leading Bloxam on. Pugin gave vent – with complete indiscretion – to his often rehearsed complaints against the majority of his fellow Catholics; their ignorance, their failure to appreciate history or architecture or to understand ritual propriety. His opinion that 'if 200 of the ablest and best of our [Oxford] men were to go over, they would be received coldly' was duly noted.[34] Pugin returned to Birmingham, characteristically unconscious of the mixed impression he had created. He reported to Shrewsbury that the visit had been 'deligtful', adding, 'I feel *perfectly* satisfied that these are the men who will catholicise England.'[35]

There was also now a stirring among the English Roman Catholics. Kerril Amherst later remembered 1840 as a time of 'sudden change for the better . . . like the effect of the first fine days of spring after a long and dreary winter'.[36] This thaw was the culmination of the process of debate at Rome. Propaganda, still uncertain what to do about the troublesome English mission, declined to restore the hierarchy. While Shrewsbury urged it, there were other voices, notably Gentili's from Leicestershire, raised against it. Gentili was disparaging about the English bishops – except Walsh – finding them ambitious and far too insistent on national independence. A compromise was reached. It was decided to increase the number of the districts to eight, thereby creating four new bishops. In the discussion of nominations for these new posts the English Vicars Apostolic showed themselves in such a poor light as entirely to vindicate Gentili's opinion. At first they made no answer at all to Propaganda's request for names, for there was a terrible shortage of candidates and a high degree of animosity among the possible contenders. Bishop Briggs made out a list of possible names but, as the historian and priest John Lingard pointed out to him, drily: 'If your Lordship look over the list again you will find there is not one of the whole number of 15 against whom you do not make some objection, actual or implied.'[37]

Little Dr Weedall of Oscott was dismayed to be offered a bishopric. He dithered, he panicked. Eventually he went all the way to Rome to ask to be excused the appointment, and when he came back found that Nicholas Wiseman, the former Rector of the English College, had been installed in his place at Oscott, leaving Weedall with no job and nowhere to live. Not for nothing have these years been called 'the knock-about phase' of the Catholic revival, but its end was in sight.[38] Wiseman's arrival in England with a permanent post as Walsh's coadjutor in the Midlands and President of Oscott marked a turning point. He had no doubt of his mission. 'Never never did I waver,' he recalled, 'in my conviction that a new era had commenced in England.'[39] His attempt to make Oscott 'the rallying point of the yet silent but vast movement towards the Catholic church' began at eleven o'clock on the morning of 9 September, when he arrived at the college lodge (designed by Pugin) as Bishop of Melipotamus.[40]

Wiseman had been born in Seville in 1802 of Irish parents and had lived mostly on the Continent, but he had been educated in England and had visited several times since, making a considerable impression beyond the Catholic Church. He gave well-received lectures in London. He was co-founder and editor with Daniel O'Connell of the *Dublin Review* and he was a scholar and a brilliant linguist, a man to command respect. Newman and the Tractarians, if they mistrusted him, took him seriously. Wiseman was a long-standing friend of Rock and the Shrewsburys, sympathetic to their antiquarianism and to the Oxford Movement. He had considerable charm and humour and a flamboyant, highly emotional personality. His arrival was a great, if not for everyone a good moment. Wiseman gave the English Catholics an intellectual and social presence in national life, a sheer respectability that the somewhat motley clergy had hitherto largely lacked. His influence made Oscott a place that both Daniel O'Connell and Henri de Bourbon wanted to visit. But, as Mary Arundell pointed out tartly, 'with all his Hebrew and erudition' Wiseman knew little about the realities of English Catholic life, and what he knew came to him through the peculiar filter of the Shrewburys and their circle.[41] Wiseman's ambition was to make Catholicism part of the mainstream of English culture again. In the Tractarians, whom he was anxious to win over, he saw the making of a Catholic intelligentsia and in Pugin the man whose buildings would 'fix the decided transition from chapel to church architecture amongst us'.[42] At the same time he was in no doubt where his first loyalty lay. Whatever Wiseman failed to understand about England, he completely understood Rome. On the eve of his appointment he wrote to Rock setting out his position. He complained that Rock

spoke of the Pope merely as 'Patriarch of the West' and thought that no more authority should be allowed him than what was barely necessary for keeping up communion . . . such opinions if acted upon would lead directly to schism . . . I would rather see all the splendid cathedrals on earth levelled to the ground, than a jot or a tittle of Catholic truth allowed to pass away & I would rather hear the pure doctrines of the church preached in barns than dangerous theories or principles that would weaken unity preached under richly fretted and gilded vaults . . .[43]

Soon after he arrived at Oscott Wiseman had Pugin's vestments cut down to the size sanctioned by Rome.

The Shrewsburys now left Alton for Italy. In Paris they heard the news that had passed them on the road and been brought again from England. Their elder daughter Gwendalyn, Princess Borghese, was dead from a fever. She and her husband had been in England in September and had visited Pugin at home in Chelsea. Her death was a quite unexpected blow. Then, as her parents were preparing to go to Rome, more terrible news came to the Earl. Two of Gwendalyn's sons had also died, of measles. Rather than tell his wife straight away, he kept the disaster to himself while they were en route, bearing alone the double burden of grief and concealment. Pugin was 'distressed beyond measure' when he heard, especially having seen the young family so recently, 'all Life & gaity'.[44] He was almost equally distressed to learn that the Shrewsburys had changed their plans and decided now to remain in Italy, not returning as intended the following summer. It was a 'desperate disappointment'.[45] The loss of Shrewsbury's daily support and protection would leave Pugin vulnerable: 'pray do not abandon us who Look to you as the centre of the important Movement,' he wrote.[46] The sudden deaths, the absence of his patron, all reawoke Pugin's old fretful dread of accidents, his mother's nervous fears: 'For heavens sake my Lord be careful. I always live in fear of these winter expeditions. I think such a journey is attended with great danger when rivers are swollen and bridges carried away . . .'[47]

But the Shrewsburys kept to their plans and from now on, partly for reasons of economy, lived mainly abroad. Their absence and Wiseman's presence altered the complexion of English Catholic affairs.

*

Pugin was generally unsettled. In London the family's quarters were once again becoming too small. Plans were in hand to move to 42 Cheyne Walk, a 'small but comfortable house . . . facing the river', on which Pugin took a lease.[48] The move, however, was only completed the next spring. From the middle of November the family was at Ramsgate for the winter. Between lodgings there and two houses in London, with St Marie's Grange standing empty and unlet, it was not only a hectic but also a somewhat makeshift household. In December Pugin decided to sell St Marie's Grange.

That winter brought his first prolonged illness since childhood and a return of the eye trouble he had first suffered five years earlier. On 7 November he told Bloxam, 'you will be grieved to hear that my eyes are very bad. this is a dreadful calamity for me who cannot bear to Lose a moment – & who have so much to do – but I must hope for relief.'[49] Soon after that he was ill with what he described as 'rheumatic fever'. Rheumatic fever is a streptococcal infection, now rare, which then haunted the damp, riverside parts of towns causing swollen joints and sweats. The term was widely used for any kind of feverish illness and in Pugin's case it seems likely that there was another cause. The blindness and the bouts of fever from now on began to recur more often and more severely. His diary for the rest of November is just a list of weather. On 30 November Wiseman reported to Shrewsbury in Rome that Pugin was still 'laid up in bed . . . and perhaps will not be able to move for some time'.[50] In fact he was up and about again soon, too soon, in early December.

Wiseman, though concerned for Pugin's health, cannot have been entirely sorry he was *hors de combat*. He was looking critically at the interior of St Chad's as it neared completion. He thought the rood screen should be removed. 'I think it of the utmost importance to throw our ceremonies open to all,' he told Shrewsbury. 'In Catholic countries where the people have faith in the divine mysteries, and where they do not care about seeing, and where the choir is 100 feet long, it may do to screen it off. but here, and in a small chancel 30 feet long, the effect is one of concealment & separation to which neither catholics nor protestants have been accustomed.'[51] He was taken aback by the violent reaction to this suggestion, first from old Mr Hardman, who had given £500 for the screen, and then from Pugin, who wrote at once to say that if it was altered he would resign. Wiseman backed down but, as Pugin told Rock, 'it augurs badly for the future'.[52] Wiseman did not mean to hurt anyone's feelings but he was used to the modern Catholic churches of Italy, which had shallow chancels and no screens. They suited the post-Tridentine forms of worship of which Pugin at this stage knew nothing. Wiseman was apparently still unaware of the extent to which his English friends saw Catholicism as a pre-Tridentine, medieval tradition.[53] Screens were soon to become the symbol of division, not between priest and people, but between English Catholics and Ultramontanes, those who looked to Rome rather than to history and local tradition for their authority. The issue also divided high and low Anglicans and, more generally, as it still does, those for whom mystery and symbolism are essential elements of faith and those who see inclusiveness and clarity as the way forward for the Church.[54]

Pugin was utterly dejected and wrote to Phillipps: 'we nearly *stand alone* if we except the Oxford men, for among them I find full sympathy of feeling. But the real truth is the churches I build do little or no good for want of men who know how to use them . . .'[55] His despair, however, lifted as usual with the first gust of fair wind. He was already working, he told Bloxam, on 'some publications which I expect will produce a great sensation amongst us'.[56] A week after his despondent letter to Phillipps he wrote buoyantly to Shrewsbury, 'I feel quite well again & my eyes are better. I am going to make great exertions this spring.' Land for a new church had been bought at Nottingham and on 31 December he finished the drawings for St Giles's, Cheadle, 'the *first really* good thing I have done'.[57]

22

True Principles and Tract XC

1841

Everybody here is turning Puseyite. Having worn out my black
gown, I preach in my surplice; this is all the change I have
made, or mean to make.
  – Sydney Smith, Combe Florey, Somerset, 31 January 1841

The rest of the winter was spent at Ramsgate, where Pugin, having decided to sell St Marie's Grange, was now beginning to think of settling. The town had altered in the seven years since he had first brought Louisa to live at St Lawrence. The streets were paved and lit by gas and there was a new Town Hall. The elegant Georgian resort Selina Welby had known, with its stucco-fronted Royal Crescent and one handsome, if wildly 'incorrect' Commissioners' Gothic church, was giving way to a brisk Victorian town. Chapels and meeting houses sprang up to cater for the nonconformists and with urban growth came urban troubles. There were more back streets and in them more poverty and more crime. The seaside towns were growing as fast as the industrial cities, and in both the expanding population was made up mostly of working people attracted by the prospect of employment. They were Low Church in religion, for reform in politics and for town against land. Pugin thought Thanet a 'most baren spot for Catholic ideas in these days'.[1]

The local luminaries were professional men whose churchmanship was low to middle, men like Lieutenant Hutchinson, an Evangelical Anglican who would do everything he could, just short of vandalism, to thwart Pugin, and Thomas Whitehead, proprietor of a respected boys' school, Chatham House Academy. Whitehead lectured Pugin one evening on the evils of Catholicism and the Oxford Movement and the virtues of '*Glorious Queen Bess*'.[2] Pugin was, for once, silenced.

'Argument with such a person was out of the question,' he told Bloxam. He was shocked that a man 'who I certainly regard as a blasphemer against the holy Ghost' should be 'considered the oracle of the place & *associate of the Clergy*'.[3] But so it was. Pugin was to find life at Ramsgate fraught with difficulties of the kind that his encounter with Mr Whitehead portended.

For the present, however, he settled down, in the lodgings in the Plains of Waterloo, to work on the publications he had told Bloxam would make such a 'sensation'. In the first six weeks of 1841 he all but completed a long article and a book. These, along with *Contrasts*, which he now substantially revised, were to be his most influential and enduring works. They were the publications that ensured his reputation at the time and were the basis on which his later fame, albeit sometimes questionably, rested. Pugin's great burst of literary energy was, in large measure, the reason why George Gilbert Scott remembered 1841 as the time of his own and many others' professional call to arms, the moment when Pugin opened the eyes of the rising generation and architecture was 'morally awakened'.[4] Scott felt that until then he had been sleepwalking through his daily round of uninspiring contract work and recalled that he was excited 'almost to a fury' by what he read, 'like a person awakened from a long feverish dream, which had rendered him unconscious of what was going on about him'.[5] The article that most struck Scott appeared in Wiseman's *Dublin Review*. It was presented under the heading: 'Elevation of the Cathedral Church of St Chad, Birmingham. By A. W. Pugin London: 1840'. In fact there was no picture and scarcely any mention of St Chad's, whose Germanic style was now a source of embarrassment to Pugin. The subject was the English parish church, illustrated entirely with examples of his own work.

The parish church happened to be the subject most on Pugin's mind as he planned Cheadle, but it was on many other minds too, Anglican as well as Catholic. The Established Church, as it endeavoured to maintain its authority, knew that the parishes were of the essence. It was there that the issues raised by the Tractarians were being fought out until even a sceptical Whig like Sydney Smith was obliged to take notice. It was there that the effectiveness of religion as a social force was on trial. All could agree with Pugin that 'It is, in fact, by parish churches, that the faith of a nation is to be sustained and nourished.'[6] Thanks to the efforts of the Commissioners in the expanding cities, many new churches and new parishes were appearing, but by now the very motley design of the buildings and their uneven quality were causing increasing dissatisfaction. The more people became aware of the efforts of the Cambridge Camden Society and the more they considered the state of the Church of England, the more critically they looked at new churches. It was not good enough any more, indeed it was scarcely decent, to have a square preaching box with a few plaster crockets on it. Pugin's article dealt with every element of church building, from siting, to interior decoration, from tower to altar to font, describing the ritual significance and proper form for each. It offered plans and sections, and other forms of 'reality', and it held out also, as a backdrop to all of this, a vision of England full of associative resonance, 'the venerable yew trees, the old grey towers' and the sweet melancholy of chancels lit by stained glass, a fusion of the mystical and the natural, a sacred Picturesque.[7]

For many readers, especially architects, the greatest impact came from the plates, which were almost instantly taken up and copied. These showed the churches with which Pugin was most satisfied. Cheadle and St George's, Southwark, took pride of place. Keighley and Southport were also shown as examples of the modest single vessel design, an honourable way of working with a small budget to stave off what Scott called 'cheap church mania'.[8] They were the first pictures of what became the Victorian church, modelled on an idealized past, entirely of its own time. A comparison with the illustrations in the survey of new churches in the *British Critic* which had prompted Pugin's own essay shows what a leap in conceptual sophistication he had achieved. His *Dublin Review* woodcuts are of solid complex buildings, their forms possessed of a sculptural integrity. Those in the *British Critic* are toy-like and incoherent. Pugin's interiors were visions of harmony, the details in proportion and 'correct'. The piers have mass, the windows depth, the roofs solidity. From the outside these buildings with their little bellcotes or solemn broach spires sang out their architectural and religious credo. Nobody, not even Pugin, doubted it was his drawings rather than the buildings they represented that made the impact. Of those illustrated, Cheadle and Southwark were scarcely begun. St Oswald's and St Wilfred's, Warwick Bridge, were not finished. Macclesfield would never have its spire and Stockton would never progress beyond the nave. Keighley appeared as it would have looked had the belfry not fallen down.

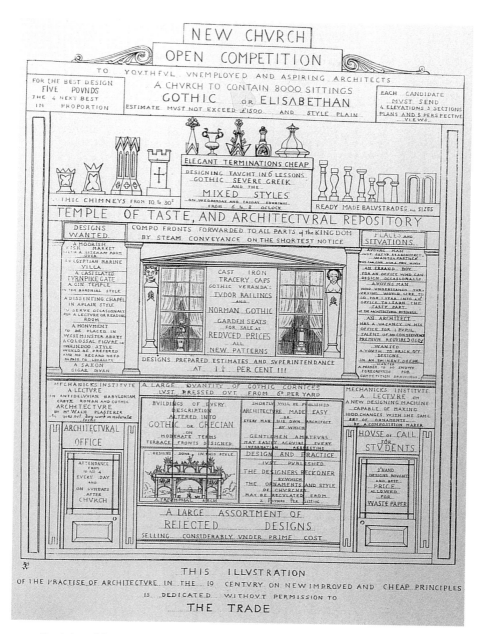

15. Pugin's reckless satire on modern architecture opened his manifesto *Contrasts* in 1836 and ensured that before his career had even begun he was *persona non grata* with the profession. John Nash, the leading architect of the Regency, is set up as a bust in a shop window, a glazing bar running impudently through his nose.

16. (*left*) 'St Edmund's Procession', from the Ideal Scheme of 1832, *The Shrine*. In the aftermath of his first wife's death Pugin made several fantastic sequences of drawings in which Gothic architecture revived and was restored and inhabited.

17. (*below*) St Marie's College, a scheme of 1834, is full of details like those Pugin provided for Charles Barry's competition entry for the Palace of Westminster. It was the basis of the claims made after Pugin's death by his son Edward that Pugin was the true architect of the building.

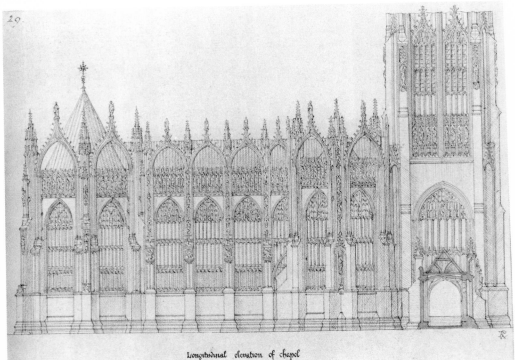

Longitudinal elevation of chapel

18. (*above left*) John Hardman, Pugin's closest friend and collaborator.

19. (*above right*) George Myers, Pugin's phlegmatic, loyal builder.

20. (*below left*) Ambrose Phillipps – Eustace de Lyle in Disraeli's *Coningsby*
– a leading figure among the Romantic Catholics.

21. (*below right*) John Talbot, 16th Earl of Shrewsbury, Pugin's greatest patron, in a
lithograph from a painting by Carl Blaas.

22. and 23. St Mary's, Derby, was Pugin's first major church, designed in 1838 when his taste was still for late English and German Gothic.

Only Southport and Uttoxeter, two very modest churches, bore a close resemblance in 1841 to their portraits.

The second of the publications completed that month became, with *Contrasts*, Pugin's most famous. This was the work 'on the Principles of Design in Catholic Architecture' in which, Pugin promised Bloxam, 'I shall be able to prove the transcendant merit of the antient architects & at the same time set forth the fundmental errors of modern buildings'.[9] The text comprised two of Pugin's Oscott lectures and appeared in a single volume, as *The True Principles of Pointed or Christian Architecture*. In *True Principles* Pugin moved beyond architecture into an account of what Gothic meant as a total system of design. He showed how it could be applied on any scale, in any medium and to every artefact from a cathedral to a curtain rail. This newness, of course, was presented entirely in terms of its opposite, conformity to pre-existing and immutable laws. The title page showed Pugin as a medieval architect at work in a panelled room and the prospectus explained that

Hitherto architectural criticism has been little more than mere capricious opinion, and few persons could give a satisfactory reason for their approval or dislike of a Building. The laws of Architectural Composition are based on equally sound principles as those of Harmony or Grammar, and that they can be violated with greater impunity is simply owing to their being less understood. It is humbly hoped that this Work, which is the result of long experience and patient research, will supply in a great measure the want of *sound information*.[10]

The prospectus offered six guiding principles. The book itself, which was neither as objective as was promised nor at all humble, opened with two: '1st, that there should be no features about a building which are not necessary for convenience, construction, or propriety; 2nd, that all ornament should consist of enrichment of the essential construction of the building.' 'Strange as it may appear at first sight,' Pugin continued, 'it is in pointed architecture alone that these great principles have been carried out.'[11] Pugin began with architecture, showing how in a classical building construction was concealed, buttresses hidden behind parapets, and domes within domes. He was particularly savage about Wren's St Paul's, 'in the revived Pagan style' with its 'fictitious dome'.[12] '*The dome that is seen* is not *the dome of the church*, but a mere construction for effect.'[13] 'Modern pointed buildings' also came under fire.[14] It is hard not to think that Pugin had Barry's new Palace of Westminster in mind when he wrote that 'many architects apply the details and minor features of the pointed style to classic masses and arrangements; they adhere scrupulously to the regularity and symmetry of the latter, while they attempt to disguise it by the mouldings and accessories of the former. They must have two of every thing, one on each side ... What can be more absurd?'[15]

Always more convincing on the attack than the defence, when Pugin came to establish his claims for the purely functional nature of Gothic he invoked a highly elastic idea of 'function', which stretched to include metaphor. In defending crockets and pinnacles, features which he supposed were generally 'considered as mere ornamental excrescences, introduced solely for picturesque effect', he explained that they 'should be regarded as answering a double intention, both mystical and natural'.[16] Mystically, by pointing upwards, they symbolized the Resurrection, practically they served as an 'upper weathering' to throw off rain. As in his *Dublin Review* article Pugin was appealing as much to the romantic, picturesque power of association as to history or practicality. Rain and resurrection in the English countryside meant as much to him as function and constructive principle. *True Principles* was a plea to preserve the landscape as well as to reform church building: 'England is rapidly losing its venerable garb,' he lamented, as Payne Knight had, 'all places are becoming alike ... Factory chimneys disfigure our most beautiful vales.'[17]

Despite the palpable effort to organize his thoughts, *True Principles* proceeded like all his writings by way of a number of digressions and numerous long footnotes. Pugin proposed in the first lecture to discuss construction in three media: stone, metalwork and wood. As he went on, however, although he still talked only of history and authority, the discussion became increasingly involved with practical matters of design. Of the jointing of stone, he noted that 'Large stones destroy proportion', while the positioning of mouldings must be considered 'with relation to the eye of the spectator'.[18] His study of the effects of light, form and distance was pure Picturesque in its methods, and for all the inconsistencies in his argument the aesthetic he was advocating was now clear, though rather more so from the illustrations than the text. Keeping hold of the idea of function, however defined, and the intrinsic qualities of materials, denouncing stucco, blind windows, false fronts and all other such artifices as unreal 'deceptions', Pugin was producing designs both for architecture and the applied arts, hinges, textiles, tiles and firedogs, which, while taken directly from medieval models, looked, *in toto*, quite different from anything that had gone before.

In his theories, as in his practice, Pugin considered nothing too big or too small to attempt. He discussed at one extreme the highest form of architecture, which was of course church-building. This should be done without extravagance or pretension but soberly and if necessary in stages, an argument that was likely to appeal to the young architects among his readers more than to a building committee: 'Let every man build to God according to his means, but not practise showy deceptions; better is it to do a little substantially and consistently with truth, than to produce a great but fictitious effect. Hence the rubble wall and oaken rafter of antiquity yet impress the mind with feelings of reverent awe, which never could be produced by the cement and plaster imitations of elaborate tracery and florid designs which in these times are stuck about mimic churches in disgusting profusion.'[19] While at the other end of the scale: 'To arrange curtains consistently with true taste, their use and intention should always be considered: they are suspended across windows and other openings to exclude cold and wind, and as they are not always required to be drawn, they are hung to rings sliding on rods . . . Hence all the modern plans of suspending enormous folds of stuff over poles, as if for the purpose of sale or of being dried, is quite contrary to the use and intentions of curtains, and abominable in taste; and the only object that these endless festoons and bunchy tassels can answer is to swell the bills and profits of the upholsterers . . .'[20] Pugin illustrated each point with examples of upholstery, tiles, hinges, parts of a panelled room. To forget, as far as possible, the rest of Victorian design and look at Pugin's illustrations as Scott saw them, against the faded fussiness of the Regency, is to see how fresh and dignified they looked in 1841. They had the qualities the younger generation longed for: 'repose, solidity, space'.[21]

True Principles, like all Pugin's writings, was laced with satire. There were cartoons of overblown pelmets and the products of 'those inexhaustible mines of bad taste, Birmingham and Sheffield', crocketed oil lamps, fire screens in the shape of an Eleanor cross and fire irons very like the ones his father had designed for Ackermann's *Repository*, 'the fender . . . a sort of embattled parapet, with a lodge-gate at each end; the end of the poker is a sharp pointed finial; and at the summit of the tongs is a saint'.[22] 'Neither relative scale, form, purpose, nor unity of style, is ever considered by those who design these abominations; if they only introduce a quatrefoil or an acute arch, be the outline and style of the article ever so modern and debased, it is at once denominated and sold as Gothic.'[23] Pugin had to admit that at Windsor 'he perpetrated many of these enormities' himself, but 'At that time I had not the least idea of the principles I am now explaining.'[24] He drew a fashionable modern castle, its turrets smoking chimneys, which had a conservatory at the side making it literally and hence architecturally indefensible: *the external and internal appearance of an edifice should be illustrative of, and in accordance with, the purpose for which it is destined.*[25] All the 'unrealities' of the Georgians were held up to ridicule, the optical illusions portrayed as moral delusions.

In the critical energy of its humour *True Principles* caught exactly the young Victorians' idea of amusement, which was more cerebral and decorous than their parents'. This was the year that the Vauxhall Gardens closed and *Punch* magazine first appeared. Young men like Scott and William Butterfield, Pugin's contemporaries in age but his successors in practice, saw, in *True Principles* and the *Dublin Review* article, how their earnest but laborious study of medieval buildings, the measured drawings, the tables 'showing the duration of the styles', could be animated and turned into something new and serious for the nineteenth century. 'A new phase had come over me,' Scott wrote. 'I was in fact a new man.'[26] Scott had begun his career, like many of his generation, designing the workhouses required by the controversial Poor Law. Suddenly he saw a 'truer sense of the dignity' of architecture as a social, spiritual force.[27] Butterfield designed his first church within months of *True Principles* appearing, the masonry round the windows jointed as Pugin illustrated.[28] Charles Eastlake, writing a generation later, remarked that *True Principles* had 'passed almost into a proverb' among Gothic architects.[29] Short as the book is, and light on practical information, the brevity, the humour and the pictures ensured that while young men pored doggedly over details of contracts and quantities, it was Pugin who went into the bloodstream.

The theoretical arguments in *True Principles* were not new, any more than the historical ideas in *Contrasts* had been. It was their application that was original. Despite this, 'much of twentieth-century Functionalism' has been seen in *True Principles* and its opening statements have been said to constitute 'the core of Pugin's long-term significance as a theorist'.[30] His first principle was a version of Vitruvius's 'firmness, commodity, delight', which Pugin passed on to his students at Oscott as he had learned it from his father. It is the second, that decoration should be secondary to construction, that has been made to bear the burden of Pugin's quondam status as a protofunctionalist. Yet this was also little more than a truism. John Nash had said the same thing before Pugin was born and many had said it since. Nor was Pugin, in applying this idea specifically to Gothic architecture, introducing the theories of the French rationalists to England. It is most unlikely that he knew them. If he had a French source it was more probably Victor Hugo's *Notre Dame*, in which the same point is made, than Laugier.[31] But neither is necessary. By 1841 it was a long time since anybody had seriously thought that medieval architecture was irrational, that Gothic buildings were 'wonders unknown to rule' raised only by 'inspiration'.[32] It would be possible, if tedious, to give many examples going back to the early nineteenth century, but one telling instance is in the works of the Cambridge historian Robert Willis, a founding vice-president of the Camden Society. Willis had written six years earlier, without any suggestion that he was breaking entirely new ground, that:

The Romans attempted concealment, and hence introduced discordance between the decoration and the mechanism of the structure. The Gothic builders in later times more wisely adapted their decoration to the exact direction of the resisting forces required by the vaulted structure.[33]

In 1840 Alfred Bartholomew's *Specifications for Practical Architecture* had rehearsed the same argument, and Pugin was later accused of plagiarizing Bartholomew.[34] Nobody, reading *True Principles* in 1841, thought the theory itself very remarkable, except for its exclusive advocacy of Gothic. In his thinking in fact Pugin was rather backward, as Mozley had made him realize. It was in his application of his ideas as an architect and designer, as a satirist, polemicist and romantic Christian visionary, that Pugin inspired his age. He brought the English antiquarian tradition into practical architecture and thus transformed it, but purely as a theorist he has no 'long-term significance' at all.

After a brief trip to London at the end of January, Pugin went back to Ramsgate. Against a background of spectacular winter weather, heavy gales and one day a scene from Coleridge, a 'brig encased with ice', he went on with his third new work, a revised edition of *Contrasts*.[35] Being a second edition, though it sold well, it attracted few reviews, which was, perhaps, fortunate. As the critic in the new Catholic newspaper, the *Tablet*, felt obliged to point out, there was 'more than the usual amount of variation from a first to a second edition'.[36] In fact Pugin substantially contradicted what he had written in 1836. His new text took full account of 'revived paganism', as he called the Renaissance, and argued that the English Reformation did not destroy Gothic but was itself the result of a general decline in faith. Thus he adjusted his theories to what he had already accepted in his practice, the general antiquarian view later known as the 'biological fallacy', that Gothic had blossomed and flourished and then declined, like a living thing. Pugin accommodated his dislike of the modern Catholic Church and his new-found warmth towards the Tractarians by explaining that the critical distinction was not between Catholics and Protestants but between 'the ancient spirit and the modern practice of Catholicism'.[37] *Contrasts* now came to quite a different 'Conclusion', namely that it was a good thing the Catholics had lost the churches at the Reformation or, instead of being merely neglected, they would have been ruined: 'we might have had the lantern at Ely terminated by a miniature dome.'[38]

The most important addition to *Contrasts* was a pair of plates. One showed 'Contrasted Residences for the Poor'; the other, illustrating Montalembert's essay 'De l'attitude actuelle du vandalisme en France', which Pugin reprinted as an appendix, showed 'Contrasted Towns'. These plates made an argument more powerful than Pugin could ever make in words, setting out, better than any other contemporary images, the Condition of England question. The town of 1440 is set on a river, bounded by protective walls. Beyond them lie fields, an abbey, a half-timbered inn and a chapel. It is a fertile, hospitable landscape. In 1840 the town has lost its walls and burst its bounds. Wharves and warehouses line the river; chimneys, bottle kilns, gasworks and ruined spires like broken teeth make up the skyline. The legend lists the chapels of the multiplying religious sects. The forefront is dominated by a panopticon prison.

The other plate, 'Contrasted Residences for the Poor' made Pugin's contribution to the battle against the Poor Law. In the early months of 1841 *The Times* waged a concentrated campaign against the abuses of the workhouse, the flogging of girls, the separation of husbands and wives, and the fact that convicted prisoners were better fed than the paupers. Pugin depicted all this, although he (or his publisher) removed the image of a bare-breasted woman being beaten. The modern workhouse is another panopticon. Beside it the 'Antient Poor House' is a medieval hospital such as Pugin himself was building at Alton. Here the argument through architecture required no special pleading or selective quotation, it drove straight to the point. The panopticon was the built expression of one view of the human condition, the utilitarian, materialist view; the medieval hospital, with its large kitchen, its chapel and neat vegetable gardens, the conscious expression of another, that man should not live by bread alone, that the spirit should be fed and social and family ties preserved. Pugin, like his mother, had become a Radical conservative. He was not alone. The *British Critic*, which had also just carried an article on 'Ancient and Modern Ways of Charity', pointed out how close the Tractarians too now were, despite their horror of 'liberalism', to the Radicals. 'Philosophically speaking,' it noted, 'there is but a single step between catholicism and revolution.'[39]

With *Contrasts* nearly finished, Pugin set off on a round of visits. He went to Oxford, where Tom Mozley's brother James, who took to Pugin, found him 'infinitely amusing, in his peculiar way'.[40] His talk was torrential: 'From six o'clock to eleven on Saturday he was on the move, never stopping, and when he left off he was quite the same as he was when he began.'[41] Mozley introduced Pugin to Newman and thought him somewhat subdued during the encounter, but Newman (who had nothing to compare with) found him an 'immense talker'.[42] Newman was, from the beginning, at best ambivalent to Pugin, whose earthy language, emotionalism and lack of social polish grated on his more refined sensibility. At times both the man and his art would overwhelm Newman's reserve, but not often. He said he 'could not help' liking him, but described him to Tom Mozley as Gerard Manley Hopkins might have done: 'rough tongue-free unselfgoverned'.[43]

The mood at Oxford now was ever more volatile. Overtures to and from Catholics were increasing. Bloxam and Phillipps were in correspondence. Phillipps published a letter in the *Tablet* putting the case for reunion. 'Take the Church of England as her canons and her liturgy testify her to be, and I declare that the chasm which separates her from the Catholic Church is but small.'[44] It was not an isolated or extreme view just then. Gladstone thought it a 'beautiful letter'.[45] Within a fortnight of Pugin's visit the tensions reached a crisis with the publication of Tract XC. The Tract, of which Newman soon acknowledged authorship, took a view close to Phillipps's. It argued that the Thirty-Nine Articles, to which all members of the Church of England must subscribe, were compatible with the Catholic faith. It was a watershed and the last of the *Tracts for the Times*. The university condemned it. Phillipps wrote excitedly to Montalembert that 'never was there a more interesting moment . . . in the whole history of the church of God', and the unhappy Bishop of Oxford was forced to agree.[46] 'Never since the Reformation has there been such a crisis of danger to the church,' Bagot wrote miserably, 'and the peace and unity of the Church may, and I fear does much depend upon the course of so humble an individual as myself – who took this diocese solely from its smallness, quietness, and the little anxiety it need give one.'[47] Pugin naturally was thrilled with the uproar. 'The prospect at Oxford is most glorious,' he told Shrewsbury.[48]

At the beginning of March Pugin and his family left Ramsgate for London, where they cleared out their lodgings at Church Row and settled into their new house. Cheyne Walk was, as the Scottish writer David Masson observed, 'a quaint riverside street of shops and antique houses, looking down upon the unembanked shore – pleasant enough . . . when the stream was full, but not so pleasant when the low tide left its margin of mud and ooze'.[49] The Pugins' house was the middle of a terrace of three, facing the river, 'set back with small gardens in front'.[50] It seems to have suited them, although in the 1840s, when the Thames served as an open sewer and the 'mud' was noxious as well as odorous, it was not an entirely healthy situation. Almost as soon as they had moved in, Pugin was off again to look at work in progress at Alton, Cheadle and Birmingham and to see Wiseman at Oscott. Until June, when he was in London for a fortnight, he was travelling almost constantly, spending only sixteen nights at home in ten weeks.

His travels were facilitated by the ever-expanding railways. These were not an evil of the modern world for Pugin. Significantly there was no station in the 'Town of 1840'. The Great Western opened all the way to Bristol that summer, the Manchester and Leeds at the beginning of March and the Great North of England between York and Darlington at the beginning of the year. Within months Pugin had travelled on them all. It was not only Ferrey who thought of Pugin himself in these years as a kind of machine. Hardman's nephew, John Hardman Powell, saw him for the first time about now, in Birmingham. Not knowing who he was, Powell observed a man whose appearance was 'very like that of a sailor', running down the street towards him, his lips 'moving rapidly in talk to himself' as he shot past. 'There was no time to notice more before he was gone . . . The impression left upon my mind was as if a fire engine had passed me.'[51]

As he hurtled to and fro, Pugin was taking on new commissions, most of them small. At Cambridge a site was bought, against fierce local opposition, for a Catholic church to be built the next year, but there were scant opportunities to realize his vision of the ideal English parish church on any scale. Pugin's ideas were now developing very fast, giving rise constantly to new and prescient designs, few of which, for one reason or another, attracted much attention. In April he went down to Spetchley in Worcestershire to set out the ground for a charity school for a local Catholic landowner. Like the Oscott furniture, this was an obscure masterpiece, a prophetic little piece of design, destined to bloom unseen, for it was never published and its location is remote. The village school became one of the most characteristic features of the Victorian landscape, but in 1841 it had no particular architectural identity. At Spetchley, where a schoolmaster's house was required in the same build-ing as the school itself, Pugin allowed the elevation to arise from the plan. It became an H shape with the two-storey house in one arm, the double height schoolroom in the other and a linking single-storey wing. Set on a slight rise at an angle to the road, the red-brick building with its wasp-waisted bell turret in one angle looks too typical now to be remarkable, yet it was the first of its type.

At Handsworth he furnished the convent simply with 'nothing', he thought, 'to merit particular notice'.[52] Yet Catherine McAuley's descrip-tion of the interiors gives a startlingly clear view through from *True Principles* to the later nineteenth century: 'Mr Pugin would not permit cloth of any kind in the rooms – rush chairs, oak tables – but all is so admirable . . . no want can be felt.'[53] The spare furnishings, the swept floor, the natural materials, are the Arts and Crafts interior in embryo. In this case Pugin himself thought too little of what seemed an obvious solution to a simple problem to draw any attention to it.

Architecturally he was learning to think, increasingly, in three dimensions. He had begun by trying to build his drawings. Now he thought more of architectural form. He began to realize, too, that a church need not be symmetrical. In his description of his church of St Wilfred's at Hulme, near Manchester, in the *Dublin Review*, he started by excusing its asymmetry, the tower placed to one side instead of centrally, as a necessity of the site, but as he wrote he changed his mind.

... this expedient is usually resorted to in churches built in towns and confined situations, where there would not be sufficient space for a tower to project at the western end ... To those whose ideas of architectural beauty are formed on the two and two system of modern building, this argument will appear very singular; but building for the sake of uniformity never entered into the ideas of the ancient designers; they regulated their plans and designs by localities and circumstances ... To this we owe all the picturesque effect of the old buildings: there is nothing artificial about them ... One of the greatest beauties of the ancient churches is this variety.[54]

Asymmetry had gone in the space of a page from an occasional permitted expedient to a great beauty. The change was typical of the way Pugin worked, thinking as he wrote and developing his buildings in dialogue with his theories rather than theorizing first and building afterwards. From now on he developed the possibilities of this idea, first of all in two small churches, the Jesus Chapel near Pontefract and St Augustine's, Kenilworth. Both, like Spetchley, were private commissions for old Catholic families, the Tempests and the Amhersts. There were no 'Romanizing' ideas or building committees to deal with and the commissions went well. Materials also interested him more and more. In Ireland, where local stone was cheap and the masons skilled, he was learning a great deal. That year he made the drawings for a convent at Waterford, one of his best buildings and one of the few, at the time of writing, to survive intact. The stone is pale gold uncut rubble, laid with the intuitive logic of craftsmen, with a natural beauty of form and texture. From now on Pugin began to consider increasingly the properties of different stones, of flint, granite and rubble. He began also to want an ever greater solidity of outline in his buildings, a tough, more muscular bulk. He got a chance that year to try out several of his new enthusiasms in a group of farm buildings in Surrey commissioned by the young Viscount Midleton, his first Anglican patron. Midleton was a member of the Cambridge Camden Society, rich and sympathetic. On his land at Peper Harow near Godalming Pugin designed a barn, a gatehouse and a well. There was enough money for the job, indeed the barn is more solidly built than many of Pugin's churches and the gatehouse is vaulted in stone. As a group, these buildings allowed him to push further the idea of the modern Picturesque that he had begun to develop at St John's Hospital, with trees carefully chosen and planted to enhance the scene. The buildings themselves are rugged, practical and 'real'.

Since the beginning of the year he had paid about a dozen visits to Birmingham, where work was going ahead steadily and the opening of St Chad's was fixed for June. Wiseman was conscious of the importance, at this moment in the tide of religious affairs, of having the first Catholic cathedral since the Reformation – a cathedral in all but name and often referred to as such, although until the restoration of English bishoprics it remained, technically, a church – opened with great éclat and in use as a national focus of Catholic life and worship. He was also changing his mind about screens, perhaps because he was getting to know the Tractarians and to understand the English Catholic tradition to which they appealed. He was now prepared to wear the Gothic vestments and what Pugin deemed 'a proper Mitre'.[55] The consecration, which had been 'so long and so anxiously looked forward to by the Catholics of the British empire', began on Saturday the 19th, with a fast.[56] The ceremonial continued for five days and was full of echoes of medieval Christianity. The relics of St Chad were brought from Oscott to the cathedral, encased in a jewelled shrine designed by Pugin. They were accompanied by Bishop Walsh. At the door of the cathedral he was greeted by the elder John Hardman, who surrendered, on behalf of himself and the other donors, all that they had given for the building. Walsh replied with a blessing and at that moment 'the great doors of the church were . . . thrown open', the choir sang out and, for the first time, the deep bells began to ring as the shrine was slowly carried on the shoulders of four priests to the Lady Chapel. There it was set amid candles and 'venerated like the ark of old' by members of the Guild of St Chad, who kept watch over it all night.[57] The occasion was attended by thirteen bishops, including representatives of America and Australia. The cathedral's own clergy wore Pugin's vestments of cloth of gold and the altar frontal, 'worth three hundred pounds', was of the same stuff, a gift from the Earl of Shrewsbury.[58] After the sacred part of the proceedings was completed with High Mass on the Wednesday there followed a grand dinner in Hansom and Welch's severely neo-classical Town Hall. Pugin disliked these occasions, the descent from the sublime of the Mass to the banal of Victorian civic life, the earnestly applauded toasts, and the 'sumptuous repast, supplied by Mr Lisseter, of New-street, in his usual complete and excellent style'.[59] On this occasion he was too over-wrought to do more than acknowledge the thanks of the company and was, the *Orthodox Journal* regretted to observe, 'evidently labouring ... under indisposition, produced by his unceasing mental and bodily labour'.[60] The words suggest more than tiredness. As the pressure of work increased and his health was undermined by recurring bouts of fever, he was more frequently reported, or reported himself, over-whelmed by emotion, prone to bursts of uncontrollable excitement and fits of abandoned weeping.

At the consecration the changing complexion of the English Catholic community was evident. Shrewsbury's absence in Italy was from now on to be more frequent, as was the presence of the Tractarians, rep-resented at the ceremony by young Bernard Smith, a recently ordained clergyman and a new friend of Pugin. Equally indicative was the fact that, despite fears of disruption from anti-papists, the only significant trouble was created by a Catholic priest, Thomas McDonnell. McDon-nell had been the incumbent of the nearby St Peter's chapel for ten years and he hated the new St Chad's. Wiseman had tried to dismiss him but McDonnell, infuriated, refused to be treated like 'a head of cattle or a ninepin' by this 'celebrated personage, this polyglot prelate, this acquain-tance of the learned'.[61] He advertised a bazaar, as a rival attraction to keep people away from the opening of the new cathedral. Having been prevented from holding it, he turned up at the dinner and made a scene.

While the celebrations and the attendant disruptions were going ahead, Pugin noted in his diary: 'Salisbury sold.'[62] St Marie's Grange, his first house, his first complete building, one of the most interesting houses in the history of English architecture, had been put up for auction. Most ignominiously it was bought by Mr Staples, the original owner of the land, for a mere £500, a quarter, perhaps, of what it had cost. In July *True Principles* appeared. It did not create the *succès de scandale* of *Contrasts*, although it was reviewed more quickly. Opinion divided along predictable lines. The *Tablet* admired it hugely. The *Christian Remembrancer* thought it 'utterly preposterous'.[63] Those who criticized it found it variously too Gothic, or too Catholic, or that its supposed arguments were mere assertions.

The summer brought a general election that saw the Whigs heavily defeated. So ended the government that had brought in the reforms of the 1830s, the government that, but for a few months, had been in power all Pugin's adult life. The new regime, under the prime minister Phillipps called 'expediency Peel!', held no brief for the Catholic cause. The new Parliament, however, marked the birth of Young England. Three young men who had been friends at Eton and Cambridge, George Smythe, Alexander Baillie Cochrane and Lord John Manners, all took their seats that year. They and a few others (including Phillipps) were transformed by the wizardry of Disraeli's rhetoric into a movement: 'a picturesque episode in the history of political ideas'.[64] They were all High Church men, and Cochrane and Manners, who had pledged themselves to the revival of ancient chivalric ideals in 1838, had become members of the Cambridge Camden Society and admirers of Pugin. Now there was within Parliament, as at Oxford, a significant sympathy for the English Catholic ideal. Wiseman was encouraged. Phillipps had made his first visit to Oxford in April and was also encouraged. Pugin, typically, thought the matter as good as settled and formal reunion of the English Church with the wider Catholic communion a certainty. Shrewsbury, on the Continent, took a longer view.

At the end of July Pugin set off to meet his patron, who had summoned him to Spa in Belgium. There they spent three days together in unseasonably stormy weather discussing, as the gales battered the woods, the work in progress at Alton and Cheadle. The pattern of their exchanges was by now established, with Shrewsbury suggesting savings here and there, Pugin pointing out why such economies were false. They talked, too, about a new church to be built at Nottingham – where Edward Willson's brother Robert was the priest – on land bought the year before. This was to be Pugin's third cathedral, St Barnabas's, a very different building from his first and different indeed from the long, low and extremely modest design that Shrewsbury thought had been agreed when Pugin left Spa for Antwerp at the start of his usual summer tour. Writing, on his return, to Shrewsbury, Pugin allowed Louisa, now about six months into her fourth pregnancy, to make one of her tantalizing, brief appearances in her husband's correspondence. As usual she is too cloaked in convention to be distinctly visible. Pugin merely passed on her 'grateful acknowledgements' for Lady Shrewsbury's 'kind presents' with which she was 'quite deligted'.[65] The social status of the architect's wife, like the artist's, was lower than that of her husband. He might, on the strength of his profession, gain entry to the highest circles, but the same invitations would not usually extend to her. Lady Shrewsbury's gifts, like the visit of the Prince and Princess Borghese to Chelsea, suggest the degree to which Louisa was acknowledged and, from the fact that she seems never to have come to Alton as a guest, the limits of the Shrewsburys' condescension.

The Earl meanwhile had been thinking over the design for Cheadle and had some alterations to suggest: less stained glass to make the interior lighter, pews – or benches as he called them – instead of chairs and an organ gallery across the west window. Pugin was aghast. Shrewsbury (whose loose grasp of church architecture led him to refer to the aisles as 'corridors') was proposing to ruin the design. Pugin sent back a plea from the heart: 'pray give me scope this once my own way that is the (old way) & if I do not suceed I will resign for ever'.[66] The Earl gave in. When Cheadle was finished there would be, Pugin realized, a much larger body of informed opinion to assess it than there had been at Derby. The Cambridge Camden Society was gathering members and publishing numerous well-informed leaflets. Pugin was as impressed now by the Camden men in their way as by the Tractarians. The Society's 'A Few Words to Churchwardens', which Pugin thought 'the best Pamphlet they have yet issued', went through eight editions in 1841.[67] It explained the 'correct', that is the historical, arrangement for a church and denounced utterly the Georgianisms of galleries and box pews. The Ecclesiologists were men of many 'Few Words', all of them dogmatic. Churchwardens, clergy, young enthusiasts of all sorts and both sexes read them ever more eagerly. 'Taking' or surveying medieval churches was becoming a popular pastime, with the help of the forms that the Society sent out along with an 'orientator', for finding true East. By 1841 a kind of ecclesiastical mass observation was under way. More than 150 churches were surveyed in the Society's first year and the new science – there was much insistence on its being a science – of 'ecclesiology' was catching on all over England.

Pugin was in Leicestershire in August when he noted in his diary, 'eyes bad', but he went on to Leadenham in Lincolnshire to visit Bernard Smith, who was the priest there. He arrived back in London 'almost blind' and 'very ill'.[68] The autumn brought a recurrence of the fever. In order, it was said, to save the sight in his right eye he was given a high dose of mercury, '3 grains . . . every four hours for *some time*'.[69] Mercury is an effective anti-inflammatory whose catastrophic side-effects were only partially understood in the 1840s. It was prescribed for many conditions, but most often for syphilis. Pugin was bled and blistered, which was thought to provide a counter-irritant. The treatment left him 'very feeble', his teeth felt loose, his face was 'covered with Leech wounds Blister scars etc.'.[70] Despite this, only a week after he had got out of bed he was off. At the end of September, taking medicine to counteract the mercury, he still had severe pains in all his limbs and was in dread of a relapse. He resolved to 'Lay by During the whole winter at home', despite Shrewsbury's invitation to Rome.[71] As usual, however, necessity was bent to his own will to work. Shrewsbury's offer was declined in a letter written not from home but from Alton, where Pugin had arrived having left London a week before. He continued on a tour of work at Scarisbrick, Liverpool, Kenilworth and as far north as Scarborough, not reaching home until mid October. At such a pace it was impossible that he should fully recover his health. Nor was home especially healthy. There was no decampment to Ramsgate this year and Chelsea, in a winter of storms and floods that brought the filthy river up over the road, was far from salubrious.

While he 'lay by', working on detail drawings for Nottingham, the to-ings and fro-ings between Tractarians and Catholics at Oscott and Oxford continued, until another crisis came. Richard Sibthorp, Bloxam's friend, on whose behalf he had approached Pugin for liturgical advice, came up from his parish on the Isle of Wight to visit Bloxam at Magdalen. He asked, on behalf of 'a friend', for an introduction to Wiseman. As Sibthorp left he met Newman and there took place a short exchange that passed into the mythology of the Oxford Movement. Newman asked Sibthorp what his plans were. 'I am going to Oscott,' came the answer. 'Mind you don't stop there,' said Newman, and went on his way.[72] On 27 October at Oscott, Wiseman, without hesitation and indeed without offering him any preparation or instruction, received Sibthorp into the Catholic Church and the storm that had rumbled since the publication of Tract XC broke. Sibthorp, the unlikely hero of the hour, was nearly fifty. He had been an Anglican priest for twenty-six years and was the first of the Tractarian clergy to convert. It seemed for a moment that the Establishment might totter, the Reformation itself be undone. There were editorials in *The Times* and the President of Magdalen, old Dr Routh, broke down in tears. Pamphlets and counter-pamphlets ricocheted around the university and up and down the country, culminating in 'A Serious Remonstrance' from the clergy of Hull.

The shock, the sense of outrage and betrayal, was immense. As far as its opponents were concerned the Oxford Movement was now un-masked as a subversive, proto-Catholic fifth column. Within its ranks there were mixed feelings – grief, foreboding and excitement. To Bloxam it came as a thunderbolt and it caused him to reconsider other friend-ships. His relationship with Pugin survived, just. Within days of the news Pugin, who had been to call on Sibthorp at his London hotel and taken him to Mass, wrote a wildly excited and tactless letter to Bloxam asking ingenuously for a reply to tell him 'how the inteligence is Likely to be received at oxford'.[73] Having realized how wounded Bloxam was, however, Pugin wrote again. He could be careful of others' feelings when he valued them. Bombastic in print, he hardly ever quarrelled seriously with anyone who had become his friend: 'all things are in the hand of God,' he wrote gently, '& will he not work for the best may he not reveal one course to one individual and another course to a second – yet both tending to the same end.'[74]

But with Sibthorp's conversion the campaign for Anglo-Catholic reunion passed its meridian. For Bloxam 'it vanished like dream'.[75] The parting of the ways among the Tractarians and the Romantic Catholics had begun. Pugin's own position was, to himself, quite clear. He never considered leaving the Catholic Church, but at the same time his view of himself as an English Catholic, 'of the old school of our Edwards Anslems Thomass Englishmen to the back bone' left him increasingly awkwardly marooned between the 'Catholic' Anglicans and his own co-religionists, who acknowledged the ultimate authority of Rome.[76] Pugin's position was, and always had been, entirely personal. In that too he was a romantic, for nothing ever meant as much to him as his own experience. By now he had if anything more sympathizers and admirers in the Church of England than among Roman Catholics. The Cambridge Camden Society felt unable to invite him to join: they were in enough trouble already with the university for their suspected Puseyite leanings. Unofficially, however, they followed his activities closely. There was a lecture at Cambridge on *True Principles*, and in their journal, the

Ecclesiologist, it was recommended to the members, 'which' Pugin reported, 'increased the sale amazingly'.[77] Benjamin Webb, one of the Society's founders, now began a correspondence with Pugin, of which sadly very little has survived, and also a lifelong friendship.

On 9 November Pugin noted the birth of a Prince (later Edward VII) in his diary. He did not much care for the Queen and her family, whom he considered nothing but a set of Lutherans, but he continued his childhood habit of following royal events. Just over two weeks later in the early hours of moonlit morning his own fifth child was born and named after her grandmother. This second Catherine Pugin survived her royal contemporary and, like her brother Cuthbert, lived to see the First World War and the General Strike.

By the end of the year Pugin had formed his ideas for his cathedral at Nottingham. He realized that he could do better than the 'miserable outline' and 'mere Long barn' he and Shrewsbury had planned at Spa.[78] He designed a cruciform building which could command the rising, open ground. It was to be plain on the outside in a severe Early English lancet style, but with the 'outline and breaks' that Pugin needed to relieve it. To have attempted the more elaborate Decorated, though it was now his preferred style, would have been impossible within the budget. Perhaps by way of compensation for its exterior plainness, St Barnabas's was to be more complex in plan than any of his previous churches. The interior was an unfolding vista of 'intricate perspective views, pillar beyond pillar, screen beyond screen', all to be densely decorated. The choir and sanctuary, just north of the crossing, comprised a freestanding space within the larger volume. It was the perfect Picturesque interior landscape, the three-arch effect he had learned at Covent Garden from the Grieves, made solid, sacred, 'real'.

The effect was somewhat too impressive for Shrewsbury, who wrote in horror from Rome to Pugin, Wiseman and Walsh separately. To Walsh he complained that: 'at Spa we agreed to erect a Church *complete*, for £10,000 . . . Now Pugin sends me a design for a Church, *109* feet in the nave, *40* in the choir, with transepts, with *3 extra* chapels & an *extra* corridor & a *tower* in the centre.'[79] Who, the Earl wanted to know, was to pay for all this? Certainly it would not be him. The reaction was a kind of compliment. Pugin had, as he explained, costed the whole building, with Myers's help. He had learned a great deal since Derby. He claimed he could build 'certainly 30 & nearer 50 per cent Cheaper than 3 years ago'.[80] He had gathered a reliable team of workmen and since 'everybody is now used to the work' they got on with it and with each other 'daily better'.[81] Pugin never shook off the reputation for extravagance acquired with his first churches, but he had indeed learned to work more or less within his means, unlike many architects – unlike, for example, Charles Barry who was notorious for overspending.

Pugin had had little contact with Barry since the estimate drawings for the Palace of Westminster were finished. It is possible that he had made a few designs for him in the intervening years but he was too absorbed in his own career to have done much, and Barry himself was immersed in the difficulties of embanking the Thames and laying the foundations for the new Palace. This had proved enormously difficult, the difficulty compounded by the fact that Parliament continued to sit on site, in temporary accommodation, throughout the building work. By 1841 the Palace should, according to Barry's first calculations, have been finished. In fact it was only in February 1840 that the foundation stone was laid quietly, not to say furtively, by Mrs Barry. The work was vastly complex, but the new government was impatient for the Palace to proceed and to anticipate the finished effect it set up a commission for 'considering whether the interior decoration of the new house of Parliament can be made conducive to the encouragement of British Art'.[82] The Prime Minister wrote to the Earl of Shrewsbury to know whether he would be a member of it. Shrewsbury, although he would be unable 'to give much personal attendance', told Peel he would.[83]

23

Reunion and Division

1842

Ours is pre-eminently a partisan age.
  *– W. Cooke Taylor, Notes of a tour of the manufacturing
    districts of Lancashire, 1842*

'From the end of 1841,' Newman wrote, 'I was on my death-bed, as regards my membership of the Anglican Church.'[1] The protracted throes of Newman's spiritual agony lasted another four years. During that time those around him, and those thousands of others whose tides of thought and belief ebbed and flowed with the pull of Oxford and Littlemore, found themselves in a similarly uncertain state, and religious anxiety mingled with wider unease. 'Distress' now in all its forms 'dominated the whole mood of the nation'. 'There was no gloomier year in the whole nineteenth century than 1842'.[2] This was a year of crisis in the textile industry, riots and strikes in the mill towns and unrest in the potteries. The poverty of the country, the numbers of people living in 'a state bordering on absolute starvation', as one Carlisle newspaper put it, led to more insistent calls to repeal the Corn Laws, which controlled the import of wheat and therefore kept the price of bread artificially high. The protests were led by the Anti-Corn Law League, under the direction of the Manchester manufacturer Richard Cobden and the Quaker industrialist John Bright, but their campaign was about more than food prices. Repeal was a social and moral as much as an economic issue. In 1841 the League had put up candidates for Parliament and it was now a significant force in the Commons, arguing for free trade on behalf of the manufacturers and the poor against 'the bread-taxing oligarchy'.[3] It was another battle in the war between land and trade, old and new money, old and new order. Mass meetings were held in Glasgow and Derby in support of repeal, which to conservatives like Shrewsbury, Pugin and Phillipps appeared as much as Chartism and Radicalism to be a threat to the benign and godly social hierarchy they sought to establish.

The year began violently in their own immediate circle when, in the early hours of 4 January, a mob attacked Kenelm Digby's house near Southampton and set it alight, believing that Sibthorp was there. Sibthorp, who had lost many of his friends, had been taken in for Christmas by the Digbys but had left the day before. The family escaped, 'in their nightclothes', according to Newman.[4] Their home was reduced to ashes, the furniture and many of Digby's manuscripts destroyed. The attack had been prompted by a sermon preached by a local minister, in which he said that the apostate deserved to be burned. Scarcely anywhere in Britain was calm, yet each part of the country was troubled in its own way, and as the unease spread a new kind of tourist embarked on a new kind of picturesque tour to try to understand the strangely troubled condition of England and its causes. Pugin's neighbour Thomas Carlyle went to East Anglia to examine 'such a Platitude of a World in which all horses could be well fed and innumerable working men could die starved'.[5] Young England was also out and about. In the parliamentary recess John Manners and George Smythe undertook a tour to the manufacturing districts of the north, which they combined with visits to Pugin's works in progress and to Wiseman at Oscott. 'You might get hold of him,' Wiseman wrote urgently to Shrewsbury of Manners, 'he is a great Puginite ... & ... It could not but be useful to him & us.'[6] In November another observant visitor, Friedrich Engels, arrived in Manchester.

Amid such uncertainty, divisions multiplied. Among Pugin's closest friends there were now scarcely two whose opinions coincided. Pugin himself, who longed for unity and security above all things, was increasingly disturbed and divided in his loyalties. On the one hand, rereading the works of Strype and others for another *Dublin Review* article, he felt less certain about reunion. 'I never went so minutely into matters before,' he told Phillipps, 'but the result has been that I am convinced the present Church of Engld. is 10 times more protestant than I thought it.'[7] Yet many of his friends were Anglicans. Bloxam, at Magdalen, was the closest, but Pugin was also coming increasingly to know and like the young Camdenians, who visited him in London. With them, as with

Bloxam, he shared a love of England's Gothic architecture and a devotion to the historic English church. Shrewsbury, by contrast, was still causing Pugin anguish with his devastating suggestions for modifications at St Giles's. The Earl was also on bad terms with his querulous chaplain, Rock, who had been writing 'very silly, if not impertinent' letters to his employer in Rome and stirring up the local Anglicans at Alton. 'He has ... a very weak mind,' Shrewsbury told Pugin, 'which study and seclusion seem to have altogether over powered.'[8] Rock left Alton and was found another position, with the Throckmortons at Buckland in Berkshire, from which distance he and Shrewsbury stayed on civil terms although Rock, who had still not published his magnum opus on the Church of Our Fathers, was becoming increasingly jealous of Pugin's reputation and was inclined to criticize his work to the Earl.

For his part Wiseman was discreetly exasperated by Shrewsbury's political activities, the wordy pamphlets and bombastic open letters he was turning out against the 'radical-reform movement'.[9] In this Shrewsbury included the Chartists, the anti-Corn Law lobby, and principally the 'GREAT AGITATOR' himself, Daniel O'Connell.[10] Shrewsbury had been a Whig in the 1830s, but now, he felt, reform had gone far enough. Unfortunately, as Mary Arundell knew, the 'poor good well-meaning Earl' was not articulate or concise: 'alas! for Lord Shrewsbury's abilities as a politician and an orator.'[11] The Earl wrote a long-winded open letter to Phillipps which received an answer in February from O'Connell, entitled 'A meek and modest reply . . .', that effectively refuted Shrewsbury's arguments. It also signalled O'Connell's resumption of the campaign against the Act of Union. Repeal, which would have allowed Ireland to reorganize the system of land ownership that was at the heart of many of the country's troubles, became from now on 'a sort of mystical goal' for the Irish.[12] It was not a campaign for full independence, but it united the country in a growing sense of nationhood, of which O'Connell was the inspiring genius.

'What desperate struggling is going on,' Pugin wrote to Rock, unhappily, when he read O'Connell's letter.[13] Wiseman, who despite having been born in Spain of Irish parents always described himself as English, was ambivalent about O'Connell, his co-founder of the *Dublin Review*, but he saw that Shrewsbury's dogmatic reiteration of divisive opinions was not helpful. He tried to 'ménager' as best he could, urging the Earl to work for the good of the Catholic cause and leave political differences unspoken. 'Repeal & its agitation, Universal Suffrage, democracy etc etc I have all along hated and detested them,' he reassured him. However, Wiseman doubted the 'expediency' (a word he understood as Pugin and Shrewsbury never did) of alienating O'Connell. 'Were [he] to denounce us . . . it is difficult to say how far his unexampled influence over the minds & prejudices of his country men might prevail.'[14] Much of the support for Oscott, and indeed for the English Catholic revival, came from prosperous, middle-class Irish men and women. They were the parents of Wiseman's pupils. They included Liberals such as Edward Challoner, the Liverpool timber merchant, with whom Pugin dined in March, a donor to the church at Old Swan and a personal friend of O'Connell. Such people were not to be alienated. Nor, however, was the Shrewsbury set. Wiseman was making efforts to placate them too. When Pugin was at Oscott for Easter he observed that Wiseman was using the Sarum Rite, aware of its appeal to Young England and the Oxford men, especially Sibthorp, who had now been ordained as a Catholic priest. Wiseman was anxious to encourage him, for he was a great trophy for the Catholic cause, both in himself and in his considerable private means.

Despite Wiseman's heroic diplomacy, however, division bred division. Pugin, always volatile, was subject to ever more extreme moods of elation and despair. In his second article in the *Dublin Review*, describing his buildings at Alton, he explained that 'When viewed from the opposite hills' across the Churnet Valley, St John's Hospital seemed to 'form but one group with the more venerable tower of the parochial church'.[15] What he had hoped would be a true architectural and theological reunion of Christendom seemed now at times no more than that, a trick of picturesque perspective. On visits to Cambridge where Webb 'Lionized Pugin about' he seemed at moments full of confidence, creating a favourable, as well as a powerful impression by his 'geniality and vigour'.[16] He was enthusiastic about the Cambridge Camden Society's restoration of St Sepulchre's, the round church. But the next day, on a visit to Ely, Webb found Pugin in the Lady Chapel after evensong 'weeping passionately' and thought him in 'an awful state of mind', a phrase which at the time might be a euphemism for actual mental illness, certainly something more than mere distress.[17] Pugin had not been to Ely since 1834. Perhaps it was the contrasts in his own life that overcame him as he saw it again, its overpowering beauty enhanced by the last light of a summer afternoon. Seven years before he had been an ardent but obscure young man on the brink of great things. Now, at thirty, he was famous, successful as an architect, but disappointed. The vision of Catholic, Gothic England seemed ever further off.

Through elation and despair he continued to work at full speed and when in the grip of neither was as cheerful and robust as usual. He was up until midnight each night, through the first weeks of the year, sending off designs to Alton and detail drawings for his proposed extension of the Benedictine monastery at Downside. He was also completing the article for the *Dublin Review*. It was, like its predecessor, a long essay cast as a review. It dealt with several of the Camden Society tracts and the first numbers of the *Ecclesiologist*. Pugin liked the pamphlets and was even more enthusiastic about the journal. The *Ecclesiologist* was pugnacious and opinionated in a way he admired. The editors had been forced to withdraw the first issue because of a violent attack in it on Ambrose Poynter, architect of a new Commissioners' church in Cambridge, St Paul's. St Paul's was denounced with that immense condescension that was to characterize the journal's editorial tone, as being 'of no particular style or shape . . . constructed of very red brick indeed' and epitomizing the 'CHEAP CHURCH OF THE NINETEENTH CENTURY'.[18] In his article Pugin reprinted the whole of the suppressed passage. He was now completely opposed to brick churches except out of 'extreme necessity' and had apparently put the very red brick of St Chad's down to experience as part of its – now discredited – foreign style.[19]

In practice he was still often obliged to use brick. His only building in Cambridge, the little Catholic church of St Andrew's, begun later this year and situated just off Hills Road within sight of Poynter's St Paul's, was an unmistakably cheap church, in red brick. As usual it was what Pugin meant, more than what he built, that had the effect. Writing of his work in progress in the *Dublin Review* Pugin held out the serious aesthetic the young Ecclesiologists wanted, denouncing 'the senseless uniformity of modern design', which he now, of course, as a reader of the *British Critic*, found 'unreal', and upholding the 'plainness, simplicity, severity' they craved in architecture.[20] He described what he had learned to do at St John's with big tough details. 'Roofs and chimney shafts,' he wrote, 'stand forth undisguised in all the unadorned grandeur produced by their extent and solidity; and . . . furnish an admirable proof of the vast superiority of effect that is produced by the *natural architecture of our catholic ancestors*.'[21] The adjective 'natural', rather than 'Catholic' or 'Christian,' applied to Gothic architecture was new and significant, the first suggestion of a different direction in his thinking. At the end of his essay, however, having warmly praised the Anglican Camdenians, Pugin returned, for no obvious reason, to the horrors of the Reformation. He wrote, or raved, in a language of apocalypse that recalled Edward Irving and which spoke more eloquently of his own fears of loss and disruption than of history: 'a dark speck soon appeared on the horizon, and a whirlwind of destruction arose, and the foundations of this vast fabric were undermined, and the choirs ceased to echo with the sound of praise, and soon they were roofless . . . and the altars of God were overthrown, and the image of Christ was defaced, and strange ministers stood in the temple of God and mocked the olden solemnity.'[22]

The writing of these last pages, which he worked at incessantly over several days and nights, both exhausted Pugin and made him frantic. The nightmare images that he conjured up would not leave him. They preyed on his mind until he was not always able to separate them from reality and for days afterwards he was 'exceedly bad' in the head.[23] For weeks he was only 'better & worse at – intervals' and 'dreadfully harrassed'.[24] It was apparently the first instance of the 'nervous fever' that he suffered from time to time after this, what is now called a manic or psychotic episode, when the mind races out of control and behaviour becomes excessive, impulsive and erratic. It was from about this time that his behaviour began to strike even casual observers as something more than eccentric and his 'habits and disposition' as Talbot Bury put it, began to 'limit his circle'. Yet to the young Camdenians it was his very intensity that was so admirable. He approached more closely than anyone to their ideal of the architect: 'a single pious and laborious artist, alone, pondering deeply over his duty to do his utmost for the service of GOD's holy religion, and obtaining by devout exercises of mind a semi-inspiration for his holy taste'.[25] Nobody else, certainly not Scott or Ferrey or even Butterfield, attempted this, to practise architecture as a vocation.

By now the Gothic Revival was spreading out across the empire. The Oxford and Cambridge Societies received many enquiries from overseas and had an authoritative answer for all of them, including the appro-

priate style for New Zealand (which was Norman), Gothic was being
'revived' where it had never before been seen, from northern Canada,
whence the Bishop of Newfoundland wrote for suitable designs for
churches, to India, where the Revd J. Tucker begged leave 'to spread
before you the wants of the Diocese of Madras'.[26] Closer to home the
university societies bred local imitators at Exeter, Lichfield and Salisbury. The rising generation of architects, Butterfield, Scott and the ever-
assiduous Ferrey among them, recruited their ecclesiastical patrons to
the societies and submitted proposals to them for approval. The Gothic
idea permeated society at many levels. While high-minded young people
beavered away with their 'orientators' and 'schemes', the Queen and
Prince Consort held their own Gothic Ball in May, at which they
appeared as Edward III and Queen Philippa. Although Victoria looked
'hot and oppressed' and her dress was thought 'not becoming', the event
was a success.[27] The royal family – increasingly it was as a young model
family that they were portrayed – confirmed the association between the
Christian Gothic past and the respectable present. It was a very different
kind of dressing up from George IV's extravagant coronation, or at least
it was differently understood.

Taste and sensibility were moving rapidly. That summer the contents
of Walpole's Strawberry Hill came up for sale and Pugin went to view
them. The house and its interior, largely unvisited then and to most
people of Pugin's age only a distant curiosity, looked hopelessly dated
and both inauthentic and cavalier in its use of Gothic sources and motifs.
'Disgusted', he wrote in his diary. But when Webb and Scott went to
look at the work in progress at Barry's new Palace of Westminster, Webb
was equally 'disgusted with the design'.[28] Architecture had changed so
fast and building at the Palace had been so slow that when at last the
structure began to emerge from the foundations it looked old-fashioned
already. It was too symmetrical, and its late Perpendicular style was now
generally considered inferior to the Decorated. The *Ecclesiologist* gave
its decided opinion that Barry 'had no feeling for ancient art' and would
need Pugin's advice to finish the building.[29] It was the first time their
names had been publicly linked and already the implications were
invidious.

At the end of February Pugin set off on the usual round of site visits.
At Cheadle, St Giles's was up to the springs of the arcade on the south
side. Bishop Walsh came to lay the cornerstone. Shrewsbury's latest

unhelpful suggestions included a clerestory for ventilation, although the windows, Pugin pointed out, would not appear on the outside of the building unless the whole roof was redesigned, and he still liked the idea of a gallery. Not for the first or last time, Pugin lost his temper with his noble patron:

... here are no Less than 5 protestant archdeacons pulling down gallerys of every kind. all the works of the Camden & oxford societies denounce them & now after I had ingeniously got rid of the organ Monstrosity your lordsip proposes to erect a gallery in the only perfect revival that has been accomplished. what Can I say or do. the gallery would not hold 20 people if crammed full & it would utterly ruin the church. all the Learned men will flock to this church as a Model & then they will see this Monstrosity. what a miserable fate awaits every architect of this wretched country. I have Lived to see almost every building on which I have set my heart either upset or ruined & now a gallery at Cheadle. perfect Cheadle. Cheadle my consolation in all my afflictions. Mercy I entreat.[30]

Under this battery Shrewsbury gave in. He was perfectly well disposed to the ecclesiologists, but he was distant, mentally and physically, from the ethos of Oxford and Cambridge. It was in Leicestershire, under Phillipps's aegis, that Pugin got the chance to explore what he was beginning to think of as 'natural' architecture. He went to Grace Dieu directly from Alton and found Phillipps and Gentili doing what they could in the face of the ever-increasing poverty in the countryside around them. Gentili was anxious to get out and work independently among the people; Phillipps had agreed to build a church at the village of Shepshed and a school nearby at Whitwick to give the Rosminians permanent local bases. Pugin designed both buildings, probably on this visit. The church, St Winefrede's, was finished, for £626, and ready for use that winter. These two small attempts to stem the flow of human misery were impressive in their modesty and effectiveness, and they also embodied a new architectural idea, Pugin's first practical demonstration of natural architecture. Built in local stone, laid in random rubble in the traditional way, rather than cut into blocks, the church stands on a corner and – as built – appeared to grow naturally out of the rubble walls that bound the site. Here again, as with his furniture, Pugin was going back to a medieval tradition, but in a way that was extraordinarily daring and imaginative, bringing the old techniques that survived among the most humble country builders into the repertoire of architecture.

The school was a long low building, also rubble built, its presence made dramatic by one or two massive blocks laid into the small walls. Ruskin would later explain that small buildings should not be built of small stones but should have one or two 'massy' elements which would give them 'nobility'. Pugin knew this already. As usual he was working largely by eye, developing theories as he built, writing the theory down and then developing it again when he went back to build. On a practical level he was bringing home to England the lessons he had learned in Ireland about stone and working out the ideas of Lord Midleton's farm buildings, adopting traditional means as well as materials. Nash and others had used thatch and half-timbering, but these buildings for Phillipps were a new kind of estate architecture. They were not prettified, like Nash's Blaise Hamlet or the cottages and lodges in pattern books; there was nothing toy-like about them. They grew in style as well as substance from the bottom up. It was arguably the first attempt at a vernacular revival.

For several weeks after Easter Pugin was at home in Chelsea. His life there is visible in glimpses only, through Webb's diaries and a few letters. There were five children now in Cheyne Walk. Anne, the eldest, was ten. Edward was eight, Agnes six, Cuthbert two and Catherine, the baby, not yet six months. There were no servants living in and Louisa must have been much occupied, though she had the help now of a friend and neighbour, Ann Greaves, the daughter of the family of boat-builders who lived next door. Ann was about twenty-five and unmarried and she liked to spend her time with Louisa and the children. Louisa's name occasionally occurs in her husband's letters, going to dine with the Camden men, too preoccupied at home, according to Pugin, to go and stay with Dr Rock, though possibly also disinclined to spend several days listening to disquisitions on liturgy.

While he was in Chelsea Pugin was working on three new churches. St Mary's, Newcastle, conceived as a 'Large parochial church', was his second essay in the three-aisled, hall church style he had adopted for St George's.[31] His church at Woolwich, St Peter's, was a much smaller affair. It was another measure of troubled times that the Board of Ordnance was prepared to cater, for the first time, for the needs of Catholic servicemen who found themselves isolated in unfamiliar surroundings. Woolwich's 3,000 Catholics were mostly in the military and poor. The third new church of the spring was the largest, a cathedral for Killarney, in County Kerry. The donor was Lord Kenmare, a local landowner. Pugin's design was intended to impress through scale, a massive cruciform church in the Early English style.

The pattern of Woolwich was repeated with variations for St Mary's, Liverpool, designed the same year, a west front composed of tower, nave and gabled aisle making a dramatic, zigzag roofline. It was Pugin's latest attempt at the urban church and another prescient design. Later moved to another site and then destroyed by bombing in 1941, St Mary's, Liverpool, is one of the greatest losses to Pugin's œuvre, for it sounded themes that were to recur in the debates on urban church architecture later in the century. The west front ran along the street line, the tower in bond with the walls giving the elevation an imposing presence. A surviving photograph shows the interior as long and narrow, a tall nave with low aisles, high clerestory and no chancel arch. The design was flawed, for the aisle windows, just feet from the neighbouring buildings, must have been all but useless. Yet the effect of the principal light source being the clerestory must have added to the effect of height and solemnity creating an impression of stasis rather than upward rush. St Mary's, Liverpool, was a precursor of the sort of town church later advocated by G. E. Street, and although Pugin was never to build another city church, he lived long enough to enter into the debate on urban churches that ushered in the High Victorian age.

At Nottingham, meanwhile, St Barnabas's was 'getting on Gloriously . . . & rappidly rising out of the Ground'.[32] Shrewsbury had been pacified about the cost and Sibthorp was there, 'full of zeal for the work' and about to have 'splendid vestments made' at his own expense.[33] The interior, with its densely patterned walls and intricate cross views, complicated by sixteen carved oak screens, would, Pugin promised, 'be far the richest thing attempted since the old time . . . 3 times the solemnity of St Georges – or Birmingham'.[34] The foundation stone was laid on 10 May on a morning 'serene and bright' but, as at Southwark, at an hour early enough to prevent a crowd from gathering: 'in the midst of heaps of bricks and stone' this was felt to be inadvisable.[35] There had been unpleasant anti-Catholic demonstrations at the Cambridge site on 5 November.

Pugin was nine days in Ireland in June, laying out the church at Killarney and seeing the foundation stone laid for the Waterford convent. He had found a builder, Richard Pierce, who if not quite another

Myers, was 'an invaluable man for Irish business' who 'perfectly understands all the material manners & prices of the country & my drawings
as well'.[36] Pugin's architecture had an influence on the Catholics of
Ireland such as he never achieved in England. His arrival there coincided
with the great wave of romantic nationalism that had carried the Gothic
Revival forward over Europe and which now crossed the Irish Sea.
Gothic was a nationalistic style, and in Ireland Catholicism and nationalism could be identified with one another as they never could be on the
mainland. Pugin's ideas spread rapidly via his buildings and his articles
in the *Dublin Review*. Despite the poverty of the country and even
through the desperate times that followed, the Irish continued to build
Gothic churches, Pugin's and others. They built them stone by stone,
penny by penny, with a commitment few English Catholic parishes ever
felt. Thus Gothic took on its local colouring in Ireland as everywhere
else. The rationale had its contradictions, but rationale was not important. The ideal of Gothic as a true, just style, a once-lost birthright now
redeemed, was the consistent theme of Gothic apologists from Paris and
Cologne to Killarney and Oxford.

Yet Pugin never liked or understood Ireland. Like many politically
more sophisticated Englishmen, he was often at a loss to fathom the
currents of national and religious sentiment flowing through it. The
resistance of the Church of Ireland to Tractarian influence, which it
feared would make it seem Popish, disappointed him. He found few
sympathizers beyond his personal friends among the prosperous ruling
class: 'for the rich I can say . . . Little,' he wrote to Bloxam, 'I think they
are in a miserably Low state of catholic feeling.'[37] Of the poor, especially
at Killarney, he formed a higher opinion and was impressed by their
devotion and enthusiasm for the new cathedral. Like Thackeray, Pugin
was filled with mixed emotions: horrified by the poverty, impressed by
the piety, depressed by the Church of Ireland's bigotry and inwardness.
Neither man could understand how the country worked. 'How do all
these people live?' Thackeray wrote, 'one can't help wondering; – these
multifarious vagabonds, without work or workhouse . . .';[38] 'the poor
people,' Pugin reported to Bloxam, 'it is heartrending to see them in the
last state of misery and destitution – only potatoes & often a scanty
supply of them. there must be something rotten in the Irish affair for
these very people appear patterns of pious resignation quite different
from the turbulent Irishmen of Dublin.'[39] By the next year, when the

agitation for repeal was reaching a climax, the Duke of Wellington was predicting civil war in Ireland but Pugin was surprised to find the country, in reality, quite peaceful, not 'the Least sign of commotion and tumult'.[40] On Lord Midleton's estates, he told his patron, the crops looked well and 'the farmers spirits' were 'fast reviving'. Pugin's observations are no more naive or contradictory than those of most of his countrymen.[41] Nobody fully understood the condition of Ireland, and for the catastrophe that was soon to overwhelm it all were unprepared.

Pugin based himself at Alton for most of the summer, travelling out to inspect work in the Midlands and the North. He was there in July when the unrest that had menaced the country all year erupted into violent protest across Britain. The trouble began almost on Lord Shrewsbury's doorstep. Just as the price of corn rose, the Staffordshire mineowners announced a wage cut. The colliers struck, bringing the Potteries to a standstill. The strike spread to the mines of South Wales and Lancashire and throughout the depressed cotton industry. There was machine wrecking and some arson and looting. The strikers had no way of feeding themselves except from charity or theft. It was less a political movement than 'a movement of despair, a revolt of hunger'.[42] For the rest of the summer, as Pugin travelled to meet the building committee at Newcastle and visit Bishop Walsh, who was staying at the convent at Caverswall, he was passing through some of the worst disruption. At Stoke the colliers were attempting to march on Macclesfield, and Minton told him the Chartists were active in the town. Walsh had seen several houses in ruins and at Newcastle 'the town is full of soldiers . . . prisoners are being constantly brought in, who are become so numerous that the authorities hardly know how to dispose of them'.[43] It looked to many like the start of a revolution. Walsh, however, distinguished between the rioters and the strikers. He was full of sympathy for those who came 'half starved' to Caverswall, where he made sure they were fed.

Pugin, easily alarmed and excited by any threat to public order, assumed command at Alton in a highly theatrical manner. Walsh temporarily changed his nickname for Pugin from Bishop to General. In late July the General wrote to Lord Shrewsbury from Lancashire reporting on the state of the country and instructing his Lordship firmly that he 'should not by any means relax in vigilance and have all made fast at night till things are really settled'.[44] He ordered brass guns for Alton, and built a barbican tower, a dry moat and the second working drawbridge of his career, with perhaps a little more justification than there had been at St Marie's Grange. He pursued the architectural and military campaigns with similar zeal, working 'As *hard as possible & travelling as fast possible* so as to *return to head* quarters *as soon as possible*'.[45] His churches at Stockton-on-Tees and Old Swan opened in July. The building committee at Newcastle, undeterred by the events unfolding around them, continued to query the estimates for St Mary's, wanting detailed costings for the font. He was also at Kirkham in Lancashire, where the priest, Thomas Sherburne, had a considerable legacy to spend on building a new church, just outside the little town in a pleasant, rural spot known as the Willows. St John's was a pure 'Dublin Review' church in simple decorated Gothic with a broach spire, built in Longridge stone. The steeple is a fine composition, its corner buttresses and deep stair turret angled into the body of the tower.

Towards the end of the summer Pugin went to Scotland for the first time since 1835. As at Ely, the recollection of the intervening years may have given rise to mixed feelings. Work was in progress on Gillespie Graham's church of Tolbooth St John's in Castlehill. Pugin, who still found it difficult to refuse a friend, had given Graham a design for the spire, a copy of the one he had just made for St George's, Southwark, where work was still going slowly for lack of funds. Thus it was that the spire that Pugin had intended to see rising over London's first post-Reformation Catholic cathedral was going up instead in Edinburgh above the intended meeting place for the Assembly of the Church of Scotland, John Knox's kirk, the 'abomination of desolation' as Pugin considered it.[46] When finished the spire became one of the great landmarks on the skyline of Scotland's capital, as it still is, and an ironic tribute to Pugin's frustrated talents, a design for which he neither got, nor wanted, any credit. Later he described the spire as 'far from good in itself but much too good for its purpose'.[47]

In August he went on to Perth to visit the work in progress at the Breadalbanes' great house, Taymouth. Activity there was reaching fever pitch in anticipation of the Queen and Prince Albert's visit. Taymouth was Alton Towers writ even larger, the country house as Gothic domain and dynastic propaganda. For Victoria and Albert's arrival in this year of strikes and near starvation, there were pipers and oarsmen, fireworks, barges and special Highland costumes for the Breadalbanes. Her Ladyship's 'sylph-like' figure made a piquant contrast to the 'swarthy

Lochaber axemen' who formed up around her when the royal party arrived.[48] The Queen admired the 'newly and exquisitely' furnished house and the spectacle, the firing of salutes, the lively dancing in Pugin's Banner Hall. She chose the rooms designed by Pugin and Graham for her own apartments, noting in her journal 'the picturesqueness' of the costumes and 'the beauty of the surrounding country, with its rich background of woods and hills'. She entered, too, into the Waverley drama enacted for her: 'It seemed as if a great chieftain in old and feudal times was receiving his sovereign.'[49] This Scottish tour marked the beginning of the royal family's love affair with the Highlands, later consummated with the purchase of Balmoral.

In the strange summer of 1842, with its violent and curious contrasts, Victoria and Albert were not the only royal persons to be living out the mythology of the olden times in Scotland. Pugin left Taymouth and travelled north, where he found another pair of masqueraders much more to his taste. He went to Inverness-shire to visit the Frasers of Lovat, an old Catholic family on whose land were the ruins of the thirteenth-century Beauly Priory, which Lord Lovat hoped Pugin would restore. The first Mass sung there would, Pugin thought, 'gladden the bones of the old monks'.[50] This was romantic enough, but there were also on the Fraser estate two living manifestations of the Catholic Gothic inheritance: the brothers John and Charles Sobieski Stuart. Tall, dark, handsome, now in their forties, they were habitually clothed in Highland dress of their own design. Their hair fell long and straight on to their shoulders and their beards were trimmed like Van Dyck portraits. The Stuarts had taken up residence, under Lord Lovat's protection, on the lovely islet of Eilean Aigas on his estate. Here they had built a house, partly furnished in Gothic style, in which they passed their time in the pursuit of antiquarian research. That year they published their *Vestiarium Scoticum*, the dubious source for many tartans still in use today. Each Sunday they sailed to Mass in a barge flying the royal standard, for they were, they said, the grandsons of Charles Edward Stuart.

Pugin was wildly excited to meet them: 'the Eldest is one of the most glorious men I ever knew', he told Shrewsbury, 'he is perfect in his ideas on Christian architecture etc & draws beautifully. they Live on a most romantic Island surrounded by waterfalls & rocks – in a vast glen between the mountains. I was quite delighed I could fight for him . . . they are *both edifying Catholics*, there is a prophecy in the highlands that the stewarts are yet to be restored what a grand thing a *Gothic* king & a catholic would be.'[51] He was not the only person to take the Sobieski Stuarts at their own self-estimation, though few went so far as offering to take up arms. The brothers, sons of an English naval officer, were not what they said they were, but it would be wrong to call them frauds, exactly, for they were not cynical. Perhaps they are best described as manifestations of the Gothic imagination, expressions of the Picturesque personality. To Pugin, who also lived out the romance of his life in a physical, literal way, these Catholic figures in a Waverley landscape of wild woods and torrents were perfectly real.

It was a heady meeting for Pugin, and a heady time. Travelling incessantly from the end of May to the middle of September, he was at home for little more than two weeks. His work was going well. 'I am ... extending my *orbit* every year...' he told Clarkson Stanfield, 'it is a great Privilege.'[52] He was continuing to earn considerable sums. He bought £1,030 of stock in August. His religious position remained clear at least to himself: 'we have had an *English* church from the days of Blessed Austen,' he told Stanfield, 'never acknowledge yourself a Roman Catholick.'[53] The question, of course, was how much if any of the English Catholic Church could be found in the Anglican establishment. By the end of the year Pugin had come round again to a more optimistic view: 'on all sides we see restorations ... men are filled with veneration for Catholic antiquity – & when we see the Glorious works which are daily put forth by the oxford men can we doubt that God has great things in store for us & all this will be brought about by the anglicans.'[54]

The extension of Pugin's orbit began to include commissions from the Church of England and these increased with time, as the men who had been Tractarians and Camdenians in their undergraduate days became clergymen with livings of their own or came into family inheritances. Lord Midleton commissioned a mortuary chapel to be added to his parish church of St Nicholas, Peper Harow. At Beverley the Archdeacon of the East Riding, Robert Wilberforce, recommended that Pugin be employed for the restoration work of St Mary's, a church he knew well and loved, 'one of the most beautiful parish churches of England', where Pugin continued to work for the rest of his life.[55]

With his Tractarian friend Bernard Smith, he was now planning an encyclopedic work, a glossary of Gothic design. Pugin's developing friendship with Smith alarmed Newman, who advised Smith not to let

Pugin come and stay with him in Lincolnshire. The advice was ignored. Bloxam too feared that Smith was on the brink of conversion and was keeping his eye on him, intending to do all in his power 'to keep him back'.[56] It was to no avail. In December Smith followed Sibthorp's path to Oscott and on the 18th, five days after he and Pugin had begun work on their book, Pugin noted in his diary: 'R.B. Smith reconciled.'[57]

24

A Shift in the Wind

January to September 1843

*... remember the Power of women is infinite beyond the screw
wedge or lever they throw out a grappling iron & tow away a
man as strong as a 79 gun ship like a wherry ... it is as old as
St John the Baptist nay older – perhaps antediluvian ...*
— Pugin to John Hardman, n.d., *c.*1847[1]

Pugin, who hated ambivalence, now found himself increasingly torn on
all fronts between his feelings for individuals and his ideals. Outside his
immediate circle his fellow Catholics were mostly indifferent or hostile to
his work, and within there was discord. Those who shared his artistic
and theological vision remained, for the most part, Anglicans. Even in his
home, that necessary pivot for all his constant activity, he was now less
than entirely happy. Pugin's diary for 1843 is missing. Almost certainly
he destroyed it himself. It seems that some estrangement had developed
between him and Louisa, and this year it became explicit. Louisa was
not, if Hardman Powell's hint is to be believed, a long-suffering woman.
She was lively, she had a temper. The fact that Pugin, who spoke so
freely of his feelings and intermingled the personal with the professional
in all his correspondence, mentions her so little in his letters suggests that
she was not quite the complete companion, the soulmate that he sought
who would share admiringly in all he did. She was not apparently by
temperament naturally pious and so perhaps despite her long-delayed
conversion she had never entered fully into his spiritual vision.

After ten years of marriage, with a stepdaughter and four children of
her own, Louisa had reasons to be discontented. She found herself often
alone. Her husband, immersed in a career that he regarded as a sacred
calling, was home just often enough to ensure she was almost constantly

pregnant. His fame brought nothing to his wife beyond reflected glory. He was not rich and he had no interest in pursuing the social opportunities which his reputation might have brought him and which might have enlivened Louisa's daily round. On both sides therefore there may have been some disappointment and a lack of that sympathy so necessary for Pugin's mental equilibrium. By the end of the year his affections had certainly been drawn away from his wife. Before that, however, it is possible that, increasingly isolated and prey to 'nervous fever', he suffered another manic episode. In a state of mania inhibitions are lowered and libido, characteristically, is increased.

In 1884 a man called Byron Pugin emerged in Charlottesville, Virginia, practising as an architect and claiming to be Pugin's illegitimate son. If he was born when he said he was, on 14 February 1844, he would have been conceived in about May of this year. Byron Pugin was possibly known, after Pugin's death, to Pugin's family. An address in Chicago for 'Welby' is noted down in one of his sons' sketchbooks.[2] Much in Byron's story is unprovable. He claimed to have been the son of Pugin and one Mary Burns, of whom nothing has yet come to light. He said that she had been sent to America and that he himself was born at sea, that he was a 'remittance man', sent money regularly from England. Pugin would not have abandoned a woman in this situation any more than he had abandoned Anne Garnett. If there was such an arrangement it would probably have been John Hardman who undertook it. Hardman often took care of practical or troubling business for his friend and it would not be the last time that he helped to get him out of difficulties with a woman. Some twenty-five years later, when both Pugin and Hardman were dead, Pugin's son Edward, who was himself by then increasingly unstable and paranoid, took it into his head that his father had been cheated by Hardman. He seems to have found discrepancies in the accounts. Hardman's nephew John Hardman Powell warned him not to pursue his discoveries, in quite specific terms:

Let your Father and my Uncle sleep in peace they were fast friends through life and respected each others integrity family dishonour may come but no good to you can by bringing their money affairs before a court. This I have means of knowing that you have not.[3]

Hardman Powell was sixteen in 1843, old enough to understand what was being said around him. Edward was only nine.

Nothing can now be proved, but Byron's story was passed on through his own family, who have made attempts over several generations up to the present to establish its truth or otherwise. Byron was something of a fantasist. He gave various accounts of his age, made a mystery of his early years and elaborated or invented a role for himself in the American Civil War. But whether this counts against the likelihood of his being Pugin's son or adds to it is a moot point. A degree of mythomania ran in the family, after all. Moreover, of all Pugin's living descendants, of whom there are more than a hundred at the time of writing, it must be said that Byron's great-grandson, the present Welby Pugin, is the only one to bear a resemblance to Pugin himself.

These scant facts form the background to the events of the following months.

Pugin was at home in January, when building was stopped, working on another book. *An Apology for the Revival of Christian Architecture in England* was dedicated to the Earl of Shrewsbury. It was to be Pugin's last extended statement of his ideas but it has been largely overlooked. He described it to Bloxam as a Tract for the Times and to Benjamin Webb as a work on domestic architecture. It was both and much – too much – else besides. Like all Pugin's writing it was an outpouring of his most recent ideas. The text grew up round individual points, charged abruptly down dead ends and spawned footnotes, some of which sprouted notes of their own. In among all this lay scattered, like seeds, ideas that amounted to a radical new definition of Gothic.

The *Apology* was another unacknowledged volte-face, like the second edition of *Contrasts*, in which the concept of 'natural architecture', raised in the *Dublin Review*, reappeared and was taken further. Pugin defined it now to mean any design that conformed to his true principles of construction and the correct use of materials. Thinking of the farm at Peper Harow and the masonry of Waterford and Leicestershire, Pugin urged his readers to admire not just ancient churches or houses, but also timber barns, gates and 'the mere essentials' of construction.[4] 'The rubble stones and flinty beach furnish stores as rich for the natural architect, as the limestone quarry.'[5] By this account the architect need no longer look to the actual buildings of the past for precedents, only for principles. Just a year after he had written that he sought nothing more than to 'revive' the art of the Middle Ages and denounced all innovations – 'We seek for *authority* not *originality*' – Pugin had changed his mind.[6] 'The whole history of pointed architecture is a series of inventions,' he wrote blithely; 'time was when the most beautiful productions of antiquity were novelties.'[7]

In a single bound, he was free of the limitations of literal revivalism. As Shrewsbury put it, summarizing his architect's ideas: 'it is no proof a thing did not exist because no perfect specimen of it is come down to our days.'[8] In other words, anything that was designed by someone with a thorough understanding of the principles of Gothic was Gothic even though it was not in appearance like anything made in the Middle Ages. It was a theory that allowed Pugin to do exactly as he liked in practice. As ever he was working out his ideas in dialogue with his architecture, his personal experience dictating his theoretical pronouncements, and from that point of view his change of mind was quite explicable. *Contrasts* had been the work of a young antiquary, looking to the past because it was all he knew. The *Apology* was written by an architect just entering his thirties, with seven years' experience, longing to spread his own creative wings.

Pugin had as yet no thought of reinventing the Gothic church; it was the urban and the secular that were on his mind. He had just designed a group of buildings attached to St George's, Southwark, which took up the theme of the Birmingham bishop's house, the play of rooflines, the use of a huge chimney stack brought right down on to the pavement across a corner. It was a bold, inventive and entirely urban scheme, 'the only correct examples of antient domestic architecture in the metropolis'.[9] In pursuit of these ideas the *Apology* returned to the theme of the modern town, offering this time patterns for houses, shops and a railway station. 'There is no reason in the world,' Pugin explained, 'why noble cities, combining all possible convenience of drainage, water-courses, and conveyance of gas, may not be erected in the most consistent and yet Christian character . . .'[10] The plates of the *Apology* foreshadow thousands of later buildings, the insurance companies, offices and banks that still characterize Victorian town centres. Pugin never built them. The closest he came was in planning a little model town for Lord Midleton on his Irish estate east of Cork, though almost nothing was realized. It would be Butterfield, Scott and dozens of obscure but thoughtful provincial architects who created the High Street Gothic Pugin now proposed.

Linked to this change of mind, Pugin's new belief that architecture could be truly Gothic without being imitative of the Middle Ages, was another resonant idea, that of 'development'. 'Catholicism,' he concluded in the *Apology*, 'is so interwoven with every thing sacred, honourable, or glorious in England . . . It clings to this land, and developes itself from time to time.'[11] Development was a theological doctrine, relatively new to England, which described the belief that while divine revelation is complete, human understanding of it grows and therefore changes in its expression over time. It is not clear how Pugin lit upon this theme, which was to become important to both the theology and the architecture of the following decades. Newman was soon to make it his own but Wiseman, certainly, was already familiar with it; he had preached on the subject at the opening of Pugin's church of St Mary's, Derby, in 1837. Such 'German notions' were regarded as unorthodox by some of Wiseman's fellow Catholics (and most Anglicans), but Pugin was not so theologically nice and his way with arguments was to seize on what suited him rather than to work through detailed implications.[12] Certainly 'development' offered a way of considering Gothic that could justify his claim that while he might build differently from the architects of the Middle Ages, he built just as truly. When it came to considering modern secular architecture, Pugin could argue that as houses had changed in the past so they might change again: 'as the castle merged into the baronial mansion, so . . . the smaller detached houses which the present state of society has generated, should possess a peculiar character'.[13] Development, in religion and in architecture, became such an important idea in the mid-nineteenth century because it offered a solution to questions that troubled most thoughtful people. Pugin was not alone in his need to rethink a fixed view of the past. To many of his contemporaries, alarmed and exhilarated by the pace of change in their lifetime, it was becoming clear that creation itself was not as they had imagined. The geologists uncovered fossils that told a different story from Genesis, a story of change and, indeed development. On the eve of Darwinism this idea, this view of the passage of time as a gradually deepening understanding of a pre-existing divine truth, was one that could reconcile faith with progress, God with evolution. Wherever he came upon it, and Wiseman is a likely source, it seems Pugin was the first to apply the theory of development to architecture.

In so far as the *Apology* was a Tract for the Times, it was Pugin's

Tract XC, in that it dwelt on the Catholic nature of the existing Anglican Church. Pugin explained that the Church of England was already in its 'present acknowledged doctrines' Catholic and pleaded for 'that union to which . . . we may even begin to look forward'.[14] The violent anti-Anglicanism of his earlier writings had gone. Reconciliation of past and present, faith and art, in an unfolding of divine providence were what he longed for, a healing of all rifts and wounds. The *Apology* evoked again the elusive England of the watercolourist's idyll: 'the grey tower of the parochial church rising by the side of the manorial house', a scene of once and future tranquillity in which Pugin himself might again move at ease and worship once more in the church.[15] Ill-organized as it is, the *Apology* holds in embryo almost every theme that was to be important in English architecture for the next two generations: development, nature as a model, the return to the vernacular, the escape from mere copyism, the creation of a Gothic idiom that could produce railway stations, grocers' shops and gas-lit town houses without incongruity, all of this is there.

Unfortunately it was the frontispiece for which the book became known. It was unfortunate, for it is an image that does not show Pugin at his best either in art or in argument. A 'somewhat coarse etching', it depicts a landscape crowded with spires representing 'The Present Revival of Christian Architecture' in the form of twenty-five of Pugin's own works.[16] All appear in an idealized state, St Michael's, Gorey, in particular not so much transfigured as reincarnated as a different, much better building. The plate was aimed at Pugin's current *bête noire*, the Professor of Architecture at the Royal Academy, C. R. Cockerell. Pugin's violent dislike of Cockerell, who, though he did not build in Gothic, had a sympathetic and scholarly understanding of medieval architecture, was scarcely rational and it did Pugin no service. The etching was a riposte to Cockerell's watercolour of 1838, *Tribute to the Memory of Sir Christopher Wren*, which showed Wren's works in a similar composition. Pugin put St George's, Southwark, in place of St Paul's. It was a comparison that struck many people as preposterously vain and egotistical. Egotistical it was, but not vain. Pugin's sincere belief that his work was God's work gave him a kind of overweening self-effacement. His intention was not to set himself up as an individual in competition with Wren, only to set the Gothic against the classical.

One of Pugin's chief objections to Cockerell, architect of such an

'unsightly pile of pagan details' as the new Ashmolean Museum, cur-
rently under construction, was that he 'paganized' in the universities
where Pugin, now so warmly disposed to the Oxford and Cambridge
men, was longing to 'christianize'.[17] Oxford especially he loved, and
now, it seemed, an opportunity opened up there. But Pugin, though he
knew the buildings of the city by heart, still understood nothing of the
university and the elaborate machinery of its politics. His next encounter
with it was a bruising and bitter experience. At Balliol College plans
were already under discussion for repairs and alterations. The Master
was the elderly Richard Jenkyns, a gentleman 'of the old school, in
whom were represented old manners, old traditions, old prejudices . . .
without much literature but having a good deal of character . . . [and]
shrewd commonsense, though deficient in delicacy of touch'. Jenkyns
was expecting to arrange the new buildings, to which he was making a
substantial financial contribution, himself.[18] He called in George Basevi,
architect of the Fitzwilliam Museum in Cambridge, to provide designs
which Jenkyns assumed would get the college's approval on the nod.
He had no idea what forces of architectural and religious enthusiasm
had been welling up around him. Balliol had a number of Tractarian
fellows, including Ward, who had lost his tutorship in the furore of
1841, and Frederick Oakeley, who also knew Pugin. Basevi, who had
been 'weighed in the balance' at the end of *Contrasts*, was everything the
rising generation disliked. A former pupil of Soane and now approaching
fifty, his designs for Balliol were Gothic, because the site required it, but
they were of the competent off-the-peg sort. Ward and Oakeley asked
the Master if they might approach Pugin for an expert opinion on the
design, at which point Jenkyns's shrewd common sense seems to have
deserted him, for he agreed.

Pugin was scathing: 'not bad enough to be rediculous, nor good
enough to be commendable', was his verdict.[19] Ward and Oakeley then
wildly exceeded their brief and as good as offered Pugin the commission.
Pugin told Shrewsbury in February that he had 'every confidence' of
getting 'a *great work* at oxford'.[20] Back at Balliol, where several of the
fellows were unenthusiastic about Basevi's designs, Ward and Oakeley
rehearsed Pugin's criticisms with the result that, to the astonishment of
the architect and the embarrassment of the Master, the scheme was
rejected. From then on a disaster course was set. Balliol has, on Magdalen
Street, the longest front of any college in the university and opposite it

now stood Scott's Martyrs' Memorial, of which Jenkyns had been an active supporter. It was inconceivable that the author of the pamphlet on the Martyrs' Memorial could be given so prominent a commission in the present climate of opinion without a row, probably on a national scale. After some discussion in the college, Pugin heard, early in March, from Ward that a compromise had been reached. Pugin was asked to provide drawings on the understanding that he was to work anonymously. On consideration, and with Bloxam's support, Pugin decided the end was more important than the means and that this was 'not a case where I ought to stand on conditions but make the best of it as it may be a great means by the blessing of God of reviving the real spirit of antient collegiate architecture'.[21] He was egotistical, but not vain.

Jenkyns then showed just how deficient he was in 'delicacy of touch'. He had apparently relied on the stipulation of anonymity to put Pugin off. The gambit having failed, he simply changed his mind, informing the college 'calmly and deliberately but with firmness' that he would withhold his consent from any plan that emanated, however distantly or partially, from Pugin.[22] The fellows saw this as a challenge to their own rights and authority, whereupon even those who had no interest in architecture and were opposed to Tractarianism nevertheless united behind Ward and voted to allow Pugin to go ahead. At this point the local press got hold of the story and the *Oxford Chronicle* began to make sarcastic remarks about the 'extraordinary liberality' being shown by Balliol in employing the Roman Catholic opponent of the Martyrs' Memorial.[23]

At the end of March, after a brief visit to Alton, Pugin threw himself into the scheme. He had less than two weeks to complete it and worked harder, he thought, than ever before in his astonishingly productive life. He had Myers's help with the costings, which he was determined should be exact; 'convenience and necessity', he insisted, 'dictated every feature', but the excitement of the project of 'working for the first time on one of the Old Buildings' seemed 'almost too deligful to bear'.[24] He made, for Ward, a little illuminated volume. Over page after page of this architectural missal there unfolds a vision of scholastic peace and material and intellectual orderliness from library to kitchen, from chapel to undergraduate room. It was another Ideal Scheme, but rational now as well as romantic. Despite the artistic, antiquarian way in which he presented his ideas, his proposals were practical and sensitive. He took as his starting point David Loggan's 1675 bird's-eye perspective of Balliol. Where the buildings had been classicized in the late eighteenth century, he proposed re-Gothicizing them (as had Basevi), restoring the library and dining hall, cladding the exterior of the east range and part of the north with stone and replacing sash windows with mullions. Pugin made drawings for the interiors as well. They show how by now he had learned to design furnishings, form after form, out of his principles of construction in a style both consistent and various. Every necessity of daily life is met: braced washstands, folding stools and individual wall-mounted bookshelves; a big plain wall clock for the kitchen and, in the undergraduate's room, with its plain wood floor, a little rug beside the bed to comfort bare feet.

Pugin scarcely slept or ate while he worked. Ferrey heard from two clergymen who called at Chelsea that they found him surrounded by dozens of drawings, everything from details to large watercolour perspectives all entirely from his own hand. He sent off the designs early in April; 'whatever may be the present result,' Pugin wrote to Bloxam when he had finished, 'it must be of imense service to place such a building designed quite in the old spirit before the members of the university. it must do good.'[25] It didn't. Although he had some 'very satisfactory Letters' from fellows describing themselves as 'quite delighed', these were merely stray shots from the fierce battle at Balliol that had raged out of control over the two weeks that Pugin had been at work.[26] It was no longer about Popery or Pugin but the fellows' authority against the Master's, and this aroused such passions that it was later agreed to remove several pages from the college records.

Pugin, oblivious, waited and wondered why he did not hear when he was to start. He had worn himself out and 'worked beyond my strength'.[27] He was finding it difficult to concentrate on the text of his Glossary. It had been going well in February but by April he was finding it 'a most Laborious work'.[28] His usual intense concentration eluded him. It may have been now that a period of dangerous restlessness began, during the course of which he embarked on some brief liaison with the woman who became Byron Pugin's mother.

The battle at Balliol resulted in a hard-fought decision to do nothing. The building committee was dissolved. Nobody, it seems, dared tell Pugin. He continued to believe his drawings were under consideration. In June he was in Ireland, where he received a 'most perplexing' letter from Ward, who was trying to retrieve something from the wreck, asking permission to give his drawings to another architect.[29] It was an outrageous suggestion. However, more embarrassed than annoyed, Pugin hesitated over his refusal. 'The Balliol men have been so kind,' he told Bloxam. 'I [would] do much to get them out of their present painful position but this amounts to a sort of suiced & I do not think I ought to consent.'[30] When he realized there was no hope he was mortified. 'I cannot conceive who can have come against me,' he wrote to Bloxam, 'except the master as the fellows have always appeared Most friendly.'[31] The whole miserable business dragged on until 1845, when Balliol added insult to injury by writing to ask for a reduction in Pugin's bill.

It was his books, rather than his buildings, that brought him satisfaction that summer. He had completed the illustrations for the *Glossary*, the encyclopedic work he had planned with Bernard Smith, using chromolithography to give the plates their peculiar vividness – golds and crimsons, shocking pinks and grass greens that turned every ecclesiastical form into pattern. The figures of vested priests repeat until they become motifs; altars are flattened into mosaics. The effect is dazzling, almost hallucinogenic, conveying something of the heightened intensity of Pugin's perceptions at the time. Even the alphabets are patterns, 'characters', as Dickens complained, conceived so that 'nobody on earth shall be able to read'.[32] Most of the pattern designs are symmetrical around the vertical axis and often the horizontal as well. The combination of solid colour and symmetry enabled Pugin to create dense elaboration, where he wanted it, without confusion. Interlacing circles around Catherine wheels; dodecafoils in quatrefoils in circles around squares containing crosses with more crosses inside; intricate figures bursting from the page fully formed. In the designs for decorative borders the eye seems to move along lines of a strange music, running from one tempo into another.

In his buildings he had never yet succeeded in creating such an intense effect. Pugin, at this stage in his career, saw painted decoration as an integral part of church design, enhancing the effect of the interior and complementing the stained glass. His intention was to use surface pattern to articulate and differentiate the space, elaborating roof beams or window reveals, but all too often the money had run out by the time the interior was ready to be painted. The richly elaborate scheme he had hoped to create at Nottingham was never completed. Elsewhere patrons economized by discharging Pugin and getting in a local painter, who usually misunderstood the scale and disposition of the decoration. Only at St Giles's, Cheadle, the Drummond chantry at Albury in Surrey and in Bernard Smith's Anglican church of St Swithin's, Leadenham, in Lincolnshire, is it possible to see what Pugin intended the effect of a painted interior to be.

As well as the *Apology* Dolman published the two *Dublin Review* articles in a single volume in 1843 as *The Present State of Ecclesiastical Architecture in England*. The books received mixed reviews but nobody apparently noticed how mixed, indeed contradictory, a view they themselves presented. The majority of critics simply wrote according to their prejudices, about Pugin and about Catholicism and about the arguments of his earlier work. Some were irritated by his style. His old enemies at the *Civil Engineer and Architect's Journal* thought his antiquarian bird's-eye views 'affectedly rude' and found his illustrations mere 'architectural farragos, instead of designs'.[33] Pugin had never been on terms with the professional establishment, and now his autodidactic, antiquarian style was starting to look increasingly odd as that establishment became ever larger and better defined. The *Builder*, the illustrated magazine in whose bound volumes it is possible to watch the story of Victorian architecture unfold, began publication this year. It did not think much of *The Present State*. From now on it might be said that Pugin and his reputation began to go their separate ways. On the one hand the growth of the architectural press added to his fame. He was well enough known for William Leeds to write about Puginism without inverted commas. But most people thought they knew what Puginism was and were firmly for or against it without knowing much about how Pugin himself had changed and would continue to develop. It began to seem as if he was being left behind while architecture as a whole raced ahead at a pace that was generally considered 'not less remarkable than that which has been exhibited in respect to locomotive science as affecting railroad coaches'.[34] The steam-age architect now entered the public imagination in the unattractive shape of Mr Pecksniff, with the appearance in instalments of *Martin Chuzzlewit*.

Pugin was sanguine in the face of criticism of his latest book, concluding that 'Both the infidel & protestant party [begin] to find out that this revival of Catholic architecture is producing a great moral change.'[35] He was right. Although Catholicism did not prevail, the Gothic Revival as a moral and religious conception of architecture had achieved a now unstoppable momentum. His confidence was further restored by the possibility of recovering something from the disappointment of Balliol. Down in Leicestershire the clash of wills between Phillipps and his unwilling chaplain continued. Gentili had now moved out of Grace Dieu and gone to Loughborough. He wanted Phillipps to fulfil his promise to build a house for the Rosminians. Phillipps agreed. It was to be in the countryside nearby, at Ratcliffe on the Wreake, and it was built with the help of Phillipps and a new Rosminian brother, William Lockhart, a young Tractarian. Lockhart had met Gentili at Oxford, and, like many people, was profoundly struck by this gently spoken, iron-willed intellectual. Lockhart began, 'little by little', to feel his soul being won for Rome. His conversion in August 1843 was a terrible blow to Newman, who soon afterwards gave up the living of St Mary's. Phillipps and Gentili were delighted both with Lockhart himself, who became a close friend, and by the fact that he gave £1,000, a quarter of the cost, to the building of the new college. The project was marred, however, and marked by the disagreements that increasingly characterized the English Catholics' efforts. Phillipps wanted Pugin to build Ratcliffe. Pugin wanted to build his Balliol scheme, in several stages if necessary. Gentili wanted something practical finished as quickly as possible. The foundation stone was laid without any clear agreement about how much would be built or whether the house was to be a noviciate, or to function as a college as well.

The building that was opened the following year consisted of a single ninety-foot range with only about half a dozen rooms downstairs and tiny cells above. Gentili complained that the fires smoked, the ceilings were too low, the corridor too narrow, and that there was no way of reaching the far side of the oratory except by passing through it. He told Rosmini that he was hoping to dismantle the building and use the bricks for something else. He was dissuaded, however, and Ratcliffe, which is now a school, still sports a front that is a modest, red-brick version of Pugin's Balliol.

Between visits to Ireland Pugin was at Alton completing the new apartments for the Shrewsburys' daughter and son-in-law, the Prince and Princess Doria. He was also restoring and extending the ruined castle opposite St John's. There was never any practical reason for doing this, it was simply a prospect that Pugin found too tempting to resist, while the Earl made attempts to turn it to some use. The work went on fitfully and Pugin and his patron were often at cross-purposes. Shrewsbury now produced what he thought was an economical proposition. He suggested curtailing work at St John's, abandoning the parts of it intended for elderly priests and using the castle to lodge them instead. It was a feasible idea, but an architectural anathema, for it would spoil both buildings, truncating one and travestying the other.

'I would sooner jump off the rocks than build a *castelated residence for Priests*,' Pugin wrote from Killarney; 'the hospital as designed would be a perfect building . . . & everybody looking forward to it. I can bear things as well as anyone but I would almost as soon cut my throat as to cut that hospital to pieces for heavens sake my dear Lord Shrewsbury.'[36] Shrewsbury backed down again, but the hospital and the castle continued to be bones of contention. Work on them was from now on intermittent and interrupted by changes of mind and intention. At Mount St Bernard's, Phillipps's monastery, the Prior, Bernard Palmer, was also thinking of saving time and money. Despite a successful fundraising bazaar he had only £800 at his disposal to build a church. Pugin's design was on a much larger scale.

Although he continued to be busy and apparently successful, there would be more incidents like this, for in truth Pugin's career as an architect had now just passed its high-water mark. At Nottingham St Barnabas's was rising fast; 'the spire . . . can now be seen sixteen miles off!!!' as Pugin told Bloxam excitedly, adding that it still had another thirty-six feet to go.[37] Newcastle and Southwark were progressing, but these were to be almost the last of Pugin's big churches. At Downside there was panic when the monks saw the splendidly idealized illustration in *The Present State* of what Pugin planned to build there. They cancelled the commission. At Southport the Revd J. Newsham wrote with frantic sarcasm to his bishop, Dr Brown, to explain that his church of St Mary on the Sands had a congregation small in number and mostly poor. Newsham himself was ill and his total funds were £114 short of what was owed to Pugin and the workmen: 'I have built Saint Mary's and paid a thousand pounds,' Newsham wrote, 'supported in the back ground always by one prop: viz, if I want Brass I will sell my watch. Now it is a capital gold watch and depend upon it, come the worst, off goes my watch. Pardon me, I forget for a moment your dignity.'[38]

At the end of July Pugin set off for his summer tour. He was overtired and overworked, possibly hypomanic, but travel was refreshing and he was soon 'better in Mind and body'.[39] He set off expecting to find 'glorious details for the Cheadle windows among the early works at Antwerp, Louvain etc.'.[40] He was also at Cologne, which he had not visited since 1838, and where the vision of Gothic Revival was being animated on a vast scale. The great unfinished cathedral's mute appeal across the centuries had been answered. In 1840 work began to complete it as a gesture of national and stylistic propaganda: 'Religion, Fatherland and Art' were the banner under which the work was undertaken. By now the Gothic Revival was as international as it was nationalist. Pugin and the Camdenians were in touch with events in France and Germany. Publications were circulated and visits exchanged to works in progress. Pugin was delighted with what he found at Cologne. 'They are actually restoring the *painting on the pillars* & vaulting. I shall return quite rich in new/old devices,' he wrote to Shrewsbury.[41] He remembered Cologne when he came to design the intense patterning of the interior of St Giles, the one building that remained his 'consolation'.

25

The Grange, Ramsgate

September to December 1843

Keep far our foes, give peace at home:
Where thou art guide, no ill can come . . .
– *Veni Creator Spiritus*, from the Ordering
of Priests

The church at Cheadle represented the culmination of one phase of Pugin's ideas, the ideal parish church. Even before it was finished, however, he had begun typically to pursue the next. He was now to take up the idea he had outlined in the *Apology*, the development of a modern kind of Gothic suitable for the nineteenth-century family house. It was to be worked out first in a new home for himself which he intended to build on a plot of land he had bought on the West Cliff at Ramsgate.

This second Grange was to be a 'folio edition' of the first, another manifesto, but one this time that would be more than a curiosity full of potential.[1] Pugin's house at Ramsgate was a prototype and it became a model for the English family house that was used in various ways by three generations of architects.[2] Such a model was needed because, as a building type, the middle-class detached family home, something less than a mansion and more than a cottage, was relatively new. It was to become as characteristic a product of the Victorian age as village schools and railway stations. There were already some such houses, of course. Since Pugin's childhood, when the Ruskins and the Ackermanns had retreated to villas in Camberwell, the professional classes had begun to commute, but before the railways most people below the level of the gentry, needing to be involved in trade and business, found it easier to live in towns. Now, as Pugin wrote in the *Apology*, the 'smaller detached houses' of the suburbs were becoming a particular feature of the age.

They proliferated over the decades as 'the branch lines infiltrated into deepest Surrey' until, by the end of the century, they were ubiquitous; the red brick rectories, the substantial middle-class houses and gardens that dot the Home Counties and the commuter belts of cities now typify the English landscape.[3] They were all prefigured in Pugin's new project at Ramsgate.

His theories of natural architecture and development allowed him this time to think the subject through from first principles of convenience, instead of trying to adapt medieval models, as he had at Salisbury. He told Bloxam about his plans for 'a most substantial catholic house not very Large but convenient'.[4] The house was not to stand alone but to be part of a group of buildings such as he often evoked in his writings. 'There is every prospect of a small church on the same ground,' he told Bloxam, 'which will be deligtful when this is finished I shall hope to induce you to come to me & enjoy what is so rarely to be attained the delight of the sea with catholic architecture & a *Library* (not a *circulating* one).'[5] At the bottom of the letter Pugin sketched his idea of what the new house would look like. Barely two inches square, the little ink outline shows it, in all essentials, as it was built.

In the years since he had drawn out his fantastic scheme for the house at Salisbury, Pugin had designed over a dozen small houses, most of them for priests. They had been cheap buildings and Pugin had learned by working on them to do more and more with less, until he had come not only to master but to prefer the 'plainness, simplicity, severity' he had achieved. The new Grange was to have no exaggerated anti-quarianism about it, no drawbridge or garde-robe. In appearance it was plain to the point of austerity. It was arranged over two storeys with attics, built in yellow brick for economy. It was not entirely stark. It had a tower – for looking out to sea – and a double-height bay window that marked the principal rooms on both floors, yet it was of its place and of its time, made up, as the *Apology* advised, of 'brick fronts, adapted perfectly to internal convenience . . . and terminated by the natural form of the gable'.[6] The effect was in the event so plain that Charles Barry's son, a young architect himself, thought the house 'uninviting and indeed . . . ugly' on the outside.[7]

When it came to the interior Pugin developed a new plan that seems to have come to him, like most of his ideas, in a single insight. It combined the plan of a modern villa – the sort of thing John Nash or his own father would have designed, with rooms grouped round a central hall – with the ethos of the Gothic mansion. There was a drawing room, a library, a dining room, with a long kitchen wing directly opposite, and a small oratory. Above were three principal bedrooms, nurseries, a little tower room and attics. What gave this arrangement its particular effect was the central, double-height staircase hall, from which the stairs rose round two sides to a gallery. This central space, large enough to serve as a room in its own right, echoed the medieval great hall, but without a dais or a minstrels' gallery, which would have been an affectation in a small modern house. The living rooms opened directly off it and between the drawing room and the library where Pugin worked there was no door, only a curtain. A door, Pugin said, would always bang. More importantly, perhaps, he liked interconnecting spaces both visually and symbolically, as much in houses as in churches, for they allowed for framed sequential views and made a distinction, but no separation, between the areas devoted to work and those for family life.

Looking back at it across the twentieth century, the plan of the Grange seems scarcely remarkable, for it is prescient of so much that was essential to the Arts and Crafts house. The inglenook fireplace in Pugin's dining room with its 'cosy sea lockers', the 'living hall' that had become by 1904 'the most English' of all rooms are there in the design of 1843.[8] Yet at the time the Grange, if it was not thought ridiculous as Salisbury had been, was unorthodox and to conventional tastes almost improper. A central hall in which family and servants would constantly meet one another, for there was no other way between rooms; an open gallery that gave a clear view of the bedroom doors; no separate nursery wing; all of this offended the developing Victorian sense of domestic propriety. Servants, family, children and guests were all supposed to be kept apart. Charles Eastlake later found the Grange scarcely decent; it was 'a picturesque arrangement, but open to objection'; it would not suit the 'modern requirements of an ordinary home' if nobody could pass between rooms without 'coming within sight of the entrance door'.[9]

This Victorian horror of transgressing the domestic hierarchy wore off. Today Pugin's desire to draw his home together, parents and children in a single harmonious whole, seems entirely proper. The arrangements he made around the house, however, would have been eccentric in any age. He surrounded it with a double courtyard and a gate lodge, all crammed into a tiny area. If he no longer wanted a drawbridge outside his front door, he clearly still felt the need, aesthetic and psychological, to defend his home. The courtyards prevented any near approach to the house except on foot. There was no door on the garden side. The defences were also a picturesque device which diverted any visitor on a winding route from a side gate round to the front. The house was alternately concealed and partially revealed until, passing through the last gate, it would suddenly appear, its height exaggerated by contrast and proximity, towering up.

That autumn, as work on the Grange began, Pugin's sixth child, a daughter, was born, on 25 September. She was called Mary. Was Pugin thinking of another Mary, who had been dispatched, pregnant, to America? Possibly. But Mary is an ancient English name, always popular, especially with Catholics. Although the domestic ideal his new house represented was less than fully reflected in his own marriage and home life, the prospect of the Grange put Pugin into high spirits. His other work was also going well. 'I am making great progress in the church way in all directions,' he told Bloxam, '& have 3 new buildings only Last week.'[10] At Ushaw, the seminary of the Northern District, the idea of a new chapel, long under discussion, was now about to be realized, and at Salford there were plans for a large church.

Meanwhile Bloxam and his allies at Magdalen were determined to find some way of compensating Pugin for his disappointment at Balliol and showing Oxford a little of the 'true thing'. They gave Pugin a commission for a gateway for the college, which he began at once, organizing the project with theatrical discretion. He refused to write down, even in a letter to the Earl of Shrewsbury, the exact nature of this job; 'it must not be talked about'.[11] The gate was made, by Myers's men, in London, finished the next summer and transported to Oxford in pieces to be assembled as quickly as possible on site, a fait accompli. Elsewhere in Oxford conversions and rumours of conversions continued to circulate. Newman, who had retreated to Littlemore in 1841, now gave up the living of the university church. Pusey had been suspended. As the agonizings of the Tractarians went on, a certain irritation began to be felt in many quarters at what seemed like spiritual valetudinarianism. Mary Arundell was 'out of patience' with the 'Puseyites' and what she saw as their spiritual pride, while Dickens found himself feeling 'horribly bitter' about men who could equivocate so long about 'what priests shall wear' while the distress and unrest in the country at large continued.[12] The great religious debate of the day was teetering on the edge of farce and in October it tipped over the edge. Sibthorp, who since his ordination as a Catholic priest had been increasingly unhappy, lonely and disillusioned, wrote to Dr Routh at Magdalen with the news that he had 'received the Holy Communion' in his old church on the Isle of Wight 'as declaratory of my return to the Church of England'.[13] Wiseman was aghast. He took to his bed for two days, sick with self-reproach for having encouraged Sibthorp to become a priest. Bloxam told Pugin, who was 'quite upset', but the two friends who had nearly quarrelled over Sibthorp's first conversion were of one mind about his second.[14] Both maintained some sympathy for him. They were too generous, too secure in their own faith, to feel any effect from the aftershocks. Pugin never quite forgave Sibthorp but he was pragmatic. Within a fortnight he was writing to Shrewsbury about Nottingham: 'by far the grandest thing we have done the Bishop is going to build the boundary wall etc . . . very fortunate we got Mr Sibthorpes 3000 just in time.'[15] Poor Sibthorp had lost his money, his dignity and most of his few remaining friends.

The Earl and Countess of Shrewsbury, assisted by Wiseman, meanwhile did their best to promote a more elevating idea of Catholic society in England and of the English Catholics abroad. That winter, while Shrewsbury continued to drag his feet over St John's Hospital and the restoration of Alton Castle, Pugin hurried ahead with work at St Giles's, where the chancel roof was on and Minton, at Stoke, was working on the tiles. The Earl's immediate anxiety, hence at once his architect's, was the visit to Alton Towers of Henri de Bourbon, Duc de Bordeaux, the pretender to the French throne. Of all the pretenders, impostors and the genuinely dispossessed who wandered Europe in those years, Chambord was less romantic but more authentic than many. The son of Caroline de Berry, he had been a child when Pugin was in France with his parents and Auguste and Louis Lafitte inhabited the fringes of the Bourbon circle at Villeneuve l'Etang and Rosny. Pugin was now very much in his uncle's professional position, rushed off his feet arranging 'fire engines' (to make light rather than fight fire), finding matching silver sugar basins, building collapsible awnings and trying to prevent the Earl from using old-fashioned 'illuminators' which would 'look like a Vauxhall night'.[16]

The results were spectacular. In the late November dusk the carriages of the royal party made their way through the great landscape gardens by rocky declivities along winding drives, until the towers and battlements of Alton reared up with seeming suddenness against the winter sky; then, all at once, every tower and window, every arrow slit and rampart, was brilliantly lit from behind. The great doors were flung open and the procession passed in to meet the Earl and Countess. It moved along the grand route, past the armour and the heraldic glass, the figure of the Great Talbot and the almost equally artificial figure of Edward Jervis, the Earl's blind harpist in his minstrel costume, into the octagon where an orchestra struck up 'Vive Henri IV'.

The Duke was more than willing, like Victoria and Albert, to don the trappings of Gothic romance, so flattering to royalty. His party later inspected Minton's works at Stoke and Hardman's at Birmingham. Their admiration for all the Earl's endeavours, including the school and hospital, must have been pleasing and perhaps encouraged Shrewsbury to overcome his misgivings. But for Pugin the Duke's visit had a further significance. It was now, at Alton Towers, that he met Mary Amherst, probably for the first time. It was certainly now that they began a friendship. She was the daughter of the Mrs Amherst who had been Pugin's patron at Kenilworth, the sister of Kerril whom Pugin had taught at Oscott and a distant cousin of the Shrewsburys. She was nineteen or twenty, intelligent, lively and very pretty. She was a devout Catholic and much under the influence of Gentili, who was her confidant and spiritual adviser. Whatever may or may not have happened earlier in the year, it is certain that in November Pugin fell in love.

26

A Return of Grief

January to August 1844

Sorrow passed, and plucked the golden blossom;
Guilt stripped off the foliage in its pride . . .
Emily Brontë, *Death*, 1846

Pugin could neither act on his feelings for Mary Amherst nor forget them. He wrote to her from time to time on general subjects and she answered. 'He was a married man with many children,' she later explained to Gentili, 'I never thought for a moment . . .'[1] Meanwhile Bernard Smith was staying at Chelsea, helping Pugin with the 'dry study' necessary to organize the text for his *Glossary* and translating the various Latin texts. He translated the French as well, for although Pugin was bilingual he found translation tedious.

Pugin's refusal, or his inability, to do what he found boring, to make detailed drawings, adopt modern professional practices, or humour committees, was beginning to count against him. From now on his headlong rise to fame and the constant flow of commissions that had begun seven years before started, almost imperceptibly at first, to slow. There were other reasons besides his volatility. First it was noticeable, quite suddenly, that he was no longer a lone star. His own writings, public taste and the many Few Words of the Cambridge Camden Society were shaping a new generation of architects. Some, like Scott and Butterfield, were Pugin's contemporaries, only now beginning to emerge. Scott's London church of St Giles, Camberwell, was just finished. It was larger, more expensive and in every way a fuller realization of Pugin's ideal parish church than Pugin had yet completed. As Scott wrote, immodestly but truthfully, it was, as far as the Gothic Revival was concerned, 'the best church by far that had then been erected'.[2] It would have been impossible without Pugin, but it was not by him.

As Pugin and his public persona moved yet further apart, Puginism went marching on, spreading little broach-spired churches all over the towns and villages of Britain and the Empire. These symmetrical English Gothic churches would soon start to look clichéd and contribute to the impression that Pugin himself had lost momentum and run out of ideas. Meanwhile, at the forefront of architecture, the High Victorian style began to emerge, a tougher, bolder, more eclectic kind of Gothic, thought both at the time and since to mark the end of Pugin's influence. This is quite untrue, for he himself had been moving for some years in the same direction. High Victorianism is there in embryo at St John's Hospital and yet more boldly in the farm buildings at Peper Harow. Pugin continued to develop as an architect in his early thirties and he passed his thoughts on, quite directly, to the rising generation. In January 1844 Benjamin Webb recorded in his diary that Pugin met William Butterfield in a party of Camdenian and Tractarian friends. This may have been their first personal encounter, although Butterfield had followed Pugin's career closely for some time. Webb gave no details of the conversation but in such company it must have revolved largely around architecture. Pugin, who always talked a great deal, mostly about his own work, would surely have expounded his latest ideas about domestic and vernacular buildings and the value of humble barns and gates, as demonstrated in his own farm buildings for Lord Midleton and in his new house at Ramsgate. He may well have brought drawings with him to show.

It was just weeks after this meeting that Webb was one of the judges for a competition to design a church at Coalpit Heath in Gloucestershire. He noted on 8 February that they 'Chose the *laus Deo* designs'.[3] This was Butterfield's entry, and the buildings that resulted, house, church and boldly chamfered lychgate, have generally been considered by historians as marking the dawn of the High Victorian age in architecture, the end of Puginism. They do indeed mark a new departure in the Gothic Revival, but one in which Pugin, far from being marginalized, almost certainly played a direct role. The gateway recalls the Peper Harow buildings while the parsonage house that Butterfield built beside the church, which has been seen as the great breakthrough into modern domestic planning, was organized, like the Grange, around a central hall that was a real room. It was an idea Butterfield immediately afterwards abandoned and tried only once more. It was too outré, presumably, for most of the clergy. The wonder is that he tried it at all and it is difficult not to think that it was Pugin who gave him the example.

For all his influence, however, the flow of work away from Pugin towards his imitators and followers continued. Richard Carpenter, whom he had met with Butterfield, was soon being hailed by the Ecclesiologists as the 'Anglican Pugin', though he had also ideas of his own. Among the Catholics there was Charles Hansom, five years Pugin's junior and an imitator more than a follower, who started to tread uncomfortably close on his heels. In 1844 Hansom was building a Puginesque church at Coventry for the Benedictines. Gothic was now so much the norm for church buildings that Catholics were increasingly willing to adopt it, but they preferred a cheaper, more pliable architect. It was Hansom who carried out the work at Downside that Pugin had hoped to do and it would be Hansom who eventually finished Ratcliffe College. Matthew Hadfield, whose employment at Macclesfield had been so brusquely set aside by Lord Shrewsbury, got the job at Salford for which Pugin had been consulted but where he had refused to give way on 'some point of principle'.[4] Hadfield's career grew from now on as Pugin's declined. An uninspired architect who copied shamelessly, his work, especially his cathedral at Sheffield, owed more to Pugin than it could repay.

None of Pugin's own commissions, meanwhile, was lucrative or prominent. He continued to do the jobs that he liked, rather than those that might advance his reputation. He was more than happy to help Edward Willson's brother Robert, the priest at Nottingham, who had recently, much to his dismay, been appointed Bishop of Hobart in Van Diemen's Land, now Tasmania. For his mission Pugin provided him with '40 large chasubles!!! several tombs 2 altars compleat, fonts &c tiles & 3 models of small churches all to take to pieces with the roofs &c framed, simple buildings that can be easily constructed',[5] all of which Willson carried with him aboard the *Bella Marina* on the hazardous five-month voyage to the most desperate and degraded of the British penal colonies. Pugin was sorry to part with him but excited about the prospect of sending work out to proclaim the gospel in a strange land. 'It is quite delightful to start in the good style at the antipodes. It is quite an honour,' he wrote to Shrewsbury.[6] Willson was a devout man but also practical, humane and effective, and he did much to improve the lives of the convicts. It was a long time before he managed to build a church. Pugin's work in Tasmania was an honour that nobody in England would know of for more than a century.[7]

Another unlikely commission to come Pugin's way just now was from Henry Drummond. Drummond, like Henri de Bourbon, was a revenant from Pugin's childhood. A Tory MP, founder of the Chair of Political Economy at Oxford and heir to Drummond's Bank, he was, according to Carlyle, a man 'of elastic pungent decisive nature; full of fine qualities and capabilities, – but well nigh cracked with an enormous conceit of himself'.[8] Like Scarisbrick, he felt a rare warmth towards Pugin, who liked to tease and argue with the older man: 'vous etes un homme inconcevable,' Pugin once wrote to him, 'but I will do my best to get the right thing for you, even at the risk of being scolded.'[9] Drummond had been a founding member of Edward Irving's Catholic Apostolic Church, whose genesis Pugin had reluctantly witnessed as he sat through the interminable sermons that had so stimulated Catherine Pugin. Irving had latterly become a sad figure. His mind had been unbalanced by public attention and private unhappiness and he had died insane a decade earlier. The Church he had founded by now owed more of its character to John Bate Cardale and Drummond.

Under their influence the Catholic Apostolic Church had lost its Calvinist ethos, and while it waited for the imminent millennium it devoted itself to the same ideals of Christian architecture and the reunion of the Catholic Church that Pugin, the Tractarians and the Cambridge Camden Society all in varying degrees advocated. Thus the curious cranks and quirks of the Early Victorian religious debates had brought Pugin into a closer sympathy with the Irvingites than he felt now for most Roman Catholics. Even the *Ecclesiologist* was forced to admit with some embarrassment that this 'strange anomalous sect . . . amid all its wild delusions has grasped . . . much of ancient truth'.[10] Pugin restored the Saxon parish church on Drummond's estate at Albury in Surrey, from which Drummond had driven the parishioners. He also created a mortuary chapel there as a burial place for Drummond's sons, all of whom had died young. Drummond was difficult and the commission dragged on for years, but the chapel was eventually one of Pugin's best works. Lovely and harmonious in itself, vividly patterned but restrained, it is also a curiosity of its time, combining as it does the iconography of

Catholic and Catholic Apostolic beliefs in an Anglican Church. But it was another obscure work, on the fringes both of architecture and of society.

At Newcastle, meanwhile, where the church of St Mary's was nearly finished, Pugin and Myers were running into difficulties of an ominously modern kind. The building committee wanted a contract, the kind of detailed arrangement that seemed to Pugin hair-splitting and bureaucratic. Difficult as such a contract might have been for Myers had it been signed before work started, it was utterly impossible to comply with now that it was nearly finished. The letters he and Pugin wrote to William Dunn and his committee are the first record of their working relationship and the correspondence shows their strengths and weaknesses. On the one hand they were clearly in the right. On the other neither was tactful or urbane enough to allay the fears at Newcastle that the committee was dealing with tradesmen, who were not to be trusted. Myers wrote to them typically:

Your letter this morning is not at all satisfactory. I wrote you the fore part of November for some money on act. of the Building, the answer I receve [sic] from you are when do you mean to sign the contract or words to this effect, you being well aware there is three or four Payments due . . . you also know that the former payments have been made without refference [sic] to the contract – I stated my objections when together three hours in your office – now I must beg once more of you for a remittence [sic] according to the order of the architect without saying more I hope you will see the justice of my application
I remain sir your very obd st
Geo Myers[11]

The committee complained about Myers's language to Pugin, who agreed that his builder was wrong to have been 'imputing motives' to the committee, but then weighed in on his behalf over several pages of furious reproach: 'in all the other works in which I have been engaed we never had occasion for official notices about anything much Less for trifles which are not worth the paper. Churches should not be built on the same principles as barrack contracts.'[12] If Myers's grammar was shaky, his spelling was no worse than Pugin's and his handwriting much better. Neither appeared like a conventionally educated person and consequently, Pugin complained, he was 'called in & ordered out like a pork contractor in a workhouse'.[13]

Nevertheless Pugin felt that 'we progress'.[14] His relations with the Tractarians continued warm. Pusey came to see him that month and commissioned designs for windows for his new church, St Saviour's, Leeds. Pugin began the illustrations for the series of *Lives of the English Saints*, edited by Newman. Wiseman was roused from his depression about Sibthorp by the arrival of another promising convert, the young Charles Scott Murray. A graduate of Christ Church and a Camdenian, he was one of the Young England generation of Tory MPs to enter Parliament in 1841 and the first sitting member to become a Catholic. The event caused such a stir in the press that Murray was almost afraid to return home from the Continent, where he had made his profession of faith. Wiseman wrote to Shrewsbury alerting him. 'He knows no Catholics – his own friends & party all are Tory, & he expects no cordiality from them he is uncertain consequently whether to resign . . . it would be a pity to lose him in the house as a Catholic.'[15] Furthermore Wiseman pointed out: 'Mr S. Murray . . . is come into a fine fortune by his father's death & his mother with whom he lives is very strongly Prot. The hands he first falls into will have of course an influence, & it would be a pity that they should not be the best.'[16] Wiseman's care was repaid. When Murray finally returned some months later he fell into Wiseman and Shrewsbury's hands. That autumn he commissioned a church from Pugin.

As well as new churches there was now a great movement for restoration of the old. Under the admonishing eye of the Cambridge Camden Society more and more Anglican clergymen looked with embarrassment at their tumbledown Georgianized aisles. The box pews, the looming three-decker pulpits, the monuments jammed anyhow across the windows, were ever more painful eyesores to readers of the *Ecclesiologist*. In the spring Pugin started work on the third restoration job he had been given that year, for the Vicar of Wymeswold in Leicestershire, Henry Alford. Alford could no longer stand the sight of the commandment boards in his church, on which the names of the churchwardens were written larger than the verses from Exodus. He and Pugin were as one in their ideas. To Alford, later Dean of Canterbury, the restoration was an act of worship, a project to 'begin, continue, and end . . . on the high distinct principles of faith and obedience'.[17] To these sympathetic qualities he was able to add a methodical, determined character and a great deal of money.

Although the restoration of Wymeswold was the sort of job that would later incense William Morris and his contemporaries, it was not invasive by the standards of the day. Pugin loved and understood medieval buildings and treated them with increasing sensitivity. Nevertheless, a later generation would not have decided, as he and Alford did, that the fourteenth-century corbels should be removed 'to replace their rude workmanship by better'.[18] Nor would it have decided that the chancel arch was 'mean and low' and that something 'very lofty, and the pitch exactly equilateral' would do better.[19] Such questions were now being raised internationally as the campaign to preserve and restore the architecture of the Middle Ages moved on. In May Pugin went to look at the most influential project in progress, Félix Duban's restoration of the Sainte-Chapelle in Paris. It was the first French renovation to be conducted on archaeological principles and the eyes of Europe were upon it. The Sainte-Chapelle by now looked significantly different from the building Pugin had drawn in 1829 for his father's views of Paris. 'The restoration . . . is worthy of the days of St Louis,' Pugin told Shrewsbury. 'I never saw Images so exquisitely painted. I worked incessantly the whole time I was away & got most interesting sketches. I have also purchased a great many casts of the most beautiful character, which will be just the thing for the images on the spire at Cheadle & also for the reredos & chancel.'[20] He decided to go back to Alton straight away in order to put his ideas into practice while they were fresh in his mind. What thrilled Pugin was the detail. He made no mention of the constructional questions raised by the work, indeed he never seems to have felt much interest in the philosophical debate generated by Duban's restoration. He left no comment on its legacy of functionalism as interpreted by Viollet-le-Duc. Viollet published his rationalist manifesto *De la construction des édifices religieux* that year in the *Annales Archéologiques*. Pugin would certainly have seen it, but if he read it he said nothing about it.

With the opening of Nottingham and Newcastle cathedrals due in the summer and work resumed at St John's Hospital and going at full speed at Cheadle, along with all the other smaller jobs he had in hand, Pugin was even more than usually stretched. He was beginning to look for assistance to his eldest son, Edward, known in the family as Teddy, as his own father had looked to him at about that age. 'I began working in my father's office when I was but seven years old,' Edward, who was ten that summer, later recalled.[21] By his own reckoning he was already quite a seasoned workman and Pugin was beginning to take him about on site visits. Teddy was an enthusiastic draughtsman, 'a bright ... miniature of his Father', with the same 'quick perception and energy'.[22] From now on Pugin had a child beside him taking notes and the impressions Edward formed of the events of 1844 had far-reaching consequences: it was now that the Palace of Westminster, the building destined to be the site of Pugin's best-known work but also, in many ways, his nemesis, came back into his life.

The Royal Commission of Fine Arts, set up in 1841, on which the Earl of Shrewsbury sat, was advising on the decoration of the Palace. The Commissioners were anxious that this should be an improving as much as an artistic project, one that would exercise a 'beneficial and elevating influence' on the country.[23] It marked the real beginning of state patronage for the arts in Britain and the Victorians expected a lot for their money. The Palace was intended not only to educate and civilize, it was also to be a boost to craftsmanship and manufacturing by 'creating new objects of industry and enjoyment ... adding ... to the wealth of the country'.[24] As England under George IV had looked to France for inspiration for its great public buildings, Victorian England looked to Germany, and not only because the Prince Consort, chairman of the Commission, was German. German art and architecture, and especially the work of the Nazarene painters already patronized by Shrewsbury, were immensely popular and seen to be the most interesting in Europe. The Nazarene artist Peter Cornelius was consulted on fresco technique, considered the most suitable medium for painted decoration for a Gothic building. In order to choose the best artists for the murals there had been two exhibitions of cartoons, one of them judged by Pugin's friend Etty.

Yet although his friends and acquaintances were involved, none of this had yet affected Pugin directly. It was the vast amount of furnishing and finishing that the Palace still required – stained glass, metalwork, wood carving, tiling, panelling, wallpaper, carpets, lighting and furniture – that put his name into several minds. He was not only the obvious person to carry out the work, he was almost the only person who could contemplate it, for while the Gothic Revival had moved ahead so rapidly in architecture the applied arts had lagged behind. An exhibition of Decorative Works was held in April to select designers. The exhibits made Charles Barry's heart sink. The wood carving in particular was lamentable. Typically, a single door panel for the House of Lords was intended to depict 'Alfred the Great receiving an illuminated missal as a reward for learning to read from his mother Osburgha', the conception as excessive as the execution was inadequate. Barry himself, though he had a strong idea of the effect he wanted, was no designer of decorative detail and was now under growing pressure to get the building ready for use. Shrewsbury, of course, was lobbying for Pugin to get the job of designing the interiors, but as so often he had misunderstood his architect. When Barry himself approached Pugin that summer Pugin, once again 'pulled down' by illness, over-committed to his architectural practice and in all his circumstances changed from the tyro of a decade before, turned him down.[25] 'I am sure I can never do you real service except in absolute detail; you should fully make up your mind as to every arrangement and then turn the small work over to me . . . Remember, I never made a drawing which was of any real use to you yet, and it is a dreadful loss of time to me, incessantly occupied as I am with Church work, to attempt it.'[26] He was willing to point Barry towards 'authorities' and to introduce him to the carvers doing the best Gothic work, who were at Louvain. Beyond that he was not interested.

The illness Pugin complained of was this time described as 'English cholera', another elusive diagnosis, but the combination of fever and mental exhaustion was a familiar one. The attack left him 'excedingly indisposed'.[27] It was not just in body but in mind that he was ailing, for he was unhappy and thinking constantly of Mary Amherst. To Bloxam he explained, 'I have been lately so very unwell through overwork that I have been seriously advised to go as far as Cologne to relieve my mind & I trust by the blessing of God to go on all the faster for this little relaxation.'[28] Relaxation was not, however, in Pugin's nature. He was setting off in pursuit of Mary. She and her mother were travelling on the Continent and Pugin went, with Kerril, Mary's brother, to join them at Godesberg on the Rhine. He stayed a week. They visited Cologne Cathedral and Ernst Friedrich Zwirner's much discussed new Gothic church at Remagen, but Pugin's real object was Mary herself, who could not but notice that his attentions to her were now 'very marked'. 'I am the one to blame,' she wrote, later, to Gentili; 'my pride was flattered and I encouraged him . . . whatever he may have done wrong since I am the one to blame.'[29] In her strenuous efforts to exonerate Pugin, Mary was unjust to herself. She was not a flirt. 'When he left us . . . I found that my affections had been drawn from the almighty & given to him I may say he was the constant object of my thoughts.'[30] She, too, was now in love.

In whatever turbulent state of mind he returned home, Pugin was at once immersed in his 'church work'. The labours of the last few years were coming to fruition. Nottingham and Newcastle were nearly finished. Cheadle was moving towards completion and a new, larger, design for the spire was made out that summer. By August, with Newcastle nearly ready to be opened and Nottingham to be consecrated, Wiseman was having to juggle dates. In the event Pugin's second and third cathedrals opened within a week of each other. Newcastle was internally 'but half completed' and at Nottingham there were finishing touches and decoration still to do.[31] Both events required preparations for the processions and ceremonial dinners. There were press releases, invitations and much else to be arranged. Even by his own frantic standards Pugin was travelling at a hectic pace. On the 5th he went from London to Nottingham and then to Derby, from where he travelled through the night to York, going on to Ushaw, back to Derby and Birmingham, then overnight again to Liverpool, forty-eight hours' constant travel. He was to and fro at Alton, where the Duke of Cambridge was expected, and he was there on the 10th when old Mr Hardman, his partner John's father, died. He was an old man, ill for some years, but it was a sad loss. No one, not even Shrewsbury, had been a greater supporter of Pugin's vision of religious art. Pugin knew what he owed to Hardman and went to Birmingham for the funeral at St Chad's to see him laid to rest in the crypt of the cathedral he had so greatly helped to bring into existence.

Pugin then went back to London, spending a couple of days at home. Louisa was unwell. This time it was she who was diagnosed with rheumatic fever and this time it seems likely that the diagnosis was correct. On the 20th Pugin returned to Alton, leaving his wife in the care of their friend and neighbour Ann Greaves. The next day saw the opening of St Mary's, Newcastle. It was a grand affair, with nine bishops and a Beethoven Mass, which Pugin would not have cared for. At the usual 'excellent dinner' afterwards the usual healths were drunk. That of the Building Committee came straight after the Pope and the Clergy, Pugin's rather crushingly towards the end, after the Ladies. Pugin himself, however, was not there. That day Benjamin Ferrey, busy as ever with his expanding and somewhat slapdash practice, found himself on Derby station where he met Pugin, greatly agitated. He had decided, he told Ferrey, to set off for London, having dreamed the night before that Louisa's illness had worsened. On the way from Alton he had met a messenger sent to tell him that she was indeed gravely ill. His worst fears, rational and irrational, bore in on him, intensified by terrible guilt. 'In conversation during the journey,' Ferrey remembered, 'he constantly expressed his belief that he should find his wife dead, though when he parted from her a few days previously she was in tolerable health.'[32]

At Chelsea he found Louisa 'in extremity'.[33] She had lapsed into unconsciousness and never recovered. On 22 August he wrote in his diary: 'This morning at ½ to 3 a.m. departed my good and dear faithful wife Louisa whose dear soul may God in his mercy assoil.'[34] The next day he wrote to Gentili, begging him to come and hear his confession, for he said: 'I have a weight on my heart. I cannot help viewing this sad affliction as a judgment of almighty God . . . I Long . . . to Lay my heart open to you.'[35] He wrote to Rock, who had prepared Louisa for her conversion, 'by you she was grafted to the church of christ. oh pray think of her soul.'[36] He also wrote to Mary Amherst.

Part Five

27

The New House and the New Palace

Autumn and Winter 1844

> *. . . the age of ruins is past . . .*
> – Benjamin Disraeli, *Coningsby*, 1844

At Nottingham on 27 August Bishop Gillis, who was to preach at vespers, spent an unhappy morning 'at the basin'. He was sick with nerves at the thought of such a distinguished congregation. As usual the day before he had been in 'black despair, not a syllable thought of', and as usual, he rose to the occasion. 'The whole thing was so fine I was carried off my legs and went off like the aerial steam engine at fifty miles an hour.'[1] The consecration of St Barnabas was magnificent. Sixteen bishops and more than 100 priests, watched by large and largely friendly crowds, processed in Pugin's vestments. The Mass was celebrated with only the 'plaintive and monotonous chaunting' of plainsong, which recalled the 'ancient glories of the Papal worship' to the minds of the press correspondents.[2]

It was a far cry from the little procession in Derby in 1838 when George Myers had carried the trowel to lay the foundation stone of Pugin's first important church. As Lord Shrewsbury said at the inevitably 'splendid' cold collation afterwards, 'When we look back on the condition of Catholicity in this country ten . . . years ago . . . and now see that we occupy the reverse of our once degraded position, we never ought for a moment to forget to thank God.' They ought also, he continued, to thank 'him whose noble views of church architecture have of late been developed, and whose indefatigability is, in my opinion, the very life and soul of the restorative movement now going on'.[3] Wiseman followed suit. 'The architectural taste of Mr Pugin has enkindled a light the rays of which will cover the present era with a halo of brightness . . .

[he] has done more than execute great works – he has founded a school; he has formed public taste.'[4]

Their tributes had a distant air, and indeed Pugin's career was nearer its effective end than anyone can then have imagined. The immediate reason, however, for the elegiac tone was that the architect was not present to enjoy his triumph. Pugin was on his way from London to Birmingham to prepare for Louisa's funeral. When the ceremonies at Nottingham were over, Gillis and Shrewsbury, along with George Myers, went to join him there. Louisa was buried in the crypt of her husband's first cathedral, St Chad's. Her funeral was gorgeous and solemn; a dark reprise of the festival of flowers Pugin had created for her reception into the Catholic Church. The coffin was draped in a black velvet pall and placed in the chancel. Above it soared a great canopy of flame, a *chapelle ardente*, which Pugin had designed and Myers had made over the previous few days. This 'chapel of fire' was Pugin's version of a late medieval custom. Bearing row upon row of candles, it rose fourteen feet, a lambent catafalque, blazing amid the gloom of the cathedral. After the requiem the coffin was carried, to the sound of the 'In Paradisum', into the crypt. John Hardman's nephew, who was acting as thurifer, heard Pugin as he stood beside it crying out aloud and sobbing passionately. Pugin paid for the medieval funeral charity: a dole of bread for 200 paupers and a shilling each to thirty-one widows, one for each year of Louisa's life. Yet as so often he did not complete all he set out to do. His first intention was to decorate the crypt chapel and build a tomb for Louisa there. Later he planned to move her body to Ramsgate. In the event nothing was done and her body remains in Birmingham, her grave marked by a modest, not to say mean, brass plate.

After Louisa's death Cheyne Walk was intolerable. 'I cant bear to return to or remain in it,' Pugin told Shrewsbury.[5] He sent the children with a governess, Miss Keats, down to Ramsgate. Only Edward came to Birmingham, for he was 'inconsolable' and would not leave his father's side.[6] When he came back from the funeral Pugin cleared out the Chelsea house. He never lived in London again and visited it with increasing reluctance. His heart was, from now on, in Ramsgate in the Grange and the self-contained community, human and architectural, that he intended to create there. For the moment, however, the house was only a shell. Pugin took lodgings for himself, the children and Miss Keats. Then he was off again on his professional travels. At Ramsgate,

Anne, the eldest of the children, having at twelve, in effect, lost two mothers, became the hub of domestic life.

With the end of his second marriage and the 'almost overpowering care' placed upon him as a widower, Pugin re-emerges as a family man.[7] After a gap of eleven years in his domestic correspondence, it resumes in letters to his daughter which reveal him as a father very much in the mould of his own mother and his Aunt Selina, anxious, especially now, affectionate, admonitory. He took a close interest in the clothes, the illnesses and the food of his six children. He sat up at night if they were ill. He was, as he later said, as good as a mother in many ways. If he was often absent or preoccupied, he had nothing in him of the remote Victorian papa.

My dear Anne I was very much pleased with your letter and its contents you are a very good girl & a great comfort to your father . . . I sent the dresses for Cath. Cuthbert etc. . . . I am pretty well . . . kiss all for me & keep some for yourself . . .[8]

. . . tell Miss Keats that I wish you to have puddings as often as you like and if you want broth or beef tea or boiled chicken you can have it . . .[9]

. . . I fully hope to come down to you on Saturday by the steam boat so you can be looking out for me but pray take care the children do not fall over the pier kiss them all for me.[10]

As he settled his family into their new motherless life, while working and travelling at his usual hectic pace, Pugin was also writing 'continually' to Mary Amherst, who was writing back as regularly and as fondly.[11] The correspondence became 'more & more familiar'.[12] The love affair that had begun illicitly in the last year of Louisa's life could now be allowed to blossom. As far as Pugin was concerned it was only a matter of time before he and Mary married and settled together at Ramsgate to build the ideal Christian community of which they both dreamed, and impulsive as he was, he had perhaps reason to think that at thirty-two he had found the love of his life. Anne Garnett can by now have been little more than a distant, poignant memory; Louisa was a more present but more troubling one. Mary, unlike them, was a cradle Catholic, an educated woman and an admirer of architecture. She knew and loved Pugin for what he had become in his maturity. In her he might hope to find a companion to share his home and his ideals as Laura Phillipps shared Ambrose's at Grace Dieu. Ventures such as Pugin planned for Ramsgate, Ideal Schemes to set right, by example, all that was rotten in the state of nineteenth-century Britain, were much in the air in 1844. This was the year of *Coningsby*. Disraeli's novel popularized the idea of Young England, of the rising generation, purer, braver than their parents, who would transform society. It was a vision that incorporated much of what the Romantic Catholics had believed in and nurtured for the last decade. Disraeli's three-decker *roman à clef* included friends and admirers of Pugin: Lord John Manners was the original of Henry Sidney, Ambrose Phillipps was Eustace Lyle. Even if *Coningsby* were, as Thackeray thought, 'a glorification of dandyism far beyond all other glories which dandyism has attained'; it was, as he also predicted, wildly popular. Edition succeeded edition, carrying the vision of Young England ever wider across the reading public.

Pugin's urgency to begin the new life at Ramsgate and his hoped-for impending marriage both spurred him on to get his house ready. Work proceeded at breakneck pace. The finishing and furnishing of the Grange were professionally and personally of the greatest importance to him. It was to be not only his home but also the proving ground for his ideas, so recently crystallized, about modern domestic Gothic. Its decoration was a manifesto. The furniture, the carpets and wallpapers, tiles, roller blinds, everything was to be – eventually – to his own design. Candlesticks, dinner plates, a tea caddy, no detail was too small to merit discussion. 'I send you the size of a plug for my wash basin,' he wrote to Hardman, 'do you think it better be plated or made of some metal that will not verdigris like brass?'[13]

His true principles had developed, now, beyond antiquarian revivalism to embrace 'any modern invention which conduces to comfort, cleanliness or durability'.[14] In this second house for himself he copied nothing *'merely because it is old'*.[15] He used plate glass rather than Gothic leaded lights so as not to lose the sea view. He had water closets and bidets. He left his woodwork unpainted to show, as Etty put it, the 'natural and consequently beautiful transparency of the wood'.[16] Ramsgate was another step away from revival towards reality. There were no 'tapestry hangings round the walls' as at Ellington Cottage, for the intention was no longer to transport the inhabitants 'back to the fifteenth Cent.' but to show them the nineteenth in a new light.[17] For Pugin, too, the age of ruins was past.

His ideas on decoration and furniture were not only visionary, they were also far-sighted in a pragmatic way. Just as he saw in the 'smaller detached residence' of the early Victorian years a new and important building type, so he sensed with a typical mixture of commercialism and idealism that the furnishings for such houses, if well designed and carefully presented to the public, would find a large market. The age of middle-class interior decoration was beginning: 'if this sort of thing takes we may do wonders,' he wrote to John Gregory Crace, who was supplying him with textiles and wallpapers.[18] Crace, whom he had met only recently, was, from now on, with Myers, Minton and Hardman, one of Pugin's closest collaborators. Between them, now that Hardman's sister Lucy Powell was producing embroidery, this informal network of craftsmen and manufacturers could make everything, except stained glass, that Pugin designed. Pugin entered into the technical details of Crace's business in order to know what could be done and how, and theirs was a frank and humorous relationship, if never of such intimacy as Pugin enjoyed with Hardman. In his correspondence with Crace, Pugin wrote as he must have talked to him. 'If I could *rely* on the Drawing room furniture etc coming on Saturday I might manage,' he told him at the end of October, 'but if it does not leave on that day I shall be *done brown* . . .'[19]

Like the rest of Pugin's collaborators, Crace expected to take the rough with the smooth. Pugin's criticisms were never spiteful and his praise was quick and generous. Crace soon found himself doing much more than supplying furnishings; he was acting as a poste restante and running errands across London. Crace was the elder by three years. He, like Minton and Hardman – and in a sense Pugin himself – represented the rising generation in manufacturing. They had each come into a family business which they had decided to transform in accordance with modern ideas about art. As Minton researched encaustic and Hardman turned his father's button-making factory over to the production of ecclesiastical metalwork, so Crace, whose family had been decorators to the aristocracy for generations, wanted to address the new taste for Gothic. The Craces' business had been much reduced by the time John Gregory bought his partnership in 1830, but he had built it up again. The Duke of Devonshire was a regular customer and the firm were now once more a byword for good taste and high quality. Like Minton, Crace was as cultivated as he was entrepreneurial. He had travelled on the Continent and studied German fresco technique. In 1843, no doubt with a professional eye on the forthcoming opportunities at the Palace of Westminster, he had lectured to the Institute of Architects on his researches into the 'processes employed in Fresco and Encaustic Painting'. Crace worked as hard as his staff and for long hours. He lived, with his wife Suzanne, over their showroom in Wigmore Street in London and he appreciated what Pugin, as a designer, had to offer him. His own taste was for the 'old French' style, but he had the romantic penchant of his generation for the Gothic and it was clearly the coming thing. He and Pugin worked together for the rest of Pugin's life.

Throughout the autumn the decoration of the Grange hurtled on towards completion. On a single day in October Pugin sent to Crace for twenty-one items including '3 sets of oak drawers . . . My coat of arms framed . . . 2 oak bidets . . . [and] an easy bedroom chair to cover'.[20] The house began to emerge, rising from the sea of workmen and packing cases. The interior was warm and vivid. There were the sea lockers in the dining room, bright textiles, dazzling wallpapers with patterns of repeating diagonals, the same design in different colours for each bedroom and Pugin's monogram everywhere on furniture and curtains and tiles.[21] If with its inglenook and central staircase hall-room the house looked forward in significant ways to the architecture of the Arts and Crafts movement, the overwhelming effect of the decoration was peculiar to Pugin himself. To live in the Grange must have been like inhabiting the pages of his *Glossary*, surrounded by a décor both brilliant and restless, like its designer. There were of course compromises. As his own client Pugin behaved like all clients. He changed his mind, he complained, and he insisted on decorating before the building was dry enough so that two rooms had later to be redone. His friends in turn behaved like all suppliers. Two of the roller blinds that Crace sent had faulty springs, the linings of Hardman's stoves burned through and Myers made the iron window frames wrongly. Pugin sent them to Hardman in Birmingham to be modified ('Help help help I send them by fast train & they must come back the same way'), guessing that this would be quicker than getting Myers to put them right.[22]

In the midst of all this, while the family were still in lodgings, Pugin received another letter from Charles Barry. Barry too was under pressure. The Westminster job was vast and complex and one of the more peculiar difficulties just now was the state of war that existed between the architect and the heating engineer, Dr David Reid, whose enormous ventilating apparatus threatened to overwhelm the building. The Commons was inclined to support Reid, the Lords, Barry. The press found the quarrel very funny and there were many jokes about the 'aerial Guy Fawkes' whose infernal engine was likely to blow up Parliament. The Lords, however, squashed and sweltering in their temporary accommodation in the Painted Chamber, were furious. 'I don't want explanation,' Lord Brougham puffed, 'I want air.'[23] Barry had promised to finish the House of Lords for him as soon as possible, but he was in a quandary about it. The chamber must be elaborate and rich. It required stained glass, metalwork, woodcarving, upholstery, furniture including a royal throne and much else, and in addition to his other anxieties Barry had just joined a rising statistic of the 1840s, having been injured in a railway accident. He was at Brighton to recuperate when he wrote the letter that was later to be much quoted and argued over.

Dear Pugin

I am in a regular fix respecting the working drawings for the fittings and decorations of the House of Lords, which it is of vital importance to me should now be finished . . . Although I have now made up my mind as to the principles, and generally, as to the details of the design for them . . . I am unfortunately unable to get the general drawings into such a definite shape, as is requisite for preparing the working details, owing to a lameness in one of my legs . . . I know of no one who can render me such valuable and efficient assistance, or can so thoroughly relieve me of my present troubles of mind in respect of these said drawings as yourself.[24]

Would Pugin come to Brighton and spend a few days at Marine Parade to help him out? Barry's proposal was a well-dressed lure. He wanted more than temporary help. He sought, he explained, to come to a 'permanent arrangement' with Pugin 'enabling me to consult you generally . . . as to occasional assistance for the future in completion of the great work'.[25] He tried to make his suggestions sound as congenial as possible and Pugin's future obligations as little onerous as he could.

I feel quite sure, that, if we were here together quietly for a few days, we should be able to make out definitively every portion of the design of the House of Lords' fittings etc. in general drawing so that you might be able to supply me with the details subsequently, from time to time, according to your leisure and convenience.

Playing on everything he could think of from friendship to professional vanity, Barry did not stop short of suggesting that at this difficult time Pugin might find a trip to Brighton 'would do you good'.[26]

It was the letter of an honest man in a tight corner, driven to some dissembling. Barry was not, as Edward Pugin later claimed, calling Pugin in to finish the building for him. He was, and remained, the architect and final arbiter of every detail. Yet the letter is contradictory. It reveals that he knew his difficulties had to do with more than a bad leg. Even when he was fit he could not possibly design Gothic detail of the quantity and quality required and in so many media. Nobody except Pugin could, though Barry would then revise and edit what he did. Distracted by domestic upheaval, open, always, to a personal appeal and with interior decoration at the front of his mind, Pugin agreed to go to Brighton. Thus began a commitment that lasted and, he often felt, blighted the rest of his life.

By the end of October the family were able to leave their lodgings. Hardman came down to help them move and Ann Greaves agreed to come and live with them, for the children were used to and very fond of her. Pugin explained that it would be merely a temporary arrangement, for he intended soon to be married. Ann Greaves and Anne Pugin now found themselves in charge of the works at the Grange while Pugin was away, and in receipt of such peremptory instructions as to 'make Olvirer [have] *the baize on the bookshelves*' or to find out 'if the man can *really* make a good job of the tap in the kitchen range . . . Miss Greaves should question him closely before he begins & see it is well done',[27] though whether Miss Greaves was qualified to undertake such a cross-examination seems doubtful.

With the house nearly ready, Pugin began to consider the next phase of his Ideal Scheme, the church. St Augustine's was so named both for Pugin's patron saint and because it was in Thanet that Augustine had landed in 597, bringing Christianity back to England. It was the kind of coincidence between the personal and the historic that Pugin, like Phillipps and the other Romantic Catholics, relished. Pugin bought the piece of land beside his house but soon discovered that his artistic vision was at odds with both the planning regulations and his neighbours. He could not build the church as he had hoped, truly oriented, without broaching the designated building line. To fit it in behind the line he needed more land, which he tried to buy from the Bings, a firm of carpenters, who owned the adjoining plots. Mr Bing, however, would only sell if he got the joinery work for Pugin's buildings. Pugin informed him – through his solicitors – that he would sooner see Bing 'pegged down at low water mark' than give him so much as a privy seat.[28] He resolved instead to go ahead on his 100ft plot and decided to build right out to the boundary, hoping thereby to reduce the value of the Bings' land. It was not a wise decision, but Pugin was upset by the undignified row. It underlined the difficulties, not to say the absurdity of his attempt to construct a romantic Catholic paradise in the middle of an expanding seaside resort – Young England, hemmed in by bathing-machines and lodging-houses. The dispute was to have several unhappy consequences. Not least, as the *Buildings of England* noted with some puzzlement, that it left Pugin's nave 'seeming very short'.[29]

Pugin wrote to the Bishop, Griffiths, explaining his plan: 'to erect a Parochial church . . . a revival of the old Catholic kentish churches stone & flint & . . . to afford room for a Priests house & a cemetery . . . I purpose a chantry chapel . . . which may be the burying place of my family . . . my intention is to compleat it with plate vestments & furniture of every description & then to transfer it in a legal manner to the vicars apostolic of the London district . . . as far as human means are concerned I shall *rely entirely on myself* . . . all I beg of your Lordship is your benediction – I . . . will take the whole charge and expense of the church & clergy on myself.'[30]

It was a munificent gesture and one that was to cost him dear in many senses. It was also a declaration of independence. By this arrangement there could be, for once, no interference from clergy or donors or committees. Pugin would design the building, the fittings and the vestments. By the time St Augustine's was given to the Vicar Apostolic, every important aesthetic and ritual decision would have been taken. Even then Pugin would support the priest and determine the exact form of the liturgy. Without such control it was 'depressing' to see what the clergy did to his buildings. St Barnabas's, Nottingham, soon 'looked like a penny theatre cotton velvet at 10s a yard hung up against the pillars . . .' Pugin had never seen anything 'so detestable'.[31] The sketch Pugin sent Griffiths showed the church and cloister configured more or less as they were built, though the scheme became more complex and the details more sophisticated. It was not, even to begin with, purely Kentish or medieval. Pevsner's description of it as 'simple and solid and antiquarianly correct – no more' was his worst misjudgement of Pugin.[32]

In the design of St Augustine's, Pugin's interest in asymmetry was taken much further than at Pontefract or Kenilworth. Since the nave and aisle are of almost equal width, the church is in fact nearly symmetrical but the focal point is not the altar, it is the south tower opening. Thus Pugin set up a tension between the actual and the expected centre of his plan that gives a sense of constant movement to the space. The effect struck the *Ecclesiologist* as 'complex and novel'.[33] The *Buildings of England* thought it 'strangely intricate'.[34] It is certainly powerful, atmospheric and perhaps uneasy. It forcefully recalls Payne Knight with its 'unequal varieties of space divided but not separated'. Ramsgate showed how far Pugin had moved from the still unfinished St Giles's, Cheadle, from the popular idea of 'Puginism', the symmetrical, Middle-Pointed parish church with nave and matching aisles. Even in its 'Kentishness' St Augustine's was far from straightforward. It is built of flint, as many Kent churches were. But medieval flints were left uncut. Only for emphasis, on battlements or a showpiece chancel or chapel, did the builders use 'knapped' or cut flints, for these were laborious to obtain and to set.[35] At St Augustine's all the flint is cut. The faceted surface sparkles darkly. The whole church is a showpiece of nineteenth-century design.

As in its dedication, as in everything Pugin did, his church included much that was personal. Some of the tracery patterns came from Kent sources, but in the details he used Pugin ranged widely over the places he knew. The piers and mouldings are typical of Lincolnshire and the capitals characteristic of the East Midlands.[36] These were the places he had known best and longest, the scenes of his childhood and some of his happiest working years. Whether consciously or not, he was building autobiographically; setting his own history and associations into the narrative of his church. He was to create in St Augustine's a modern Gothic church both scholarly and romantic.

Progress on the house meanwhile continued. 'Dining Room finished,' Pugin noted with satisfaction on 3 November.[37] But just then he received a setback. Mary Amherst's mother wrote to him enclosing his letters to her daughter and explaining that she wished the correspondence to cease. Pugin, who had been encouraged both by Mary herself and by her brother Kerril, decided that it was time to make clear his seriousness and explain that his intention was marriage. On 10 November he 'sent proposal to Mrs Amherst'.[38] He wrote also to Mary a love letter that 'enflamed' her affection for him still further.[39] That same day Charles Barry left Ramsgate after three days' intense collaborative work on the sovereign's throne for the House of Lords. The final design, which Barry had claimed almost to have finished in September, would not be decided until the middle of the next year. This painstaking process whereby Pugin worked, Barry reworked, Pugin revised and then revised and revised again would be repeated for every single detail of the interior.

For some time after Barry's departure Pugin remained in a state of suspense, waiting to hear from Mary. At Fieldgate House, the Amhersts' home near Kenilworth, relations between mother and daughter were strained. Mrs Amherst, a widow, had no intention of giving Mary, who was under age, the necessary consent to marry Pugin. He was much older than she, he had six children and no assured income, he was not a gentleman and his clothes and his manners were peculiar. Which of these facts counted most forcefully with Mrs Amherst is not clear, but the cumulative effect was decisive. Mary, however, felt by now that all her happiness 'was centred in him'.[40] She felt responsible, too, for having encouraged him. 'I knew he was attached to me & that I had gained his affections & . . . the idea of leaving him as soon as it was a little known seemed to me so unkind . . .'[41] She refused, for the moment, to refuse him.

Some news of what was going on reached Pugin, probably via Mary's brother. He complained to the Earl of Shrewsbury that he had heard that Mary 'is suffering dreadfully & it is a monstrous sin to think of keeping her from me'.[42] He needed Mary, he argued, as well as wanting her. 'I could make this a most Catholic spot . . . with her cooperation I could do wonders . . . Mary would deligt in everything I have. She is an admirable sacristan.'[43] It was an unusual compliment, but one his lover would have appreciated. She was as serious as he in her devotion to the Church and its revival. Shrewsbury wrote back ambiguously that 'if it is for the best it will be Please God'.[44] He and his wife took a close interest in their young cousin and supported her mother, agreeing that the marriage would be a scandal and a humiliation for the family. The social disparity between Pugin and the Amhersts, more difficult to appreciate a century and a half later, was certainly considerable. The Shrewsburys had once been firmly discouraging to the undoubtedly genteel Ambrose Phillipps when he showed an interest in one of their daughters. Friendship was one thing, kinship by marriage quite another. Yet Kerril Amherst was on Pugin's side and Shrewsbury himself, left to his own devices, might not perhaps have been so opposed to the marriage, but the Countess domineered over him and she was a snob.

Anxiety was now exacerbated by and no doubt contributed to a return of Pugin's illness: 'sometimes I feel so unwell & weak that I am quite dejected,' he told Crace.[45] Eventually Mary, after days of careful thought and prayer, found that the 'Blessed Virgin . . . obtained grace for me & I told Mama I would give him up for ever.'[46] She wrote to Pugin to tell him that she would not defy her mother. Almost at once Pugin's health declined further. He complained of 'cold', of pains and weakness. An eminent Catholic doctor, Sir Arnold Knight, examined him and attributed much of the trouble to his being overworked. Pugin promised to rest. He told Lord Midleton he would not go to Ireland for him. He was in such constant pain that he said he would not go anywhere before the middle of March. As the winter closed in Pugin felt his loneliness all the more. He began to remember Louisa and to feel her absence. 'I have been accustomed to return home for winter & miss my wife at every turn . . . it is almost insupportable,' he told Midleton.[47] Visits to London became unbearable for their associations: 'when I go there I feel as if I ought to see my poor Louisa', for if she had not sympathized with what he had become, Louisa had at least known what he had been.[48] She had known Great Russell Street, his parents and his aunt. With her death another link, one of the last, to the world of his childhood was gone.

He told Hardman that he no longer cared for Mary. He was bitter and unsympathetic about her refusal to stand up to her mother: 'if she has not pluck enough to cut her stick she is not worth the powder & shot . . . it is not my fault – anything like hapiness is a mere delusion – women soon get sick & uncomfable. All the fun is in the idea.'[49] Without a companion, that necessary sympathetic female eye and mind, he seemed distracted, what psychiatrists call 'depersonalized'. He lost something of his sense of self. It was from this time that Talbot Bury, who still worked for him engraving illustrations and saw him often, later dated the period of illness and intermittent mania, 'an excitability most distressing to his friends' that lasted until 1848.[50]

It was thus of little immediate consolation to Pugin when in December Barry secured an official post for him at the Palace of Westminster. Shrewsbury, perhaps sorry that he could not support his architect in his love affair, was much more enthusiastic about it. '[Pugin] is unquestionably far ahead in his profession,' the Earl wrote to his former chaplain, the querulous Dr Rock, who had been criticizing him again. 'Barry has completely settled this . . . by picking him out from the whole kingdom as the only man to carry out the details of the Parliament Houses.'[51] What the Earl said was true. Pugin's actual appointment, however, as Superintendent of Woodcarving on a salary of £200 a year, gave no indication or recognition of the real scope of his brief. The nature of his employment made it invidious from the beginning for both Pugin and Barry. It ensured that while Pugin would never, in his lifetime, get the credit he deserved, Barry would always be suspected of owing him more than he did. Pugin was now so famous and such a hero to the young generation that even before he was officially employed, as Charles Voysey, the father of the architect, later recalled, it was 'considered an acknowledged fact that Mr Pugin was the real Architect of the houses of Parliament, and that . . . Barry was behaving shabbily'.[52] Among the first things Pugin designed were the vanes, the sparkling gilded shafts that give the outline of the Palace, especially in sunlight, a glamour and verticality. It was a device he had used at Salisbury and at Scarisbrick, the first flicker of his decorative genius to enhance Barry's design. Hardman made a prototype.

Despite his loneliness, Pugin, as he settled down at Ramsgate to the winter's work, was seldom alone. His household numbered a dozen. As well as six children there were Miss Keats, Miss Greaves, who now prepared to stay indefinitely, a nurse and two maids. Pugin also engaged a domestic chaplain, an Italian priest, Luigi Acquarone, who, though an implacable classicist, nevertheless struck Pugin for the moment as admirable, and a 'Learned ecclestic'.[53] He was to act as a tutor to Edward. Before Christmas there was another arrival. Hardman's nephew, the seventeen-year-old John Hardman Powell, who had observed the violence of Pugin's grief at Louisa's funeral, was sent from Birmingham as a pupil-assistant. Perhaps it was the prospect of the work at Westminster that made Pugin and Hardman consider such an arrangement, or possibly Hardman was worried about his friend's state of health and mind. Pugin was less than enthusiastic about the prospect. He disliked strangers in the house, although Hardman Powell, whose mother Lucy ran the textile department of Hardman's works, had been known to him for years. 'It would be as well for you to speak seriously to him,' Pugin warned Powell's uncle, 'he is the only person I have ever consented to take as a pupil . . . I hope he will apply most earnestly to study he will have immense advantages . . . explain to him that I have a very small establishment . . . & therefore he must in a great degree wait on himself for I dread servants.'[54] It was an understandably nervous young man who arrived, dripping wet, on a stormy December night at Ramsgate.

28

The New Life

December 1844 to April 1845

Forty-five is a critical age for men, maidens and centuries.
— *The Spectator*, January 1845

'Power was the first impression he gave as he came towards you,' Hard-man Powell recalled of the man who, after a great deal of shouting and elaborate unbarring of the door, let him in, for the first time, to the Grange; 'strongly built, with a muscular frame . . . hands and feet broad, forehead high and massive . . . eyes quick pale grey and restless . . . a sonorous trumpet voice, and long dark hair.' Pugin's illness had so far taken no obvious toll of his physique. In other ways, however, his appearance had become more remarkable since Kerril Amherst described him at Oscott. He now habitually wore a working costume of his own devising that comprised, Powell noted, 'a very short sailor's jacket of pilot cloth with pockets outside, well worn and greasy, an ample double breasted waistcoat, a pair of roomy trousers up at the ankles and show-ing between them and a pair of large thick shoes about four inches of coarse grey socks, and a shiny hat with a very low crown and damaged brim.' He told Powell to get rid of his own 'rather stylish' overcoat at once and to go into town and get kitted out similarly.[1] Pugin, Powell discovered, was as unselfconscious in his manners as in his dress. When work went well he would sing loud snatches of opera in a 'powerful baritone' and, when it went badly, he would swear like a sailor.[2]

As a child of nine, commandeering the porters at Dover, Pugin had seemed remarkably adult. As a man of thirty-two he was still childlike – enthusiastic, vulnerable to disappointment, completely absorbed in his own ideas. In this intense, passionate and unconventional presence it is easy to imagine what Mary Amherst found to love and also what her mother might dislike. Powell's memories of Pugin were set down in the 1880s. As befitted a late Victorian 'memory offering to lay on the Tomb of his Master' they were idealized, softened by time and family piety as well as by the naïvety of Powell's youthful impressions. The picture of Pugin 'sparkling with good humour' is not false, but partial.[3] Pugin was often elated, but he was also often depressed, ill and sometimes manic over the years that Powell knew him, and although he was, as Powell remembered, affectionate, he was also domineering. To live at the Grange was to inhabit his vision and to live by his rules. He dictated every detail of domestic life, from Powell's overcoat to his daughters' shoes. Powell remembered the girls, when they grew older, crying as their father drew around their feet in front of the 'shocked Bootmaker' to indicate the large outlines of soles, designed on true principles to allow for a 'fair margin for growth'.[4]

The memory offering did not include Powell's own unhappiness in Ramsgate or his stormy passages with 'the governor', as he called him, of which there were many. He did, however, remember being astonished by the routine to which the household ran. Like nothing that would have obtained in the Middle Ages or since, it was part monastic, part shipboard and partly a re-creation of Pugin's mother's regime at Great Russell Street. Each day before dawn young Edward toured the house with a bell, waking the inhabitants. Throughout the day more bells rang to announce the offices. There were prayers at eight in the morning and Compline at eight at night, 'supper at 9, bed at 10', when 'all ingress was stopped, and every door and window bolted and barred for the fear of burglars'.[5] The family ate simply and, when alone, in the kitchen. Pugin loved order for its own sake and as a means of shoring himself up against the dark unknown, without and within. The chapel in the house was ready before Christmas and Acquarone celebrated the first Mass. The little oratory was warm, intimate and dark, its stained glass windows including images of Pugin himself, Louisa and the children, kneeling like medieval donors below their patron saints; here again the personal narrative was built into the architecture. If the window was symbolic, in romantic portraits, of the divided self, the meeting between interior and exterior realities, then the stained glass window was perhaps the epitome of Victorian romanticism, more serious and more sacred than the Georgian. Set at the meeting point of material and immaterial worlds, as a body is animated by a soul, so the visible glass is animated by invisible and unreflected light.

The first Christmas since Louisa's death cannot have been happy but it was somewhat cheered by a visit from Pugin's friend, the painter J. R. Herbert. From now on Herbert came nearly every Christmas, and this time he made a drawing of Louisa, a profile à la Holbein, the only image of her known to survive. He also finished a portrait in oil of Pugin. Herbert had been working on it for some time in fits and starts, for Pugin loathed sitting still. The picture shows him, too, in the Holbein manner, the attributes of his profession clearly on view. He holds the compasses Gillespie Graham gave him at the start of his career and wears the 'ample black velvet gown', another of his own designs, that he assumed for formal occasions.[6] The painting suffered perhaps from the interruptions. Pugin's face has a doughy, lifeless quality that it can never have had in reality. Nevertheless the portrait was shown at the Royal Academy and engraved for publication, marking another step in Pugin's emergence as a public figure.

His friendship with Herbert, like that with Etty and Clarkson Stanfield, has left little trace in the correspondence. They were three of the leading painters of their day, although now, with the exception of Etty, largely forgotten, all Academicians and all well known to each other. Pugin's relations with them were easier and more boisterous than with the Oxford and Cambridge men. The painters had known Pugin longer. Etty and Stanfield were considerably older and they too had been formed by the commercial art world of Pugin's childhood and in Stanfield's case by the theatre, rather than by public schools and universities. All of them shared Pugin's views on art and religion as well as his enthusiasm for the stage. Herbert and Stanfield were Catholics, Etty a High Anglican, and Stanfield, who had become a marine painter, loved the sea and would come to Ramsgate to sail with Pugin. The few surviving letters reveal a mutual admiration and warmth from the artists towards Pugin, the 'dear boy', as Etty called him. Discussions of ecclesiology did not preclude robust exchanges on other older interests, such as stage design. 'What did you mean by sending me to see that execrable humbug at the Princes Theatre . . .' Pugin complained to Stanfield on one occasion. 'The man who caricatured the town Hall of Ghent ought to be stifled in Priming . . . Who is the property man? . . . & that humbug Herbert says it made him giddy . . . Giddy indeed I certainly felt rather sick.'[7]

Exuberant in all his moods and emotions, 'Pugin in his home', Powell discovered, was at first an overwhelming experience. The new pupil was not happy and Pugin, who never entered easily into other people's states of mind, seemed baffled by the obvious symptoms of homesickness: 'we can make nothing of little Powell,' he told Hardman, 'he wont come to breakfast or anything. I never saw such a curious boy.'[8] His tendency to spend all evening writing home irritated Pugin 'dreadfully': 'what can all this mean . . . I cant understand a young man of his age without business or love affairs writing so much I hope he is not plotting.'[9] It was a joke, but in his fretfulness a streak of paranoia was beginning to show in Pugin, not for the last time. His fears – of loss, of the dark, of ghosts and the unknown – all haunted him more than ever. His Catholicism apparently did nothing to counter his dread of the supernatural in its tritest, most theatrical forms. He was terrified to discover that Powell was a sleepwalker. 'You should have told me and prepared me for [his] . . . being a somnambulist . . .' he wrote in horror to Hardman. 'I had no idea of such a dreadful thing in practice.'[10] He was in a nervous state all round, missing Louisa and no doubt his parents, his aunt and all the others whom he loved but saw no longer. No wonder Powell was homesick. Miss Greaves too began to suffer with headaches and to talk of returning to Chelsea. Gradually, however, Powell settled down. Pugin became fond of him, found he had talent and was 'a very good soul' even though he had no idea of principles, having always worked by eye and got into bad habits.'[11] The time that it took to teach Powell to draw and model astonished and exasperated Pugin, who took his own quickness for granted, but he decided on the whole he could make a 'fine fellow of him'.[12] Soon he was treating him like a son, which meant that Powell came in for a great deal of criticism, regular 'blowing up' and unwanted advice. He in return regarded the Governor with a degree of nervous awe that led him to imitate him in everything from his turn of phrase to his handwriting.

On 2 February Pugin noted: 'Began carving for the Palace of Westminster.'[13] At the Thames Bank site, where the woodwork for the Palace was produced, he established a system to train the craftsmen that was essentially his father's drawing school writ large. He provided casts and 'squeezes' of medieval details for use as models, and wrote to Willson in Lincoln, an infrequent correspondent these days, explaining that he wanted 'crockets stall finials elbows of stalls sub sellae &c heads of kings' for the House of Lords, adding that 'Linclon stalls will furnish me with all this.'[14] Through Willson he found a supply of facsimiles, and so a touch of Lincoln cathedral, another of Pugin's earliest memories, was woven into the Palace of Westminster. As soon as he got started on the House of Lords Pugin, typically, became completely absorbed in it. Forgetting his first reluctance, he now prepared to devote 'all my energy' to it.[15] He forgot, too, for the moment, his own career and even the great Catholic revival. Barry had got an extension of the deadline for the Upper House but he was still under pressure. 'Mr Barry looks ill & harassed,' Pugin reported to Hardman; 'it is a very difficult work & I think he finds me a great comfort to him . . . I must give up almost everything else.'[16]

Anticipating 1,000 detail drawings for the woodcarving alone, Pugin built a studio in the outer courtyard of the Grange where Powell worked and where Pugin could have 'all the figures and difficult parts modelled under my own eye': 'this will cost me about £200,' he told Barry, his entire year's salary, 'but I don't mind expense and trouble if we can obtain a good result.'[17] In addition he was to make drawings for 'glass, metal works, and tiles, &c', receiving a percentage of the total cost of the designs. Pugin worked so quickly when he had no one to please but himself that he cannot have realized what a poor bargain he was making.[18] The work was constant and constantly revised, the payments often delayed. On one point, however, he was adamant. Barry would have to face the Office of Woods, the Commissioners, the clerks of works, committees, MPs and peers alone. 'I am only responsible to you in all matters connected with the work. I act as your agent entirely, and have nothing to do with any other person.'[19] Although his refusal to deal with the administration saved Pugin a great deal of annoyance, it also ensured the obscurity of his position.

The first interior metalwork, for which Hardman was sub-contracted, was the brass railing for the gallery of the House of Lords. The design took almost a year to settle. The correspondence about this one fitting makes agonizing reading and is indicative. Barry and Pugin were both perfectionists, with different ideas of perfection. Barry's alterations tended to simplify, clarify and secularize what Pugin did. He made the work overall more consistent than it might have been but he lacked Pugin's technical knowledge and so was unable to visualize a design until it was made. Pugin acceded to Barry's ideas but could not anticipate them. The difficulties of communication were multiplied by distance. Pugin, Barry and Hardman, at Ramsgate, London and Birmingham, were often at cross-purposes. Hardman made up a section of the railing to Pugin's design. Barry, once he saw it, realized he would prefer it solid, rather than tubular. The frieze was to be simplified. The petals of the metal roses had to be turned over to reflect more light. The number of decorative shields was to be reduced. The branches for the lighting had to be extended and, since it was not yet decided how the House was to be lit, the whole thing must be adaptable for either candles or gas. Not until November were the final measurements decided. 'I send you a sketch which will explain to you the alteration . . .' Pugin wrote to Hardman. 'I also send you a full size drawing of the iron stanchion . . . you will observe a nut drawn on the screw part this nut will be Let into the bottom part of pendant so as to screw on & draw the stancheon down tight . . .'[20] Soon, however, he had to report that 'The railing is quite altered in proportion . . . & I do not think a single pattern will do excepting the bottom Roses which will remain . . . I warned you of the alterations that might be expected till Mr Barry had finally pronounced – however all will be setled this time.' Sadly it was not.[21] 'I now find we shall have to begin quite afresh with the railing for Last night Mr Barry altered all the rose work at bottom . . . he says it cannot be helped for he must have perfection to his mind.'[22] And so it would go on, for the rest of Pugin's life.

When he did consider his own practice, Pugin had at present only one new church to think about. It was at Marlow, for the gentleman convert Charles Scott Murray, whom Wiseman had so thoughtfully steered in his direction. The design for St Peter's brought together elements of St Augustine's and St Mary's, Liverpool. A small, rural church, gently redolent of medieval England, it was built in flint, not so much because that is a local tradition in Buckinghamshire, as because it was the material most on Pugin's mind. The plan is asymmetrical to an extent that neither the site nor the function of the building require, with the Lady Chapel shorter than the chancel and the tower built, as at Liverpool, in bond with the west front of the nave, making one continuous west wall. Unlike St Mary's, which stood on the street line, St Peter's is set in a spacious churchyard. The only reason for repeating this element of the Liverpool design can have been that Pugin liked the effect and wanted to try it again.

Scott Murray was a sympathetic patron with adequate funds, so Pugin was allowed to complete the design with sedilia, piscina and screens.

There is an arch between side chapel and chancel and through it the cross-views are multiplied and complicated, making the building feel larger than it is. From every point in the body of the church there is a view into another space and the impression of more space beyond that. Scott Murray, possibly on the advice of Pugin, followed his example in ensuring he kept control over St Peter's. In return for an endowment he obtained from Pius IX the right for himself and his heirs to present the living to a priest of their own choice, 'restoring in this almost unique instance so far as England is concerned, the condition of things in pre Reformation times'.[23] Thus the church was used and cared for as Pugin would have wished while the Scott Murrays remained nearby. Even today, having been tactfully extended, St Peter's is remarkably unspoilt.

Easter fell early in 1845. It was the second great religious festival to be celebrated at the Grange and the sacred 'functions' went off 'gloriously', with the members of Pugin's monastic-domestic household performing their dual roles in the two spheres.[24] Powell now doubled as sacristan and was learning to sing, although for the moment Pugin had to do nearly all of it by himself. The organ had arrived and was played most agreeably by Miss Greaves, who had decided, for the moment, to stay. There was an element of amateur dramatics, an echo of Pugin's model theatre at Great Russell Street, in the religious life of Ramsgate. The solemn procession from the chapel round the hall and back again would have struck an unsympathetic eye as absurd. Yet for Pugin it was the ideal, home and God all together. The completeness of the celebrations extended to dinner, for which Hardman managed to get the salt cellars made and posted in time.

Outside his own home the wider world, especially the Catholic world, was growing ever colder. As well as Rock's personal grievances and the antipathy of men like Lingard, who thought the Gothic Revival simply silly, resentment among the clergy was growing. There was a feeling that Pugin was a show-off, opinionated and – especially – expensive. It was unfortunate, from this point of view, that as Wiseman had observed Pugin had indeed founded a school. Many people, including Wiseman himself, were happy with work 'à la Pugin'.[25] Pugin was told as much by a priest with whom he fell into conversation on the train. The priest turned out to be 'the most prejudiced and determined opponent I have ever met,' Pugin told Hardman, '– he . . . says he is building a church like one Myers built for HALF PRICE . . . he says as soon as it is done he is going to make Myers prices public . . . he ran us all down to nothing. I said a great deal I hope it will do him good.'[26]

Pugin might have found patronage elsewhere. He might have developed a country house practice of the sort that kept many middle-ranking architects, including the ever-busy Ferrey, afloat. Wealthy patrons sometimes approached him, but nothing ever came of the overtures. Pugin was temperamentally and professionally ill-equipped for work that required specialist knowledge and a fully staffed office with several clerks. Even when he had got Powell into 'firmness of hand', Pugin did all his own drawings, for 'designs are generally spoilt by the vile way in which they are set out by mechanical clerks all the soul is Lost like a bad translation of a book'.[27] He also made all his own site visits, which cost, in time and money, more than they earned. To Lord Champernowne, who was considering some work at his home, Darting-ton Hall in Devon, Pugin ingenuously suggested that in order to justify the expense of his visits he should be allowed to build more: 'I do hope next time I come you will give me something more to do for in the same time & expense I could have arranged for 6 times the quantity of building.'[28] It was an odd idea of economy from a client's point of view. At Scarisbrick Hall there was still, after seven years, 'not a single room finished'.[29] Pugin, on one of his now rare visits, found two men looking at the work and a foreman who could not read the designs. Charles Scarisbrick, who was used to getting Pugin cheap, was not receptive to the idea that he should have '5 per cent if I superintend the work and 2½ for the drawings and my journeys, expenses etc.' even though, as Pugin pointed out, 'this is what you would have to pay any other architect and certainly I am well worth the sum'.[30] No more came of it, while at Albury Henry Drummond, having been stirred up by Rock to doubt Pugin's scholarship, started quibbling with him about details of heraldry. Work at Albury slowed to a halt while that at the Palace of Westminster gathered momentum.

Pugin never made any systematic attempt to develop his career. His practice veered with the wind of circumstance, his state of mind and home life affecting it as much as anything. But the domestic ideal always eluded him and life at the Grange was an uneven mixture of the sublime and the ridiculous. Acquarone, the chaplain who had seemed in January to be 'a man of Piety & Learning of a retired & studious disposition', was soon giving cause for anxiety.[31] Perhaps it was Pugin's continual attempts to educate him about Gothic architecture, conducted, Powell recalled, 'in rapid French at meal times' that irritated the priest.[32] As Acquarone spoke no English they must have been almost his only social exchanges. Whatever the reason, Pugin was soon in 'a good deal of alarm' about his chaplain, who had taken to visiting public houses in Ramsgate and drinking spirits. 'I find . . . he has a bottle under *his bed*!!!' he wrote, aghast, to Hardman.[33]

Another, unacknowledged, factor in his vacillating moods was Mary Amherst. He had not forgotten her, despite his protests to Hardman, nor had he given up the idea of marrying her. Mary had told him that she would not defy her mother, but had since apparently written to him in terms that implied that when she came of age and could act independently she would marry him. This would now be only a matter of months. Pugin certainly believed they had a secret understanding. The Amhersts were abroad for the first part of the year, in Belgium and Germany, where, like Pugin, they went to look at medieval art and architecture. Mrs Amherst, however, was uneasy; indeed she had been uneasy for some time about the third of her four daughters, the prettiest as well as the cleverest. All her children seem to have been profoundly religious. Mary's eldest sister had already become a nun and Mrs Amherst had taken this very badly, especially as it had seemed ever since that Mary would like to follow her sister's example.

Mary had confided this, along with much else, to her confessor, Luigi Gentili, the Rosminian priest. Gentili had left his uncongenial chaplaincy at Grace Dieu three years before and was now running the Rosminians' mission at Loughborough near Sileby, where the first stage of Pugin's college had just opened. Mrs Amherst, like Lord Shrewsbury, John Lingard and others, mistrusted him for his asceticism, his highly emotional manner and his powerfully charismatic effect on women. She had stopped his correspondence with Mary, whom she had then sent to stay at Alton Towers, so that she might at least see something of the world before she gave it up. Unfortunately, from her mother's point of view, the only person Mary had found interesting among the Shrewsburys' wide and glittering circle was Pugin. Now, with her passionately pious daughter in thrall in different ways to two unsuitable men, it seemed to Mrs Amherst that Gentili was the lesser of two evils. She positively encouraged Mary to resume her correspondence with him in the hope that he would destroy Pugin's case. To judge from the letters, Gentili seems never to have put pressure on Mary to become a nun, telling her merely to pray and discover God's will. On matters of family duty and sexual propriety, however, he took a rigorously conservative line. He had disapproved of the Phillippses' village school because it allowed boys and girls to be taught under the same roof. He would certainly not countenance Mary disobeying her mother, even if the law allowed it. As her twenty-first birthday approached, and Mrs Amherst and the Shrewsburys remained united in their view that marriage to Pugin would be a scandal, Mary also came to believe it would be a sin. She wrote to Gentili from Brussels asking him to intervene. 'I am so afraid he still hopes that when I am 21 I shall accept him could you discover this & if he does tell him you know I shall *never* do such a thing. He will doubtless think that I am changed . . . This I must bear as a punishment . . . but I have not altered my opinion of him the least I *esteem him* as much as ever & religion alone made me reject him.'[34]

It is hard now to enter into the social and moral scruples of the 1840s, especially the internal and external forces that played on the minds of women, whose scope for action was so limited and over whom the threat of moral censure always hung. It could fall easily and with catastrophic results. The choice that Mary faced was a real and painful one and she made it with courage, blaming nobody else for her decision and 'still . . . grieving much for him & for myself'.[35] Gentili wrote to Pugin in April, asking to see him. Pugin, travelling as fast as ever, en route to Alton where Lord Shrewsbury was threatening economies at Cheadle, wrote back that he was too busy to come and asked Gentili to put whatever he had to say in a letter, adding that although he had been 'very ill indeed this winter' he was much better now.[36] He was, however, 'lonely beyond description' at Ramsgate 'when all are gone to bed & I am left to work'.[37] He missed Louisa and he longed for Mary. Gentili wrote to him, explaining that Mary wanted him to know she would never marry him. The news had a devastating effect. Pugin replied at once, enclosing a letter to Mary. He warned Gentili that he would not accept Mary's refusal: 'if there is a spark of truth honour or fidelity left in her she must know that she is solemnly bound to me and . . . I will never release her.'[38]

29

A Battle of Wills

May to October 1845

... and at the last he swore
That he would send a hundred thousand men
And bring her in a whirlwind ...
— Alfred, Lord Tennyson, *The Princess*, 1847

Mary, now home again in Warwickshire, handed Pugin's letter un-opened to her mother. Mrs Amherst told her that it contained a torrent of reproach for her deceitfulness, at which Mary, briefly, lost her temper. Pugin was in no position to talk about deceit when 'he himself ... set me the example with regard to his own wife'.[1] Yet at the same time she begged Gentili to put in a good word for Pugin with her mother. Far from being, as Mrs Amherst had hoped, the end of the affair, Gentili's letter to Pugin was the beginning of more than a year of intermittent struggle that divided friends and family on both sides. Mary's own feelings were horribly mixed. She was torn between Pugin, whom she loved, her mother whom she also loved but frequently quarrelled with and her fluctuating sense of her vocation. Her brother Kerril was firmly for Pugin and went, without their mother's knowledge, to stay in Rams-gate to support him while Mrs Amherst took her daughter back to the Continent. The Shrewsburys too were abroad, but Mary heard from Lady Shrewsbury's half-sister, Anne Talbot, that Pugin had been at Alton speaking 'in a most determined manner'.[2] He had Mary's letters and was threatening to publish them to prove breach of promise. It seemed now to the embattled Mary that whatever course she took she would bring grief and scandal on her family.

With the return of the longer days and warmer weather Pugin began to travel again. He had work to oversee at Ushaw, at Liverpool, at

Wymeswold, and at Bilton Grange in Warwickshire, the home of Captain Hibbert, a relative by marriage of the Shrewsburys. In East Anglia he was on the lookout for authorities for the Palace as well as for his own work. Yet only some of his travel was really necessary. From the beginning of April until the end of August he was at home for less than five weeks altogether. He was simply too agitated and unhappy to keep still. As the war of nerves went on, with Mary refusing to read his letters, Pugin grew increasingly bitter. He could not bear to be thwarted in anything and he insisted on his right to Mary at the same time as, increasingly, he seemed to dislike her. Possessiveness, always a powerful element in Pugin's affections, had now it seems entirely overtaken love. At the eye of the storm was Gentili, the only person untroubled by mixed feelings – on this or any other subject. For her own good he told Mary some of the things Pugin now said about her. 'I am very glad you told ... me for they will make a lasting impression,' she replied sadly, 'but for a time they really made me miserable for I cannot help loving him.'[3] Gentili used his authority as a priest and as a friend to make Pugin return Mary's letters. Much relieved, Mrs Amherst destroyed them. Gentili insisted that for her part Mary should dispose of anything that Pugin had given her and she dutifully complied; 'a little drawing of his own which I used to like very much I have burned & also his hair which he sent me to Munich,' she reported.[4]

Mary had become more convinced with the passing weeks that God's purpose in all this was to allow her to return to her first intention and become a nun. Gentili believed that she had a vocation and should follow it, and it now began to dawn on Mrs Amherst, to her dismay, what price she might have to pay for the priest's co-operation. She turned once more against Gentili and asked Bishop Walsh to write forbidding Mary to make any commitment; in particular not to the Rosminians' convent at Loughborough, which she wanted to enter so that she might continue under Gentili's guidance. Surrounded by so many people all sure of God's will for her, Mary became ever more unhappy and uncertain, and in this uneasy state matters rested for some months.

Despite the mental and emotional turmoil that engulfed him, Pugin managed between his travels to carry on working, keeping up the flow of designs for the House of Lords. He was busy with Crace designing the ceiling panels and making alterations to the floor, which was to be covered in Minton's encaustic tiles. Pugin had now not only to meet

Barry's specifications but to incorporate the ideas of the increasingly irritable peers. 'I wish Lord Brougham had to set it out himself,' he complained as he rearranged the tiling patterns again. By this time news of Pugin's involvement at Westminster had inevitably begun to get about. He was now well known, as Wiseman remarked, 'not to the learned alone ... but amongst the people who have anything to say to them. This is real fame.'[5] He had many admirers and many detractors, and if in some circles it was thought that his role was being hidden, in others it was said that he exaggerated it. As the rumours surrounding the nature of his employment began to break out in the press, a crisis in his relations with Barry began to be inevitable. It came as a result of an article in the *Artizan* on 'Charles Barry and his right-hand man', which accused Pugin, 'the busy champion of Romanism in all its most besotted superstitions', of 'boasting in the most egotistical and uncalled-for ... manner of the important share he has in the decoration of the Palace of Westminster'.[6]

Pugin, who had certainly been talking, as he always did, and possibly boasting a bit, now produced a refutation, published in the *Builder*, which seriously misrepresented the true situation. In it he stated that he was 'not engaged in any work connected with that building on my own responsibility, but am simply superintending the practical execution of the internal details and decorations of Mr Barry's design'.[7] The first part of the denial was true. Barry's was the ultimate responsibility. But the second was not, for Barry designed no details or decorations himself, he only modified Pugin's. This letter and the circumstances of its composition became one of the most fiercely disputed points in the later pamphlet war over the authorship of the Palace. Did it, as Edward Pugin said and as history shows, understate Pugin's importance, and if so was it Barry who forced him to write it in these terms? Talbot Bury remembered seeing Pugin in London at the time and that he was quite sanguine about the letter. Ann Greaves recalled it as the occasion of much distress. She remembered Pugin returning from London distraught: 'he said, "I have been up all night. Barry is in an awful state respecting the reports which have oozed out about my being the architect of the Houses, and he wants me to write a letter to save his reputation; it is gone if I do not, and I have no alternative." '[8] Given Pugin's temperament and his particularly volatile state of mind just now, it is quite possible that both accounts are true. As for Barry, he was certainly becoming increasingly nervous about Pugin's involvement. He very possibly did dictate the terms of the letter. Certainly from now on he made sure, when he could, that Pugin's name was kept out of reports of the work.

The row about the Palace, the rapid development of his own architectural ideas, the decline in his practice and his intermittently irrational state of mind as he raged and fretted over Mary all combined to make 1845 a critical year in Pugin's life. Yet again his personal fortunes coincided with a change in the wider world that magnified and intensified his own experience. The mid 1840s were a turning point for the nineteenth century itself and from now on Pugin would begin to find himself less in sympathy with the spirit of the age. The tide of religious and political events that had borne him along so rapidly since the publication of *Contrasts* was turning. The young Victorians were growing up and starting to go their separate ways. Some of their youthful confidence and urgency was lost and a more sober Victorianism was starting to dawn. Religious tensions were running even more than usually high throughout the country this year and hostility to Tractarianism was building up to another crisis. In January at Exeter the congregation of St Sidwell's had walked out in protest against their priest, Mr Courtenay, wearing a surplice to preach. When the service was over and Courtenay attempted to leave the church he found his parishioners and an angry mob of 2,000 protesters waiting for him outside. At Oxford in February the university authorities, who had been longing for years to take action against Newman and his circle, had stripped W. G. Ward, author of *The Ideal of a Christian Church*, of his degrees. After this Newman, who voted neither for nor against his friend's 'degradation', found his *via media* had narrowed still further. At Littlemore he was working on his *Essay on the Development of Christian Doctrine* but by the autumn it seemed unnecessary to complete it, for he could see the way ahead. On 27 September one of his companions, John Dobrée Dalgairns, left Littlemore. Two days later, at Pugin's little chapel of St Anne at Stone in Staffordshire, the Passionist priest Dominic Barberi received him into the Catholic Church. Soon after that Barberi came to Littlemore. On 8 October Newman, with his unfailing sense of dramatic occasion, wrote letters to 'a number of friends'.[9] The death-bed agonies of the last four years were over. The next day he too was received into the Catholic Church with three others. Several more followed and within a few months they had all left Littlemore for Oscott.

At Cambridge, meanwhile, the mood was equally tense. The Camden Society had long been suspected in many quarters of Catholicizing tendencies, its ecclesiological principles, it was alleged, a mere excuse for imposing the liturgical and ritual arrangements suitable for Catholic worship. By 1845 there was a feeling even among some of the members that the Society had gone too far, that 'The Church had enough enemies already, what with Romanism without, and something like Romanism within.'[10] There were several resignations, including those of two bishops, and a proposal for the dissolution of the Society. The annual meeting on 8 May had to be held in Cambridge Town Hall, so great were the numbers wishing to attend, and the final result of the stormy debate was a change of name and headquarters. As the Ecclesiological Society it transferred operations to London. From now on the Society gained a more national scope, but its heyday, in terms of energy and numbers, was past.

Thus the Oxford and Cambridge movements, from which Pugin had hoped for so much, were fragmented by the events of 1845, and Young England too, which had never been much more than a bubble on the surface of troubled waters, was broken up. It also failed over the politics of religion, in this case the question of increasing the grant for Maynooth, the Catholic college and seminary near Dublin, and making it permanent. Peel brought a bill before Parliament proposing three new secular colleges in Dublin and £30,000 to rebuild and extend Maynooth. It was one of his hard-fought attempts to relieve the distress and address the grievances of Catholic Ireland, but there was national outrage at the idea of Englishmen paying for the teaching of Popery, which in Ireland it was said meant sedition and treachery; 'petitions against the Bill poured in, by the hundred at first, later by the thousand.'[11] It eventually went through, amid furious protests. Among the opponents in Parliament was Disraeli. Lord John Manners supported it, George Smythe had reservations and so, only months after it had been formally named, Young England was divided and set on a course towards dissolution, another sign of changing times.

In April, while the Maynooth controversy was going on, Pugin was far too preoccupied with Mary to take much notice. Once the grant had been agreed, however, it became a matter for his immediate concern. An architect had to be found and the college's choice, not surprisingly given his reputation in Ireland, fell on Pugin. He visited in July and began his drawings at the end of August but the grant, so grudgingly given, was from the outset inadequate. Maynooth, had he completed it, would have been the largest commission of his career, but again, as at Southwark and Westminster, his involvement in one of the most prominent buildings of the day was doomed from the outset to bring him little credit. His first design was for a stark new quadrangle and accommodation block. Only the chapel, intended to occupy the east side of the new court, had any grandeur. The Board of Works nevertheless estimated the cost at £57,400, which was unacceptable. It was a bad beginning to a long, unsatisfactory job.

Yet while circumstances began to turn so markedly against him Pugin was in his creative prime, thinking along new and exciting lines as he worked out the implications of what he had said in the *Apology* about natural architecture and construction. Ideas were now unfolding in his mind with tremendous speed. He was abroad that summer for over three weeks, mostly in Germany, travelling at his usual hectic pace. He drew constantly, 'taking a fresh supply from the fountain of antiquity' as he wrote back to Barry, who was hard at work on the House of Lords. 'I thought you would be glad to know where I was,' he added, rather cheekily, explaining that he was looking at brass and iron work that would be of use at the Palace.[12] But he was also looking at new buildings. Those which most impressed him were not the churches but the railway stations on the line from Mannheim to Strasbourg. 'The stations are beautiful – all constructive principle,' he told Barry.[13] Mannheim at that date consisted of two train sheds with colonnades of round arches, a clerestoried roof and gable ends filled with simple scrollwork patterns. It was not Gothic in any way, not even in the way that Pugin's proposed station in the *Apology* had been Gothic. He was beginning to see much further into the idea of architecture as a system of principles and an expression of the modern age. It was now that he began to be – in some respects – what Pevsner might have called a protofunctionalist.

At the same time that he was casting off literal imitation of historic architecture he was also moving away from a narrow sense of national style. Perhaps it was his loss of respect for Dr Rock, who constantly now tried to undermine him, or perhaps he simply felt he had done all he could in a purely English idiom, but after this trip unmistakably Continental features began to make their way back into Pugin's architecture. In his eclecticism, too, he was becoming a High Victorian. This critical change in his thinking, the move away from English precedents and copyism, the working out of 'constructive principle', has never been discussed, because he never published it and had few chances to build it, but it was decisive. From now on he moved ever further and faster away from the popular idea of 'Puginism' as he had established it in 1841, discovering for himself most of the developments that would characterize English architecture in the decades after his death. In an undated letter to Bishop Sharples, written probably this winter, Pugin set down his latest thoughts:

. . . my impression is that something even grander than most of the old things can be produced by simplicity combined with gigantic proportions I think the old buildings are for the most part too much cut up by detail which perishes in a few years & destroys the idea of permancy I think all sort of lace work in stone is bad in principle & lofty arches & pillars, huge projecting buttresses grand severe lines are the true thing.[14]

It was the embryo of another manifesto, one never fully developed either in theory or in practice. Pugin did, however, publish some of his thoughts in an open letter to Herbert that summer. It was prompted by the public debate about the National School of Design, which had been set up at Somerset House in 1837, and which was singularly failing to produce any improvement in English art. Pugin set out his own view of art education and the need to create a new art for the age: 'a school of national artists, not mere imitators of any style' was what he wanted, '. . . founded on the old principles, and yet a true expression of our period. I must own I have long entertained a most sanguine hope that Christian art and architecture may be carried to a far higher degree of perfection than they ever attained during the middle ages.'[15] What Pugin meant by national art now was only that it should be 'adapted . . . to our country . . . our wants . . . our faith . . . our Government'.[16]

That autumn the handful of buildings he designed or began showed what he meant in practice. In September he went to the college at Ware to set out the ground for the chapel. It was never completed, but St Edmund's Chapel is one of Pugin's best and best-realized buildings, a tantalizing indication of what he could now do with his scarce opportunities. Based on the T-shaped Oxford college chapel plan, the ante-chapel is divided from the choir by a spectacular stone screen, five bays wide and two deep, internally vaulted with altars against the east wall. The effect of the altars within the screen, of buildings within buildings, is the Grieves' old three-arch device from Covent Garden, but made dramatic, not merely theatrical. The decade or so that separated the screen at St Edmund's from that at St Chad's had seen stage carpentry transformed into architecture and craftsmanship. Pugin's constant efforts to find and train carvers were now bearing fruit. The carving at Ware has reality and requires no distance to lend enchantment.

Later in the month Pugin went down to Leicestershire, where Ambrose Phillipps's father had been persuaded to pay for some additions to Grace Dieu. The proposal was only for a two-storey service range, necessary for the rapidly expanding family, but it was interesting. Pugin designed a low, plain, rendered building. It has square mullioned and transomed windows, dormers and a polygonal stair turret set off centre with three small windows, one on each turn, each on a different face. As a subordinate wing to Railton's mansion Pugin's building subtly upstages the house, for in its very plainness it speaks a new language. This was the modern vernacular that grew out of Gothic when it had been stripped of the last antiquarian reference and became purely traditional, but part of a living tradition capable therefore of development and variety.

There were also two churches that autumn, in the designs for which Pugin was able to take further the play of symmetry and asymmetry which he was meditating in the design for his own church at Ramsgate. The first survives only as a design. It was intended for St Peter Port, Guernsey, but never built. As at Ramsgate, Pugin devised a nave with a single aisle almost as wide. This time he set the chancel arch off centre too. The spaces he was now imagining were more complex than any he had previously conceived and quite original, mysterious and uneasy.[17] In so far as he was still thinking of the Middle Ages he was perhaps moving towards the idea of a double-aisle church, one of the strangest and loveliest of medieval plans that was to appeal, decades after his death, to the architects of the late Gothic Revival. The designs for Guernsey broke away too from the Decorated style, using the supposedly 'debased' Perpendicular for the nave windows. Pugin had gone beyond symmetry and Englishness and the Decorated, all the essential principles of Puginism. He had by now absorbed the language of Gothic so well that he could vary it and play on it with ease, discarding conventions and breaking rules, even his own. Whether the priest in Guernsey thought the design too peculiar, or too expensive, he turned it down and Pugin fell back on the reliable and relatively economic three-aisle plan he had used at Southwark and Newcastle. Something of the Guernsey scheme was realized, however, on a smaller scale in the other new church, St Mary's at Rugby, for the Shrewsburys' relative by marriage Captain Hibbert. St Mary's was Pugin's first complete post-Puginian church. Un-English, unsymmetrical, tough and blocky, it was a pure exercise in High Victorianism. The chancel arch was set against the north wall of the nave, making an asymmetric two-bay arcade with the lower arch into the lady chapel, as in the design for Guernsey. Externally the composition was a complex, satisfying whole, the distinct volumes fitting neatly yet surprisingly into one another. The tower had buttresses continuous with the wall-plane, as at Marlow, adding to its solidity, and it had a strikingly Continental saddleback roof.

Rugby would never receive much attention. It was a small church in a small place and has since been altered beyond recognition. It would have no significant successors in Pugin's œuvre, for he would not build very much more. From now on his energies were increasingly directed towards the applied arts and in particular to that most difficult and unpredictable of them, stained glass. Stained glass was becoming increasingly popular. It was obviously appropriate for Gothic churches and in its appearance and effects it was conducive to the spiritual and meditative. It was also an ideal way of disposing of the demand for intrusive wall monuments in churches, what Pugin called 'blisters'. Glass in the medieval tradition allowed a memorial to be personal without being worldly.[18] It was, to Victorian eyes, more respectable than the statues of weeping women, less pagan than cherubs and less pompous than the marble slabs, engraved like *Times* obituaries with a list of appointments held. Stained glass manufacture, however, was difficult. The dense colours and rich textures of medieval windows remained elusive, to the frustration of Pugin and the handful of other pioneering glassmakers. As with encaustic, the entrepreneurial and the antiquarian sides of the nineteenth-century mind were required to be equally engaged, but here the steam age found itself lamentably wanting: 'with all our machinery, and facilities which they never possessed, we are hardly able to imitate the commonest of their productions,' Pugin had complained in 1839.[19] After six years, collaborations with three different makers and many dozens of window designs, he was still dissatisfied. He decided to take matters into his own hands.

The immediate spur to set up his own glassworks was probably the prospect of a commission at the Palace of Westminster. Stained glass was integral to Barry's scheme, but Ballantine and Allen, the Edinburgh firm who had the contract for windows in the House of Lords, were unsatisfactory. They had no idea of design and their medievalizing was ludicrous and literal. Their windows had texts as long as *Punch* cartoons and often unintentionally funnier. Barry would not take much persuading to hand the job to Pugin and Hardman. In the spring Pugin told Hardman that 'I have some great schemes in my head which I will tell you by & by it does me good to scheme. I am scheming a stained glass shop but this is only between ourselves.'[20] Just as Pugin could not keep an idea secret for more than the length of a sentence, so it was not long after he thought of it that Hardman was putting the plan into practice. It was typical of their relationship that Pugin should imply he was letting his friend in on a secret, when in fact the whole project depended on Hardman setting up a manufactory in which his would be the principal financial risk. It was typical too that Hardman was eager to fall in with the idea. Glass became a major part of the firm's business, bringing the last of the applied arts in which he worked within Pugin's immediate circle of collaborators. In July Hardman bought the equipment and the first window was made in November. Over the following months Pugin set about pushing stained glass design forward, or rather backward to the Middle Ages, undoing all that the intervening centuries had done to make glass lighter, thinner and easier to decorate. He bought thick uneven flint glass instead of crown 'to make the windows doubly rich in effect', and an engraving tool 'like the old', which 'doubles the labour ... but ... is the true thing & it is impossible to produce a good effect otherwise'.[21]

All the while that his involvement with the glassworks and his latest architectural ideas carried Pugin's practice ever further away from his public reputation, that reputation nevertheless continued to grow. Herbert's portrait of him, now available as an engraving, gave Pugin a public face to which *Punch* promptly held up the mirror of caricature. 'I figure . . . every week,' Pugin told Shrewsbury in October.[22] The satires were fairly friendly, dwelling on 'Pugsby's' Gothicism, his legendary speed and versatility ('Designs for cathedrals made in five and forty minutes') and his habit of putting his monogram all over his work.[23] The jokes were mainly concerned with the dramatic interest provided by the work on the Palace of Westminster and the various debates and delays that surrounded it. These, much to Barry's chagrin, continued to feature regularly in the press and *Punch* paid tribute to Pugin in his role there 'FOR HIS DETERMINED ZEAL IN KEEPING UP THE BAD DRAWING OF THE MIDDLE AGES'.[24]

The events at Oxford and Cambridge as they unfolded through the summer and autumn, while they naturally interested Pugin, did not touch him as profoundly as they would once have done. His relations with the Oxford men had not exactly cooled, but they had become more distant. He wrote to Bloxam as affectionately as ever, but less often. Preoccupied with his own unhappiness about Mary and his work for Barry, his reaction even to Newman's conversion was muted. Four years earlier the news would have driven him wild with delight. He would have been the first to tell the Earl of Shrewsbury, who was still abroad. Instead Shrewsbury seems to have read the news in the papers and to have been much more excited about it. Pugin wrote laconically to confirm the facts: 'It is quite true about Newman & several more I believe Father Dominick reconciled him nobody seems astonished & very little is said in the newspapers several more will soon follow.'[25] There was, in fact, a great deal said, yet Pugin was right that his own sense of anticlimax was general. Even to Manning and Henry Wilberforce, two of Newman's closest friends to remain for the moment Anglican, there was sorrow but there could be no surprise. The emotional and intellectual tension of the high Tractarian years in which Pugin had flourished had dissipated.

As winter approached, the second that Pugin would have to face as a widower, the prospect appalled him. His health was still uneven and the row with the Amhersts had demoralized and embarrassed him. 'I know in your heart you think me as great a fool as the rest,' he wrote to Hardman, 'but are too kind to express it.'[26] He was so embarrassed at having told so many people that he was going to marry Mary, especially Bishops Walsh and Griffiths, that he was reluctant even to go out. 'I have fastened up the outer gate,' he went on, 'and no one can get in.'[27] He also said that he had been in physical agony for several days. He suffered from pains in his back and hands as well as headaches and wondered if his old 'rheumatic' trouble had returned. His moods were as variable as his health. When low he was ravaged by disappointment – in his work, his house, which he now complained had been shoddily built, the Gothic Revival and the Catholic Church. Financially he was feeling the drain of his building work, and while he had paid out hundreds of pounds for casts to use at the Palace of Westminster, his payments there were delayed. He talked of giving up everything and going abroad. Yet he could never resist a trophy for his collection, boasting to Hardman of a manuscript 'about 8 inches by 6 . . . the finest I have ever seen', 'for 60 guineas!!!!!'.[28] Within the space of a single letter he would rally, regain his confidence and optimism, and then relapse. He was in a precarious, at times probably hypomanic, state of mind. More than anything he needed a companion. He must have a wife, and now he decided to take desperate measures to secure one.

30

Entre Deux Femmes

October 1845 to June 1846

And I have asked to be
Where no storms come,
Where the green swell is in the havens dumb
And out of the swing of the sea
  – Gerard Manley Hopkins, 'Heaven-Haven:
                    A nun takes the veil'

'[Y]ou will be deligted to hear that Miss Greaves has made her profession of faith & received the holy communion Deo gratias. send me my lock handles you vagabond. I have orders for 2 more windows for you wanted directly simple design just the thing. I am very bad.' Thus Pugin concluded one of his typically inconsequent letters to Hardman.[1] Ann Greaves's reception into the Catholic Church drew her yet further into the Pugin family circle. The boatbuilder's daughter had lived at Ramsgate now for more than a year. The children loved her, she played the organ and she ran Pugin's house in 'the most admirable manner'.[2] Miss Keats had left shortly before Acquarone arrived as tutor, and there was no new governess. Ann Greaves, it seems, took charge of the younger children's lessons as well. Pugin decided to propose to her, a marriage of convenience, and she accepted. For a working-class woman it was a brilliant match. She was devoted to the family and, reading between the lines of Pugin's letters, it seems likely she was in love with him. From Pugin's point of view the arrangement was, in a sense, pragmatic. Many Victorian widowers might have done the same. But Pugin was not a pragmatic man. He was behaving now with all the cynicism he could muster, which was not a great deal. He wrote at once a most 'upsetting' letter to Mary Amherst telling her of his plans. Mary felt guilty and miserable. 'How can I ever . . . forgive myself,' she asked Gentili, 'if . . . P . . . is going to take the step he is from exasperation . . . I fear . . . it is not for his happiness & that he will repent after. A Protestant too.'[3] Pugin had clearly not mentioned Ann Greaves's conversion. He was punishing Mary in a childlike way by threatening that he would ruin his life and be miserable and it would be all her fault. Mary begged Gentili to be allowed to write to him to express her concern and assure him of her affection.

Filled with new resolve, Pugin began laying out the ground for his church and cloisters. He started with the north cloister range that would serve first as a temporary church and in time become a school. He decided that he would indeed spite the Bings by building out as far as the boundary of his site. He was, altogether, in a savage mood and just now he found an unfortunate confidante in Lady Shrewsbury's meddlesome half-sister. Anne Talbot, to Mary's annoyance, had wormed some confidences out of her and taken it upon herself to act as a go-between for the unhappy lovers. Pugin met her in London on 15 November. Whatever she said to him, it caused him the next day to pronounce himself, in a letter to Lord Shrewsbury, 'full of work and energy', adding, 'I hope your Lordsip will not give credit to any reports you may hear about me. Several persons have been circulating that I am about to be married but such *is not the case*.'[4] Miss Talbot's conversation, combined with the two letters Mary could not resist writing to him, had convinced Pugin that her love had been 'merely concealed', that it now 'burst forth in all its force' and she would, after all, marry him.[5]

His strategy had worked, but he was not a good strategist and he had succeeded in putting himself in an impossible situation with Ann. From now on he was 'a stranger to rest even for an instant. I lost sleep energy appetite, strength everything.'[6] So he continued for some months. Still he worked. The largest building, apart from his church, to be begun that winter was a convent beside the cathedral at Nottingham for the Sisters of Mercy. Meanwhile in the studio Powell, who was modelling metalwork designs for Westminster and other buildings, was settling in, though his progress went by fits and starts. 'I am getting on famously,' he wrote to his uncle in October, 'as you will see by the moddles [sic] in capital spirits and working very hard'.[7] A month later he was in the depths again, having received a 'regular blow up' from Pugin, and wrote, crestfallen: 'I am very sorry to hear that my carelessness has caused you so much trouble . . . the Governor has put me right . . . you never [sic] find it so again uncle.'⁸ This was to be the volcanic pattern of Powell's working life. He had talent and application but neither of them on the scale Pugin expected, and while he took his work seriously, he did not see it as a sacred vocation.

Herbert came again for Christmas, as did Bernard Smith. A German priest, James Jauch, visited too and met a Cambridge student 'just about to enter the Catholic church' who was also staying.⁹ It is clear from other references in Pugin's letters that he frequently had more guests, some making lengthy visits, than he made mention of in his diary and that the household was run so as to accommodate a large and shifting population. Yet in the midst of his hospitality he was lonely and anxious. It must have been a peculiarly uncomfortable Christmas as Pugin, tortured by who can say what mixture of guilt, embarrassment and doubt, presided over the festivities with his supposed fiancée. As the year turned he struggled to conceal his dilemma, but he was never able to conceal anything for long; 1846 is the second year for which his diary is missing and, as in 1843, it seems likely he destroyed it himself, though it is unclear exactly why, for there were many and various unhappinesses.

The first blow came from a quite unexpected direction. The January number of the *Ecclesiologist* carried a violent attack on Pugin. It was cast as a review of *The Present State*, two prints of St Chad's and *St Edmund*, a frontispiece for the *Lives of the Saints* series. Of these only the last was a recent work and it was a very minor one. The design for St Chad's was eight years old. The buildings illustrated in *The Present State* had been conceived four or five years earlier but the author had deliberately chosen to avoid Pugin's more recent work. The article, on 'The Artistic Merit of Mr Pugin', had picked its subjects, or rather its targets, invidiously, to make a particular point. The unnamed author was Alexander Beresford Hope, who later became a friend and vocal admirer of Pugin. Exactly what possessed him to make this attack is debatable. A wealthy and imperious man, he had recently assumed command of the reconstituted Ecclesiological Society. He had ideas of his own about 'development' in architecture, which he was about to publish, and he also had it in mind to commission a church from Butterfield. Possibly he was seeking to clear the field of competition before he started. His argument was that Pugin was burned out, that, 'clever and enthusiastic as he is, [he] has not answered the expectations which were formed of him';[10] Pugin now, Hope wrote, merely repeated himself. The article made some fair points. It was true that the *Dublin Review* illustrations showed Pugin's buildings 'in a state of ideal perfection'.[11] It was arguable that in St Chad's and St Barnabas's Pugin's ideas were too big for his site. But Hope had more in mind than selective criticism; he wanted to undermine Pugin totally. 'Time was,' he noted with condescension, when Pugin's ideas had been 'useful . . . But we are now past them . . . They are, in truth, old churches made easy . . . with their . . . flow of diaper their symmetrical roods, their transparent screens . . .' He suggested that Pugin should concentrate on the Palace of Westminster for the moment: 'it will be a good discipline.'[12]

Pugin himself was also long past the buildings he had drawn for the *Dublin Review*, yet the flood of Pugin-by-numbers churches would flow on, in a stream of often hackneyed imitations, to the eve of the twentieth century. Patronizing, insulting and partial as it was, Hope's view was persuasive. His attempt to fix Pugin in the past by tying him for ever to his earliest and weakest work met with considerable success, and the perception of Pugin as a man of one idea, artistically exhausted and overtaken in the mid-1840s, has currency still. The article took Pugin aback. He was hurt. 'It quite surprised me,' he wrote to Bloxam, 'the publication must have changed hands.' The 'Ecclesiologist people' had always been so friendly to him, and he had 'designed their seal for them gratis & served them in every way'.[13] The next annoyance was Maynooth. The Board of Works wrote asking that the estimate be cut. With the *Ecclesiologist*'s criticisms of his cheap buildings, 'unfinished towers and undiapered walls' fresh in his mind, Pugin decided that for once he would not attempt the impossible:[14] 'the funds are inadequate to procure even a respectable building', he told the Board. If built it would be 'utterly unfit for its intended purpose' and Pugin would get the blame.[15] He declined a fee for the drawings, preferring 'the lesser evil of losing money and time, to the greater one of being architect of an unworthy building'.[16] On which dignified note he resigned, for the moment.

All the while Miss Greaves remained at the Grange, under the impression that she was soon to be married. By now Hardman was aware something was very wrong and insisted on knowing what was going on. Once apprised of the facts, he took a characteristically practical line. He suggested they should go to Chelsea together, explain all to Miss

Greaves's father and ask him to persuade his daughter to release Pugin from the engagement. Pugin duly went to Cheyne Walk to undertake the delicate task of telling the boatbuilder what had happened and asking for his help in releasing his daughter from the unhappy situation in which Pugin had placed her. Charles Greaves, that most 'sensible worthy man', seems to have grasped the essentials of the case, and he, Pugin and Hardman set off for Ramsgate to break the bad news to Ann that she was not after all to become the third Mrs Pugin.[17] It came, not surprisingly, as 'a most severe blow' to her.[18] Once everything had been explained, however, it was generally agreed that after this she could remain at the Grange no longer. Sadly she packed her bags and went home with her father. It must have been a shock for the whole family. The younger children can have had no idea of the reason why this kind woman they had known nearly all their lives, their mother's particular friend, had suddenly to leave them. They were extremely upset to see her go and Pugin too found it 'went to his heart', for he was fond of her and thought she behaved in 'a most kind & christian manner', but 'under existing circumstances' the marriage would have been a miserable mistake.[19]

Pugin did not seem to feel that the mistake was entirely his. He was regretful more than personally repentant, but nonetheless he felt obliged to make financial provision for Ann Greaves, indeed her father may have insisted on some compensation. To have lived under a single man's roof for over a year, part of the time as his intended bride, and to leave abruptly and still unmarried would cast a shadow over Ann's reputation. Pugin paid out, he said, probably with some exaggeration, 'the price of a church . . . thousands' to extricate himself.[20] For her part Ann felt no bitterness. Indeed she continued to nurture a *tendresse* for Pugin and kept in touch with the family for the rest of her life.

All that now remained was to secure Mary Amherst, but this was no easy matter. Mary was still divided within herself and surrounded by more and more conflicting advice as news of her peculiar situation spread. Bishop Walsh favoured the marriage. So did Wiseman, who told Mary she should be true to her feelings for Pugin. Lady Shrewsbury, on the other hand, told her that the Earl would never employ Pugin again if he married Mary, though it seems most unlikely that her husband had said any such thing. Mrs Amherst was immovable. She would rather see her daughter dead, she said, than Pugin's wife. Pugin was wretched, ill, unable to sleep and longing for 'a little Domestic peace & comfort'.[21] He wrote to his patron, appealing to Shrewsbury for support: 'I entreat of your Lordship if you value my life to let Mrs Amherst know that you will not oppose the marriage.'[22] Shrewsbury, who was in Italy, caught between his snobbish wife and his own good nature, sent ambiguous replies.

Confusion became worse confounded with the passing weeks. Pugin was now barely rational, but even if he had been it was no easy matter to tell what was going on. The more people heard about the situation the more rumours and misunderstandings were put into circulation. In March Pugin heard from Bishop Walsh that Mrs Amherst had, at last, consented. Within a fortnight another letter came denying that she had ever agreed. Mary then asked to go on a retreat to the Sisters of Mercy at Nottingham. Gentili was in Nottingham and she wanted be under his 'kind care'.[23] She also seems to have had it in mind to try out her vocation, but she had reached no final decision. Word somehow, however, reached Pugin that she had entered the convent permanently. It was a terrible shock. He went at once to Nottingham to try to dissuade her but Walsh and Gentili met him and – at Mary's request – turned him away. He left 'brokenhearted without even being allowed to see her'.[24] Crushed and desperate, he poured out his feelings to Shrewsbury: 'sleep has quite forsaken me I cannot tire myself out. I cannot rest. I cannot work. as soon as I can settle my mind to arrange all the works I have in hand I purpose quitting England & giving up my profession . . . I am a broken man & it is no use trying to go on.'[25]

He veered between pitying Mary and blaming her: 'if Mary had stabbed me it would have been charity but to lead me on to the last & then abandon me . . . is insupportable . . . she was frightened by her mothers violence & sacrifices herself & me I never felt affection till I knew her . . . pray forgive this wretched letter my dear lord Shrewsbury.'[26] Ten days later he had begun to be bitter: 'I break up everything that I had done for her sake go through a world of distress & agony, then at last without a single line without a word I *hear* she is to be a nun . . . I have at last been made very angry & that has done me some good . . .'[27] Mary meanwhile left Nottingham and went home, where she continued to fight her mother, not now for Pugin, but for her vocation. Over the following weeks Mrs Amherst came, eventually, to accept that she would be a nun but, with Walsh's support, insisted that she should not go to Loughborough. The order there was not yet established. Most of the sisters were Italian and, of course, Gentili was a constant presence among them. Mrs Amherst was convinced that Mary's 'vocation' was intimately bound up with her feelings for the Italian priest. She was not alone in her suspicions, for Gentili had a reputation. Lingard, who disliked him for his 'declaiming and exaggerating', which confirmed Protestants' worst suspicions of Catholic extravagance, observed the effect of his 'female retreats' with caustic amusement.

[He] has . . . carried off a number of young ladies to Loughborough . . . Dr Rochell went off poste haste, and brought back his sister. A protestant lady in Liverpool in a letter to me laments greatly the loss of a female neighbour . . . are not all these religious missionaries . . . so many Ciceros pro domu sua?[28]

Uncertain what was happening, half-crazed from lack of sleep, Pugin forced himself to keep up with as much work as he could but on all sides he was frustrated, his mental state rendering the days as nightmarish as his troubled nights. At Cheadle, to his horror, he found that the cement on the interior walls of St Giles's was peeling off and destroying the newly painted decoration. Some 'optical delusion' made all the white glass in the windows look yellow.[29] He arranged to replace one at his own expense. Lord Shrewsbury had already had clear glass installed in some of the windows to get more light, which, as Pugin said, looked 'beastly'.[30] The view to the outside of the building ruined the integrity of the interior and the undiffused light bleached the decoration. Pugin told Hardman to make quarries, small plain squares of glass, for the windows, 'greenish glass with a little ornament just to give character without obstructing light'.[31] Visiting Alton, he passed 'one of the most dreadful nights of my life'. Always subject to bad dreams, he found the great Gothic house terrifying when the Earl was away. On stormy nights the wind would toll the chapel bell, which rang mournfully across the Churnet Valley and frightened Pugin to death. He fell asleep exhausted but woke in the small hours with 'the most horrible feelings . . .' too frightened to go back to bed.[32]

From Alton he went on to Ireland, where the famine which had begun the previous autumn was deepening into a catastrophe and the Irish Coercion Bill was brought in to override the normal process of law. The staff of Maynooth were anxious to find some way forward with their building. They wanted Pugin to design it and proposed a compromise to persuade him to change his mind. The senior Dean wrote: 'We have £30,000; let us begin with that sum, and when exhausted, Providence will not be wanting.' It was Pugin's own argument, if one in which he was losing confidence. As ever, though, he could not resist a personal appeal and it was agreed that he would take the job with drastic modifications to his designs. At the time he was depressed by the thought, but by the summer, when he came to make the drawings, he could muster some enthusiasm. Maynooth was to be 'an enormous building, very plain, but on a grand scale, vast rooms, a refectory 120 feet long'.[33] Vastness and sombre grandeur were the qualities he now sought in architecture and saw, wherever he could, in his own work. As St Giles's neared completion and the school beside it was roofed in, he wrote to Shrewsbury that with the church it would form 'a grand mass of building ... it is so plain'.[34] 'Plain', like 'natural', had become one of Pugin's highest terms of praise, though it is the last adjective anyone else would think of applying to Cheadle, where brilliantly elaborate detail is the most striking feature.

As the situation in Ireland worsened, Sir Robert Peel brought forward, in May, the repeal of the Corn Laws. Landowners, fearing for their own interests, began to retrench. Lord Shrewsbury was gloomy. Mr Champernowne at Dartington, never an enthusiastic patron, gave up any idea of building. Repeal, Pugin noted, was 'playing the devil with architecture among landed proprietors . . . I hope the manufacturers will take to building.'[35] Between reluctant patrons and dissatisfied workmen he was at his wits' end. That month he reported that 'the men have struck on every job I have in hand'.[36] There was no new Catholic church work either. Pugin could not now fail to notice the pattern that been developing over the last couple of years. He had 'litterally nothing but Protestant business . . . there are so many catholic architects now . . . I believe I design for all of them for I see actually my own casts & figures used and they abuse me afterwards these men can afford to sell cheap for they steal their brooms ready made however the movement progresses and the right sort of thing becomes general & that is a great point.'[37] The greatest broom-stealer was Bishop Ullathorne's protégé Charles Hansom. This year saw the completion of his church at Hanley Swan in Worcestershire. It is a competent, slightly literal, Puginesque church, one of those sometimes misattributed to him. With the building

30. The House of Lords, opened in 1847. This was the first part of Charles Barry's new Palace of Westminster to be completed. Pugin, who had designed all the interior details, including the royal throne, was not present at the opening and his name was left out of the press reports.

31. (*top left*) Window in Ely Cathedral, designed by Pugin and made by Hardman's. Of all the medieval crafts, stained glass was the most difficult to replicate.

32. (*top right*) Encaustic tiles from St Giles's, Cheadle, another lost medieval technique which Pugin helped Herbert Minton to revive.

33. (*above left*) Wallpaper for Captain Washington Hibbert for his house, Bilton Grange, Warwickshire, which Pugin extended. It was a successful design for a difficult client.

34. (*above right*) Plate, decorated with a transfer print by Pugin, made by Minton's. It was shown at the Great Exhibition in 1851 as part of a display to demonstrate the domestic uses of Gothic.

35. (*top left*) Vestments from the *Glossary of Ecclesiastical Ornament* of 1844, in which Pugin used chromolithography to get the intense colours he wanted.

36. (*top right*) One of the patterns from the *Glossary*, intended for stencil decoration.

37. (*above left*) A page from *Floriated Ornament* of 1849, a gothic flora based on the plants and flowers of Britain.

38. (*above right*) Jewellery, including a headband, designed in 1848, probably for Pugin's third wife, Jane Knill.

39. The Blessed Sacrament Chapel of St Giles's, Cheadle. The effect of this complete Pugin interior made John Henry Newman exclaim '*Porta Coeli*', 'heaven's gate', when he saw it.

40. The Parsonage house at Rampisham, Dorset. Designed in 1845, just after his own house, here Pugin improved on his first thoughts to create a more mature, gentler version of the same idea. It is the quintessential English country rectory.

41. (*top*) The Banqueting Hall at Lismore Castle, County Waterford, the interior by Pugin and J. G. Crace for the 6th Duke of Devonshire, 1849–50. This sort of Gothic decoration became fashionable when illustrations of the Palace of Westminster began to appear.

42. (*above*) The Mediaeval Court at the Great Exhibition of 1851, lithograph by Joseph Nash. Here Pugin broke the official categories, showing work in all media and presenting himself, uniquely in the Exhibition, as a designer rather than as an artist or a manufacturer.

43. (*right*) The Rolle Chantry at Bicton, Devon. This small mortuary chapel with its fine carving and delicate stained glass was one of Pugin's last and loveliest buildings.

44. (*below*) Chimneypiece from Eastnor Castle, Herefordshire, 1849–50, another grand commission brought to him by the decorator J. G. Crace. Pugin complained that it was too much trouble and that 'to be architect … to one fireplace is worse than keeping a fish stall'.

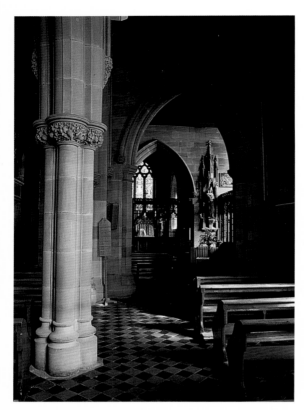

45. (*left*) Pugin's own church of St Augustine's, Ramsgate, begun in 1845. Here he rejected the brilliant colours of St Giles's, Cheadle, in favour of plain stone and the complex, asymmetric interior spaces that interested him increasingly towards the end of his life.

46. (*below*) The tomb at St Augustine's. Pugin was the first to be buried in the family chapel he had created. His son Edward designed the monument on which Pugin's children and his widow appear as weepers.

complete, Pugin was called in to design the furnishings, metalwork, tiles, lights and a lychgate built like one of his plain tables, a massive, springy construction of curved braces that gives the church its one thrilling note of particularity. This too was to be a pattern from now on. Pugin worked increasingly as a decorator and furnisher for other architects. His own ideas remained unbuilt.

Among Pugin's Anglican commissions the most distinguished was at Jesus College, Cambridge, where work had already begun to restore the medieval chapel, which had suffered badly during the eighteenth century. Pugin's restoration began a new phase and it continued for the rest of his life, culminating in a group of stained glass windows for the east end. There were a few other, secular, commissions, including the restoration and decoration of 'a very curious house called Chirk Castle', one of Edward I's defences in the Welsh Marches.[38] Chirk had been relentlessly improved by successive generations of the Myddelton family until by the end of the eighteenth century, with its elegant neo-classical interiors, it was not nearly Gothic enough to satisfy a Victorian eye. Most of the work was decorative and Pugin recommended Crace to carry out his designs. It was, eventually, a lucrative commission, stretching over years, but it was tedious and Pugin's heart was never in it. He saw it chiefly as an opportunity to create fabric and carpet designs that could become part of Crace's stock range.

More satisfactorily, Frederick Rooke of Rampisham in Dorset, a young clergyman whose time at Oxford had coincided with the headiest days of Tractarianism, wanted a new parsonage. The result was Pugin's best, most fully realized house. A variation on the theme of the Grange and benefiting from that experience, it is built in rubble stone instead of brick and with the gable breaking forward to give more light and shade. This was something Pugin wished he had done in his own house and often he drew it as if he had. Rampisham is perfectly poised between revival and invention. There is nothing quaint about it. Its windows are square-headed, except for the one over the front door which indicates a little oratory. It is the Grange matured and softened. Set amid a garden and open on all sides, each face of the building is different, the whole composition compact and easy, without contrivance. 'As progressive as Butterfield's Coalpitheath parsonage of the same year,' John Newman wrote in *The Buildings of England*.[39] This is as close as architectural history has come to revising Hope's view of Pugin as an early Victorian, burned out by the mid-1840s. Yet in fact Rampisham is more 'progressive'. It is Pugin's third house on such a pattern and the pattern itself was, almost certainly, the model for Butterfield.

It was a poignant contrast. Pugin's domestic architecture had reached a peak, while his domestic circumstances had never been more miserable and lonely. He had not loved Ann Greaves, but hers had been a cheerful, friendly presence in the house and he must have missed her. So must his children, who now had no motherly figure in their young lives. After a row about Ann the unsatisfactory Acquarone had also left Ramsgate, for Oscott, where he became chaplain to Newman and his fellow converts. His departure occasioned little regret on either side. In his role as tutor he was replaced by Mary Holmes, a woman of about thirty, who, if she was not as comfortable a soul as Ann Greaves, could boast accomplishments much superior to the general run of governesses. A friend and correspondent of Newman and of Thackeray, and later of Trollope, Miss Holmes had converted to Catholicism and had indeed published a book, *Aunt Elinor's Lectures on Gothic Architecture*, which appeared in 1843, anonymously. It was a hugely popular work of genteel ecclesiology dedicated to 'the ladies of London'. Pugin and Hardman Powell were somewhat in awe of Miss Holmes at first, until the awe gave way in Pugin's case to irritation. Although she seemed so ideally suited to her new post, Miss Holmes did not elicit much warmth at the Grange or elsewhere. None of her appointments lasted long.

Pugin was still brooding on Mary Amherst. He continued to hope, sometimes at least, that she would after all come to him. At others he felt defiant: 'it shall never be said that one or 20 women have upset me . . . it is a bad job but I shall survive it.'[40] With Miss Holmes's arrival, however, he could begin to think again of going abroad to recover his spirits. He was 'so wretched that I am not fit to transact business . . . I feel as if I were ten years older in the last four month.'[41] The usual cure, a sight of the 'magnificent old works in France' seemed the only answer.[42] He decided to set off early in June. At exactly the same time Mary's difficulties resolved themselves. Mrs Amherst, worn down by months of argument, conceded defeat. She wrote wearily to Gentili on 1 June that she would go 'on Saturday next' to the convent at Loughborough 'with my dear Mary to leave her there'.[43] This final resolution to the long, protracted battle for Mary Amherst's heart and soul caused consternation and dismay to Pugin's friends. Wiseman was deeply shocked and wrote to Shrewsbury that he thought '[Pugin] has been most unjustly & cruelly treated, and as to Mary Amherst's going to Loughbro' I have had no share in it certainly. I have been distressed beyond measure at the entire business . . . it is wearing Pugin to death.'[44]

Mrs Amherst honoured her promise, however, and Mary wrote to Gentili soon afterwards from the convent to thank him for bringing her at last 'safe into the Ark'.[45] She had found peace. Walsh saw Sister Mary Agnes, as she became, some months later and thought her 'happy and settled'.[46] Indeed she remained at Loughborough for the rest of her life, becoming in time Superior of the convent. Pugin, in despair, set off for the Continent.

31

Improving the Taste of Young England

June 1846 to February 1847

The chapel . . . is on entering a blaze of light. I could not help
saying to myself 'Porta Coeli'.
— John Henry Newman at St Giles, Cheadle, July 1846[1]

Pugin was home before the end of the month. Perhaps it was a determination to throw himself back into life that made him invite his oldest – and most distinguished – friends, the painters Etty, Herbert and Clarkson Stanfield, to stay in July. They came down by train, for the railway had reached Ramsgate a few months earlier. Etty wrote two accounts of the visit, describing Pugin's house and his life. He made of it a scene as idealized as his own pictures and, like them, sincere if sentimental and highly wrought. He saw Pugin's ideal community as Pugin himself envisaged it, a tranquil landscape of human and divine love, a romance of piety and longing. 'Here I am,' Etty told his brother, 'breathing pure oxygen the breath of nature, from off cornfields golden with plenty – and seas azure and green – the organ sounds the song of praise in the chapel – and the lark sings over our heads, there was one this morning singing and sustaining his flight in the most extraordinary way . . . it is wonderful the admirable way in which every thing is done, so solid, good, and truly comfortable, without nonsense and frippery – he is a marvellous man there is only one Pugin'; 'he is building a chapel, a church, cloisters and school';[2] 'he will have a little town'.[3]

The only sad note in Etty's letters was on the subject of the children, who reminded him so much of their mother. Louisa had not been dead two years and she was a vivid memory for Etty, even if she had been all but eclipsed in her husband's mind. He was pleased, however, to see his friend so much better settled and, as he thought, much happier than on his last visit, shortly after the move to Ramsgate. He had clearly disapproved of Ann Greaves and noted with satisfaction that Miss Holmes was 'a very different person . . .'[4] Pugin was less serene. There was always something to worry about. Crace had failed to send the new chairs he had designed, 'oak & crimson utrech velvet', and the old ones, 'wretched Louis 15 things', were 'all broken . . . a disgrace to the place'.[5] 'I have had a home full of people,' Pugin wrote crossly to Wigmore Street, 'if you sent them by rail I could get them in a night . . . pray let me have my chairs before all my bigwigs go.'[6]

Soon after his guests had gone Pugin too was off. He was away, as usual, for much of July and August and on his return he was pitched into preparations for the long-awaited opening of St Giles's, Cheadle on 1 September. There was to be no scope for critics, this time, to say that the building or its decorations were unfinished, that Pugin's reach exceeded his grasp. So much had already been said and written about the church and its architect that it was an object of national and international curiosity. Shrewsbury was delighted with it now and long past regretting the gallery and pews. He thought it would 'improve the taste of young England' and was often to be found showing visitors round.[7] George Gilbert Scott came and was ravished by the interior: 'the stencilling absolutely made the water run down both sides of his mouth,' the Earl reported, with more glee than dignity.[8] Another visitor was Newman. Shrewsbury had invited him to spend a few days at Alton Towers. Newman, 'though no aesthetic', was impressed with the splendour of Alton and after a tour of Pugin's buildings found them 'enough to convert a person, certainly enough to make a convert twice over a Catholic'. At Cheadle he was overpowered by 'the most splendid building I ever saw . . .'[9]

St Giles's was the culmination of Pugin's first ideas about Catholic architecture, the ultimate 'Dublin Review' church. Like the Young England Shrewsbury hoped to impress, it had already somewhat passed its moment. In its elaboration, its Englishness and its predominant symmetry it no longer represented his thinking, yet it was the epitome of 'Puginism'. The church cost over £30,000 and in the five years of its construction the design had been modified. The most immediately impressive features were the last to be included, when the Earl had decided to spend more money: the 200-foot spire, the intensely patterned interior decoration and the Nazarene paintings by Edouard Hauser on the chancel arch and in the Easter Sepulchre. The effect was spectacular and no 'mere revival'. There was never anything quite like Cheadle in the Middle Ages. It is a full-blown work of high romantic art. For Pugin it marked the point, perhaps the first, certainly the last, where his religious and aesthetic ideals were seen to be equally fulfilled. It convinced architects and Catholics alike and it remains his best known and most loved building. Charles Barry was among the important visitors who came up for the consecration, which took place on the day before the opening. That night he was a guest of the Earl at a banquet at Alton. The Towers's full ceremonial forces were mobilized for a dinner that brought together the leading figures of the Gothic Revival in Europe and beyond. For that moment the whole attention of Catholic christendom was on Pugin. Montalembert was there. So were Adolphe-Napoléon Didron, editor of the *Annales Archéologiques*, the French equivalent of the *Ecclesiologist*, and August Reichensperger, editor of its German counterpart, the *Kölner Domblatt*, who now met for the first time, as well as the French glass artist Henri Gérente. Clarkson Stanfield and Herbert came. Wiseman was present, of course, as was Archbishop Polding from Australia.

It was shrewd, as well as generous, of Shrewsbury to include Newman and the other Oxford converts. If they were ever to be won over to his and Pugin's ideal of romantic English Catholicism, this was the moment. Newman, however, remained aloof. He declined to stay as long as the Earl would have liked. Impressed as he was by St Giles's, he was repelled, like many of the converts, by what he saw as the emotionalism of the generality of Catholics, their lack of education, intellectual rigour and 'reality'. He was horrified by Gillis's sermon at the consecration. It was another of the Bishop's steam-driven efforts, 'half screaming and bellowing, half whining', but as Newman noted with exasperation, 'ladies of quality were in raptures with it'.[10] Indeed most people were in raptures. What the opening lacked in oratory it more than made up for in ceremonial. The effect of Cheadle was not to be realized by argument, it was to be understood in sublimation of the self, in surrendering 'the thoughts and feelings of the soul' to the overwhelming power of the totality.[11] As Frederick Lucas, evoking the scene for his readers in the *Tablet*, wrote, this was a demonstration of 'the indissoluble connection between Art and Faith; the external beauty and the inward principle from which it springs . . . the universality of the Catholic Church in both space and time'.[12]

The climax for Pugin of so much that he had worked and prayed for was tremendous, and so was the anticlimax. After the opening he went straight home, exhausted, overwrought and unwell with an 'internal complaint'. By the winter he was seriously ill. One person who did not go home was Frederick Faber, another of the Oxford converts. Faber was a romantic, somewhat histrionic young man, now in his early thirties. A fellow traveller with Young England, a friend of Manners and Smythe and of Wordsworth, who had remarked, when Faber became a priest, 'England loses a poet,' he had followed Newman to Rome.[13] He had since founded his own brotherhood, the Brothers of the Will of God of the Congregation of St Wilfrid, known as the Wilfridians. Lord and Lady Shrewsbury were charmed by Faber. They invited him to stay for as long as he liked. Within a fortnight they had presented him with Cotton Hall, a house they owned near Alton, and the Wilfridians began work, cutting a swathe through the local population as they preached outdoors in their remarkably flamboyant robes. Faber built an arbour to Our Lady of Salette at Cotton and put a statue of the Virgin, whom he called 'Mamma', in the hall. Soon he was talking of 150 converts. Pugin extended Cotton Hall for Faber and designed a church, St Wilfrid's, and a school for him, for all of which the Shrewsburys paid. The foundation stone of the church was laid on 12 October. Ill as he was, Pugin had managed to make a design. It was his last church for the Earl and, though much altered, still one of his best. Built in the local stone, it has an almost double aisle plan and a tough, sculptural tower.

Pugin's state of physical and mental health was now giving serious concern to his friends. Wiseman was not the only one who feared he might actually die. Sickness, depression at the failure of his love affair, loneliness and wild restless anxiety combined in what Bury described as an 'alarming illness which affected the whole nervous system', bringing on another bout of temporary blindness.[14] As ever, as it had been with his mother, it was difficult even for close friends to tell how much of Pugin's illness was physical. What was Hardman to make of a letter that included details for fixing enamels and comments on the work at Chirk interspersed with such desperate accounts of mental and bodily anguish?

. . . thus comes the last stage of all sans teeth, sans eyes, sans everything I am very bad tonight . . . I shall never be well again – never – I am done for – you laugh . . . but I . . . shall never be a man again I doze away half my time now. I have done nothing today. I feel worse tonight than I have done yet. The medicine does not act as they expected. I am wretched beyond description I shall soon cease to even wish for life I never was so miserable I shall never get well oh dear dear dear I shall die alone neglected by all.[15]

He was obsessively, irrationally preoccupied with Mary. He had become convinced, once more, that she was held against her will in the convent, a belief to which he clung in the face of the facts. It was a stiflingly warm autumn. Ramsgate was hot and crowded and Pugin was frantic at being confined there, longing to travel in search of mental repose but too ill, quite 'unable to move from home'.[16] He worked intermittently, making plans and drawings for the restoration of an Anglican church in Cheshire, St Oswald's, Winwick. A few weeks later, however, he was writing to the rector: 'I have been so very ill since I was with you that I have not been able even to write this is the first severe illness I have had in my life & it has pulled me down so much that I can hardly sit up.'[17] Pugin's Ramsgate doctor, James Daniel, went with him to London to see a consultant, who took a serious view of his case. He prescribed something, probably mercury, which Pugin complained was unpleasant to take. It did not have the predicted beneficial effect and Pugin attributed his drowsiness to it. In view of his 'most precarious state of health', Pugin remade his will and wrote to Bishop Griffiths that he wanted to give the incomplete church and land at Ramsgate to the diocese at once, in case he did not live to finish it.[18] The deed of gift was executed in November.

Still work at the Palace of Westminster went on, remorselessly, as the House of Lords neared completion. Pugin could not get to London, so at the end of October Barry came to him. Indeed the Barry family decamped to Ramsgate, renting a house in Nelson Crescent. The Indian summer was over. The harbour was full, with two or three hundred ships driven in to seek shelter from storms in the Channel. Despite the wind and 'perpetual rain', Barry's son, Charles, found plenty to interest him.[19] At twenty-two Charles Barry Jun. had made a start in his father's profession. His diary speaks with the confidence of the younger generation, and what he recorded in Ramsgate that autumn was a microcosm of 1840s England, the interplay of architecture with politics, religious and social, that was being acted out in towns and villages across the country and at many levels of society. The Barrys went to church on

Sunday to the once genteel St George's, where the liturgy had taken on a Tractarian hue while the building itself now looked sadly out of date. 'By Mr Kendall,' young Barry noted, 'and . . . below criticism . . . in fact execrable.'[20] The congregation was sparse, for the Puseyite vicar was unpopular in the town, especially since he had been so unfortunate as to lose two of his curates to Rome.

So agitated was the moderate middle class of Ramsgate at the perceived Catholic threat from St George's on the one hand and from Pugin's expansionist plans on the West Cliff on the other, that it decided that summer to take action. Lieutenant Hutchinson, a resident of Spencer Square, only a few hundred yards from the Grange, called a meeting in the Town Hall to propose a new church to be built on the west side of Ramsgate, a more or less explicit breakwater against the tidal pull of St Augustine's. The Lieutenant's appeal raised £8,000 in short order. A site was purchased in Vale Square and Pugin's admirer, George Gilbert Scott, was commissioned to build Christ Church. So it came about that the church in Ramsgate which most directly reflects Pugin's influence was built in a deliberate attempt to counter it. Like the Martyrs' Memorial and the spire of the Tolbooth church, it demonstrates how Pugin's impact on architecture and the British landscape, though immense, was so oblique, refracted through so many turns of historical and religious circumstance, that it seldom worked for his advantage and sometimes, as here, could be deployed directly against him. Scott was always a safe pair of hands, an utterly sound and moderate Church of England man. Architecturally, however, he was still finding his feet. If he did not quite steal his broom, Christ Church is highly derivative, a leaf out of *The Present State* with a touch of the porch from Cheadle.

Standing almost within sight of each other, Pugin and Scott's Ramsgate churches make a telling contrast. To compare, for once, an expensive building by Pugin with a cheap one by Scott proves the truth of Pugin's argument against his critics, that he had rarely had the chance to show what he could do. More tellingly, it was Scott who was building the Puginian church while Pugin himself had moved on. By now Pugin had finished one range of his cloister and the room next to it, intended for the school, as well as a north tower with a pyramidal roof. This was to be his temporary church and it was designed so that externally it indeed looked like a small church, one with a nave and single south aisle, asymmetric and Continental in appearance, rather than a fragment of something incomplete. The first Mass was held in it that Christmas.

When Pugin could work he was mostly occupied with stained glass. The new business had not attracted as many orders as he and Hardman had hoped, and they had doubts about its viability. Much depended on getting the glass for the Palace of Westminster. Barry was happy to use the Hardman works, but the Fine Arts Commissioners had obliged him to use Ballantine and Allen for at least some of the work. In November Pugin and Hardman began making a sample window for the House of Lords. Technical perfection was still elusive. Charles Barry, unlike the Earl of Shrewsbury, understood the effects of light in architecture but it was difficult for him, as for Pugin, to predict how the coloured glass would transmit and diffuse it. One problem was that the uneven transparency of medieval glass, which broke up the light and rendered the surface more interesting, was partly an effect of age, what Hardman Powell called 'the glamour produced by time'.[21] Pugin and Barry could not wait for time. Hardman Powell too was now busy with the glass. He would take Pugin's sketches, clarify and scale them up into full-size cartoons. These would be sent to Birmingham for manufacture with the colours marked on. Even though they only went after inspection by Pugin, stringent criticism and subsequent revision, Powell could never be sure of avoiding a blowing up.

Pugin disliked having any aspect of his work out of his control. For the glass it was necessary to have draughtsmen and artists to assist him, and over the years half a dozen or so came to Ramsgate, some from Hardman's works, others independently. Pugin never got on with them. The first, and one of Pugin's least favourite, was Francis Oliphant, who began as a freelance at the end of the year. Oliphant was fated to be remembered principally as the husband of his novelist wife and cousin, Margaret, yet he was an artist of some skill. Pugin disliked him. The reason he usually gave was that Oliphant was a Protestant, but so were many of Pugin's friends; it was undoubtedly Oliphant's independence of spirit and drawing style that rankled. It was soon after Oliphant began work for him that Pugin's illness affected his eyes. In the short winter days he could not work after dusk. Hardman Powell wrote to Crace explaining that 'he is quite unable to read or draw by lamp light'.[22] A little later Pugin himself told Crace he was almost blind and 'very wretched'.[23] Within the month his eyes were somewhat better but everything still seemed to go wrong. He and Crace had trouble at Chirk. 'I do believe IF I had given £50 never to have seen the place I should have been a gainer...' Pugin complained; '...it is impossible making all these things hundreds of miles apart ... such a job ... is enough to drive any one mad ... it is worse than the house of Lords.'[24]

The Lords, due now to open in April, was bad enough. Only one window was ready, made by Ballantine but to Pugin's design, the first of a series of twelve depicting kings and queens, and Barry was still changing his mind about everything. 'I am about wild,' Pugin told Hardman, 'I spent 3 days on these house of Lords Benches & made a magnificent job & now Mr Barry has altered his design and all thrown away.'[25] Even more fraught was the question of the lighting. Hardman was making sample gas brackets, expecting to get the order for the whole job, which would be substantial. In November a technical trial was made. It was a failure. Michael Faraday was called in to advise, as a result of which the Hardman-Pugin brackets were abandoned in favour of gaslights designed and manufactured by Faraday's brother James. Barry had to break the bad news to Birmingham. It was not his fault but Pugin was furious and bitter. 'I am not astonished about the house Lords nothing astonishes me. Mr B is a man who does not care for anybody beyond his own interest he would see you & me ruined with the most perfect apathy. I entered into the Parliament work against my better judgement. I have every cause to regret it like everything for the last 2 years it has been a misfortune.'[26]

Pugin talked of resigning but Barry certainly and Hardman probably made efforts to calm him down and cheer him up. He was soon on good terms again with Barry. Even so, the year ended miserably. Pugin was desperately lonely, ill and terrified of blindness: 'my eyes are very bad tonight,' he wrote dejectedly to Hardman, 'I ... must sit with lotions all the evening it is dreadful worse than all & nobody even to speak to nothing but my own miseries to reflect upon.'[27]

He was wildly unhappy. 'I would sooner go before the mast than live in this dismal solitude,' he wrote.[28] His lethargy, doubtless, had a psychological element – even his poor eyesight Pugin sometimes attributed to his frequent bouts of crying – yet he was also physically extremely ill. The neurological symptoms that had first manifested more than a decade earlier were getting worse and more frequently debilitating. Pugin was now considering the possibility that he might have to give up his practice and told Hardman he had enough savings to live on the income if he had to. Powell and Oliphant held the fort in the studio. Powell wrote the business letters and rather enjoyed being able to cheek Crace in the person of the Governor: 'the curtains arrived to day safely but Mr Pugin thinks one of your foremen must have sent them . . . for with them was packed 3 rods and a number of wretched hooks which as he says are not fit to put in a stable.' But of course when Pugin regained his sight he was far from satisfied with his assistants' efforts: 'Oliphant has been finishing a lot of things he sketched in while I was blind – vile they must all be torn up – I never saw anything like it.'[29] Powell was understandably depressed and working slowly. The weather continued bitter. At the end of February Pugin went to London for another medical consultation. The doctor gave it as his opinion that Pugin's latest sufferings were the effect of cold combined with the mercury rather than 'a return of the original disorder'.[30] With this slight reassurance, but still very ill, he went home. Gradually after this it seemed his health improved, as did his state of mind, both of them yielding to perhaps the only possible cure, a sympathetic and attractive woman.

32

The House of Lords

February to Autumn 1847

...a hall worthy of this advanced age and this opulent empire...

– *The Builder*, 1847

Helen Lumsdaine was twenty-one. She was the niece of Pugin's neighbour, Mrs Benson, and her father was a clergyman, rector of Upper Hardres near Canterbury. That winter she and her parents made a long visit to their relatives in Ramsgate, during which Helen met Pugin. She began to call on him and her visits became more frequent and protracted until she was spending 'a great part of the day' at the Grange.[1] She was a bright and prepossessing young woman. Her father's family were Scottish gentry, cultivated but conservative, and Helen, like so many of her contemporaries, took an informed interest in theology and religious affairs. After her return home she began to correspond with Pugin, who sent 'various Catholic works' to the Rectory for her perusal. Feeling now much better, he started the job that had been hanging fire since the autumn, the restoration of St Oswald's, Winwick. It was one of his happiest commissions and although architecturally a minor work it is remarkably complete; '. . . it is a real pleasure to work for one like yourself,' Pugin told the Revd James Hornby when it was finished. 'If all employers were like you the exercise of the architectural craft would be the most delightful pursuit possible.'[2]

Hornby was an Anglican parson squire in the old, Georgian mould. He was everything Pugin had once in principle most disliked and yet now, thanks to the many and curious changes in the religious climate over the last decade, he was the most sympathetic possible patron. He was a High Churchman who understood the antiquarian tradition of

Dugdale that lay so close to Pugin's heart. He was financially independent, with a wealthy living, and he treated his architect with a mixture of frankness, respect and personal warmth that suited Pugin's temperament. The inscription Hornby composed to commemorate the work summed up its peculiarly early-Victorian nature, its political and theological meaning and its spirit of workmanlike collaboration:

This Chancel, impaired by time and injured in the Great Rebellion, was rebuilt on its old foundation and restored to its original form, in more than its original beauty, in the years of Our Lord MDCCCXLVII and MDCCCXLVIII. James J. Hornby, Rector. A. Welby Pugin, Master of the Work. George Myers, Builder. Laus Deo.

The counterpoint to Pugin's warm relations with Hornby was the increasing strain felt among his co-religionists. The Romantic Catholics, like the Oxford and Cambridge men and the heroes of Young England, had come to a parting of the ways. The great gathering at Cheadle in the autumn would not be repeated. No one felt the pressure more than Wiseman, who was in a state of 'constant mental tension'.[3] Running Oscott, managing Newman and the other converts who were still uncertain of their best course within the Church and dealing with the enormous number of 'distressing perplexing matters that are thrown upon me from all sides' tried his always delicate nerves.[4] In particular he was becoming impatient with the Earl of Shrewsbury and his frequent peremptory queries and complaints. He wrote the Earl a long, decorous letter whose unmistakable purpose was to put him in his place. Wiseman stated clearly that he would not account for himself to 'any but my ecclesiastical superiors . . . reflect what would be the case were this to become a general practice & were Mr Phillipps and Lord A B C . . . to take his three or four points of attack . . . In France in Belgium in Italy such things are not known . . . But I fear that with us the Bishop . . . is held for little more than a public officer and functionary of the Catholics.'[5] So indeed it had been in the penal days. Still, when Wiseman first came to England, the emerging Catholic Church had looked to the laity for leadership and patronage. But those days were passing ever further into history and with them went the influence of men like Phillipps and Shrewsbury.

No doubt some of these questions were discussed between the Earl and his architect when Shrewsbury came to Ramsgate in March to cheer

Pugin on in his recovery. He was well enough now to get to London, where he was overseeing preparations at the House of Lords; 'everything is coming out magnificently,' he told Hardman.[6] As usual, when he felt back on form, he expected everyone else to speed up too: 'send up the brass for the floor,' he wrote to Birmingham, 'for they are waiting for that – you better send up grates [fire] dogs everything as fast as you can for they are hanging curtains & fixing stuffed seats . . . there is great cry for the gates . . .'[7] Pugin was at the Palace when the Queen came to inspect the chamber and 'expressed her great Satisfaction'. Hardman's painter, Thomas Earley, was also present and reported that Pugin was in 'tip top spirits'.[8]

The much delayed opening finally took place on 15 April and public reaction was favourable. The *Illustrated London News* ran a series of articles over five weeks describing the interior, which was, it thought, 'the finest specimen of Gothic civil architecture in Europe'.[9] It savoured every detail of materials, colour and design in this 'stupendous whole'.[10] Hardman, Crace and John Webb, who had made the furniture, were all singled out for praise. Together the articles ran to eleven pages. Nowhere was Pugin's name mentioned in any of them. It is difficult, at this point, not to think that Barry suppressed it. That he could do so was due to Pugin's complete lack of instinct for public life. The House of Lords did not interest him much personally, certainly not as much as Winwick, and as soon as his work there was done he left London for the Continent. By the day of the opening he had got as far as Carcassonne.

He was on the move almost continuously until the middle of June, his 'tip top spirits' the exaggerated nervous excitement that often followed his bouts of depression and illness. He travelled further and longer this year than he had since 1834 in the aftermath of his parents' deaths. Perhaps not since then had he been so disturbed. He carried almost no luggage but wore his sailing clothes and bought a new shirt only when the one he was wearing fell to pieces. His appearance was becoming something more than eccentric. As his mental disarray began to show itself he was often wildly dishevelled and sometimes markedly dirty. This trip took him for the first time beyond northern Europe. His knowledge had deepened vastly since his childhood travels with his parents but now he would widen it. He would face up to the Renaissance and go to Italy, that 'test act of a Goth's faith' undreamed of in the Great Russell Street school.

As he travelled, Pugin's agitation was further stirred by the letters he was writing to Helen Lumsdaine recounting his adventures and by the regular and enthusiastic replies she sent to various postes restantes. Helen's family belonged to the solid centre of the Anglican Church, inclining towards the Evangelical. Her aunt was a supporter of Lieutenant Hutchinson's Vale Square venture and decidedly anti-Catholic. Helen's letters, thoughtful but naïve, peppered with exclamation marks, bespeak her excitement at toying with forbidden fruit as her religious feelings and her attraction to Pugin became ever more intertwined. For a country rector's daughter to correspond with a man so famous, so controversial, so clearly half in love with her, was indeed an adventure. 'How magnificent the service at Amiens must have been!' she wrote in April. 'What would I not have given to have the same privilege! I never wished to be a Catholic more than on Easter Sunday.'[11]

Thus encouraged, Pugin went on his way, travelling first over familiar ground. He made an excursion to Abbeville, whose medieval wooden buildings had figured prominently in *Antient Timber Houses*. Although he had not attempted timber-framing since he had made a lodge design, which was never built, for Charles Scarisbrick a decade earlier, he was still fascinated by wooden construction. The evidence of this tour is that he was reconsidering it, if not for whole buildings then for elements of them, in combination with stone. Such a use of half-timbering was prescient, another High Victorian theme, developed notably by Burges, stated thus early by Pugin. He was looking at secular architecture as much as ecclesiastical, seeking to expand and vary the model he had been developing since the Grange. His drawings show him continuing to ponder the question of street architecture and urban building types. Several times he drew courtyard houses such as had inspired the bishop's house at Birmingham. His preference for sculptural blocks of building and 'grand severe lines' continued. Full of such hints, the drawings of 1847 are tantalizing, for Pugin was considering possibilities he would have scarcely any chance to build.

After a quick visit to Blois, where he looked at the restoration of the château, begun by Duban two years before, Pugin was back on the train the same day en route to Tours. From now on he was travelling through unknown country. At Carcassonne he noted that there was restoration work going on, carried out by 'Violet le Duc'.[12] He reached Marseilles on 20 April. This was his first taste of the south, his first sight of the

Mediterranean. 'It is quite summer in this part of the world,' he wrote to his daughter Anne, 'the trees are in leaf asparagus colliflowers artichokes as common as possible', but he missed the north, with its green, particular landscape. 'I never saw a more miserable country . . .' he went on, 'it is burnt up no trees no fields nothing but rocks dust & glare.'[13] The following day he embarked for Livorno and the great adventure of Italy: 'to go to Rome and come back unchanged', this was the challenge.[14] Many would have said the same in the 1840s, but for Pugin of course it was architectural, rather than religious, seduction that he had to risk. Ever since he had published *Contrasts*, and the most obvious flaws in its argument, the fact of the Renaissance, the classicism of St Peter's, the complete lack of any connection at the heart of Catholic Christendom between faith and Gothic architecture, had been pointed out to him, this was a journey he had been bound to make.

There could be no resolution of the inherent contradictions in his position, and typically he made no attempt either to justify or to modify it. Rome held no temptation to forsake his architectural faith, it was 'quite disgusting and depressing'.[15] He loathed the 'pagan' Renaissance and even more the Baroque, the 'attitudinising of Saints, Theatrical Virgins' and 'Brobdignagian sculpture killing the scale of the church'.[16] In his ten restless days in the Holy City he was not short of company. Newman was there, preparing for ordination. Newman had decided that the best course for himself and his friends would be to create an English version of the Oratory. This was a post-Reformation religious body, founded by St Philip Neri, comprising independent houses made up of secular priests. Such a community offered Newman and his circle scope to work together to relieve the intellectual poverty of the English Catholic Church. Living together, celibate but not monastic, would be congenial, indeed it would be very much like being in an Oxford college. When they met in Rome, Newman asked Pugin if he would consider designing an oratory. But Pugin, despite his latest ideas on 'development', had no interest in such an un-English, un-medieval institution and in his over-excited state responded rudely to the effect that he would as soon design a mechanics' institute.[17] Newman was offended. From now on he began to dislike Pugin and to undermine him when he could.

Others were more pleased to see him. Prince Doria, Shrewsbury's son-in-law, invited Pugin to dinner and Richard Simpson, a young Oxford clergyman who had converted the year before, took him to meet his hero, the Nazarene painter Friedrich Overbeck. Pugin immediately took the artist over 'and rattled into his ears a voluble torrent, which had no break, and scarcely allowed Overbeck to get in a word . . . Pugin's active pencil kept forming a running commentary on his precepts.'[18] His usual ebullience was straining the limits of self-control. Bishop Gillis, also in Rome, was amused by Pugin's invective and his habit of 'abusing everything' at the top of his voice to everyone, including 'two prelates in immediate attendance on the Pope', whom he told that he expected St Peter's to be rebuilt in the Gothic style.[19] The priests, Pugin wrote to Lord Shrewsbury, 'quite agreed with me'.[20] Perhaps they did not like to disagree with this agitated, unkempt Englishman.

Pugin had an audience with the Pope, to whom he presented a specially bound copy of *Contrasts*. He was no more likely to convert Pius IX to the Gothic Revival than he himself was to be seduced from it, yet he extrapolated from the pontiff's polite interest a complete commitment to the cause. He told Simpson, who lent him some respectable clothes for the occasion, that he had seen His Holiness 'in the distance seated under a Gothic canopy, shining in gold and purple', rather than in the plain audience chamber where they had, in fact, met.[21] Simpson enjoyed Pugin's company, even when he was manic, but found him naïve, scandalized by the nudity in Michelangelo's *Last Judgement*. His patchy education also meant that he was completely astonished to find, once he left Rome, that there was a great deal of Gothic architecture in Italy. John Lingard, who received news of Pugin's adventures via Ushaw, was caustically unimpressed by this excited discovery of what Lingard, Willis and many others had always known.

As usual Pugin lagged, intellectually, behind the antiquaries and for that matter *Murray's Guide*, but he was ahead of his fellow architects. It was still true, as Willis had written twelve years earlier, that Italian Gothic was the subject of 'undeserved neglect'.[22] Classicists went to Italy, Goths did not. Ruskin had yet to open their eyes: the great vogue for Italianate Gothic in England began only after the publication of his *Stones of Venice* in 1851. As Pugin travelled north from Rome he was in a state of amazement to find himself in 'a perfect mine of medieval art . . .' and wrote home rapturously of the beauty of Assisi and 'enchanting' Florence.[23] If the architectural ideas he was forming had few occasions for expression, the textiles he saw in Italy had a direct and instant effect on him as a pattern designer. Damasks and velvets, 'a vast number of beautiful & antient patterns', were incorporated into designs for Crace, for fabrics and wallpapers.[24] The grandest patterns at the Palace of Westminster, where the drama of scale could be fully deployed, are Italian.

From Florence he made his way to Venice, of which, disappointingly, he said almost nothing, although Venetian Gothic made enough of an impression for him to try a touch of it in his own work, some four years before it began to be the vogue among English architects and a decade or more before it became the preferred style for banks, insurance offices and shops in high streets across the country.[25] From Venice he went on to Verona and from thence by night train to Milan. It was early June when he set off for home by way of Switzerland, taking the quickest route up to northern France, pausing little and drawing less than on the way down. He was in Ramsgate on 16 June and the next day in London to meet the Phillippses and Lord Shrewsbury, whom he showed, with Barry, round the House of Lords. As soon as he was able to spend a few days at home, Helen Lumsdaine came to the Grange. She told Pugin she had decided to become a Catholic. She then announced her decision to her family, with consequences as unpleasant as they were predictable. Her brother was furious, while the reactions of her parents, her father 'so grieved, and yet so mild' and the agonizing sadness of 'darling mamma' were even harder to bear.[26] The following weeks saw many stormy scenes in the Rectory.

The Lumsdaines had no doubt of Pugin's role in Helen's decision. For a while, in letters that reflected a predicament horribly reminiscent of Mary Amherst's, she furtively reassured him. 'Matters are worse than ever: believe nothing you hear except from me.'[27] Eventually, however, the family prevailed. Another letter came in mid-July explaining that 'However painful it may be, I must NEVER write to you or any body belonging to you again . . .'[28] Pugin immediately went abroad. Helen arranged for the return of the books he had lent her and Pugin asked his daughter Anne to 'tell Miss Holmes to open the parcel . . . before I come I hate all unpleasant things'.[29] Clearly, although Pugin considered he had been discreet, the family and servants knew about his relations with Helen, which probably meant that the affair was common gossip in Ramsgate. Helen had not – for the moment at least – broken his heart as Mary had, but he was hurt and disappointed and once again alone.

What was left of his architectural practice was as varied and fragmented as the faltering English Catholic revival. He had two new churches to work on now and these, between them, embodied the changes that had come over English Catholic life and worked to his disadvantage. One was a happy commission from an old friend. The other, from a friend of Newman, was to prove unsympathetic both artistically and personally. The first, which he had designed the year before, was at Salisbury, where Pugin had not been forgotten by his earliest Catholic companions. John Lambert was sufficiently prosperous now to be the principal donor for a modest new church and St Osmund's was built near the city centre, within sight of the cathedral spire. The conception of the church and its dedication were a testament to the English Catholic ideal. Osmund, founder of Old Sarum, is depicted in the east window between St Martin and St Thomas of Canterbury, the patron saints of the other medieval churches of the city. Far from being an attempt to further 'some sort of competition between the denominations', as has been suggested, the iconography was symbolic of the unity and continuity of the Catholic tradition in England and its special significance in Salisbury.[30] The design of St Osmund's was also perhaps intended to acknowledge Pugin's own connection with the city where he had begun the world as a Catholic and an architect, for it was laden with personal references. It was a close relative of the cloister buildings so far completed at Ramsgate, which looked from the outside like a little flint church with a nave and one aisle. That is what St Osmund's actually is. Pugin used uncut flint with stone dressings, and in the tracery of the west window he made an anthology of his designs for St Augustine's, combining elements from its east window and his own chantry chapel. In the interior he tried out again the possibilities of asymmetry, setting the chancel arch even further off-centre than at Rugby, drawing the south aisle into a nearly equal relation with the nave.

There were no such personal touches at his other new church, St Thomas's, Fulham, in London, where relations with his patron Elizabeth Bowden broke down altogether. The difficulties of the commission were an indication of things to come, of the obstacles that the Oxford converts, from whom he had once hoped for so much, would create for him now they were Catholics. Mrs Bowden was herself a convert and a close friend of Newman, who was now rapidly changing his mind about Pugin and all that he represented. 'P. is notorious for making people spend twice or thrice what they intend – so you must set out with that clear expectation,' he warned her, ensuring an element of mistrust in the relationship from the outset.[31] In fact Pugin produced his well-tried three-aisle plan, which he could build perfectly to a budget by now. Even so, he and Mrs Bowden never saw eye to eye. Like most of the Oxford converts she had left not only the Church of England but the English Catholic tradition behind. She wanted an orthodox Roman Catholic church, without a rood screen.

The ideal of *Contrasts* lived on here and there, however, between the old Catholics and the new. It flickered into life this year when poor Richard Sibthorp, who embodied in his own unhappy person all the permutations of the Anglo-Catholic crisis, produced a commission for Pugin. Sibthorp had gone back to Lincoln, his native city, where the Bishop allowed him to minister 'in an individual fashion'.[32] This latest project was perhaps the only real success of his strange life. He decided to build fourteen 'bede houses' in which the poor were to be lodged, paying their rent by bede, or prayer. The little houses Pugin designed for him, four small rooms each, set round a cloister garden, are still in use, still lived in by elderly women, a rare fulfilment of Pugin's vision of Christian charity and architecture.

All this time the work on Pugin's cathedral at Southwark continued to drag on fitfully, as it had for nearly a decade. That summer a committee was formed to try to resolve matters. They calculated with Myers how much money was needed to bring the cathedral to a point where it could be opened and set about raising funds. There was £7,000 still owing and much work needed. It was not a good time to ask for help: 1847 was a year of hunger, of bad harvests, business failures and short-time working in the cotton mills. As well as the catastrophe of Ireland there was also near famine in Western Scotland and food riots even in Exeter and Taunton. All classes and degrees were affected: 'do you think you can muster me a little money,' Myers wrote to John Hardman, 'I am very short or I not [sic] have asked you'; and the Earl of Shrewsbury explained to Dr Rock that 'I am continually reproached by those to whom I have made . . . promises . . . Had times continued as they were, all wld [sic] have been right – but between the abolition of the Corn laws, free trade in cattle etc & the Income Tax, I have the greatest difficulty in getting thro'.'[33] As the year wore on, the glorious summer weather was in stark contrast to the misery of many thousands. In Ireland the famine was reaching its crisis. By March 1847 it was calculated that 240,000 had already died; 300,000 emigrated that year. Pugin sent donations and the offertory from his services. All over England Catholics – and others – held benefit events but the horror of the situation was hard to understand and even harder to redress. The famine cost Pugin work. Lord Midleton gave up his model town in Cork, his philanthropy apparently evaporating with his income. His estate accounts for August tell a terse but common tale of death, eviction and forced emigration:

No 368 Received notice to quit
No 369 Two of the tenants, Jeremiah and John Hegarty, sent to Canada, their portion of arrear will be lost.
No 370 Tenant dead; notice to quit given to his widow
No 372 Tenant removed; arrear lost
No 373 Arrear lost; tenant sent to Canada[34]

Lord Shrewsbury at least, who was perhaps never quite as badly off as he imagined, continued work at Alton. If building progressed unevenly there it was not so much for want of funds as want of agreement between the Earl and his architect. Of the castle they had always had different and incompatible conceptions. For Pugin, whatever he said about function, this was principally a romantic eye-catcher, a fragment of Continental Gothic perched above the Churnet Valley, its purpose, if any, notional. The more pragmatic Earl was determined to find a use for it. Beside the chapel, a Staffordshire Sainte-Chapelle, a more prosaic three-storey range was also going up, intended as a warden's lodgings though, as Shrewsbury noted, it was far bigger than was necessary. The central portion of the castle, it had been decided, was to be a residence for Wiseman. An episcopal palace in a castle, like Durham, functional and medieval, came as close as anything could to reconciling Pugin and Shrewsbury's ideas. When Shrewsbury tried to enter into Pugin's vision with suggestions, he generally made matters worse. Now, browsing through his library, it occurred to him that the accommodation could be expanded if the wing was taken up another storey, modelled on Linlithgow Palace. Pugin wrote back testily, 'There is no comparison between this building & Linlithgow ... if carried up so high with dormers [it] will look like ... a row of houses. Nothing can be more dangerous than looking at prints of buildings & trying to imitate bits of them. These architectural books are as bad as the scriptures in the hands of the Protestants.'[35] The Earl was understandably offended by this and insisted on having his way, but Pugin won the aesthetic argument, for the resulting block joins awkwardly to the rest and does indeed look barracks-like.

While the wrangling went on, Wiseman had to be told that his residence would not be ready 'before Easter or midsummer next'.[36] It was not an immediate concern, as he was now in Rome, on another mission to Propaganda to discuss the establishment of an English hierarchy. He met with no very sympathetic hearing. Propaganda had received numerous complaints about the Vicars Apostolic from laymen, in addition to which they now had regular unflattering bulletins from Gentili, advising them not to confide in the English bishops. 'It is one of the weaknesses of this nation,' he explained, 'that they cannot keep a secret.'[37] Propaganda, furthermore, did not want to do anything just now to antagonize the British government. The Papal States, uncomfortably aware of the need to assert themselves against both the Austrians and the gathering forces of Italian unification, wanted all the international diplomatic support they could muster and were hoping to establish an embassy in London. Then, as matters rested thus uneasily, news came from England in August of the death first of Bishop Mostyn of the Northern District and then, the next day, of Bishop Griffiths of London. These were bad blows, the second especially for Pugin. Griffiths, who had been so wary of him once, had become one of his few supporters among the clergy. While Rome continued to deliberate a permanent solution for the vacant posts, Wiseman returned to England in September as acting Vicar Apostolic of the London District. He would never return to Birmingham, or live in Alton Castle, which remains unfinished and unfulfilled to this day, like the romantic Catholic vision it represents.

33

Many Hands

Autumn 1847

Mr Hardman seems to supply the hundred hands, Mr Pugin the one dominant head.

– Journal of Design, September 1849

Ten years after it had begun at breakneck pace, Pugin's architectural career had stalled. From now on an increasing proportion of his work was in the applied arts, finishing and furnishing his own buildings and others. If he did not always have much taste for the work, he had an undeniable and unique talent for it. He had also developed remarkable technical resources. The opening of the House of Lords had revealed him as a designer without rival. While Barry's architecture already looked out of date to the cognoscenti, the interiors of the Palace were of the moment. Gothic was established as the taste of the Victorian age and the Palace of Westminster style began to be in vogue. Crace's wealthy clients wanted it for their houses, while church architects came to Pugin, as he complained, for the 'difficult bits' of their buildings, the metalwork, stained glass and wall decoration.[1] Private customers, clerical and lay, could buy Pugin's metalwork, wallpapers and fabrics from Hardman in Birmingham and Crace in Wigmore Street, or order tiles from Minton at Stoke.

Pugin himself was now at the centre of an extensive if somewhat improvised production network. There were several dozen men and women employed in Birmingham and Ramsgate on vestments, metal-work and glass, as well as a team of peripatetic craftsmen, based in Hardman's factory, carvers, decorative painters, gilders and carpenters, busy all over England. Crace had his own men who worked on the more expensive jobs, as had Myers, who himself stumped the country seeing to work in progress. The enterprise had grown up in an ad hoc way to meet Pugin's requirements but it pointed the direction that 'art manufactures' would follow. Pugin was not the first architect to work with a regular team of craftsmen and manufacturers; the Adam brothers, notably, had done the same. But he was the first to realize his designs over such a wide spectrum and on such a scale, from large public commissions to middle-class houses and small chapels. He was the first whose work was available to any extent in shops, the first architect designer in the modern sense, exploiting the manufacturing and transport capabilities of nineteenth-century England to cater, if not for a mass market, then for a much larger and more socially various market than his predecessors.

The story of this enterprise is told in the Hardman company archives from the late 1840s in several voices besides Pugin's, voices not often heard in history, those of workmen. One of the most distinctive is that of the foreman, Thomas Earley. Earley, who turned twenty-eight in 1847, was a painter and gilder. He took pride in his work, was anxious to improve himself by study, but was no model of Victorian deference. Hardman cared no more than Pugin for excessive formality. They treated the men as frankly as they did each other. 'I am very sorry that Mr Drummond has commenced his annoying letters to you so early in the Work,' Earley wrote drily this autumn from Albury, where painting at the mortuary chapel was again in hand, 'as it is only a foretaste of what you may expect to receive.' The irascible Drummond wanted the niche in his chapel painted without the statues in it being removed. This, Earley pointed out, 'is about as reasonable [as] to expect a man to paint a cupboard inside when the door is locked'.[2]

Earley's was a demanding job. He was responsible for finding lodgings for the men as they travelled and ensuring that wages and expenses were paid. His letters are full of the consequent ups and downs. On one occasion his belongings were stolen, but he traced them and bought them back. On another he took all the stencil patterns from Ushaw to Albury by mistake. Sometimes he got lost, and money was always a worry. Funds came from Birmingham in the form of five pound notes cut in half, the pieces sent by separate posts for security. When Earley's wife pasted two wrong halves together by accident there was a temporary cash crisis. But if the operation was not always smooth or harmonious it was benign, at a time when conditions for many working people were harsh. Earley and Hardman, like Pugin himself, tried to deal with arguments and bad behaviour as honourably as possible. When one of the workmen at Albury was short of money 'owing to his love of Drink & low Company', Earley tried the experiment of paying him more.[3] This unfortunately only led to his drinking more. Earley then sent him home, suggesting to Hardman that 'he perhaps might do better in Birmingham amongst his own people if you can employ him at the factory'.[4] It was rare for anyone to be sacked. All Hardman's men were Catholic (the firm did not employ a non-Catholic until the 1960s), though Earley was by his own reckoning 'a bad hand at Devotion' and resented Hardman's enquiries about his attendance at Mass while away from home.[5] He was more engaged with his ambition 'to improve myself considerably in my work'.[6] That summer he had been to look at Gothic architecture in Belgium and France, and in September Pugin promised to let him come to Ramsgate 'to receive instruction'.[7]

As Earley and his team shuttled to and fro across England, their paths crossed from time to time with those of Pugin and Myers. Myers's work overlapped with theirs, for he supplied some furnishings, as well as wood and stone carving. Occasionally he fitted glass. He was at Rampisham, Ramsgate and Manchester that winter. 'I saw Mr Pugin on Saturday morning for ½ an hour only,' he reported to Hardman, 'he could not stop as the wind was blowing so hard.'[8] Pugin was always in a hurry, both to arrive and to leave, and he demanded the same of everyone: 'you may expect me . . . by the *Derby* train that gets in at ¼ past 10 . . .' he warned Hardman typically, 'so don't go to bed till I get there.'[9] Pugin had always got on with workmen. He was impatient with everybody, but he was no testier with Earley than he was with Lord Shrewsbury. Myers's phlegmatic deliberation annoyed him, as did Hardman's embarrassment about asking for payment from important clients: 'you leave me to get all the money & fight out everything & never speak yourself.'[10] Hardman in turn got flustered when he lost track of people, as could happen easily with the erratic communications of the 1840s. Myers explained in early December that 'this as [sic] been to me the most uncertain journey that I have ever had . . . I never could get to a post when I expected'; 'you should be like me,' he went on irritatingly, 'take things coolly.'[11]

Sometimes he was rather too cool. On one occasion he reported that 'the Rector' liked the stained glass, even though part of it had been put 'in the top lytt [sic] instead of the bottom – but it can't be altered now

& looks very well'.[12] But if he did not have a refined eye or a sensitive
temper, Myers, like the others, entered into Pugin's ideas as much as
his business. 'Just like what a Grecian man would do' was a phrase
that came naturally to him, and in Manchester, where he saw Hadfield
and Weightman's new Catholic church of St Mary, the final outcome of
the project on which Pugin had worked ten years earlier, he was contemptuous.[13] 'I can't speak what I think,' he told Hardman, '. . . it is full
20 years behind Mr P and no mistake.'[14]

Stained glass was now the largest part of the Pugin-Hardman business.
With the work for the Palace of Westminster which Barry was now
putting their way, the turnover more than doubled. It was a mixed
blessing. It enabled Pugin to work in a medium for which he had a great
affinity and by 1850 the firm 'set the standard' for England.[15] But it cost
him a great deal in time, money and frustration. The rapid technical
progress in stained glass design and manufacture at the end of the
1840s meant that a window that seemed successful one year looked
unsatisfactory by the next. Pugin was usually unhappy with his work
when it was completed, but never more so than with glass. He constantly
revised as he went along, and since profit margins were lower anyway
than for architecture the business was as unrewarding economically as
artistically. The increased volume of orders also required more hands to
draw up the cartoons, and life at Ramsgate began to change accordingly.
That autumn saw the arrival in England of Enrico Casolani, Overbeck's
'best pupil', according to Pugin, who had presumably met him in Rome.[16]
All Pugin's geese were swans. Hardman Powell cast a more critical eye
on the new arrival. Like many easel painters Casolani was oppressed by
the demands of an applied art and did not after all turn out well. Powell
reported that he was 'fearfully slow' and doubted he would make a
living at piecework.[17]

Powell was anxious to have help and he was longing for company.
He was still not very happy at Ramsgate. Between his work in the studio,
his duties as chorister and sacristan and his regular blowings-up, he was
alternately overworked, overwrought and bored. Pugin would not hear
of his moving out into lodgings. Soon Powell and Casolani were joined
by two young men from Birmingham, Frederick Hill and Edwin
Hendren. Powell wrote anxiously home to pave their way: 'the Governor
says it is all right [Hendren] will be usefull [sic] . . . so that the only thing
left is whether he can make himself happy . . . represent it well to him

uncle I will do anything I can to make him comfortable both for his sake and my own'; '[but] be sure and tell him how dull he must be here Uncle so that he may know the worst.'[18] Life for the young men in the studio was often dull and always demanding. They were much less happy than their colleagues on the road or even the much-criticized Oliphant, who at least lived in London, for Pugin drove them as hard as he drove himself and expected them to enter fully into his vision of Catholic life. The long hours they spent in the studio drawing and modelling were relieved only by the religious offices.

He was all the more demanding for being, himself, in a constant state of depressive agitation. Without a companion he could neither work nor rest. He did not get on with the book he had started on 'floral ornament'.[19] His efforts seemed to mock him: 'I feel like a mariner without a compass . . . night after night I have sat alone in my library too unhappy to study . . . I have expended thousands & I cant enjoy what I have done for very loneliness.'[20] Feeling at times 'abandoned, lonely & miserable', he told Hardman that he would often 'cry for hours like a child'.[21] The only new architectural work was a job that the Shrewsburys put his way for their friends the Duke and Duchess of Leeds, the rebuilding of Hornby Castle in Yorkshire. Pugin went to Hornby, where he spent the night terrified and sleepless with the bed-clothes over his head 'in an enormous room where the moment I entered with my candle I saw myself reflected in glasses on all sides'.[22] Apart from that, he told Shrewsbury, the job was going well. He had handled his noble clients tactfully, balancing their various ideas and steering carefully between 'Scylla and charybdis', a vision of his architect as diplomat which must have caused the Earl to raise his eyebrows.[23] Pugin's surviving drawings for Hornby are not impressive. He aimed for mass and grandeur, but, at least in the drawings, he achieved only monotony. The plan for the rebuilt house was as unsuccessful as the elevations. Pugin complained that classical architects had two of every-thing, one on each side, just for the sake of symmetry, but he too was at the mercy of his plan and had one and a half of everything on the same side. There was a long gallery, a small gallery, a great drawing room, a small drawing room and so forth. The principal rooms were largely en suite and inconveniently situated. In truth he was out of his depth. With a commission like this he reached the point where his lack of training and the absence of an office began to tell. By the late 1840s, as Jill

Franklin wrote, 'the components of the country house plan had become so complex that assembling and relating them conveniently was a very real test of an architect's skill'.[24] The social conventions, separating family, servants and children, which Pugin had so daringly ignored in his own house, had here to be respected as well as many other proprieties and the all important 'dinner route'.

For the moment, however, he was full of confidence, and as he started on the drawings in late October his spirits were lifted further by a letter from Scotland, where Helen Lumsdaine was staying with relatives, away from the watchful eye of mama and papa. She apologized for what she had been forced to write earlier, asked Pugin to forgive her and assured him of her unchanged commitment to the Catholic faith. Pugin, as easily moved to hope as to despair, at once forgave everything and poured out his heart. 'When you abandoned me I felt more lonely than ever,' he wrote straight back, indeed 'except for that unhappy matter which I explained to you' – so much for Mary Amherst – 'I never felt anything so much.'[25] On the point of her conversion he struck a sterner note. He warned her that now she had seen and understood the truth of the Catholic faith her soul was in peril if she continued to deny it. Over the following weeks their correspondence gathered pace, the emotional temperature rising steadily. Although there had still been no absolutely plain declaration on either side, Pugin dwelt in his letters on his loneliness and his longing for love.

Once he had seen the whole world as his field of action; now he found that it held neither hope nor help for pain. His sphere had dwindled to his own small fortified house and church, while his disdain for all things worldly, for 'ostentatious displays & parties full of every hollowness & deceit', was becoming as great and as Puritanical as his mother's in her latter years.[26] All he wanted was one faithful, female heart. Pugin suggested coming on from his next visit to Hornby to Edinburgh, where they might meet. Helen thought the idea 'delightful . . . !' She went on to commiserate with his domestic difficulties as a widower, adding, boldly, 'I wish I were so situated that I could prevent your having a moment's anxiety on such subjects; then my happiness would indeed be perfect.'[27] He wrote by return proposing marriage. Helen suggested a rendezvous in Aitchison's, a grocer's shop in Queen Street, which Pugin objected to, 'cheesecakes and mock-turtle!' being unconducive to romance, but it was a place Helen could visit alone without arousing suspicion.[28] They met on 30 November and agreed that they would marry, whereupon Edinburgh's classical New Town was infused for Pugin with Gothic glamour. When Helen had left, he told her, 'I followed you as long as I was able & gazed after you I felt so proud of you you rode like one of the ladies of the old time to a tournay.'[29]

The engagement was, of course, a secret. Helen was of age and Pugin urged her to come to Ramsgate and be received into the Church and then married at once privately. 'If you expect to obtain any sanction to our union from your parents beforehand, you will be miserably mistaken,' he warned.[30] Once again Hardman, up in Birmingham, realized there was something afoot. Oblique references in Pugin's letters ordering new dessert dishes and other items for the refurbishment of the Grange suggest that Hardman had understandable misgivings about his friend's latest romance. 'I know you blame me in your heart but I assure you it is all for the best,' Pugin told him, 'I know you think I was a fool for all this but . . . remember if I am comfortable in my mind I can do twice as much work for you.'[31] Yet Pugin was not comfortable in his mind. He continued anxious all winter, worried about Helen, about his work, about money and about the political disturbances abroad and at home. In England the financial crisis that had been threatening for over a year came to a head that autumn. The massively inflated market in railway shares collapsed and, as the effects spread through the economy, 'Firms of the highest standing and repute failed.'[32] There was, the diarist Henry Reeve recorded, 'Remarkable depression in the last months of this year, general illness; great mortality; innumerable failures'.[33] For Pugin there was almost no new work and, struggling with the designs for Hornby Castle, he found himself, for almost the first time in his life, stuck.

At Westminster he and Crace were designing the interiors for the libraries, some of the best and best preserved of Pugin's work in the Palace, as well as decorations for the corridors and refreshment rooms. Pugin was anxious to harvest the fruit of his Italian trip. In working out textile and wallpaper patterns he allowed Crace a degree of freedom that he did not give to Hardman or the young men in the studio. He trusted Crace's colour sense. 'This first pattern is Venetian I send it to you coloured exactly like the original but I think you can move colours & vary it with . . . effect if done in gold & flock it will be like the drawing.'[34] He was working on a ready-made range of textiles and furnishings, some of which would be sold by Hardman as well as in Crace's Wigmore Street showroom, and he was thinking of moving on to other soft furnishings. It was all something of an innovation for Crace, who needed persuasion to do anything so déclassé as advertise. 'I am very anxious to get lots of ground patterns for papers . . . but when you get a stock you should make them known,' Pugin urged him, 'we must have a turn at CARPETS next – let us reform them altogether.'[35]

As the year closed in with bitter cold and terrible storms, Pugin began to contemplate another new enterprise that had nothing to do with upholstery. From the tower on his house he watched with anguished fascination as ships struggled and foundered at sea around the treacherous Goodwin Sands: 'at day break I observed with my glass a large ship on the goodwins with the crew in the rigging,' he told Crace, 'by 8 o'clock not a stick of her was left & all hands 16 in number perished a Dover boat who went to try & take the poor fellows off was also lost with all hands & a large brig went on the goodwins this morning & went to pieces in 20 minutes . . . there is every appearance of a dreadful night.'[36] Considering what to do in the face of such distress, he decided to start a hospital for shipwrecked mariners, for whom he had a great, if somewhat sentimental affection. He rented the lower floor of a house in King Street, a poor part of Ramsgate, for temporary premises. His doctor James Daniel helped him and a number of injured seamen were soon receiving attention. It was, of course, a Catholic charity and too small to accommodate many patients. Its principal effect was to provoke Lieutenant Hutchinson and Mr Hoare, the new, Evangelical vicar of Vale Square, into a campaign of competitive philanthropy. The next year they began to raise funds for their own – non-denominational – Seamen's Hospital.

To Helen, in whom he now confided all his news and hopes, Pugin unfolded his plans for the mariners' refuge and told her of the hard lives that sailors lived on board ship, even under ordinary circumstances. With a lover's desire to impress and a touch of his father's bravado he added that he knew all about it, having himself been 'at sea for several years'.[37] Catholic sailors, whether injured or not, were always welcome at the Grange, for it gave Pugin, he told Helen, the greatest happiness, 'when I see these poor seamen assembling for mass under the roof I have raised'.[38] Hardman Powell was not so romantic: 'we had lots of sailors up to the chapel from all countries,' he wrote to his uncle in November, 'among them were some herring fishermen who distributed a most fearful smell throughout . . . fortunately the incense helped to counteract it or we should have nearly been stifled.'[39]

Pugin was also boasting to Helen, with more justice, about his work at Ushaw. The chapel there had been 'five years in progress' and was now nearly finished, 'one of the most satisfying buildings I have ever produced'.[40] Unfortunately, as the same storms that hit the Goodwins swept over the open moorland of County Durham the building began to leak. 'I am sorry to tell you there is not one of the Stain [sic] Glass Windows but what the Rain pours through,' Earley reported in December. 'Dr Newsham was unfortunately in the Church at the time he says something must be done with them.'[41]

34

Helen Lumsdaine

December 1847 to May 1848

Woman's faith, and woman's trust,
Write the characters in dust;
Stamp them on the running stream,
Paint them on the moon's pale beam . . .
— Walter Scott, *The Betrothed*, 1825,
quoted in Pugin's *A Statement of Facts*

Despite his anxieties, this was the most cheerful Christmas Pugin had spent for some years. Herbert came as usual and, as Pugin told Helen, now that he was sure of her he had a heart for celebration and 'carried out the Xmass festivities in my way'.[1] His way was to combine Catholic piety with Dickensian jollity, both in their most vivid forms. The offices began with vespers on Christmas Eve, then Midnight Mass. The church was decorated with 'bunches of yew and holly'. Anne played the organ 'exceedingly well'.[2] There was Mass at daybreak, High Mass at ten, vespers again at three.

After this 'the festivities at the house' began.[3] Tables were laid in the library for thirty-four people and there was 'a tree 10 feet high candles & variegated lamps in the branches': 'it was very pretty indeed', Pugin told Hardman, 'there was a hoard of children'. Typically he was just as pleased when it was over. His sense of the dramatic allowed for no tailing off. The curtain should fall leaving not a rack behind; 'by ½ past 10 & before I went to bed I saw everything washed up & put away. table reduced etc. so that next morning you would not have known that anything of the kind had taken place.'[4] The bright hearth, the loving family of children, were as necessary to Pugin as they were to Dickens and to his readers, the more precious for being fugitive, glowing bright against the darkness beyond. This new year, 1848, was to be the year of revolutions. They began almost at once, on 12 January, with a rebellion in Palermo that spread quickly across Italy. Pugin was not surprised. As usual he felt confident that he had seen it coming, nor was he entirely sorry: 'did you see that the Roman Republicans threatened to blow up St Peters,' he asked Hardman, 'I am afraid they have not spirit to do it.'[5]

He was too happy to take trouble seriously. Helen was still in Scotland but wrote reassuringly. 'I cannot express to you the happiness [your letters] afford me,' he replied, 'since I know you love me I feel quite another man, indeed dearest Helen you have saved me, litteraly saved me. I was rapidly falling into a misanthropic state of mind.'[6] His hair, which had been coming out, was growing again. His confidence returned and he felt sure that he would resume his architectural career and complete his book on floral ornament. Meanwhile he urged Helen to keep everything secret until it had been 'irrevocably settled at the altar . . .'[7] She, however, had qualms about deceiving her parents. She decided to be received into the Church in Edinburgh 'and then, after I get home, I would tell papa and mama that I was engaged to be married to you; they could not reproach me with having taken such a step without their knowledge, and . . . as I should then be a Catholic, a great part of their objections would be removed. It strikes me that, although my plan requires an immense deal of courage on my part, yet it is the right one to pursue . . . You are my all in all.'[8] If the argument is not quite logical, it is hardly surprising. Helen's situation, like Mary's, had become hopelessly invidious.

Pugin foresaw more clearly than she just how much courage she would need, warning her, without irony, that 'where religion is concerned there is no knowing to what length people go'.[9] He sent her a pair of letters setting out the promise of marriage cut in zigzag like an apprentice's indenture, one for each party, agreeing to marry 'as soon as conveniently may be after Easter'. Each was to keep half of each.[10] Helen signed hers on 25 January. With this security he continued making practical arrangements. The refurbishment of the Grange continued, 'panelling the best rooms, putting new stained glass in the windows, redecorating the ceilings . . . I am fitting out in every department'.[11] He also set in train the design and manufacture of jewels and clothes suitable for a Gothic bride. Miss Holmes, who had irritated Pugin as much as she had irritated her other employers, and had come back after Christmas against his wishes, was ordered to leave after Easter. The children were told, for the third time in four years, that their father was about to be married. Little Polly (as Mary was known) was pleased, remembering that Miss Lumsdaine had given her sweets, but Polly was only four. Anne, who was now fifteen and, her father reassured his prospective bride, 'useful' about the house and good at accounts, had perhaps more mixed emotions.[12]

As preparations were under way there was another revolution, this time a domestic one. In the middle of January, Hardman Powell announced that he should like to leave in March. He would be twenty-one and he wanted to go back to Birmingham and work for his uncle while he developed a career of his own as an artist. This, too, Pugin had predicted, much more specifically than events in Italy, but the reality came as a shock. He took Powell's decision, as he took all his dealings with people, absolutely personally. Though he strove to respond more in sorrow than in anger, he revealed a disappointment histrionic and bitter to the point of unreason: 'of course I have nothing to complain of in this he is quite right,' he wrote to Hardman, '. . . of himself I have not a syllable of anything but praise . . . he will now have his ammunition against me & I shall have to contend against another enemy this is natural it is human nature & I do not complain for an instant (he that is not with me is against me) etc however it will bring about one great change that I am not sorry for. I shall give up stained glass entirely you have now an artist of your own . . . & you will be able to carry out the work independently of me . . . of course after what he told me I would not detain him an hour.'[13]

Hardman was horrified, not least at the thought of Pugin withdrawing from the glass business, which would ruin it. He was also hurt. Pugin reassured him that there had been 'no row whatever', yet his possessiveness, his fears of loss and betrayal, his conviction that the Protestant Oliphant had corrupted Powell, were barely rational.[14] 'I know a great deal & I know I think how he has been worked upon & when I tell you which I do in confidence he is a Pagan in heart you will not wonder at anything . . . he is [a] capital man very good etc but no Pagan lives with me. say nothing to him on this score . . .'[15] Powell was sent home, a first class railway ticket heaping coals of fire on his head. Hendren went with him, with undisguised relief. 'I feel I have done a good action in freeing 2 prisoners,' Pugin wrote, 'perhaps later in life when things appear in their true light he will regret not sticking to the ship but this is no affair of mine . . .'[16] Hardman came down to Ramsgate, where no doubt he had to listen to much more in the same vein before Pugin could be pacified. Whatever Hardman said to his friend, and to his nephew, he succeeded in restoring good relations. Pugin was persuaded that Powell was not a Pagan, and Powell was no doubt made to realize that it would be the end of the glass business if he stayed in Birmingham. In little more than six weeks he was back at Ramsgate. The rebellion was over, for the moment.

Now preparations for the wedding sped along. 'I have between thirty and forty people working,' Pugin boasted to Helen. 'There are five at your jewellery at Birmingham . . .'[17] The centrepiece of the trousseau was, of course, the dress. It is the only one of Pugin's garment designs known to survive.[18] Crace was making it, with Hardman doing the buttons and Mrs Powell, presumably, responsible for the embroidered girdle. Pugin had it made up in calico first and sent the toile to Helen to check the fit. It was plain by the standards of the time, round-necked, waisted with long close-fitting sleeves, modest but utterly feminine. The lines were pure. There was some scalloping but the outline was unblurred by frills or lace and it accorded as much as one of his tables with Pugin's true principles of design. The rich effect would have come from the materials, the fabric itself and the accompanying jewels, which included a band for the forehead, studded with gems. Helen's suggestion that the waist might be pointed was rejected. Pugin replied that 'it does not accord with the natural shape of the waist . . . nature is the true form'.[19] In other words Helen should not construct her ornament but ornament her own construction. She was to be 'the first woman that has had a true dress for centuries' and, of course, his muse, dwelling with him 'at the fountain head of pattern making'.[20]

Yet there were certain ominous signs. Helen was getting nervous. Her sister had found out about her correspondence with Pugin, who, unwisely perhaps, harped on the trouble to come when the news finally broke, warning his fiancée she must be 'prepared for the worst'.[21] Soon he was complaining that 'it seems so long between your letters & they are so short'.[22] He himself, most unusually, had moments of doubt. 'I know you think me a fool,' he told Hardman, '& I half think so myself. I can see it in your letters though you try to hide it.'[23] Then another blow struck the household at Ramsgate. The children caught measles, which, in the 1840s, was not infrequently fatal. Pugin was beside himself with anxiety. As he told Shrewsbury, who had lost two of his grandsons to the illness, 'they have no mother I look after everything & I cant trust to anybody'.[24] Pugin nursed his children, seeing each of them one by one past the crisis. All six survived.

While he was still watching over them news came from France on 27 February that Louis Philippe had been dethroned. It was, for the moment, almost a bloodless coup but one that shocked England by its suddenness and its proximity. The spirit of revolution had reached the Channel and might not stop there. Remembering 1830 and the unrest events in France had triggered then, bearing in mind the poverty and hunger of large parts of the population, it was not surprising that many Englishmen and women feared trouble at home. In Pugin the news awoke all his earliest and deepest fears. 'I am so upset by this French news I am hardly myself,' he told Crace;[25] 'it has completely frightened me,' he wrote to Hardman '– it will play the devil with everything.'[26] In between complaining about a brooch for Helen which he wanted remade, 'a regular Houndsditch affair poor & vulgar', he prophesied terrible things to come, 'adieu to art & architecture ... 10 per cent property tax & no trade ... what are muskets at Birmingham we shall need a supply soon ...'[27] Pugin was quite serious about defending himself with firearms at St Augustine's, though who else would have wielded the muskets apart from himself and Hardman Powell is questionable; there were only the children, the maids and the highly refined author of *Aunt Elinor's Lectures*.

If few of Pugin's friends took fright to the same extent, everyone was exercised. Shrewsbury's only hope was that this latest French revolution would create some unity among the Catholics and 'bring some of them to their senses'.[28] If not, 'we shall soon be in as mischievous a state as they are in Ireland – the Clergy against the Laity, & all divided amongst themselves'.[29] It was the question of Ireland more than anything that was now drawing the Romantic Catholics out of sympathy with one another. From the Continent the Irish appeared simply as a suffering Catholic people. Montalembert was one of many who pleaded their cause with Rome. From England matters appeared in a different light. Shrewsbury thought Montalembert 'wild' on the subject, and was terrified he would persuade the Pope to throw his weight behind the Irish.[30] Ambrose Phillipps's father-in-law, Lord Clifford, was 'the mouthpiece of the mouthpieces of the Irish party at Rome', while Phillipps himself agreed with Shrewsbury and disliked what he saw as the French tendency to mythologize Ireland and O'Connell.[31] Few of the English landowners could see anything in proposals for reform in Ireland but a threat to the structure and survival of society itself.

The revolutions continued with uprisings in Vienna and Prussia; 'Prussia too', Carlyle lamented, 'solid Germany itself'.[32] 'Ireland will be free,' Gavan Duffy, the journalist and leading member of Young Ireland, promised, 'before the coming summer fades into winter . . .'[33] At Enniscorthy, where work continued, slowly, on Pugin's church of St Aidan, the Irish tricolour, the orange, white and green, was flown for the first time. The clergy, Shrewsbury claimed, 'openly preach sedition and treason', while at the Vatican, where Montalembert had done 'infinite mischief', the Irish gained every point by 'misrepresentation & effrontery'.[34] Pugin was in agreement with the Earl. He was thus even more agitated than usual when suddenly Helen, unwilling to continue her life of subterfuge, decided that she would not wait until after Easter to be received into the Church. Pugin set off for Edinburgh to arrange matters. He half-explained to Hardman that 'circumstances . . . oblige me to go to Scotland next week', adding ungallantly that in courtship 'the diplomatic part is a horrible waste of time'.[35] Bishop Gillis, a ready ally, received Helen in St Margaret's, Gillespie Graham's church for which, at the start of his career, Pugin had designed some of the details. He reported back to Anne that he had 'never heard anyone make the profession of faith in a finer manner . . .'[36] But if he thought the 'diplomatic part' of his love affair was over he was wrong. He was never a diplomat and Helen's Scottish relatives took the news of her conversion very badly indeed, giving Pugin, when he visited her at their home afterwards, 'the most inhospitable reception I ever experienced north of the Tweed'.[37]

Helen was now to return south. She went first to an uncle in London. Knowing what train she would catch, Pugin joined it at Rugby and travelled with her. It was a romantic gesture and the journey would have given them their first chance to talk privately since the meeting in the grocer's. If they were alone in the compartment it would offer a chance for complete privacy, for there were no corridors on trains in the 1840s. After this intimate journey Helen came back to a family predictably united in opposition to her and her lover. They had all Mrs Amherst's objections to Pugin, his age, his class and his large family, as well as an intense dislike and mistrust of his faith. Pugin waited in agonies of suspense, writing to Helen first in London then following her down to Kent. His letters went unanswered; he assumed they were intercepted, until one evening his neighbour, Henry Benson, Helen's uncle by marriage, brought him a reply. In the letter Helen declared that she would 'never, under any circumstances, unite herself in marriage with me, or see me, or receive any letter or communication from me'.[38] When Pugin read it he fainted.

The next two weeks saw him join battle with the Lumsdaines in an almost exact recapitulation of his fight for Mary Amherst. He refused to believe that Helen was speaking for herself and argued that she could not be released by her parents from her binding promise. Once again friends and relations were divided. Henry Benson believed Pugin had acted honourably and supported him, and Helen's uncle, the Revd Mr Sandys, an Anglican clergyman, was at first not unsympathetic. Pugin, however, did not help his own case. Wild with fury, he wrote to Mr Sandys that he knew Helen loved him. Her latest letter could not be her own, it could not express her true feelings towards a man 'to whom she has pledged herself . . . & who but a few days since was the object of her affectionate embraces'.[39] Were it really the case, he went on (suggesting that perhaps they had been alone on the train), 'I would cast her from me with as much disgust as I would for the lowest prostitute in the street.'[40] 'Europe does not contain the spot to which she can be removed without my knowledge,' he warned.[41]

Neither the tone nor the content was calculated to reassure a responsible and now somewhat flustered clergyman that the author was a suitable husband for his niece. He replied that he thought 'the union would not be for the happiness of either party', and accused Pugin of taking advantage of Helen's feelings for himself to influence her religious opinions.[42] From 1 April to the 18th Pugin's diary is a litany of one syllable: 'Hardres, Hardres, Hardres'; every day for more than a fortnight he merely wrote the name of Helen's home. He cannot have been in the Rectory all this time, if he was allowed past the front door at all. Perhaps he merely waited within sight of the house, the very picture of a hopeless lover. At last Henry Benson arranged to meet Helen in Canterbury to plead Pugin's cause. After this she wrote saying that much as she loved him she would not marry him, out of duty to her parents.

She begged to be released from her promise. Pugin refused. He asked for a chance to talk to her. Her reply was cold and final and possibly dictated by papa. He never saw or heard from Helen Lumsdaine again.

This last rejection prompted a complete collapse. He went to bed – unable even to work. His reaction was extreme, but in this latest return to the emotional loneliness that oppressed and petrified him who knows how much he thought of his other, earlier losses. He desperately needed female sympathy, a companion and a lover, and yet every woman he had ever cared for, his mother, his aunt, Anne Garnett, Louisa, Mary Amherst and now Helen, each had been taken from him by death or circumstance. Powell, who can scarcely have been relishing his return to the Grange, wrote business letters on Pugin's behalf. When he was somewhat better Pugin explained to Crace that he was 'worn out with distress & anxiety ... I wish to give up business altogether as far as possible I can't do it all in a minute but it might be managed gradually.'[43] He wrote to the Duke of Leeds resigning the job at Hornby.

By May he was at work again. His first desperate grief had subsided and he was less agitated about the political unrest in England and Europe, as were most people. At home the Chartist demonstration of 10 April had been an anticlimax, while in Ireland Duffy's prophecies remained unfulfilled. Britain was once again a stable port in the international storm. At Ramsgate the 'late occurrence in France' drove in 'a number of persons' and so was good for business after the poor season of 1847.[44] The *Kent Herald* noted that several houses had been taken by families from Paris and 'the paint pot was to be seen all over the place'.[45] Lord Shrewsbury was trying to shake off the exiled Duke of Parma: 'we would not have such a mad-cap for a neighbour for the world', he told Wiseman, suggesting the Duke might go and stay with Louis Philippe.[46] There he would find 'Guizot, Metternich & all the other ex-kings and ex-ministers whom these wild times may throw upon our shores.'[47] Only Ambrose Phillipps remained determinedly pessimistic, predicting that '8 millions of human beings must be immolated before peace to the Church can be secured'; 'he reads it in the Apocalypse!!!' Shrewsbury wrote exasperatedly to Wiseman.[48]

Yet Pugin continued to brood obsessively on his wrongs and now made an extraordinary decision. He resolved to write a pamphlet about his affair with Helen, naming her and publishing her letters and his own. Such public exposure of a woman was, by any standards, brutal and in

Victorian England amounted to an act of social violence. Pugin admitted that he hoped she would be forced to leave the country. His friends were appalled but he was past listening. He said he wished to establish the facts of the case, but his reasoning was a thin crust beneath which resentment, humiliation and sexual frustration boiled; 'what punishment does not this faithless woman deserve,' he wrote to Hardman, 'but they are all alike there is no such thing as real affection it is all humbug impulse mere impulse transient as possible humbug deception.'[49] Pugin's *A Statement of Facts relative to the engagement of marriage between Miss Selina Helen Sandys Lumsdaine of Upper Hardres, Kent and Augustus Welby Pugin Esq of St Augustins, Isle of Thanet* was sent to the printers on 25 May. Composed in the same white heat as his architectural books, it was cast as a mixture of formal treatise and popular tract. On the title page he printed eight lines of verse from Scott's *The Betrothed*. At the end he turned directly on Helen. 'I find one who has either acted a most deceitful part from the beginning, or whose character has so little fidelity and fortitude in its composition, as to render her unworthy of honourable love . . . Such lightness of conduct is extremely dangerous . . . I trust that if she indulges in a repetition of it, she may not fall into the hands of a man who may act with less prudence and integrity than I have done, and involve her in a more lasting dishonour.'[50]

The ugly, misogynist tone of the conclusion misrepresented Pugin, in his usual character, as much as it maligned Helen. Pugin of course thought it all quite justified: 'it is a strong case for me I must convince all honourable people,' he told Hardman.[51] Scarcely, if at all, in his right mind, he began distributing the pamphlet as widely as possible. He sent a copy to Lord Shrewsbury and posted six to Hardman to pass round Birmingham, one for John Moore at Oscott, who was almost the only one of his friends to endorse Pugin's actions, one for Bishop Walsh and anyone else he might think interested. Hardman could not bring himself to mention it. 'I wonder you do not say anything about it,' Pugin wrote, adding that it was making a 'great sensation' in Ramsgate.[52] No doubt it was, and no doubt Mr Hoare, Lieutenant Hutchinson and the rest of the Spencer Square and Christ Church set shook their heads in pious sorrow and wonder at seeing all their prejudices about Catholics in general and Pugin in particular confirmed in such a lurid piece of scandal. Shrewsbury was embarrassed, but gave Pugin a vague impression of support. Crace was horrified to receive a bundle of copies and told Pugin straight out he should not have written it: 'you are quite mistaken' came the reply, in among designs for the Palace of Westminster libraries, 'it is indispensable to counteract the lies . . .'[53]

Most of his friends destroyed their copies and to date only one is known to survive.[54] Finally it was Talbot Bury who decided to take matters in hand. In July he persuaded Pugin to send out no more pamphlets and to hand over those he had left. Pugin and Bury destroyed them together. In Pugin's desperate quest for a bride, history had repeated itself as near farce. His enemies were gratified and caustically amused, his friends mortified as this second love affair in two years ended in tears and smoke.

35

'One affectionate heart'

May to 10 August 1848

A perfect Woman, nobly planned,
To warn, to comfort, and command;
And yet a Spirit still, and bright
With something of angelic light.

– William Wordsworth,
'She was a Phantom of delight', 1807

Once again life seemed hollow, his efforts all seemed to mock him. Pugin disconsolately took any job that came his way, however unsuitable. He designed a Gothic veranda for Henry Drummond, which was a predictable failure, and a coronet for a Miss Fox to wear with a medieval costume in 'some fooling on 6 of July': 'it must be copper as light as possible,' he told Hardman, 'with a mere wash of gold & false stones as cheap as it can be made.'[1] It was a travesty of his principles and a parody of the bridal jewels he had made for Helen. In his present mood he found a grim satisfaction in it. Not surprisingly, given Pugin's state of mind and Powell's temporary absence, what work he had in hand was tending to go awry. The files at Birmingham contain complaints about spelling mistakes in inscriptions, problems with deliveries and other graver errors. The window for St Mary the Virgin, the university church at Oxford, proved unsatisfactory when installed. Exactly what was wrong is not clear but it was serious: 'this place of all others where I wished to do well,' Pugin lamented to Hardman. 'I will pay everything – I may as well be ruined altogether . . .'[2]

The question of financial responsibility for mistakes was complex with so many people involved. It became urgent when the east window for Winwick was found, on arrival, to be two feet two inches longer than the opening. Pugin blamed Myers, who blamed his clerk Jackson, who said he took the measurements from a piece of paper written by a Mr Piddock, 'which paper is not forthcoming'.[3] In the end Myers felt he should take the blame: 'it is quite clere [sic] that the dementions [sic] that we sent Mr Pugin is not the same as the window therefore it rests with me,' he wrote to Hardman, but 'the charge for alterations becomes so heavy upon me that I must say what possition [sic] I am to be in,' he added. 'I hope you will not think this wrong of me to say so for you see what a loss I subject myself to.'[4]

Pugin's pessimism was further fed by a realization that the decline in support among his fellow Catholics was accelerating, due to the very people in whom he had once had such hope, the 'Oxford men'. His two most recent churches, St Wilfrid's, Cotton, and St Thomas's, Fulham, were opened early that summer. Both commissions had arisen from the Tractarian conversions and Newman preached at both ceremonies. Yet he and his followers, now they were Oratorians, were falling ever further out of sympathy with Pugin and his ideas. The Oratory, into which Faber and his colleagues at Cotton had now followed Newman, was a Roman, post-Reformation religious body. From now on there was an ever-widening gulf between the Roman or Ultramontane Catholics and the English, or 'Gallicans' as their opponents called them. The already contentious issue of rood screens was the small point on which the whole weight of the dispute was brought to bear. Mrs Bowden did not want a screen at Fulham. Pugin explained that his design would be spoiled without one and started to build it regardless. Mrs Bowden sacked him and had the screen demolished. At St Wilfrid's Faber also declined to build the screen Pugin had designed. Pugin and Phillipps went to Cotton and demanded to know why. All three men lost their tempers and a hysterical row ensued, with shouting, threats and foot stamping. As soon as it was over Phillipps and Faber both rushed to put their respective sides of the quarrel to Newman.

Newman answered Phillipps that:

Mr Pugin is notoriously engaged in a revival – he is disentombing what has been hidden for centuries amid corruptions; and, as, first one thing, then another is brought to light, he, like a true lover of the art, modifies his first views, yet he speaks as confidently and dogmatically about what is right and what is wrong, as if he had gained the truth from the purest and stillest founts of continuous tradition . . . Gothic is now like an old dress, which fitted a man well twenty years back but must be altered to fit him now . . . I wish to wear it, but I wish to alter it, or rather I wish him to alter it . . . I, for one, believe that Gothic can be adapted, developed into the requisitions of an Oratory. Mr Pugin does not.[5]

Yet behind this reasonable objection to medieval architecture for a post-medieval building lay personal hostility and perhaps some uneasiness about what he and Pugin had in common: '. . . you must not be surprised, My dear Mr Phillipps,' Newman went on,

at my taking the views above expressed . . . It is no new thing with me to feel little sympathy with parties, or extreme opinions, of any kind . . . I advocated what are called High Church principles, while I believed them to be the teaching of the English Church; I first gave up my living, then left that Church as it broke upon me that they were not. I never joined the Camden movement . . . I did not even join in Dr Pusey's movement for the London Churches . . . there seemed to me something excessive and unreal in it.[6]

There is a striking symmetry between what Newman complained of in Pugin and what he boasted of in himself. His progress from St Mary's to Littlemore to Rome was an attempt, like Pugin's, to disentomb the truth from centuries of corruption, at each stage of which Newman had been full of conviction. And if Newman was not a party man, then neither was Pugin. They were both too egotistical. Each was at the centre of a circle over which they exercised influence by sheer force of personality. Now, within the Church, each was trying to recover what he had most loved and lost. For Pugin it was the coherence of his childhood, domestic love and emotional security amid Gothic buildings. For Newman it was Oxford, the life of the mind and spirit lived among a group of celibate men. Phillipps realized that architecture was only the ground on which Newman had chosen to fight. 'No one expected,' he wrote to him, 'or had any right to expect, that the Oratory was to be a Congregation of Architects . . . we all knew you had a higher and holier work to perform; yet we did not expect you or your disciples to preach a crusade against us, to denounce us as mere Puseyites (Faber's words to me) . . . or to divide the Catholick Body, already too much divided, by throwing the weight of your talents, your zeal and your piety in the scale against the noble efforts of that admirable man Pugin.'[7] Newman denied the suggestion, but it was true. From now on the Oratorians were actively, if discreetly, hostile.

Soon the row spread to the press. Pugin was furious to read an account of his Fulham church in the *Tablet* that congratulated him on the absence of a screen and the 'magnificent . . . view' thereby afforded of the altar.[8] He wrote to deny any responsibility for the 'light communion rails', which were, he said, an entirely Protestant feature.[9] The *Tablet* and its rival, the *Rambler*, ran letters over the next six months which rehearsed in tedious detail the historical, liturgical and theological arguments for and against screens. What was said matters little now. What was done was to achieve an open breach between elements within the Catholic Church that had sat uneasily together since Emancipation but for which, in the early days, there had been enough elbow room for all to rub along. Shrewsbury did not involve himself in the rood screen row. He was engaged with larger issues and probably sensed the absurdity of such a quarrel while revolutions convulsed the Continent and threatened the Holy See itself. He too, however, found Newman increasingly unsympathetic. Shrewsbury's only domestic campaign just now was for the Jewish Disabilities Bill, to admit Jews to Parliament. Like many Catholics who had so recently benefited from similar laws he felt honour bound to do so. Newman did not. 'I cannot say I feel any desire to give the Jews privileges,' he told Phillipps.[10]

As the summer wore on Pugin was increasingly involved in arrangements for the opening of St George's, Southwark. The building had been so much interrupted and the design so compromised that there was a sense of ennui about the whole thing. What should have been the climax of his career so far, the opening of his first important London church, the largest Catholic church in the capital, had lost momentum. 'Like every other work that remains long unfinished,' Thomas Doyle noted, discouragingly, 'when its completion does at last arrive, one feels almost unconcerned and indifferent.'[11] As Hardman, Myers, Earley and his men worked to get the building ready for opening, though it would be far from finished, lines of command were unclear and progress dogged by misunderstanding: 'there will be a row' Pugin predicted, accurately.[12] Earley's team were painting the chancel and in answer to anxious enquiries from Birmingham about progress Myers wrote back that he was taking no responsibility for them, or the glass, and furthermore 'I don't know anything at all about the gas fittings I never see them – I do not wish to interfere for I see there is a many of them without me.'[13] The general bickering that dogged the work extended to the preparations for the opening. The choristers, who were being directed by the distinguished Herr Meyer Lutz, used breaks in rehearsal to taunt Earley about the rival choir at St Chad's, in which he, like Hardman, sang. Earley lost his temper with 'a little brat of a tenor' and 'told him if he was a sample of the London choirs they were not very remarkable for talent – it was only out of regard to mr Burton or I would have punched him'.[14] All this was duly reported back to Hardman, who was more anxious to hear about the gilding.

So matters progressed, unsteadily, towards the opening, which was fixed for 4 July. Pugin entertained Lord Arundel, one of the principal donors, at Ramsgate along with Lord Dormer. He had almost daily meetings now with the patrons and committee members, one of the more congenial of whom was John Knill. Knill, who had become a Catholic in 1842, was a prosperous wharfinger and fruiterer with farms in Herefordshire. His London home, Walworth House, an eighteenth-century town house on the Walworth Road, was not far from St George's. Pugin became a regular visitor. The household comprised Knill's wife and grown-up children as well as his two nieces Mary and Jane. Their father, Knill's elder brother, had died in 1833, whereupon John had inherited the estate and responsibility for the widow and her daughters. Jane, the younger, turned twenty-three that summer. She was dark-haired and strikingly good-looking, handsome rather than pretty, with well-defined features and large eyes. Almost at once Pugin fell in love with her. His heart was indeed an elastic organ. Within weeks of his denunciation of Helen Lumsdaine in particular and her sex in general he was sending affectionate messages via her uncle to 'Sancta Johanna'.[15]

On the appointed day St George's was finally opened. The ceremony, like the building, represented a compromise. Pugin and Shrewsbury, who ten years before had stormed out of St Mary's, Derby, in protest against the Beethoven Mass, sat and listened to 'several of the leading Italian vocalists of the day', accompanied by the recalcitrant Southwark choir.[16] The occasion brought together, for the moment at least, old and new, Ultramontane and English Catholics. About 3,000 people were inside the church. The 240 clergy included Passionists, Oratorians, Dominicans, Cistercians, Benedictines, Franciscans, Redemptorists and Rosminians. Dominic Barberi walked in the procession with George Spencer, who had joined the Passionists and taken the name of Father Ignatius, their crucifixes and sandals great 'objects of public observation'.[17] At vespers Bishop Gillis preached for an hour and a half, and the London Catholics, who had not cared for Newman's series of closely argued sermons, heard his flights of declamatory prose with 'breathless attention'.[18]

There was one notable absentee, the Archbishop of Paris, Monsignor Affre. In France the revolution had entered a new and bloody phase in June, and Affre had been shot and killed while trying to mediate at the barricades. In London, however, all was calm. The precautions taken at the laying of St George's foundation stone scarcely seemed necessary for the opening a decade later. 'Strange, indeed, are the mutations of localities in this vast metropolis,' as the *Illustrated London News* noted, 'and not the least remarkable of them is, that the focus of the No Popery Riots of 1780 should, within a life-time, become the site of a Roman Catholic church – the largest erected in England since the Reformation.'[19] Pugin was aware of the weaknesses of St George's. But once again the failures and disappointments of the last four years were giving way to the power of love. He was writing a furious reply on the rood screen question to the *Rambler*, 'scarce able to touch a morsel of food all day from the excitement'.[20]

Jane Knill had given him back his courage. In her he believed he had found at last a perfect bride; 'you have saved me,' he wrote to her, as he had written to Helen, 'you have no idea of the wear which a constant strain upon the mind produces when unrelieved by affectionate kindness, you have saved me & a life of tender care & affection cannot repay you what I owe you for giving me your love.'[21] His letters to her are almost verbatim reiterations in places of those to Helen. Jane, now, was to be the muse, the companion, 'the main spring of the revival'.[22] It was not that Pugin was fickle. He was always sincerely in love. But his need to love and be loved were much greater than his attachment to any one woman. This time, at last, he had found a bride as suitable as she was lovable. There would be no opposition from her family; on the contrary, they were delighted. They were Catholics and Jane, though baptized an Anglican, had converted and been educated in Catholic schools. Socially too there was complete equality. The Knills, like the Pugins and the Welbys, could trace their family back through many centuries, in their case 'to the pre-Norman Earls of Orkney', and they too had a family crest, which Pugin duly quartered with his own 'arms'. And yet, however ancient the name, an address in the Walworth Road, home to John

Wemmick and already a busy omnibus route, was not genteel. The mixture of romance, aspiration and commerce in the background of bride and groom was pretty exactly equal. Pugin proposed and was accepted. John Knill offered to settle some money on Jane. Pugin gallantly but rashly refused on the grounds that 'a money transaction would tarnish the glory of the whole thing'.[23]

What he told Hardman and when is not clear. Crace suddenly received orders for a new dress and a cape. Adjustments were made to some of the jewellery. Pugin was desperately impatient. 'My marriage will be a dreadful blow to the modern men,' he promised Jane, 'I shall come out like a giant', 'we shall accomplish wonders'.[24] They were formally engaged on 22 July and yet again the children were prepared for a new mama. 'Anne,' Pugin reported, 'is quite pleased she says she shall be very happy indeed with you.'[25] As he rushed into his third marriage, as he had into the previous two, the few of Pugin's friends who knew what he was doing must have wondered what the outcome might be. In the event his luck was finally in. In Jane he had found the 'one affectionate heart in whom I can really rely,' a devoted but by no means passive wife, whose devotion would be much tried.[26] Pugin's letters to Jane, for all the similarity of their content, have a warmer tone than those to Helen, with whom he was always somewhat courtly. He did not watch Jane from afar as if she were a lady of the olden time but longed to catch her up and carry her home. Travelling back to Ramsgate the day after their engagement, across the Kentish countryside, he saw the world transformed; 'how one person can change the face of things,' he wrote when he got home, 'the suns rays were thrown obliquely on the new mown meadows bright green . . . with yellow tints of ripening corn . . .' But there was a note too of melancholy and foreboding: 'already the sun sets nearer to the west and the days though long are shortening rely on me, & my experience we shall find time fly, & we must not lose a day.'[27]

Theirs was the first marriage to be celebrated in St George's, on 10 August 1848. Pugin's premonitions would prove true. As he and Jane left by the west door they would have seen the Bethlem Hospital for the insane opposite them, the shaven-headed inmates wandering in the grounds. They did not linger, however, but set off for Ramsgate where, when they arrived, the flag on the tower was flying, for the first time.

Part Six

36

'A first rate Gothic woman'

11 August 1848 to August 1849

Are you not surprised at me?
– Pugin to Talbot Bury, 12 August 1848

'By the enclosed card you will perceive that I am married & have got a first rate Gothic woman at last who perfectly understands & delights in spires chancels screens stained windows Brasses vestments etc.'[1] Thus Mr Hornby at Winwick learned of Pugin's third marriage. The card announcing it, a delicate quartering of the crests of bride and groom, was sent to friends and patrons, most of whom were astonished. Combining courtesy with frankness, the Earl of Shrewsbury replied, on behalf of himself and the Countess, that 'nothing has given us more pleasure for a long time than the announcement of your sudden & happy marriage'. To his good wishes he added congratulations, tinged perhaps with amusement, on Pugin's 'new armorial bearings'.[2] These, the Earl realized, meant as much to Pugin as the whole heraldic panoply of the Talbot Gallery at Alton.

Pugin and Jane spent ten days at the Grange before setting off for a five-week tour up the east coast of England to Scotland, returning by the Lakes down the coast, then to Birmingham, the West Country and home. This extended wedding journey was a picturesque tour of Pugin's life and work. It retraced in part that first journey of which he could 'remember particulars', with his parents in 1818, to the great Gothic churches of Lincolnshire and Yorkshire. He took Jane to Lincoln Cathedral, under whose vaults his vision of Christian architecture had been born, to Oxford, which he had drawn with his father, and to Wells, where, with his mother, he had conceived the idea of *Contrasts*. Pugin, who could enjoy nothing when he was lonely, was rekindling his enthusiasm after the despondency of the last four years, reanimating the familiar sites with the touch of a new love. 'Northumberland from Whitby Cliff My dear wife with me,' he wrote on one of the sketches he made as they travelled.[3] At Lincoln they no doubt saw the Willsons, who must have recalled meeting Pugin's first bride on the short winter honeymoon of 1832. But though he revisited the past and although his work and his writings were saturated with a longing for it, Pugin would never express anything like retrospection. He was always looking *en avant.*

He was pleased to find that Jane had 'the true & right feeling on all ecclesiastical matters' and was a 'capital traveller'.[4] He hated feminine paraphernalia and elegant indolence, speaking with horror of an acquaintance whose new wife went to London with 'a maid & 5 boxes for herself & 2 for the maid & did not turn out till 12 of a day'.[5] Jane, luckily, could keep up the pace. For the last week in August Pugin's diary, typically, records visits to sixteen places:

24 London to Cambridge, Ely, Wilburton
25 Ely, Peterborough, Stamford
26 Stamford, Melton, Grantham, Lincoln
27 Lincoln
28 Lincoln to Nottingham and back
29 Lincoln, Boston, Wainflete, Skegness
30 Skegness, Louth, Hull
31 Hull, Beverley, Filey[6]

On 23 September they returned to the Grange to begin married life. It was an Indian summer and Jane's first experience of Ramsgate was at its full-blown seasonal best, or worst. The town was lively, but as it expanded it did not grow in gentility. Steamers took day-trippers from Ramsgate to Dover or across to Boulogne while 'cries of prawns shrimps and lollipops', barrel organs, German bands and men 'in their shirt sleeves . . . at open windows eating shrimps' were among the spectacles that rendered Ramsgate, in Jane Carlyle's opinion, 'truly disgusting'.[7] A less delicate constitution might find in it, as Frith did in his hugely popular painting *Ramsgate Sands,* a vivid portrait of Victorian England at play. Nobody, however, found it spiritually elevating. The local papers describe the steady march of improvement as the town followed the ever broader path of civic progress. The town clock was now illuminated by gas and, from 1 November, it ran to Greenwich Mean Time. The *Kent Herald* carried a notice of Pugin's marriage but otherwise continued steadfastly opposed to his efforts. Lieutenant Hutchinson's Seamen's Hospital was making headway. That summer the foundation stone for new church schools was laid by Mr Hoare of Christ Church, 'the devil incarnate' as Pugin uncharitably referred to him.[8] The schools were designed 'in the early English style of the 14th century' by the well-known local architect W. E. Smith.[9]

Inevitably the homecoming had an element of anticlimax. Pugin was obliged to confront difficulties that his new happiness might mitigate but could not cure. While he was away he had received a 'most distressing' letter from Captain Hibbert.[10] There were problems with the newly completed wing at Bilton Grange. 'I see clearly the captain is preparing to throw all the blame on me so pray be very careful,' Pugin wrote to Crace, who was decorating there, 'it makes me almost wild. I assure you I would pay anything rather than have all these rows.'[11] He set off gloomily for Bilton. Nor was there much work in prospect. '£40 a week at best going out [and] the business I have at present is not worth doing a little painting a frame a lock all sorts of little bothering things.'[12] Work at Westminster was slow. After the opening of the House of Lords and in view of the general economic climate Parliament was reluctant to spend any more: 'they will not grant any money,' Pugin warned Hardman, 'I am going to discharge a great part of the men from Thames Bank it is a very sad look out.'[13] It seemed now that with every change of political and ecclesiastical circumstance, Pugin's opportunities diminished. Wiseman's move to London had shifted the centre of gravity in English Catholicism. He was still friendly to Pugin, but he had his eye on wider horizons. Pugin's early stamping ground in the Midland District was now closed as a source of support, for Bishop Walsh, old and ill as he was, had been transferred, much against his will, with Wiseman and his assistant, to London. He was enthroned as bishop in September, but he was too frail now to be an effective advocate. From Dublin came news of another loss. Gentili was dead. He had succumbed to the cholera that was ravaging Europe. At forty-seven his health had long been undermined by his ascetic way of life. For all the difficulties of their relations, Pugin, who had always felt a respect bordering on awe for Gentili, thought it 'an impossible loss'.[14]

Meanwhile the new religious orders, prominent at the consecration of St George's, were establishing themselves in the capital. The Redemptorists had made their home in Clapham, at the heart and indeed in the teeth of the Evangelical movement. They commissioned a large church, Our Immaculate Lady of Victories, from William Wardell. Pugin thought it 'really almost ludicrous' as a parody of his work.[15] Pevsner, more reasonably, called it 'one of the best Victorian churches in South London' but it would have been unthinkable without Pugin's example.[16] In English architecture that autumn his influence was apparent everywhere, while he himself made a poor showing. In London Benjamin Ferrey's St Stephen's, Westminster, in the 'Middle Pointed style', was rising steadily above the slums of Rochester Row. 'The fruit of Miss Burdett Coutts's munificence', it sat at the heart of a group of schools and other buildings.[17] The church was a direct product of Pugin's 'Present State' models, the whole ensemble a scene from *Contrasts*. At Salford, Weightman and Hadfield's St John's was opened in August with great pomp. It too would have been impossible without Pugin, but it brought him no credit and neither did his own work.

His chapel at Ushaw was remote, the church at Salisbury small, and it had not been built by Myers. Pugin thought its construction 'a disgrace'.[18] The reviews of St George's, Southwark, were at best mixed. The most the *Ecclesiologist* could offer was sympathy. It could 'readily conceive how great must have been Mr Pugin's well-founded disgust at having so much to mar his own creation'.[19] Other critics were less forgiving. His old enemy William Leeds, writing as Candidus in the *Civil Engineer and Architect's Journal*, concluded that it 'does not say very much for Mr Pugin's artistic talent and taste'.[20] To a disinterested observer it might seem that Leeds and Beresford Hope had been right after all. Pugin's precocious genius had blown itself out in a decade. The long summer at last gave way to a stormy autumn. Pugin was caught in gales and snow as he made his way from Thetford to Lyndford to talk to Sir Richard Sutton about the restoration of the church at West Tofts. This was the most productive part of his journey, 'a nice job & will do me some credit'.[21] At Cambridge Pugin found work at Jesus College went on 'capitally'. For the rest there was little new. He was overseeing the slow progress of Alton Castle. On a visit to the Towers he had the pleasure of telling the Earl and Countess 'the whole history' of his marriage and the satisfaction of suspecting that Shrewsbury was now sick of his old buildings, realizing that the alterations had been more expensive than letting Pugin start afresh.[22] He was to start work on a new dining room there at Easter. Pugin went on to the convent at Nottingham, where Earley was working against the background din of the goose fair to an impossible deadline. 'I do not think the chapel will be ready for the 14th,' he wrote nervously back to Birmingham. 'I dare not tell Rev Mother perhaps you might drop a gentle Hint.'[23]

Though he was 'dying to get home', Pugin had to go and talk to Barry about the work at Westminster.[24] Then he was with Hardman at Birmingham. It was humdrum stuff and he missed Jane. For the moment he was tired of wandering. 'It seems such a time since I have been away from you & last night I dreamt I was at home ... It is miserable work travelling alone,' he wrote to her.[25] Even so he was away for most of October, leaving Jane to grapple alone with the peculiarities of life as chatelaine of the Grange. Pugin told Shrewsbury that 'my wife manages everything most admirably & is a great comfort & assistance to me'.[26] But as usual there was more light and shade in reality than in Pugin's roseate view. At twenty-three Jane found herself responsible for running a large household, including six stepchildren ranging in age from four to sixteen, two servants and Hardman Powell, all of them bound together by the shared experience of years from which she was excluded. Pugin's letters home are full of advice which tells by implication the story of her difficulties. He is sorry that she is not eating; if she is cold she must have a fire lit in her room early in the evening; she cannot always hear from him – 'you could not imagine a letter could come 386 miles in one night even by railway' – and she must be firm with the children: 'Edward is not to make fire works on any account.'[27]

The fireworks were averted but Agnes, Louisa's eldest daughter, who was twelve, did not take to her stepmother. In October she went away to school at the convent at Caverswall, adding another £60 a year to Pugin's expenses. The gentle Anne was more of a comfort, while Hardman Powell saw in Jane's arrival and the Governor's new cheerfulness his chance to make a bid for freedom. He asked Jane to ask if he might move into lodgings. Pugin agreed. It would be a saving in the household budget, 'but he is a flat for doing it ... you cannot give experience to young people'.[28] Powell's lodgings were to be a continual source of argument. He would occasionally try to work at home, which Pugin could not bear. 'I find the study left for hours together,' he complained to Hardman, 'if this fine room which I have built at so much expense &

fitted with such fine things is not good enough for him & if he does not like to work under my eye there is an end to everything if he is to begin the independent artist let him to go to London & fight his way by himself for I will not have it.'[29] Powell wrote sulkily to his uncle that he had only been at home one afternoon, 'the governor only wants a trifle to make him suspicious'.[30] The wrangling, as Powell struggled for his independence and Pugin fought to keep control, was interminable. There was no doubt that Pugin was increasingly self-absorbed and suspicious. His disappointments caused him to take an ever narrower view of life. In early November the public was scandalized by the suicide of Lord Midleton at Peper Harow. 'I gave up all hopes of him when he put up the old pews in the new aile I built for him,' Pugin remarked, 'I thought he would come to a miserable end.'[31] But then, as he also said, 'we live in such times that unless one is actually shot oneself it makes little impression'.[32]

The winter brought worse news from Italy. The Romans had become increasingly hostile to Pius IX, disappointed by his refusal to declare for the forces of Italian unification. On 24 November the Pope, wearing a plain cassock and dark glasses, slipped down the back stairs of the Quirinal Palace and fled to Naples. 'I am not surprised,' Pugin of course wrote to Hardman, 'I was considered half a lunatic for my opinion of the Romans but it was a correct one';[33] 'we must give up our . . . visions & make ourselfs as happy as we can by creating an atmosphere you will have to come under the shadow of St Augustines yet mark my words'.[34] This Christmas Pugin was more determined than ever to make sure that those gathered into his ark should be merry and safe. He invited neighbours and friends and held a party on Twelfth Night with charades. Thus, snug in the Grange while floods and gales raged over the Kent cliffs, Pugin and his family saw out 1848, 'this most awful & eventful year'.[35]

In January Pugin began the next stage of his buildings at Ramsgate, setting out the ground for the church itself. St Augustine's was to be, as he half knew and sometimes said, his last important work. A vast undertaking, both physically and financially, it became a symbol of his battle for existence as an architect, a struggle to the death. On every side his support now seemed to dwindle by the month. 'I have nothing but enemies & I dont know why,' he complained.[36] In February Bishop Walsh died, a sad if not an unexpected loss, and as old friends departed new adversaries arose. Pugin and Shrewsbury found themselves increasingly under attack in the Catholic press. Once again the issue was Ireland. Pugin shared the Earl's views on the subject, views that were conservative, though not extreme. Shrewsbury believed that Ireland had 'one monster grievance' on the point of religion. He thought the English guilty of 'great sin & folly' in their dealings with the Irish.[37] Yet like many of his countrymen he could not countenance repeal of the Union or reform of the land laws.

His former friend Thomas Doyle, the priest at Southwark, was now one of his loudest critics. As 'Fr Thomas' he had become a columnist in the *Tablet* and this success had rather gone to his head, leading him to indulge 'his anti-aristocratic tendencies' in his regular 'Letter'.[38] Wiseman, to whom Shrewsbury complained, was apologetic but helpless: 'I have spoken to him before & . . . the very same day he has concocted another of his foolish letters. It seems to have become a sort of madness . . . & people flatter him up about the nonsense which he writes . . .'[39]

The *Tablet*, like the *Rambler*, was now consistently hostile to Shrewsbury and his circle. Both papers were Liberal in their politics, loud and influential in their views, and both were edited by converts. John Moore Capes at the *Rambler*, a former Tractarian, was the wittier and more good-natured; at the *Tablet* Lucas, an ex-Quaker, was more violent and politically extreme. Shrewsbury thought Lucas a covert communist, while Lucas found in the 'noble Earl' with his 'broad acres . . . ancient earldom, moderate abilities, and . . . judgement very liable to be led astray' the epitome of the *ancien régime* and everything he most disliked.[40]

Not all Pugin's difficulties, however, could be put down to Catholic factionalism. His unwillingness to adapt was an increasing limitation. Four years earlier, when Shrewsbury had been angling to get the Jesuits' London church for him, the priest there had complained that if he employed Pugin, Pugin would insist on Myers and accept no competition for tenders. 'I know it is more convenient for him to employ one builder but people generally do not like it.'[41] He was right, but Pugin still not only preferred Myers, he depended on him. He found it difficult to make full detail drawings, specifications and estimates without him. A small but revealing failure this year was the station at Alton, where the North Staffordshire Railway was due to open in July. Pugin feared that 'the greatest horrors' would occur 'under the very walls of the old castle . . .'

413

if he did not design it himself.[42] The railway company was happy to employ him, but on their usual terms, a commission in return for complete drawings and specifications. These he declined to provide. 'I was afraid . . . they would expect me to go through all the routine of railway building . . . supplying detailed specification of the modern work inside . . . I work altogether on different principles . . .' he explained.[43] Principles were part of it. He was also at the limits of his capability.

Myers, on the other hand, could get on perfectly well without Pugin. He was on his way to becoming one of the great master builders of the Victorian age. On the strength of Pugin's generous references he was winning large contracts. As a result he had less time for Pugin's work when Pugin had any. It was a vicious circle. One way and another it seemed, Pugin thought, the devil was 'particularly busy' just now but, as he pointedly reminded Shrewsbury, 'Building is a great consolation under all troubles.'[44] Work started in the spring on the new dining hall at Alton Towers. It went slowly and Shrewsbury was impatient: 'all good works are laborious to produce,' Pugin wrote back briskly, 'your lordship ought not to look at it going on but see it compleat it is as bad as looking at plants growing.'[45] Neither Pugin nor Shrewsbury saw the hall complete, and little remains of it now, but photographs show it was once a splendid room. As the chapel at Ware stood to St Chad's, so the dining hall at Alton was to Scarisbrick, a richer, more coherent, incomparably better crafted version of the same idea. Pugin also built a little lodge at Alton. It is a toughly asymmetric building that derives from the gateway at Peper Harow but incorporates later ideas. It steps steeply down in blocks from two storeys to one beside the gate, rugged but well controlled. Fine heraldic carving adds a delicate touch, bringing to the modesty of the house the dignity of the estate, like livery on a servant.

What Pugin did, he now did with deft confidence, but what he did not do he would not learn. To make up his diminishing income he embarked instead on a very different venture. In February he wrote excitedly to Hardman that he and a neighbour, Alfred Luck, were going to buy a boat, 'the finest lugger in the port'. 'He has got the tin and I the knowledge,' as Pugin put it.[46] The *Caroline* was theirs for £70. Luggers are open boats designed to be launched easily from shingle beaches like those on the Kent coast, and rigged with square 'lug' sails. The *Caroline* was thirty tons and just over forty feet long. Pugin planned to hire her out for fishing in spring and autumn and for day trips in the summer, but the chief purpose, the most profitable and exciting, was the winter work of wrecking. In the days before lifeboats, wreckers went out to ships in distress. They rescued crew and passengers and under the watchful eye of the Revenue Cutters they salvaged the cargo, for which they received a percentage of the value. Wrecking was not illegal, but it was certainly not respectable; it was a dangerous and shady business with overtones of smuggling. No one would insure the boats and not all of them, it was said, put the saving of life above the taking of salvage. Pugin gave no thought to the effect this venture would have on his reputation in Ramsgate, but the clifftop settlement with its Popish goings-on, romantic debacles and many foreign visitors must now have assumed something of the character of a pirate's lair in the narrow eyes that watched it from Spencer Square.

Pugin was thrilled with the *Caroline* and she was soon fitted up with 'every requisite – from chains for heaving up anchors, tools for breaking up wrecks – and instruments for raising sunk cargoes'.[47] Crace was applied to for cushions 'for the top of the lockers for the men to lie on'.[48] There cannot have been many luggers upholstered by the royal decorator. Pugin, supplying the instructions, was thinking the design out as he wrote: 'a sort of light sail canvass cover that will take off & wash what would you stuff them with? horsehair there must be a strong leather strap with a hole at y y [sketch] to fasten on to a pin to keep them from rolling off . . . youve no idea of the pitching of these boats.'[49] He hired a crew and occasionally went out himself with his boat. It was an exciting business. Anxious as Pugin was for the fate of seafarers, even the most humane wrecker must have mixed feelings: 'it is thick at sea,' he wrote to Hardman one evening, 'so perhaps something will run on the sands . . . a homeward bound Batavia man would be just the thing . . . we should do a good action and get something sold as well.'[50] The salvage value of gin, ebony, tea and coconuts began to figure in his letters. Like all Pugin's enterprises the *Caroline* did not entirely fulfil his expectations, but as a source of income she seems to have more than earned her keep.

Pugin's friends, meanwhile, would have liked to see him find some more respectable way out of the hiatus in his career. Herbert, Etty and Stanfield persuaded him to stand for election to the Royal Academy. Somewhat reluctantly Pugin began work on four watercolour drawings for the annual exhibition. They were 'good drawings in their way', he thought, 'but an immense deal of work'.[51] He showed a view of the spire of St George's, the dining hall at Alton, Bilton Grange, surrounded with vignettes of St Marie's, Rugby, and a bird's-eye perspective of his own house and church. They hung among works by Ferrey, R. C. Carpenter, the Ecclesiological Society's own preferred architect, and Cockerell. The *Ecclesiologist* devoted the longest section of its review to Pugin and its criticisms were shrewd. The design for St Marie's, Rugby, was admired, its bold use of foreign sources noted. The 'True Prospect' of St Augustine's was discussed in some detail. The church's 'complex and novel plan' was carefully described, but 'The mass so produced will, we suspect, be found, (particularly in the interior,) to be too complex for the scale of the building – a mistake to which more than any other Mr Pugin is liable.'[52]

The 'eclectic use of Perpendicular' which he had adopted for parts of the building was disapproved of.[53] Here, as with the saddlebacked tower at Rugby, Pugin was looking ahead, but in this case further than the *Ecclesiologist* could see. He was now fluent enough to use the Gothic of any period or country as he liked and to achieve a synthesis, rather than the undigested medleys of his earliest Ideal Schemes. Other architects would follow suit, but it would take another generation to achieve on any scale the confident eclecticism Pugin had already mastered. The 'True Prospect' is a lovely drawing, a Victorian book of hours with the cycle of the year and of human birth and death, all present or implicit in the scene. In the garden of the Grange children play while next door, in the churchyard, a funeral takes place. Yet if true in the highest sense, it is not realistic. Pugin altered the shape of his house, making the bay break forward, and also its position, so that it appeared on the same line as the church. He placed the vignettes carefully so as to cover Mr Benson's Grecian villa and other signs of modern life. The 'fields' were in reality marked-up building plots.

Elsewhere in the Academy Millais was showing his first Pre-Raphaelite picture. The Brotherhood, formed the previous year, brought to England many of the Nazarene ideals and something of both the spirit and the style of Pugin himself. Millais exhibited his *Isabella*, based on Keats's poem. 'That's going to be the man,' Pugin said when he saw it, 'he has got the Mediaeval spirit in him.'[54] *Isabella* is set in a room that Pugin might have furnished. The flat Italianate pattern stencilled on the wall behind the diners, the majolica plates (of which Pugin had a collection) and Isabella's rich but simple dress falling in elegant natural folds, all obey his true principles of design.

Despite his friends' best efforts, however, Pugin was not elected. He was embarrassed and annoyed by the failure: 'it is cause of a good deal of ridicule,' he told Jane, 'you remember I was opposed to it but was persuaded.'[55] But he never cared much about institutions and soon he was philosophical. 'There is no likelyhood of my ever having any letters after my name,' he told Crace, 'unless V.P. (very pointed).'[56] He was much more upset by the opening, that month, of the London Oratory. Faber and his confrères had decided that they too would become Oratorians and leave Cotton. To Shrewsbury's astonishment, after he had spent over £3,000 on the church and house, they announced that they no longer wanted St Wilfrid's. They intended to abandon the mission and rent out Cotton Hall to add to their income. The Earl, who had left the details of the tenancy to their 'honour and conscience', was as shocked as he was angry.[57] Meanwhile Faber took a lease on the Lowther Rooms off the Strand. It was a seedy place, in fact, as he wrote excitedly to Newman, 'It is a gin shop.'[58] The Lowther Rooms, built in about 1830 in King William Street, were the epitome of the stucco-fronted late-Georgian style that Pugin most detested. The Oratorians' move to London was a page of *Contrasts* in reverse. They had left a handsome Gothic church and chosen instead to fit up a meeting-room behind a commercial façade. Faber was having a lovely time getting it all ready ('calls – walks – bustle – hardly time to say Office') and found a thrill in slumming.[59] It was rather fun, he reported to Newman, 'to borrow a few chairs from a policeman'. Pugin could, just about, see the funny side.[60] He made a sketch for Hardman in his old satirical style, showing bonneted ladies entering at the 'Narthex or Porch' of this 'modern temple of Bacchus and Terpsichore'.[61]

In May he went over to Ireland to inspect work at Maynooth. Like many people he was puzzled by the prosperity that persisted amid the destitution, both during the famine and after. He found Dublin 'very gay balls, concerts, bands . . . No one would think it a ruined country.'[62] Writing home he complained, for almost the first time in his life, of tiredness. He often still felt 'poorly', suffering from that 'lowness' which was partly mental but also physical.[63] Maynooth was not turning out as well as he had hoped. Rather than being grand and plain, as Pugin intended, the *Ecclesiologist* found its 'vast uniformity' monotonous and oppressive, as have many people since.[64] His other Irish work was even less promising. The cathedral at Killarney stood unfinished and unused 'although long since roofed in and slated'.[65] At Enniscorthy the new bishop had boarded up the choir of St Aidan's and allowed the building to fill up with rubbish. Pugin would make several more visits to Ireland but each one seemed drearier than the last.

He was unwell once more and in Dublin feverish, which terrified him as the city, like much of Britain and France, was ravaged by cholera. He recovered and went on, dosing himself with powders as he travelled. Away from home he was often overwhelmed with misery. The latest instalment of *David Copperfield*, the account of the death of David's mother, left him distraught: 'beautifully written but so much the worse to read it made me cry a deal,' he told Jane.[66] The description of Clara's death and funeral, told by her orphaned son, is one of the most affecting passages in Dickens, and for Pugin it must have recalled especially those four deathbeds at which he himself had watched and the graves beside which he had stood. 'I dont like reading melancholy things when I am away from you,' he told Jane, 'when I am at home it is all right I feel perfectly safe & happy when I am near my own & always nervous when I am a long way off.'[67] Jane herself, newly pregnant, was fretful at Ramsgate and feeling perhaps as Louisa had done: 'what can I do,' Pugin wrote back, 'I must look after the business or everything would stop I assure you I do not lose a moment but the jobs lie a long way apart.'[68]

Pugin's third marriage is the only one of which any significant record survives. His correspondence with Jane in this first year, despite his absence and their several ailments, is full of warmth. It bespeaks a playful and still flirtatious affection. Perhaps if he had married Helen Lumsdaine, Pugin would have come to feel the same easiness with her, but it seems unlikely that the genteel rector's daughter would have been as entertained as Jane evidently was by stories about the watchmen at St George's getting drunk, by cartoons of people being seasick or by the items of sensational gossip for which Pugin had lost none of his childhood relish ('& now the young woman is dead having apparently poisoned herself – and the man tried to kill the priest with a poker').[69] They teased each other about Pugin's eye for female charm: 'a clean smart looking girl sets off the grub ha ha ha,' he wrote to her, 'I think I hear you say disgusting but in your heart you think as I do.'[70] She wrote to him: 'I suppose you march about in your mackintosh you will therefore not look over bewitching you have therefore my permission to take your walk in Oxford Street any time you like.'[71]

Jane reported on Powell's comings and goings, on the weather at sea, the position of the *Caroline*, the health of the children and the doings of neighbours. She entertained the many visitors who came to see her husband's collection and Pugin encouraged her efforts in all directions: 'when a schooner loses her bowsprit . . . she is said to carry it away not break it,' he explained, 'mind this for the future I must make you a good sailor at least in knowledge.'[72] He fussed over her, especially now that she was pregnant. 'You must have all sorts of nice little things for breakfast.'[73] He arranged for Hardman Powell's mother to come and stay, which was not necessarily such a boon to Jane as he imagined. She was not entirely pleased to discover that the Hardmans were so close to Pugin that she had, in effect, married into their family as well as his. Between her and Pugin, however, there were no disappointments yet. 'You are my second existence,' he told her, and over and over again he thanked God for her.[74] That month they went to London for a few days and heard a different opera every night, 'which I was much pleased with,' Jane recalled, 'as I had never been allowed to go before I was married.'[75]

But relaxations were rare and professional setbacks constant. At Nottingham Pugin had a row with the Mother Superior. 'I dislike nuns more & more,' he grumbled, 'no fine feeling about them,' and he was terribly short of ready money.[76] To leave the church at Ramsgate unroofed through the winter would be 'ruinous' but he had already paid Myers £1,000.[77] He now wished, often, that he had never begun his clifftop citadel: 'this great building like a millstone sinking me'.[78] His mission did not thrive, the church congregation was 'a most fluctuating set & very few'.[79] The school which he had started cost £1 a week to run. Pugin's charity was famous, as no doubt was his naïvety, and it was mostly the poor and the opportunistic who made their way to his door. At Christ Church, Vale Square, the Archbishop of Canterbury came to preach a fund-raising sermon in June, while Pugin at St Augustine's had to 'stand alone for everything with a congregation who expect to be paid for coming to mass so much for the state of Christendom in 1849 in Thanet'.[80]

Everyone but Jane let him down and even she was sometimes unsatisfactory as her pregnancy progressed. Pugin wrote to Hardman, with his usual lack of imagination about other people, 'women are never well my wife has not moved off the sofa for a week except to go to bed I never saw the like they are always ill it is dreadful'.[81] The still devoted Ann Greaves came to stay, which Pugin found a great help but Jane, perhaps, did not. At the end of June they had a visit from the ebullient Bishop Gillis, who came to discuss his ambitious plans for a Catholic college and cathedral in Edinburgh. He was anxious to make a good impression on Jane 'as I had so nearly been the means of putting her nose out of joint in re Miss Lumsden' and found her 'a very nice person indeed & a very nice family to look after, all the children uncommonly well brought up & every thing apparently going on very well . . .'[82] He seems to have been surprised, as others perhaps were, by the contrast between Pugin's dishevelled personal appearance and the neatness and cleanliness of his home.

Gillis and Pugin agreed that Pugin would make a tour of Scotland to look at the important Scottish ruins, 'Arbroath, Elgin etc', with a view to beginning work that autumn and starting the building in the spring. He went to Scotland but the designs he made for Gillis bore no relation to what he had seen. The building in the presentation drawings was a thirteenth-century English cathedral, with a touch of France about it. It made no reference to local precedents or even to its immediate site. It was his fifth cathedral but the first he had conceived on the scale of a Lincoln or a Salisbury. Gillis was expecting the building to cost £400,000, though it was never clear where the money would come from, and Pugin planned accordingly. Yet there is something remote, detached, about the drawings. As Pugin knew, the cathedrals of the Middle Ages usually grew up piecemeal, 'like cities, from particular causes, and without some such great moving cause it is as difficult to erect the one as to establish the other'.[83] He came back via Birmingham, where he talked to Hardman about business in general and about stained glass in particular. It was the only part of his practice where demand was increasing and the one that engaged his interest most, after architecture. 'I owe it entirely to you,' he told Hardman, 'it was a capital job your starting it . . . I should never have had the courage.'[84] Pugin's selective memory did not always work for purposes of self-justification; it was he who had urged his friend to take it on. The results, however, were still unpredictable, artistically and technically. The windows that had been so far installed in St Augustine's, Pugin's own church and artistic laboratory, had disappointed him. There was more to the problem than getting the right colour, it was necessary to understand the physics of light as well as the chemistry of glass. Colours that looked beautiful in separate pieces changed in situ in relation to each other, 'pale ruby & yellow 5 become a regular gin shop orange'.[85]

Pugin and Hardman now found they had a serious competitor in Henri Gérente, the glass designer who had been at the consecration of Cheadle. Gérente, like Pugin, was half French. He had set up his works in Paris in 1846 and won the competition to restore the glass in the Sainte-Chapelle. Pugin had visited his studio and found him 'a first rate artist in the old way'.[86] Never mean-spirited, Pugin saw Gérente as a rival to be emulated rather than an enemy to be beaten. Gérente's approach was empirical. At Wells he spent eight days making a tracing of the west window, giving him a complete reference for the lead lines as well as the detail of the painting. Pugin had, he admitted, 'never troubled' with such technical notes, something he now regretted.[87] 'I saw glass & drew it but not with the idea of making it & I am sure there is a deal to learn.'[88] He went to France to make more technical drawings and to try to buy medieval specimens. He probably intended to visit Gérente, but while he was in Dublin fearing for his own life amid the cholera news came that Gérente had succumbed to it in Paris: '. . . after a few hours is it not sad,' Pugin wrote to Jane, '– it is awful.'[89]

Nevertheless Pugin did well in his twelve-day trip. He got his hands, by questionable if thoroughly antiquarian means, on a collection of samples he had heard about. They belonged to an old glass mender who had accumulated fragments as they dropped out of windows over time. He had no intention of selling, but he was out and Pugin was able to talk his way into the house: '. . . his wife a most curious old woman at first she would not let me see his pieces but you know I can gammon old women . . . & at last she let me into a place full of Fragments I got all I want I was there till 11 at night.'[90] He emerged filthy with the dust and came home laden with medieval glass and full of enthusiasm. Jane had managed all the comings and goings in his absence. There had been many visitors, including the now well-disposed Beresford Hope and his wife, and some impatient enquiries from clients, which Jane dealt with firmly, as well as domestic difficulties. Cuthbert had caught fleas and Agnes, who was unhappy at school as well as at home, had become extremely 'tiresome' towards the end of the holidays. Pugin wrote anxiously to know if his daughter was really well enough to go back to Caverswall, but Jane replied briskly that Agnes was perfectly fit and she was glad she had gone. 'I hope she will alter very much before she leaves for good or else I do not know what I shall do.'[91]

Only weeks now from her confinement, Jane was ill and fearful. Her husband reassured her that 'every mother has gone through the same thing & look what large families many people have & live to a great age . . . you are just at the right time of life'.[92] Yet they both knew that this pregnancy would never have come about had not Anne Garnett succumbed to post-puerperal fever sixteen years earlier. Had she lived she would have been forty. In Pugin's study, carefully preserved, was the box which held her death mask. Then, to add to their domestic anxieties, the Pugins became aware of a threat from outside. The world that could be blotted out in a bird's-eye perspective with a well-placed vignette could not be so easily effaced in reality. The land next door to St Augustine's had changed hands since 1845. It now belonged to the Habershons. Matthew Habershon was an established architect twenty-three years Pugin's senior, a Low Church Protestant and militant no-Popery man. He knew all about Pugin. Thirteen years earlier he had published a long and detailed riposte to *Contrasts*, arguing that the Reformation was the making of England, for it had freed it from the Catholic Church and thereby 'broke the spell of architecture as an engine of oppression and superstition'.[93] It was bad enough to have him as a neighbour. Much worse was the fact that he proposed to build a terrace of houses, right out to his own boundary. Pugin had hoped that by building to the edge of his land he would detract from the value of the next-door site. But, incapable of real malice or cynicism, Pugin's occasional attempts to behave badly always backfired. Habershon was not deterred. He did not mind if the blank end wall of his terrace was jammed right up against the east window of St Augustine's. On the contrary, he rather relished the idea. His houses would not only shut all the light out of Pugin's building, they would block access to the churchyard. Pugin's model church, his great statement of true principles, would be made to look ridiculous with a row of modern houses pushed in its face. He and Jane faced 'destruction', and it was no less a tragedy for the considerable element of comedy that enemies – and even friends – must find in it.[94] From this pathetically weak position Pugin had no choice but to open negotiations with Habershon.

37

Design for the Middling Sort

September 1849 to January 1850

I consider everything up to this time an experiment . . . it is the beginning of another half century 1850 just the time for a start . . .

– Pugin to John Hardman

The Habershons at first refused to sell. Pugin refused to give up trying to persuade him. But while he brooded on the fate that menaced his church, he managed at last to write the text for the book on 'vegetable and floral ornament' that he had begun four years earlier. It was finished on Michaelmas day, 29 September. *Floriated Ornament* was published by Bohn, 'uniform with the glossary . . . [and] rather a nice book' in Pugin's opinion.[1] It is a beautiful book, now rare, having been used to destruction in drawing offices, a stylized English flora.[2] Each plate shows five designs arranged in a quincunx within a gold border, the individual patterns symmetrical round one or two axes. The common plants of field and garden, primrose, ivy, thistle and wild geranium, are transformed into crystalline shapes, 'principally intended for stencilling'.[3]

The plates, however, as the *Ecclesiologist* noted, had little to do with the text. They had been completed some time ago. The short introduction Pugin wrote in 1849 reflected his change of mind over the last four years. The phrase 'true principles' turned easily now into 'first principles'; nature not art was the model: 'if we go to the fountain head, we shall produce a multitude of beautiful designs treated in the same spirit as the old, but new in form'.[4] The *Ecclesiologist* hoped he would develop this theme, which offered a theoretical route out of the dead end of revivalism, a subject which concerned architects and their critics more and more now that Gothic was so well understood and mere imitation of the past seemed inadequate. The reviewer was to be disappointed. He was disappointed too that Pugin had used as his source for the plant names a 'beautiful old botanical work ... "Tabernae montanus eicones Pantarum" printed at Francfort in 1590'.[5] The review complained that to use pre-Linnaean names was mere archaism; there could be nothing in Pugin's principles that required him to practise Gothic botany. Perhaps Pugin thought differently. More probably he had never heard of Linnaeus, any more than he had heard of the Renaissance when he wrote *Contrasts*. The *Ecclesiologist* also pointed out that there was a mistake, which it charitably described as a misprint, in the Latin on the title page.[6]

Intellectually, as well as practically, Pugin had in some directions reached his limits. He was no more likely to work at his Latin than to learn how to specify for a railway station. And while his conceptions of design and architecture continued to grow and develop, the theoretical ground he had won with *Contrasts* and *True Principles* was falling away from him. It was falling to John Ruskin. Ruskin's *Seven Lamps of Architecture* had appeared in May and by the autumn, when the *Ecclesiologist* reviewed it, it was already an important book. One of the defining works of the Victorian age, its appearance marked an epoch in English art and architecture. Although Ruskin himself came to dislike this 'wretched rant', it was, as *Contrasts* had been, the right book at the right time.[7] As the turbulent, uncertain decade of the 1840s came to an end and a new, more confident age dawned, Ruskin offered a moral creed for architecture, 'some constant, general, and irrefragable laws of right' and an urgent call for action.[8] He spoke to his readers in the same apocalyptic terms that Pugin had used in 1836. 'The aspect of the years that approach us is as solemn as it is full of mystery,' he wrote, 'and the weight of evil against which we have to contend, is increasing like the letting out of water ... The blasphemies of the earth are sounding louder, and its miseries heaped heavier every day.'[9]

Ruskin, like Pugin, had spent his childhood Sundays listening to Evangelical sermons. The prophetic books of the Old Testament echoed through his writings. Pugin was the elder by seven years, but they had much in common. Ruskin's prose, however, still noticeably veined with the involutions of Carlyle, was rich and flexible enough, as Pugin's was not, to deal with the more sophisticated debates of the later 1840s. Ruskin too offered his readers a way out of 'servile imitation', but his argument for a style for the age was more developed and more persuasive than Pugin's. *Seven Lamps* was, as *True Principles* had been, another reinvention of the Picturesque. Repton's 'pleasing associations' became the Lamp of Memory, his 'variety' the Lamp of Life. It was more moral, of course, than Repton, more subtle than Pugin, but it was essentially the same aesthetic philosophy, recast for the High Victorians. Like *Contrasts* it was a firm push at a half-open door, and it had immediate effect. Its publication came just a month before Beresford Hope and Butterfield agreed the details of the church they were to build at Margaret Street in London. All Saints was to be the Ecclesiological Society's model church and by August, when they had read Ruskin, Hope and Butterfield had revised their plans as a result. Margaret Street would be the first Ruskinian building in so far as its decoration in stone and brick was a part of its construction rather than a surface application of pattern. It owed something to Pugin too, as Butterfield knew him. The bishop's house at Birmingham in particular and German Gothic in general were important in the design. But to those familiar only with the general idea of Puginism, the English, symmetrical 'Present State' churches, All Saints would mark the end of Puginian architecture.

While Ruskin's ideas were taking hold, Pugin himself was becoming ever more entangled in contradiction. The *Rambler*, which took a lively interest in architecture, continued to criticize him and the whole Gothic Revival as 'an utter waste of toil and talent'. 'Church architecture', the editor Capes argued, had never been different from 'the ordinary architecture of the day' and it should continue to engage with the modern world, it should be economical and up to date.[10] Pugin's reply, a long open letter, 'Why This Waste', published in the *Weekly Register*, took its text from the gospel story of the woman who anointed Christ with precious ointment and was reproached by Judas for her extravagance. To his protest Christ replied: 'Let her alone . . . for the poor always ye have with you; but me ye have not always.'[11] Pugin argued that the House of God should stand as 'one green spot in the desert' of the modern city.[12] The argument that churches are for everyone, that to beautify them is to offer the poor a share of beauty and art, is a powerful one that found much favour among High Anglicans and is still invoked persuasively today. The article as a whole was not, however, well argued – or tactful. The title, by implication, cast the *Rambler* in the role of Judas, which provoked a wounded response and a plea for 'christian charity in discussion of questions of architecture'.[13] On points where Capes had criticized Pugin for views he no longer held, such as strict adherence to precedent, Pugin did not expound his recent ideas but went back and defended his earlier position: 'the Catholic religion is not of the nineteenth century it is the religion of antiquity'.[14] Ruskin could rejoice in contradiction. Pugin hated it. He had painted himself into a rhetorical corner.

When it came to practice, however, he was more sophisticated than Ruskin would ever be. What Ruskin was arguing for – the importance of craftsmanship in architecture – Pugin and Hardman had long been working to realize. Now they began to reap the rewards of their efforts in the applied arts. That autumn they showed their metalwork in an exhibition at Birmingham. It was one of a number of local exhibitions that were giving the new generation of 'art manufacturers' a chance to show what they could do. They were part of a general stirring of interest in the idea of 'design' in manufacturing. It was still a new idea. The notion of preferring one object to another on the basis of its appearance was quite novel to most people. It was the debate over the inadequate government schools, the decoration of the Palace of Westminster and in particular the growing flood of mass-produced goods, many of them very shoddy, that carried it along. One of the most influential figures in what would soon be called the 'design reform movement' was Henry Cole. Four years older than Pugin, a pragmatist, an administrator of genius and the inventor of the Christmas card, he was poised on the verge of his peculiarly Victorian career.

In March Cole had founded a magazine, the *Journal of Design*. It was a Victorian successor to Ackermann's *Repository* – much more didactic and professional. Like Pugin the *Journal* argued that the best model for design was nature. It reviewed the Birmingham exhibition and was impressed by Hardman and Pugin: 'locks, keys, hinges, screws and nail-heads', nothing, it remarked, was too small to benefit from Pugin's 'vivifying hand', while to traditional forms Pugin and Hardman's products brought 'the all-important elements of freshness and originality'.[15] Pugin was immensely cheered. 'It has been very hard work for many years,' he wrote, 'but it will repay all the toil, our exposition . . . has attracted a deal of attention & done much good.'[16] Henry Cole was a utilitarian. He had little time for religion and less for the Gothic Revival. Yet he and Pugin shared an understanding of practicalities. The *Journal* thought Ruskin's book unrealistic, with its 'dreamy blotches' of illustration and its 'very lopsided view of railways'.[17] Cole from now on kept his eye on Pugin. Despite their differences they were thinking along similar lines. Pugin was chivvying Crace to produce a range of moderately priced, plain furniture for retail. 'The great sale will be in articles that are within the reach of the middling class,' he explained.[18] Crace, whose firm had not been accustomed to catering for anything less than the gentry, certainly not for 'clergymen furnishing parsonage houses etc.', needed pushing to make the plain oak tables and washstands such as Pugin had designed for Oscott and Handsworth. Pugin was sure, however, that furniture in 'a sensible style . . . of good . . . construction that shall compete with the vile trash made & sold these days' would be a success.[19] The designs looked daringly stark: 'dont let your Father see them,' Pugin warned Crace, 'he will say they are only fit for a Tap room . . . but I know the feeling that is arising for simple good things.'[20]

On 17 October Jane's confinement began. Pugin, as so often, was not at home, but Hardman Powell's mother had come down. Dr Daniel was also on hand. After nearly five hours' labour a daughter, 'dear little Margaret', was born. Daniel wrote at once to Pugin, who replied that it was 'quite delightful to have a good little girl . . . they are far easier managed than boys & as no Estates are depending on male heirs we cannot be better off'.[21] Generally, however, his mood continued low. The buildings at Ramsgate drained him financially and emotionally. 'I have taken on a work greater than my strength,' he confessed to Hardman, who kindly offered to pay for the glass in the Lady Chapel.[22] Sometimes, in a rare flash of insight, Pugin would compare himself with Micawber, always on the brink of ruin then finding something turn up. At others he was sombre, realizing that he had, figuratively and literally, dug his own grave at St Augustine's. On the day of Margaret's baptism he noted that 'the great stone was lowered on the entrance of our vault this afternoon to remain until it is required . . . a sad and solemn consideration'.[23]

His fortunes as an architect continued to founder. He read 'insulting' accounts of Hansom's superior abilities. 'By George it is too Bad a man who entices the men away to work what is done, I should like to see him locked up till he drew out a niche.'[24] Myers was working more all the time for other architects, who thereby benefited from Pugin's casts and the craftsmen he had trained. '[Myers] will become a great builder

& a rich man & I shall be knocked down to nothing as it is I am the servant of every ... architect that turns up ...'[25] Pugin complained, with some justice. Nevertheless he was always busy. There was a new decorating commission, brought to him by Crace, a Gothic dining room for Earl Somers at his home, Eastnor Castle in Herefordshire. The scheme survives and is a rich and rare example of Pugin's late decorative style, one of only two domestic interiors by him to have remained almost intact. Yet for all its glamour – Earl Somers had plenty of money – Pugin was not much interested in the project. He visited Eastnor only once, when work was nearly finished. He therefore did not realize – until it was too late – that it was not a medieval castle like Chirk but a vast piece of Regency neo-Norman by the much-detested Smirke. Crace, perhaps understandably, did not mention this as Pugin was working on the great chimney-piece, complete with painted armorial overmantel with figures of the Earl and Countess in medieval dress. When it arrived on site the fireplace was far too deep for the thin, Georgian construction. Pugin was aghast when Crace told him. 'I thought it was a very old place with tremendous thick walls,' he explained.[26] Myers – who was doing the fitting – refused to make adjustments. Not for the first or the last time Pugin remarked that there 'was not a greater Pig in christendom ... when he takes it into his head nobody can do anything with him', and in the end he split the cost with Crace.[27] It was annoying. The whole way that he worked now depressed him: 'this is all very well if one is architect to the whole job or builder to the whole job but architect to one grate or one fireplace is worse than keeping a fish stall'.[28]

That Pugin should thus be caught out by sham Gothic, by Smirke of all people, whose career he had insisted in *Contrasts* had already 'gone on too long', was sadly ironic. More ironic still, he was now in his father's position, in exactly the line of work he had rebelled against in 1827, designing decorative details. 'I am reduced to a mere mechanick a maker of handles to other mens buildings,' he complained, and it was literally true.[29] Dr Gillis had not answered his enquiry about money on account; 'this cathedral is all moonshine', Pugin told Hardman.[30] 'I am worn out with one thing & another,' he wrote, 'the expense the loss of time the agony of mind is unbearable it seems hopeless ... everything goes wrong.'[31] The young men in the studio were a mixed blessing. In theory 'the only way to bring up lads & make a catholic school' was to have them trained under his eye.[32] The reality was more often reminiscent of the ramshackle regime at Great Russell Street and Pugin began to sound very like his mother: 'the truth is I am surrounded by a set of fools who lose the little brains they have as soon as I leave home ... Powell's forgetfulness is dreadful ... he literally cannot think of anything.'[33] Earley was slow at learning to carve, Casolani had taken to smoking cigars and going about with women, Hendren had not much talent and sang so badly in church that Pugin could have 'stabbed him on the spot'.[34] By far the worst of all that winter's troubles, however, was the threat to St Augustine's. 'I shall reproach myself day & night,' Pugin told Hardman, 'my church is ruined.'[35] To prevent any more such disasters he bought the two plots opposite his house on the other side of the road. He must have sold stock to do it, and at £750 it was an expense he could barely stand. 'I hope I have done right ... I could ill afford it but buildings are ... more on every side & a row of vile houses or a terrace would have been dreadful.'[36]

Eventually in December the Habershons were forced to give in, for Pugin discovered that he owned the road in front of his own land and could refuse permission for the water pipes to be laid to the new houses unless he got his way. It was a costly victory. He paid £450 for '15 feet of ground' when the whole plot had cost only £700.[37] He had to borrow £200 from the bishop, Dr Waring. 'I am one of the most unfortunate men in these things,' he told Hardman.[38] He was certainly one of the most unbusinesslike. Habershon built his Chartham Terrace just yards away from Pugin's church. A tall, rather grim block, it is in a flint Gothic style and not unsympathetic to St Augustine's. Pugin would be mortified to know how many visitors to Ramsgate over the years have thought that it is by him. He concluded that 1849 was 'the worst year ever'.[39] Financially this was true. Myers's account showed Pugin owed him £3,000. He instituted a new regime of strict economy: 'you must not make anything for me next year,' he told Hardman, adding, realistically, 'even if I order it'; 'the completion of the church and the purchase of the land have beggared me for years to come unless something wonderful turns up'.[40] Jane took it all 'most beautifully' and was 'quite prepared for the worst', but she was ill and so was the baby;[41] 'you talk of comfort here,' Pugin reproached Hardman, who was presumably trying to get him to count his blessings, 'Jane was scarcely in bed last night why for 2 days and 2 nights that poor child has scarcely ceased screaming.'[42]

Edward, at fourteen, was growing up. His father sent him around to look at Gothic buildings and make drawings. Pugin was delighted one night to find his son working away on 'a splendid crucifixion' long after he had thought he was in bed.[43] Not every parent would have thought this an unqualified sign of promise. Edward's constant efforts to please his father met with alternating praise and furious blame that can have done little to stabilize an already intense adolescent temperament. He must still have missed his mother very much, although in time he formed a close and happy relationship with Jane. This year there would be no Christmas festivities, no party for the neighbours and only beef, not turkey. No more entertaining and no travel, unless the expenses were paid, such were Pugin's resolutions for the New Year. He also began keeping notes of his postal costs, and those of Hardman and Crace, who from now on received regular homilies on extravagance: 'the letter . . . had a 2d stamp I enclose the envellope as proof this could not be an urgent letter I think you must allow me something for looking after your interests.'[44]

But despite his resolutions the new year began badly. Pugin discharged all but two of the workmen from St Augustine's and could not bear the mockery of the deserted workshops; 'I shall pull them down,' he told Hardman.[45] Jane's health was 'quite gone'; she seemed 'altogether changed in constitution' since Margaret's birth.[46] There were 'black and threatening prospects' on all sides.[47] Hardman Powell was in constant trouble: 'you will hardly believe what I am going to tell you,' Pugin wrote to Birmingham, 'Powell who is a first class fool A1 in everything but his art' had allowed the studio chimney to catch fire.[48]

Then in January Pugin went up to London to learn from Barry that 'the rascally commissioners' had reduced his salary at Westminster by half:[49] 'it is almost an insult to pay such a man as me 100 a year,' he told Jane, 'I have a great mind to throw up the whole thing but my spirit is so broken by poverty that I hardly know what to do.'[50] For the immediate future he borrowed £400 from Hardman, that 'capital good man'.[51] It was not in fact the Commissioners' idea to reduce Pugin's salary, it was Barry's. He was hard pressed to cut costs and the bulk of the work was over. Even so it was a small, mean saving. Pugin had received a total of about £800 for his work so far, Barry £24,735. Barry had of course done much more, but Pugin's payments in no way reflected his contribution. The cut in his salary was symptomatic, however, of the mess that Parliament had got itself into over the New Palace. Public opinion and rising prices dictated that the budget should be curbed. The MPs were impatient for the work to be finished but implacable in their refusal to pay for it. Half measures and false economies were the result. Pugin at times swore he would never draw another line. In the end he carried on. The Commons was to be ready for members to try by May. A squarer, plainer chamber than the Lords, it still required Pugin's skill to design clock faces, railings, glass, benches and carving.

His moods were now more volatile even than usual, like scudding clouds. He swung from optimism to rage to despair, sometimes within a single paragraph of a letter, and his savagery with the unhappy young men in the study made them 'run like rabbits'.[52] He more than once threatened to turn Edward out of the house if he did not mend his ways. He complained now of no physical illness, but commented that his memory had suddenly failed and he needed to write everything down. Whatever his mood or health, however, he remained a child of the Picturesque. The internal and the external worlds, nature and human nature, interacted as powerfully as ever in him. Winter sunlight slanting through stained glass, as it might be in one of his father's watercolours, never failed to touch him. 'I have been frantic all day,' he wrote to Hardman, complaining that some bolts he had sent were the wrong size, 'but a Ray of the setting sun striking on the chancel arch has restored tranquillity to my soul. ever thine vade in Pace.'[53]

38

The High Victorians

1850

Honor had grown up among those who fed on Scott, Words-worth, and Fouqué, took their theology from the British Critic, *and their taste from Pugin; and moulded their opinions and practice on the past. Lucilla and Phoebe were essentially of the new generation, that of Kingsley, Tennyson, Ruskin, and the* Saturday Review. *Chivalry had given way to common sense, romance to realism . . . the past to the future.*

— Charlotte M. Yonge, *Hopes and Fears*, 1860

The new half-century saw a new mood stir in England. In architecture and the arts signs of change had been in the air the year before, in Henry Cole's magazine, Ruskin's book and Hope and Butterfield's church. Now they came together in a debate that raised questions not only of aesthetics but of purpose, of social responsibility and meaning. The argument centred on the question of the town church, for it was in urban areas, especially in the industrial cities, that the tensions of modern life were most acutely felt and it was in the design and construction of churches, buildings which through their use and their very presence would act as unifying, civilizing forces, that the moral arguments about the value of architecture being developed by Ruskin could be worked out. These concerns blended with the ever-increasing anxiety about finding an idiom for the age, a modern Gothic. From the discussions of 1850 was born what came to be called the High Victorian style, and although he was not in the vanguard of this shift of sensibility, Pugin and his ideas were very much at its heart. Indeed it was Pugin who began the whole debate in 'Why This Waste'.

The *Rambler* duly retaliated in January 1850 when it published an article showing a model design for a town church. Intended to be cheap and practical, it was also intended, by implication, as an alternative to the supposed extravagance of Pugin and the Ecclesiologists. The design was by Hadfield, Pugin's old rival at Macclesfield, who was now by far the more successful, or at least the busier, of the two. Hadfield's design was for a brick church in a Germanic Byzantine style. It was not a bad building, nor a very good one. What is striking about it is how up-to-date it looked. Given that Hadfield was not an original thinker, it seems likely that he – or Capes – had been reading Ruskin. Pugin responded with a twenty-five-page pamphlet, *Some Remarks on the articles which have recently appeared in the Rambler*. He picked on the weaknesses of Hadfield's design – the round windows like 'the cosmoramic walk in a popular tea-garden', the interior 'very like the Hungerford Market, only not quite so handsome', and so on.[1] After that the rest of the *Remarks* turned into a kind of apologia for his own career, the closest Pugin had come since his adolescent notes to autobiography. The disappointment of the last six years poured out on to the pages. 'I believe, as regards architecture, few men have been so unfortunate as myself,' he complained.[2] 'I have passed my life in thinking of fine things, studying fine things, designing fine things, and realising very poor ones. I have never had the chance of producing a single fine ecclesiastical building, except my own church, where I am both paymaster and architect, but everything else, either for want of adequate funds or injudicious interference and control . . . is more or less a failure.'[3]

There was truth in what he said, as well as a characteristic degree of exaggeration. It was neither fair nor prudent to criticize his patrons so severely, especially not the long-suffering Earl of Shrewsbury, who, Pugin now announced, had spoiled both St Barnabas's, Nottingham and St Giles's, Cheadle. Four years after it was finished, 'perfect Cheadle' looked highly imperfect to its designer. In particular the size of the spire and the density of the painted decoration seemed ill-judged. These had been the last additions to the design; 'it was quite an afterthought of its noble founder to cover it with coloured enrichment,' Pugin wrote, 'hence there is a great anomaly between the simplicity of its walls and mouldings and the intricacy of its detail.'[4] No evidence suggests that Pugin, who argued with Shrewsbury about many things, ever protested about the stencilling. He had been thrilled by the patterns he found to copy at the Sainte-Chapelle. Whatever he now considered to be the weaknesses of

Cheadle, they were not the Earl's fault. Pugin was, once more, changing his mind, and as usual he could not admit it. His growing preference for plain surfaces and the natural qualities of stone and brick which created the effect of his own church, flint without and ashlar within, made him dislike applied decoration. Less than four months after he had published the stencil patterns of *Floriated Ornament*, he wrote in the *Remarks* that: 'As for stencilled walls, I dislike them exceedingly.'[5]

This question of colour and decoration had come to seem critical in the debate about the emerging style of 1850. The *Ecclesiologist*, which rallied warmly to Pugin's cause, reprinting long extracts from the *Remarks*, regretted only his failure to give an opinion on 'constructional polychrome'.[6] This was the latest architectural in-phrase. It meant the use of natural materials, marbles, stones and brick to create the sort of integral decoration admired by Ruskin and planned for All Saints, Margaret Street. Pugin in effect was moving in the same direction, but he never explicitly said so. Polychrome, however, came to characterize the architecture of the next decades, not only churches but houses, schools and shops. It signified an attitude as much as an aesthetic. Like High-Tech in the twentieth century, it was seen to indicate honesty and modernity. The *Ecclesiologist* was 'more and more convinced' that polychrome was 'one of the problems, which the revived Pointed architecture of the nineteenth century, enterprising and scientific as it is, will have chiefly to work out, if it means to vindicate its position of being a living and growing style'.[7]

Enterprise and science, growth and progress, this was the new mood in architecture and in England. It was the age of applied utilitarianism, 'a time when Bentham's name was being forgotten . . . [but] his language was in everybody's mouth'.[8] It was, most notably, in Henry Cole's. His *Journal of Design* could not sympathize with Pugin's religion or his revivalism but it took the *Remarks* seriously as it took the art of the Middle Ages seriously because it was 'a genuine thing . . . it was based upon principles'.[9] Pugin disliked utilitarianism as much as Cole disliked Catholicism, but the two men were now being drawn into one another's orbits. In January Herbert Minton came to Ramsgate to talk to Pugin about Cole's latest and greatest venture, the plan for an international exhibition. The scheme, officially announced that month, had its origins in the Paris Exhibition of 1849, where members of the Society of Arts, including Minton and Cole, had met to discuss it. With the support of the Prince Consort and by means of a Royal Commission, London would 'act the part of host to all the world at an intellectual festival of peaceful industry ... a festival, such as the world has never seen before'.[10] It was to be the Great Exhibition.

The prospect of showing what he and his collaborators, Minton, Myers, Crace and Hardman, could do aroused Pugin's enthusiasm. He made sheaves of drawings on the spot and with Minton arranged 'a great deal'.[11] He discussed it all with Crace and felt sure they could 'produce an effect'.[12] Yet at the same time he continued to be far from well, and life at home still fell short of his ideals of love and harmony. He was in a most 'aggravating state of mind', while Jane, whose nurse-maid had left, was finding her baby hard work:[13] 'she has no experience & no one to advise her & it is very miserable indeed.'[14] Pugin told Hardman she was 'quite fading away'.[15] Jane, who had been so robust on her honeymoon journey, seems never fully to have recovered from the birth of her first child and she complained of poor health for the rest of her life. Complications of childbirth that would today be reckoned minor could often, in the nineteenth century, undermine a woman's health for many years or indeed permanently. In addition to which she was discovering, as Louisa had, that to be Pugin's wife meant to be often alone. If Louisa had been made angry by her husband's absences and directed her frustrations towards him, Jane did not have her prede-cessor's temper. Although she sometimes made her displeasure felt and wrote him letters that Pugin complained were cold, her unhappiness was mostly turned in on herself. She fretted and was nervous.

While Pugin was away at Birmingham and Lincoln, where Sibthorp and Myers had got at cross purposes over the bede houses and his intervention was required, Jane was miserable at home. Margaret was sickly and her own hair was falling out; 'do all you can to keep it in,' her husband wrote back, unhelpfully, 'for you had beautiful hair I cant bear to think of it coming off.'[16] He was more stoical about the baby, his seventh, 'they often look poorly & all right again in no time'.[17] In her weakened state, however, Jane found the other children, even with Agnes away, too much for her and wondered if a couple more could not be sent to school. Pugin was reluctant to send them away, partly out of affection and partly because of the expense. He never seems to have lost his temper with Jane, but perhaps her difficulties made him lose it more often with poor Powell, in whom hope continued to triumph over increasingly bitter experience. His latest scheme was moulding. Rather than send models to Birmingham it would be safer and cheaper, he suggested, to make moulds in Ramsgate from the plaster models and send those instead. 'I am afraid he will fail,' Pugin noted glumly, and sure enough he did.[18] Having used about half of Pugin's supply of decorating glue for his Patent Gelatine, it exploded, 'burst the case broke the clay models & covered about 40 square feet of the study with glue [so] stiff that we have been obliged to scrape the very boards up to get it off.'[19] Powell himself was no doubt blown up soon after.

Captain Hibbert continued to terrorize Pugin with complaints about his house at Bilton Grange and was now threatening to go to law. Pugin took the disarmingly direct method of writing back saying that he was too frightened to come to Bilton. 'I . . . told [him] I dare not come & that is the truth I tremble at the thought of his folded paper of remarks. I will not go.'[20] This had an emollient effect on the Captain, who promised that he would not be cross, and Pugin agreed to go in the spring. Exactly what was wrong with the house is impossible to discover, though one problem was damp. The 'remarks' sound like a tedious snagging list, the sort of finishing details that no other architect of Pugin's eminence would have expected, or needed, to deal with personally. Hibbert was not too dissatisfied to allow Pugin to undertake another job, a new college and novitiate for the Rosminians at Rugby, where the Captain had offered them the chance to take over the mission, promising to pay for new buildings behind the church. Thus the familiar process began whereby Pugin was asked by the Father Provincial, Pagani, to produce drawings for a building with a series of rooms 'lofty and well lighted' and of course extremely cheap.[21] Pugin, it was afterwards recalled, 'in his quaint way exclaimed "you may as well ask me to build a factory"' and so it went on until a compromise was reached that satisfied nobody.[22]

The best of the few commissions that came his way this year and were to be his last works was the smallest of all, a funerary chapel at Bicton in Devon. It is one of the loveliest things Pugin ever did. The commission came through the Shrewsburys, who had either not read or not minded about the Remarks, and were wintering in Torquay in what Pugin considered a 'wretched modern house something like Brighton'.[23] They arranged an introduction for Pugin to Lady Rolle, a widow 'with £10,000 a year', who was fortunately just now in want of an architect.[24] Pugin found Louisa Rolle a 'cheerful happy sort of woman'.[25] At first she wanted a 'mausoleum' for her late husband in the Soanian style with 'light coming in from the top'.[26] Pugin quickly made her realize that a Gothic chapel with '2 painted glass windows a proper ceiling with armorial bearings a brass & tiles' would be much better.[27] It was to stand next to the new village church on the edge of Lady Rolle's grounds. He built it amid the remains of the old, fifteenth-century church, which was almost entirely demolished. The tower and a single arcade still stand next to the memorial chapel, creating an effect that is truly picturesque. The setting is melancholy and tender, the interior rich and solemn. Between the vivid ceiling, painted with one of the finest patterns from the *Glossary*, and the brightly tiled floor, the tomb itself is almost monochrome, white stone, beautifully carved, black marble and brass. Sunlight through the stained glass chequers it from time to time with colour. The Rolle chapel bears out, quietly, Pugin's loud complaints about the way that he had travestied his ideas and his abilities elsewhere.

Soon after Pugin began work on the chapel, early in March, more details of the Great Exhibition were released for the benefit of entrants. Prince Albert's philosophical vision of a display that would be 'a living picture of the point of development at which the whole of mankind has arrived . . .' had been translated through the Commission and the committees and subcommittees which successively formed, divided and subdivided, into a system of categories.[28] Within these the applied arts were divided by materials. Metalwork, glass, furniture and so forth were each to be shown separately. This was a blow, for Pugin's romantic conception of the arts as a continuous whole could never fit into such a system. Hardman proposed mounting a rival show of their own but Pugin realized that was out of the question. 'I do not know what can be done,' he wrote back, 'I believe they will rigidly enforce the classification of articles.'[29] His by now usual gloom and mistrust returned. Hardman might enter some things in the metalwork section but otherwise it was hopeless, just another 'castle in the air'; 'we shall never get any particular space allotted or anything of the kind . . . I rather think that some whom we might imagine to be our supporters will do all in their power to prevent us having any opportunity of showing our things to advantage – I have lived to doubt everybody but you,'[30] Pugin confided in Hardman. It seems he was afraid that Barry, who was one of the Commissioners, might not want the public to see the full extent of what Pugin could do on his own. Crace suggested that Pugin send in an outline of what he intended to see if they might get an exception made, but Pugin, who had suffered so much from plagiarists, was wary of showing his hand: 'there will be some vile IMITATION got up.'[31]

In fact almost every exhibitor wanted special arrangements, 'convenient to himself, but inconvenient to everybody else', as Cole wearily noted.[32] His organizing genius accommodated most of them and in Pugin's case he was willing to make every allowance. Still Pugin had his doubts: 'the time is now so very short,' he protested to Crace 'that I am quite certain we can never get the stone work ready . . . I really do not think it is worth while applying for so large a space . . .'[33] In the event, although the final allocations were not made until the beginning of the next year, Pugin and his collaborators were assured they would be given the space they wanted and allowed to exhibit together, Cole having bundled them somewhat incongruously into Class XXVI: 'Decorative furniture and upholstery, paper hangings, papier mache and japanned goods'. Many details had yet to be decided. There was still no building for the exhibition or a design for one decided. The idea hung fire for several months.

At the *Rambler*, meanwhile, the architectural dispute went on well into the spring. Pugin, of course, felt confident that he got the better of the argument, which he conducted with his usual mixture of high-flown rhetoric and knockabout comedy. Capes finally drew matters to an amicable close in April: 'I hit him hard because he hit me hard, and because he is a strong man. I now cordially, though figuratively, shake hands with him and bid him farewell.'[34] It was not the same thing at all with Oratorians. Pugin loathed them more than anyone. 'I never looked on a Puritan with half the disgust,' he told Hardman.[35] Newman now returned this loathing. Pugin infuriated him. Mary Holmes, who still followed her former employer's activities, received a voluble response when she asked what Newman thought of the *Remarks*.

'What Mr Pugin writes I do not know, and do not much interest myself about . . . I speak as a simple looker-on, who never has been able to bear extreme views of bigots; and I see that he is a bigot.' Newman protested his indifference at great length. 'He who makes orthodoxy consist in any thing but truth in faith and morals . . . goes far towards being a heretic . . . The truth is this,' he went on, 'Catholics have been under-educated. They are waking up – and the first beautiful thing that they meet with is Gothic architecture, so they take it, and fall into raptures (as they well may), and, it being the only thing they know or have heard of, they ride it like a hobby . . . When I hear of a thorough Puginian, I am quite sure he is a "dandified", under-educated man – always excepting Miss Holmes and dear Mr Phillipps who is by nature an enthusiast.'[36] Newman used Pugin's own argument, reasonably enough, against him: 'if the rites of the Church have *changed*, let architecture *develop* – let it modify and improve itself to meet them.'[37] Pugin, however, did not accept that the rites had changed. He stayed loyal to the English Catholic ideal that had once been Newman's too, and it was an ideal that still flourished sufficiently among the Anglicans for Pugin to continue to hope for a reunion with the church of his childhood. Visiting Pusey's foundation, St Saviour's, Leeds, he was impressed. 'What capital men . . . quite like monks, living in community, reciting office etc What an immense amount of catholicism there is among the anglicans. Every day I am more & more convinced that immense results will come from that Quarter.'[38]

By the end of April the new House of Commons was being fitted up for trial sittings in May, amid complaints from a sizeable and vocal section of members. The costs of the building continued to rise and now it transpired that the new chamber was not large enough to seat all the MPs on the floor, but would require some of them to sit in a gallery behind the Speaker's chair. In addition to this annoyance, relations between Barry and Dr Reid, the ventilating expert whose apparatus had already required the construction of several additional turrets and the large central lantern, had deteriorated still further. The two men had now fallen out over sewers and drainage and Barry had started legal proceedings against Reid for defamation. Mr Osborne, the MP for Lancaster, was not alone in thinking that unless this 'squabbling' was resolved they would 'never get into the new building'.[39] He proposed dismissing both men. Some of these difficulties were chickens coming home to roost. The estimates of 1835 had been wildly speculative and they had never included the costs of decoration and furnishing. Pugin was furious about Parliament's attitude. It confirmed his worst suspicions of the Radicals, especially Cobden, whom he thought a 'traitor' in general and most particularly for his views on the Palace:[40] 'we have all been sold to a Manchester mill,' he reported to Hardman, 'the wretched government, the vile wigs dare not grant a few thousands for decorating the largest national work they have cut our stencilling.'[41]

439

In May the Institute of British Architects presented Charles Barry with its gold medal. The President, Lord de Grey, one of the Commissioners of the Palace of Westminster, commented pointedly on the difficulties that had been 'unnecessarily created' there for Barry, a remark which was noted and resented by the House of Commons, where members were becoming restive as they waited for their new Chamber.[42] Barry's estimates, they complained, were 'moonshine', the cost of decoration (£497,400) exorbitant and the lack of seating unforgivable. Henry Drummond, Pugin's imperious patron, demanded to know why the Commissioners could not just 'take the fattest member they could find and multiply him by 658'.[43] Another suggestion, that it would have been better to have had a building in the classical style, was warmly seconded, but as the Chancellor of the Exchequer pointed out wearily, it was 'all very well to say hear hear' now but it was much too late to change and anyway Parliament itself had chosen the style.[44] The debate was not very elevated and the trial sittings saw members joking, larking about and generally behaving in a way scarcely 'creditable to the sense and seriousness' of the House.[45] When the trials were over Barry began work to address the more reasonable objections.

Pugin meanwhile carried on glumly with his part of the business, complaining regularly about his reduced salary and the difficulty of getting his expenses. Hardman and Crace were anxious to make plans for the Great Exhibition, due to open in exactly a year. But Pugin was unenthusiastic. The pessimism of his *Remarks* was still with him. He thought it was too late for the Exhibition, too late perhaps for everything. '12 months are nothing gone like a week the days are now light till ½ past 7 soon the longest day. then decline & candles at 4 . . . no use making great sacrifices for there will be no returns . . . the serious men are in a nut shell the million are humbugs . . . if that oratorian movement spreads it destroys all we have been building up for years . . . & there are men who say that pointed architecture is allied with Heresy . . . it is all miserable miserable.'[46] It seems that Miss Holmes had passed on something of Newman's reply to her about Pugin's pamphlet. Of course the Oratorians had nothing to do with the Great Exhibition, except in Pugin's mind, but they and the rood screen question loomed larger than anything else just now. He set off for Paris on 14 May and was away in France, Germany and the Netherlands until early June, making drawings of the great screens of Germany for his long-meditated book on the subject. No letters to Jane from this trip seem to have survived. Maybe she resented his absence and said so.

On his way home Pugin stopped in Bruges. The Low Countries had, in his youth, inspired him and he was now in turn the subject of enthusiastic and not entirely welcome imitation there. The Gothic Revival had come to Belgium late, but it found many followers in a country not only rich in medieval architecture but also, as a nation, itself a creation of the 1830s looking for a national style. The Belgians had gifted craftsmen, but few designers of merit. They looked to England and especially to Pugin. Among his greatest admirers was the Baron Béthune, a leader of the revival who had visited him in Ramsgate. More problematic was Thomas Harper King, an Oxford graduate and Catholic convert who had settled in Bruges and was producing Pugin's designs and reprinting parts of his books without permission. Pugin had some sympathy with King, as a supporter of the true thing, but he was not pleased to discover that he had full-size tracings of stained glass cartoons and was receiving casts for metalwork from Birmingham. He warned Hardman to be careful about whom he let into the factory.

The more famous Pugin became – and he was now famous enough to be listed in the papers under 'fashionable arrivals' when he travelled ('ha ha ha,' he wrote to Jane) – the more common was this sort of piracy.[47] His fame, it seemed, only made him a loss or a laughing stock. He was now the butt of *Household Words*, Dickens's magazine, which took in Pugin in the course of an attack on Millais. The Pre-Raphaelites, heralds like Ruskin and Butterfield of the new mood in the arts, were beginning to be noticed. At this year's Royal Academy exhibition Millais's *Christ in the House of his Parents* shocked many people by its realism. It showed Mary as a simple peasant woman and Joseph with a carpenter's dirty fingernails. Dickens was one of many who thought it blasphemous, plumbing the lowest depths 'of what is mean, odious, repulsive, and revolting'.[48] If a Pre-Raphaelite Brotherhood, he wondered, why not a Pre-Newtonian or Pre-Galilean. Why not a 'Pre-Laurentius Brotherhood ... for the abolition of all but manuscript books. These MR PUGIN has engaged to supply in characters that nobody on earth shall be able to read. And it is confidently expected by those who have seen the House of Lords, that he will faithfully redeem his pledge.'[49] Luckily for Pugin, Dickens had not noticed the Pre-Linnaean *Floriated Ornament*.

In Ramsgate at least he was not burdened with celebrity. The *Kent*

Herald commented with great enthusiasm on the new houses next to his church, noting 'the enterprise of [Messers Habershon] the eminent architects of Bloomsbury Square, London' in building this 'very picturesque' terrace.[50] Mr Hoare and Lieutenant Hutchinson's Seamen's Infirmary opened with a great flourish. Pugin, having given up his own hospital scheme, subscribed, with typical largeness of character, to theirs – for it would benefit the sailors and that was the important thing. Meanwhile his own charitable enterprises floundered. As he told Hardman, 'nobody gives a shilling they are desperate Prayers but wretched payers in our congregation'.[51] With no prospect of finishing his church as he would wish, Pugin decided to get it ready for consecration anyway. This meant that the school could move into its permanent premises. The school was one of his most troublesome endeavours. The children were 'a set of young villains' who swore and fought, in addition to which he later discovered that 'the little beasts' had been quietly stealing his coal, and had made off with about thirty tons in all.[52] The expense was a drain and the parents were sometimes worse than the pupils. With only one schoolmistress, Miss Bridge, the elder children taught the younger. It was a common arrangement in schools at the time, but one father, 'an Irishman', was not satisfied and 'came to blow up because his children were taught by monitors'.[53] Pugin was livid: 'a beggar a beast a fellow without a penny & I paying about £1 a week to keep the school going it does indeed cost me that I detest the Irish.'[54]

In an attempt to cheer himself and Jane up he took her on a brief trip to France. He had promised, in the early days of their marriage when he missed her most, that she should come with him in future and now, perhaps to make up for his long absence earlier in the year, he kept his word. The tour was not a great success. Jane was still not strong, Pugin himself was ill, and this journey was not bathed in the honeymoon glow that makes adventures out of every difficulty. Jane liked Paris. Bourges was less attractive. 'I was never in such a dirty place in my life . . . the food was disgusting,' she recalled, while her chief impression of Amiens was that the Hôtel de Postes was 'a very nice clean house'.[55] All in all she was glad to be home and confessed that it was not 'a very delightful trip'.[56] Her husband returned 'very poorly indeed . . .', which did not prevent him setting off again almost at once.[57] Despite his many resolutions to travel less, he was away for much of the summer. On his brief visits home he had a great deal to attend to, for the pattern of his family life was changing once again. This year marked the end of Edward's short and troubled childhood. His father had decided that he should, from now on, be paid for his contributions to the office and work there regularly. He was sixteen, slightly older than Pugin had been when he started to earn his own living. Cuthbert, now ten, was, to Jane's relief, going away to school in the autumn and Anne, at eighteen, was also leaving home. She was to be married, to Hardman Powell. They had been playmates since childhood and had apparently grown easily into lovers. By July the matter was decided and they took a house nearby in St Lawrence's, where Pugin himself had first settled with Louisa in 1833.

If it was not a marriage of convenience, it was certainly a very convenient marriage to both families. Pugin was sure that it would settle Powell down. He would forget his hankerings for London and the artist's life once he had a wife and family, while the revival would be further strengthened by ties of kinship between Birmingham and Ramsgate. The more disillusioned Pugin became with the world and the Catholic Church, the more he depended on his friends. Hardman was the only man he trusted. 'I hope you will take care of yourself and live a long while,' Pugin wrote to him, 'for I should never carry on without you.'[58] The friends of one generation would become the siblings of the next. Pugin set about decorating and furnishing the young couple's new home at 3 Southwood Terrace. He supplied 'all the furniture earthenware china & glass Prints Papers etc etc', much of it designed by himself. Mrs Powell supplied the linen and Hardman the metalwork, 'so between us 3 he will be fitted out completely'.[59] The furniture and upholstery were made by Crace. Everything was to be 'as simple as possible', both for economy and for propriety; the Powells were a young couple in a modest walk of life, yet every detail was considered:[60] 'no fringe on the curtains but some little weights sewed in to make them hang well',[61] 'a stuffed couch of the simplest principles ... 4 oak chamfered legs will be sufficient & I think it should be covered with utrecht velvet plain with some nails along the edge.'[62] However much Pugin had contradicted himself on paper, there was now no faltering or false note in his design. From an upholstery nail to a rood screen, everything had physical and metaphysical integrity. Form and meaning, what an object was, how it was made and what it was for, all were interwoven. This 'little job', his first child's first house, must have been, when finished, a perfect epitome of Pugin's plain domestic style.[63]

Southwood Terrace interested him much more than the other commission he was working on with Crace, a Great Hall for the Duke of Devonshire at Lismore Castle in County Waterford. He complained of lack of information about the castle and the family, yet when he was in Ireland he made no attempt to see it. Indeed he never saw it or followed up the opportunity of an introduction to the Devonshires. He merely supplied designs for heraldic glass, painting and a great brass chandelier, giving Crace a very free hand: 'I have just sent you up my ideas to make the best & alter as you judge . . . there is nothing to be done but decorate as well as we can what is already there.'[64] Despite Pugin thinking it was 'a horrid job', the result has great clarity as well as richness, the splendour of the coloured decoration set off by dark linenfold panelling below.[65] But as so often with his grandest work, and the Lismore banqueting hall is very grand indeed, it engaged him little.

In Ramsgate the church and the Powells' house were speeding towards completion together. In between ordering Anne's dressing table and some good down pillows, Pugin was also applying for sedilia cushions. Crace, not surprisingly, sometimes confused the two jobs, and to Pugin's fury made the altar canopy in a domestic floral pattern by mistake. The consecration of St Augustine's took place quietly on 15 August, the Feast of the Assumption. Pugin told Shrewsbury that it had gone well. For the service of Benediction, when the Holy Sacrament is exposed for veneration, it had been displayed beneath a canopy and veil reaching from the roof and extending the whole width of the chancel, the splendour of this grail-like display enhanced by a sense of mystery for its being partly obscured by the rood screen.[66] To Hardman Pugin confessed the difficulties. He explained about Crace sending the wrong material. The altar had looked 'dreadful', the chairs 'beastly' and outside the church 'that horrible row of houses' compromised the setting.[67] Father Costigan, the priest from Margate who officiated, 'literally bellows in the confessional it is impossible to use it in the way he goes on at the highest pitch of his voice it is ridiculous'; Pugin despaired again.[68] 'I have been a great fool ever to begin on such a large work without better materials.'[69] He was now, on medical advice, taking constant baths to try to cure the sweats that had begun to afflict him but 'nothing stops this constant perspiration night & day'.[70] Jane too was ill, 'worse every day', and having to take 'beastly cod liver oil'.[71] Pugin, as usual, forced himself on. His wife, meanwhile, repined. Dimly he sensed that there was more than physical weakness in Jane's case. She was weighed down with domestic duties, often alone and with no outlets for her natural energy. Pugin, though not usually imaginative about other people's difficulties, was more sympathetic than some Victorian husbands whose wives took to the sofa; 'you and I get on capitally,' he told Hardman, 'because we are always employed & have lots of real work to do. if we were idling about it would not be half so delightful.'[72]

They were far from idle now, for Pugin had finally been persuaded by Crace and Hardman to make an effort for the Great Exhibition. In July the design of the Exhibition building by Joseph Paxton, soon to be known as the Crystal Palace, was published. Pugin had decorated buildings by Paxton at Bolton Abbey, Burton Closes and now Lismore, none of which he liked. He was no enthusiast for the 'vert monstre', as he called the Crystal Palace, in an Anglo-French play on glasshouse and greenhouse. Nevertheless by August he was writing to Hardman that 'I think the space at the exhibition will do very well indeed.'[73] It seems to have been Hardman who finally arranged with Cole the sort of display Pugin wanted. Cole gave them a prime site. On the plan of the Exhibition published the following March, it was the only area to bear the names of individuals: Pugin, Minton, Myers, Crace and Hardman. The display itself, the Mediaeval Court, was to be unique in the Great Exhibition. Unlike the rest of the Crystal Palace exhibits, its contents were linked not by their materials or their country of origin but by an abstract idea, the idea of design. Every object in the Court was the product of one man's creative invention. In the House of Commons the Crystal Palace now took over from the Palace of Westminster as a subject for argument and criticism. For the Commons itself a sum of £3,129 had at length been voted to get the chamber, committee rooms and a temporary house for the speaker ready. Enormous numbers of fittings and decorations were wanted quickly. Pugin supplied them resentfully: 'it don't pay the cabs,' he grumbled to Crace as they worked on the decoration of the Bishops' Corridor at the House of Lords.[74] At the same time he was doing another job for Barry, who was enlarging a house in Dorset, Canford Manor, for a wealthy iron founder. Barry still had no feeling for Gothic detail and sent Pugin rough, unready sketches: 'as for the doors,' Pugin confided to Hardman, 'you never saw such things.'[75] So he spent his time spinning Barry's straw into gold, for Barry. His own fees were modest.

At the end of September Pugin and Jane made another journey together, hoping to improve their health and raise her spirits. They went to Salisbury, but this trip was an even worse failure than the last. The cholera that still haunted England broke out in Wiltshire and Jane fell victim to it. Six days later, though much 'reduced', she was able to come home.[76] They were a sad pair. Pugin was now almost constantly ill, often feverish, sweating, racked with pain. He suffered bouts of diarrhoea. He was afraid that his eyes were failing again and as his health declined his expenses continued to mount. 'Cuthbert has had everything new for going to school Anne everything new to be married ... Miss Bridge struck for wages & obliged to give her 4s a week more.'[77] New vestments were needed in the church, even the *Caroline* needed a new foresail. 'I never at any point of my life felt the anxiety I do now,' he told Hardman, 'I have only a few years to redeem myself in all probability I never felt so weak before for expenses encrease on every side they will soon be terrific with all the children growing up & if anything happens to my health I am a ruined man ... I must turn over a new leaf.'[78] As usual Pugin's new leaf meant drastic reform of the studio, starting with yet more attempts to drill Hardman Powell into efficiency. Now that the house in Southwood Terrace was ready, Powell was living there and so 'throwing his time away' by spending half an hour walking to and fro.[79] Pugin found this for some reason astonishing. After the wedding no doubt he would want to work there all the time. 'This is very natural,' Pugin noted, taking the histrionic high ground again, 'how singularly things turn out what we expected would bind him to the work will be the means of taking him away from the study & perhaps eventually forcing us to give up the glass trade ... it is wonderful what changes take place as people grow up ...'[80] As pragmatic about other people's love affairs as he was passionate about his own, on 20 October Pugin noted that 'the wedding is tomorrow a good job over it will be quite private and as quiet as possible'.[81] It was the first wedding celebrated at St Augustine's, a modest affair, yet Pugin noted that 'the costumes [were] perfect'.[82] Jane, though so unwell, 'looked magnificent it was difficult to tell who was the bride'.[83] Afterwards the young couple set off for a short honeymoon, though not until Pugin had made Powell go back and get a mackintosh. After three days of heavy rain in Maidstone they came home to begin their married life.

While still meditating his book on rood screens, Pugin produced a short pamphlet on his other *idée fixe*, plainchant. In the years since he and Shrewsbury had stormed out of St Mary's, Derby, in protest against the Beethoven Mass, Pugin had not changed his mind about the use of music in churches. As usual he stayed up all night, writing in a fever of excitement to produce a 'strong dose' of invective against the *Rambler*, which was campaigning to introduce English hymns.[84] For Pugin there was no point in Catholic architecture unless the buildings were filled with the sound of Latin plainchant, the 'simple and divine song . . . which alone assimulates and harmonises with its lofty vaults and lengthened aisles'.[85] Here he and his friend John Lambert of Salisbury were out on a limb. The Ecclesiologists agreed that professional singers and singers' galleries, with their theatrical overtones, were not suitable for churches. But the use of English hymns, many of the greatest of which were written by the Tractarians, was an important part of their attempt to draw worshippers. It was the Oratorians with their modern Italianate services who most enraged Pugin, however. Newman shuddered when he read *An Earnest Appeal for the Revival of the Ancient Plain Song* and recommended to Faber a 'profound silence' as the best response.[86] Newman's horror was understandable. For all that Pugin lamented the divisions within the Church, he drew attention to them with his attacks on the Ultramontanes. Long passages from his pamphlet were reprinted by the Protestant magazine *English Churchman* under the title, 'Present State of public worship among the Roman Catholics'.

It was a particularly unlucky time to give such a hostage to fortune, for in the autumn of 1850 Catholicism became a national issue in England as it had not been since Emancipation. In April Pius IX had returned from exile to Rome. The once liberal-minded Pope was now 'a resolute conservative'.[87] By the summer the English Catholic press was full of predictions that Wiseman would be made a cardinal. He set off for Rome in August and many were glad to see him go. He was not, as Lingard wryly observed, 'in the odour of sanctity' in London.[88] His energy, his conspicuousness in public life and his growing impatience with the old English ways, as well as his high-handedness at times, had made him enemies. He was, however, determined to return. He had a mission to complete in England and no desire to stay at the Vatican for long. At the end of September it was announced that Rome had decided to restore the English hierarchy. Wiseman was to be Cardinal Archbishop of Westminster. He was fêted on a magnificent scale in Rome by 'all the tip top nobility who only mix amongst each other', as his proud mother put it.[89] The effect of the news on the English Catholics was less happy. Pugin and Newman for once agreed and many others were of the same mind. They thought the Church was not able to support a hierarchy: 'we are not ripe,' Newman wrote, 'they can't fill up the sees positively can't.'[90] To Pugin the Archbishopric was 'a dignity without support without a church . . . a grand elevation without anything to back it up'; 'the more I think of the hierarchy the more I feel dismayed . . . we have no materials for such a structure it is an assumption of a giant with the weakness of a dwarf'.[91]

Wiseman, however, was feeling neither weak nor dwarfish. He issued a pastoral letter, *From Without the Flaminian Gate*, which made matters infinitely worse. As the new Cardinal made his stately progress home across Europe, stopping to be congratulated en route, his letter was read, by his orders, from all the pulpits in the new Archdiocese: 'his Holiness was . . . pleased to appoint us, though most unworthy, to the Archiepiscopal See of Westminster . . . giving us at the same time the administration of the Episcopal See of Southwark. So that . . . we govern and shall continue to govern, the counties of Middlesex, Hertford and Essex, as Ordinary thereof, and those of Surrey, Sussex, Kent, Berkshire, and Hampshire, with the islands annexed, as Administrator with Ordinary jurisdiction.'[92] When Queen Victoria read it she is said to have enquired whether she was still Queen of England or not.[93] The Prime Minister, Lord John Russell, wrote to *The Times*, protesting at this 'aggression of the Pope' as 'insolent and insidious' and the press, lacking much other news, went wild in an orgy of anti-Popery.[94] Many Catholics were furious with their new Cardinal: 'this was not the work of Rome,' Shrewsbury wrote to Pugin, '[Wiseman] flattered himself that it would please Lord John to have a subject of the queen a Prince of the Church & . . . within sight of her Royal Abbey of Westminster.'[95] Anti-Catholicism burst out all over England, across all social classes, in the cities and in the provinces. There were popular gatherings on street corners and mass meetings in most towns. Editorials in *The Times* and caricatures in *Punch*, week after week, carried the same message. Lord John Russell warned that England might lose its right to 'freedom of opinion, civil, political and religious' if the 'fetters' of Catholicism were once more fastened upon it.[96] Lists were published of Catholics in positions of power, the governor of the Mint and the governor of Malta, all, it was implied, potential traitors.

Some of this was hysteria that would subside as quickly as it arose. But behind it lay mid-century England's growing sense of itself as a liberal Protestant power. The England of Prince Albert and the Great Exhibition did not feel the romantic pull of the olden times so strongly. The dream of 'reunion' with Rome that had faded through the 1840s now vanished. Between the Evangelical and High Church parts of the Established Church, a Liberal, Broad Church movement was emerging anxious that England, having escaped the Continental revolutions of 1848, should now avoid the reaction to those revolutions which had seen the Catholic Church reassert itself already in Belgium and Austria, as it would soon in France. In March the Judicial Committee of the Privy Council had delivered the 'Gorham Judgment', a direction to the Dean of Arches to induct the Revd George C. Gorham into the vicarage of Brampford Speke, in spite of his denial of the High Church doctrine of baptismal regeneration, a doctrine to which his Bishop insisted he should subscribe. Beyond its doctrinal significance the broader implications of the case were, as Lord Shrewsbury and many others realized, 'most *most* interesting'.[97] At issue was the State's right to overrule the Church. This was the issue which had prompted Keble's sermon on National Apostasy in 1833, the point of principle that had launched the Oxford Movement. There were fierce protests from the High Church party against the judgment itself and the assertion of secular authority, and although the protesters struck Shrewsbury as 'stronger & bolder than I had any idea of, as well as far more extensively organised', they did not prevail.[98] As he predicted, several of them would soon find they had no room left for manoeuvre in the Establishment.

The 'papal aggression' controversy began in late October. By 5 November the national mood was ugly. English Catholics were physically afraid. Pugin, who was in London, reported that the brewers' drays went round with 'no popery' on the casks.[99] On the bonfires that night Pius IX and Wiseman were burned alongside Guy Fawkes. So was Faber, who refused to close the Oratory, although he came to no harm as there was a police guard on the building and he rather enjoyed giving the officers dinner. Jane was at Ramsgate. There were anti-Catholic posters plastered everywhere 'like an election', and 'groups of people on the streets' loitered menacingly as dusk fell.[100] After dark a mob carrying an effigy of the Pope began to make its way towards the Grange. They were turned back by the police but Jane was 'much frightened'.[101] At

St Lawrence the Powells' house was splattered with excrement and daubed with graffiti. The worst of the hysteria blew itself out before long. Wiseman issued an emollient explanation of his pastoral which won many people round. The paper war, however, went on. *Punch* kept up its attack on Wiseman for months. The local press in Kent was vocal and there, as elsewhere, as Pugin had feared, it was his Catholic-minded Anglican friends who came in for the worst of it. Now was the time many people thought to kick out the High Church party and the Puseyites for good. 'The Church of England – if it is worried – should look to itself . . .' the *Herald* advised, 'let the Reformation be perfected . . . let the semi-popish pomps' be abandoned.[102] Public opinion was still sufficiently inflamed to demand legislation. In Ramsgate an open meeting generated 500 signatures for a petition to outlaw the hierarchy. Pugin issued a pamphlet of his own, taking the line that this was a question not of religion but of 'civil freedom'.[103] Thus, like many Catholics, he found himself, briefly, in agreement with Cobden and the Radicals. The Catholic press responded largely by becoming more Ultramontane, arguing that if England would always be hostile it was important to ally itself as closely as possible with Rome. 'Roman worship is the order of the day,' Pugin lamented. 'I will never live to finish my church & no one will do it after me.'[104] On 21 November Wiseman was enthroned at Southwark and the state did not totter, but the row was far from over.

Pugin's depression and agitation were deepening, intensified by the fear that his health was really broken. He was falling asleep '20 times of an evening' and his digestion was failing, 'I feel as if I [had] no inside like a wasp.'[105] He suffered now not only from sweats but from agonizing sore throats. Medical advice from 'a regular consultation of first rate men' was that he must avoid anxiety and overwork.[106] There was little chance of that, though Pugin said he would try. His desire to recover was at odds with his increasing desire to fit as much as possible into what might be left of his life. He took 'posset', a mixture of warm milk and spirits, and a cold bath every morning and the symptoms seemed to abate. By the winter he was working '17 hours a day'.[107] In the same letter he wrote, to Hardman, 'my days are numbered'.[108] He drove himself now as hard as he could, as if trying to get ahead of the death which, at thirty-eight, he could feel unmistakably approaching. Beside his house his church, incomplete, the tower still scaffolded, seemed to mirror its architect's perilous condition. On 25 November a great gale came up from the south-south-west. It loosened the scaffolding on the tower and Pugin to his horror saw 'the whole thing lifting up to windward', about to break away and crash through the roof at the east end.[109] It was a Sunday and there were no workmen on site. While they waited for help, Pugin and Edward pulled up 'at least 15 tons of stone' to weigh the planks down.[110] They carried it by hand across the cliff in the driving rain until with cold and exhaustion they were hardly able to walk. At the height of the storm Pugin was horrified to see Jane soaking wet and struggling to carry a huge stone. They may not yet have realized that she was pregnant, but her health in any case made it a rash attempt. Help arrived just in time. It was 'a wonderful sight' to see the men up by the tower struggling to make the scaffold fast as it rocked violently 'as if every moment was the last'.[111]

At sea the scene on the West Cliff was mirrored in the struggle of crewmen to save their ships as they drove on to the Goodwins and broke up. There were five on the night of the gale and not a trace of any of them by morning. The *Gazelle*, a brig of 242 tons, homeward bound from Sydney, was lost with all hands. The wreckage on land and sea was terrible and the *Caroline* was out, looking for salvage. Next day everyone was exhausted, stiff but unharmed, though Jane was 'poorly'.[112] Pugin was if anything exhilarated by the victory over the elements. The storm still raged. The house was leaking badly, Pugin complained he might as well live in a sieve, but the church was safe and the *Caroline* had salvaged eighteen tons of Russian tallow, which would pay for the damage. As the year approached its end, Pugin got down to work on the Great Exhibition and was now disappointed that there was not time to do more: 'it has wonderfully reduced itself,' he complained to the ever-patient Hardman, who had struggled to talk him into doing it at all.[113] '[It] reminds me of a story of a man who began to make a great image out of a tree but he got tired of it & said well I think I better give up this job & only work it into a *gate post*.'[114]

For the rest of the year the papal aggression controversy, as it had become known, went on in the press. Pugin's own opinions would have done nothing to reassure that part of middle England that doubted Catholics' loyalty: 'as for Loyalty I see very little left if thing go on as they do & if any Restrictions are placed on religious liberty I shall have none at all we have no attachment to any dynasty or house the Queen or King are useful people as a centre to keep things in order but nothing more & as long as I have my service I care not a farthing for any government I am ashamed of this country I am disgusted surely the wrath of God must be poured out and so it would before this only the Catholics themselves are such a wretched sort ... if I was a younger man I think I should emigrate.'[115] The Earl of Shrewsbury, who was in Italy, wrote that 'All Europe is astounded at the folly & bigotry of England.'[116] The disturbances had lost nothing in their retelling in the Continental press, and the Earl was glad to know his architect still had a head on his shoulders. He himself had lobbied Lord John Russell but thought there was no chance of winning him round: 'he has a soft pillow & a hard heart.'[117]

As Christmas approached there was not much seasonal spirit at Ramsgate. Relations with the studio were very low. The men wanted to go back to Birmingham for two weeks for the holidays, which Pugin thought an unwarrantable interruption. On the other hand, if he made them stay 'they will be like pigs and do nothing'. 'I daresay you will not believe me,' he told Hardman, 'I often entertain serious thought of selling all my property & trying to realise enough just to live on anywhere for I am worn out & sick of the whole thing.'[118] Jane in the early months of pregnancy was often tired, 'she fluctuates in the most extraordinary manner & generally dozes all the evening', Pugin commented.[119] His sore throat was agony and Jane thought Christmas in every way 'not so merry' as before.[120] Ever one for extremes, from his *Christmas Carol* of 1848 Pugin had transformed himself into Scrooge: 'I dont care,' he wrote, 'the less festivities the better a waste of money & vexation of spirit.' He faced the new year with grim resolve, 'intense exertion or death'.[121]

39

The Great Exhibition

January to October 1851

> *A blazing arch of lucid glass*
> *Leaps like a fountain from the grass*
> *to meet the sun!*
>
> — W. M. Thackeray, 1851

On New Year's Day Pugin was in London. He had arranged to meet Crace in Hyde Park and get his first sight of the Crystal Palace. The structure had been largely prefabricated off-site and had risen with eerie quietness through the summer and autumn. The iron columns, cast at Smethwick and brought to London by train, fitted together like sections of a telescope, rising in three identical storeys, all now glazed and ringing to the sound of 2,000 workmen making haste to finish. The Palace covered nineteen acres and was more than twice the length of the Palace of Westminster. Pugin realized it had been a mistake to try to meet Crace there, 'like making an appointment on Salisbury Plain', he wrote, having come home without finding him.[1]

The Crystal Palace was one of the most successful and admired British buildings ever. It has fascinated historians, who have seen in its innovative use of prefabrication an early example of what would become the preferred practice of modernism, and like Pugin himself it has been seen, misleadingly, as a pioneering example of the functionalist aesthetic. Pugin loathed the Crystal Palace. Although he had admired the railway stations in Germany he would not have cared to exhibit works of art in them. The Palace was, he thought, 'a great failure' because it was unsuitable for its purpose: 'the great length should have been arched . . . it is a capital place for plants but one might as well show pointed things in Trafalgar Square . . .'[2] He had doubts about the construction too. 'I can think of nothing but those angles at the transept,' he wrote to Crace, 'the braces they have put up are worth nothing I am very glad we have got a place a good way off . . . dont stand in that part.'[3]

The Exhibition was now eagerly anticipated all over Britain and far beyond. Lord Shrewsbury, who was wintering abroad, wrote with his usual ingenuous enthusiasm to ask how the 'glass palace' was coming on. 'I should have liked to have seen it filled with the works of the world . . . tell me all about it.'[4] On learning what Pugin thought of Paxton's efforts, in the course of a request to borrow back some of his work at Alton to exhibit, the Earl became rather discouraged, but agreed on condition that Pugin would be answerable for the damage to Shrewsbury's property if, as he predicted, the building was 'blown down altogether'.[5] Pugin now began to concentrate his mind on the question of filling the Mediaeval Court. He and Hardman made a selection of pieces, secular and ecclesiastical, that were either already in progress or could be borrowed back from sympathetic clients. The chandelier for the new dining room at Alton Towers was one of the grandest. Another, which showed off the joinery and carving skills of Pugin's operation, was a staircase designed for a house Pugin was fitting out, Horsted Place in Sussex. The wedding jewellery he had designed for Jane, a cabinet from the Grange, textiles, tiles, ceramic jardinières and garden seats all helped Pugin in his intention at the Great Exhibition, which was to promote his belief in Gothic as a style suitable for domestic as well as church use and affordable by the 'middling sort' as well as the upper ten thousand.

Since there was neither time nor money to make many pieces on spec, in the event the bulk of the display was ecclesiastical. It included altar plate and vestments, fittings from churches in progress, a large display of stained glass and the chancel screen for St Augustine's. Pugin was tempted, of course, despite his shortage of funds, to have things made that he could later buy for Ramsgate. Hardman did his best to restrain him. Among the objects that were created especially for the Court were two great tiled stoves made by Minton and Hardman and two pianos, commissioned by Burns and Lambert, a London firm that sold Hardman and Pugin's designs. Even Pugin found it difficult to Gothicize pianos and they became one of the leitmotivs in his litany of complaint about the Exhibition. Time was now short and so were tempers. Pugin and Hardman came as close to quarrelling as they ever could – 'What do you mean by saying *if* we had a factory of men to look after? . . . how many men do I look after? . . .' 'I have not the least idea about what to do about the catalogue it is too bad to come to me . . . what am I to say?'[6] – for all of which Pugin rather enjoyed the bustle and the theatrical aspect of the whole thing.

At the same time he was busy with London's other new Palace at Westminster. There was much to do if the Commons was to open in February 1852. The decorations for the corridors, the refreshment room, the libraries, the Commons lobby and the conference room as well as more furniture and sundry small items, letter racks, coat hooks and umbrella stands were all to be designed and made this year. Barry, at 'the nadir' of his fortunes in the whole troublesome job, was effecting, with Pugin's help, alterations to the ceiling of the Commons chamber which the MPs insisted would improve the acoustics, while Barry argued they would merely ruin the design.[7] Pugin rifled his library for emblems suitable for every corner of the building. Historic kings, boroughs, sees, seaports, for all of these he found crests, badges and images. Not all of them were historically correct but they gave the New Palace a depth of allusion, a richness of visual texture that nobody else could have achieved. It was very hard work. The patterns for the tiles were in themselves a huge task and Pugin got his children to help him with filling in the colours.

In newspapers and magazines and around the dinner tables of England, the Great Exhibition was now joined as a talking point by the Ecclesiastical Titles Bill. This was the tangible result of the previous year's anti-Catholic furore. It proposed to impose fines on any Catholic bishop or archbishop who claimed a see in British territory. Hastily conceived and objectionable in many ways, it passed its first reading on 14 February. A week later the government resigned in 'the oddest Cabinet crisis England has known'.[8] For ten days it proved impossible to form a new administration. The Whigs and the Conservatives were united in their support for the anti-Catholic legislation, but the Peelites, the supporters of Sir Robert Peel who had resigned in 1846 after the repeal of the Corn Laws, held the balance of power between the parties and they were opposed to the Ecclesiastical Titles Bill. While various attempts were made to form a government, pamphlets and open letters to Lord John Russell poured off the presses. Pugin and Shrewsbury were naturally among the authors. Shrewsbury was particularly pleased with his 'long and strong' letter 'to Johnny himself in propria persona', in which, he told Pugin, 'I give him the Devil in his wig. It seems to me the best thing I ever wrote.'[9] The letter is certainly long, 125 pages. Shrewsbury's most persuasive point, that the bill was an attempt to reassert control over religion at a time when 'every other state is relaxing its grasp', was submerged in a rehearsal of the wrongs of Mary Queen of Scots and the wickedness of Cranmer.[10] It seems unlikely that Lord John Russell would have had time or inclination to read much of it. Pugin's *Earnest Address on the Establishment of the Hierarchy* created a rather greater stir. He too argued against state control over religious affairs. Beyond that, however, he touched hardly at all, directly, on the bill. His main subject, one which was coming once again to dominate his ideas, was the reconciliation of Catholics and Anglicans, 'our separated countrymen' as he called them, among whom were so many of his closest friends and most of his supporters.[11]

The *Earnest Address* was a return to the High Church view of the Reformation that Pugin had first absorbed in childhood from the 'truly edifying and reverent works' of Dugdale and the other Stuart antiquaries who had never considered their Church 'a newly created body' but part of 'a strictly continuous succession'.[12] Setting out the argument he had learned from the *Monasticon Anglicanum*, Pugin explained that it was not Protestants but the Catholic bishops themselves who had 'sacrificed the liberty of the English church at one blow' by giving in to Henry VIII.[13] Unlike Shrewsbury, however, he did not dwell on the past. To count up the 'burnings and bowellings' that had been carried out by both sides was only to fuel resentment and 'lead men to become cruel . . . from a very hatred of cruelty'.[14] Like all Pugin's writings, this apparent disquisition on history and theology was a highly personal statement of faith and intent. In his religious as in his artistic creed, Pugin no longer wanted to look back to the past. He knew now that his first view of the Middle Ages had been sentimental and he abandoned it with typical abruptness. Indeed the whole vision of *Contrasts* – 'pleasant meadows, happy peasants, merry England . . . bread cheap and beef for nothing, all holy monks, all holy priests – holy everybody such charity, and such hospitality, and such unity, when every man was a Catholic' – was rejected. 'I once believed in this utopia myself,' he noted, as if with surprise, 'but when tested by stern facts and history it all melts away like a dream . . . the people were barbarous, the customs were barbarous, the traditions were barbarous.'[15] In one sense it was a declaration of disillusionment. The ideal on which he had once based his life's work had vanished. But it was also a cry of liberation. It looked forward to an age in which religion might be freer and better, in which Catholics might be united with 'those good and earnest souls who yet man the shattered bark of England's church'.[16]

Contrasts had caught the mood of 1836 when England was 'dinned with philanthropy and revolution'. The *Earnest Address* was as much a reflection of 1851, of High Victorian confidence and optimism. It was also, however, unorthodox. Pugin refused to believe that 'the Church of England, since the accession of Elizabeth, is a mere imposture and a sham', and he thereby implied that Anglican orders were valid, that Anglican priests were as much part of the direct apostolic succession as their Catholic counterparts.[17] This was a question on which the Vatican did not pronounce until 1896 and it was certainly not one for a layman to decide. Perhaps the only thing that could have alarmed the beleaguered Cardinal Wiseman just now more than the pamphlet itself was the promise on the inside front cover of Pugin's next work 'preparing for press': 'A new view of an old subject the English Schism impartially considered'. Pugin finished the *Earnest Address* in his usual state of feverish excitement: 'all the difficulties the doubts the anxiety I had to understand the decay of the church ... are now removed everything is explained all is cleared away ...' he told Hardman, 'nobody knows what I have suffered till I could clear up all the difficulties of the Reformation etc.'[18] The pain that he had felt as he saw the Catholic Church move away from the Gothic Revival was terrible. It was for him the agony of seeing division where there could be no distinction, only the terrible tearing apart of all that he loved and hoped for. His was, he told Phillipps, if 'a new view', nevertheless 'true as scripture'.[19]

The pamphlet provoked instant and violent reaction among his co-religionists. 'A Catholic Priest' in the *Tablet* accused Pugin of being a 'Puseyite'.[20] The patronizing Father Thomas reprimanded him as 'a nice young man' who had got out of his depth.[21] All his opponents were Catholic and all his supporters, beyond his own friends, Anglican. Gladstone wrote to congratulate him. Benjamin Webb and Butterfield supported him. Among 'our people', as Pugin grumbled to Hardman, who was himself rather nervous about the *Earnest Address*, most were 'narrow-minded'.[22] 'I have been told from very good authority that I am marked out . . . as a troublesome person to be put down . . .'[23] Newman certainly was now actively manoeuvring to get some official steps taken against Pugin. None were, and it seems likely that it was Wiseman who protected him. Without his intervention the *Earnest Address* might have been put on the Index of books forbidden to Catholics. Perhaps Wiseman came to an agreement with Pugin that he would not publish his proposed sequel. Certainly it never appeared.

Instead it was Ruskin who once again took the initiative. The first volume of his *Stones of Venice* appeared at the beginning of March, at the height of the cabinet crisis. In the debates that dominated the early months of 1851 design and politics, religious freedom, architecture and the modern city were all intermingled, for all were expressions of England's growing self-consciousness on the world stage. In *The Stones of Venice* Ruskin presented a study not just of art but of a great secular city state of the past, offering it as a model to the present. To the surprise of many readers he also included a violent attack on Pugin. Since the publication of *Seven Lamps*, people had commented on the similarity between Ruskin's ideas and Pugin's. Ruskin in fact owed almost nothing to Pugin, though they had much in common, and he was infuriated by the comparison.[24] He was, at this stage of his life, militantly anti-Catholic. Moreover, he resented the suggestion that his intensely subjective writings, the outpourings of his own curious inner life, were anything but original.

The Appendix to *The Stones of Venice*, 'Romanist Modern Art', was extraordinarily spiteful. 'One might have put this man under a pix, and left him, one should have thought; but he has been brought forward, and partly received, as an example of the effect of ceremonial splendour on the mind of a great architect. It is very necessary, therefore, that all . . . should know at once that he is not a great architect, but one of the smallest possible or conceivable architects.'[25] Ruskin made the mistake Newman had so carefully avoided. He lost his temper with Pugin in public and as a result drew attention to the very thing he wanted to deny, the similarity between them. Reviewers disliked his tone. Henry Cole's *Journal of Design* thought that 'Mr Ruskin has followed out a course of analysis very similar to that adopted by Mr Pugin' and so was in no position to make 'such unnecessarily disparaging remarks'.[26] It dismissed his architectural writing as 'complicated second-rate analysis'.[27] Even Ruskin's friend Coventry Patmore protested at the 'unmixed 'wrath' against Pugin, whose precursorship 'might be considered as constituting a claim to more merciful treatment'.[28]

Pugin apparently paid little attention. It was remembered in the family that when asked about Ruskin, 'he merely said: "Let the fellow build something himself" and then turned back to his work'.[29] The story has the ring of truth. Pugin was much more exercised about the Oratorians, against whom he continued to wage war, and about rood screens. The early spring saw the publication of his long-planned book on the subject, *A Treatise on Chancel Screens and Rood Lofts, Their Antiquity, Use, and Symbolic Signification*. Involving itself in an always obscure and now almost opaque controversy, it is one of his least-read works. It too, however, made a contribution at the time to the questions that exercised so many minds. It contained Pugin's latest thoughts on the subject of urban churches, the debate about which continued and had now spread across the fence from the *Rambler* to the *Ecclesiologist*. There it had elicited a letter on 'The Proper Characteristics of a Town Church' from the young George Edmund Street. Street was a pupil of Scott and one of the brightest of the rising generation. His letter was one of the most influential architectural statements of the century. In it he complained that the Puginian model which was multiplying at such a rate was essentially rural and neither practical nor impressive in a city. He suggested instead the use of height and light from clerestories and continuous rooflines with no external division between nave and chancel.

Whether Pugin had read Street or not before he wrote his *Treatise* is unclear, but he largely shared his views. Indeed these were the ideas he had begun to put into practice in his own church of St Mary's, Liverpool, of 1842. He too dismissed the Puginian model of 'Low churches built of rubble walls with broach spires' as rustic and 'quite out of place ... among the lofty mansions and scenery of a great city', arguing instead for height and power in urban architecture.[30] He had never built such a church in a city himself, but many of his followers had and his explicit rejection of the idea marked another point at which Pugin and Puginism were out of joint.

The *Treatise* was also, like everything else he wrote now, an attack on Newman. Adapting Montalembert's classification of different kinds of Vandal, Pugin described the four sorts of 'Ambonoclast' or screen destroyer: the Calvinist, the Pagan, the Revolutionary and the Modern. The Moderns were the Oratorians, whom he characterized as 'several old women of both sexes', who, sitting in 'an edifice . . . like a fish-market', attempted to 'realize a somewhat Italian atmosphere' in England.[31] He had as usual been conducting his polemical activities in the midst of all his other work. Crace was canvassed for his opinion about a review of Pugin's *Earnest Address* in the *Morning Post* at the end of a letter about stencil patterns for Westminster. Hardman, who was flustered both by the Exhibition and by the uproar which his friend had once again created, was lectured on the virtues of Archbishop Parker, on whose consecration in 1559 much of Pugin's argument depended, in among suggestions for a new catalogue of metalwork designs.

Eventually the government crisis was resolved. Lord John Russell formed a new, if fragile government and the Ecclesiastical Titles Bill pursued its tortuous course. Each reading was passed eventually and each time as the rhetoric of the bill was inflated its actual scope was reduced. At Ramsgate meanwhile, despite Pugin's confidence in his visions for the future of the greater Catholic Church, he was finding it difficult to support his own efforts. The costs were rising and controversy was not cheap. His printing expenses for the year came to £150. Father Costigan's lack of refinement continued to grate. He used a pocket handkerchief for a chalice veil, changed his boots in the sacristy and used the sacrarium as a chamber pot. He preached the same sermon four times running: 'it is dreadful', Pugin complained to Hardman, 'the same sermon the same anecdotes & everything'.[32] When the Bishop of Clifton came to take vespers Father Costigan suddenly varied his repertoire and preached on 'stomachs and food', which Jane found embarrassing.[33] Pugin wanted his own resident priest as soon as the presbytery he was building between the church and the house was finished. In the studio Powell was more than usually vague. 'It is a most curious thing I cant get [him] to think at all about what he does,' Pugin noted, 'he makes beautiful drawings but they dont fit the places they are intended to fill & he does all sorts of extraordinary things.'[34] Perhaps Powell's abstraction was due to his wife's being newly pregnant. Casolani was another cause for concern. He was, now Pugin reported, actually 'starving', and 'in a state of despair', having run up debts locally until he was afraid to go out, for he had fathered a 'poor illegitimate child'.[35]

Pugin was slow to condemn, perhaps in no position to, and ready with help, but he was dismayed by the situation. 'I have relieved his present wants but I must try to get him clear I will never have anything to do [with] a foreigner as long as I live.'[36] But it was no time for reflection. The Exhibition deadline was drawing on and as Pugin reminded Hardman, 'the month is flying by'.[37] The Mediaeval Court, which was under construction by the beginning of March, took Pugin back to his days at Covent Garden. It was essentially a stage set. Made of framed canvas and papered, it was designed to screen out the rest of the Palace as much as to form a backdrop for the work itself. Pugin was too busy to worry about his True Principles. The hanging pieces went in first to get them out of the way and, in another echo of Covent Garden days, the boatman from Ramsgate was seconded to Hyde Park to 'set the Landyards up & make all taut'.[38] Myers made the prefabricated glass cases, which Pugin designed so that they would go up 'like clockwork' on site.[39] Hardman was now working so hard on the Exhibition that his other orders were suffering. Barry was finding it increasingly difficult to get the fittings for the Palace of Westminster out of the Birmingham works. The lobby windows were urgently wanted and Pugin was having to 'lie . . . like Figaro' on his friend's behalf: 'it is dreadful,' he wrote to him, 'if you could send him up half a design it would quiet him a little'.[40] Myers was going slowly and Pugin could do nothing to budge him. 'I might as well try to work on the Rock of Gibralter,' 'I begin to think [he] will never be finished,' he moaned to Hardman.[41] 'I cant get him to finish a single thing there they lie day after day uncarved, undecorated, & then it all spoiling at the last.'[42] The worst offender, however, was Minton, who suddenly announced that he would not be showing very much in the Mediaeval Court after all. He had left his preparations too late and was concentrating on his own exhibit in the ceramics section. The tiles for the great stoves, which Pugin had designed to be a major feature of the Court, were so much delayed at Stoke that Hardman had to tell Pugin there would be no time to galvanize the iron frames. Should he, he asked in a moment of panic, gild them instead? 'It would be rediculous . . . rediculous,' Pugin wrote back, to have such large structures gilt; the effect would be elephantine.[43]

'It is infamous of Minton . . . I am the only man that looks ahead Myers would not be in the mess he is in if he had taken my advice Minton is the worst I ever met for getting on . . . the stoves must go in the iron & they better be black leaded up . . . we shall look like fools if we have nothing to show finished after all the boasting . . . those humbugs Burns and Lambert have not got the guts of that infernal Piano in the place so . . . I expect that job will be doomed . . .'[44] This was not exactly the smooth operation that Cole had envisaged in the *Journal of Design*, the hundred hands and the single controlling head, but neither were matters so bad as Pugin painted them. Indeed, having been for so long under-employed, he was rather exhilarated. Even the pianos had their humorous side. Lambert threatened to exhibit the grand in the musical instrument section rather than the Mediaeval Court: 'he says there will be nobody to play on it,' Pugin explained to Crace, 'unless you stop there all day & give selections from Rossini etc.[45] I can't play nor Myers either & I don't think Minton would be very brilliant so it falls to you to delight the astonished circle of admirers.'[46]

It was a stormy spring and Pugin was half dreading and half hoping that the Palace would leak. It did, but not too badly. The setting up of the Mediaeval Court began later in March, and the difficulties and anxieties of Pugin and his collaborators were then merged in the greater tumult, the near pandemonium that reigned throughout the building. At the eye of the storm was Henry Cole, directing exhibitors, cajoling the police, who wanted 750 men on site but were argued down to 400, and seeing to the vast number of other arrangements. In its organization, as in so many of its aspects, the Great Exhibition was a model for the new age. In Pugin's childhood public events were not expected to be either safe or sanitary. Two people were killed at the peace celebrations in St James's Park in 1814 when Nash's pagoda caught fire, but very little was said about it. Pugin's father had produced an aquatint to commemorate the festivities with no reference to their disastrous end. This was not to be the Victorian way. At the Crystal Palace there were fire precautions, public lavatories, refreshment rooms and press facilities.

Most exhibitors complained about the spaces they were given. Cole was assisted by one Colonel Reid, whose almost permanent job it was to pacify 'enraged and frantic' participants, '(the foreigner particularly)', and reconcile everyone to the various places they thought to be too dark, too small or too far from the centre.[47] The Mediaeval Court was in a prime position, but even so Earley had to deal with the Coalbrook Founders on one side, whose fenders were encroaching on Pugin's space, and complaints from the other side that Crace's hangings were blocking out the light. The Queen's several visits to the Palace were highly gratifying. Earley was one day overwhelmed to find himself 'a dirty painter holding conversation with our Sovereign Lady the Queen for some five minutes or more' but at the same time the protocol involved meant that they tended to hold up preparations.[48] Myers still failed to deliver the larger pieces: 'I have done all that a human being can do,' Pugin told Hardman, 'but you know what a Pig he is . . .'[49]

As the set-up went on, reviews of Pugin's *Earnest Address* were still appearing while the debates continued in Parliament on the Ecclesiastical Titles Bill. Many of the protagonists, including Lord John Russell himself, sat on the Exhibition Royal Commission, and distant echoes of the controversy were audible amid the clangour in the Crystal Palace. Among the hanging objects that Pugin had installed first was the rood for St Edmund's, Ware. The sight of the great crucifix in the otherwise empty Court lit a trail of rumour that a Roman Catholic chapel was being built in the middle of the Great Exhibition. 'We have just escaped a regular break up,' Pugin wrote in panic to Hardman. 'If I had not been in London I don't know what would have happened.'[50] But for Cole the row was all in a day's work. 'Lord Granville came & said A Kinnaird had reported to Lord Ashley who had written to Lord John Russell abt the Crucifix. Reid sent Ld G my letter to Pugin . . .' he noted in his diary.[51] The next day he wrote, 'Pugin & Crace came & agreed to lower the Cross.'[52] Another minor crisis had been defused.

Less than a week before the grand opening, Earley reported that Lord John himself had visited the Court. Despite all the invective that he and Pugin had poured out against one another in principle, they got on perfectly well in person. They talked 'for ¾ hour' and the Prime Minister 'expressed his delight at the Beautiful production of our manufactory'.[53] At the end of March there was a strike at the Palace, and in the middle of April Cole threatened to use the army to take down the scaffolding whether the decorators had finished or not. In the Mediaeval Court there were other difficulties. When Myers finally produced his contribution it transpired that the centrepiece was an oak cabinet of his own design. This 'elaborate' object, a present for his son, was carved with 'various tools used in masonry, ornamentally disposed with foliage'.[54] In order to ensure that nobody should mistake his masterpiece for a work of Crace's firm, Myers nailed his trade card (one of 10,000 he had had printed especially for the Exhibition) prominently on the front. Crace was furious to see his cabinet-making upstaged by Myers's heftier handiwork and large advertisement. Myers as usual would not budge and so Hardman and Pugin had to volunteer to move their own work round instead.

In the end, although the ceremony did not go quite without a hitch, it was all right on the night, or rather the warm May day of the opening. Three hundred thousand people made their way to Hyde Park. The Queen, with the somewhat over-tired Prince Consort at her side, declared the Exhibition open and the strains of Handel's Hallelujah Chorus filled the Crystal Palace.

The press and public opinion were overwhelmingly favourable to the Mediaeval Court. The *Illustrated London News* was especially lavish in its tributes. 'To Mr Pugin . . . who furnished the design for this gorgeous combination, is the highest honour due; and he has marvellously fulfilled his own intention of demonstrating the applicability of Mediaeval art in all its richness and variety to the uses of the present day.'[55] During the first week of the Exhibition Crace rearranged and thinned out the display, which, after all Pugin's fears of there being nothing to show, was actually rather crowded. Once that was done the wallpapers and hangings in rich colours and bright patterns, Minton's jardinières planted with red and white roses and the glass cases of domestic china and jewellery were a fine spectacle. There was nothing like it in the Crystal Palace, or in the world. No other designer had such a coherent understanding of so many forms and media and the overall effect was striking. The solemnity of vestments and the glow of stained glass beside the cheerfulness of tea cups and drawing room carpets embodied Pugin's vision of home and hearth and God. It was a vision that appealed powerfully to the mid-Victorian mind. The great social upheavals of the first half of the century, the life of the cities, 'a system of life constructed on a wholly new principle' and the worrying condition of England had posed difficult questions to the expanding middle class.[56] Morally and socially they were finding reassuring answers in church-going and church-building, in the creation of respectable suburbs, the upholding of family life and even more perhaps the ideal of home, a warm and comfortable haven, reassuringly bright amid the smoke and the fog. At the beginning of his career, in *Contrasts*, Pugin had been among the first to put these questions and over the succeeding fifteen years he had answered them, creating in his architecture not only the Victorian church, but a new kind of family house for the modern railway age. Now, at the Great Exhibition, he showed that he could furnish it as well.

On the train to Birmingham he overheard people talking about the Court and praising it, 'I sitting as a perfect stranger.'[57] After years of rejection and failure he was genuinely surprised by the response his work aroused. It was, in fact, the first time that the public had seen it on any scale. His role at the Palace of Westminster had been obscured; the houses he furnished were for priests or private clients. Now, as a designer, he appeared to burst forth fully formed. The *Annales Archéologiques*, from the distance of the Continent, envied Pugin's apparent ability to rise above religious differences: 'Catholique, il est recherché des anglicans et des puseystes', while pointing out that of course he was, by birth and talent half French.[58] The *New-York Ecclesiologist* paid Pugin the backhanded compliment that summer of complaining that he was too influential, too much copied for the health of modern architecture.[59] It was a very different view of him and his position from that which Pugin himself, short of work, short of money and surrounded by critics, usually took. Once open, the Exhibition had to be judged and prizes and medals awarded. There was a system of juries and Pugin was appointed as a judge for Class XXX: Sculpture, Models and Plastic Art. This was to be the most important of the judging committees. At its meetings over the first weeks of the summer Pugin was, for the first time, playing a role in public life commensurate with his achievements and abilities.

In between meetings, however, old troubles beset him and new ones arose. Jane's second pregnancy was far advanced and had been even more difficult than the first. She had been depressed, 'below par' as well.[60] Pugin had reported to Hardman that she 'gives way to the lowest spirits & does not rally all day . . . I cant rouse her at all.'[61] While Jane dozed much of the time, Powell and Anne drove Pugin 'wild' with their carelessness about paperwork and he began to fear that Edward was getting ideas of his own and thinking of leaving his father.[62] Pugin's health had only just held up during the preparations for the Exhibition. He had been put on a reducing diet, which he felt made him worse. 'I am so weak that I fall asleep at all hours with pains in all my limbs . . . I am helpless at night by 8 o clock.'[63] Myers, whose own appetite was legendary, advised him to go back to 'regular and constant supping'.[64] Pugin was suffering still from 'perspirations', getting through three shirts a day: 'literally dripping I cant understand it the moment I begin to walk the water pours off me,' he complained.[65] Money was a perpetual and growing source of anxiety. 'I was mad ever to make so large a house & place as I have – someday I shall have to leave it altogether,' he lamented, not for the first time.[66] Meanwhile he decided to take drastic measures. 'I have made up my mind to get rid of a lot of useless & costly things tending only to vanity . . . I now regret most bitterly all the foolery & delusions under which I previously laboured as long as things are clean & warm in winter & cool in summer the rest is indifferent.'[67] He decided to let the garden, which had been one of his greatest expenses, run wild.

With the Exhibition work completed there was nothing much new in prospect. At Northampton the bishop had been obstructed in his attempt to buy land for the new cathedral. Charles Scott Murray had fallen out with Pugin about a chapel in his house because 'he expected so much for so little', while the heirs of Lord Midleton were threatening to sue him for not building the model town in Ireland.[68] Apparently 'an architects estimate is a contract in . . . the Emerald Isle of thieves & humbugs', Pugin told Hardman.[69] As the weeks went by he blew hot and cold about the Mediaeval Court. Sometimes it seemed splendid, at others a waste of time. It 'cost me no end of money . . . which will never earn a copper farthing'.[70] The *Caroline* had also earned little recently; every post brought the threat of a letter from Captain Hibbert and the stained glass orders were behind. In between meetings of the Jury the early summer passed as usual on the road. Pugin was at Alton and Birmingham. There was talk of a new cathedral at Shrewsbury and there was the usual trip to Ireland, to Dublin and Maynooth. Pugin wrote somewhat wanly to Jane from Holyhead, 'no husband can love his wife dearer than I do & I believe I have the most affectionate wife possible'.[71] It was a rough crossing and a trying visit. He felt weak and decided that he really must 'give up this Irish business'.[72] He never went back. When the prizes for the Exhibition were announced, the Jury for Class XXVI, in which the Mediaeval Court was included, gave it no award. Myers, Hardman, Crace and Minton were all prizewinners in their own categories but Pugin's display got nothing. This was a result of the classification system, into which Pugin, as a designer rather than a manufacturer, did not fit. He did not feature as the maker of any single object, but he was terribly disappointed. His moment of triumph he thought was over, another bubble burst. 'The court is cut out altogether as not containing a single object worthy of any consideration and our glass is . . . not even worth looking at . . . just what I expected,' he reported to Hardman.[73]

In his capacity as a judge, however, he was able to do some cutting of his own, which pleased him. The Jury for Class XXX included the hated Cockerell, who, Pugin complained, swore classical oaths, 'by the body of Bacchus, etc.' There was also John Gibson the sculptor, Anthony Panizzi, Keeper of Printed Books at the British Museum, and the artist Richard Redgrave. Redgrave was Henry Cole's closest friend and ally in the campaign for national art education and design reform. He was also a great, if not uncritical, admirer of Pugin. They found they had much in common and when the final decisions were made Pugin and Redgrave 'beat the Pagans hollow':[74] 'lots of sculptures were set on one side dont hint at this as we are sworn to secrecy,' Pugin at once told Jane.[75] There was only one more meeting and then a grand dinner at Holland House, to which Pugin after this 'great victory' was rather looking forward. The last meeting was 'very stormy' but no ripple of dissent was allowed to show in the Jury's final report.[76] It did, however, include a special note to the effect that 'The Jury gladly seize the opportunity which now offers itself of rendering justice to the taste displayed by their colleague Mr Pugin in the arrangement of the Mediaeval Court in the Exhibition.'[77] Under the present system it was the most that could be done, but Redgrave, Cole and others were already looking beyond the Exhibition and its narrow classifications. They had ambitious plans for the arts in Britain, plans in which Pugin figured prominently.

On 29 June, after an anxious delay, Jane gave birth to a son, Edmund Peter, Pugin's eighth child. 'My dearest Jane doing well,' he noted in his diary, 'for which thanks be to God for this and all mercies.'[78] Edmund, later known as Peter Paul, was the last of Pugin's children, the baby in an extensive family. His eldest half-sister, Anne, was now nineteen and settled at St Lawrence. The rest were still at home. Louisa's children, Edward, Agnes, Cuthbert, Catherine and Mary, were sixteen, fourteen, ten, eight and seven, while Edmund's only full sibling, Margaret, was just twenty months old. With Pugin's dislike of servants and her own fragile health, it was no wonder that Jane often felt overwhelmed by her domestic responsibilities. Two weeks after the birth Pugin was in London for the dinner at Lord Holland's, which was 'very good' but he did not care for 'such fine cooking'.[79] The next day, when he was planning to set off for the Continent with Hardman, he felt so ill he could not think of travelling, 'I have no strength in my legs,' he reported, yet in the event he was off almost immediately and spent two weeks in France and

Belgium looking at glass and metalwork.[80] The sketches he made on this trip tended to simplify and smooth out the medieval originals, making them easier to reproduce and more acceptable to Victorian taste. His success at the Exhibition and his continuing failure as an architect combined to make him think of himself, increasingly, as a designer for manufacture. When he sent the drawings to Hardman in the autumn he was quite specific: 'you will distinctly understand that you are to leave out such details as are too costly & do exactly as you like with them transposing the feet or knops . . . to suit your means & the readiness with which you get them up . . . they are sent to you as material which the master hand of the goldsmith will arrange and distribute . . . add or omit everything according to the customers & the price.'[81] From now on Pugin urged Hardman, as he urged Crace, to work on ready-made lines: 'in addition to things absolutely ordered we have to create a stock of useful articles which are constantly required in churches & only want making to sell . . . The whole of this could be managed in a small shop quite independent of anything else 2 joiners & a carver would do everything . . .'[82] His failing health was another reason to build up the design side of his practice, for 'though . . . crippled in body' he could still draw '& I can keep up the supply in every way'.[83] He seems by now to have lost any hope of a complete recovery.

While Pugin was away, the Ecclesiastical Titles Bill finally passed its third reading. Its provisions were now much reduced and no prosecutions were brought under them. Yet the effects of the legislation and the controversy that surrounded it were palpable. Together with the Gorham Judgment of the previous year, the new law made it clear that there was little future now within the Church of England for the Puseyites. There was another wave of conversions, the greatest since 1845. The Archdeacon of Chichester, Henry Manning, later Cardinal Manning, was the most prominent. He was joined by many of the clergy at Pusey's own church of St Saviour's, Leeds. It was in one sense a great advance for English Catholicism. For those who welcomed all conversions, like Shrewsbury, it was cause for simple rejoicing. But these latest converts would do nothing to heal the internal divisions among Catholics. In Manning Newman would find a rival far more formidable than Pugin. For Pugin himself, and those like him who hoped for a closer union between Anglicans and Catholics, it was a reverse that amounted to defeat. Pugin's last unfinished pamphlet, for which he left some notes, was to have been an *Apology for the Separated Church of England*. Had he lived to complete it it would anyway have come too late. The High Victorian Church of England was predominantly the Broad Church, the Liberal-Protestant faith of Prince Albert. Wiseman found himself after 1850 less welcome in London society than he had been in the 1840s, while the converts of 1851 by their departure from the Established Church stepped outside the stream of national life. Theirs has been called 'a self-elimination, a secession, an emigration at home'.[84]

In August Pugin went up to Alton, where Shrewsbury told him to go to St Wilfrid's and clear out all the Italianate 'trash' the Oratorians had left there.[85] After a fraught correspondence with Bishop Ullathorne it had been agreed that the church should be handed over to the Passionists, who would use it as the Earl wished. Shrewsbury, now as disgusted with Newman and Faber as Pugin was, felt he had been exploited. As Pugin went to reclaim St Wilfrid's he also went to look, for the first time in three years, at St Giles's, Cheadle. Yet again he changed his mind about it: 'it looks magnificent,' he told Jane, 'it is a very glorious building & stands capitally I assure you it quite astonished me . . .'[86] But it was a cold, rainy summer and to that, or to sleeping in a damp bed, Pugin attributed the terrible pains in his back and legs and the fever that dogged him as he went. He knew, however, that this was something worse than a chill. He admitted to Jane that he was in a 'wretched state of health altogether as soon as I leave home something comes on'.[87] One minute he would feel 'capable of starting for any point of the inhabitable globe' and a couple of hours later be on the sofa 'done brown', the exhaustion coming and going with strange suddenness.[88] By now his whole system was 'so shaken' by what was diagnosed as 'nervous fever' that he could hardly work.[89] The doctors made various suggestions. He declined to take up riding but agreed to consider walking – though it seemed a waste of time. He began to have violent headaches and what he described as slight 'fits' of narcolepsy. He would fall suddenly unconscious for a short period, once blotting a letter to Hardman as he fell on it for a moment or two. One day without warning he lost his memory. For about two hours, Jane reported, he had no idea of who or where he was. Despite these puzzling and alarming symptoms, Pugin carried on as much as possible regardless. Dr Daniel and Hardman recommended rest, but got little thanks for their trouble. 'If I was to follow your advice

& lie by reading novels . . . I should soon come to an end,' Pugin snapped back.[90]

The more ill he became, the more restless he was and the more frantic to impose order on his work. His anxiety was vented on those around him. The beam in the Mediaeval Court fell down and Earley got the blame, which he felt was so unfair that he actually took the rope down to Ramsgate to prove it had been perfectly good. Hardman was lectured on 'procrastination', and Pugin was at his wits' end with Edward, who was doing his best but got into scrapes and miscalculated the postage and was, his father thought, 'wholly unfit' to carry out any kind of business.[91] Two of the servants left, creating more disorder. 'The whole place is turned upside down & we cant get settled or even eatable victuals.'[92] Then the nurse went too. With two babies and no help, Pugin discovered the practical disadvantages of his design for the Grange, with its interconnecting spaces. 'I have made a horrid mistake in building this house,' he complained to Hardman, 'there are no nurseries cut off from the rest the consequence is that living in a Pig market is less terrible the perpetual screams that proceed in succession from every room in the house are distracting . . . incessant powerful screeching . . . oh dear. & to design gas fittings in this.'[93] The church was as difficult to maintain as the house. Father Costigan, who if unsophisticated was no fool, pointed out with justice that it was all very well having 'the feasts of Constantine the great' but it was a pity Pugin had 'not his means of raising funds'.[94]

It was not until September that Jane felt well enough to go up to London and see the Exhibition. It was to close on 11 October and it was starting to look tired. There was a general sense of anticlimax. Hardman Powell also went up for a 'last look'. 'I had scarcely seen it before our time was so short. It looks very shabby now and the people seem very careless everybody is quite tired and wishes it done.'[95]

40

The Whole Machinery of the Clock

October 1851 to February 1852

*I know it is all over with me . . . but I will draw for you till the
break up as they coil up ropes till the ship strikes . . .*
                                                    – Pugin to John Hardman, late 1851

In London the dispiriting work of taking down the Exhibition went on,
while life at Ramsgate offered little consolation. With the approach of
winter Jane's health declined. She was too weak to breastfeed and Pugin
enquired anxiously of Suzanne Crace about the merits of manufactured
baby food. He himself continued to suffer, 'tumbling asleep' on his
drawing board every half hour.[1] Dr Daniel was mystified and like many
doctors at the end of their diagnostic resources began to blame the
patient: 'all [his] comfort is that I am an Example of a man who has
lived 60 years in 40 & is now suffering for it,'[2] Pugin wrote wearily to
Hardman. His mother had said the same when he was twenty, a long
life in a short one. His general health must have suffered from his refusal
to rest. He had worms and piles. A degree of self-neglect had been
manifest for some time in his dishevelled, sometimes dirty appearance.
How much this aggravated his condition, how much it was itself symptomatic, is impossible to know, but Pugin's interludes of health were
getting shorter and the episodes of illness more severe. His symptoms
also suggest that he was suffering now from a hyperthyroid condition.
Writing to Hardman about where the Crystal Palace exhibits were to
go, he signed himself 'ever thine most miserably' adding a pathetic
postscript in a weak hand: 'I cant design anything just now,' and ending
simply 'oh dear'.[3]

He had told Henry Cole that he was too unwell to contribute to the
supplementary reports which the Jury for Class XXX was to produce,

despite which, when the reports appeared in September and November, Pugin's name figured prominently in them. The reports were a manifesto for design reform that made it clear that the closure of the Exhibition was not an end but the springboard for a great new beginning. Lessons were to be learned. It was apparent, the jury reported, that for all Britain's pre-eminence in industrial production, its manufactured goods were sadly lacking in quality of design. 'It is in the "Crystal Palace" that the great truth has been impressed upon us that art and taste are hence forth to be considered as elements of industry and trade of scarcely less importance than the most powerful machinery.'[4] 'The foundation of a permanent industrial Museum in the heart of the metropolis [would be] the logical and practical consequence.'[5]

To launch this national programme it was decided that a selection should be made of the best objects in the Exhibition. These would be purchased by the government for the new Museum. It was the beginning of what became, in time, the Victoria and Albert, which was itself the hub of the greater South Kensington project, the national complex of museums and schools for the arts. On 7 October, just before the Exhibition closed, Pugin managed to get up to London, feeling for the moment slightly better. There he discovered that he was one of the selectors responsible for choosing the national collection. He was surprised and terribly excited: 'what was my astonishment,' he wrote straight away to Hardman, 'to find myself regularly appointed one of the 4 men who are [to] decide what is to be purchased ... the others who are with me most reasonable men & we shall get on but it shows well after all I have written and said that I should [be] selected to fill so important an office we have 20000 to lay out but this is between ourselves – by George if you were [to] see how they cut about & bow when we approach it is astonishing I am very weak to day but not worse & I dare say I shall pull through'.[6] As he added in a postscript, 'Cockerell is out of this.'[7] A new generation, Pugin's generation, was taking over. His fellow selectors were his slightly older contemporaries: Cole, the driving force of the Exhibition, his friend Richard Redgrave the artist, who was Inspector General for Art and who later became Principal of the Government Schools of Design, and Owen Jones, the architect best known for his skill in interior decoration and for the colour theory which had dictated the appearance of the Crystal Palace. Their ideas were largely in sympathy with Pugin's and had been to some degree formed by them. A decade after *True Principles* was published, its readers were moving into positions of influence. Pugin's time, it seemed, had come.

Redgrave's *Supplement* to the second Jury Report underlined Pugin's importance. As he surveyed the Crystal Palace for good examples of his various points Redgrave found himself turning often to the Mediaeval Court. As a whole, Pugin's works, he concluded, 'deserve commendation for their illustration of truth, and as showing what one man, by earnest and well-directed attention, can achieve in the reformation of taste, and in the training and forming of other minds to assist in his truthful labours'.[8] Elsewhere Redgrave's praise for the 'true constructive treatment of wood', his insistence that 'utility and construction' should never be 'secondary to decoration', revealed how far Pugin's *True Principles* had been absorbed and how well they sat with the attitudes of 1851.[9] Like Cole, Redgrave was no apologist for the Gothic, but he shared the now general perception that the principles of design could be deduced from the architecture of the Middle Ages, that 'when the style was purest the construction was most scientific'.[10]

Redgrave's essay also goes beyond Pugin's *True Principles* in one important direction. He was beginning to consider, as Pugin scarcely had, the question of the means of manufacture and the division of labour. This issue, which lay at the heart of nineteenth-century debates about social organization and of Marx's view of history, was, from now on, to be part of the design reform movement too. William Morris, who was sixteen that year, refused in a fit of adolescent temperament to go into the Great Exhibition. His family left him to sulk on a bench outside. Yet he owed the impetus of his own vision of manufacture to the discussions that began inside in the Crystal Palace in the autumn of 1851. In considering the relations of handicraft to machine manufacture Redgrave turned again, in his concluding paragraphs, to Pugin: 'our own Mediaeval Court and the clever revivals it contains will show the influence on manufacture of an educated designer acquainted with the various processes of the manufactures for which he designs.'[11] What the reformers had to discover was how this was done, 'whether the workmen have any, and what amount of education in design, and whether their inventive powers have been stimulated'.[12] What Hardman Powell, Oliphant or Earley would have said had they been asked about the 'blowing up' process whereby Pugin stimulated their efforts or the ferocity with which he discouraged their occasional attempts at invention can only be imagined.

The preliminary selection of objects had to be made rapidly in the last days before the Exhibition closed. The crowds of people anxious for a last chance to see it were huge, swelled by the rainy autumn weather: 'we can only really work by meeting at 7 in the morning,' Pugin explained to Jane, '& then we get 3 hours before the people are let in.'[13] He was thrilled not only by the 'very great honour' of being chosen but, even more astonishing in his own experience, 'on dit that we are to be paid for expenses time & trouble but this remains to be proved – it is very singular them selecting me for this office but it does good, for . . . they must in their hearts believe I am right . . .'[14] Pugin was not, however, too over-awed to complain when the others arrived late and was soon taking command. On the second morning he insisted on getting everyone together at 6.30. 'I kicked up such a row that they were all there in time – we have selected a great lot of things . . . we have 4 police and 2 soldiers to clear the way . . . you should have been there to see the girls run to see us . . .'[15] In the selection process Pugin was quite willing to see his 'true principles', or, as he now preferred, 'natural principles', in the work of any culture, Christian or not. Like his fellow Commissioners he was particularly impressed by the 'Oriental productions'. Pugin thought these would be of 'infinite service' to students.[16] One of only two pieces of furniture purchased was his own Gothic bookcase cabinet and the Commissioners also chose metalwork, ceramics and carpets from the Mediaeval Court. A third of the budget for British products was spent on work designed by Pugin, which thus went to make up the core of the national collection.

Between meetings and despite his fluctuating health he continued to shuttle to and fro from London to Ramsgate. His other work was mostly for Westminster, but he was also designing fittings for a Catholic church by Wardell at Greenwich, Our Lady Star of the Sea. He had to admit that this was 'not much of Daniels Quiet' and could only answer Hardman's protests with his own peculiar sense of vocation: 'we must work for the cause while we have breath.'[17] He was in London with his fellow Commissioners when his daughter Anne gave birth, the day after her first wedding anniversary, to Pugin's first grandchild. 'Powell has got a little girl thank God,' Pugin wrote to Hardman when he heard, '& Anne all right.'[18] Soon, however, Anne fell ill. She was in great pain and sometimes feverish. Pugin was terrified '& thought of her poor mother'.[19] He watched her 'lingering agony' and it seemed that yet again death would rob him of a life he loved.[20] Jane moved over to St Lawrence to nurse her stepdaughter. Pugin's anxiety about Anne put him in 'a state of constant excitement'.[21] He had 'no digestion' at times.[22] At others, as he did not forbear from telling Hardman, he was painfully constipated. He began to suffer from insomnia, 'even here at home where I slept like a top'.[23] His restless nights were dogged by feverish dreams of devils, 'a gigantic figure on a spike . . . & a truncated church tower in a lurid light', this last presumably his own, unfinished, church at Ramsgate.[24] When awake he seemed also to be haunted by misfortune. Myers's men suddenly struck in November and all of Pugin's work in progress was halted '& everything thrown into the greatest confusion'.[25]

As the opening of the Commons approached they had, Pugin told Hardman, just '50 days to finish the job Carpets and all'.[26] He felt now the work was 'murdering' him and, perhaps because of the respect with which he was treated at the Crystal Palace, he began for the first time to express a resentment of his position in relation to Barry.[27] 'I am now nearly 40,' he complained, '& am handled as a boy as a clerk upon work of which I only have the key.'[28] At the same time he began to worry that Barry would dismiss him before the opening to avoid his getting any credit. 'I have every suspicion . . . of certain great men. Useful men to great men were usually poisoned or put in a sack when the enterprise was nearly ready.'[29] Almost every post now brought orders to Birmingham: 200 coat-hooks, quantities of glass, the 'quarry lights with small emblems for the 29 lights at intersections of long cloister', gas fittings, ventilator grills and so on and on, all accompanied by Pugin's increasingly peremptory instructions.[30] Hardman, who was himself unwell, finally answered back. 'I have just received your astonishing letter,' his wounded friend replied, 'you talk about me why [what] have you done but blow up for 3 successive posts however for the future I will conceal all my ideas from you.'[31] As usual Pugin's determination to 'say nothing' ran to considerable length. It was not long before the quarrel was resolved though and Pugin apologized: 'mea culpa mea culpa mea culpa,' he inscribed in Gothic letters at the top of the paper.[32]

Anne was beginning to recover and this made her father calmer. Yet all the time his own condition worsened. Jane had to write to Crace about the carpet designs on his behalf, her letter obviously a paraphrase of Pugin's own words, but the last lines her own. 'I am sorry to say Mr Pugin is very poorly to day having had a very bad night, the truth is he has worked too hard lately and unless he has more rest and less anxiety I am very much afraid he will be very ill.'[33] Barry continued to press for designs and to threaten that if Pugin 'did not get on' then other 'inferior' suppliers would have to be used.[34] This provoked a furious response from Pugin, who, despite his steady litany of complaint, had worked so hard for so long for so little. He still submitted every detail to Barry, which not only made the work less rewarding, it made it slower. Barry's temperamental 'tendency to alteration' was increasing with time and anxiety.[35] 'Always fastidious', he was becoming with age 'morbidly sensitive' about every detail.[36] Pugin told Hardman what he had told Barry:

. . . that when I brought beautiful old patterns to select from that he never even deigned to notice them. I asked him if he settled nothing how we were expected to get on . . . I have also told him there can be no steam without heat and no heat without fuel & that I have no fuel to keep up steam . . . I have never seen any expenses since this commons began . . . my expenses are far away far beyond the Salary . . . & you know it, you smile murder but it is true £2 a week & . . . send in some acres of drawings all full size . . . the time alone exceeds the salary. the splendid Salary.[37]

By the end of November Anne was out of danger, but her father was much worse. The nightmares 'of visionary things' persisted.[38] He was weak and distraught and began, for the first time in his life, to think of delegating his work. As he contemplated a journey to Exeter in the cold winter weather he quailed. Could not Edward or someone be 'brought on' to take some of this burden from him, he asked Hardman.[39] He managed to get up to Birmingham, from where he wrote to Anne that he had taken a vow to the Virgin to complete the lady altar at Ramsgate in thanksgiving for her recovery.[40] On the outside of the letter, which Anne sealed on 17 October the following year, she wrote: 'my poor dearest papa's last letter to me'. He went from Birmingham to Exeter. On the way he was seized 'with intense pain it was dreadful'.[41] He came back up to London and was again taken ill, with a high temperature. He was now so weak that he had to accept Daniel's orders not merely to rest but 'to live altogether on a different system'. He was to stay at home, for at least six months.[42] 'I am going to turn over a new leaf I shall not undertake half so much,' he told Hardman. He felt he was getting better, though he could still hardly 'put one foot before the other'.[43] In the same letter he mentioned that Myers was at the Grange, having resolved his strike, and they were discussing their business arrangements. This year's settlement of accounts left Pugin still deeply in Myers's debt and he was desperate to undertake any work he could get. On 11 December, however, Jane was sending off the rug designs for the Palace of Westminster to Crace, begging that 'you will send for nothing more at present that is not indispensable as the least exertion is very injurious to my Husband'.[44] Having resolved at last to obey doctor's orders, Pugin threw himself into recuperation as he threw himself into every venture. There was 'great activity' set in motion at the Grange to make the house as warm and draughtproof as possible: extra curtains, three new stoves and a new door to the porch.[45] 'I have 12 thermometers & we regulate our atmosphere beautifully,' he told Hardman.[46] Having, as he said, never really 'lived' at home before, he immediately started to reform domestic arrangements.[47] He designed a laundry list and asked Hardman to get two quires printed so that Jane need not write out all the items every week but could just tick them off. He drew up 'written rules for everything'.[48] No doubt, as Pugin suspected, Hardman laughed at all this, but it was a hopeful sign.

Meanwhile in London the selectors, now that the Exhibition had closed, continued with their work. Pugin was notified of the various choices, one of which infuriated him. It was an ornamental shield by Antoine Vechte in the Renaissance style. Pugin wrote 'to present myself as the uncompromising opponent of that purchase, to which I have never by word or deed consented'.[49] Enraged by illness and a sense of his powerlessness, his behaviour towards the committee became unmanageable, 'cruel and wild', as Cole recalled.[50] 'I deeply regret having anything to do with that doubly cursed jury business,' Pugin told Crace, adding that perhaps it was the 'Paganism & debasement' at the Crystal Palace that had made him ill.[51] Daniel still talked of cold and 'nervous fever', Pugin talked of rest and quiet, but he continued to receive visitors and make designs, not only for Westminster, but for furnishings of two more private commissions for Crace: 'my hours are from 6 till 10 with an hours walk in the day by the sea,' he told Hardman.[52] He meant of course six in the morning until ten at night.

On 17 December the Bishop of Southwark, Thomas Grant, came to

St Augustine's to give confirmation. Grant placed a relic of the Holy
Cross on Pugin's forehead and Pugin pronounced himself at once cured.
It was 'instantaneous . . . a few minutes'.[53] He made a series of drawings
to prove the point. One that survives, in ink, a textile design, is as firm
of line and crisp as anything he ever drew. He wrote at once to Crace
and Hardman of his delivery, although the letters are less lucid than the
drawing: 'it is a curious thing to write about but between friends like us
we may talk like Doctors,' he told Hardman, 'my water which has been
thick for years (disease of the kidneys) & latterly in that disorder more
like Peas soup for the last few days became perfectly clear When I
showed it to Daniel he said you are all right you are better than you
have been for years your kidneys are relieved & the regular digestion is
going on.'[54] Pugin was, by now, 'an altered man half the size I was', but
he was convinced that the illness had passed.[55] Still weak, he worked
while Jane helped by making tracings of the designs. From now on
whatever element of lethargy or depression had underlain her own illness
evaporated. She quit the sofa and addressed herself energetically to
helping her husband, who was once again looking forward: 'what we
have already is nothing to what is to come.'[56]

Yet as he prepared once more to hurtle *en avant*, Pugin was willing
for the first time to look back as well. In his illness, he said, he had
thought of many things. He remembered his parents and his devoted
aunt, now nearly twenty years in their neglected graves. He decided to
repair the vault at Islington. He told Hardman he would 'make something of a good tomb' of it and a brass for his father.[57] His father's sister
Sophie Bernard died that winter in Paris at the age of seventy-eight.
Although he had drifted more or less out of touch with his French family
he ordered a brass for her too. 'I am endebted to my father my mother
& aunt,' he wrote. It was if anything Selina whom now he seemed to
appreciate the most, for her modesty, her goodness and her generosity,
the qualities which a happy child may take for granted but which Pugin
now realized were rare and precious. He remembered her 'at daily
prayers & weekly communion . . . a holy woman giving all to her
relations & the poor. I must see her tomb restored it is a duty a deal
came on me in my illness about this . . . My grandfather & grandmother
lay in that vault too. I will have it well put to rights.'[58] He became
anxious not just for the mortal remains but also for the souls of his
family. Of his mother there was perhaps nothing to be said, but his

father, who, as Pugin had remarked only months before, 'never spoke to me about Religion or minded it himself', had at least been baptized a Catholic.[59] Pugin now 'made enquiries' among friends of Auguste, who reassured him: 'they all say he always said he was a Catholic & would die one,' he told Hardman.[60]

From France Pugin received, apparently via his cousin and childhood playmate Antonia Molinos, an impression of the Pugin seal. It had 'lion supporters & mantling & the whole thing done before the revolution. This shows a noble family,'[61] Pugin told Hardman. He must have realized over the years, as he learned more about heraldry, that the crest his aunt had first shown him in Paris when he was a child was not a coat of arms. He was delighted with what he took to be incontrovertible evidence of his noble lineage and arranged to get the documents framed, though they do not seem to have survived. Equally delightful and surprising was the possibility of a small legacy. Yet whatever he said about recovery, Pugin's last letters show that he was increasingly haunted by the prospect of death, by regret, disappointment and an almost equal horror of past and future: 'how wise how providential we only know the past but there is so much in that that it makes me tremble,'[62] he wrote to Hardman. 'If my time was to come over again you would not see the church at St Augustine – it is a hopeless undertaking.'[63] Still he struggled to make Christmas merry, giving a feast for sailors' widows and another for the young men in the study. There was a turkey, 'the finest in Ramsgate', and 40lb of beef, 'a splendid pudding & wonderful mince pies'. Pugin himself ate almost nothing,[64] 'but as I am getting better I must not complain'.[65] Jane was not deceived and remembered that Christmas as 'very miserable'.[66] The next day Pugin was ill again, but the day after back at his drawing table working at details for Barry's job at Canford Manor and panelling for the House of Commons. Against doctor's orders he went to London for the meeting of the Purchase Committee on 5 January. He was delighted to find he was not alone in his views on the Vechte shield, which was being foisted on them by higher authorities. Cole suggested the committee should 'buy the shield and exhibit it as a monument to the Board of Trade's ignorance'.[67] Pugin set off, feeling much better, for Beverley.

On 7 January he wrote to Cole that he would like to publish an article in the *Journal of Design*. He had 'a great lot of mss' written before he was ill, 'a sort of lecture on the principles of constructional design';

'what will you give a sheet,' he asked anxiously.[68] Cole wrote back to explain he had given up the *Journal* but would try to get the lecture published elsewhere. No trace, however, of what might have been Pugin's last statement of his still developing theories seems to survive. Cole also promised to speak to the Board about Pugin's expenses for the Selection Committee, which like all expenses were taking their time to appear. Pugin was desperate to regulate his accounts. It was difficult to know how much he was owed for work at Westminster. The tangled question of who was subcontracting whom, when he was employed directly by Barry and when by Crace or Hardman, was further complicated by the various loops and tucks Barry had made in the arrangements in order to appease both Parliament and Pugin: 'is it you or Mr Barry,' Pugin asked Crace, 'who pay for the shields round the house also those for ceiling etc. . . .' Some of it was piecework, some on commission.[69]

In mid-January Pugin was pleased to get a letter from the Irish builder and architect with whom he had worked at Maynooth, J. J. McCarthy, asking for drawings for a church in Dublin. It was the sort of arrangement that Pugin would never have tolerated a few months, even weeks earlier, but now it seemed to offer a solution to some of his difficulties. He wrote warmly back, agreeing that he would undertake 'finishing all the drawings details & anything required you superintending'.[70] Finally the work for the Commons ceased. On 3 February Queen Victoria opened Parliament and the new chamber was inaugurated. The alterations to the ceiling had, in Barry's opinion, ruined the design and he never looked at it again. The ceremony itself, however, 'passed off a merveille', he told Pugin, who did not attend.[71] A few days later Barry was knighted by his admiring sovereign. He had not dismissed Pugin, he could not afford to, but as far as the public accounts of the building were concerned he might as well have put him in a sack. Although Pugin's involvement at Westminster was common knowledge, the details to which Barry's office gave the press 'ready access' made no mention of him.[72] There were gracious references to the 'taste and skill of Messers Crace'.[73] Even Gough and Co., suppliers of 'indiarubber floor cloth', received their due.[74] Pugin's name appeared nowhere.

He got no credit and he got no rest. 'I am now anxious,' Barry wrote to him, 'to add farther to the glories already accomplished, and farther to invoke your aid towards the attainment of that object. Would it be perfectly convenient and agreeable to you to give me bed and board if I was to be with you until Monday or Tuesday?'[75] While he waited for Barry, Pugin was working on Crace's two commissions, designs for Leighton Hall in Montgomeryshire and Abney Hall in Cheshire. Crace had sent Pugin his own first thoughts for Abney, which Pugin dismissed as 'the worst heresy I ever saw since Wyatts times . . . leave it to me & for £50 I will make every detail . . .'[76] It was not Crace's fault that the work put Pugin under such strain but Jane, who was now constantly at her husband's side, could barely conceal her annoyance when she answered Crace's enquiries. 'Every exertion has possibly been made to finish the drawings . . . Everyone has been at work as the time was so short. I must beg that in future you will make some better arrangement as really after Mr Pugin's severe illness it is very injurious to his health to be so driven.'[77]

Jane helped, too, with Pugin's attempts to reconcile himself with his past. She was often anxious, her journal shows, that as a stepmother she would be suspected and misjudged. She persuaded her husband to send to Anne Powell at St Lawrence the few 'trinkets' of her mother, Anne Garnett, that he had kept.[78] Pugin himself now spoke at times openly of death and quite calmly: 'you know,' he told Hardman, 'I have learned to love God to that degree that death has nothing dreadful in my eyes . . . I felt as resigned as if I had a journey to perform.'[79] This serenity came in part from his work in progress, his 'great . . . apology for the church of England'.[80] He had seen wonderful things, 'almost revelationary', in his illness and believed that in the end all should be well, that he had found the means to reconcile the true faith with the English Church, to bring together past and present in his own life and in divine truth.[81]

Barry duly arrived and he and Pugin talked over the next phase of work at the Palace. There was still a great deal to do. The building itself was incomplete; the work would continue into the 1860s and beyond. What Barry wanted now was more glass and fittings and, most particularly, a design for the upper part of the great clock tower, including the clock itself. This, too, would not be built for years, but discussions about it had been going on since 1844 and in 1851, when there were several design proposals, none of them satisfactory, 'the controversy rose to its height'.[82] That the design of the clock stage, the most prominent feature of the Palace, one of the most famous landmarks in the world, was, essentially, Pugin's, has never been seriously disputed. Even Alfred Barry, in his biography of his father, while he denies Pugin any direct credit, avoids attributing the design entirely to his father, writing ambiguously of 'an example' and a 'suggestion' on which the final design was based.[83] The clock is pure Gothic and Barry, who still could not design a door knob in the medieval style, was entirely reliant on Pugin for the conception. Pugin had first toyed with the form in the competition drawings and had developed it again in his unbuilt schemes at Scarisbrick Hall. The final design is very like one he had contemplated there. Thus his last and most famous work was a recapitulation of one of his first.

Although the Barry family later tried to minimize Pugin's contribution to the crowning glory of the Palace, and Barry himself almost certainly destroyed letters and drawings that would have proved his involvement, Pugin's own account survives. During Barry's visit he wrote, full of enthusiasm, but barely lucid, to Hardman: 'Mr Barry is here & has ordered for 10000 thousands we begin the great hall window immediately – he said everything a man could of you & says without us he would not have the drive ... I never worked so hard in my life for Mr Barry for tomorrow I render all the designs for finishing his bell tower & it is beautiful & I am the whole machinery of the clock.'[84] The letter, parts of it firmly written, others scrawled, blotted and illegible, shows Pugin slipping in and out of coherence. He had been so ill in the morning he thought he would die, but with hot brandy and water had brought himself round again and gone on drawing: 'you [will] find me much altered,' he wrote to Hardman, 'but a fine fellow in every way ... I am like a man risen from the grave ... ever thine till death.'[85] If Barry now drove Pugin cruelly, Pugin drove himself just as hard. Both men sensed perhaps that time was short and that Pugin was indeed the machinery in the clock. What he meant to write, in his deluded state, was that he was to design the mechanism; later he suggested they get a patent for it. But what he actually wrote was the truth. He had always been the projector of his vision of the Gothic. As he broke down so it came falling in around him. Soon after Barry left Ramsgate, with Pugin's drawings, Pugin collapsed. 'I am sorry to inform you,' Jane wrote to Crace, '... the medical men have had a consultation they say the only thing to save his life is to give up his profession which Thank God he has done ...'[86] Barry was telegraphed to know he could expect no more drawings and wrote back, 'Do not, I beseech of you think of anything you have offered to do for me, except so far as it may afford you amusement ... I have

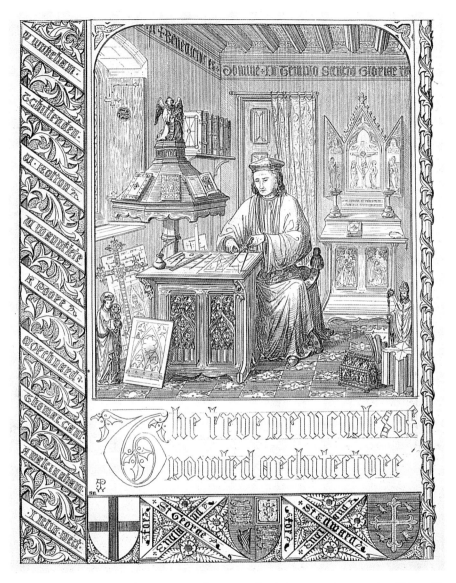

47. The Frontispiece of *True Principles*, 1841. Pugin's romantic portrait of himself as a medieval architect expressed his longing to inhabit the world of his own visual imagination.

48. (*left*) St John the Evangelist, Kirkham, 1842, was one of the first of Pugin's English Gothic churches, a model used for the rest of the nineteenth century across Britain and the Empire.

49. (*below*) St Augustine's, Kenilworth, designed in 1841, was the type of small but dignified church that inspired Pugin's contemporaries as they tried to build on limited budgets in poor industrializing areas.

50. (*top*) Alton Castle, Staffordshire. Built by Pugin for the Earl of Shrewsbury out
of a ruin, it was destined to remain incomplete, a monument to the failure of the
Romantic Catholic ideal.

51. (*above*) Ratcliffe College, Ratcliffe-on-the-Wreake, Leicestershire. When his
designs for Balliol College, Oxford, were rejected Pugin had to settle for building
them in Leicestershire instead. They are the main inspiration for the principal front,
designed in 1843–4.

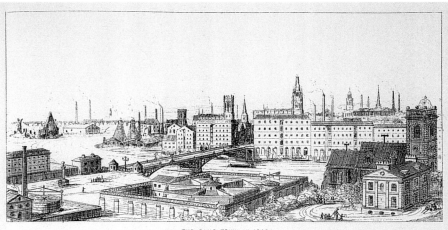

THE SAME TOWN IN 1840

1. St Michaels Tower, rebuilt in 1750. 2. New Parsonage House & Pleasure Grounds. 3. The New Jail. 4. Gas Works. 5. Lunatic Asylum. 6. Iron Works & Ruins of St Maries Abbey. 7. Mt Evans Chapel. 8. Baptist Chapel. 9. Unitarian Chapel. 10. New Church. 11. New Town Hall & Concert Room. 12. Wesleyan Centenary Chapel. 13. New Christian Society. 14. Quakers Meeting. 15. Socialist Hall of Science.

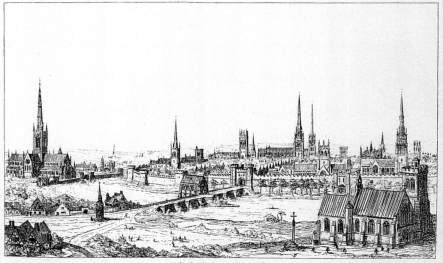

Catholic town in 1440.

1. St Michaels on the Hill. 2. Queens Cross. 3. St Thomas's Chapel. 4. St Maries Abbey. 5. All Saints. 6. St Johns. 7. St Peters. 8. St Alkmunds. 9. St Maries. 10. St Edmunds. 11. Grey Friars. 12. St Cuthberts. 13. Guild hall. 14. Trinity. 15. St Olaves. 16. St Botolphs.

52. 'Contrasted Towns' was one of the plates Pugin added to the second edition of *Contrasts* in 1841. These new images turned his manifesto from an architectural *cri-de-coeur* into a wider protest against the callousness of the Victorian city.

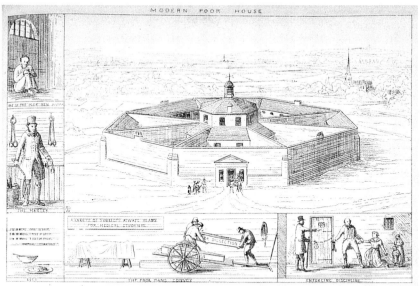

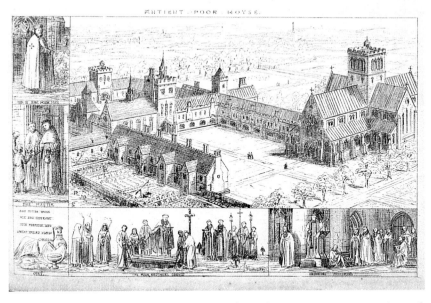

53. In 'Contrasted Residences for the Poor', from the 1841 *Contrasts*, Pugin made an unanswerable case for the connection between architecture and ideology, setting the Christian monastery against the Utilitarian panopticon.

54. (*far left*) Anne Pugin Powell, Pugin's eldest child, wearing jewellery designed by her father, in a photograph of the 1860s.

55. (*left*) John Hardman Powell was the only pupil Pugin ever formally took. He survived a stormy apprenticeship and married Pugin's daughter, Anne, in 1850.

56. (*below far left*) Louisa Button, Pugin's second wife, in a drawing probably by J. R. Herbert. It was not an entirely happy marriage, and little trace of Louisa's life has survived.

57. (*below left*) Jane Knill, Pugin's third wife, photographed as a widow in the 1870s wearing jewellery her husband had designed for her.

58. (*above right*) One of the carvings Pugin made for Scarisbrick Hall in about 1838 shows a design for a clock tower that clearly resembles the one at the Palace of Westminster, commonly known as 'Big Ben'.

59. (*below right*) The clock tower as built was modified by Charles Barry, but the essential design was undoubtedly Pugin's.

60. (*left*) St Mary's church, Rugby, designed in 1847 and photographed in the 1860s before it was altered. A tough little building with a strong French influence, it shows how Pugin's ideas continued to develop in the last years of his life as a pioneer of the High Victorian style.

61. (*below*) Grace Dieu Manor, the home of Ambrose and Laura Phillipps. The wing on the right was added by Pugin in 1848–9 in a style of plain, modern Gothic that had shaken off the last traces of revivalism.

been very glad to shake hands with Hardman this morning on his way to you.'[87] Within days Pugin had written back to him announcing that he was well again, but he was not. The 'mind mists' that increasingly obscured his judgement now became opaque.[88] The nightmare visions invaded the daytime too. One day he thought he saw a wreck at sea, when there was no ship at all. On 25 February, Ash Wednesday, he set off with Edward for London. It was four months before Jane saw him again.

41

Bethlem and Ramsgate

26 February to September 1852

God accept him Christ receive him . . .
– Alfred, Lord Tennyson, Lines on the death of the Duke of
Wellington, 1852

The precise sequence of events over the next few days is unclear. Those most intimately involved were too shocked and preoccupied perhaps to recall them exactly afterwards. What is certain is that by the time Pugin arrived in London he was psychotic. Unaware of his surroundings, unable to recognize anyone, he was excitable and occasionally violent. He went or was taken either to George Myers's house or to the Golden Cross Hotel in the Strand, where his friends tried to calm him. His son Edward, Myers and Herbert were with him and others came from time to time. Edward remembered that it was Charles Barry who sent for Dr Tweedie, a well-known physician. Under Tweedie's orders Pugin was taken to a private asylum, Kensington House. He was to remain there for nearly four months, with only moments of semi-lucidity, restless and liable at times to attack his visitors. On one such occasion a few days later Myers tried to distract him by reminding him of the work they had in hand at St Mary's, Beverley. Pugin made out a drawing for the wind vane, inscribing it weakly and incoherently, 'March 1st my 40th Birthday & the English nation.'[1]

Jane, at first, was told nothing. The account she left of the last terrible months of her marriage is shot through with resentment at the treatment she received from some of her husband's friends and her own family. She was much younger than most of them and a woman. Hardman in particular, who had seen Pugin through two wives and at least three affairs, was inclined to be dismissive of her. He too was frantically worried and meant perhaps to be protective, but she found him obstructive and overbearing. Certainly he underestimated the determination and decisiveness of which Jane was capable, now that she had quit the sofa. For a while, perhaps, Hardman and Myers hoped to shield her from the spectacle of her husband's madness until it had passed off. Yet by leaving her in ignorance they could not but increase her alarm. After some days with no news, Jane came to London by herself. Hardman told her where Pugin was, but despite her 'repeated entreaties' refused to allow her to see him.[2] For the moment she accepted his prohibition and went back to Ramsgate. Hardman and Edward followed. Over the next few weeks they cleared out Pugin's study. Taking the drawings and papers they needed for the work in hand, they moved the business up to Birmingham. Powell, Hendren and the others who had been working at the Grange went with them. It was the only way to keep the practice going in Pugin's absence, but it left the house sadly empty. The church had lost its choir and Jane was left alone with the youngest children to worry and grieve.

A letter arrived in March from the Earl of Shrewsbury in Palermo, where he had heard from Pugin in January of his complete recovery. The Earl was delighted and full of plans for a new cathedral at Shrewsbury. 'Please God, we shall be laying the foundations about this time next year. I hope it stands upon a rock & will stand firm till the last day.'[3] His optimism must have rung particularly hollow by the time the letter reached Ramsgate. In June, having heard from Ambrose Phillipps of Pugin's collapse, the Earl wrote again, to Jane, with the warm support of the Countess, begging that Pugin (Jane, it was made politely but firmly clear, would be too busy with the children to accompany him) might be sent to them at the Villa Belmonte as soon as he could travel: 'if he wld make up his mind to remain a whole 12 month with us, so much the better.'[4] The Shrewsburys had often invited him before, but Pugin always excused himself. He had disliked his brief experience of the south. He dreaded the heat and had heard that there were snakes and lizards in the Shrewsburys' garden, which terrified him. Now, however, there was no need for polite evasion. His mind continued as disordered as it had been in February.

By the middle of June he was no better. It was decided to try to get him admitted to the Bethlem Hospital at Southwark. Bethlem, which stood opposite his cathedral of St George's, was a public hospital, principally for paupers, but its staff were among the best qualified in their field. Only a few weeks earlier Dr Charles Hood had been appointed resident superintendent. His regime had begun with alterations to the building, the removal of bars from the windows and other improvements to make the patients' environment more humane. The works were being carried out by Myers, whose own house in Laurie Terrace was only yards away, while at St George's there was Thomas Doyle. Doyle's irritation with Pugin had evaporated as soon as he heard of his illness and he was anxious now to help. At Bethlem Pugin would be close to friends and, as Edward and others believed, he would receive 'the best professional treatment'.[5] One of the governors, Samuel Sharwood, who lived in Ramsgate, wrote on Pugin's behalf to the committee, begging them to 'sympathize with the truly deplorable case of my neighbour Mr Pugin the eminent architect . . . [and] his afflicted family'.[6] In order for him to be admitted Pugin had to be certified insane. On 17 June in Ramsgate Jane signed the certificate. Sharwood arranged his admission four days later.

The doctors who observed Pugin on his arrival described his condition as 'mania'.[7] He had no 'particular delusion but general confusion of ideas', and had been until recently 'very dirty in his habits'.[8] He was also remarkably restless, even for someone in a state of manic psychosis. 'It is extraordinary,' the notes go on, 'to observe his incessant activity of mind and body.'[9] For years he had been driving himself faster and faster. Now it seemed as if the process of acceleration had run out of control. News of his plight soon spread. There was an outcry at his being in Bethlem. It was known as a paupers' hospital, and the shadow of 'Bedlam' as it had been in the eighteenth century, where the mad were mocked and degraded, still hung over the name. Letters appeared in the press. It was assumed that Pugin was destitute and had been abandoned. He would have been astonished to know that Lord John Russell himself, who had clearly not forgotten their meeting at the Crystal Palace, wrote to *The Times* offering ten pounds to start a public subscription for his treatment. Not everyone behaved so well. Dr Rock, who was now, as Pugin had observed, positively 'spiteful' to his former protégé, wrote to Shrewsbury recommending William Wardell to finish the work in hand at Alton.[10] The Earl wrote back loyally that 'young Pugin & Powell hope to be able to carry on the business' and that he believed they would, for Edward had inherited all his father's talent.[11]

The public reaction to Pugin's illness showed how much he was valued. Yet, as his friends and family struggled to do what they could in intolerable circumstances, divided in their own minds and among themselves, the implied criticisms were hard to bear. In July Edward wrote to *The Times*, protesting that his father was receiving the best possible care. Jane meanwhile made up her mind to take matters into her own hands. She went to Bethlem with John Glennie, one of the Oxford converts of 1845 who was now a priest and had long been a friend of Pugin. She was at first refused entry but she persisted and was eventually allowed to see her husband for the first time since February. What she saw dismayed her: 'he did not know me he looked half the size he was his hair was shaved off in fact he was so much altered that if he had been with others I should not have known him he looked certainly 70.' His voice too was 'quite altered'.[12] Jane managed to conceal her emotions. She 'neither spoke nor cried' but 'kissed him several times'.[13] After a few minutes she was told to leave, although Glennie remained a little longer. Men, it was assumed, could bear more of such reality. Pugin drew a rough sketch of a church for Glennie, but he had no idea who he was.

Appalled by what they had seen, Jane and Glennie decided to re-move Pugin from Bethlem. By now it seems unlikely that anything could have saved his life, but Jane was determined to try another course. Glennie suggested Samuel Dickson. Dickson was a London doctor who had made his reputation with a book, *Fallacies of the Faculty*, which had run through many editions since the first in 1839. He was a controversial figure, popular with the public and unpopular with many of his profession for his denunciation of bloodletting, which was still common practice in cases of fever. He advocated chloroform instead, which had only come into general use for anaesthesia in the last two years. 'Mania' or 'brain fever' was then assumed to be a feverish inflammation of the brain – Pugin's head had been shaved in an attempt to lower his temperature – so Dickson recommended using chloro-form to achieve a temporary lull in the 'delirium' during which a fever remedy could be applied. He had not seen Pugin but was confident that if he was removed from Bethlem and placed under his care he could cure him.

Jane and Glennie confided their plans to her uncle and aunt. The Knills thought it a 'mad scheme' and the next day, when he found Jane alone, Hardman made strenuous efforts to persuade her to leave Pugin where he was.[14] The discussion ended in a quarrel and from now on Jane and Hardman were increasingly at cross purposes. A few days later an anxious impromptu 'committee' of friends and family was convened. Jane, her uncle, Glennie, Herbert, Hardman and Hardman Powell all met at the House of Lords. Surrounded by the patterns that had poured torrentially from Pugin's hand until only a few months earlier, his presence must have been almost as palpable as his absence. They struggled to decide what to do. John Knill at last told his niece that it must be her decision: 'we cannot take the responsibility'.[15] If he meant to intimidate her by this he failed, for Jane was more than willing to take the initiative. 'I immediately said . . . "everything has been tried instead of getting better he is much worse . . . if he remains in Bethlem I am quite sure he will die so this is the only chance left I will take the responsibility upon myself." '[16]

Herbert and Glennie supported her. A house, 16 The Grove, Hammersmith, was rented and on 29 July Jane arrived there in disguise, wearing a cap and false hair. She had, it seems, been told that her husband must not recognize her, as her presence might disturb or excite him. Pugin was brought to Hammersmith in a cab from Bethlem. On arrival he began to eat. His appetite was gargantuan, diseased. He consumed a whole loaf, chops, ten cups of tea, far more than 'a person in health'.[17] In the evening the doctors came to administer the chloroform. Jane, terrified, went into the next room to pray. When it was over she came in and saw him asleep, he was 'quite calm and comfortable' but terribly 'old and changed'.[18] For some days the strange routine continued. Pugin received regular doses of chloroform. Glennie and Jane looked after him, Jane telling him that her name was Mrs Knight and she was a housekeeper. Pugin at times accepted this. At others he thought she was Mary Amherst.

Dr Dickson was then obliged to go to Ireland. In his absence the chloroform was discontinued and Pugin became violent and uncontrollable. He had physical fits or 'paroxysms' and called out, occasionally for Mary Amherst, a fact that Jane recorded without comment. The two men hired as minders were rough with him, tying him to a chair or holding him down under bedclothes. Jane could not bear to watch. She insisted on intervening and managed to pacify him herself by conversation. When she put her head on the pillow beside him he would sleep.

The men complained to Glennie that she was making their job more difficult and tried to persuade him to send her away. Dickson too, on his return, said that Jane's interference did not give 'fair play' to his methods.[19] Undaunted, she sent for the carpenter from Ramsgate and when he arrived she dismissed the others, though Dickson remained in charge of the case. Pugin recognized his workman and was pleased to see him. Over the following days, although he still suffered fits, he seemed, between times, to become more lucid.

Gradually Jane left off her disguise. One day as they walked together Pugin stopped and asked if she was his wife; she admitted she was. 'How kind you are to come and take care of me,' he went on, 'I will never leave you again. Have we not got a house at Ramsgate why do we not go there.'[20] He also asked Jane why, if she was his wife, she would not sleep with him. This the doctors had strictly forbidden. Jane herself felt 'a little nervous' at the prospect 'but I was his wife . . . We went to bed and much to my surprise he fell asleep without his medicine saying how happy he felt.'[21] Over the weeks the improvement continued. Relations between Jane and Hardman, meanwhile, deteriorated. He too seemed to regard her presence in Hammersmith as obstructive and he doubted her competence. He sent money, but annoyed her by telling her not to be extravagant with it and even more by suggesting she should go home, 'for fear I should forget how to take care of the house and my children'. Jane replied that her husband was her 'first care' and 'best love' and that she would stay with him.[22]

By September, as the autumn damp set in, Pugin seemed physically less well at Hammersmith. Dickson agreed with Jane that she could take him home. It was a difficult and frightening journey by cab and train, for part of which Pugin had to be sedated, but when he arrived at Ramsgate he seemed pleased to be back and wanted to know where his drawings had gone. On the Sunday after his return 'he gathered a rose which was growing near the Library window drew it and wrote . . . "Drawn in presence of my dear wife the XII sept 1852." '[23] The next day he was well enough to go for a walk. Looking back from inland across the fields towards the house he had built, the disillusionment of recent years seemed to leave him. He turned to Jane and said, 'it is a beautiful place is it not? it is all yours my dear wife.'[24] They went on as far as St Lawrence. As they returned, the sounds of the last weeks of the summer season reached them on the air. In Spencer Square they could hear a band playing. The holiday music, Jane remembered, 'fell like a dead weight' on her spirits.[25]

They reached home in the early evening. Pugin went into his church and found that beautiful too. Then he and Jane sat together in the garden, for the weather was warm, until, at about eight o'clock, he went to bed. At eleven he woke and got up, his eyes 'fixed'. Jane called to him and he answered her that he was going. She sent for the local doctors, who said he must be bled, despite Dickson's instructions. Jane argued with them but they told her it was necessary to save his life and applied leeches. Dickson, who had received a telegram, arrived at three the next afternoon. He gave Pugin brandy and told Jane she should not have allowed the bleeding. 'I had done my best but I was no doctor,' she wrote, 'and the doctors were all against me.'[26] Pugin was now unconscious. Father Costigan came and administered the last rites; on 14 September 'at 10 minutes to 5 he died.'[27] Jane felt that she was left 'to every body's mercy' on that 'first dark day of nothingness' that began her long widowhood.[28]

A few miles away along the Kent coast, within a few hours, the Duke of Wellington also died, at Walmer Castle. Born in 1769, his life had spanned almost exactly those of Pugin and his parents. The hero of Waterloo had grown into an eminent Victorian. At eighty-three he was still in command of the army and 'in possession of his great and powerful mind'.[29] His death plunged England into mourning and drove the news of Pugin's to the further corners of the newspapers.

Six days later, on a bright moonlit evening, Pugin's coffin was carried from his house across the garden to his church in a small candlelit procession. It was a 'solemn sight', Jane recalled, a scene like many he himself had drawn, the cycle of life and death against the backdrop of Christian architecture.[30] Matins and Lauds for the dead were sung that night. The next day Thomas Doyle celebrated the Solemn High Mass of Requiem. The church was full. Hardman of course was there, as were Herbert, Crace, John Lambert, Myers, Talbot Bury and Sir Charles Barry. Other local people and passers-by came in, including two young architects, W. E. Nesfield and Norman Shaw, who happened to find themselves in Ramsgate that day. For Hardman Powell, who like Doyle had long forgotten his differences with the Governor, it was 'the most melancholy day I have yet known'.[31] Jane, with her two small children 'looking on unconscious of their loss', felt as she watched her husband's coffin lowered into the vault he had built that they might as well have followed, for 'God alone knows who will take care of them.'[32]

Bishop Grant preached, taking his text from Ecclesiasticus: 'rich men in virtue, studying beautifulness: living at peace in their houses.'

Epilogue

Of a death as sudden and premature as Pugin's something must be said both of the cause and of the immediate consequences. As far as the first is concerned, the cause of Pugin's death, as given on the death certificate, was 'convulsions followed by coma'. The underlying condition that had afflicted him over the years can never now be determined with certainty. What the evidence suggests to modern medical opinion is as follows.[1]

In the last year or so of his life he probably suffered from a thyroid condition. Hyperthyroidism would account for the perspirations, the exaggerated appetite and restlessness and the dramatic weight loss as well as the 'dropping asleep'. But it would not explain the many earlier episodes of illness that had afflicted him periodically from 1835, when he first recorded trouble with his eyesight. These episodes were, it seems reasonable to suppose, due to the same disease. In the nineteenth century the only condition that could cause such recurring incidence of illness involving the nervous and ocular systems and ending in death was syphilis. The circumstantial evidence supports this conclusion. To manifest when he was twenty-three the disease would need to have been contracted in his late teens or early twenties. At that age Pugin was certainly sexually active and in a milieu, at Covent Garden, where venereal disease was endemic. On the nights when he stayed there, 'sleeping in private boxes', he may have had other partners as well as Anne Garnett.[2] Perhaps he had some suspicion of the cause of his illness. His exaggerated horror of anything 'theatrical' in a church, his insistence on the depravity of the opera singers hired to perform the Mass, his complicated dread of the past, might suggest that he had.

At the time of his death, however, it was generally agreed that his collapse was the result of exhaustion and overwork. When the press came to notice it at more length, their verdicts were as various as they had been in his life, from the eulogy in the *Ecclesiologist* to 'the most eminent and original architectural genius of his time', to the bathos of the *Builder* and its opinion that in his prodigious output 'he overdid it'.[3] The *Kent Herald* grudgingly conceded that 'his peculiar style obtained many admirers', the *Illustrated London News* remembered 'a great architect . . . in every respect a wonderful man'.[4] Pugin's posthumous reputation was duly launched on its peculiar course. Among architects he was never entirely forgotten. W. E. Nesfield and Norman Shaw, who by chance attended Pugin's funeral, developed his legacy in their own work and Shaw remained an admirer of Pugin all his life. Like Scott and Butterfield, Street, the young architect whose ideas on town churches had so closely chimed with Pugin's, built much of what Pugin had only had time to draw. Street at Boyne Hill in Berkshire, Butterfield at Baldersby in Yorkshire, realized the vision of *Contrasts* in groups of houses, church and schools that celebrate the English landscape and hold out an ideal of social and moral harmony. Butterfield's offices for the Society for the Propagation of the Gospel, illustrated in the *Builder* in 1871, show him, nearly thirty years later, still working out the implications of the designs Pugin had published in his *Apology*.

The influence of his contemporaries took Pugin's ideas on to another generation less familiar with, or less responsive to his name. Street's office, where William Morris trained and where he met Philip Webb, became the nursery of the Arts and Crafts movement, which was to work out much that had been implicit in Pugin's career as a designer in the applied arts. His name by then, however, was fading. The Arts and Crafts saw itself as a reaction to the age of the Great Exhibition and its mentor was Pugin's rival Ruskin, who outlived and out-talked him by half a century. 'If Ruskin had never lived,' Kenneth Clark wrote, 'Pugin would never have been forgotten.'[5] As it was he was largely forgotten by the end of the century. When Hermann Muthesius published *Das Englische Haus* in 1904–5, Pugin was all but invisible. Muthesius's influential study of English domestic architecture traces its modern form to Philip Webb, Eden Nesfield and Norman Shaw. It was they, Muthesius wrote, who had broken away from the 'axial and symmetrical plan' in houses, who had broken the 'cold grip of classicism' and 'false Gothic' that merely imitated church buildings.[6] It was they, too, who had begun to look to vernacular models and 'to design more freely'.[7] Shaw and Nesfield, of course, were Pugin's direct inheritors, and Webb may have owed him something by way of Street. Altogether these three had done much to develop Pugin's legacy, but it was he, not they, who invented the English House that Muthesius so admired.

Privately, for the intimate circle of friends and family whose orbit had been so entirely fixed by the force of his personality, Pugin's death was a catastrophe from which none of them perhaps entirely recovered. Without him they had no unifying force, and the mistrust that had developed between Jane and Hardman during Pugin's illness was never dispelled. Hardman advised Jane to take her own children and go to live near her uncle, while the rest of the family came up to Birmingham. John Knill for his part suggested she go to the Hardmans. Nobody, she felt, really wanted her. To prevent the family being broken up and to thwart what she believed was Hardman's plan to marry off the eighteen-year-old Edward Pugin to one of his daughters, Jane went with the others to Birmingham. Edward and the Hardmans ran the practice from there while the Grange was let out to tenants until 1861, when the family returned. Jane seems at first to have feared she would be destitute, although shortly before Pugin's death she was awarded a Civil List pension of £100 a year. In fact Pugin's financial situation had never been as bad as he sometimes said and his estate was valued at £10,000. The hardship the family suffered after his death was principally due to his having made no legal will. There was a letter leaving everything to Jane to dispose of among the children as she chose, but it had no force in law. Under these circumstances it was a legal requirement that the property be divided among the male heirs and to achieve this everything, except the house, had to be sold. Unbusinesslike to the end, Pugin left his family with no choice but to disperse his valuable and much-loved collections. This they did in three long auction sales the following spring, each lasting several days. The books, pictures and antiquities that Pugin had spent his life acquiring were all sold off, and Jane was heartbroken, and angry, as she watched Pugin's friends carrying off bargains. '2 fine Albert Durers', worth £500, 'John Hardman bought them for £52 the pr.!!!'[8]

While all these matters still hung in the air, however, just weeks after Pugin's funeral shocking news reached England of another sudden death. The Earl of Shrewsbury had contracted malaria and died at Naples, on 9 November. His body was brought back to England. It lay in state first at St George's cathedral and then in the chapel at Alton Towers. The ceremony was designed and fitted out by Edward Pugin and Hardman as Pugin himself would have done it. The coffin under its black velvet pall stood in the centre of a great *chapelle ardente*. It was a magnificent occasion, and afterwards an immense funeral procession wound its way along the Churnet Valley from the Towers to St John's church, where the Earl was buried. It was the last great pageant at Alton, the funeral, to all intents and purposes, of the English Catholic romance. Shrewsbury's heir, Bertram, who wrote touchingly to Edward of his desire that they should continue the work begun by their predecessors, survived him by less than four years, dying childless at the age of twenty-four in 1856. Despite complicated provisions in the wills of both the 16th and 17th Earls to try to keep the title and the estate in Catholic hands, both passed after many legal suits to the Anglican branch of the family. The 18th Earl was Henry John Chetwynd-Talbot. He had no interest in Alton or what it had stood for and from then on the estate's decline, if unsteady, was sure. By the time the Tussauds Group bought Alton Towers in 1990 it was a ruin.

All Pugin's children survived to adulthood and all three of his sons became architects, although only Edward achieved any real distinction. He began by completing or extending his father's work but in time developed a significant practice of his own. He went into partnership first with George Coppinger Ashlin, an Irish architect, and later with his brother and half-brother as Pugin and Pugin. Edward undoubtedly had talent, but his was a troubled inheritance both personally and professionally. As volatile as his father and as inclined to exaggerate, he lacked Pugin's warmth and self-confidence. Over the years Edward became a conspicuous, if not always respected figure in Ramsgate, known for his flamboyance, his litigiousness and a wildly over-ambitious hotel development on the East Cliff, which bankrupted him and broke up his relationship with Ashlin. Like many sons of overpowering fathers he was touchy, torn between filial pride and a desperate need to assert himself. He was propelled by both at once into his battle with the Barry family.

Sir Charles Barry died in 1860 and was buried in Westminster Abbey. In 1867 the news that his son Alfred was on the point of publishing a biography of his father seems to have been the immediate spur for Edward to launch his pamphlet war, but resentment between the families had simmered since Pugin's death. Although the claims that Edward later made were grossly exaggerated, for Pugin was certainly not the 'true' architect of the Palace of Westminster, what he had witnessed in his teens of his father's treatment more than justified Edward's passionate sense of wrong. The Barrys for their part were defensive to the point of shiftiness. Alfred Barry's book, written before the controversy broke out, nevertheless devotes five pages to asserting the entirely subordinate nature of Pugin's position, which, as he admits, had often been questioned. As well as his oddly vague account of the authorship of the clock tower, his tone overall is insufferably patronizing. '[Pugin's] suggestions and criticisms,' he gushed, 'freely given and freely received, were invaluable; and his enthusiasm, even in its eccentricities, was inspiring and irresistible.'⁹ If he spoke to Edward as he wrote, then it was no wonder Edward felt aggrieved. After his pamphlet war Edward's brief moment of national fame was passed. His later life became a kind of parody of his father's, history repeating itself if not as comedy then with considerable elements of farce. Increasingly quarrelsome and paranoid, he turned against the Hardmans after John Hardman's death in 1867 and fell out with the Benedictines who came to Ramsgate to run Pugin's church. He remained close, however, to Jane, who seems always to have felt a protective affection for her eldest stepson. He never married. By his late thirties his chief enthusiasms were Turkish baths and chloral hydrate, which in combination almost certainly contributed to his death from heart failure at the age of forty-one in 1875.

Pugin's eldest daughter, Anne, having survived the difficult birth of her first child, went on to have eleven more. She outlived her husband, Hardman Powell, dying in 1897 at the age of sixty-five. Hardman Powell never did become an artist but worked instead as the principal designer in the family's stained glass business in Birmingham. Agnes, Louisa's troubled eldest daughter, married Louis Peniston in 1862 but he died ten years later and she seems, to judge from family correspondence, to have had a penurious and unhappy widowhood. Catherine, Mary and Margaret all married, Margaret twice. Mary's husband was Edward's partner George Ashlin. She was the last survivor of Pugin's children, dying in 1933 at the age of ninety. Peter Paul Pugin, as Edmund was known, was the only one of Pugin's sons to marry and have children. Cuthbert lived on alone at Ramsgate after the rest of the family had left until his death in 1928. John Summerson remembered visiting him there in about 1926, 'a frail, wistful little man' surrounded by family memorabilia, his conversation 'not in the slightest degree memorable'.[10]

Pugin's collaborators all survived him. The Hardman works flourished and its windows can be found in Victorian and medieval churches throughout Britain and beyond. Although the firm later passed out of the family, it continues to make stained glass today. John Gregory Crace also passed the firm on to the next generation and his son, John Diblee, presented his collection of Pugin's drawings to the Victoria and Albert Museum. George Myers's business flourished. Among his regular clients were the Rothschilds, for whom he built Mentmore. He died in 1875. On his deathbed he cancelled the debt still outstanding to him for St George's, Southwark.

Of the women whom Pugin had loved and who loved him, three, apart from his widow, survived. Mary Amherst, having become Superior of the convent at Loughborough, died there of tuberculosis in 1860. She was thirty-six. Ann Greaves retained her affection for Pugin's memory and for his eldest children. The year after his death she married John Mares, a widower in the upholstery trade, and they both rallied to Edward's support in his battle with the Barrys. When she died, in 1896, Ann left half her estate to the surviving children of Pugin's first two marriages, in repayment perhaps of the settlement she had received in 1846. Helen Lumsdaine became an Anglican again and in 1850, at Upper Hardres, she married Forster George Simpson, a clergyman of irreproachably Broad Church views. She spent much of her married life at Overstrand in Norfolk, where her husband was incumbent. Widowed in 1892, she retired to Parkstone, near Poole in Dorset and died there in 1916.[11]

Frederick Hugh Thomas, whose descendants believe that he was Pugin's illegitimate half brother, the son of Auguste Pugin and Margaret Harries, was transported to Australia in 1834 at the age of fifteen, having stolen a hat. Sentenced to hard labour in Van Diemen's Land, he was taken on as a clerk in 1846 by the architect William Porden Kay and developed a career in the Public Works Department. In 1852 he was granted a conditional pardon. Bishop Willson wrote to him in December asking 'on what terms you would undertake the carrying out of Mr Pugin's design' for a church in Hobart.[12] Thomas, who much admired the 'master spirit' of the 'late and lamented Pugin', took the work.[13] If he was really Pugin's half-brother, which seems plausible in light of his family's research, that he should build Pugin's churches in Tasmania was a coincidence of Dickensian proportions.

The other putative member of Pugin's family, his supposed son Byron Augustus, was still a child at the time of Pugin's death. By 1884, however, he was working as an architect on a Gothic chapel for the University of Virginia. He spent some years in Durham, North Carolina, where his practice seems to have flourished, and settled ultimately in Atlanta, Georgia, dying there in 1907. His recorded age at death is at odds with the account he gave of his date of birth. His son, Byron Welby Northmore Pugin, also became an architect, and his current descendants are attempting at the time of writing to establish the truth of their family history by means of DNA testing.

Bishop Willson returned to England, where he died in 1866 and was buried in Pugin's cathedral of St Barnabas, Nottingham. His brother Edward, whose antiquarian Catholicism had so largely formed Pugin's own, died in 1854. Rather than a modern Catholic burial place, he chose the graveyard at St Mary Hainton in Lincolnshire, a medieval church he had restored, believing to the last that the stones of the old buildings were imbued with the ancient faith. John Britton outlived most of his contemporaries and much enjoyed writing their obituaries. He took the opportunity of Willson's to mount one last assault on the Pugins, father and son, complaining of Auguste's lack of business sense and Pugin's 'inveterate' Catholicism. He died in 1857.[14] Pugin's uncle, Adlard Welby, with whom he had long since lost touch, also outlived him, dying in Islington in 1861, his will a long tangle of acrimonious codicils. By the time Richard Sibthorp died in 1879 he had become a Catholic yet again. He too is buried in St Barnabas's, the cathedral for which he had partly paid.

Jane Pugin never remarried. She continued to live in Ramsgate after 1861 and did everything possible to keep her husband's memory alive. Although her health always troubled her, she outlived both her own children and three of Pugin's. She died in 1909, in St Edward's, the house Pugin built as a presbytery, at the age of eighty-four, and is buried with him in the vault at St Augustine's.

Abbreviations

Autobiography	Pugin's autobiographical notes, transcribed in Wedgwood, *V&A*
BAA	Archives of the Archdiocese of Birmingham
BAL	RIBA British Architectural Library of Drawings & Archives Collection
BCL	Birmingham City Library and Archives, Hardman archive
BL	British Library
Bloxam Letters	Letters of John Rouse Bloxam in the archives of Magdalen College, Oxford
BoE	*The Buildings of England*
CoE	Church of England
Diary	Pugin's diary, transcribed in Wedgwood, *V&A*
NAL	National Art Library, Victoria and Albert Museum
NRO	Northumberland Record Office
PC 304	Letters in a private collection, available on microfilm in the House of Lords Record Office, HOLRO 302
PC 339	Letters in a private collection, available on microfilm in the House of Lords Record Office, HOLRO 339
Powell PC	Manuscript memoir of Pugin by John Hardman Powell, in a private collection
PRO	Public Record Office (National Archives)
RA	Royal Academy
RC	Roman Catholic
SAA	Archives of the Archdiocese of Southwark
SRO	Scottish Record Office
Stresa	Centro Internazionale di Studi Rosminiani, Stresa, Italy
Ushaw	Ushaw College, County Durham
V&A	Victoria and Albert Museum
WAA	Archives of the Archdiocese of Westminster
Wedgwood, *RIBA*	A. Wedgwood, *The Pugin Family*
Wedgwood, *V&A*	A. Wedgwood, *A. W. N. Pugin and the Pugin Family*
Yale	Pugin papers in the Yale Center for British Art, New Haven, Connecticut

List of Works

The nature of Pugin's practice makes it difficult to establish a complete list of works. This is merely an attempt to improve on what has been previously available. Included are all known buildings, major additions to buildings, unbuilt designs and major decorative schemes. The list does not include the many buildings to which Pugin contributed smaller decorative elements or furnishings. For a complete gazetteer of the stained glass designs, see Stanley Shepherd, 'The Stained Glass of A. W. N. Pugin'.

The secondary literature and manuscript sources listed here are confined to those dealing exclusively or substantially with an individual work. Sources already listed in the Select Bibliography are given only short titles. Many other references to Pugin's works will be found in his correspondence and in the more wide-ranging works in the Select Bibliography, as well as those in Margaret Belcher's *Annotated Bibliography* and the *Buildings of England, Scotland* and *Wales*.

Pugin's ideas developed rapidly. I have therefore dated buildings where possible according to the year of their design, even though in some cases construction began later, as this gives a more realistic impression of their place in Pugin's development as an architect.

Entries are arranged geographically, with the buildings (or schemes) first, followed by the dates, patron where known, further details of the work, location of primary material and secondary sources.

Buildings
EXECUTED WORKS (NEW BUILDINGS, RESTORATIONS AND ALTERATIONS)

Great Britain

Albury, Surrey

Albury House, 1846–c.1856, Henry Drummond
Alterations to an already much altered house of Tudor origin, including stained glass, decorations, recasing of the exterior, new porch and a new office wing. The work was mostly carried out by George Myers without Pugin's supervision and continued after Pugin's death. Some of the decoration but none of the glass survives. Now flats.

Arthur Oswald, 'Albury Park, Surrey', *Country Life*, 25 August and 1 September 1950

SS. Peter and Paul's church (CoE), 1843–7, Henry Drummond
Mortuary chapel for the Drummond family.

Material relating to both Albury commissions: V&A; BAL; Albury Park; Archives of the Duke of Northumberland, Alnwick Castle, Northumberland

Charles Walmsley for the Redundant Churches Fund, *Notes on the old parish church, Albury*, n.d., c.1988; Charles Walmsley, *Drummond's Chapel, being the story behind the mortuary chapel in the old parish church*, Albury, n.d.

See also: Maurice Burton, *Albury: a short guide to the parish*, Albury, 1994

Alderbury, Wiltshire

St Marie's Grange, new house, 1835–7 (alterations c.1839–41), A. W. N. Pugin
Winterthur Library, Delaware

Gatehouse, Clarendon Park, 1836, Sir Frederick Bathurst

Alton, Staffordshire

Alton Castle, ?1841–c.1847, 16th Earl of Shrewsbury
Rebuilding and extension of a ruined medieval castle.
Mark Girouard, 'Alton Castle and Hospital, Staffordshire', *Country Life*, 24 November 1960; Fisher, *Pugin-Land*

Alton Towers, 1839–52, 16th Earl of Shrewsbury
Alterations and additions.

Two lodges, Counslow, 1841, and Station Lodge, 1848, 16th Earl of Shrewsbury
Fisher, *Alton Towers* and *Pugin-Land*

St John's Hospital, 1839–52, 16th Earl of Shrewsbury
It is possible that E. W. Pugin continued the work after his father's death until 1856.
Mark Girouard, 'Alton Castle'; Fisher, *Pugin-Land*
Staffordshire Record Office: archives of the Talbot Earls of Shrewsbury contains estate papers bearing relation to these buildings

Banbury, Oxfordshire

St John the Evangelist's church (RC), 1839–1846
Addition of a chancel and decoration to a building by Hickman and Derick (1838), c.1841

Presbytery, 1839

School (altered), 1846
A Heritage Preserved: the story of the Parish of St John the Evangelist Banbury Oxon, c.1978

Barnstaple, Devon

Church of the Immaculate Conception (RC) (attrib.), 1844–55, Sir Bourchier Palk Wrey
This attribution from a contemporary source, repeated in BoE, is unsupported by documentary evidence and seems unlikely on stylistic grounds.

Beverley, Yorkshire

St Mary's church (CoE), 1844–52, Diocese of York
Repairs and restoration of a medieval building.
>Yorkshire Archaeological Society; East Riding of Yorkshire County Archives; Humberside County Archives

Bicton, Devon

Rolle Chantry, 1850–52, Lady Rolle
Mausoleum, incorporating fragments of a medieval church (CoE). Nineteenth-century Anglican church adjacent, designed by John Hayward.

Bilston, Staffordshire

Holy Trinity church (RC), 1846
New chancel added to existing building.
>BAA; Myers Family Trust
>O'Donnell, *The Pugins and the Catholic Midlands*

Birmingham

St Chad's church, later cathedral (RC), 1837–56
First design, 1837; revised design, 1838–41; minor alterations, 1850; south-west spire completed, 1856. NW chapel added by Sebastian Pugin Powell, 1933.
>BAA; BAL
>Michael Hodgetts, *St Chad's Cathedral*; Gavin Stamp, 'Ambonoclasm Redeemed', *True Principles*, 2, 4, Summer 2002

Bishop's House, 1840–41 (dem. 1960)
>BAL; BAA

Birmingham: Aston

St Joseph's church (built as a mortuary chapel), 1850, John Hardman
Incorporated into a later, larger chapel by E. W. Pugin, 1872.
>O'Donnell, *The Pugins and the Catholic Midlands*

Birmingham: Handsworth

Convent, 1840 and 1844, church and House of Mercy, 1845, Hardman
family
  BAA, BCL, Sisters of Mercy
  The Handsworth Sisters of Mercy, Handsworth, n.d.; McAuley, *Correspondence*

Birmingham: Oscott

St Mary's College, 1837–41
*Alterations to and decorations of the chapel by Joseph Potter (c.1834–7),
1837–8; gate lodges, 1840; furnishings, c.1838–41.*
  Oscott Archives, BAA
  Judith F. Champ, *Oscott College*; Judith F. Champ, *Oscott College
Chapel*, Oscott, 2002; Williams, *Pugin's Furniture at Oscott*; O'Donnell,
The Pugins and the Catholic Midlands

Blithfield, Staffordshire

St Leonard's church (CoE), 1846–51, Revd H. Bagot
Restoration and decoration of a medieval building.

Brewood, Staffordshire

St Mary's church (RC), 1843–4, Revd Robert Richmond
  BAA
  The Very Rev. F. C. Husenbeth, *Life of the Rev. Robert Richmond*,
Norwich, 1845

Presbytery, 1843–4

School (altered), 1849

Burton Closes, Bakewell, Derbyshire

1846–9, John Allcard
*Alterations to and decorations in a house by Joseph Paxton and John
Robertson. Further additions 1856–8 by E. W. Pugin and T. D. Barry; in
1888 and 1949 some demolition. Now a residential home.*
  V&A; BCL

Cambridge

Jesus College Chapel (CoE), 1846–9
Restoration, decoration and furnishing of medieval fabric. Restoration begun by Anthony Salvin; later repairs and decoration by G. F. Bodley, 1864–7, and largely re-glazed by Morris & Co. 1873–7.
> Robert Willis, *The Architectural History of the University of Cambridge*, ed. John Willis Clark, Cambridge, 1886

St Andrew's church (RC), 1842–3, Huddleston family
The church was dismantled and moved to St Ives, Huntingdonshire, in 1902, where it was rebuilt with the addition of a clerestory by Morley of Cambridge and Robb of St Ives.
> P. S. Wilkins, *Our Lady and the English Martyrs, Cambridge*, Cambridge, 1955

Cheadle, Staffordshire

St Giles's church (RC), 1840–46, 16th Earl of Shrewsbury

St Joseph's Convent, *c.*1846–9, 16th Earl of Shrewsbury

Presbytery, 1842, remodelling of an existing building, 16th Earl of Shrewsbury

School, *c.*1845–6, 16th Earl of Shrewsbury
> Brittain-Catlin, *Pugin's Residential Architecture*; Michael Fisher, *Perfect Cheadle*, Stafford, 2004; Higham and Carson, Pugin's *Churches of the Second Spring*

Chirk, Denbighshire

School, 1846, Col. Myddelton Biddulph

Chirk Castle, 1846–9, Col. Myddelton Biddulph
Alterations and decorations to a medieval castle. Some work after 1852 by E. W. Pugin.
> V&A; private collection
> Michael Hall, 'Chirk Castle, Denbighshire', *Country Life*, 16 July 1992, 54–7

Cotton, Staffordshire

St Wilfrid's church (RC), 1846–8, 16th Earl of Shrewsbury
Altered and lengthened 1936–7 by George Drysdale.
   V&A

Cotton College, 1846–8, 16th Earl of Shrewsbury
Adaptation and extension of an existing manor house. Many later additions during the years it was used as a school: 1874–5, 1886–7 and 1931–2.
   Very Rev. Canon W. Buscot, *The History of Cotton College*, London, 1940

Derby

St Mary's Church (RC), 1838–9

Presbytery (dem. *c.*1967), 1838–9
   Canadian Center for Architecture; BAL.
   Dan Cruickshank, 'Building with Principle', *Architects' Journal*, July 1990

Dudley, Warwickshire

Church of Our Lady and St Thomas (RC), 1838–41, George Spencer and William Fletcher
   WAA; Yale

Glasgow

Catholic Apostolic (Irvingite) church (dem. 1970), 1852, Henry Drummond
Built by James Salmon without Pugin's supervision from drawings supplied by him, c.1850.
   Frank Worsdall, *The City that Disappeared*, Glasgow, 1981

Grace Dieu, Leicestershire

>Grace Dieu Manor House, 1841, 1845 and 1848–9, Ambrose Phillipps
>*Additions and alterations to an existing house and chapel by William*
>*Railton.*
>>BAL
>>Leicestershire Record Office
>>Pawley, *Faith and Family*; Purcell, *Ambrose Phillipps*; O'Donnell, *The*
>>*Pugins and the Catholic Midlands*

Halstock, Dorset

>St Mary's church (CoE), 1845–7
>*Rebuilding of the body of the church to replace an eighteenth-century*
>*structure, but incorporating the late medieval tower. Later nineteenth-*
>*century alterations to the chancel.*
>>Dorset Record Office; Lambeth Palace Library

Keighley, Yorkshire

>St Anne's church (RC), 1838–40
>*Later extended and altered.*

>Presbytery, 1838

Kenilworth, Warwickshire

>St Augustine's church (RC), 1841, Amherst family
>*Extended 1851 by William Blount.*
>>BAA

King's Lynn, Norfolk

>St Mary's church (RC) (dem. 1896), 1844–5, Revd John Dalton
>*Replaced by new church by W. Lunn.*
>>Norfolk Record Office; typescript history of the church in the archives
>>of the Catholic Diocese of Northampton

Kirkham, Lancashire

St John the Evangelist's church (RC), 1842–5, Fr Sherburne
F. J. Singleton, *Mowbreck Hall and The Willows: A History of the Catholic Community in the Kirkham District of Lancashire*, Kirkham, 1983

Lanteglos by Camelford, Cornwall

New Anglican rectory house, 1847, Revd Roger Bird
Built without Pugin's supervision. Altered, now a hotel.

Lincoln

St Anne's bede houses, 1847–50, Revd Richard Sibthorp
Built to Pugin's design, largely without his supervision. Chapel by William Butterfield, 1853–4.

Liverpool

New house, Oswald Croft, 1844–7, Henry Sharples

Our Lady of the Annunciation, chapel (RC) (Bishop Eton), 1845–50, Bishop George Brown
Incorporated in a larger church by E. W. Pugin, built to replace it in 1857.

Gate lodge, attributed to Pugin on stylistic grounds.
The Rev. George F. Drew, *Bishop Eton and its Shrine: the story of the Redemptorists in Liverpool (1851–1951)*, Liverpool, 1951

Convent of Mercy (dem.), 1841–3

Orphanage (dem.), 1844–5 and 1847, Henry Sharples

St Mary's church (RC) (dem.), 1843–5
Originally built in Edmund Street, the church was moved to make way for the enlargement of Exchange Station. It was rebuilt in Highfield Street in 1885 by Peter Paul Pugin, but destroyed by bombing in 1941.
V&A

St Oswald's church (RC) (Old Swan), 1839–42
Destroyed, except for the tower and spire, during the Second World War; new church by Adrian Gilbert Scott, 1951–7.

School, *c.*1840–44, Edward Chaloner

Convent of Mercy, 1844–6
  V&A
  Brittain-Catlin, *Pugin's Residential Architecture*; Colin Harrison, *A Woolyback's Journey through Old Swan*, 1990

London: Bermondsey

Convent of Mercy, 1838–9
Destroyed by bombing 1945.
  L. E. Whatmore, *The Story of a Dockhead Parish*, London, 1960

London: Chelsea

Cadogan Street, Convent and schools, 1841–4, Joseph and Mary Knight

St Joseph's almshouses, *c.*1848–55
Only fragments of this scheme now survive within the later fabric.

Cemetery chapel, 1845
Now SE chapel of St Mary's church (RC), 1863, by J. F. Bentley.

Cemetery cross (attributed to Pugin), 1845
  BAL
  William James Anderson, *A History of the Catholic Parish of St Mary's, Chelsea*, London, 1938

London: Fulham

St Thomas's church (RC), 1847–8, Elizabeth Bowden

Schools, 1847–8, altered

Presbytery, 1848–9
  Denis Evinson, *St Thomas's Fulham*, London, 1976

London: Hammersmith

Convent of the Good Shepherd (dem. *c.*1921), 1848–9
Church and additions to an existing convent by J. J. Scoles.
Denis Evinson, *Pope's Corner: An historical survey of the Roman Catholic institutions in the London Borough of Hammersmith and Fulham,* London, 1980

London: Southwark

St George's church, later cathedral (RC), 1838 (unbuilt scheme) and 1839–48
Largely destroyed by bombing, April 1941, rebuilt by Romilly Craze, 1953–8. Adjacent presbytery and schools, 1839–43, rebuilt by F. A. Walters, 1886–7.
BAL; SAA
Bogan, *The Great Link*

London: Wandsworth

Church of St Thomas of Canterbury (RC) (dem.), 1847
Pugin provided designs for a building that could be used both as a school and a church.

London: Woolwich

St Peter's church (RC), 1842–3

Presbytery, *c.*1842
Yale
WAA

Macclesfield, Cheshire

St Alban's church (RC), 1838–41
Cheshire Record Office (church accounts); St Alban's church
Michael J. Ullman, *St Alban's, Macclesfield*, Macclesfield, 1982

Manchester

St Wilfred's church, Hulme (RC), 1838–42
Converted to other use.

Unitarian Chapel, Upper Brook Street, 1837–9, by Charles Barry
Pugin probably contributed details and a design for the west front. Now ruinous.

Marlow, Buckinghamshire

St Peter's church (RC), 1844–50, Charles Scott Murray
Large extension 1968–70 by Francis Pollen.
  V&A
  Pat Taylor, *St Peter's Church, Marlow*, Marlow, 1996

Medmenham, Buckinghamshire

Grounds of Danesfield House, Chapel of St Charles Borromeo (dem. 1901), 1850–53, Charles Scott Murray
Finished by E. W. Pugin. There may have been other estate buildings and the BoE attributes one surviving gate lodge to Pugin. Fittings from the Danesfield Chapel survive in the church of the Sacred Heart, Henley.
  Myers Family Trust

Mount St Bernard, Leicestershire

Cistercian Abbey, 1839–44, and calvary, 1847, Ambrose Phillipps and 16th Earl of Shrewsbury
Since extended. Chapter house by E. W. Pugin, 1860; Abbey church 1843–4, enlarged 1935–9 by F. J. Bradford.
  Mount St Bernard
  Leicestershire Record Office
  Lacey, *Second Spring*

Charnwood Lodge, house, 1843, Mr Collier
Attributed to Pugin. The only known house of this name has been demolished.

Neston, Cheshire

St Winifrede's church (RC) (later a school) and adjacent house, *c.* 1841–3
Attributed to Pugin.

Newcastle upon Tyne

Church, later Cathedral, of St Mary (RC), 1842–4.
Tower and spire by Dunn and Hansom, 1872.
V&A; BAL; Yale; Northumberland Record Office, Hexham and New-
castle Diocesan Archives
P. McGuinness, 'Pugin and St Mary's Cathedral, Newcastle upon Tyne',
Northern Catholic History, 28, 1988

Sexton's cottage
Possibly demolished, possibly never built.
BAL

Newport, Shropshire

Church of St Peter and St Paul, by Joseph Potter, 1838 and 1840
Alterations and repairs.

Northampton

St Felix's church, now Cathedral of St Mary and St Thomas (RC), 1843–4
*Pugin made designs for a new building in 1851 but no work was done
until 1863, when the church was enlarged and altered by E. W. Pugin. In
the course of this and further additions and alterations, Pugin's original
building has been rendered all but invisible.*
BAL
Fr Kenneth Payne, *The Cathedral of Our Lady and St Thomas,* n.d.,
after 1990

Nottingham

Church, later Cathedral, of St Barnabas (RC), 1841–4, 16th Earl of
Shrewsbury

Presbytery, 1844–5

Convent of the Sisters of Mercy, 1844–8, John Exton
Now converted for domestic use.
> Monsignor Martin Cummins, *Nottingham Cathedral, A History of Catholic Nottingham*, Nottingham, 3rd edition, 1994

Old Hall Green, Ware, Hertfordshire

St Edmund's College Chapel (RC), 1846–52
> St Edmund's College; BAL; WAA

House, adaptation of an existing building, *c.*1846, W. G. Ward
Much altered, now part of the school.
> Bernard Ward, *History of St Edmund's College*, Old Hall, London, 1893

Oxford

Magdalen College, entrance gate (dem. 1883), 1843–4
Replacing gateway of 1635.
> Magdalen College
> *The Buildings of Magdalen College 1458–1958*, Oxford, 1958; Roger White and Robin Darwall-Smith, *The Architectural Drawings of Magdalen College, Oxford*, Oxford, 2001

Peper Harow, Surrey

Barn and gatehouse, 1841–3; Spring House, 1843; Mousehill House alterations; 5th Viscount Midleton
> Drawings: BAL
> Correspondence: Surrey History Centre

St Nicholas's church (CoE), 1844, 5th Viscount Midleton
Restoration and extension.
> Surrey History Centre

Pontefract, Yorkshire

Jesus Chapel, Ackworth Grange (RC) (dem. 1966), 1841–2, Tempest family

Radford, Oxfordshire

 Chapel, c.1839–41

Rampisham, Dorset

 New Anglican Rectory House, 1845–7, Revd F. J. Rooke
 Now private house: 'Pugin Hall'.
  Salisbury Cathedral archives; Yale

 St Michael's church (CoE), 1845–7
 Rebuilding of chancel.

Ramsgate, Kent

 New house, The Grange, 1843–5, A. W. N. Pugin
 Subsequently altered by E. W., Peter Paul and Cuthbert Pugin; altered for use as school boarding house after 1928; restoration by the Landmark Trust completed 2006.
  BAL: foundation plan

 St Edward's Presbytery, house, 1850–51, A. W. N. Pugin
  Hill, *Pugin and Ramsgate* and 'Pugin's Home Restored', *Apollo*, August 2006

 St Augustine's church (RC), 1845–93, A. W. N. Pugin
 Work continued after 1852 by E. W. and Peter Paul Pugin.
  BAL
  Newman, *St Augustine's Ramsgate*; Libby Horner and Gill Hunter, *A Flint Seaside Church*, Ramsgate, 2000

 West Cliff Lodge, 1847–8, Henry Benson
 Porch for an existing house.
  Rosemary Hill, 'West Cliff Lodge', *True Principles*, 1, 8, Summer 1999

Ratcliffe-on-the-Wreake, Leicestershire

 Novitiate and College for the Rosminians, 1843–4 and additions 1846–7, William Lockhart, the 16th Earl of Shrewsbury, Ambrose Phillipps, Lady Mary Arundell
 Only the east (front) range is by Pugin. The building was continued

1849–54 and 1857–8 by Charles Hansom, using Pugin's designs with further additions by E. W. Pugin in 1862 and 1867–8.
Rosminian archives: Derry's Wood and Stresa
The Very Revd C. R. Leetham, *Ratcliffe College, 1847–1947*, Ratcliffe, 1850; O'Donnell, *The Pugins and the Catholic Midlands*

Reading, Berkshire

St James's church (RC), 1837, James Wheble
Altered and extended 1926.
John Mullaney, *St James's Catholic Church and School*, Reading, 1987

Rugby, Warwickshire

St Mary's church (RC), 1847, Captain Washington Hibbert
Greatly enlarged and altered by E. W. Pugin, 1864; tower and spire by Bernard Whelan, 1872.
Rev. S. E. Jarvis, *A Short History of St Marie's Rugby: 1844–1914*, Rugby, 1914; Derek and Lucy Thackray, *A brief history of St Marie's church 1844 to 1986*, Rugby, 1987

St Mary's College (altered), 1849–52, Captain Washington Hibbert and the Rosminians
Rosminian archive: Derry's Wood

Bilton Grange, 1844–51, Captain Washington Hibbert
Large additions and alterations to an existing house.
V&A; BAL

St Peter Port, Guernsey

St Joseph and St Mary's church (RC), 1845–51
Drawings of the first, unbuilt, design: St John's College within the University of Sydney, Australia

Salisbury, Wiltshire

Hall of John Halle, 1834
Restoration of fifteenth-century merchant's house. Converted into the foyer of the Gaumont cinema by W. E. Trent, 1931.

St Osmund's church (RC), 1846–8, John Lambert
North aisle added 1894 by E. Doran Webb.
>   Wiltshire Record Office; St Osmund's church
>   Raleigh St Lawrence, *St Osmund's and Catholic Salisbury, a short history*, Salisbury, 1997

Scarisbrick Hall, Ormskirk, Lancashire

>   Alterations to an existing house, decorations, furnishing, 1837–45 (and possibly later), Charles Scarisbrick
>   *E. W. Pugin worked for Charles Scarisbrick's sister Anne Scarisbrick from 1861 to about 1865, continuing with the decoration and adding the tower.*
>   >   BAL; V&A; Lancashire County Record Office
>   >   Hasted, *Scarisbrick Hall*; Rosemary Hill, 'Scarisbrick Hall Revisited', *Country Life*, 8 August 2002, 44–9 and 15 August 2002, 44–7

Shepshed, Leicestershire

>   St Winefrede's church (RC), 1842, Ambrose Phillipps
>   *Much altered and converted to domestic use.*
>   >   Lacey, *Second Spring*

Solihull, Warwickshire

>   St Augustine's church (RC), 1838–9
>   *Extended by Hansom and Sons 1878, altered 1884, 1897 and 1904, extended and reorientated by Brian Rush, 1979; only Pugin's south wall survives.*

Southampton, Hampshire

>   St Joseph's church (RC), 1841–3
>   *The church was begun as an extension to an existing building to Pugin's designs. It is not clear whether Pugin ever supervised the work. Whatever personal involvement he had was short-lived. The plans were redrawn by a local architect, J. G. Poole, in 1850 and the church was further altered and extended in 1888 by Leonard Stokes, who left intact the sanctuary, which is all that can now properly be attributed to Pugin.*
>   >   Paul Beaumont, *St Joseph's Church Bugle Street: 1830–1980*, ?Southampton, 1981

Southport, Lancashire

St Mary's church (RC), 1840–41
Extended, to Pugin's designs, 1852; extended and largely rebuilt 1875.
Lancashire County Record Office

School, 1842

Spetchley, Worcestershire

Village school, 1841, Berkeley family

Stockton-on-Tees, Co. Durham

St Mary's church (RC), *c.*1840–42, Revd Joseph Dugdale

Presbytery and schools, *c.*1840–41
Only the nave was completed when the church was opened in 1842.
All that survives now of Pugin's design is the west front. Tower, 1866;
extensions by Goldie and Child, 1870, and C. & C. M. Hadfield, c.1908.
Brittain-Catlin, *Pugin's Residential Architecture*

Stone, Staffordshire

St Anne's, combined chapel (RC) and school, 1843–4, James Beech
Norman A. Cope, *Stone in Staffordshire: The History of a Market*
Town, Hanley, 1972

Tubney, Berkshire

St Lawrence's church (CoE), 1844–7, Magdalen College, Oxford
Drawings and correspondence: Magdalen College, Oxford
Roger White and Robin Darwall-Smith, *The Architectural Drawings of*
Magdalen College, Oxford, Oxford, 2001

Ushaw, County Durham

St Cuthbert's College

Chapel (RC), 1843–8
A scheme for a chapel and exhibition room of 1840 was not built. Pugin's
Chapel was rebuilt and expanded using original material by Dunn and

Hansom, 1884; Lady Chapel rebuilt and redecorated by J. F. Bentley, 1894; extension 1925–8 by Sebastian Pugin Powell.

Cloister, 1852–3

St Joseph's chapel, 1852–4
Completed by E. W. Pugin.

   V&A; BAL; Ushaw

Uttoxeter, Staffordshire

St Mary's church (RC), 1838–9
Altered by Peter Paul Pugin in the 1870s; greatly extended 1913 by Henry Sandy.
   Paul F. Wilson, *St Mary's Catholic Church*, Uttoxeter, *c.*1989

Presbytery, 1838–9
   Drawings: Getty Center, Los Angeles
   Hill, *Pugin's Small Houses*

Warwick Bridge, Cumbria

Our Lady and St Wilfred's church, 1840–41, Henry Howard

Presbytery, *c.*1840
Built by George Myers to Pugin's design but without his supervision.
   Myers Family Trust

West Tofts, Norfolk

St Mary's church (CoE), 1846–52, Revd Augustus Sutton and the Sutton family
Restoration and extension of an existing medieval building. Work continued by E. W. Pugin, largely to Pugin's designs, 1855–9.
   Myers Family Trust; Norfolk Record Office
   Roy Tricker, *St Mary's West Tofts, Norfolk, History and Guide*, 3rd edn, 1987; Anthony Barnes, 'A Pugin Rediscovered?', *True Principles*, 2, 2, Summer 2001

Whitwick, Leicestershire

School, 1842, Ambrose Phillipps
Later used as a convent.

Wilburton, Cambridgeshire

Wilburton Manor, 1848–51, Sir Albert Pell
New house, built without Pugin's supervision.
    Private collection
    John Kenworthy-Browne et al., *Burke's and Savills Guide to Country Houses, 3, East Anglia*, London, 1981

St Peter's church (CoE), *c.*1848, Lady Pell
Restoration (attr.) of medieval church.

Winwick, Cheshire

St Oswald's church (CoE), 1847–8, Revd J. Hornby
Rebuilding of chancel of medieval church.
    Cheshire Record Office
    Revd W. A. Wickham, 'Pugin and the Rebuilding of Winwick Chancel', *Transactions of the Historic Society of Lancashire and Cheshire*, 1907

Wymeswold, Leicestershire

St Mary's church (CoE), 1844–50, Revd Henry Alford
Restoration and additions.
    Anonymous [Henry Alford], *A History and Description of the Restored Parish Church of St Mary Wymeswold, Leicestershire*, London, 1846; G. K. Brandwood, *Bringing them to their knees: church-building and restoration in Leicestershire and Rutland 1800–1914*, 2002

Australia

For all of the following, see Andrews, *Creating a Gothic Paradise* and *Australian Gothic*.

Berrima, New South Wales

> St Francis Xavier's church (RC), designed 1842, built 1849–51, Archbishop Polding

Brisbane

> St Stephen's church (RC), designed 1842, built c.1848–50

Ryde, New South Wales

> St Charles Borromeo's church (RC), designed 1842, built 1852–c.1857
> *Much enlarged 1934, with most of the original fabric reincorporated in the new building.*

Sydney

> St Mary's church, later cathedral (RC), 1842, Archbishop Polding
> *Pugin supplied designs for a temporary bell-tower and major extensions to the existing church as well a school. Some of this was built but the cathedral was largely destroyed by fire in 1865. The rest was demolished in the early twentieth century.*

Sydney: Balmain

> St Augustine of Hippo's church (RC), designed 1842, built c.1848–51, Archbishop Polding
> *Altered and extended in nineteenth century, converted 1907 to use as a parish hall.*

Sydney: Parramatta

> St Patrick's church, now cathedral (RC), designed 1842, built 1854–9, Archbishop Polding
> *Rebuilt and expanded 1936 by Clement Glancey.*

St Benedict's, Broadway (RC), design supplied 1842, built 1845–56
Dismantled and rebuilt 1940s.

Pugin also supplied at least five designs for churches of which Polding made use between 1843 and 1859.

Tasmania

St Patrick, Colebrook (RC), designed 1844, built 1855–7, Bishop Robert Willson
Built by Frederick Hugh Thomas from a model and drawings by Pugin.

St Paul, Oatlands (RC), designed 1844, built 1850, Bishop Robert Willson
Built by Frederick Hugh Thomas from a model by Pugin.
Archdiocese of Hobart Museum and Archives; Archives Office of Tasmania

St John the Evangelist, Richmond (RC), designed 1844, built 1858–9
Built by Frederick Hugh Thomas from Pugin's model as an extension to an existing church of 1836 by Henry Goodridge.
Tasmanian Museum and Art Gallery

Eire

For all of the following see Scott-Richardson, *Gothic Revival Architecture in Ireland* and Williams, *Companion Guide to Architecture in Ireland.*

Adare, Co. Limerick

Adare Manor House, *c.*1846–7, 2nd Earl Dunraven
Designs for alterations and extensions to the existing house, some carried out.
RIBA [75] is a design of 1838 which may have been a first conception for the Great Hall.

Barntown, Co. Wexford

St Alphonsus's church (RC), 1844–8

Birr, Co. Offaly

Convent, 1845, Sister Anastasia Beckett
*The building was extended from 1852 onwards by George Ashlin and
E. W. Pugin.*

Bree, Co. Wexford

Church of the Assumption (RC), *c.*1837–40, John Hyacinth Talbot

Cobh, Co. Cork

Two villas for 5th Viscount Midleton
Possibly not built.

Enniscorthy, Co. Wexford

St Aidan's church, later cathedral (RC), 1843–50

Gorey, Co. Wexford

St Michael's church (RC), 1839

Convent, *c.*1839

Killarney, Co. Kerry

St Mary's church, later cathedral (RC), 1842–50, Lord Kenmare
Extended after 1852 and drastically altered in the early 1970s.

Maynooth, Co. Kildare

St Patrick's College, 1846–51
Chapel added 1875 by J. J. McCarthy, further additions 1895 and 1902–5.
St Patrick's College archives; BAL
O'Dwyer, 'A. W. N. Pugin and St Patrick's College, Maynooth'

Midleton, Co. Cork

Midleton Arms, pub and shop (attrib.), 1861, Midleton Estate
*Built 1861, possibly by E. W. Pugin. Pugin's commission to build a model
town for Lord Midleton was abandoned during the famine. It is possible,
however, that these buildings were adapted from his designs.*

Portarlington, Co. Offaly

Church (attrib.), *c.*1845
*Pugin received more than one commission from Lord Portarlington, but
little work was carried out because of the famine. It has been suggested
that this church was built from a design supplied by Pugin.*

Ramsgrange, Co. Wexford

St James's church (RC) (attrib.), 1835–48
*Exactly what Pugin's involvement was in this design is unclear. Whatever
he contributed is now largely masked by later additions and alterations.*

Rathfarnham, Dublin

Loreto Abbey (RC) chapel, *c.*1839
Designs of c.1839 modified in execution by Patrick Byrne and J. B. Keane.

Tagoat, Co. Wexford

St Mary's church (RC), 1843–6, John Hyacinth Talbot

Waterford

Convent of the Presentation, 1842–8

School, *c.*1842–8

St John's Manor, house, after 1845, Thomas Wyse
*Alterations to an existing house. Wyse, an MP and long-standing friend
of Pugin, wanted a Great Hall, which Pugin considered too elaborate for
a house of this size. Exactly what was built remains unclear.*
*References in PC 339 including an account by Winifrede, Wyse's niece,
and one letter in a private collection.*

Wexford

Chapel of St Peter's College (RC), 1838

France

Douai, Nord

St Edmund's College Chapel, designs 1840
The chapel as built seems to have been based on Pugin's designs.
  Douai Abbey, Woolhampton, Berkshire
  Roderick O'Donnell, 'Pugin in France: Designs for St Edmund's College
  Chapel, Douai (Nord), 1840', *Burlington Magazine*, October 1983

UNBUILT SCHEMES

Dartington, Totnes, Devon

Dartington Hall, 1845, Mr Champernowne
Designs for alterations to Dartington Hall, a fourteenth-century house.
  Devon County Record Office

Edinburgh

Cathedral and college, 1849–50, Bishop Gillis
  Drawings: BAL and copies of some drawings now lost, Catholic
  Cathedral House, Edinburgh
  Sharples, 'Pugin and Gillis'

Holyrood Abbey church, 1836–7
Proposal for restoration (drawings for Gillespie Graham).
  Royal Commission on the Ancient and Historic Monuments of Scot-
  land; Macaulay, 'Gillespie Graham and Pugin'

Glasgow

Restoration of Glasgow cathedral (Church of Scotland), 1837
Drawings for Gillespie Graham.
  Royal Commission on the Ancient and Historic Monuments of Scotland
  James Macaulay, 'The Demolition of the Western Towers of Glasgow
  Cathedral', in Deborah Mays, ed., *The Architecture of Scottish Cities:
  Essays in Honour of David Walker*, East Linton, *c.*1997

Hobart, Tasmania

Design for a cathedral (RC), *c.*1847, Bishop Robert Willson
BAL
Andrews, *Creating a Gothic Paradise*

Hornby, Yorkshire

Hornby Castle, proposed alterations, 1847
Yorkshire Archaeological Society, Borthwick Institute
Giles Worsley, 'Hornby Castle, Yorkshire', *Country Life*, 29 June 1989,
188–93; 'A. W. M. Pugin's scheme for Hornby Castle, Yorkshire',
Burlington Magazine, cxlvi, 1217, August 2004, 550–53

Liverpool

Our Lady Immaculate, scheme for a pro-cathedral at Everton, 1845

Manchester

Proposals for a church and clergy house in Ducie Street, 1837–8
BAL; V&A

Milford

Mousehill Manor, design for a cottage
Liverpool Record Office
Brittain-Catlin, *Pugin's Residential Architecture*

Oxford

Balliol College, designs for restoration and extension, 1843
Balliol College archives
Colvin, *Unbuilt Oxford*; Leon B. Litvak, 'The Balliol that might have
been: Pugin's crushing Oxford defeat', *Journal of the Society of Architectural Historians*, 45, December 1986

Magdalen College, designs for a new college school, 1843–4 and 1848
Drawings: Magdalen College
Roger White and Robin Darwall-Smith, *The Architectural Drawings of
Magdalen College, Oxford*, Oxford, 2001

Stratton-on-the-Fosse, Somerset

Downside Abbey, 1839, 1841, 1842
Roderick O'Donnell, 'Pugin Designs for Downside Abbey', *Burlington Magazine*, April 1981

Stroud, Gloucestershire

Woodchester Park, designs for a manor house and monastery, 1845–6, William Leigh
A church and monastery were built by Charles Hansom, 1846–9 and 1861–5. The mansion, by Benjamin Bucknall, was begun in 1858 based on Pugin's drawings but also much influenced by Viollet-le-Duc. It was never finished.
Gloucestershire Record Office; BL
Duff Hart-Davis, *Woodchester Mansion*, Stroud, 1999

Major Decorative and Furnishing Schemes

Birmingham

King Edward VI Grammar School by Charles Barry
Designs for furnishings, 1835–6. The original school, which stood in New Street, was demolished in 1936, but the chapel was preserved and moved to the site of the new school in Edgbaston and re-erected 1952.
BAL; King Edward VI School
Anthony Trott, *No Place for Fop or Idler: the Story of King Edward's School, Birmingham*, London, 1992

Cheadle, Cheshire

Abney Hall (villa of 1847, extended 1849 by Travis & Mangnall), 1852, James Watts
Decorations and furnishings, most now dispersed, carried out post-humously by J. G. Crace, 1852–7.
V&A

Eastnor, Herefordshire

Eastnor Castle by Robert Smirke (1812), 1849–50, Earl Somers
Drawings: V&A
Giles Worsley, 'Eastnor Castle, Herefordshire-I', *Country Life*, 13 May 1993, 82–5; Clive Wainwright, 'Eastnor Castle, Herefordshire II', *Country Life*, 20 May 1993, 90–93

Edinburgh

Heriot's Hospital (George Heriot's School)
Furnishings for the chapel, re-ordered by Gillespie Graham, 1837.

St Margaret's Convent
Chapel furnishings, shrine and some architectural details, 1835.
Sharples, 'Pugin and James Gillis'

Leadenham, Lincolnshire

St Swithin's church, 1841, Revd Bernard Smith
Painted decoration in the chancel.

Lismore, County Waterford

Lismore Castle, 1849–50, 6th Duke of Devonshire
Banqueting hall and other furnishings.
Drawings, V&A
Mark Girouard, 'Lismore Castle, County Waterford', *Country Life*, 6 August 1964, 336–40 and 13 August 1964, 389–93

Little Horsted, East Sussex

Horsted Place (house by Samuel Dawkes), 1851
Fittings and decorations, staircase still in situ. The house is now a hotel.

London

Palace of Westminster, 1835–7 and 1844–51
Designs for interiors, details and furnishings.
BAL; V&A; House of Lords Record Office
Port, *Houses of Parliament*; Crook and Port, *King's Works*; Alexandra

Wedgwood, 'The throne in the House of Lords and its setting', *Architectural History* 27, 1984

Melton Mowbray, Leicestershire

St John the Baptist (RC) (church by E. J. Willson), 1840, John Exton
Pugin supplied fittings, since removed.

Perthshire

Murthly Castle, new building (by Gillespie Graham), 1829–32 (dem.), Sir William Stewart
Pugin designed a suite of interiors including a Great Hall and a French ballroom which survive in part in the old castle.
Macaulay, *Gothic Revival*; Ian Gow, *Scotland's Lost Houses*, London, 2006

Taymouth Castle, 1837–42, Lord Breadalbane
Designs for decorations and fittings for Gillespie Graham's refurbishment and extension.
Royal Commission on the Historic and Ancient Monuments of Scotland; SRO
Alistair Rowan, 'Taymouth Castle Perthshire', *Country Life*, 8 October 1964, 912–16, and 15 October 1964, 978–81

Welshpool, Montgomeryshire

Leighton Hall (house by William H. Gee), 1851–2, John Naylor
Fittings and decorations, mostly carried out posthumously by J. G. Crace, 1852–5.
V&A; Queen's University, Kingston, Ontario
Megan Aldrich and Barry Shifman, 'Crace, Pugin and the Furnishing of John Naylor's Leighton Hall', *Furniture History*, 2005

Weston, Warwickshire

Weston Park, furnishings for a house (by Edward Blore), *c.*1830–31, George Philips
Michael Warriner, *A Prospect of Weston in Warwickshire*, 1978; Peter Reid, *Burke's and Savill's Guide to Country Houses 2, Herefordshire, Shropshire, Warwickshire, Worcestershire*, London, 1980, 185

Select Bibliography

Adams, Bernard, *London Illustrated: 1604–1851*, London, 1983.

Aldrich, Megan (ed.), *The Craces: Royal Decorators 1768–1899*, Brighton, 1990.

Anderson, William James, *A History of the Catholic Parish of St Mary's Chelsea*, London, 1938.

Andrews, Brian, *Australian Gothic: the Gothic Revival in Australian Architecture from the 1840s to the 1950s*, Carlton South, Victoria, 2001.

Andrews, Brian (ed.), *Creating a Gothic Paradise: Pugin at the Antipodes*, Hobart, 2002.

Anstruther, Ian, *The Knight and the Umbrella, an account of the Eglinton Tournament – 1839*, London, 1963.

Architect-Designers Pugin to Mackintosh, Fine Art Society, London, 1981.

Arundell, Lady Mary, *Letters*, ed. with a memoir by the Very Rev. Joseph Hirst, Ratcliffe College, 1894.

Atterbury, Paul, and Wainwright, Clive (eds.), *Pugin: A Gothic Passion*, New Haven, 1994.

Atterbury, Paul, and Wainwright, Clive (eds.), *Pugin: Master of Gothic Revival*, New Haven, 1995.

Barry, Rev. Alfred, *The Life and Works of Sir Charles Barry, RA FRS*, London, 1867.

Barry, Rev. Alfred, *The Architect of the New Palace: a reply to a pamphlet by E. W. Pugin*, London, 1868.

Basset, Bernard, S. J., *Newman at Littlemore*, Warley [1984?].

Belcher, Margaret, *A. W. N. Pugin: an annotated critical bibliography*, London, 1987.

Bellenger, Sylvain and Hamon, Françoise (ed.), *Félix Duban, 1798–1870, Les couleurs de l'architecte*, Paris, 1996.

Bogan, Bernard, *The Great Link: A History of St George's Southwark*, London, 1948.

Bogan, Peter Paul, *Beloved Chapel: the story of the Old Chapel of St Peter's, Winchester*, Winchester, n.d.

Bolitho, Hector, and Peel, Derek, *The Drummonds of Charing Cross*, London, 1967.

Bonython, Elizabeth, and Burton, Anthony, *The Great Exhibitor: The Life and Work of Henry Cole*, London, 2003.

Bossy, John, *The English Catholic Community, 1570–1850*, London, 1975.

Brendan, Piers, *Hurrell Froude and the Oxford Movement*, London, 1974.

Briggs, Asa, *The Age of Improvement: 1783–1867*, 2nd impression with corrections, London, 1960.

Briggs, Asa, *Victorian Cities*, Penguin edition, London, 1990.

Brittain-Catlin, Timothy, *A. W. N. Pugin's Residential Architecture in Context*, unpublished PhD thesis, Cambridge, 2004.

Brooks, Chris, and Saint, Andrew (eds.), *The Victorian Church, Architecture and Society*, Manchester, 1995.

Brooks, Michael W., *John Ruskin and Victorian Architecture*, London, 1989.

Bury, J. T. P., *France 1814–1940*, New York, 5th edition, 1985.

Bury, Shirley, Wedgwood, Alexandra, and Snodin, Michael, 'The Antiquarian Plate of George IV', *Burlington Magazine*, 121, June 1979.

Caledonia Gothica: the Journal of the Architectural Heritage Society of Scotland, VIII, 1997.

Carlyle, Thomas, 'Chartism', in The Shilling Edition of Carlyle's Works, London, n.d.

Carlyle, Thomas, *Past and Present*, Everyman edition, London, 1912.

Carlyle, Thomas, *Selected Writings*, ed. Alan Shelston, Penguin English Library, Harmondsworth, 1971.

Carter, George, Goode, Patrick, and Laurie, Kedrun, *Humphry Repton, Landscape Gardener 1752–1818*, Norwich, 1982.

Chadwick, Owen, *The Victorian Church: Part One*, London, 1966.

Chadwick, Owen, *A History of the Popes: 1830–1914*, Oxford, 1998.

Champ, Judith, *Oscott*, Birmingham, 1987.

Champ, Judith (ed.), *Oscott College 1838–88: a volume of commemorative essays*, Birmingham, c.1988.

Chandler, John H., *Endless Street, a history of Salisbury and its people*, Salisbury, 1983.

Chateaubriand, François-René, Vicomte de, *The Memoirs of Chateaubriand*, ed. and trans. by Robert Baldick, London, 1961.

Christiansen, Rupert, *Romantic Affinities: Portraits from an Age 1780–1830*, London, 1988.

Clark, Kenneth, *The Gothic Revival*, 3rd edition, London, 1962.

Clarke, Michael, and Penny, Nicholas (eds.), *The Arrogant Connoisseur: Richard Payne Knight 1751–1824*, Manchester, 1982.

Colvin, Howard, *Unbuilt Oxford*, New Haven, 1983.

Colvin, Howard, *A Biographical Dictionary of British Architects, 1600–1840*, 3rd edition, Oxford, 1995.

Crook, J. Mordaunt, 'John Britton and the Genesis of the Gothic Revival', in John Summerson (ed.), *Concerning Architecture, Essays on architectural writers and writing presented to Nikolaus Pevsner*, London, 1968.

Crook, J. Mordaunt, *John Carter and the Mind of the Gothic Revival*, London, 1995.

Crook, J. Mordaunt, and Port, M. H., *A History of the King' Works: Vol. VI 1782–1851*, London, 1973.

Daniels, Stephen, *Humphry Repton*, New Haven and London, 1999.

Daniels, Stephen, and Watkins, Charles (eds.), *The Picturesque Landscape, Visions of Georgian Herefordshire*, Nottingham, 1994.

Dent, Robert K., *The Making of Birmingham*, Birmingham, 1894.

Digby, Kenelm, *The Broad Stone of Honour or the True Sense and Practice of Chivalry*, London, 1829.

Digby, Kenelm, *Mores Catholici or Ages of Faith*, London, 1831–42.

Dixon, Roger, and Muthesius, Stefan, *Victorian Architecture*, London, 2nd edition, 1985.

Dodds, John W., *The Age of Paradox*, London, 1953.

Eastlake, Charles, *A History of the Gothic Revival*, London, 1872.

Evans, Joan, *A History of the Society of Antiquaries*, London, 1956.

Evinson, Denis, *Catholic Churches of London*, Sheffield, 1998.

Faber, Frederick William, *Faber, Poet and Priest: Selected letters by Frederick William Faber from 1833–1863*, ed. and selected by Raleigh Addington, Glamorgan, 1974.

Faber, Richard, *Young England*, London, 1987.

Ferrey, Benjamin, *Recollections of A. N. Welby Pugin and his father Augustus Pugin*, London, 1861, reprinted with an introduction by Clive Wainwright and index by Jane Wainwright, London, 1978.

Fisher, Michael J., *Alton Towers, a Gothic Wonderland*, Stafford, 1999.

Fisher, Michael J., *Pugin-Land: A. W. N. Pugin, Lord Shrewsbury and the Gothic Revival in Staffordshire*, Stafford, 2002.

Fisher, Michael J., *Staffordshire and the Gothic Revival*, Ashbourne, 2006

Flegg, Columba Graham, *Gathered Under Apostles: a study of the Catholic Apostolic Church*, Oxford, 1993.

Ford, John, *Ackermann 1783–1983*, London, 1983.

Fox, Celina (ed.), *London World City, 1800–1840*, New Haven, 1992.

Franklin, Jill, *The Gentleman's Country House and Its Plan 1835–1914*, London, 1981.

Freeman, Michael, *Railways and the Victorian Imagination*, New Haven, 1999.

Garrioch, David, *Neighbourhood and Community in Paris, 1740–1790*, Cambridge, 1986.

Germann, Georg, *Gothic Revival in Europe and Britain, sources, influences and ideas*, London, 1972.

Gilley, Sheridan, *Newman and His Age*, London, 1990.

Girouard, Mark, *The Victorian Country House*, New Haven, 1979.

Girouard, Mark, *The Return to Camelot: Chivalry and the English Gentleman*, New Haven, 1981.

Gomme, George Laurence, *Sacred and Medieval Architecture: a classified collection of the chief contents of The Gentleman's Magazine from 1731–1868*, 2 vols., London, 1890.

Goodall, Frederick, *The Reminiscences of Frederick Goodall RA*, London, 1902.

Gwynn, Dennis, *Lord Shrewsbury, Pugin and the Catholic Revival*, London, 1946.

Gwynn, Dennis, *Fr Luigi Gentili and his Mission*, Dublin, 1951.

Halévy, Elie, *A history of the English People in the nineteenth century*, 6 vols., paperback edition, London, 1961.

Hall, Michael (ed.), *Gothic Architecture and its Meanings 1550–1830*, London, 2002.

Hardie, Martin, *Water-Colour Painting in Britain*, 3 vols., London, 1966–8.

Harrison, J. F. C., *Early Victorian Britain, 1832–51*, Fontana edition, London, 1979.

Harrison, Martin, *Victorian Stained Glass*, London, 1980.

Haskell, Francis, *History and its Images*, New Haven, 1993.

Hasted, Rachel, *Scarisbrick Hall, a guide*, 1987.

Hayes, John, *Rowlandson watercolours and drawings*, London, 1972.

Hazleton, Nancy J. Doran, 'The Grieve Family, patterning in 19th-century scene designs', *Theatre Survey* 32:1, New York, 1991.

Hesketh, Christian, *Tartans*, London, 1961.

Higham, David, and Carson, Penelope, *Pugin's Churches of the Second Spring*, Uttoxeter, 1997.

Hill, Rosemary, 'Bankers, Bawds and Beau Monde, A. C. Pugin and Ackermann's "Microcosm of London"', *Country Life*, 3 November 1994.

Hill, Rosemary, 'A. C. Pugin', *Burlington Magazine*, 1114, January 1996.

Hill, Rosemary, '"To Stones a Moral Life": how Pugin transformed the Gothic Revival', *Times Literary Supplement*, 18 September 1998.

Hill, Rosemary, *Pugin and Ramsgate*, Kent History Federation and the Pugin Society, Ramsgate, 1999.

Hill, Rosemary, 'Reformation to Millennium, Pugin's *Contrasts* in the history of English Thought', *Journal of the Society of Architectural Historians*, 58:1, March 1999.

Hill, Rosemary, 'Pugin and Ruskin', *British Art Journal*, 2, Spring/Summer 2001, republished in a revised and expanded version in *Ruskin and Architecture*, ed. Rebecca Daniels and Geoff Brandwood, Victorian Society, 2003.

Hill, Rosemary, 'Pugin's Small Houses', *Architectural History*, 46, 2003.

Hill, Rosemary, 'Pugin's Churches', *Architectural History*, 49, 2006.

Hitchcock, Henry-Russell, *Early Victorian Architecture in Britain*, 2 vols., New Haven, 1954.

Hobhouse, Hermione, *Thomas Cubitt Master Builder*, London, 1971.

Hunt, Leigh, *Dramatic Criticism*, ed. Lawrence Huston and Carolyn Washburn, New York, 1949.

Kee, Robert, *The Green Flag, Volume 1, The Most Distressful Country*, Penguin edn, London, 1989.

Kelly, Alison, *Mrs Coade's Stone*, Upton-upon-Severn, 1990.

Ker, Ian, *John Henry Newman, a biography*, Oxford, 1988.

Kerney, Michael, 'The stained glass commissioned by William Butterfield', *Journal of Stained Glass*, 20, 1996.

Kerney, Michael, 'All Saints, Margaret Street: a glazing history', *Journal of Stained Glass*, 25, London, 2002.

Knight, Richard Payne, *An Analytical Enquiry into the Principles of Taste*, London, 1805.

Kremers, Hidegard et al., *Marie Caroline de Berry, Naples, Paris, Graz, itinéraire d'une princesse romantique*, Paris, 2002.

Lacey, Andrew C., *The Second Spring in Charnwood Forest*, Loughborough, 1985.

Lafitte, Louis, *Catalogue des tableaux, dessins, estampes, livres, médailles et curiosités du cabinet du feu M Louis Lafitte, peintre*, Paris, 1828.

Langlois, E.-H., *Stalles de la Cathédrale de Rouen*, Rouen, 1838.

Leach, Terence R., and Pacey, Robert, *Lost Lincolnshire Country Houses*, vol. 1, Burgh le Marsh, Lincolnshire, 1990.

Leetham, Very Rev. C. R., *Ratcliffe College 1847–1947*, Ratcliffe, 1950.

Liscombe, R. W., *William Wilkins, 1778–1839*, Cambridge, 1980.

Macaulay, James, *The Gothic Revival, 1745–1845*, Glasgow, 1975.

Macaulay, James, 'The Architectural Collaboration between J. Gillespie Graham and A. W. N. Pugin', *Architectural History* 27, 1984.

McAuley, Catherine, *Correspondence, 1827–1841*, ed. Sister Angela Bolster, Dioceses of Cork and Ross, 1989.

Mathews, Charles, *Memoirs, 1776–1835*, 2 vols., 1838.

Mayer, David, III, *Harlequin in his Element, The English Pantomime, 1806–1836*, Cambridge MA, 1969.

Mays, Deborah (ed.), *The Architecture of Scottish Cities: Essays in Honour of David Walker*, East Linton, c.1997.

Meara, David, *A. W. N. Pugin and the Revival of Memorial Brasses*, London, 1991.

Mercier, Louis Sébastien, *Tableau de Paris*, ed. Jean-Claude Bonnet, 2 vols., Paris, 1994.

Middleton, R. D., *Newman and Bloxam, an Oxford friendship*, Oxford, 1947.

Milner, John, *A Dissertation on the Modern Style of Altering Antient Cathedrals as Exemplified in the Cathedral of Salisbury*, London, 1798.

Milner, John, *Letters to a Prebendary*, London, 1800.

Milner, John, *The History Civil and Ecclesiastical and survey of the Antiquities of Winchester*, 2nd edn, 2 vols., London, 1809.

Mozley, Revd Thomas, *Reminiscences, chiefly of Oriel College and the Oxford Movement*, 2 vols., London, 1882.

Muthesius, Hermann, *Das Englische Haus* (Berlin, 1904–5), ed. and trans. Dennis Sharp, St Albans, 1979.

Myers, Harris, with a foreword by Brian Allen, *William Henry Pyne and his Microcosm*, Stroud, Gloucestershire, 1996.

Newman, John, *St Augustine's, Ramsgate as a Kentish Church*, Ramsgate, 1996.

Newman, John Henry, *Apologia Pro Vita Sua* (1864), Everyman edition, London, 1912.

Newman, John Henry, *Diaries and Letters*, ed. with notes and an introduction by Charles Stephen Dessain et al., London, 1961–77.

O'Donnell, Roderick, *The Pugins and the Catholic Midlands*, Leominster and Leamington Spa, 2002.

O'Dwyer, Frederick, 'A. W. N. Pugin and St Patrick's College, Maynooth', in *Irish Arts Review Yearbook*, 12, 1996, 102–9.

Oliver, W., *Prophets and Millenialists*, Oxford, 1978.

Olney, R. J., *Lincolnshire Politics 1832–1885*, Oxford, 1973.

Pagani, Very Rev. Father (ed.), *Life of the Rev. Aloysius Gentili, 1801–48*, London, 1851.

Pawley, Margaret, *Faith and Family: the Life and Circle of Ambrose Phillipps de Lisle*, Norwich, 1993.

Peniston, John, *Letters of John Peniston, Salisbury architect, catholic and yeomanry officer, 1823–1830*, ed. Michael Cowan, Trowbridge, 1996.

Pevsner, Nikolaus, *The Sources of Modern Architecture and Design*, London, 1968.

Port, Michael, *The Houses of Parliament*, London, 1976.

Powell, Christabel, *Augustus Welby Pugin . . . The Victorian Quest for a Liturgical Architecture*, Ceredigion, 2006.

Powell, John Hardman, 'Pugin in his home', ed. Alexandra Wedgwood, *Architectural History*, 31, 1988.

Price, Uvedale, *An Essay on the Picturesque, as compared with the Sublime and the Beautiful; and on the use of studying pictures, for the purpose of improving real landscape*, 2 vols., 1794–98.

Pugin, Auguste Charles, and Britton, John, *Specimens of the Architectural Antiquities of Normandy*, London, 1828.

Pugin, Auguste Charles, Rowlandson, Thomas, et al., *The Microcosm of London*, 3 vols., London, 1808–11.

Pugin, Auguste Charles, and Willson, Edward J., *Specimens of Gothic Architecture selected from various antient edifices in England*, 2 vols., London, 1821 and 1823.

Pugin, Auguste Charles, and Ventouillac, L. T., *Paris and its Environs*, 2 vols., London, 1829–31.

Pugin, Auguste Charles, Willson, E. J., Pugin, A. W., et al., *Examples of Gothic Architecture*, 3 vols., London, 1831–36.

Pugin, A. W. N., *Gothic Furniture in the style of the 15th century designed & etched by A. W. N. Pugin*, London, 1835.

Pugin, A. W. N., *A Letter to A. W. Hakewill, architect, in answer to his reflections on the style for rebuilding the houses of parliament*, Salisbury, 1835.

Pugin, A. W. N., *Contrasts or a parallel between the noble edifices of the fourteenth and fifteenth centuries, and similar buildings of the present day; shewing the present decay of taste; Accompanied by appropriate Text*, Salisbury, 1836.

Pugin, A. W. N., *Designs for iron and brass work in the style of the xv and xvi centuries*, London, 1836.

Pugin, A. W. N., *Designs for Gold & Silversmiths*, London, 1836.

Pugin, A. W. N., *Details of Antient Timber Houses of the 15th & 16th centries selected from those existing at Rouen, Caen, Beauvais, Gisors, Abbeville, Strasbourg, etc drawn on the spot*, London, 1836.

Pugin, A. W. N., *An apology for a work entitled 'Contrasts;' being a defence of the assertions advanced in that publication, against the various attacks lately made upon it*, Birmingham, 1837.

Pugin, A. W. N., *A reply to observations which appeared in 'Fraser's Magazine,' for March 1837 on a work entitled 'Contrasts' by the author of that publication*, London, 1837.

Pugin, A. W. N., *A letter on the proposed protestant memorial to Cranmer, Ridley, & Latymer, addressed to the subscribers to and promoters of that undertaking*, London, 1839.

Pugin, A. W. N., *Contrasts*, 2nd revised edn, London, 1841.

Pugin, A. W. N., *The True Principles of Pointed or Christian Architecture: set forth in two lectures delivered at St Marie's, Oscott*, London, 1841.

Pugin, A. W. N., *The Present State of Ecclesiastical Architecture in England*, London, 1843.

Pugin, A. W. N., *An Apology for the Revival of Christian Architecture in England*, London, 1843.

Pugin, A. W. N., *A Statement of Facts relative to the Engagement of marriage between Miss Selina Helen Sandys Lumsdaine of Upper Hardres, Kent and Augustus Welby Pugin, Esq. of S. Augustins, Isle of Thanet*, London, 1848.

Pugin, A. W. N., *Floriated Ornament: A Series of Thirty-one Designs*, London, 1849.

Pugin, A. W. N., *An address to the inhabitants of Ramsgate*, London, 1850.

Pugin, A. W. N., *An Earnest Appeal for the Revival of the Ancient Plain Song*, London and Edinburgh, 1850.

Pugin, A. W. N., *Some Remarks on the articles which have recently appeared in the 'Rambler,' relative to ecclesiastical architecture and decoration*, London, 1850.

Pugin, A. W. N., *An Earnest Address, on the Establishment of the Hierarchy*, London, 1851.

Pugin, A. W. N., *A Treatise on Chancel Screens and Rood Lofts, Their Antiquity, Use, and Symbolic Signification*, London, 1851.

Pugin, A. W. N., *The Collected Letters, vol. 1, 1830–1842*, ed. Margaret Belcher, Oxford, 2001.

Pugin, A. W. N., *The Collected Letters, vol. 2, 1843–45*, ed. Margaret Belcher, Oxford, 2003.

Pugin, A. W. N., and Smith, Bernard, *Glossary of Ecclesiastical Ornament and Costume, compiled and illustrated from Antient Authorities and Examples . . .* , London, 1844.

Pugin, A. W. N., and Smith, Bernard, *Glossary of Ecclesiastical Ornament*, 2nd extended edition, 1846.

Pugin, E. Welby, *Who was the Art Architect of the Houses of Parliament, a statement of facts*, London, 1867.

Pugin, Jane, *Dearest Augustus and I: the journal of Jane Pugin*, ed. with an introduction by Caroline Stanford, Reading, 2004.

Purcell, Edmund Sheridan, *Life and Letters of Ambrose Phillipps de Lisle*, 2 vols., London, 1900.

Réau, Louis, *Histoire du Vandalisme*, Edition augmentée par Michel Fleury et Guy-Michel Leproux, Paris, 1994.

Repton, Humphry, *Sketches and Hints on Landscape Gardening*, London, 1795.

Repton, Humphry, *Observations on the Theory and Practice of Landscape Gardening, including some remarks on Grecian and Gothic architecture*, London, 1803.

Riding, Christine, and Riding, Jacqueline (eds.), *The Houses of Parliament, History, Art, Architecture*, London, 2000.

Roberts, Hugh, *For the King's Pleasure: the furnishing and decoration of George IV's apartments at Windsor Castle*, London, 2001.

Roskell, Mary Francis, OSB, *Francis Kerril Amherst DD*, London, 1903.

Rottmann, Alexander, *London Catholic Churches: a historical and artistic record*, London, 1926.

Ruskin, John, *Works*, ed. E. T. Cook and A. Wedderburn, 39 vols., London, 1903–12.

Saint, Andrew, *The Image of the Architect*, New Haven, 1983.

St Aubyn, Fiona, *Ackermann's Illustrated London*, Ware, 1985.

St Lawrence, Raleigh, *St Osmund's and Catholic Salisbury, a short history*, Salisbury, 1997.

Schiefen, Richard J., *Nicholas Wiseman and the transformation of English Catholicism*, Shepherdstown, 1984.

Schinkel, Karl Friedrich, 'The English Journey', *Journal of a Visit to France and Britain in 1826*, ed. David Bindman and Gottfried Riemann, New Haven and London, 1993.

Scott, Sir George Gilbert, *Personal and Professional Recollections*, ed. Gavin Stamp, Stamford, 1995.

Scott-Richardson, Douglas, *Gothic Revival Architecture in Ireland*, New York, 1983.

Sharples, Joseph, 'A. W. N. Pugin and the patronage of Bishop James Gillis', *Architectural History*, 28, 1985.

Shepherd, Stanley, 'The Stained Glass of A. W. N. Pugin, c.1838–52' unpublished PhD thesis, Birmingham University.

Simond, Louis, *Voyage en Angleterre pendant les années 1810 et 1811*, 2nd edition, 2 vols., Paris, 1817.

Southerwood, W. T., *The Convict's Friend (Bishop R. W. Willson)*, George Town, Tasmania, 1989.

Spencer-Silver, Patricia, *Pugin's Builder, The Life and Work of George Myers*, Hull, 1993.

Stuart, John Sobieski and Charles Edward, *Tales of the Century or Sketches of the Romance of History between the years 1746 and 1846*, Edinburgh, 1847.

Stuart, John Sobieski Stolberg and Charles Sobieski, with an introduction by Nancy Foy Cameron, *The Highland Lady's Colouring Book, reproduced from The Costume of the Clans*, Blair Atholl, 1988.

Suggett, Richard, *John Nash, Architect*, Aberystwyth, 1995.

Summerson, John, *The Life and Work of John Nash*, London, 1980.

Sykes, Christopher, *Two Studies in Virtue*, London, 1953.

Thompson, Paul, 'All Saints Church, Margaret Street, Reconsidered', *Architectural History*, 8, 1965.

Thompson, Paul, *William Butterfield*, London, 1971.

Timmins, Samuel (ed.), *The Resources, Products and Industrial History of Birmingham and Midland Hardware District*, London, 1866.

Tóibín, Colm, and Ferriter, Diarmaid, *The Irish famine, a documentary*, London, 2001.

Tracy, Charles, 'The Importation into England of church furniture from the Continent of Europe from the Later Middle Ages to the Present day', *Journal of the British Archaeological Association*, 152, 1999.

Tracy, Charles, *Continental Church Furniture: a Traffic in Piety*, Woodbridge, 2001.

Trappes-Lomax, Michael, *Pugin: a Mediaeval Victorian*, London, 1932.

Trott, Anthony, *No Place for Fop or Idler, the Story of King Edward's School, Birmingham*, Birmingham, 1992.

Trott, Michael, *The Life of Richard Waldo Sibthorp*, Brighton, 2005.

True Principles, the Journal of the Pugin Society.

Ullathorne, William Bernard, with an introduction by Shane Leslie, *From Cabin Boy to Archbishop, the Autobiography of Archbishop Ullathorne*, n.p., 1941.

Vaughan, William, *German Romanticism and English Art*, London and New Haven, 1979.

Wainwright, Clive, *The Romantic Interior*, London and New Haven, 1989.

Walsh, Vicomte, *Relation du voyage de Henri de France en Ecosse et en Angleterre*, Paris, 1844.

Ward, Monsignor Bernard, *The Sequel to Catholic Emancipation*, 2 vols., London, 1915.

Warton, Revd T., et al., *Essays on Gothic Architecture*, 2nd edition, London, 1802.

Watkin, David, *The Life and Work of C. R. Cockerell*, London, 1974.

Webster, Christopher, and Elliott, John (eds.), *A Church as it Should Be: the Cambridge Camden Society and its Influence*, Stamford, 2000.

Wedgwood, Alexandra, with a contribution by Christopher Wilson, *The Pugin Family: Catalogue of the Drawings Collection of the Royal Institute of British Architects*, Farnborough, 1977.

Wedgwood, Alexandra, *A. W. N. Pugin and the Pugin Family: catalogue of architectural drawings in the Victoria and Albert Museum*, London, 1985.

White, James E., *The Cambridge Movement*, Cambridge, 1962.

Williams, Jeremy, *A companion guide to architecture in Ireland 1837–1921*, Dublin, 1994.

Williams, Simon, 'The Birth of Functionalism: Pugin's furniture designs for St Mary's College, Oscott', unpublished dissertation, Cambridge, 1991.

Wintermute, Alan (ed.), *1789: French Art During the Revolution*, New York, 1989.

Worsley, Giles, *Architectural Drawing of the Regency Period, 1790–1837*, Washington DC, 1991.

Young, Fr Urban, CP, *Life of Father Ignatius Spencer CP*, London, 1933.

Zigrosser, Carl, 'The Microcosm of London', *Print Collectors Quarterly*, 24, 1937.

Notes

Prologue

1. It is in fact the bell that is called Big Ben.
2. Scott to General Grey, 20 December 1869, RA, ADD H2, 2867.
3. T. E. Hulme, 'Romanticism and Classicism', reprinted in *Art, Humanism and the Philosophy of Art*, ed. Herbert Read, London, 1936, 113–40, 117.
4. Catherine Pugin to Selina Welby, 13 June 1832, Yale 52.
5. Scott, *Recollections*, 89.
6. J. D. Sedding, *Art and Handicrafts*, London, 1893, 144.
7. Virginia Woolf, *Orlando* (1928), World's Classics edition, 1992, 222.
8. ibid.
9. Clark, *The Gothic Revival*, 2.
10. Nikolaus Pevsner, 'A Short Pugin Florilegium', *Architectural Review*, 94, August 1943, 33.
11. Pevsner, *Sources of Modern Architecture and Design*, 7.
12. *BoE, Staffordshire*, 1974, 97. This was the last volume of the series that Pevsner completed and his remark refers to St Augustine's, Ramsgate, Pugin's last important church.
13. Robin Middleton, 'Viollet-le-Duc's influence in nineteenth-century England', *Art History*, 4:2, June 1981, 203.
14. David Watkin, *Sir John Soane, Enlightenment Thought and the Royal Academy lectures*, Cambridge, 1996, 342.
15. The point is made very well in the preface to A. N. Wilson's *God's Funeral*, London, 1999.
16. Quoted in Briggs, *Age of Improvement*, 3.
17. Sketchbook now in the NAL, 86.mm.36.

Chapter 1: Auguste Charles Pugin

1. Ferrey, *Pugin*, 2.
2. If the information about A. C. Pugin's age recorded on his entry to the Royal Academy and on the burial register after his death is correct, he was born between 20 December 1767 and 27 March 1768. In the surviving Paris archives, many of which were destroyed during the commune in 1871, the Etat-civil des français réfugiés en Angleterre, register R baptêmes et mariages (1801–3) (Londres) gives the names of his parents. That it was a second marriage and the number of children are suggested by a note, in Benjamin Ferrey's hand, of 'particulars forwarded to me by Madame Molineux née Lafitte, cousin of Mr Welby Pugin', PC 339/332 and supported by a document referring to Sophie Pugin in the Archives de Paris (6A2.676).
3. Archives de Paris, collection Christian de Parrel (cote provisoire D49Z).

4. ibid.
5. The little principality of Salm, in what is now Lorraine in France, had many princes. Pugin's employer was not, as the *Oxford Dictionary of National Biography* suggests, the Prince de Salm-Kybourg. It was probably Prince Maximilian (1732–73) and possibly his successor Konstantin Alexander (1762–1828). The Principality lost its independence and was absorbed into France under the treaty of Luneville in 1801.
6. Extrait des registres des baptêmes, mariages et sépultures de l'église Paroissiale de S Jacques–S Philippe-du-haut-pas à Paris, recording the baptism of A. C. Pugin's sister Marie Félicité, 11 October 1771.
7. Archives Nationales, Paris, fichier notaire.
8. *Cabinet des Modes*, 15 Avril 1786, planche II.
9. *Catalogue des tableaux ... M Louis Lafitte*. Simon Mathurin Lantara (1729–78) was famous for his moonlight scenes and his laziness; a heavy drinker and an even heavier eater, he was too apt to give his work away in exchange for a dinner. He died penniless despite the efforts of many friends to help him.
10. *Cabinet des Modes*, 4, 21 July 1789: 'circonstances trop fameuses et trop malheureuses'.
11. ibid., 5, 25 March 1790.
12. *Memoirs of Chateaubriand*, 18.
13. ibid., 109.
14. A. C. Pugin to Thomas Cubitt, 10 August 1827, BL Add. Mss. 39577 f.39.
15. Unsigned letter to an unnamed correspondent, 1803, possibly from Louis Lafitte to A. C. Pugin, Yale 215.
16. Quoted in Fox, *London World City*, 167.
17. Quoted in Worsley, *Architectural drawing of the Regency Period*, 23.
18. Quoted ibid., 8.
19. See Suggett, *John Nash*, which sets out all that is now known of Nash's sad and curious marriage. His wife feigned pregnancy, twice, passing off adopted babies as her own. Nash realized the deception and abandoned her. He married again but he never had children of his own, although he adopted the Pennethorne children, relatives of his second wife.
20. Mathews, *Memoirs*, I, 171.
21. ibid., II, 19.
22. Ferrey, *Pugin*, 51.
23. Thomas Rees, *The Beauties of England and Wales*, 18, London, 1815, 342.
24. It is impossible to trace the source of an idea to a single date. Much of what was said in the 1790s had been anticipated by Vanburgh. The word 'picturesque' was first used by Winckelmann and in English by Pope, albeit it in a difference sense from that which it later acquired. The development of the romantic Picturesque, however, can reasonably be confined to the period 1790–1805.
25. Price, *Essay on the Picturesque*, 86.
26. ibid., 124.
27. ibid., 19.
28. Quoted in Clarke and Penny, *The Arrogant Connoisseur*, 47.
29. Quoted in Suggett, *Nash*, 67.
30. ibid., 67.
31. ibid., 69.
32. Quoted in Carter, Goode and Laurie, *Humphry Repton*, 135.
33. Auguste Pugin to 'Dear Sir', 'Saturday morning 7th May', PC 339/315. 7 May was a Saturday in 1791 and 1796, but the latter is a much more likely date for the commission.
34. See for example Girouard, *The Victorian Country House*, 30: 'Pugin ... proclaimed two iconoclastic doctrines that plan should come before appearance, and that buildings should be what they seemed.'
35. PC 339/315.
36. ibid.
37. ibid.

38. Quoted in Suggett, *Nash*, 85–6.
39. Nikolaus Pevsner, 'Richard Payne Knight', *Art Bulletin*, 31, 1949, 297.
40. Knight, *Analytical Enquiry*, 177.
41. Rees, *The Beauties of England and Wales*, n.23, 821.
42. The Society of Antiquaries paid A. C. Pugin £50 for the drawings. It is suggested (Evans, *History of the Society of Antiquaries*, 210) that this was to avoid employing the increasingly outspoken Carter, in the event that engravings were made.
43. *Gentleman's Magazine*, 1804, reprinted in Gomme, *Sacred and Medieval Architecture*, I, 238–9.
44. See Hill, 'A. C. Pugin'.
45. Summerson, *Nash*, 31.
46. Colvin, *Unbuilt Oxford*, 89.
47. Two views of the ruins of Chelmsford church, Essex, which fell down in January 1800, drawn by John Claude Nattes and coloured by Merigot, published 25 March 1800 by Colnaghi, Sala & Co., London.
48. Sketchbook in the Fitzwilliam Museum, Cambridge (PD86–1993).

Chapter 2: Catherine Welby

1. Only fragments now survive, but an engraving of the window was published by William Fowler in 1808, which Michael Whiteway kindly brought to my attention.
2. *Notices of the Family of Welby collected from ancient records . . . by A Member of the Family*, Grantham, 1842.
3. For this information and much help in researching the Welby family I am grateful to Mrs Rippen of the Lincolnshire Record Office.
4. Monument by Thomas Green of Camberwell (*c.*1659–*c.*1730). The Welbys built a succession of houses at Denton. The biggest, by Arthur Blomfield, built in 1883, was destroyed by fire in 1906.
5. *Universal British Directory*, 1791 and later.
6. Ferrey, *Pugin*, 5.
7. The burial records give her age at death in 1833 as sixty-four.
8. Until Nicolas Walter's death in 2000 this was, fittingly, the home of the Rationalist Press Association and I am grateful to Mr Walter for letting me explore the house.
9. Founded by Major John Cartwright in 1812, the Hampden Club, named after the seventeenth-century Parliamentarian, brought together Radicals of all classes in opposition to the repressive measures being used by government against demands to extend the franchise. Other Hampden Clubs were formed outside London.
10. Northmore showed MacEnery the cave in 1825. MacEnery spent four years excavating it and examining animal bones preserved there. He died in 1841. His papers, discovered in 1859, revealed him to have anticipated Darwin.
11. Selina Welby to Catherine Welby, April 1799, Yale 98.
12. Adlard Welby to Catherine Welby, 6 August 1797, Yale 67.
13. ibid., 25 July 1797, Yale 65.
14. See above, n.12, Yale 67.
15. ibid., 17 May 1798, Yale 75.
16. ibid., 1 March 1801, Yale 81.
17. Adlard Welby to William Welby, 28 June 1798, Yale 78.
18. Catherine Welby to Selina Welby, 19 October 1798, Yale 18.
19. ibid.
20. ibid.
21. Selina Welby to Catherine Welby, 3 August 1801, Yale 100.
22. Adlard Welby to Catherine Welby, April 1799, Yale 98.
23. Other references in her letters show that Catherine was well aware of Wollstonecraft and Rebecca Christie, whose daring style of dress she found shocking.

24. Catherine Welby to Adlard Welby, 19 April 1799, Yale 21.
25. Catherine Welby to Selina Welby, 18 June 1799, Yale 25.
26. ibid.
27. ibid.
28. ibid.
29. Catherine Welby to Adlard Welby, see above, n.24, Yale 98.
30. Will of William Welby, PRO, Prob 11.1498.
31. Catherine Pugin to William Welby, 28 January 1802. This was the date on which the licence was granted. Another hand, possibly William Welby's, has annotated the letter 'reced. Tuesday morning 2 Feby'.

Chapter 3: The Microcosm of London: 1802 to 1812

1. Selina Welby to Catherine Welby Pugin, 16 September 1802, Yale 102.
2. Quoted in Briggs, *Age of Improvement*, 144.
3. A draft of Catherine's description survives, Yale 193.
4. ibid.
5. There is a copy in the Guildhall Library in London and a copy of the earlier version in the Metropolitan Museum, New York. The original watercolour is in the Museum of London.
6. Draft in Catherine's hand for the text published with the aquatint by Ackermann, Yale 174-5.
7. ibid.
8. Draft of a letter to an unnamed correspondent, *c.* July 1803, Yale 56.
9. Richard Earle Welby to an unnamed correspondent, presumably Auguste Pugin, 17 December 1804, Yale 169.
10. Goodall, *Reminiscences*, 14.
11. Catherine Welby Pugin to Auguste Pugin, October 1807, Yale 39.
12. Auguste Pugin to Catherine Welby Pugin, 27 September 1810, PC 339/318.
13. Catherine Welby Pugin to Auguste Pugin, 26 October 1804, Yale 40.
14. Yale 102, see above, n.1.
15. Catherine Welby Pugin to Selina Welby, 29 October 1802, Yale 35.
16. ibid., 29 June 1805, Yale 36.
17. Draft prospectus, attributed to Auguste Pugin but clearly in the style and hand of his wife, Yale 176. See Hill, 'Bankers, Bawds and Beau Monde'.
18. ibid.
19. ibid.
20. ibid.
21. Pyne had also published a book called *Microcosm* in 1803, depicting thousands of groups of figures illustrating trades, sports and occupations. It seems likely that this was where Ackermann took the idea for the title of Auguste Pugin's book.
22. Quoted in Hayes, *Rowlandson*, 45. The original is now in the Art Institute of Chicago.
23. ibid., 14.
24. Myers, *William Henry Pyne and his Microcosm*, 10.
25. See above, n.17, Yale 176.
26. St Aubyn, *Ackermann's Illustrated London*, 146.
27. St Mary's, Islington, was bombed in the Second World War and during rebuilding the vaults, including the Welbys', were cleared.
28. Colvin, *Dictionary*, 199. The house is now demolished.
29. Selina Welby to Catherine Welby Pugin, 24 October 1809, Yale 106.
30. Catherine Welby Pugin to Selina Welby, 26 October 1809, Yale 42.
31. Catherine Welby Pugin to Adlard Welby, 20 December 1809, Yale 43.
32. I am most grateful to Jill Ford for extracting Auguste Pugin's accounts from her unpublished transcription of Ackermann's business records.
33. Simond, *Voyage en Angleterre*, 2, 201.

34. *Journal des Luxus und der Moden*, quoted by Simon Jervis in Fox, *London World City*, 108.
35. *Lady Anna*, quoted in Victoria Glendinning, *Trollope*, London, 1992, 4.
36. See above, n.11, Yale 39.
37. I have found no record of Pugin's baptism, beyond a reference in the International Genealogical Index to his having been born in London. On the certificate of insanity completed by his wife Jane in 1852, his place of birth is given as Islington, suggesting that Catherine returned to Pullins Row to be with her mother and Selina for the birth.

Chapter 4: Waverley: 1812 to 1821

1. Catherine Welby Pugin to Selina Welby, September ?1824, Yale 45.
2. Adlard Welby to Catherine Welby Pugin, 5 September 1813, Yale 88.
3. The drawing was until recently in the Victoria and Albert Museum, department of Prints and Drawings.
4. Most of the biographical information about Louis Lafitte in this chapter is taken from the *Catalogue des tableaux . . . M Louis Lafitte*.
5. ibid.
6. Archives de Paris, fichier général, noms des personnes, 6AZ 676, 9 Vendémiaire An IX (2 October 1800) refers to Marie Marguérite Duchène as a widow. The document renounces any claim by Sophie Pugin on her mother's estate – a measure usually taken when the inheritance was likely to be less than the cost of claiming it.
7. Several notes among family papers of the memories of Sophie Pugin Bernard and Antonia Lafitte Molinos or Molineux give roughly the same account.
8. Catherine Welby Pugin to Selina Welby, 14 October 1824, Yale 46.
9. I am grateful to Dr Emily Cole of English Heritage for giving me the details of this commission.
10. *Repository of the Arts*, 75, 288.
11. Halévy, *History*, 1, 193.
12. *Autobiography*, 24.
13. ibid.
14. ibid.
15. ibid.
16. Pugin, *Some Remarks*, 18.
17. John Britton to Revd J. E. Jackson, 6 October 1854, Britton collection, Devizes Museum, Devizes, Wiltshire.
18. Quoted in Crook, 'John Britton', 108.
19. E. J. Willson, 'Remarks on Gothic Architecture and Modern Imitations', in A. C. Pugin, *Specimens*, II, [ix].
20. *Kenilworth* (1821), Centenary Edition, Edinburgh, 1871, 62.
21. A. C. Pugin, *Specimens*, I, xiv.
22. *Kenilworth*, 140.
23. A. C. Pugin, *Specimens*, I, Preface.
24. ibid., I, xx.
25. Royal Society of Antiquaries, Willson Collection, 786/1 and 786/3.
26. John Prebble, *The King's Jaunt, George IV in Scotland*, London, 1988, 73.
27. Fox, *London World City*, 48.
28. See above, n.1, Yale 45.
29. Auguste Pugin to Rudolph Ackermann, 8 November 1824, BL Add. Mss. 19/263.
30. ?'Langdon' to Catherine Welby Pugin, October 1812, verso, Yale 137.
31. I am grateful to Margaret MacDonald, a descendant of Frederick Hugh Thomas, whose family believe he was the son of Margaret Harries and Auguste Pugin, for sharing her considerable if inconclusive research with me.

Chapter 5: 'My first design': 1821 to 1824

1. It has been said that Pugin himself was the model for Pecksniff, and although this is certainly untrue, for there is no resemblance, there may be some connection. Dickens was certainly aware of and unsympathetic to Pugin, and there is no reason for the purposes of the plot why Pecksniff's house should be where Pugin's own first house, the much mocked St Marie's Grange, was, just outside Salisbury. It is possible too that Dickens had heard from their mutual friend Clarkson Stanfield something of Pugin's early life and of the Great Russell Street drawing school and its peculiarities. If so, then Pecksniff, the architect who never built anything but whose 'genius lay in ensnaring parents and guardians, and pocketing premiums' for young men who came to live in the family home where 'in the company of certain drawing-boards, parallel rulers, very stiff-legged compasses and two, or perhaps three, other young gentlemen' they spent several years drawing Salisbury cathedral from every possible angle, may owe something to the late Auguste.
2. Catherine Welby Pugin to Selina Welby, n.d., c.September 1821, Yale 44.
3. ibid.
4. ibid., n.d., c. September 1824, Yale 45.
5. ibid.
6. See above, n.2, Yale 44. Catherine was told that Auguste's brother had been a commissioned officer, but this seems to have been another attempt to boost the family's status. The Archives Militaires at Paris, which survive intact, have no record of him.
7. *Autobiography*, 24.
8. Drawing now in the British Museum.
9. Walter Scott, *Waverley* (1821), Centenary edition, Edinburgh, 1871, 33.
10. John Britton and A. C. Pugin, *Illustrations of the Public Buildings of London*, 2 vols., London, 1825 and 1828, II, 188.
11. *Autobiography*, 24.
12. ibid.
13. Shide Ledger, BAL.
14. Ferrey, *Pugin*, 26–7.

Chapter 6: Metropolitan Improvements: 1824 to 1826

1. Ruskin, *Works*, 12, 311.
2. ibid.
3. *Autobiography*, 24.
4. Catherine Welby Pugin to Selina Welby, n.d., c. September 1824, Yale 45.
5. Réau, *Histoire du Vandalisme*, 288, 'en trois jours on a détruit l'ouvrage de douze siècles'.
6. Ferrey, 18–19.
7. *Autobiography*, 24.
8. Chateaubriand, quoted in Bury, *France*, 4.
9. Quoted in Graham Robb, *Victor Hugo*, London, 1997, 119.
10. See above, n.4, Yale 45.
11. Quoted in Anstruther, *The Knight and the Umbrella*, 78.
12. William Makepeace Thackeray, *The History of Pendennis* (1850), Penguin edition, London, 1986, 41.
13. *Autobiography*, 24–5.
14. ibid.
15. Figures taken from Brooks and Saint, *The Victorian Church*.
16. Schinkel, 'The English Journey', 175.
17. ibid.
18. John Stuart Mill, *The Spirit of the Age* (1831), Chicago, 1942, 2.
19. Charles Dickens, *The Uncommercial Traveller* (1867–8), London, Hazell, Watson & Viney, n.d., 567–8.

20. Benjamin Ferrey, *The Ecclesiologist*, 21, 1861, 368.
21. ibid.
22. ibid.
23. Powell, 'Pugin', 191.
24. Benjamin Ferrey, *The Antiquities of the Priory of Christ-Church*, 2nd edition, London, 1841, 14.
25. William Cobbett, *Rural Rides* (1830), London, 1985, 324.
26. Catherine Welby Pugin to Selina Welby, 6 September 1825, Yale 47.
27. *Autobiography*, 24.
28. ibid., 25.
29. Auguste Pugin to Mr Walton, 26 July 1825, Fondation Custodia, Paris, Collection Frits Lugt 1989–A656.
30. Quoted in Ford, *Ackermann*, 51.

Chapter 7: The King's Pleasure: 1827

1. PC/304/944.
2. Ferrey, *Pugin*, 35.
3. Goodall, *Reminiscences*, 15.
4. *Autobiography*, 26.
5. ibid.
6. Briggs, *Age of Improvement*, 186.
7. Summerson, *Nash*, 161.
8. Roberts, *King's Pleasure*, 36.
9. Much remains to be discovered about Auguste Pugin's furniture designs. He was probably responsible for some of the furniture at Eaton Hall attributed to Porden (see Atterbury and Wainwright, *Pugin: A Gothic Passion*, 129) and he seems to have designed at least one item for C. R. Cockerell, according to Cockerell's diary for 14 January 1823.
10. *The Repository of the Arts*, 10, 345. The designs were published between 1825 and 1827, when they appeared in book form as *Pugin's Gothic Furniture*. It is implied that the text is by Auguste. It may be by Catherine.
11. ibid., 9, 183.
12. ibid., 8, 245.
13. Pugin, *True Principles*, 42.
14. *The Repository of the Arts*, 10, 183.
15. *Autobiography*, 27.
16. Ex inf. Hugh Roberts.
17. *Gentleman's Magazine*, June 1826, 548.
18. The drawings for this and for the other Windsor furnishings in the Victoria and Albert Museum have all been catalogued as by Pugin, Wedgwood, *V&A*, cat. nos: 630–36. In my opinion 631 and 636, which are different in style and technique, are the work of Auguste. For attribution of two surviving cups in the royal collection to Pugin, see Bury, Wedgwood, Snodin, 'Antiquarian Plate of George IV'.
19. Catherine Welby Pugin to Selina Welby, 25 September 1827, Yale 49.
20. ibid.
21. ibid.

Chapter 8: Beginning the World: October 1827 to July 1831

1. Auguste Pugin to Thomas Cubitt, 10 August 1827, BL Add. Ms. 39577 f.39.
2. Auguste Pugin to John Britton, 7 June 1827, Edinburgh University Library ms La.II 648/199.
3. The account of the quarrel is given in 'Memoir of Augustus Pugin' in the *Magazine of the Fine Arts and Journal of Literature and Science*, I, 1833, 320–27.

4. Catherine Welby Pugin to Selina Welby, 3 September 1828, Yale 51.
5. ibid., 30 May 1828, Yale 50.
6. Auguste Pugin to Henry Walton, 11 February 1829, NRO, Brookes collection of autographs, f.230.
7. Playbill, 30 July 1829, Theatre Museum, London.
8. *Autobiography*, 27. Here and throughout I have preserved Pugin's spelling and punctuation.
9. Sketchbook in the Victoria and Albert Museum, Wedgwood, *V&A* [107].
10. Ferrey, *Pugin*, 61.
11. Quoted in 'James Gillespie Graham and A. W. N. Pugin, some Perthshire connections', by James Macaulay, in *Caledonia Gothica*. Macaulay thinks the man was Auguste Pugin, but Graham's correspondence in the SRO shows payments to Swaby, making him the more likely point of contact.
12. Thomas Grieve to E. W. Pugin, reprinted in E. W. Pugin, *Art Architect*, 9.
13. ibid., 10.
14. *Autobiography*, 28.
15. Quoted in E. W. Pugin, *Art Architect*, 10.
16. See Hazleton, 'The Grieve Family'.
17. Quoted in David Mayer, *Harlequin*, 51.
18. *Autobiography*, 28.
19. Pugin, *Letters*, 1, 3.
20. ibid., 7.
21. ibid., 4–5.
22. ibid., 5.
23. ibid., 7.
24. Gillespie Graham to John Stewart, SRO, Grantully Papers SRO/GD 121/Box 101/ Vol. XX, 149.
25. Ferrey, *Pugin*, 70.
26. *Autobiography*, 28.
27. Auguste Pugin to an unnamed correspondent, 6 July 1830, private collection.
28. G. M. Young (ed.), *Speeches by Lord Macaulay*, Oxford, 1935, 18.
29. Gillespie Graham to John Stewart, Grantully Papers SRO/GD 121/Box101/Vol.XX, 183.
30. ibid., 182.
31. Pugin, *Letters*, 1, 10.
32. Six of the dolls based on characters from *Kenilworth* are now in the Museum of London and I am grateful to Kay Stannard, who identified them, for showing them to me.
33. *Athenaeum*, 5 March 1831, 157.
34. *Autobiography*, 28.
35. Ferrey, *Pugin*, 63.
36. ibid.
37. Powell, 'Pugin', 179.
38. The Liverpool dealer Thomas Winstanley, writing in 1828, quoted in Wainwright, *Romantic Interior*, 49.
39. Diary of Marc Brunel, 23 March 1831, Institution of Civil Engineers, London. I am grateful to Andrew Saint for drawing my attention to this.
40. A. C. Pugin, *Examples*, I, 1831, xi.
41. Quoted in Summerson, *Nash*, 181.

Chapter 9: A Very Short Courtship: July 1831 to May 1832

1. For information about Anne Garnett's parents, her relationship to Edward Dayes and her age, I am indebted to Michael Egan and Alexandra Wedgwood.
2. *Autobiography*, 27.
3. Ferrey, *Pugin*, 57.

4. Hunt, *Dramatic Criticism*, 252.
5. Pugin, *Letters*, 1, 12.
6. I am grateful to Claire Tomalin for pointing out Pugin's name on the playbill.
7. Ferrey, *Pugin*, 68.
8. Quoted in Gilley, *Newman*, 112.
9. Journal in a private collection, pages unnumbered.
10. ibid.
11. ibid.
12. ibid.
13. ibid.
14. ibid.
15. *Examples*, 1, xiv. The text was completed in May 1831 but this idea occurs in a footnote, possibly added later. Clearly at the time of Pugin's visit to Lincoln the term 'Catholic Architecture' was fresh in Willson's mind.
16. ibid.
17. Sketchbook now in the Victoria and Albert Museum, Wedgwood, *V&A* [104].
18. Quoted in Chadwick, *The Victorian Church*, 38.
19. Catherine Welby Pugin to Selina Welby, 21 May 1832, private collection.
20. ibid.
21. ibid.
22. Trappes-Lomax, *Pugin*, 36.
23. Pugin, *Letters*, 1, 15.
24. Catherine Welby Pugin to Selina Welby, 13 June 1832, Yale 52.
25. ibid.
26. ibid.

Chapter 10: 'Gothic for ever': June 1832 to April 1833

1. Catherine Welby Pugin to Selina Welby, 13 June 1832, Yale 52.
2. ibid.
3. ibid.
4. ibid.
5. ibid.
6. 'The Chest' and six other Ideal Schemes are catalogued in Wedgwood, *V&A*, [108]–[114].
7. See above, n.1, Yale 52. It is possible that Pugin did provide designs for French productions. E. W. Pugin, *Art Architect*, says that Pugin worked on productions of *La Juive* and *Comte Ory*. If so it must have been soon after this date.
8. Auguste Pugin to Catherine Welby Pugin, 29 August 1832, PC 339/316.
9. ibid.
10. Two drawings by Pugin showing the bishop's palace and the deanery at Wells are in Lambeth Palace Library, ms 4201/1 and 2.
11. Catherine Welby Pugin to Selina Welby, 9 September 1832, Yale 53.
12. Pugin, *Letters*, 1, 12.
13. ibid., 12–13.
14. Nikolaus Pevsner, *BoE, North Somerset and Bristol*, London, reprinted 1995, 319.
15. See above, n.11, Yale 53.
16. Ferrey, *Pugin*, 92.
17. Halévy, *History*, 3, 58.
18. John Stuart Mill, *The Spirit of the Age* (1831), Chicago, 1942, 33.
19. See above, n.11, Yale 53.
20. Adlard Welby to Selina Welby, 21 February 1833, Yale 90.
21. Pugin, *Letters*, 1, 14.
22. ibid.

23. ibid.
24. ibid., 15.

Chapter 11: Beginning the World Again: May 1833 to October 1834

1. *Catalogue of original drawings etc . . . property of the late Augustus Pugin esq*, London, 1833.
2. Ferrey gives Louisa's name as the slightly smarter 'Burton', but the marriage register and the birth certificate of her daughter Mary both clearly read 'Button'.
3. Adlard Welby to Selina Welby, 21 February 1834, Yale 93, and 22 September 1834, Yale 95.
4. See above, n.3, Yale 95.
5. See above, n.3, Yale 93.
6. Powell, 'Pugin', 190.
7. Powell PC.
8. ibid.
9. Pugin, *Letters*, 1, 40.
10. ibid.
11. ibid., 20.
12. ibid., 21.
13. ibid., 17.
14. ibid., 17–18.
15. ibid., 23.
16. ibid.
17. John Stuart Mill, *The Spirit of the Age* (1831), Chicago, 1942, 1.
18. Mozley, *Reminiscences*, 1, 273.
19. ibid.
20. ibid., 1, 275.
21. Oliver, *Prophets and Millennialists*, 11.
22. Pugin, *Letters*, I, 23.
23. Quoted in Stewart J. Brown, *The National Churches of England, Ireland and Scotland 1801–1846*, Oxford, 2001, 270.
24. Newman, *Apologia*, 42.
25. Newman, *Letters and Diaries*, 4, xiv.
26. These are now in the Public Library, St Louis, Missouri.
27. Pugin, *Letters*, 1, 24. The 'chapel' was probably St Peter's Stonyhurst, Lancashire, by J. J. Scoles.
28. Evans, *History of the Society of Antiquaries*, 2.
29. Quoted in Crook, *John Carter*, 58.
30. A. C. Pugin, *Specimens*, I, x.
31. Pugin cites in *Contrasts* the English version of the *Monasticon* extended by John Stevens (c.1662–1726), a Roman Catholic antiquary of openly Jacobite sympathies.
32. Newman, *Letters and Diaries*, 4, 67.
33. Pugin, *Letters*, 1, 20.
34. ibid., 39.
35. ibid., 43.
36. ibid., 29.
37. ibid., 21.
38. ibid., 32. The phrase is included in Pugin's draft of the Preface to Vol. 2 of *Examples*. By the time it was eventually published he had given up the idea of following in his father's professional footsteps.
39. Robert Gittings (ed.), *Letters of John Keats*, Oxford, 1970, 203.
40. Pugin, *Letters*, 1, 32.
41. See above, n.3, Yale 95.

42. Pugin, *Letters*, 1, 37.

43. ibid., 35.

44. ibid., 38.

45. ibid.

46. ibid., 40.

47. Pugin to John Hardman, PC 304/525, n.d., *c.*1851.

48. Pugin, *Letters*, 1, 41.

49. ibid., 36.

50. ibid.

51. Port, *Houses of Parliament*, 17.

52. Quoted in Edward Wedlake Brayley and John Britton, *The History of the ancient Palace and late Houses of Parliament at Westminster*, London, 1836, 409.

53. This story was told me by the late Professor Clive Wainwright, who believed it to be true.

54. Barry, *Sir Charles Barry*, 145.

55. Pugin, *Letters*, 1, 42.

56. ibid.

57. ibid.

Chapter 12: The New World Begun: October 1834 to May 1835

1. Quoted in Port, *Houses of Parliament*, 23.

2. ibid.

3. ibid.

4. Pugin, *Letters*, 1, 44.

5. ibid., 42.

6. Quoted in Port, *Houses of Parliament*, 23.

7. Pugin, *Letters*, 1, 42.

8. Letter from John Peniston to an unnamed correspondent, 3 February 1830, in *Letters*.

9. Pugin, *Letters*, 1, 45.

10. ibid.

11. ibid.

12. ibid.

13. John Chessell Buckler, *An Historical and Descriptive Account of the Royal Palace at Eltham*, London, 1828, 3. J. C. Buckler was an antiquarian architect and an acquaintance of the Pugins. His writings are full of ideas that Pugin was credited in the twentieth century with inventing, such as the precept that a building should express its various functions in its different elements. This was a commonly accepted idea in antiquarian circles by the time Pugin was growing up.

14. Auguste Pugin to an unnamed correspondent, n.d., PC 339/315.

15. I am grateful to the present owner of St Marie's Grange, who discovered the well, for pointing this out to me.

16. Pugin, *Letters*, 1, 49.

17. ibid., 43.

18. Ferrey, *Pugin*, 73.

19. Repton, *Observations*, 162.

20. Pugin, *Letters*, 1, 48.

21. Ferrey, *Pugin*, 73 and Nikolaus Pevsner and Bridget Cherry, *BoE*, *Wiltshire*, 2nd edition, London, 1975, 84.

22. Diary, 32.

23. ibid.

24. ibid.

25. Pugin, *Letters*, 1, 45.

26. ibid., 46.

27. A copy of the prospectus issued by Ackermann, addressed to E. W. Cooke, survives in a family collection.

Chapter 13: Salisbury and Sarum: Summer 1835

1. Pugin, *Letters*, 1, 49.
2. The note in Pugin's diary for 26 August 1836, 'Mr Graham fell from baloon,' refers to the well-known balloonist of that name, not, as has been suggested, to the architect Gillespie Graham.
3. *Salisbury and Winchester Journal*, 30 March 1835.
4. Pugin, *Letters*, 1, 50.
5. ibid., 46.
6. John Milner, 'Observations', in Warton et al., *Gothic Architecture*, xvii–xviii.
7. Milner, *Antiquities of Winchester*, 1, 15.
8. Milner, *Letters to a Prebendary*, 216.
9. ibid., 218.
10. Pugin, *Letters*, 1, 46.
11. Crook and Port, *King's Works*, 195.
12. ibid.
13. Diary, 32.
14. Annotation on one of the drawings for the grammar school furniture, now in the BAL, Wedgwood, *RIBA* [24].
15. Diary, 32.
16. ibid., 33.
17. E. W. Pugin, *Art Architect*, 27.

Chapter 14: Contrasts: Summer 1835 to August 1836

1. F. Schlegel, *Dialogue on Poetry and Literary Aphorisms*, 1800, quoted in Brendan, *Hurrell Froude*, 29.
2. Diary, 32.
3. ibid., 33.
4. Pugin, *Letters*, 1, 48.
5. ibid.
6. ibid., 49.
7. ibid.
8. Quoted in E. W. Pugin, *Art Architect*, 9.
9. Quoted in Port, *Houses of Parliament*, 70.
10. Barry, *A Reply*, 7.
11. Quoted in Port, *Houses of Parliament*, 41.
12. Quoted ibid., 67. Bury's testimony in the controversy of 1867–8 is some of the most unaccountable. His reluctance overall to give his late friend even so much credit as he was due was perhaps attributable in part to Bury's dislike of Pugin's son Edward, as well as a proprietary attitude towards Pugin's reputation which caused him to clash with Benjamin Ferrey and others.
13. Quoted in Belcher, *Annotated Bibliography* [A2].
14. Pugin, *A Letter to A. W. Hakewill*, 6.
15. ibid., 6–7.
16. ibid.
17. Pugin, *Letters*, 1, 50.
18. ibid.
19. ibid., 49–50.
20. ibid., 50.
21. *Salisbury and Winchester Journal*, 3 August 1835.

22. ibid.
23. ibid.
24. Pugin, *Letters*, 1, 50.
25. ibid., 56.
26. Diary, 33.
27. ibid.
28. Quoted in Port, *Houses of Parliament*, 68. This evidence does not tally with Pugin's diary, which suggests he finished Barry's drawings on 29 November and Graham's on 5 December. It is impossible now to recover the exact sequence of events.
29. Pugin, *Letters*, 1, 48.
30. ibid.
31. Quoted in Port, *Houses of Parliament*, 73.
32. Diary, 35.
33. Note in a sketchbook now in the NAL, 86.mm.39, Wedgwood, *V&A* [123].
34. Pugin, *Contrasts*, plate between pages iv and [1].
35. *Catalogue of the designs for the new Houses of Parliament*, London, 4th edition, 28 April 1836, iii.
36. Quoted in Liscombe, *William Wilkins*, 180.
37. Pugin, *Letters*, 1, 60.
38. ibid.
39. Pugin, *Contrasts*, 15.
40. ibid., iii.
41. ibid., 1.
42. ibid., 2.
43. ibid., 7.
44. ibid., 30.
45. ibid., 18.
46. ibid., 19.
47. ibid., 20.
48. ibid., 21.
49. ibid., 23.
50. ibid., 30–31.
51. ibid., 32.
52. ibid., 31.
53. ibid., 6.
54. Pugin, *Letters*, 1, 60.
55. A. C. Pugin, *Examples*, 2, viii–ix.
56. ibid., Preface.

Chapter 15: Entre Deux Guerres: Autumn 1836

1. Unsigned prospectus, certainly by Pugin, published in *Loudon's Architectural Magazine*, 4, 1837, 145.
2. Pugin, *Details of Antient Timber Houses*, 21.
3. Quoted in E. W. Pugin, *Art Architect*, 24.
4. Quoted ibid., 23–4.
5. ibid., 24.
6. Pugin, *Letters*, 1, 62.
7. ibid.
8. 'Mr Pugin's Contrasts', by AF, *Salisbury and Wiltshire Herald*, 17 September 1836.
9. ibid.
10. ibid.
11. ibid.
12. ibid.

13. ibid.
14. Pugin, *Letters*, 1, 75.
15. ibid., 64.
16. ibid., 65.
17. *Salisbury and Wiltshire Herald*, 17 September and 8 October 1836.
18. ibid., 17 September 1836.
19. *Scenes of Clerical Life* (1858), by George Eliot, 3rd edition, London, 1860, 46.
20. Quoted in White, *The Cambridge Movement*, 15.
21. *Salisbury and Wiltshire Herald*, 1 October 1836.
22. Pugin, *Letters*, 1, 61.
23. *Salisbury and Wiltshire Herald*, 8 October 1836.
24. Pugin, *Letters*, 1, 74.
25. Quoted in E. W. Pugin, *Art Architect*, 26.
26. ibid.
27. ibid.
28. Crook and Port, *King's Works*, 595. There is now considerable evidence that medieval architects were interested in achieving symmetry, but to the nineteenth century irregularity seemed an integral characteristic of Gothic.
29. Mayer, *Harlequin*, 119.
30. Pugin, *Letters*, 1, 75.

Chapter 16: Romantic Catholics

1. The description refers to Eustace Lyle's 'Beaumanoir', which was intended to evoke Ambrose Phillipps's Grace Dieu, though there is no literal resemblance. Disraeli later used Shrewsbury's Alton Towers for his Muriel Towers in *Lothair*.
2. Mozley, *Reminiscences*, 1, 274.
3. Notes for a biography of Shrewsbury contained in an undated and unsigned letter, postmarked 8 January 1854 and addressed to the Revd Dr Winter, the Catholic priest at Cheadle. The author, who is perhaps a relative, had known Shrewsbury since at least the 1820s and is commenting from personal knowledge and documents in his or her possession on a draft biography by Winter (BAA).
4. ibid.
5. ibid.
6. Lady Mary Arundell to the Hon. Mrs Doughty, 10 January 1829, quoted in Arundell, *Letters*, 26.
7. ibid., 27.
8. ibid.
9. Quoted in Fisher, *Alton Towers*, 53.
10. ibid., 77.
11. Tussauds have made considerable efforts in recent years to maintain and partially restore the ruins.
12. Arundell, *Letters*, 26.
13. Shrewsbury to Rock, 3 April, n.d., c.1851, SAA.
14. Shrewsbury to Pugin, postmarked 28 March 1840, PC 339/101.
15. Quoted in Pawley, *Faith and Family*, 21.
16. Ambrose Phillipps to Laura Phillipps, 24 June 1835, ms in private possession, microfilm copy in the Record Office for Leicestershire and Rutland, MF477.
17. Quoted in Pawley, *Faith and Family*, 75. 'Ni riche, ni belle, ni jolie, une figure Saxone, une taille assez bonne.' Charles Phillipps kept private passages of his diary in French.
18. 'For a Seat in the Groves of Coleorton' (1811).
19. Pawley, *Faith and Family*, 76.
20. Kenelm Digby, *Mores Catholici*, 2, 1832, 265.
21. Peter Cornelius, the leading Nazarene painter who had immense influence in Europe

and particularly in England, after Victoria's marriage to Prince Albert, quoted in Germann, *Gothic Revival*, 94.

22. Kenelm Digby was a descendant of the seventeenth-century author and diplomat of the same name. Ambrose Phillipps was not, however, descended from the poet Ambrose Phillips who quarrelled with Pope and whose name was the origin of the phrase 'namby-pamby'.
23. Digby, *Mores Catholici*, 5, 1834, 265.
24. ibid., 3, 1833, 14–15.
25. Kenelm Digby to an unnamed correspondent, probably Ambrose Phillipps or Nicholas Wiseman, n.d., *c.*1840, WAA 137/4/26.
26. Bossy, *English Catholic Community*, 329.

Chapter 17: The Professor of Ecclesiastical Antiquities: 1837

1. Mozley, *Reminiscences*, 1, 273–4.
2. Quoted in Peter Dennison, 'Thomas Walsh's vision of Oscott', in Champ, *Oscott College*, 37.
3. Quoted in Champ, *Oscott*, 10, and Pawley, *Faith and Family*, 109.
4. Quoted in Roskell, *Francis Kerril Amherst*, 205.
5. ibid.
6. ibid.
7. ibid., 113–14.
8. ibid.
9. 'Mr Pugin and the students of St Mary's Address and Reply', *Edinburgh Catholic Magazine*, November 1838, 691.
10. ibid.
11. Canon William Greaney, *The Buildings, Museum, Pictures and Library of St Mary College Oscott*, Birmingham, 1899, 4.
12. *Edinburgh Catholic Magazine*, see above, n.9, 693.
13. Greaney, *The Buildings of . . . Oscott*, 5.
14. ibid.
15. Williams, 'The Birth of Functionalism'. Although I disagree with Williams's thesis about the importance of this furniture in the history of 'functionalism', I much admire his descriptions of it.
16. *Quarterly Review*, 58, February 1837, 62 and 64.
17. *Fraser's Magazine*, 15, March 1837, 339.
18. 'An Architect', *Reply to* Contrasts *by A. Welby Pugin*, London, 1837, 22.
19. *Fraser's Magazine*, see above, n.17, 331.
20. *Civil Engineer and Architect's Journal*, 2, September 1839, 351–2.
21. Quoted in Tracy, 'The Importation into England of Church Furniture', 108.
22. Pugin, *Contrasts*, 32.
23. Girouard, *Victorian Country House*, 116.
24. Pugin, *An Apology for 'Contrasts'*, 29–30.
25. Diary, 37.

Chapter 18: 'My first church': July 1837 to May 1838

1. Diary, 38.
2. Pugin, *Letters*, 1, 147.
3. Jane Carlyle, quoted in Rosemary Ashton, *Thomas and Jane Carlyle, Portrait of a Marriage*, London, 2001, 154.
4. Quoted in J. F. C. Phillips, *Shepherd's London*, London, 1976, 82.
5. Pugin, *Letters*, 1, 80.
6. ibid.
7. *The Oscotian*, 5, July 1905, 111.
8. ibid.

9. 'Lectures on ecclesiastical architecture ... by A. W. Pugin, Professor of Ecclesiastical Antiquities...', *Edinburgh Catholic Magazine*, April 1838, 196.
10. ibid., 201 and 198.
11. 'Professor Pugin's first lecture', *Civil Engineer and Architect's Journal*, May 1838, 180.
12. ibid., 181.
13. Harrison, *Early Victorian Britain*, 23.
14. Quoted in Pawley, *Faith and Family*, 92–3.
15. ibid.
16. A Cistercian Monk [Bernard Palmer], *A Concise History of the Cistercian Order*, London, 1852, 275.
17. Newman, *Letters*, 4, 379.
18. *Edinburgh Catholic Magazine*, 1838, 1–2.
19. Pugin, *Letters*, 1, 80.
20. 'The founding of a new Catholic·Church on the ruins of the Convent Abbey at Reading', *Edinburgh Catholic Magazine*, 1838, 62.
21. *Edinburgh Catholic Magazine*, see above, n.18.
22. ibid.
23. Pugin, *The Present State*, 49.
24. First Oscott lecture, see above, n.9.
25. Ferrey, *Pugin*, 185–6.
26. Scott, *Recollections*, 88.
27. Briggs, *Victorian Cities*, 92.
28. Transcribed in Wedgwood, *V&A* [573].
29. Shrewsbury to Ambrose Phillipps, n.d., early 1838, PC 339/104–5.
30. ibid.
31. Arundell, *Letters*, 125.
32. Diary, 40.
33. Quoted in Champ, *Oscott*, 4.
34. Quoted in Ullathorne, *Cabin Boy to Archbishop*, 135.
35. ibid.
36. Pugin, 'Chasuble of Cloth of gold...', *Orthodox Journal*, 14 April 1838, 225–30.
37. ibid.

Chapter 19: Birmingham and Oxford: May 1838 to May 1839

1. Thomas Roscoe esq and the resident engineers, *The Book of the Grand Junction Railway*, London, 1839, 31 and 33.
2. Le Comte de Montalembert, 'De l'état actuel de l'art religieux en France', 1837, in *Du Vandalisme et du Catholicisme dans l'art*, Paris, 1839, 196.
3. Pugin, *Letters*, 1, 80.
4. ibid.
5. Diary, 40.
6. Faber, *Young England*, 1.
7. *Mores Catholici*, 3, 1833, 12.
8. Diary, 40.
9. Shrewsbury to Revd John Hall, 14 September 1838, quoted in Michael J. Ullman, *St Alban's Macclesfield*, Macclesfield, 1982, 9.
10. Knight, *An Analytical Enquiry*, 174.
11. Pugin to an unnamed correspondent, probably Nicholas Wiseman, n.d., c.1850, PC 339/126.
12. Hitchcock, *Early Victorian Architecture*, 1, 72.
13. Pugin, *Letters*, 1, 88.
14. ibid.
15. Diary, 41.

16. Matthew Arnold, *Discourses in America* (1885), New York, 1896, 139–40.

17. Newman, *Letters*, 7, xvi.

18. Shrewsbury to Rock, n.d., March 1839, BAA B798.

19. Countess of Shrewsbury to Laura Phillipps, n.d., letter in private collection on microfilm in the Leicestershire County Record Office, M/F480.

20. Arundell, *Letters*, 119–20.

21. Pugin, *Letters*, 1, 108.

22. Quoted in Newman, *Letters*, 6, 332.

23. Pugin, *Letters*, 1, 88.

24. Pugin, *To the Subscribers and Promoters of the Martyrs Memorial in Oxford . . .*, London, 1839, epigraph.

25. The Revd Thomas Lathbury's *Strictures on a letter addressed by Mr Pugin . . .*, London, 1839, followed soon after.

26. Pugin, *Martyr's Memorial*, 29.

27. ibid., 89.

28. ibid., 102.

29. Jennifer Sherwood and Nikolaus Pevsner, *BoE, Oxfordshire*, London, 1974, 314. It was arguably illogical to choose a style that predated the event it commemorated, although presumably it was considered to be more in keeping with the surroundings.

30. Pugin, *Letters*, 1, 112.

31. ibid.

32. Shrewsbury to Rock, see above, n.18.

33. Statistics taken from Edward Norman, *The English Catholic Church in the Nineteenth Century*, Oxford, 1984. Precise figures are impossible to obtain.

34. Carlyle, *Chartism*, 18.

35. ibid.

36. Kenelm Digby to Ambrose Phillipps, 10 August 1834, WAA 137/4/14.

37. ibid.

38. Pugin, *Letters*, 1, 107.

39. Ferrey, *Pugin*, 170.

40. Pugin, *Letters*, 1, 106.

41. *Orthodox Journal*, 8, 16 February 1839, 105.

42. Pugin, *Letters*, 1, 23.

43. Quoted in Michael Hodgetts, *St Chad's Cathedral Birmingham*, Birmingham, 1987, 4.

44. Pugin, *Letters*, 1, 78. Belcher assumes that this is addressed to John Hardman Jun., but it seems more likely that it was to his father, who took the lead in fund-raising for St Chad's.

45. ibid., 77.

46. Shrewsbury to Rock, see above, n.18.

47. ibid.

48. Walsh to Shrewsbury, 6 March 1839, Ushaw, Walsh/Shrewsbury Letters, 9.

49. ibid., 27 October 1838, Ushaw, Walsh/Shrewsbury Letters, 1.

50. Letter from Fr William Foley to Provost Husenbeth, 19 September 1838, correspondence transcribed by Frank Devany.

51. ibid.

52. *Edinburgh Catholic Magazine*, June 1839, 498.

53. ibid., 336.

54. Diary, 42.

55. Pugin, *Letters*, 1, 113.

56. *Edinburgh Catholic Magazine*, June 1839, 499.

Chapter 20: Young Victorians: May 1839 to February 1840

1. Letter to Ambrose Phillipps, quoted in Purcell, *Life of Ambrose Phillipps*, 1, 169.

2. Newman *Letters*, 7, 94.

3. Manning to Newman, 17 September 1839, Newman, *Letters*, 7, 153.
4. Mozley, *Reminiscences*, 2, 150.
5. ibid., 1, 255.
6. Journal of Lord John Manners, quoted in Faber, *Young England*, 42.
7. F. W. Doyle, *Reminiscences and Opinions*, 1886, 145.
8. ibid.
9. Pugin, *Letters*, 1, 193.
10. Ferrey, *Pugin*, 244.
11. Pugin, *Apology for 'Contrasts'*, 30.
12. Carlyle, *Chartism*, 3.
13. Mozley, *Reminiscences*, 2, 274.
14. Pugin, *The Present State*, 87.
15. ibid., 90.
16. ibid., 29.
17. Nikolaus Pevsner, *BoE, Staffordshire*, 1974, 121.
18. Diary, 43.
19. Arundell, *Letters*, 125.
20. Quoted in Pawley, *Faith and Family*, 193.
21. Arundell, *Letters*, 147.
22. Phillipps to William Ullathorne, 5 July 1843, WAA, Series 7/4/8.
23. Walsh to Shrewsbury, 15 November 1839, Ushaw, Walsh/Shrewsbury Letters, 11.
24. Pugin, *Letters*, 1, 117.
25. *British Critic*, April 1837, 308. The observation is made in a long essay reviewing several books under the title 'Gothic Architecture'.
26. *British Critic*, April 1839, 481.
27. *Catholic Magazine*, March 1839, 176.
28. Kenelm Digby to an unnamed correspondent, probably Nicholas Wiseman or Ambrose Phillipps, n.d., *c.*1839–40, WAA 137/24.
29. *Orthodox Journal*, 9, 9 November 1839, 316.
30. ibid.
31. ibid.
32. ibid., 320.
33. Pugin, second Oscott lecture, *Catholic Magazine*, 2, 321–37.
34. *Orthodox Journal*, 8 June 1839.
35. Pugin, 'On the erection and adornment of Catholic churches', *Orthodox Journal*, 31 August 1839, 152.
36. Walsh to Shrewsbury, see above, n.23.
37. ibid.
38. ibid.
39. Pugin, *Letters*, 1, 130.
40. Walsh to Shrewsbury, 24 December 1839, Ushaw, Walsh/Shrewsbury Letters, 12.
41. ibid.
42. ibid., 20 January 1840, Ushaw, Walsh/Shrewsbury Letters, 13.
43. Shrewsbury to Rock, 31 October 1841, BAA R801.
44. Pugin, *Letters*, 1, 137.
45. Diary, 43–5.
46. Pugin, *Letters*, 1, 119.
47. Newman, *Letters*, 7, 206.
48. ibid.
49. Quoted in Pawley, *Faith and Family*, 111.

Chapter 21: A Vision for England: March to December 1840

1. Pugin, *Letters*, 1, 156.
2. Shrewsbury to Pugin, postmarked 28 March, PC 339/101.
3. ibid.
4. Pugin, *Letters*, 1, 133.
5. *British Critic*, April 1837, 335.
6. Quoted in Pawley, *Faith and Family*, 196.
7. ibid.
8. Kenelm Digby to Ambrose Phillipps, 3 March 1840, WAA137/21.
9. Pugin, *Letters*, 135.
10. Shrewsbury to Pugin, see above, n.2.
11. ibid.
12. Pugin, *Letters*, 1, 135.
13. McAuley, *Correspondence*, 121.
14. ibid.
15. ibid., 120.
16. The dimensions specified in the letter are identical to those Pugin jotted down in his sketchbook. See Wedgwood, *V&A* [1000].
17. Alexandra Wedgwood, *BoE, Warwickshire*, London, 1966, 182.
18. Diary, 45.
19. Pugin, *Letters*, 1,136.
20. I was told this by one of her descendants, Jacina Bird.
21. Countess of Shrewsbury to Laura Phillipps, n.d., *c.* early August 1840, private collection, copy on microfilm, Leicestershire County Record Office, m/f480.
22. Quoted in Pawley, *Faith and Family*, 84.
23. Quoted in Purcell, *Life of Ambrose Phillipps*, 301.
24. Quoted in Lacey, *The Second Spring in the Charnwood Forest*, 41.
25. Quoted in Pawley, *Faith and Family*, 96.
26. 'Catholic chapels – Mr Pugin', *Civil Engineer and Architect's Journal*, July 1840, 228.
27. Pugin, *Letters*, 1, 140.
28. ibid., 145.
29. ibid., 156.
30. ibid., 144.
31. ibid., 146–7.
32. R. W. Church to Frederic Rogers, quoted in Mary Church (ed.), *Life and Letters of Dean Church*, London, 1895, 26–7.
33. ibid.
34. Quoted in Ker, *Newman*, 213.
35. Pugin, *Letters*, 1, 161.
36. Ward, *Sequel to Catholic Emancipation*, 2, 1.
37. Quoted in Schiefen, *Wiseman*, 106.
38. Sykes, *Two Studies in Virtue*, 88.
39. Ward, *Sequel to Catholic Emancipation*, 2, 2.
40. ibid.
41. Arundell, *Letters*, 130.
42. Quoted in Roderick O'Donnell, ' "An Apology for the Revival": the Architecture of the Catholic Revival in Britain and Ireland', in Jan De Maeyer and Luc Verpoest (eds.), *Gothic Revival: Religion, Architecture and Style in Western Europe 1815–1914*, Leuven, 2000, 39.
43. Wiseman to Rock, postmarked 24 May 1840, SAA.
44. Pugin, *Letters*, 1, 167 and 169.
45. ibid., 167.
46. ibid., 179.

47. ibid., 167.
48. ibid., 178.
49. ibid., 163.
50. Wiseman to Shrewsbury, 30 November 1840, Ushaw, Wiseman Papers 843.
51. ibid.
52. Pugin, *Letters*, 1, 173.
53. 'Tridentine' refers to the Council of Trent, held in three sessions between 1545 and 1563 to reform the Catholic Church in response to the Protestant Reformation.
54. The rood screen at St Chad's continued to cause controversy well into the next century. Ultimately, in 1967, the Revd Dr George Dwyer, Bishop of Birmingham, decided to have it removed. He was opposed forcefully by the Victorian Society and Nikolaus Pevsner, who called it an act of 'vandalism unmitigated'. The screen was rescued by a High Anglican priest, Brian Brindley, who installed it in his parish church, Holy Trinity, Reading, where it remains at the time of writing. The medieval carvings which Pugin had fixed to it are still in Birmingham.
55. Pugin, *Letters*, 1, 175.
56. ibid., 171.
57. ibid., 178.

Chapter 22: True Principles and Tract XC: 1841

1. Pugin, *Letters*, 1, 164.
2. ibid., 199.
3. ibid.
4. Scott, *Recollections*, 88.
5. ibid.
6. This and Pugin's next article for the *Dublin Review* were later published together as *The Present State of Ecclesiastical Architecture in England. The Present State*, 1.
7. ibid., 2.
8. Scott, *Recollections*, 85.
9. Pugin, *Letters*, 1, 191.
10. The prospectus appears in the list of the publisher's recent works at the back of many copies of *True Principles*.
11. *True Principles*, 1.
12. ibid., 7 and 8.
13. ibid., 8.
14. ibid., 62.
15. ibid.
16. ibid., 9.
17. ibid., 56.
18. ibid., 18.
19. ibid., 45.
20. ibid., 27.
21. ibid., 40.
22. ibid., 24 and 23.
23. ibid., 24–5.
24. ibid., 41.
25. ibid., 42.
26. Scott, *Recollections*, 89.
27. ibid., 87.
28. This point is made by Paul Thompson in *Butterfield*.
29. Eastlake, *Gothic Revival*, 150.
30. Hitchcock, *Early Victorian Architecture*, 77.
31. Victor Hugo, *Notre Dame de Paris*, Nelson Edition, 2 vols., Paris, n.d., 1,165: 'Tout se

tient dans cet art venu de lui-même, logique et bien proportionné. Mesurer l'orteil du pied, c'est mésurer le géant.' (Everything in this art is consistent, logical and well proportioned. To measure the big toe is to measure the giant.)

32. E. J. Willson, *Specimens*, 1, xiv, attributes the phrase to Thomas Gray's *Ode on a Distant Prospect of Eton College*.

33. Robert Willis, *Remarks on the Architecture of the Middle Ages especially of Italy*, Cambridge, 1835, 17–18.

34. The accusation was made in the *Bristol and West of England Archaeological Magazine* and reprinted in the *Builder* for 23 March 1844. There is certainly a resemblance between Bartholomew's constructional diagrams and those in *True Principles*.

35. Diary, 48.

36. *Tablet*, 25 December 1841, 37.

37. Pugin, *Contrasts*, 1841, 42.

38. ibid., 56.

39. *British Critic*, 1841, 47.

40. Mozley's letter describing the visit is quoted in Pugin, *Letters*, 1, 212–13.

41. ibid.

42. Letter to Henry Wilberforce, quoted in Ker, *Newman*, 213.

43. Letter to Tom Mozley, quoted ibid.

44. Quoted in Pawley, *Faith and Family*, 121.

45. ibid.

46. Ambrose Phillipps to Charles, Comte de Montalembert, 6 March 1841, Archives of Magdalen College, Oxford, MD459/12.

47. Transcript in the Staffordshire Record Office of a letter from Bishop Bagot, possibly to his brother, 18 March 1841 (SRO:3259/14/21/8/1).

48. Pugin, *Letters*, 1, 226.

49. Quoted in Dodds, *Age of Paradox*, 170.

50. Pugin, *Letters*, 1, 261.

51. Powell PC.

52. Pugin, *The Present State*, 105.

53. McAuley, *Correspondence*, 255.

54. Pugin, *The Present State*, 18.

55. Pugin, *Letters*, 1, 239.

56. *Orthodox Journal*, 26 June 1841, 400.

57. ibid., 401.

58. ibid., 402.

59. ibid., 403.

60. ibid., 408.

61. Ward, *Sequel to Catholic Emancipation*, 2,15.

62. Diary, 49.

63. *Christian Remembrancer*, March 1842, 356.

64. Faber, *Young England*, x.

65. Pugin, *Letters*, 1, 263.

66. ibid., 269.

67. ibid., 1, 286.

68. Diary, 49.

69. Pugin, *Letters*, 1, 275.

70. ibid., 272.

71. ibid., 275.

72. This story recurs in several places and with variations. This one, like most of my account of Sibthorp's career, is taken from Sykes, *Two Studies in Virtue*.

73. Pugin, *Letters*, 1, 280.

74. ibid., 281.

75. Quoted in Middleton, *Newman and Bloxam*, 161.

76. Pugin, *Letters*, 1, 384.
77. ibid., 293.
78. ibid., 289.
79. Shrewsbury to Walsh, 16 November 1841, BAA, B606.
80. Pugin, *Letters*, 1, 289–90.
81. ibid., 290.
82. Peel to Shrewsbury, 14 October 1841, BL Add. Mss. 40492 f.100.
83. Shrewsbury to Peel, 13 November 1841, BL Add. Mss. 40494 f.414.

Chapter 23: Reunion and Division: 1842

1. Newman, *Apologia*, 147.
2. Briggs, *Age of Improvement*, 295.
3. J. Almack, *Character, Motives and Proceedings of the Anti-Corn Law Leaguers* (1843), quoted ibid., 314.
4. Newman, *Letters*, 8, 447.
5. Thomas Carlyle, *Past and Present* (1843), Everyman edition, London, 1912, 22.
6. Wiseman to Shrewsbury, *c.*10 November 1842, Ushaw, Wiseman Papers 467.
7. Pugin, *Letters*, 1, 317.
8. Shrewsbury to Pugin, postmarked 28 March 1840, PC 339/101.
9. *A Second Letter to Ambrose Lisle Phillipps esq from the Earl of Shrewsbury on the present posture of affairs*, London, 1841, 7.
10. ibid., 8.
11. Arundell, *Letters*, 118.
12. Kee, *The Green Flag*, 194.
13. Pugin, *Letters*, 1, 324.
14. Wiseman to Shrewsbury, Feast of St Stanislaus (11 April), 1842, Ushaw, Wiseman Papers 73.
15. Pugin, *The Present State*, 95.
16. Diary of Benjamin Webb, Bodleian Library, ms Eng.misc.e406, f.44v.
17. ibid., f.40v.
18. Pugin, *The Present State*, 90.
19. Pugin, *Letters*, 1, 373.
20. Pugin, *The Present State*, 66 and 144.
21. ibid., 112.
22. ibid., 157.
23. Pugin, *Letters*, 1, 320.
24. Ibid., 333.
25. *Ecclesiologist*, 4, 277, quoted in White, *Cambridge Movement*, 122.
26. Correspondence of the Oxford Society for Promoting the Study of Gothic Architecture, Bodleian Library, DepC.589.
27. Dodds, *Age of Paradox*, 67.
28. Webb diary, see above, n.16, f.38v.
29. Quoted in Janet Myles, *L. N. Cottingham 1787–1847, Architect of the Gothic Revival*, London, 1996, 163. Myles gives a thorough summary of the Cambridge Camden Society's various comments on Barry and his building.
30. Pugin, *Letters*, 1, 328.
31. ibid., 347.
32. ibid., 326.
33. ibid.
34. ibid., 321.
35. *Orthodox Journal*, 28 May 1842, 329.
36. Letter to Lord Midleton, 20 June 1843, Surrey History Centre, 1248/33/9.
37. Pugin, *Letters*, 1, 361.

38. W. M. Thackeray, *The Irish Sketchbook of 1842. The Works of Thackeray*, 26 vols., London, 1892, 18, 39.
39. Letter to John Rouse Bloxam, Bloxam Letters, 85.
40. Letter to Shrewsbury, PC 339/31.
41. Letter to Lord Midleton, see above, n.37.
42. Halévy, *History*, 4, 34.
43. Walsh to Shrewsbury, 25 August 1842, Ushaw, Walsh/Shrewsbury Letters/20.
44. Pugin, *Letters*, 1, 368.
45. ibid., 371.
46. Pugin to Helen Lumsdaine, n.d., *c.* December 1847, PC 339/138.
47. ibid.
48. Thomas Dick Lauder, *Memorial of the Royal Progress in Scotland*, Edinburgh, 1843, 300.
49. Quoted in 'Taymouth Castle, Perthshire – II' by Alistair Rowan, *Country Life*, 136, 1964, 978–81.
50. Pugin, *Letters*, 1, 372–3.
51. ibid., 373.
52. ibid., 384.
53. ibid.
54. ibid.
55. Nikolaus Pevsner and David Neale, *BoE, Yorkshire: York and the East Riding*, 2nd edition, London, 1995, 294.
56. Newman, *Letters*, 8, 215.
57. Diary, 53.

Chapter 24: A Shift in the Wind: January to September 1843

1. PC 304/759.
2. Sketchbook of Peter Paul Pugin, *c.*1882, Victoria and Albert Museum, Wedgwood, *V&A* [1098], f.19, lists 'Welby 323 Chicago Avenue' among other notes of addresses. Byron's descendants, however, do not know of him living in Chicago and he did not, later, use the name Welby, although it survived in the family. I am most grateful to the present Welby Pugin for sharing his researches with me.
3. Hardman Powell to Edward Pugin, n.d., *c.*1868, BCL.
4. Pugin, *Apology*, 15.
5. ibid., 21.
6. Pugin, *The Present State*, 113.
7. Pugin, *Apology*, 40.
8. Shrewsbury to Rock, 21 November 1844, SAA.
9. Pugin to Michael Forristall, Whitsun Eve, 1843 (postmarked 5 June), SAA.
10. Pugin, *Apology*, 39.
11. ibid., 50.
12. Quoted in Schiefen, *Wiseman*, 103.
13. Pugin, *Apology*, 38.
14. ibid., 25 and 51.
15. ibid., 37.
16. David Watkin, *The Life and Work of C. R. Cockerell*, London, 1974, 121.
17. Pugin, *Apology*, 3.
18. Quoted in John Jones, 'The Civil War of 1843', in *Balliol College Annual Record 1978*, Oxford, 1978, 60–68, 61.
19. Transcript by Frederick Oakeley of Pugin's letter to him, annotated 'Mr Pugin's opinion of the plans', dated 'Sexagesima Sunday', Balliol College Archives, D.21.50 A.
20. Pugin to Shrewsbury, 8 March 1843, PC 339/9.
21. Pugin to John Rouse Bloxam, 7 March 1843, Bloxam Letters, 97.
22. Jones, see above, n.18, 63.

23. *Oxford Chronicle and Reading Gazette*, 18 March 1843.
24. Pugin to Bloxam, Saturday in Passion Week, [8 April] 1843, Bloxam Letters, 93.
25. ibid.
26. Pugin to Shrewsbury, postmarked 13 April 1843, BAL, Wedgwood *RIBA* [27].
27. Pugin to Bloxam, see above, n.24.
28. ibid., postmarked 21 April 1843, Bloxam Letters, 99.
29. ibid., St John's Day [24 June] 1843, Bloxam Letters, 85.
30. ibid., 21 November 1843, Bloxam Letters, 73.
31. ibid.
32. Charles Dickens, 'Old Lamps for New Ones', *Household Words*, 15 June 1850, 267.
33. *Civil Engineer and Architect's Journal*, April 1842, 118.
34. John Weale, *Quarterly Papers on Architecture*, 2, London, 1844, 1.
35. Pugin to Bloxam, n.d., *c.* autumn 1843, Bloxam Letters, 20.
36. Pugin to Shrewsbury, St John's Day [24 June] 1843, PC 339/31.
37. Pugin to Bloxam, n.d., 1843, Bloxam Letters, 45.
38. Revd James Newsham to Bishop Brown, 21 January 1841, Records of the Archdiocese of Liverpool, Lancashire Record Office, RC/LV/63.
39. Pugin to Shrewsbury, postmarked 2 August 1843, PC 339/42.
40. ibid., NAL, Wedgwood, *V&A* [31].
41. ibid., see above, n.37.

Chapter 25: The Grange, Ramsgate: September to December 1843

1. Pugin to David Read, n.d., *c.*1844, Fitzwilliam Museum, Cambridge, Henderson bequest, I.64.
2. For a fuller account of Pugin's small houses and their influence, see Hill, 'Pugin's Small Houses'.
3. Franklin, *Gentleman's Country House*, 2.
4. Pugin to Bloxam, n.d., *c.* September 1843, Bloxam Letters, 20.
5. ibid.
6. Pugin, *Apology*, 39.
7. Diary of Charles Barry Jun., entry for 26 October 1846, ms in a private collection, on microfilm in the House of Lords Record Office.
8. Muthesius, *Das Englische Haus*, 203.
9. Eastlake, *Gothic Revival*, 164. The improper implications of this arrangement were realized in the set for Ben Travers's farce *Rookery Nook*, causing Osbert Lancaster to characterize the living-hall house as the 'Aldwych Farcical' style in *Homes Sweet Homes*, 1939. The original approach to the Grange was rediscovered by Paul Drury in his researches for the Landmark Trust.
10. Pugin to Bloxam, see above, n.4.
11. Pugin to Shrewsbury, n.d., *c.* February 1844, PC 339/78.
12. Arundell, *Letters*, 142, and the *Examiner*, 3 June 1843.
13. Quoted in Sykes, *Two Studies in Virtue*, 56.
14. Pugin to Bloxam, n.d., postmarked 4 October 1843, Bloxam Letters, 142.
15. Pugin to Shrewsbury, 17 October 1843, PC 339/60.
16. ibid., n.d., PC 339/72.

Chapter 26: A Return of Grief: January to August 1844

1. Mary Amherst to Luigi Gentili, 12 January 1845, Stresa, ASIC A.G. 62, 1135–40.
2. Scott, *Recollections*, 92.
3. Pugin, *Apology*, 55.
4. Ferrey, *Pugin*, 276.
5. Pugin to Shrewsbury, n.d., *c.* January 1844, NAL, Wedgwood, *V&A* [36].

6. ibid.
7. The pioneering scholarship of Brian Andrews finally established Pugin's oeuvre in Tasmania, culminating in the exhibition *Creating a Gothic Paradise, Pugin at the Antipodes*, which toured Australia in 2002 with an extensive accompanying catalogue.
8. Quoted in Columba Graham Flegg, *Gathered Under Apostles, a study of the Catholic Apostolic Church*, Oxford, 1993, 35.
9. Pugin to Henry Drummond, *c.* April 1845, archives of the Duke of Northumberland, Alnwick Castle, C/17/5.
10. *Ecclesiologist*, 6, 202.
11. George Myers to William Dunn, 13 December 1843, NRO 2988/AWP/47.
12. Pugin to William Dunn, 9 January 1844, NRO 2988/AWP/24.
13. ibid.
14. Pugin to Shrewsbury, see above, n.5.
15. Wiseman to Shrewsbury, n.d., summer 1844, Ushaw, Wiseman Papers, 462.
16. ibid.
17. Anonymous [Henry Alford], *A History and Description of the Restored Parish Church of Saint Mary, Wymeswold, Leicestershire*, London, 1846. I am grateful to Geoffrey K. Brandwood for providing me with a copy of this.
18. ibid., 19.
19. ibid., 20.
20. Pugin to Shrewsbury, 30 May 1844, NAL, Wedgwood, *V&A* [39].
21. E. W. Pugin, *Art Architect*, 32.
22. Powell, 'Pugin', 174.
23. F. Knight Hunt (ed.), *The Book of Art, cartoons, frescoes, sculpture and decorative art, as applied to the new houses of parliament . . . compiled from the reports of the Royal commission of Fine Arts . . .*, London, 1846, 2.
24. ibid.
25. Quoted in Barry, *A Reply*, 53.
26. ibid.
27. Pugin to Miss Ryland, 20 June 1844, Warwickshire County Record Office, CR2120/2.
28. Pugin to Bloxam, n.d., *c.* July 1844, Bloxam Letters, 59.
29. Mary Amherst to Gentili, see above, n.1.
30. ibid.
31. *Tablet*, 31 August 1844, 142.
32. Ferrey, *Pugin*, 176.
33. Diary, 56.
34. ibid.
35. Pugin to Gentili, Stresa, ASIC A.G. 62, 479.
36. Pugin to Rock, 23 August 1844, SAA.

Chapter 27: The New House and the New Palace: Autumn and Winter 1844

1. Gillis to his housekeeper Miss Maxwell, 26 and 29 August 1844, Scottish Catholic Archives, Edinburgh, ED/2/8/5 and ED/2/8/6. Henson's Aerial Steam Carriage was a proposal for a steam-powered monoplane with a 150-foot wing span. It was patented in 1843 but never flew.
2. *Morning Post*, reprinted in the *Tablet*, 14 September 1844.
3. ibid.
4. ibid.
5. Pugin to Shrewsbury, n.d., *c.* late August 1844, PC 339/80.
6. ibid.
7. Pugin to Bloxam, n.d., *c.* September 1844, Bloxam Letters, 42.
8. Pugin to Anne Pugin, n.d., *c.*28 August 1844 PC 304/240.
9. ibid.

10. ibid., n.d., *c.*29 August 1844, PC 304/251.
11. Mary Amherst to Gentili, 12 January 1845, Stresa, ASIC A.G. 62, 1135–40.
12. ibid.
13. Pugin to Hardman, n.d., autumn 1844, BCL.
14. Pugin, *Apology*, 38.
15. ibid.
16. Etty to Pugin, 3 August 1845, RA, RAJU/10/65. In fact the panelling was pitch pine stained mahogany colour, so Pugin had not entirely abandoned his Wardour Street habits.
17. Pugin, *Letters*, 1, 43.
18. Pugin to Crace, autumn 1844, BAL PUG/1/30.
19. ibid., 28 October 1844, BAL PUG/1/25.
20. ibid., October 1844, BAL PUG/1/23.
21. Powell, 'Pugin', 175.
22. Pugin to Hardman, n.d., PC 304/337.
23. Quoted in Port, *The Houses of Parliament*, 115.
24. Quoted in Barry, *A Reply*, 39.
25. ibid.
26. ibid.
27. Pugin to Anne Pugin, n.d., *c.* September 1844 and October 1844, PC 304/252 and 302.
28. Pugin to Clarkson Stanfield, transcribed by R. Stanfield, n.d., between October 1844 and October 1845, WAA SEC 20/11/23. Maps in the East Kent Archives (R/U1568/P442) show that the Bings bought their land in October 1844. Pugin began laying out his church in November 1845.
29. John Newman, *BoE, North East and East Kent*, 3rd edition, 1983, 423.
30. Pugin to Thomas Griffiths, 27 October 1844, WAA A81/2.
31. Pugin to Hardman, n.d., *c.*September 1845, PC 304/287.
32. Nikolaus Pevsner, *BoE, Staffordshire*, London, 1974, 97.
33. *Ecclesiologist*, 9, 369–70.
34. See above, n.29, 111.
35. John Newman, 'St Augustine's Ramsgate as a Kentish Church, transcript of a lecture given in Ramsgate in October 1996', Ramsgate 1996, unnumbered pages [5]. This is the best analytical account of the church to date.
36. This point is made in Newman's lecture.
37. Diary, 56.
38. ibid.
39. Mary Amherst to Gentili, see above, n.11.
40. ibid.
41. ibid.
42. Pugin to Shrewsbury, n.d., *c.* November 1844, PC 339/25.
43. ibid.
44. Shrewsbury to Pugin, November 1844, PC 339/102.
45. Pugin to Crace, n.d., autumn 1844, BAL PUG/1/35.
46. Mary Amherst to Gentili, see above, n.11.
47. Pugin to Lord Midleton, 14 December 1844, Surrey History Centre 1248/33/44.
48. Pugin to Hardman, n.d., *c.* February–March 1845, PC 304/951.
49. ibid., n.d., December 1844, PC 304/954.
50. Talbot Bury, 'Recollections of A. W. N. Pugin', *Building News*, 4 October 1861, 808.
51. Shrewsbury to Rock, 1 December 1844, SAA, box marked 'Rock'.
52. E. W. Pugin, *Art Architect*, 14.
53. Pugin to Griffiths, Feast of St Hugh [17 November] 1844, WAA A81/3.
54. Pugin to Hardman, PC 304/61.

Chapter 28: The New Life: December 1844 to April 1845

1. Powell, 'Pugin', 174 and 179.
2. ibid., 174.
3. ibid., 177.
4. ibid.
5. ibid., 176.
6. ibid., 177.
7. Pugin to Clarkson Stanfield, transcript by R. Stanfield, n.d., WAA, SEC 20/11/23 f.77.
8. Pugin to Hardman, n.d., PC 304/87.
9. ibid., n.d., c. January 1845, PC 304/954.
10. ibid., n.d., c. January 1845, PC 304/321.
11. ibid., n.d., c. January 1845, BCL.
12. ibid.
13. Diary, 58.
14. Pugin to Edward Willson, 3rd Sunday in Lent [23 February] 1845, Johns Hopkins University.
15. Pugin to Charles Barry, quoted in Barry, A Reply, 55–6.
16. Pugin to Hardman, n.d., March 1845, PC 304/953.
17. Pugin to Barry, see above, n.15.
18. ibid.
19. ibid.
20. Pugin to Hardman, n.d., c. January 1845, BCL.
21. ibid., n.d., c. February 1845, BCL.
22. ibid., c. 26 February 1845, BCL.
23. Typescript account of the history of the church by the Revd Harold Squirrell, f.2, Archives of the Diocese of Northampton.
24. Pugin to Hardman, Easter Sunday [23 March] 1845, BCL.
25. Wiseman to Shrewsbury, Ember Saturday 1844, Ushaw, Wiseman Papers, 852.
26. Pugin to Hardman, n.d.,?5 September 1845, BCL.
27. Pugin to Henry Drummond, n.d., late 1843–early 1844, Archives of the Duke of Northumberland, Alnwick.
28. Pugin to Henry Champernowne, n.d., c. October 1844, Devonshire Record Office, Z/15/37/15/1.
29. Pugin to Charles Scarisbrick, postmarked 3 March 1844, Lancashire Record Office, RO/DDSc 78/4.
30. ibid., Whitsunday [11 May] 1845, Lancashire Record Office, RO /DDSc 78/4 (15).
31. Pugin to Thomas Griffiths, 5 January 1845, WAA A81/4.
32. Powell, 'Pugin', 176.
33. Pugin to Hardman, n.d., c. February–March 1845, PC 304/951.
34. Mary Amherst to Gentili, 2 January 1845, Stresa, ASIC A.G. 62, 760–61.
35. ibid., 4 March 1845, Stresa, ASIC A.G. 62, 790–91.
36. Pugin to Gentili, n.d., c. 12–14 April 1845, Stresa, ASIC A.G. 62, 695.
37. ibid.
38. ibid., n.d., c. 16 April 1845, Stresa, ASIC A.G. 62, 847.

Chapter 29: A Battle of Wills: May to October 1845

1. Mary Amherst to Gentili, 22 April 1845, Stresa, ASIC A.G. 62, 1116–19.
2. ibid.
3. ibid., n.d., c. June 1845, Stresa, ASIC A.G. 62, 946–7.
4. ibid., n.d., c. August 1845, Stresa ASIC A.G. 62, 987–8.
5. Transcripts of letters in the Stanfield letter book, WAA SEC 20/11/23.
6. 'Charles Barry and his right-hand man', Artizan, 7, 1 July 1845.

7. *Builder*, 6 September 1845, 426.
8. Quoted in E. W. Pugin, *Art Architect*, 65.
9. Newman, *Apologia*, 212.
10. Professor Lee, quoted in White, *The Cambridge Movement*, 150.
11. Halévy, *History*, 4, 94.
12. Pugin to Charles Barry, postmarked 5 August 1845, quoted in Barry, *A Reply*, 54.
13. ibid.
14. Pugin to Bishop Sharples, n.d., late 1845–early 1846, Liverpool Diocesan Archives, Lancashire Record Office, RCVL/63.
15. 'Mr Pugin on Christian art', letter in the *Builder*, August 1845, 367.
16. ibid.
17. For a fuller description, see Hill, 'Pugin's Churches'.
18. The idea of the memorial window was not entirely new but it was widely popularized by the lawyer and antiquary J. H. Markland in a pamphlet, based on a lecture given to the Oxford Architectural Association in 1840. I am most grateful to Michael Kerney for sharing his researches on the subject with me.
19. Pugin, 'Lecture on Ecclesiastical Architecture . . . Lecture the Third', *Catholic Magazine*, 3, 1839, 97.
20. Pugin to Hardman, n.d., *c.* February 1845, BCL.
21. Pugin to Bishop Sharples, see above, n.14.
22. Pugin to Shrewsbury, 26 October 1845, PC 339/33.
23. 'A Card', *Punch*, 9, 1845, 238.
24. 'The Cromwell Statue Question', *Punch*, 9, 1845, 186.
25. Pugin to Shrewsbury, see above, n.22.
26. Pugin to Hardman, n.d., summer 1845, PC 304/952.
27. ibid.
28. ibid., n.d., October 1845, BCL.

Chapter 30: Entre Deux Femmes: October 1845 to June 1846

1. Pugin to Hardman, n.d., *c.*9 October 1845, BCL.
2. Pugin to Shrewsbury, postmarked 14 March 1846, PC 339/1.
3. Mary Amherst to Gentili, 1 November 1845, Stresa, ASIC A.G. 62, 1011–12.
4. Pugin to Shrewsbury, Feast of St Hugh [17 November], 1845, PC 339/84.
5. Pugin to Shrewsbury, see above, n.2.
6. ibid.
7. Letter from Hardman Powell to Hardman, postmarked October 1845, BCL.
8. ibid., postmarked 20 November 1845, BCL.
9. James Jauch, 'A Christmas Tale', *Tablet*, 6, 27 December 1845.
10. *Ecclesiologist*, 5, 1846, 10–16.
11. ibid.
12. ibid.
13. Pugin to Bloxam, Eve of the Purification [1 February] 1846, Bloxam Letters, 65.
14. *Ecclesiologist*, see above, n.10.
15. Quoted in O'Dwyer, 'A. W. N. Pugin and St Patrick's College, Maynooth'.
16. ibid.
17. Pugin to Shrewsbury, see above, n.2.
18. ibid.
19. ibid.
20. ibid.
21. Pugin to Shrewsbury, 22 March 1846, PC 339/6.
22. Pugin to Shrewsbury, see above, n.2.
23. Mary Amherst to Gentili, postmarked 2 April 1846, Stresa, ASIC A.G. 61, 312.
24. Pugin to Shrewsbury, postmarked 15 April 1846, PC 339/3.

25. ibid.
26. ibid.
27. Pugin to Shrewsbury, postmarked 25 April 1846, PC 339/2.
28. Lingard to the Revd Robert Tate, 10 August 1846, Ushaw, transcript of Lingard's letters, 718.
29. Pugin to Hardman, n.d., *c.* April 1846, PC 304/885.
30. ibid.
31. ibid., n.d., *c.* April 1846, BCL.
32. Pugin to Hardman, see above, n.29.
33. Quoted in O'Dwyer, see above, n.15, 106.
34. Pugin to Shrewsbury, Passion Sunday [5 April] 1846, PC 339/96.
35. ibid.
36. Pugin to William Leigh, postmarked 27 May 1846, Gloucestershire Record Office, D2258/4.
37. Pugin to Shrewsbury, postmarked 13 February 1846, PC 339/15.
38. ibid.
39. John Newman and Nikolaus Pevsner, *BoE, Dorset*, London 1972, 356.
40. Pugin to Hardman, n.d., *c.* April 1846, PC 304/300.
41. Pugin to the Revd Mr Walker, Whitsun Eve [30 May] 1846, Ushaw, PU/3.
42. ibid., postmarked 3 June 1846, Ushaw, PU/4.
43. Mary Louisa Amherst to Gentili, 1 June 1846, Stresa, ASIC A.G. 63, 445–6.
44. Wiseman to Shrewsbury, 22 May 1846, Ushaw, Wiseman Papers, 492.
45. Mary Amherst to Gentili, n.d., *c.* June 1846, Stresa, ASIC A.G. 63, 447–8.
46. Bishop Walsh to Shrewsbury, 22 December 1846, Ushaw, Walsh/Shrewsbury Letters, 38.

Chapter 31: Improving the Taste of Young England: June 1846 to February 1847

1. Newman, *Letters*, 11, 209–11.
2. William Etty to Betsy Etty, 12 July 1846, NAL ms.L.5164.2-1979.
3. William Etty to Walter Etty, 12 July 1846, York Central Library.
4. William Etty to Betsy Etty, see above, n.2.
5. Pugin to Crace, n.d., *c.* July 1846, BAL, PUG/3/8.
6. ibid., n.d., *c.* July 1846, BAL PUG/3/10.
7. Shrewsbury to Pugin, n.d., *c.* August 1846, PC 339/110.
8. ibid.
9. Newman, *Letters*, 11, 227 and 210.
10. ibid., 14, 183.
11. 'The Opening of St Giles Cheadle', *Tablet*, 7, 5 September 1846.
12. ibid.
13. Faber, *Poet and Priest*, 13.
14. Talbot Bury, 'Recollections of A. W. N. Pugin', *Building News*, 7, 4 October 1861, 808.
15. Pugin to Hardman, n.d., *c.* autumn 1846, PC 304/2.
16. Pugin to Crace, n.d., annotated 9 September 1846, BAL PUG/3/18.
17. Pugin to the Revd J. Hornby, n.d., *c.* October 1846, Cheshire County Record Office, P158/4296/30[3].
18. Pugin to Thomas Griffiths, n.d., annotated 12 November 1846, WAA A81/9.
19. Diary of Charles Barry Jun., Sunday 25 October 1846, ms in private collection, microfilm in House of Lords Record Office.
20. ibid.
21. 'Powell', *Pugin*, 184.
22. Hardman Powell to Crace, n.d., annotated 4 December 1846, BAL PUG/3/22.
23. Pugin to Crace, n.d., December 1846, BAL PUG/3/30.
24. ibid., n.d., 1846, BAL PUG/3/20.
25. Pugin to Hardman, postmarked 20 December 1846, PC 304/222.

26. ibid., n.d., *c.* November 1846, PC 304/14.
27. ibid., n.d., *c.* November 1846, PC 304/18.
28. Pugin to Hardman, n.d., *c.* January–February 1847, BCL.
29. ibid., n.d., February 1847, BCL.
30. ibid.

Chapter 32: The House of Lords: February to Autumn 1847

1. Pugin, *A Statement of Facts*, 3.
2. Pugin to the Revd James Hornby, n.d., *c.*11 November 1848, Cheshire County Record Office, P158/4296/30/81.
3. Wiseman to Shrewsbury, 29 March 1847, Ushaw, Wiseman Papers, 872.
4. ibid.
5. ibid.
6. Pugin to Hardman, n.d., *c.* March 1847, BCL.
7. ibid.
8. Thomas Earley to Hardman, n.d., *c.* March 1847, BCL.
9. 'The House of Lords', *Illustrated London News*, 10:17, 24 April and 1, 8, 15 May 1847.
10. ibid.
11. Pugin, *A Statement of Facts*, 4.
12. Note in a sketchbook, NAL, 86.mm.34, f.12, Wedgwood, *V&A* [1037].
13. Pugin to Anne Pugin, n.d., *c.*21 April 1847, PC 304/275.
14. Powell, 'Pugin', 188.
15. Pugin to Shrewsbury, postmarked 13 May 1847, PC 339/30.
16. Powell, 'Pugin', 189.
17. Newman repeated the story in a letter to Ambrose Phillipps the following year. Newman, *Letters*, 12, 219–22.
18. 'Recollections of Pugin' [Richard Simpson], *Rambler*, 3rd series, 5, September 1861, 394–402.
19. Bishop Gillis to Miss Maxwell, 28 April 1847, Scottish Catholic Archives, Edinburgh, ED/2/8/13.
20. Pugin to Shrewsbury, see above, n.15.
21. Simpson, see above, n.18, 400.
22. Robert Willis, *Remarks on the Architecture of the Middle Ages especially of Italy*, Cambridge, 1835, iii.
23. Pugin to Shrewsbury, see above, n.15.
24. Note made probably in Milan, in a volume of sketches now in the Metropolitan Museum of Art in New York, Pugin Drawings, vol.3, f.81.
25. This was in a house called Wilburton Manor in Cambridgeshire, see Hill, 'Pugin's Small Houses'.
26. Pugin, *A Statement of Facts*, 5–6.
27. ibid., 6.
28. ibid.
29. Pugin to Anne Pugin, postmarked 4 August 1847, PC 304/308.
30. John Elliott, 'Pugin, St Osmund and Salisbury', in *Ecclesiology Today*, 22 April 2000, 6.
31. Newman, *Letters*, 12, 71.
32. Sykes, *Two Studies in Virtue*, 68.
33. Myers to Hardman, n.d., *c.* summer 1847, BCL; Shrewsbury to Rock, 13 September 1847, SAA.
34. Quoted in Tóibín and Ferriter, *The Irish Famine*, 140.
35. Pugin to Shrewsbury, postmarked 30 July 1847, NAL, Wedgwood, *V&A* [52].
36. Shrewsbury to Wiseman, 30 July 1847, Ushaw, Wiseman Papers, 878.
37. Quoted in Schiefen, *Wiseman*, 185.

Chapter 33: Many Hands: Autumn 1847

1. Pugin to Hardman, n.d., *c.* autumn 1847, PC 304/288.
2. Thomas Earley to Hardman, 17 April 1847, BCL.
3. ibid., 19 September 1847, BCL.
4. ibid.
5. ibid., 2 May 1847, BCL.
6. Thomas Earley to Hardman, 19 September 1847, BCL.
7. ibid.
8. Myers to Hardman, n.d., BCL.
9. Pugin to Hardman, n.d., *c.*20 September 1845, BCL.
10. Pugin to Hardman, n.d., *c.* September 1845, BCL.
11. Myers to Hardman, 2 December 1847, BCL.
12. ibid., n.d., BCL.
13. ibid., 12 October ?1847, BCL.
14. ibid., n.d., *c.*1848, BCL.
15. Harrison, *Victorian Stained Glass*, 19.
16. Pugin to the Revd J. Hornby, 21 August 1847, Cheshire County Record Office, P158/4296/30/36.
17. Hardman Powell to Hardman, n.d., *c.*22 September 1847, BCL.
18. ibid., postmarked 27 October 1847, BCL, and ibid., postmarked 20 October 1847, BCL.
19. Pugin to Helen Lumsdaine, n.d., *c.* early December 1848, PC 339/133.
20. ibid.
21. ibid., n.d., *c.* October 1847, PC 339/137.
22. Pugin to Shrewsbury, n.d., *c.* September 1847, PC 339/79.
23. ibid.
24. Franklin, *Gentleman's Country House*, 129.
25. Pugin, *A Statement of Facts*, 7.
26. Pugin to Helen Lumsdaine, postmarked 9 November 1847, PC 339/140.
27. Pugin, *A Statement of Facts*, 10.
28. ibid., 12.
29. Pugin to Helen Lumsdaine, see above, n.19.
30. Pugin, *A Statement of Facts*, 13.
31. Pugin to Hardman, n.d., *c.* spring 1848, PC 304/18.
32. Halévy, *History*, 5, 197.
33. ibid., 200.
34. Pugin to Crace, annotated 10 November 1847, BAL PUG/4/26.
35. ibid.
36. ibid., annotated 13 December 1847, BAL PUG/4/29.
37. Pugin to Helen Lumsdaine, n.d., *c.* December 1847, PC 339/138.
38. ibid., postmarked 9 November 1847, PC 339/140.
39. Hardman Powell to Hardman, postmarked 23 November 1847, BCL.
40. Letter to Helen Lumsdaine, see above, n.37.
41. Thomas Earley to Hardman, 5 December 1847, BCL.

Chapter 34: Helen Lumsdaine: December 1847 to May 1848

1. Pugin to Helen Lumsdaine, n.d., *c.* December 1847, PC 339/130.
2. ibid.
3. ibid.
4. Pugin to Hardman, n.d., *c.* December 1847, PC 304/375.
5. ibid., n.d., 1848, BCL.
6. Pugin to Helen Lumsdaine, see above, n.1.

7. ibid.
8. Pugin, *A Statement of Facts*, 14.
9. Pugin to Helen Lumsdaine, n.d., *c.* January 1848, PC 339/134.
10. ibid.
11. Pugin, *A Statement of Facts*, 15.
12. Pugin to Helen Lumsdaine, see above, n.9.
13. Pugin to Hardman, n.d., *c.* January 1848, PC 304/132.
14. ibid., n.d., *c.* January 1848, PC 304/404.
15. ibid., see above, n.13.
16. Pugin to Hardman, n.d., *c.* January 1848, PC 304/327 and 364.
17. Pugin, *A Statement of Facts*, 15.
18. Drawing now in the RIBA collection, Wedgwood, *RIBA* [88].
19. Pugin to Helen Lumsdaine, n.d., *c.* February 1848, PC 339/139.
20. ibid., n.d., *c.* February 1848, PC 339/132.
21. Pugin to Helen Lumsdaine, see above, n.19.
22. ibid.
23. Pugin to Hardman, n.d., *c.* February 1848, PC 304/409.
24. Pugin to Shrewsbury, n.d., *c.* February 1848, PC 339/70.
25. Pugin to Crace, annotated 27 February 1848, BAL PUG/5/16.
26. Pugin to Hardman, n.d., *c.* February 1848, PC 304/376.
27. ibid.
28. Shrewsbury to Wiseman, 7 March 1848, Ushaw, Wiseman Papers, 914.
29. ibid.
30. ibid.
31. ibid., 18 May 1848, Ushaw, Wiseman Papers, 925.
32. Quoted in Halévy, 5, 237.
33. Quoted in Kee, *The Green Flag*, 264.
34. Shrewsbury to Wiseman, 13 April 1848, Ushaw, Wiseman Papers, 921.
35. Pugin to Hardman, n.d., *c.* early March 1848, PC 304/421.
36. Pugin to Anne Pugin, n.d., *c.*15 March 1848, PC 304/384.
37. Pugin, *A Statement of Facts*, 17.
38. ibid., 18.
39. Pugin, draft of a letter to Revd Mr Sandys, n.d., *c.* March 1848, PC 339/125.
40. ibid. The phrase has been crossed through, so Pugin may not have gone quite so far in the letter as sent.
41. ibid.
42. Revd Mr Sandys to Pugin, 28 April 1848, Yale 161.
43. Pugin to Crace, annotated 14 April 1848, BAL PUG/5/27.
44. *Kent Herald*, 30 March 1848.
45. ibid., 20 April 1848.
46. Shrewsbury to Wiseman, 18 May 1848, Ushaw, Wiseman Papers, 925.
47. ibid.
48. ibid.
49. Pugin to Hardman, n.d., *c.* May 1848, PC 304/432.
50. Pugin, *A Statement of Facts*, 22.
51. Pugin to Hardman, n.d., *c.* May 1848, PC 304/322.
52. ibid., n.d., *c.* May 1848, PC 304/411.
53. Letter to Crace, n.d., *c.* May–June 1848, BAL PUG/10/5.
54. It is in a private collection and I am grateful to the owner for copying it for me. Long extracts are reprinted in Ferrey, *Pugin*.

Chapter 35: 'One affectionate heart': May to 10 August 1848

1. Pugin to Hardman, n.d., postmarked 14 June 1848, PC 304/239.
2. ibid.
3. Pugin to Revd Hornby, 7 June 1848, Cheshire County Record Office, P158/4296/30/71.
4. Myers to Hardman, n.d., c. June 1848, BCL.
5. Newman, *Letters*, 12, 221–2.
6. ibid.
7. ibid., 220.
8. *Tablet*, 9, 3 June 1848, 355.
9. Pugin, 'Church of St Thomas of Canterbury', letter to the *Tablet*, 1 July 1848, 419.
10. Newman, *Letters*, 12, 212.
11. Quoted in Bogan, *The Great Link*, 120.
12. Pugin to Hardman, n.d., c. early 1848, PC 304/410.
13. Myers to Hardman, n.d., postmarked 7 April 1848, BCL.
14. Thomas Earley to Hardman, 3 June 1848, BCL.
15. Pugin to John Knill, n.d., c. July 1848, SAA.
16. Bogan, see above, n.11, 131.
17. ibid., 140.
18. *Tablet*, quoted ibid., 131.
19. Quoted in Bogan, see above, n.11.
20. Pugin to Jane Knill, n.d., c. July 1848, PC 339/269.
21. ibid.
22. Pugin to Jane Knill, postmarked 23 July 1848, PC 339/186.
23. ibid.
24. ibid., n.d., July 1848, PC 339/225.
25. ibid.
26. ibid., postmarked 1 August 1848, PC 339/185.
27. ibid., see above, n.22.

Chapter 36: 'A first rate Gothic woman': 11 August 1848 to August 1849

1. Pugin to Hornby, annotated 11 August 1848, Cheshire County Record Office, P158/4296/30/74.
2. Shrewsbury to Pugin, n.d., c. August 1848, PC 339/109.
3. Sketchbook in the Victoria and Albert Museum, Wedgwood, *V&A* [1013] f.45.
4. Pugin to Shrewsbury, n.d., c.31 August 1848, PC 339/63.
5. Pugin to Hardman, postmarked 27 August 1848, PC 304/183.
6. Diary, 64.
7. Quoted in Rosemary Ashton, *Thomas and Jane Carlyle, Portrait of a Marriage*, London, 2001, 418.
8. Pugin to Hardman, n.d., c.1851, PC 304/163.
9. *Kent Herald*, 10 August 1848.
10. Pugin to Crace, annotated 1 September 1848, BAL PUG/5/42.
11. ibid.
12. Pugin to Hardman, postmarked 27 September 1848, PC 304/170.
13. ibid., n.d., c.28 August 1848, PC 304/185.
14. ibid., n.d., c. September 1848, PC 304/146.
15. Pugin to Jane Pugin, n.d., c. February 1850, PC 339/213.
16. Bridget Cherry and Nikolaus Pevsner, *BoE, London 2, South*, London, 1983, 381.
17. *Ecclesiologist*, 9, 331.
18. Pugin to 'my lord Bishop', probably Wiseman, n.d., c.1850, PC 339/126.
19. *Ecclesiologist*, 9, 154.
20. *Civil Engineer and Architect's Journal*, October 1848, 290–91.

21. Pugin to Jane Pugin, postmarked 19 October 1848, NAL, Wedgwood, *V&A* [76].
22. ibid., postmarked 13 October 1848, PC 339/203.
23. Thomas Earley to Hardman, September 1848, BCL.
24. Letter to Jane Pugin, see above, n.22.
25. ibid., postmarked 18 October 1848, NAL, Wedgwood, *V&A* [75].
26. Pugin to Shrewsbury, postmarked 26 December 1848, NAL, Wedgwood, *V&A* [63].
27. Pugin to Jane Pugin, postmarked 17 October 1848, PC 339/174.
28. ibid.
29. Pugin to Hardman, n.d., PC 304/399.
30. Hardman Powell to Hardman, n.d., BCL.
31. Pugin to Hornby, 11 November 1848, Cheshire County Record Office, P158/4296/30/81. The implication of the extensive press coverage was that Midleton, who had separated from his wife, was involved in a homosexual scandal. He asphyxiated himself with the fumes from a charcoal brazier.
32. Pugin to Hardman, n.d., *c.*1848, PC 304/1034.
33. ibid., n.d., *c.* November 1848, PC 304/1033.
34. ibid., n.d., *c.* November 1848, PC 304/1034.
35. Pugin to Shrewsbury, postmarked 26 December 1848, NAL, Wedgwood, *V&A* [63].
36. Pugin to Jane Pugin, n.d., *c.*23 April 1849, PC 339/283.
37. Shrewsbury to Wiseman, 8 April 1848, WAA 137/3/14.
38. ibid., 9 March 1849, Ushaw, Wiseman Letters, 942.
39. Wiseman to Shrewsbury, n.d., *c.*17 March 1849, Ushaw College, Wiseman Papers, 941.
40. Quoted in Schiefen, *Wiseman*, 181.
41. Quoted in Spencer-Silver, *Pugin's Builder*, 60.
42. Pugin to Shrewsbury, n.d., *c.* October 1847, PC 339/89.
43. ibid., postmarked 10 June 1849, NAL, Wedgwood, *V&A* [65].
44. ibid., n.d., *c.* December 1848, PC, 339/50.
45. ibid., n.d., summer 1849, PC 339/53.
46. Pugin to Hardman, n.d., February 1849, PC 304/138.
47. Pugin to Crace, 22 March 1849, BAL PUG/6/2.
48. ibid.
49. ibid.
50. Pugin to Hardman, n.d., *c.* March 1849, PC 304/99.
51. ibid., n.d., *c.* February 1849, PC 304/192.
52. *Ecclesiologist*, 9, 368–74.
53. ibid.
54. Powell, 'Pugin', 182.
55. Pugin to Jane Pugin, n.d., *c.* autumn 1849, PC 339/229.
56. Pugin to Crace, annotated December 1849, BAL PUG/6/25.
57. Shrewsbury to Bishop Ullathorne, 12 May 1849, BAA B/1558.
58. Faber, *Poet and Priest*, 185.
59. ibid.
60. ibid., 189.
61. Pugin to Hardman, n.d., *c.* April 1849, PC 304/231.
62. Pugin to Jane Pugin, postmarked 31 May 1849, NAL, Wedgwood, *V&A* [79].
63. ibid., n.d., *c.*26 June 1849, PC 339/271.
64. *Ecclesiologist*, 9, 289–91.
65. 'Killarney cathedral', *Tablet*, 24 August 1850.
66. Pugin to Jane Pugin, n.d., postmarked 11 July 1849, PC 339/211.
67. ibid.
68. ibid., n.d., *c.* April 1849, PC 339/268.
69. ibid., n.d., *c.*17 April 1849, PC 339/275.
70. ibid., n.d., *c.*15 April 1849, PC 339/277.
71. Jane Pugin to Pugin, n.d., *c.*1849, PC 339/294.

72. Pugin to Jane Pugin, postmarked October 1848, PC 339/172.
73. ibid., n.d., *c.*16 April 1849, PC 339/276.
74. ibid., postmarked 18 October 1848, NAL, Wedgwood, *V&A* [75].
75. Jane Pugin, *Journal*, 56.
76. Pugin to Jane Pugin, n.d., *c.*23 April 1849, PC 339/283.
77. Pugin to Hardman, n.d., early 1849, PC 304/417.
78. ibid., n.d., *c.* February 1849, PC 304/144.
79. ibid., n.d., *c.*22 June 1849, PC 304/837.
80. ibid., postmarked 6 May 1849, PC 304/417.
81. ibid., n.d., summer 1849, PC304/297.
82. Gillis to Miss Maxwell, 1 July 1849, Scottish Catholic Archives, Edinburgh, 1/12.
83. Pugin, *Some Remarks*, 14.
84. Pugin to Hardman, n.d., PC 304/55.
85. ibid., n.d., *c.* July 1849, PC 304/395.
86. Pugin to Jane Pugin, n.d., August 1849, PC 339/212.
87. Pugin to Hardman, n.d., *c.* August 1849, PC 304/406.
88. ibid.
89. Pugin to Jane Pugin, n.d., August 1849, PC 339/212.
90. ibid., postmarked 26 August 1849, PC 339/288.
91. Jane Pugin to Pugin, 30 August 1849, PC 339/293.
92. Pugin to Jane Pugin, postmarked 12 August 1849, PC 339/184.
93. Matthew Habershon, *The Ancient Half-Timbered Houses of England*, London, 1836, xxiii.
94. Pugin to Jane Pugin, n.d., 29 November 1849, PC 339/273.

Chapter 37: Design for the Middling Sort: September 1849 to January 1850

1. Pugin to Bloxam, 14 February 1849, Bloxam Letters, 165.
2. It is suggested by Stuart Durant (in Michael Whiteway (ed.), *Christopher Dresser, A Design Revolution*, London, 2004, 48) that in *Floriated Ornament* Pugin 'unashamedly employed, unacknowledged' William Dyce's designs from the *Drawing Book of Government Design* of 1842. Having compared the two with as open a mind as I can muster, I can see no more than the broadest similarity, inevitable given the date and subject matter.
3. *Floriated Ornament* (unnumbered pages), [4].
4. ibid., [3].
5. ibid., [4].
6. *Ecclesiologist*, 10, 324.
7. Quoted in Kenneth Clark, *Ruskin Today*, Penguin edition, London, 1982, 125.
8. Ruskin, *Seven Lamps of Architecture*, London, 1849, 3.
9. ibid., 6.
10. 'Modern Church Architecture', *Rambler*, August 1849, 233–6.
11. John 12, vii.
12. 'Why This Waste?', *Weekly Register*, 6 October 1849, 145–50.
13. 'Church Decoration', *Rambler*, December 1849, 498.
14. 'Why This Waste?', 146.
15. *Journal of Design and Manufacture* [*Journal of Design*], November 1849, 54–5.
16. Pugin to J. Gibson, Dean of Jesus College, Cambridge, 5 December 1849, Jesus College Archives.
17. *Journal of Design*, October 1849, 72.
18. Pugin to Crace, annotated 1849, BAL PUG/10/6.
19. ibid.
20. ibid.
21. Pugin to Jane Pugin, n.d., *c.*19 October 1849, PC 339/223.
22. Pugin to Hardman, n.d., *c.*24 October 1849, PC 304/964.

23. ibid.
24. ibid., n.d., *c.*21 October 1849, PC 304/966.
25. ibid., n.d., *c.* September 1849, PC 304/956.
26. Pugin to Crace, annotated 1849, BAL PUG/6/16.
27. ibid., annotated 13 November 1849, BAL PUG/6/17.
28. Pugin to Hardman, n.d., *c.* November 1849, PC 304/817.
29. ibid., n.d., *c.*1850, PC 304/692.
30. ibid., n.d., *c.*1849, PC 304/816.
31. ibid., n.d., *c.* November 1849, PC 304/895.
32. ibid., n.d. autumn 1849, PC 304/822.
33. Pugin to Hardman, see above, n.31.
34. ibid., n.d., *c.* late 1849, PC 304/820.
35. ibid., n.d., *c.* late 1849, PC 304/895.
36. ibid., n.d., *c.*19 November 1849, PC 304/819.
37. ibid., n.d., December 1849, PC 304/728.
38. ibid.
39. ibid., postmarked 19 November 1849, PC 304/826.
40. ibid., n.d., *c.* December 1849, PC 304/901 and PC 304/908.
41. ibid., n.d., *c.* December 1849, PC 304/908.
42. ibid., n.d., *c.* December 1849, PC 304/899.
43. ibid., n.d., *c.* December 1849, PC 304/909.
44. Pugin to Crace, annotated 29 March 1850, BAL PUG/7/17.
45. Pugin to Hardman, n.d., *c.* January 1850, PC 304/924.
46. ibid., n.d., *c.*1850, PC 304/922.
47. Pugin to Hardman, see above, n.45.
48. ibid., n.d., *c.* January 1850, PC 304/943.
49. Pugin to Jane Pugin, n.d., *c.*9 January 1850, PC 339/255.
50. ibid.
51. ibid.
52. Pugin to Hardman, n.d., *c.*1850, PC 304/714.
53. ibid., n.d., *c.*1850, PC 304/716.

Chapter 38: The High Victorians: 1850

1. Pugin, *Some Remarks*, 4.
2. ibid., 11.
3. ibid., 13.
4. ibid., 9.
5. ibid.
6. *Ecclesiologist*, 10, 397.
7. ibid., 398.
8. Halévy, *History*, 4, 404.
9. *Journal of Design*, May 1850, 87–8.
10. Quoted in Bonython and Burton, *The Great Exhibitor*, 121.
11. Pugin to Hardman, n.d., *c.* January 1850, PC 304/929.
12. Pugin to Jane Pugin, n.d., *c.* March 1850, PC 339/173.
13. Pugin to Crace, annotated 8 February 1850, BAL PUG/7/6.
14. Pugin to Hardman, n.d., *c.* January 1850, PC 304/937.
15. ibid.
16. Pugin to Jane Pugin, n.d., *c.*24 February 1850, PC 339/243.
17. ibid., postmarked 2 February 1850, PC 339/190.
18. Pugin to Hardman, see above, n.14.
19. ibid., n.d., *c.* February 1850, PC 304/936.
20. ibid., n.d., *c.* February 1850, PC 304/224.

21. Ms 'Reminiscences of Rugby by a Priest of the Rugby Mission', unsigned [William Lockhart], Rosminian Archive, Derry's Wood, [1].
22. ibid.
23. Pugin to Jane Pugin, n.d., c.27 February 1850, PC 339/219.
24. ibid.
25. Pugin to Shrewsbury, n.d., c. March 1850, PC 339/19.
26. ibid.
27. ibid.
28. Quoted in Bonython and Burton, *The Great Exhibitor*, 130.
29. Pugin to Hardman, n.d., c. March 1850, PC 304/848.
30. ibid., n.d., c. late March 1850, PC 304/852 and PC 304/847.
31. Pugin to Crace, annotated March 1850, BAL PUG/7/19.
32. Quoted in Bonython and Burton, *The Great Exhibitor*, 140.
33. Pugin to Crace, annotated 17 April 1850, BAL PUG/7/25.
34. *Rambler*, 27 April 1850, 325.
35. Pugin to Hardman, n.d., c.1850, PC 304/922.
36. Newman to Mary Holmes, 7 April 1850, Newman, *Letters*, 13, 460–62.
37. ibid., 462.
38. Pugin to Shrewsbury, postmarked 9 April 1850, NAL, Wedgwood, *V&A* [67].
39. *Hansard*, vol. CX, 29 April 1850, 890.
40. Pugin to Hardman, n.d., c. spring 1850, PC 304/55.
41. ibid.
42. Crook and Port, *King's Works*, 622.
43. *Hansard*, vol. CXI, 24 May 1850, 341.
44. ibid., 340.
45. Beresford Hope, quoted in Port, *Houses of Parliament*, 146.
46. Pugin to Hardman, n.d., c. May 1850, PC 304/696.
47. Pugin to Jane Pugin, n.d., c.27 February 1850, PC 339/219.
48. 'Old Lamps for New Ones', *Household Words*, 15 June 1850.
49. ibid.
50. *Kent Herald*, 3 October 1850.
51. Pugin to Hardman, n.d., c. March 1850, PC 304/852.
52. ibid., n.d., c. April 1850, PC 304/691, and c. October 1851, PC 304/518.
53. ibid., n.d., c. February 1850, PC 304/224.
54. ibid.
55. Jane Pugin, *Journal*, 61.
56. ibid., 62.
57. ibid.
58. Pugin to Hardman, n.d., c. summer 1850, PC 304/749.
59. ibid., n.d., c. August 1850, PC 304/781.
60. ibid.
61. Pugin to Crace, annotated 20 July 1850, BAL PUG/7/40.
62. ibid.
63. ibid.
64. ibid., annotated 17 April 1850, BAL PUG/7/26.
65. ibid.
66. Although Benediction was largely a post-Reformation rite, which Pugin might have been expected to find inimical to his idea of English Catholicism, it has medieval origins and he seems to have adopted it readily.
67. Pugin to Hardman, n.d., c.14 August 1850, PC 304/719.
68. ibid.
69. ibid.
70. Pugin to Hardman, n.d., c. August 1850, PC 304/724.
71. ibid., n.d., 14 August 1850, PC 304/719.

72. ibid., n.d., *c*. August 1850, PC 304/724.
73. ibid.
74. Pugin to Crace, annotated 3 November 1850, BAL PUG/7/65.
75. Pugin to Hardman, n.d., *c*. September 1850, PC 304/746.
76. Pugin to Anne Pugin, n.d., *c*.28–9 September 1850, PC 304/242.
77. Pugin to Hardman, n.d., *c*. August 1850, PC 304/746.
78. ibid.
79. ibid.
80. ibid., n.d., early October 1850, PC 304/725.
81. ibid., n.d., *c*.20 October 1850, PC 304/748.
82. ibid., n.d., *c*.21 October 1850, PC 304/750.
83. ibid.
84. Pugin to Phillipps, postmarked 3 October 1850, PC 339/116.
85. Pugin, *Plain Song*, 8.
86. Newman, *Letters*, 14, 103.
87. Chadwick, *History of the Popes*, 92.
88. Quoted in Schiefen, *Wiseman*, 186.
89. Quoted ibid., 188.
90. Quoted ibid., 194.
91. Letters to Hardman, see above, n.40, and n.d., *c*. October 1850, PC 304/753.
92. Quoted in Schiefen, *Wiseman*, 189.
93. ibid.
94. Quoted ibid.
95. Shrewsbury to Pugin, 28 November 1850, PC 339/106.
96. Quoted in Halévy, *History*, 4, 369.
97. Shrewsbury to Bishop Ullathorne, 23 March 1850, BAA B1872.
98. ibid.
99. Pugin to Hardman, n.d., *c*. October 1850, PC 304/742.
100. ibid.
101. Jane Pugin, *Journal*, 60.
102. *Kent Herald*, 24 October 1850.
103. Pugin, *An Address to the Inhabitants of Ramsgate*, 8.
104. Pugin to Hardman, n.d., *c*. November 1850, PC 304/273.
105. ibid., n.d., *c*. autumn 1850, PC 304/216.
106. Pugin to Crace, annotated 3 November 1850, BAL PUG/7/65.
107. Pugin to Hardman, n.d., *c*. November 1850, PC 304/159.
108. ibid.
109. ibid., n.d., late November 1850, PC 304/784.
110. ibid., n.d., *c*.26 November 1850, PC 304/785.
111. ibid., n.d., *c*.26 November 1850, PC 304/786.
112. Pugin to Hardman, see above, n.110.
113. ibid.
114. ibid.
115. ibid., n.d., *c*. November 1850, PC 304/787.
116. Shrewsbury to Pugin, 28 November 1850, PC 339/106.
117. ibid.
118. Pugin to Hardman, n.d., *c*. November/December 1850, PC 304/791.
119. ibid., postmarked 11 December 1850, PC 304/794.
120. Jane Pugin, *Journal*, 60.
121. Pugin to Hardman, n.d., *c*.24 December 1850, PC 304/799.

Chapter 39: The Great Exhibition: January to October 1851

1. Pugin to Crace, annotated 1 January 1851, BAL PUG/8/1.
2. ibid.
3. ibid., annotated 21 January 1851, BAL PUG/8/11.
4. Shrewsbury to Pugin, 30 January 1851, PC 339/100.
5. ibid., postscript, 6 February 1851.
6. Pugin to Hardman, postmarked 27 January 1851, PC 304/455–7.
7. Port, *Houses of Parliament*, 149.
8. Halévy, *History*, 4, 312.
9. Shrewsbury to Pugin, 3 January 1851, private collection.
10. *Letter to the Rt Hon Lord John Russell by John Earl of Shrewsbury*, London, 1851, 32.
11. Pugin, *An Earnest Address*, 1.
12. ibid., 12.
13. ibid., 3.
14. ibid., 2.
15. ibid., 16.
16. ibid., 10.
17. ibid., 15.
18. Pugin to Hardman, n.d., *c*.21 February 1851, PC 304/451.
19. Letter to Phillipps, postmarked 18 February 1851, PC 339/120.
20. *Tablet*, 8 March 1851.
21. *Tablet*, 15 March 1851.
22. Pugin to Hardman, n.d., *c*. February 1851, PC 304/476.
23. ibid., n.d., *c*.15 April 1851, PC 304/201.
24. See also Hill, 'Pugin and Ruskin'.
25. Ruskin, *Stones of Venice*, 1, London, 1851, 372.
26. *Journal of Design*, September 1851, 26.
27. ibid., 27.
28. *Edinburgh Review*, October 1851, 371.
29. Quoted in Trappes-Lomax, *Pugin*, 58.
30. Pugin, *A Treatise on Chancel Screens*, 120.
31. ibid., 98.
32. Pugin to Hardman, n.d., spring 1851, PC 304/492.
33. ibid., n.d., PC 304/722.
34. ibid., n.d., spring 1851, PC 304/738.
35. ibid., n.d., spring 1851, PC 304/448.
36. ibid.
37. ibid., n.d., *c*. March 1851, PC 304/174.
38. ibid., n.d., *c*. March 1851, PC 304/481.
39. ibid., n.d., *c*. April 1851, PC 304/448.
40. ibid., n.d., *c*. March 1851, PC 304/207.
41. ibid., n.d., *c*. April 1851, PC 304/209.
42. ibid., n.d., *c*. March 1851, PC 304/480.
43. ibid.
44. ibid.
45. Pugin to Crace, annotated 6 March 1851, BAL PUG/8/23.
46. ibid.
47. Quoted in Bonython and Burton, *The Great Exhibitor*, 140.
48. Thomas Earley to an unnamed correspondent, probably Hardman, 15 April 1851, BCL.
49. Pugin to Hardman, n.d., March 1851, PC 304/485.
50. ibid., n.d., *c*.20 March 1851, PC 304/487.
51. Diary of Henry Cole, 19 March 1851, NAL.
52. ibid., 20 March 1851.

53. Thomas Earley to an unnamed correspondent, probably Hardman, n.d., BCL.
54. Spencer-Silver, *Pugin's Builder*, 44.
55. 'The Mediaeval Court', *Illustrated London News*, 20 September 1851.
56. Briggs, *Victorian Cities*, 12.
57. Pugin to Crace, annotated May 1851, BAL PUG/8/35.
58. 'Exposition universelle de Londres', *Annales Archéologiques*, 11, 1851, 294.
59. 'Originality in church architecture', *New-York Ecclesiologist*, 3 July 1851. The author, George L. Duyckinck, seems to conflate the work of Pugin and his father, a confusion that after Pugin's death became ever more common.
60. Pugin to Hardman, n.d., *c.* March 1851, PC 304/488.
61. ibid.
62. ibid., n.d., *c.* March 1851, PC 304/489.
63. ibid., n.d., *c.* March 1851, PC 304/506.
64. ibid.
65. ibid., n.d., *c.* April 1851, PC 304/584.
66. ibid., n.d., *c.* May 1851, PC 304/584.
67. ibid., n.d., *c.* April 1851, PC 304/162.
68. ibid., n.d., summer 1851, PC 304/502.
69. ibid., n.d., *c.* April 1851, PC 304/503.
70. ibid., n.d., summer 1851, PC 304/502.
71. Pugin to Jane Pugin, postmarked 9 June 1851, PC 339/191.
72. ibid., postmarked 12 June 1851, PC 339/183.
73. Pugin to Hardman, n.d., *c.*22 June 1851, PC 304/577.
74. Pugin to Jane Pugin, postmarked 24 June 1851, PC 339/200.
75. ibid.
76. ibid., n.d., *c.*15 July 1851, PC 339/246.
77. *Exhibition of the Works of Industry of All Nations, 1851, Reports by the Juries*, 2 vols., London, 1852, 2, 1538.
78. Diary, 71.
79. Pugin to Jane Pugin, n.d., *c.* July 1851, PC 339/246.
80. Pugin to Hardman, n.d., *c.*16 July 1851, PC 304/205.
81. ibid., n.d., *c.* summer 1851, PC 304/572.
82. ibid., n.d., *c.* September 1851, PC 304/652.
83. ibid.
84. Halévy, *History*, 4, 414.
85. Pugin to Jane Pugin, postmarked 24 August 1851, NAL, Wedgwood, *V&A* [92].
86. ibid., n.d., *c.* 26 August 1851, PC 339/247.
87. ibid., n.d., *c.* August 1851, PC 339/282.
88. Pugin to Hardman, n.d., *c.* summer 1851, PC 304/166.
89. Pugin to Henry Cole, 29 August 1851, NAL, Cole Papers, Box 12.
90. Pugin to Hardman, n.d., summer 1851, PC 304/578–79.
91. ibid., n.d., summer 1851, PC 304/654.
92. Pugin to Crace, annotated 15 September 1851, BAL PUG/8/49.
93. Pugin to Hardman, n.d., *c.* autumn 1851, PC 304/559.
94. ibid., n.d., *c.*1851, PC 304/572.
95. Hardman Powell to Hardman, n.d., *c.* September 1851, BCL.

Chapter 40: The Whole Machinery of the Clock: October 1851 to February 1852

1. Pugin to Hardman, n.d., late September 1851, PC 304/651.
2. ibid.
3. ibid., n.d., *c.* early October 1851.
4. *Exhibition of the Works of Industry of All Nations, 1851, Reports by the Juries*, 2 vols., London, 1852, 2, 1545 [*Report*].

5. ibid.
6. Pugin to Hardman, n.d., *c*.7 October 1851, PC 304/217.
7. ibid.
8. *Reports*, 2, 1623.
9. ibid., 1, 589.
10. ibid., 1, 589.
11. ibid., 1, 682.
12. ibid.
13. Pugin to Jane Pugin, n.d., *c*.7 October 1851, PC 339/170.
14. ibid.
15. ibid., postmarked 9 October 1851, PC 339/194.
16. Pugin to 'the Lords of the Committee for Trade, Whitehall', 10 December 1851, quoted in Ferrey, *Pugin*, 141.
17. Pugin to Hardman, n.d., October 1851, PC 304/602.
18. ibid., n.d., *c*.22 October 1851, PC 304/630.
19. ibid., n.d., November 1851, PC 304/618.
20. ibid., n.d., late October 1851, PC 304/609.
21. ibid., n.d., early November 1851, PC 304/655.
22. ibid.
23. Pugin to Hardman, see above, n.20.
24. Pugin to Hardman, n.d., *c*. October 1851, PC 304/643.
25. Pugin to Henry Cole, 14 November 1851, NAL, Cole Papers, Box 12.
26. Pugin to Hardman, n.d., *c*. December 1851, PC 304/667.
27. ibid., n.d., November 1851, PC 304/624–5.
28. ibid.
29. ibid.
30. Pugin to Hardman, see above, n.26.
31. Pugin to Hardman, n.d., November 1851, PC 304/669.
32. ibid., n.d., November 1841, PC 304/659.
33. Jane Pugin to Crace, 8 November 1851, BAL PUG/8/61.
34. Pugin to Hardman, n.d., November 1851, PC 304/617.
35. Barry, *Sir Charles Barry*, 256.
36. ibid.
37. Pugin to Hardman, see above, n.34.
38. Pugin to Hardman, n.d., *c*. November 1851, PC 304/660.
39. ibid.
40. Pugin to Anne Pugin Powell, n.d., *c*.30 November 1851, PC 304/383.
41. Pugin to Hardman, n.d., *c*.5 December 1851, PC 304/182.
42. ibid.
43. ibid.
44. Jane Pugin to Crace, 11 December 1851, BAL PUG/8/66.
45. Pugin to Hardman, n.d., *c*.17 December 1851, PC 304/111.
46. ibid., n.d., December 1851, PC 304/541.
47. ibid., n.d., December 1851, PC 304/595.
48. ibid.
49. See above, n.16.
50. Undated draft of a letter from Henry Cole to Pugin, *c*. December/January 1851–2, NAL, Cole Papers, Box 12.
51. Pugin to Crace, n.d., *c*. December 1851, BAL PUG/8/8.
52. Pugin to Hardman, n.d., December 1851, PC 304/531.
53. ibid., n.d., 18–24 December 1851, PC 304/529.
54. ibid., n.d., 18–24 December 1851, PC 304/543.
55. ibid.
56. Pugin to Hardman, see above, n.53.

57. Pugin to Hardman, n.d., 18–24 December 1851, PC 304/525.
58. ibid.
59. ibid., n.d., *c.* January 1851, PC 304/473.
60. Pugin to Hardman, see above, n.57.
61. Pugin to Hardman, n.d., December 1851, PC 304/516.
62. ibid., n.d., *c.* early January 1852, PC 304/113.
63. ibid.
64. ibid., n.d., *c.*25 December 1851, PC 304/783.
65. ibid.
66. Jane Pugin, *Journal*, 63.
67. Diary of Henry Cole, 5 January 1852, NAL.
68. Pugin to Cole, 7 January 1852, NAL, Cole Papers, Box 12.
69. Pugin to Crace, 6 January 1852, BAL PUG/9/1.
70. Letter to J. J. McCarthy, 15 January 1852, trs. of a letter in the collection of the late Phoebe Stanton.
71. E. W. Pugin, *Art Architect*, 55.
72. *Illustrated London News*, 7 February 1852, 122.
73. ibid., 14 February 1852, 138.
74. *Illustrated London News*, see above, n.72.
75. Quoted in E. W. Pugin, *Art Architect*, 55.
76. Pugin to Crace, n.d., *c.* December 1851, BAL PUG/6/68.
77. Jane Pugin to Crace, 7 February 1852, BAL PUG/9/5.
78. Pugin to Anne Pugin Powell, n.d., *c.*17 February 1852, PC 304/218.
79. Pugin to Hardman, n.d., *c.* February 1852, PC 304/538.
80. ibid.
81. ibid.
82. Crook and Port, *King's Works*, 621.
83. Barry, *Sir Charles Barry*, 255.
84. Pugin to Hardman, n.d., February 1852, PC 304/540.
85. ibid.
86. Jane Pugin to Crace, 14 February 1852, BAL PUG/9/6.
87. E. W. Pugin, *Art Architect*, 56.
88. Powell, 'Pugin', 194.

Chapter 41: Bethlem and Ramsgate: 26 February to September 1852

1. The drawing now belongs to the Myers Family Trust.
2. Jane Pugin, *Journal*, 65.
3. Shrewsbury to Pugin, 1 March 1852, PC 339/112.
4. Shrewsbury to Jane Pugin, 3 March 1852, PC 339/111.
5. E. W. Pugin, letter to *Blackwood's Magazine*, February 1862. The controversy about Pugin's illness and care had been reignited at this date by the publication of Ferrey's biography.
6. Letter from Samuel Sharwood to the House Committee of Bethlem Hospital, 17 June 1852, Bethlem Hospital Archives.
7. Pugin's case notes, Bethlem Hospital Archives.
8. ibid.
9. ibid.
10. Pugin to Jane Pugin, n.d., *c.*23 April 1849, PC 339/283.
11. Shrewsbury to Rock, postmarked June 1852, SAA.
12. Jane Pugin, *Journal*, 67.
13. ibid.
14. ibid., 68.
15. ibid.

16. ibid.
17. ibid., 69.
18. ibid.
19. ibid., 71.
20. ibid., 72.
21. ibid.
22. ibid., 73.
23. ibid., 75.
24. ibid.
25. ibid., 76.
26. ibid., 77.
27. ibid.
28. ibid.
29. John Raymond (ed.), *Queen Victoria's Early Letters*, London, revised edition, 1963, 192, Queen Victoria to the King of the Belgians, 17 September 1852.
30. Jane Pugin, *Journal*, 77.
31. Hardman Powell to William Powell, n.d., c.21 September 1852, BCL.
32. Jane Pugin, *Journal*, 77.

Epilogue

1. I am grateful to the late Sir Richard Baylis and the late Professor Ian McDonald for their opinions, on which my own remarks are based. They concurred that while a conclusive diagnosis is impossible, the overwhelming likelihood is that Pugin suffered from syphilis.
2. Talbot Bury, quoted in Powell, 'Pugin', 191.
3. *Ecclesiologist*, 13, 352–7 and *Builder*, 25 September 1852, 605.
4. *Kent Herald*, 23 September 1852; *Illustrated London News*, 2 October 1852, 281.
5. Clark, *Gothic Revival*, 144.
6. Muthesius, *Das englische Haus*, 15.
7. ibid., 15.
8. Jane Pugin, *Journal*, 78.
9. Barry, *Sir Charles Barry*, 197.
10. John Summerson, 'Pugin effigy: A Christmas Reminiscence', in *Architect and Building News*, 27 December 1940, 182.
11. I am grateful to Helen Lumsdaine's descendants Soonagh Asplin and Christopher Cork for details of her later life and death.
12. Robert Willson to Frederick Hugh Thomas, 22 December 1852, University of Tasmania Archives, Willson Papers, CAL/1. I am grateful to Margaret MacDonald, Thomas's descendant, for giving me her transcripts of the correspondence between Willson and Thomas.
13. Thomas to Willson, 14 January 1853, University of Tasmania Archives, CAL/2.
14. John Britton, 'Edward James Willson', *Builder*, 6 January 1855, 4–5.

Acknowledgements

This book has been the work of more than a decade and would not have been accomplished without the tireless help of many friends and colleagues. Like everyone who works on Victorian design I owe a great debt to the late Professor Clive Wainwright, who first encouraged my interest in Pugin and supported my research until his untimely death in 1999. Michael Hall and Gavin Stamp have been my constant friends, critics and supporters throughout and have read and commented perceptively on my typescript, as have Dr Sheridan Gilley and Emily Lane.

I owe a particular debt to Pugin's descendants and putative descendants, especially Sarah Houle, John, Jane and David Franklin, Jeremy Purcell, the late Dr James Mackey and his family, Jacina Bird, Beatrix Brooking, Joan Howkins and Welby Pugin as well as to Benjamin Ferrey's descendant, Simon Ferrey, and George Myers's relatives, Tim McCann, Patricia Spencer-Silver and the Myers Family Trust.

Several scholars have been generous enough to share their work in progress with me. I have benefited greatly from the unpublished researches of Dr Brian Andrews, Dr Alexandrina Buchanan, John and Jill Ford, Sir Hugh Roberts, who also gave me generous access to the collections and archives at Windsor Castle, and especially Dr Stanley Shepherd. Margaret MacDonald shared her considerable if inconclusive researches into the life of her ancestor, Pugin's putative half-brother, Frederick Hugh Thomas; the late Sir Paul and Lady Getty gave me the run of their Library at Wormsley, which was of immense benefit; Pat and Denys Groves gave me historical material relating to Scarisbrick Hall; Frank Devany gave me his copies of the correspondence of Fr Foley and Fr Husenbeth; the Revd Michael Fisher took me around Alton Towers; Professor Judi Loach encouraged me to publish my work in progress in *Architectural History* and edited it expertly; the Benedictine community at St Augustine's, Ramsgate, was always welcoming, and I thank particularly the Abbot, and my friends the late Dom Bede Millard OSB and Fr Dunstan Keauffling OSB, as well as my fellow members of the Pugin Society, especially Catriona Blaker, who took great trouble to answer many questions, and Nick Dermott.

For practical support I am grateful to the Society of Authors, which awarded me a grant, V. S. Naipaul's Award, in 1996 which helped to begin the work, and to the Warden and Fellows of All Souls College, Oxford, for a Visiting Fellowship in 2005–6 which helped me to finish it.

I have depended on the expertise of many archivists and librarians, some of whom have gone far beyond the call of duty: Elisabeth Fairman at the Yale Center for British Art made the Yale papers available to me on microfilm; Stephen Parks of the Beineke Library gave me a copy of Pugin's *Statement of Facts*; Ruth Gosling at the Birmingham City Library and the Revd Dr John Sharp and Jeanette Grisold at the Archives of the Archdiocese of Birmingham also made material available to me at inconvenient times and answered many questions, as did Fr Ian Dickie of the Westminster Archdiocesan Archives; Fr James Flynn, Father General of the Rosminian order, and Fr Ceschi, the order's archivist, were tireless and imaginative in their efforts to help me in Stresa and to transport material from Italy to London; the late Penny Ward shared her unrivalled knowledge of the history of Thanet with me; Malcolm Hay, curator of works of art at the Palace of Westminster, gave me access to every part of the building; Stuart Adam at Middle Temple explained the implications of what I had discovered about William Welby's career; John d'Arcy of the Wiltshire County Record Office and Mrs Rippen of the Lincolnshire Record Office used their expertise to take enquiries on my behalf further than I could have managed alone. The staff of the London Library are unfailingly resourceful.

Many other people also helped: Malcolm Airs, Soonagh Asplin, Philip Athill, Paul Atterbury, Rebecca Bailey, David Beevers, Carol Bennett, David Blissett, Geoffrey K. Brandwood, John Burrow, Francis Carlin, Judith Champ, John and Bridget Cherry, Sam Clapp, Emily Cole, Christopher Cork, Alan Crawford, Squire de Lisle, Lindsay Duguid, Charles Fane Treffusis, John T. Ferguson, Mary Finch, Aidan Flood, Richard Ford, Andrew Franklin, Robert Franklin, Simon Gooch, Ian Gow, the late Christian Hesketh, Robert Hewison, Peter Higgins, Michael Hill, Peter Howell, Sir David Hughes, Ralph Hyde, James Joll, Robert Kee, Michael Kerney, Alastair Laing, the late Mary McAuliffe, the late Charles Mann, Sister Mary Cecily of the Sisters of Mercy, Oswyn Murray, Guy Myddleton, Mark Negin, Charles Nugent, John Oddy, Roderick O'Donnell, Andrew O'Hagan, Stephen and Humphrey Osmond, Linda Parry, Fr Robin Paulson, Margaret Pawley, Jan Piggott, Craig Raine, Jane Roberts, Andrew Saint, Andrew Sanders, Philip Saunders, Diana Scarisbrick, Paul Schlicke, Kay Stannard, Tina Staples, Richard Suggett, Ian Sutton, Paul Thompson, Claire Tomalin, Peter van der Merwe, Michael Taylor, Lucy Thakray, Adam Thirlwell, Jane Wainwright, Tom Wall, the late Nicholas Walter, Marina Warner, Suzanne Waters, Alexandra Wedgwood, Richard Wentworth, Michael Whiteway, Mary-Kay Wilmers, Lucy Wood, Thomas Woodcock the Somerset Herald, Christopher Woodward and Kerry York.

Without my husband, Christopher Logue, who first took me to Pugin's church at Ramsgate, this book would have been neither begun nor finished.

Index